Empire and Modern Political Thought

This collection of original chapters by leading historians of political thought examines modern European thinkers' writings about conquest, colonization, and empire. The creation of vast transcontinental empires and imperial trading networks played a key role in the development of modern European political thought. The rise of modern empires raised fundamental questions about virtually the entire contested set of concepts that lay at the heart of modern political philosophy, such as property, sovereignty, international justice, war, trade, rights, transnational duties, civilization, and progress. From Renaissance republican writings about conquest and liberty to sixteenth-century writings about the Spanish conquest of the Americas through Enlightenment perspectives about conquest and global commerce and nineteenth-century writings about imperial activities both within and outside of Europe, these chapters survey the central moral and political questions occasioned by the development of overseas empires and European encounters with the non-European world among theologians, historians, philosophers, diplomats, and merchants.

Sankar Muthu is Associate Professor of Political Science at the University of Chicago. He is the author of *Enlightenment against Empire*.

D1528394

Empire and Modern Political Thought

Edited by

SANKAR MUTHU

University of Chicago

CAMBRIDGE
UNIVERSITY PRESS

32 Avenue of the Americas, New York NY 10013-2473, USA

Cambridge University Press is part of the University of Cambridge.

It furthers the University's mission by disseminating knowledge in the pursuit of education, learning and research at the highest international levels of excellence.

www.cambridge.org
Information on this title: www.cambridge.org/9781107460034

© Cambridge University Press 2012

First published 2012
First paperback edition 2014

A catalogue record for this publication is available from the British Library

Library of Congress Cataloguing in Publication data
Empire and modern political thought / [edited by] Sankar Muthu.
    p.   cm.
Includes bibliographical references and index.
ISBN 978-0-521-83942-6 (hardback)
1. Imperialism – Philosophy – History.   I. Muthu, Sankar, 1970–
JC359.E44   2012
325'.3201–dc23   2011045033

ISBN 978-0-521-83942-6 Hardback
ISBN 978-1-107-46003-4 Paperback

Contents

Contributors

David Armitage Lloyd C. Blankfein Professor of History, Harvard University

Mikael Hörnqvist Senior Lecturer in the History of Science and Ideas, Uppsala University

Karuna Mantena Associate Professor of Political Science, Yale University

Pratap Bhanu Mehta President, Centre for Policy Research, New Delhi

Uday S. Mehta Distinguished Professor of Political Science, Graduate Center, City University of New York

Michael Mosher Professor of Political Science, University of Tulsa

Sankar Muthu Associate Professor of Political Science, University of Chicago

Anthony Pagden Distinguished Professor of Political Science and History, University of California, Los Angeles

Gabriel Paquette Assistant Professor of History, the Johns Hopkins University

Jennifer Pitts Associate Professor of Political Science, University of Chicago

Emma Rothschild Jeremy and Jane Knowles Professor of History, Harvard University

Richard Tuck Frank G. Thomson Professor of Government, Harvard University

Acknowledgments

For their support of this book at various stages, I am very pleased to be able to thank Sunil Agnani, Richard Bourke, Greg Conti, Steve Macedo, John McCormick, Alan Patten, Alan Ryan, and Cheryl Welch. Thanks also to the Rockefeller Foundation, which sponsored a conference at its Bellagio Center at which early versions of some of the chapters were presented. In particular, thanks to Susan Garfield of the Rockefeller Foundation as well as Pilar Palacià and Laura Podio of the Bellagio Center. At Cambridge University Press, I thank the late Terence Moore for his early support of this book as well as my editor, Beatrice Rehl, both for her expert oversight of this project and for her patience. For their careful and conscientious work on this manuscript as it made its way through the production process at Cambridge University Press, I am very grateful to Maria den Boer, James W. Dunn, Asya Graf, Helen Greenberg, Amanda J. Smith, Emily Spangler, and Helen Wheeler.

Introduction

Sankar Muthu

European political thought from the Renaissance through the nineteenth century has long been associated with theorizations of a few key social, political, and economic developments: the rise of "the state" and its primary subinstitutions and practices, such as standing armies, central banks, and bureaucratic administrations; the reordering of relationships among religious institutions and political powers, at times leading to governments' greater or lesser toleration of diverse religious practices and denominations; the development of commercial systems of trade, mass manufacturing (eventually industrial production), chartered companies with transnational operations, and related debates about consumption, luxury, and the social and political effects of growing merchant classes; and the ideologies of natural (or human) rights and of republican (or democratic) forms of governance. Many of the political events that are taken to be constitutive of this period, from the Thirty Years War to the Edict of Nantes (and its revocation) to the upheavals of 1688, 1776, and 1789 were both influenced by and shaped modern political discourses. When one adds to these developments the significant impact of the rise of modern science, including the experimental sciences, on moral and political writings as well as the technological breakthroughs that made accurate oceanic navigation and industrial manufacturing possible, the profound transformations in social thought in this period cannot be underestimated.

The global and imperial dimensions of this period, however, and in particular the self-conscious theorization of them in past centuries, have been relatively neglected by historians of political thought when compared to the vast amount of scholarly work in political theory about, for example, modern political philosophies of revolution, toleration, and the state. While historians of modern political thought have occasionally turned to the global dimensions of this period, only in the past roughly dozen years has a critical mass of such scholars analyzed the importance of territorial expansion and transcontinental (often imperial) networks of direct or indirect imperial governance, naval and military activity, and trade in the writings of modern European political thinkers. In addition, such scholars have attempted to understand how, if at all, such ideologies interacted with statist, religious, commercial, republican, and revolutionary developments and discourses. To be sure, historians working in areas other than intellectual history, postcolonial theorists in various disciplines, and scholars of literature and literary theory, among others, have been working in large numbers on such global and imperial issues for a longer period of time. Only fairly recently, however, have significant numbers of historians of political thought as well as contemporary political theorists turned to global matters.[1] Given this scholarly turn in the study of modern political thought, this set of original chapters has been commissioned to offer a range of interpretations about European thinkers' writings from the fifteenth through the nineteenth centuries about conquest, colonization, and the various institutions and practices that have come to be grouped under the term "empire."

No single-volume study along these lines can come close to capturing the vast range of writings that treated such issues across a few hundred years; moreover, even the thinkers who would likely be considered to be the most philosophically astute or historically influential could not all be covered in the space of one volume. Ideally, this book will spur further scholarly analysis not only about the thinkers and writings under study, but also about the many figures and themes not covered, or only briefly mentioned, here. While the long chronology of this book cannot provide the coherence of a collection that focuses on a particular ideology or concise period, the wide range of perspectives analyzed here allows one to discern both stark differences and occasionally similar preoccupations across multiple intellectual traditions and centuries in the modern era. The chronological range of the chapters is extensive, covering political and philosophical debates from Renaissance republican writings about conquest and liberty and sixteenth-century writings about the Spanish

---

[1] For a survey of the recent imperial and global turn in the history of political thought and contemporary political theory, with an extensive bibliography, see Chapter 13 of this book by Jennifer Pitts.

conquest of the Americas, to Enlightenment debates about global empires, to nineteenth-century writings about the development of social theory in the context of imperial debates, the French colonization of Algeria, Napoleonic conquests, and British imperial activities in India and elsewhere. The emphasis in this book is on European thinkers of the modern period, but one hope that underlies this volume is that the many connections and tensions among European and non-European thinkers' perspectives about conquest, occupation, and imperial rule can be researched and investigated in ways that will be enhanced by the following chapters.

Although recent political developments and philosophical discourses – about globalization, military interventions and occupation, terrorism and responses to it, and the rise of the United States as the most powerful hegemon or, arguably, as the dominant imperial power in international relations – no doubt helped to turn the attention of some political theorists to possibly analogous debates and writings in earlier centuries, the contributors to this volume have not examined past writings primarily with a view to the present. To be sure, many dilemmas that confront citizens and states today about humanitarian intervention, national sovereignty, conquest and occupation, empire, and human rights in a global context have a long, intriguing, and complex intellectual history. Accordingly, some of the authors have occasionally noted what might or might not be reasonably seen as analogous assumptions, concepts, and arguments in the writings of modern and contemporary political thinkers and actors. A key purpose of this book, however, is to investigate what some modern European thinkers sought to analyze, to justify, and to criticize as they wrestled with what they saw as the political and intellectual challenges raised by territorial, oceanic, and commercial conquests and their aftermath.

In surveying the many ethical and political questions that the development of overseas empires and European encounters with the non-European world occasioned among theologians, historians, philosophers, merchants, and political actors in Western Europe from the fifteenth through the nineteenth centuries, what emerges most clearly is that what were perceived to be fundamental issues and concepts changed over time and were formulated in different terms and that certain perspectives gained or lost importance, depending upon shifting intellectual, political, and historical concerns. The following chapters will, among other things, investigate the distinctive and sometimes overlapping manner in which each political thinker, or set of thinkers, under study understood and assessed the social, economic, and political relationships between the occupiers and the occupied; in this book, usually this corresponds to various European powers, on the one hand, and particular non-European rulers and peoples, on the other.[2] Notwithstanding this diversity of perspectives and histories, particular instantiations of more general questions will no doubt arise in one form or another in several chapters. What moral and legal principles and assumptions were used to theorize conquest and occupation, and to what philosophical and political ends were such concepts applied? To what extent and precisely how did these thinkers' arguments draw upon the existing ethnography about foreign peoples in order to understand how European states should or should not interact with non-European peoples? What European and extra-European religious, political, and commercial developments influenced these thinkers and, in turn, how did these thinkers seek to justify, criticize, or transform such developments? Indeed, as suggested at the outset, in addition to transformations such as the formation of centralized states and disputes over the changing role of religion in political life, the creation of vast European empires and imperial trading networks played a key role in the development of modern European political thought. The rise of what we now classify as modern empires raised fundamental questions about human nature, property, sovereignty, international justice, war, commerce, trade, rights, duties across borders, sociability, civilization, citizenship, and progress – indeed, about virtually the entire set of contested concepts and ideas that are now retrospectively grouped together as "modern political thought."

If one aim of this book is to understand how some European thinkers from 1492 onward understood and evaluated the extraordinary developments by which a small group of Western European countries came to rule or to dominate much of the non-European world, then today the language of empire seems most appropriate. While "empire" is used in the title of this book for precisely this reason, it is important to appreciate that contemporary uses of "empire" and "imperial" differ markedly from the use of such terms for much of the period under study in this book, and that the cognate concept of "imperialism" emerged only in the nineteenth century. One scholar has recently noted that an "empire in the classic sense is usually believed, first, to expand its control by conquest or coercion, and, second, to control the loyalty of the territories it

---

[2] The conception of "Europe" and what ought to be thought of as properly European or extra-European was in flux and vigorously contested during this period, as indeed it is today. See Anthony Pagden, ed., *The Idea of Europe: From Antiquity to the European Union* (Cambridge and Washington, D.C.: Cambridge University Press and Woodrow Wilson Center Press, 2002).

subjugates. It may rule these subject lands directly or it may install com-
pliant native leaders who will govern on its behalf, but it is not just an
alliance system among equal partners."[3] The use of "empire" to identify
control over an extensive assemblage of lands that resulted at least in part
from conquest, occupation, and at times significant colonial settlements
("territorial empires") and/or to delineate a commercial network of trading posts, small colonial establishments, and often indirect rule over foreign populations ("maritime empires," "naval empires," or "empires of
the sea") begins to emerge only in the eighteenth century.

In the *Characteristicks of Men, Manners, Opinions, Times* (published
initially in 1711), one of the most reprinted English books of the eighteenth century, Anthony Ashley Cooper, the third Earl of Shaftesbury,
wrote of the "Advantages" that "powerful States" have found "in sending
Colonys abroad," and immediately followed this assertion by contending
that "Vast Empires are in many respects unnatural: but particularly in this,
That be they ever so well constituted, the Affairs of many must, in such
Governments, turn upon a very few[.]"[4] Edmund Burke, in 1793, referred
to the combination of British trading activities and territorial conquests
in India – at the time conducted by the English East India Company and
well before the sovereign declaration of India as a subject territory ruled
by a queen who would be declared the "empress of India" – by asserting
succinctly that "Our Empire in India is an awful thing."[5] In the *Wealth of
Nations*, published initially in 1776 with significant additions in the 1783
edition, Adam Smith discussed European activities in the non-European
world from 1492 onward, including territorial expansion, the planting
of colonies, and aggressive commercial trading networks of joint stock
companies all under the traditional heading "Of Colonization," but he
ultimately concluded his book with an assertion about the need to dismantle what Smith himself termed the "British empire."[6] This was an

---

[3] Charles Maier, *Among Empires: American Ascendancy and Its Predecessors* (Cambridge,
Mass.: Harvard University Press, 2006), pp. 24–25. See also Jane Burbank and Frederick
Cooper, *Empires in World History: Power and the Politics of Difference* (Princeton, N.J.:
Princeton University Press, 2010), chap. 1.

[4] Anthony Ashley Cooper, Earl of Shaftesbury, *Characteristicks of Men, Manners, Opinions,
Times* (Indianapolis: Liberty Fund, 2001; reprint of the 6th ed. [London: J. Purser, 1737–
1738]), p. 71.

[5] Edmund Burke, "Remarks on the Policy of the Allies," in E. Burke, *Three memorials on
French affairs written in the years 1791, 1792 and 1793 by the late Right Hon. Edmund
Burke* (London: F. and C. Rivington, 1797), p. 182.

[6] Adam Smith, *An Inquiry into the Nature and Causes of the Wealth of Nations*, ed. R. H.
Campbell and A. S. Skinner, textual ed. W. B. Todd (Oxford: Clarendon Press, 1976), bk.
V, chap. iii, p. 946.

agglomeration that, for him, included both the colonies of America and the trading outposts and territorial seizures (either as tributary states or as direct dependencies) of the English East India Company. Similarly, a contemporaneous British author analyzed the "emigrations to America, to Ireland, and other more distant settlements, belonging to the British Empire" and considered "those lost in defence of ourselves and of our colonies, and in carrying on our extensive commerce to all parts of the globe," concluding later that "an extended empire must ever prove pernicious."[7]

The eighteenth century, then, is a transitional period in the history of the concept of empire, for the traditional understanding of *imperium* as simply sovereign or military rule – or, at times, such rule over a fairly large, though contiguous, territory – increasingly became mixed with the languages of colonization, conquest, and overseas commerce.[8] Hence, given the chronological scope of this book that spans the fifteenth through the nineteenth centuries, "conquest" is a more historically apt term for this entire period, though only the contemporary use of "empire" covers the full range of activities and institutions that the thinkers under study in this volume usually theorized as they pondered what they took to be among the key transcontinental developments of their age. Among the issues that were thought to demand analysis and judgment were the seizure of many non-European lands; the establishment and escalation of vast systems of slavery, most notably (but not only) the transcontinental Atlantic slave trade; the attempted religious and cultural conversion of conquered peoples; the emerging institutions and practices of global commerce; and the increasingly complex networks of transnational alliances and modes of transcontinental governance. The impact of these developments on both European and non-European societies and global relations has been, and continues to be, profound. An examination of a substantial subset of the philosophically rich and ideologically influential modern European intellectual debates about these developments, therefore, illuminates – perhaps simultaneously in unsettling and hopeful ways – both the past and the present.

---

[7] James Anderson, *The interest of Great-Britain with regard to her American colonies, considered. To which is added an appendix, containing the outlines of a plan for a general pacification* (London: T. Cadell, 1782), pp. 86, 102.

[8] For a classic study of the languages of *imperium* and "empire" (from ancient Rome to nineteenth-century Europe), see Richard Koebner, *Empire* (Cambridge: Cambridge University Press, 1966). See also James Muldoon, *Empire and Order: The Concept of Empire, 800–1800* (New York: Palgrave Macmillan, 1999).

I

Machiavelli's Three Desires

Florentine Republicans on Liberty, Empire, and Justice

Mikael Hörnqvist

While Florence's role as the cradle of the European Renaissance and the great mediator between the ancients and the moderns in the fields of learning, visual arts, architecture, and natural science is firmly established in the scholarly community and the popular imagination alike, the Florentine republic's contribution to the history of empire and imperialist theory is less well recognized. The inclusion of Florence and the Florentine Renaissance in a volume dedicated to empire and political theory may therefore need some explaining. Needless to say, there can be no question of Florence being ranked among the great empires of history. The city on the banks of the river Arno bears no comparison to the Roman, the Spanish, the British, the French, the Ottoman, or the Soviet empires. It can hardly even be mentioned in the same breath as minor imperial powers such Portugal, the Netherlands, Sweden, or Japan. However, in the history of thinking about empire and imperial mythmaking, the Florentine republic of the late Middle Ages and the Renaissance, the self-appointed heir of the ancient Roman republic, must rank among the historically most significant and the most sophisticated. From the fourteenth to the early sixteenth centuries Florentines came to regard Florence, through a strong and intensely felt identification with the ancient Roman republic, as destined for imperial greatness and hegemonic rule over Tuscany, Italy, and, on occasion, even the entire world. As I have argued elsewhere, Florentine republican imperialism was premised on the idea that the republic had two ends: to preserve its liberty at home and to pursue empire abroad.[1] The task of this chapter is to build

---

[1] Mikael Hörnqvist, *Machiavelli and Empire* (Cambridge: Cambridge University Press, 2004), esp. chap. 2. See also Mikael Hörnqvist, "The Two Myths of Civic Humanism," in

on this research by inquiring into the role of liberty, empire, and justice in the Florentine tradition in general and in the political theory of Niccolò Machiavelli in particular. As I hope to show, Machiavelli's rejection of the humanist philosophy of justice takes on its full meaning when studied in the context of his republican imperialism.

In the history of political thought, Renaissance Florence has long been associated with the ideology of liberty and with civic humanism, the embryonic form of liberalism identified by Hans Baron and Eugene Garin in the mid-twentieth century.[2] This emphasis on liberty has highlighted important aspects of Florentine political culture but, at the same time, has made us largely oblivious of the fact that Florentine republicans spoke of their state as an empire (*imperio*), were unashamedly proud of their city's territorial acquisitions, and understood and conceptualized their republic as the modern reembodiment of its ancient forebear, the mighty Roman republic.

In fourteenth- and fifteenth-century representations of Italian city-states, accounts of conquests and victories in battle are commonplace. In the case of Florence, these panegyrics as a rule go back to the fourteenth century, when the Florentine republic began to emerge as an aspiring imperialist state in the pursuit of Tuscan hegemony.[3] As the expansive merchant families tightened their control over the city's government toward the middle of the century, Florence embarked on a series of military adventures that eventually led to the acquisitions of Colle Valdelsa in 1338, Prato and Pistoia in 1351, San Gimignano in 1354, Volterra in 1361, Arezzo in 1384, and Montepulciano in 1390. After a series of protracted wars with the dukes of Milan for supremacy in central Italy, ending in 1402, the republic succeeded four years later in subjugating its bitter rival, the seafaring city of Pisa, which for centuries had blocked its access to the sea. Florentine humanists and patriotic writers celebrated the conquest as the greatest military triumph in the history of the city,

Renaissance Civic Humanism: Reappraisals and Reflections, ed. J. Hankins (Cambridge: Cambridge University Press, 2000), pp. 105–142.

[2] Hans Baron, *The Crisis of the Early Italian Renaissance: Civic Humanism and Republican Liberty in an Age of Classicism and Tyranny* (Princeton, N.J.: Princeton University Press, 1966); Eugenio Garin, *Italian Humanism: Philosophy and Civic Life in the Renaissance* (Westport, Conn.: Greenwood Press, 1975). For a more extensive discussion of the recent scholarship on Florentine republicanism, see Hörnqvist, *Machiavelli and Empire*, pp. 41–44. See also the essays collected in *Renaissance Civic Humanism*.

[3] See, for example, *Images of Quattrocento Florence: Selected Writings in Literature, History, and Art*, ed. S. U. Baldassarri and A. Saiber (New Haven, Conn.: Yale University Press, 2000), pp. 73, 300.

and Leonardo Bruni, the humanist and future chancellor, later compared it to Rome's triumph over Carthage.

Inspired by the example of the ancient Roman republic, most Florentine humanists of the early fifteenth century refused to view liberty and empire as contradictory values or pursuits. Instead, they subscribed to the idea that the republic had two ends – one internal, centered on the classical concept of liberty (*libertas*), and one external, aspiring to acquisition of dominion (*imperium*), material goods, greatness, and glory. Prompted by this observation, I have opposed the one-sided characterization of Florentine republicanism as more or less exclusively devoted to liberty, endorsed by Baron, Skinner, and Viroli, arguing that it instead draws on two different but related vocabularies, one internal and liberty oriented and the other external or imperialist. While the language of liberty includes notions such as civic peace (*pace*), concord (*concordia*), security (*sicurtà*), rule of law, equality (*equalità* or *civile equalità*), order (*ordine*), citizenship and the rights of the citizen, and various expressions designating the republican way of life (*vivere politico, vivere civile, vivere libero*, etc.), the vocabulary of empire is made up of terms that connote growth, greatness (*grandezza*), expansion, acquisition (*lo acquistare*), riches (*ricchezze*), territorial gain, honor (*onore*), dignity (*dignitas*), reputation (*riputazione*), triumph (*trionfo*), fame (*fama*), and glory (*gloria*). These two vocabularies are distinct and based upon different sets of values, perhaps even different views of human nature, but within the overarching framework of Roman republicanism, they are inextricably connected and, in a sense, complementary. Together they constitute the nerve center of the healthy republic so that when one of the categories is neglected, the other is bound to suffer as well, with corruption and tyranny as a result. It therefore becomes paramount to devise a conceptual formula capable of balancing liberty and empire and to develop strategies and policies allowing the republic simultaneously to pursue its two aims.

As attentive students of classical political theory are bound to have noticed, I have in the preceding account omitted one of the most important concepts in the republican tradition: the virtue of justice. If we were to follow the prevailing tendency in recent scholarship, we would remedy this oversight by simply placing justice on the side of liberty, regarding it as one of the distinctive qualities contributing to the preservation of the republic.[4] This chapter will take issue with this view, arguing instead that

---

[4] Quentin Skinner, *The Foundations of Modern Political Thought*, 2 vols. (Cambridge: Cambridge University Press, 1978), I, p. 123: "The 'civic' humanists, as well as the

justice, by participating in both vocabularies, being intimately associated with empire as well as with liberty, constitutes an important link between the two concepts, the two vocabularies, and the two aims underlying Florentine republicanism. This argument will prompt us to pose the question of why Machiavelli, who wholeheartedly subscribed to the republican credo of liberty at home and empire abroad, did not also embrace the view of justice as the overarching principle holding these two contrary aims together. As I hope to show, Machiavelli's relative silence on justice in his theoretical works should not be seen as an outright rejection of the concept, but instead should be regarded as part of a radical, but never explicitly stated, redefinition of the role of justice within, or in relation to, the republican project.

The importance that civic humanists and Florentine republican writers in general attached to justice can hardly be exaggerated. Drawing on classical sources, especially Aristotle and Cicero, they saw justice generally as the chief among the civic virtues, the foundation of the *vivere civile*, and the bond that held the republic together. According to the humanist Chancellor Coluccio Salutati, justice embraces all the other virtues and serves "an almost divine end," since it contributes to the edification and utility not just of the individual but of all citizens.[5] Comparing the city that lives without justice to a band of thieves, Salutati claims that justice is the virtue that maintains peace and allows human society to thrive.[6] In his *Laudatio florentinae urbis* (c. 1404), Leonardo Bruni declares that justice is observed and "held most sacred" in the Florentine republic and that it is for this reason that Florence has the right to call itself a city, for, as he lays down, "without justice there can be no city."[7] Throughout his career Bruni continued to hold the Aristotelian and Ciceronian view of justice as the

authors of advice-books for podestà and city magistrates, had all committed themselves to the claim that the preservation of liberty and justice must be taken to constitute the main values in political life." See also Maurizio Viroli, *From Politics to Reason of State: The Acquisition and Transformation of the Language of Politics 1250–1600* (Cambridge: Cambridge University Press, 1992), pp. 16–69.

[5] Quoted from Daniela De Rosa, *Coluccio Salutati: Il cancelliere e il pensatore politico* (Florence: La Nuova Italia, 1980), p. 114: "La giustizia delle leggi, abbracciando ogni virtù, è destinata ad un fine quasi divino, non al bene di un solo, ma alla edificazione ed alla utilità di tutti."

[6] Ibid., p. 111: "Essa soltanto permette la sussistenza della società umana, crea le condizioni adatte al mantenimento della pace, vendica i delitti e remunera l'onestà"; ibid.: "Che cosa sono le città prive di giustizia se non grandissime bande di ladroni?"

[7] Leonardo Bruni, "Panegyric to the City of Florence," trans. B. G. Kohl, in *The Earthly Republic: Italian Humanist on Government and Society*, ed. B. G. Kohl and R. G. Witt (Philadelphia: University of Pennsylvania Press, 1978), pp. 135–175, at p. 169.

principal civic virtue, on one occasion defining it as "an absolute and all-encompassing sort of virtue," which in itself contains the exercise of every other virtue.[8] Against this background it was singularly fitting that justice should be chosen as the subject for the inaugural orations, the so-called *protestatio de iustitia*, held in connection to the installation of each new *signoria*, Florence's highest deliberative council.[9] In one *protestatio*, the humanist Donato Acciaiuoli defines universal justice as "an aggregate of all the moral virtues arranged for the good of others and for the common good of the republic," and goes on to claim that there can be no justice where there is not also prudence, temperance, and fortitude.[10] A similar view is taken by Giovanni Cavalcanti, who in his *Trattato politico-morale* (c. 1450) maintains that all the moral or political virtues work together toward the same end and are so closely knit together by their common origin that one cannot be found without the others.[11] Along these lines, a *Pratiche* of November 1499 states that justice is all-encompassing and "contains everything *(Justizia ha in se ogni cosa)*."[12]

Depending on whether the republic was conceived as a living organism or as an architectural structure, justice could be alluded to as the soul or the foundation of the city. Both Filippo Pandolfini and Donato Acciauoli compare in Platonic terms the role of justice in the city to that of the soul in the body. While the body lives "for the soul" and is dependent on the soul for its existence, the republic lives "for justice" and survives only as long as justice is observed.[13] If justice is absent, Bono Boni maintains, the

[8] *The Humanism of Leonardo Bruni: Selected Texts*, ed. G. Griffiths, J. Hankins, and D. Thompson (Binghamton, N.Y.: Center for Medieval and Early Renaissance Studies, 1987), p. 279.

[9] On the *protestatio de iustitia*, see Emilio Santini, "La *protestatio de iustitia* nella Firenze Medicea del sec. XV," *Rinascimento*, 10 (1959), 33–106; Anthony J. Parel, "Machiavelli's Notions of Justice: Text and Analysis," *Political Theory*, 18 (1990), 530–536; Uwe Neumahr, *Die Protestatio de Iustitia in der Florentiner Hochkultur: Eine Redegattung* (Münster: Lit-Verlag, 2002).

[10] Quoted from Santini, "La *protestatio de iustitia*," 50–51: "non può essere iusto che no sia prudente, temperato et forte."

[11] *The Trattato politico-morale of Giovanni Cavalcanti: A Critical Edition and Interpretation*, ed. M. T. Grendler (Genève: Droz, 1973), p. 149: "... virtù morali ... Tutte traggono ad uno medesimo fine ... sono congiunte & di si stretto parentado che, dove ne va una, vi vanno tutte."

[12] Quoted from Felix Gilbert, "Florentine Political Assumptions in the Period of Savonarola and Soderini," *Journal of the Warburg and Courtauld Institutes*, 20 (1957), 187–214, at 212. *Consulte* and *pratiche* were informal meetings of leading citizens, summoned to give their views *(parere)* on matters of public interest.

[13] Santini, "La *protestatio de iustitia*," 51: "chome nel corpo nostro è l'anima, così l'anima della città è la iustitia; vive el corpo per l'anima, vive la rep[ublica] per la iustitia." Cf. ibid., 62 and 73.

city will simply die.[14] Drawing on the architectural vocabulary, Poggio Bracciolini hails justice as the "queen of the virtues" and describes it as "the firmest foundation of both public and private affairs."[15] In a *protestatio* from around 1460, justice is praised as the foundation without which no government, no republic, and no single house can be erected.[16]

In around 1435, Matteo Palmieri in his *Vita civile*, a dialogue on the principles of liberal education and republican government, summed up fifty years of civic humanist teaching on justice. The practice of this virtue, Palmieri argues at the beginning of book III, completely devoted to justice, is the most honorable of all human pursuits since it contributes to the expansion and health of the patria and the well-ordered republic. Without justice, we are told once more, no city, state, or republic (*publico reggimento*) can survive, nor can any stable empire (*imperium*) be erected, because without its support every force and power is doomed to come to ruin. Justice is once more extolled as the "principal empress of all the virtues" and is made responsible for the provisions and administration of the whole body politic (*tutto il corpo della republica*). It preserves every member of the community, upholds peace, unity, and concord, and acts as a shield for the republic, protecting it from unforeseen events arising within or without its borders.[17]

Since justice in this tradition is defined as the chief among the political or civic virtues, it comes to stand in a close relation to liberty, the other principal republican value. Leonardo Bruni states this doctrine most clearly when he argues that justice and liberty are "joined (almost as a stamp or goal) to all the institutions and statutes that the Florentine government has created."[18] In Bruni's view, the Florentine republic has brought about the happy union of justice and liberty, since there is "no place on earth where there is greater justice open equally to everyone" and where liberty "grows so vigorously."[19] Bruni returns to the bond between liberty and justice in his *History of the Florentine People* in a speech by

[14] Ibid. 83: "... chosì, separata la giustitia dalla città, la città diventa morta."
[15] Poggio Bracciolini, " On Avarice," in *The Earthly Republic*, pp. 251–252 and 278.
[16] Santini, "La *protestatio de iustitia*," 104: "... non può senza iustitia, fondamento et principio di tutti i governi di ciashuna respublica, senza il quale fondamento niuna casa di sopra si può stabilitamente edificare ... "
[17] Matteo Palmieri, *Vita civile*, ed. G. Belloni (Florence: Sansoni, 1982), pp. 104–105: "... a tutto il corpo della republica insieme provede et ministra, ciascuno membro conserva ..." (p. 104); "pertanto è chiamata iustitia non parte, ma intera virtù, et perfecto è couli che vive giusto." (105)
[18] Bruni, "Panegyric," p. 169.
[19] Ibid., p. 173.

Giano della Bella, the leader of the popular faction in Florence at the end of the thirteenth century and one of the instigators of the Ordinances of Justice in 1293: "It seems to me that the liberty of the people is contained in two things: laws and judges. When these two things are more potent than individual citizens, then is liberty preserved."[20] The canonical status of Bruni's work in fifteenth-century Florence is evident from quotations and references in the *protestationes de iustitia*, where liberty is often evoked together with the common good, stability, harmony, peace, happiness, greatness, wealth, and unity as the so-called fruits of justice.[21] An unidentified orator cites Bruni's *History* when claiming that liberty is "contained in two things, that is, laws and judges," and that it is maintained when these two factors exert more power in the city than private citizens.[22] The strong bond between liberty and justice is also evoked in an unattributed *protestatio* where it is claimed that those who are not living in "just liberty (*giusta libertà*)" are, "morally speaking," more similar to brute animals than to men.[23]

As we can see, there is no lack of evidence in support of the conventional scholarly view that justice belongs together with liberty in the ideology of the Florentine civic humanists. The problem with this position is not that it is mistaken, but that it fails to account for the complexity of the tradition and tends to reduce the virtue of justice to a mere handmaiden of liberty. Even a cursory look at the texts by the Florentine fifteenth-century writers reveals that justice cannot be limited to the internal liberty-oriented side of Florentine republicanism. Time and again, Florentine humanists and patriotic writers also refer to justice in connection to war, territorial expansion, and the quest for empire. Matteo Palmieri, quoting Cicero's concept of the just war, claims that the republic should be just as scrupulous in conducting its wars according to the principles of justice as it is in administering justice for its own citizens.[24]

---

[20] Leonardo Bruni, *History of the Florentine People*, vol. I, ed. J. Hankins (Cambridge, Mass.: Harvard University Press, 2001), p. 171. Cf. Bruni, "Panegyric," p. 169.

[21] Cf. Santini, "La *protestatio de iustitia*," 50–51, 57, 68, 72, 74.

[22] Santini, "La *protestatio de iustitia*," 90: "la libertà in due chose si contiene, cioè con legge et con iudicii; inperò che quando queste due chose possono più nella ciptà che [i] privati ciptadini, la libertà si conserva."

[23] Ibid., 86: "chi sotto giustitia e libertà non vive, moralmente parlando quasi a bruto animale assimigliare si potrebbe ... quello che in giusta libertà non è per poco una bestia chiamare."

[24] Palmieri, *Vita civile*, p. 115: "In ogni republica si debbe adunque non meno considerare con che iustitia si governino le guerre che quale sia nella città il iusto vivere de' proprii cittadini. Dua modi sono di questione, l'uno per disputatione, quando legittimamente si

The conduct of war should aspire to "just victory (*iusta victoria*)," since such conquests allow the victor to take secure possession of the acquired territories, as demonstrated by Florence's past dealings with neighboring cities like Volterra, Pistoia, and Arezzo.[25] In a similar vein, Giovanni Cavalcanti argues that wise men, concerned with the greatness of the republic, always consider how they can draw strength from justice when raising their families, defending the patria against enemies, and expanding the city beyond its borders.[26]

Needless to say, this coupling of justice and empire must be seen in relation to medieval conceptions of the ancient Roman Empire and the revival of classical republicanism in the early Renaissance. Many Florentine writers regarded Romans' observance of justice as one of the main reasons for the Roman republic's unparalleled territorial expansion. Coluccio Salutati, who explains the Roman people's rise to world rule with reference to the strength of their arms, their just government, and their other splendid virtues, contends that Rome did not reduce the world to servitude but "governed it with fair laws in sweet liberty."[27] Similarly, Matteo Palmieri, echoing Livy, argues that the Romans spread their rule by benefits rather than by fear, and that they not only subdued the whole world but also gave it "the most just laws (*giustissime leggi*)."[28] Giovanni Cavalcanti claims that justice had no lesser role in Rome's expansion than the size and the strength of its citizen army.[29] For Goro Dati, the fact that Rome in seven hundred years succeeded in subjugating most of the

cerca il dovere di ciascuno, l'altro per forza, quando con armi si combatte quale sia la potenzia magiore. El primo modo è proprio de gl'huomini, il secondo è in tutto bestiale et crudo; necessario è però ricorrere all'ultimo quando non si può usare il primo … "

[25] Ibid., pp. 104, 106, and 121: "La iusta victoria ancora ha dato poi posseditori alle vincte province" (p. 106). "Molte volti poi con minore atrocità s'è combattuto co' Volterrani, Pistolesi et Aretini, solo per discernere coll'armi in mano a chi la fortuna riserbi la signoria, onde poi vincti, sono stati preservati, et i Fiorentini solo contenti riserbarsi il titolo della loro signoria" (p. 121).

[26] Grendler, *The Trattato politico-morale of Giovanni Cavalcanti*, p. 116.

[27] De Rosa, *Coluccio Salutati*, p. 95: "ricordiamo che il popolo romano, grazie alla forza delle armi, ad un giusto impero ed alle sue splendide virtù, non sottomise in maniera servile tutto il mondo … ma lo governò con leggi eque nella dolcezza della libertà … "

[28] Palmieri, *Vita civile*, p. 127: "… et infine il loro amplissimo imperio tanto gloriosamente dilatorono, che grandissima parte de' navicabili mari et quasi tutta l'abitata terra divenne loro sottoposta, onde a tutto il mondo posono giustissime leggi …"; ibid., p. 129: "sempre cercorono più tosto con benificii che per paura et acrescere et ritenere lo imperio …" Cf. Livy, XXVI, 49.

[29] Grendler, *The Trattato politico-morale of Giovanni Cavalcanti*, p. 152: "… della ciptà di Roma, però ch'ella non ampliò meno per la giustitia che pella forza della multitudine de' militi."

known world was due in part to its "just proceedings (*giuste operazioni*)" and in part to its superior virtue, its good customs, and the assistance of God.[30] In Dati's mind, there could be no doubt that the worldwide empire the Romans acquired during the republic was just and divinely ordained.[31] Vespasiano da Bisticci, repeating the conventional view that "a republic cannot endure without justice," claimed that it was because the Romans "maintained justice" that their empire grew.[32] Toward the end of the fifteenth century, Girolamo Savonarola argued that one of the chief reasons the Romans could establish their world empire was their just rule, because God is in the habit of rewarding those who rule according to justice by increasing their dominion.

The celebration of Roman justice, far from being a mere literary topos or humanist convention, had also far-reaching consequences for the way the Florentines themselves conceived their republic and their collective destiny. The importance of the Roman legacy for Florentine self-understanding and self-fashioning can be witnessed most clearly in connection to Florence's prolonged war against the Visconti dukes of Milan at the turn of the fifteenth century. Defenders of the Florentine cause drew on the city's Roman heritage to justify its claim to act as the defender of Italian liberty and its right to exercise dominion over subject peoples. The most consistent and elaborate identification of modern Florence with the ancient Roman republic is found in Leonardo Bruni's *Laudatio*. According to Bruni, it was an indisputable fact of "utmost importance" that "the Florentine race arose from the Roman people,"[33] the most virtuous and glorious people ever to have existed. The right to lordship over the world, which God originally had bestowed upon the Romans, had now, Bruni proudly declared, been passed on to the Florentine republic. As a consequence, all Florentine wars must be regarded as legitimate and just, since they were either fought in defense

[30] Goro Dati's "Istoria di Firenze" has recently been republished in Antonio Lanza, *Firenze contra Milano: Gli intellettuali fiorentini nelle guerre con i Visconti (1390–1440)* (Rome: De Rubeis, 1991), pp. 211–300; quote from p. 261: "... quando i Romani, per ispazio di tempo di settecento anni, per loro virtù ed eccellenzia di giuste operazioni e per grazia di Dio soggiogata la maggiore parte di tutta l'universa terra." On the Romans: "... l'altro per lo esercizio della giustizia e di tutte le oneste virtù e buoni costumi che di principio avevano imparati in Toscana."
[31] Ibid., p. 261: "[...] i Romani, per ispazio di tempo di settecento anni, per loro virtù ed eccellenzia di giuste operazioni e per grazia di Dio ebbono soggiogata la maggiore parte di tutta l'universa terra [...]"
[32] Baldassarri and Saiber, *Images of Quattrocento Florence*, p. 65.
[33] Bruni, "Panegyric," p. 149.

16

of Florentine liberty or in order to regain land that belonged to the free Florentine people by "a certain hereditary right."[34]

The connection between Roman and Florentine justice is also prominent in the writings produced in the aftermath of the city's conquest of Pisa in 1406. Emphasizing Florence's love of liberty and Roman ancestry, Goro Dati insists that the Florentines had done everything in their power to ensure that the acquisition was made according to "the laws of the world (*le leggi del mondo*)."[35] They had sent out ambassadors who had been able to convince their neighbors and the rulers of the leading powers in the region that the enterprise was just and the purchase of the city legitimate.[36] For Dati, the conquest of Pisa must ultimately be seen as an act of divine providence since no acquisition is possible without the grace of God.[37] In Matteo Palmieri's chronicle in Latin of the Pisan War, *De captivitate Pisarum* (c. 1450), justice is defined according to the iron law of victory, which demands that the vanquished should obey the conqueror, who in turn should show mercy to the defeated and treat them with justice. Reiterating another Florentine commonplace, Palmieri maintains that the city's conquests have been just and for the good of its subject peoples, who can have no higher aspiration than the wish to participate in the spread of Florentine power. After the recovery of Pisa in 1509, the Gonfalonier Piero Soderini exhorted his compatriots in speech, reported by Bartolomeo Cerretani, to build on their victory and to continue to "make this republic and this empire great," which "cannot be done without the observance of justice."[38] As these examples show, the Roman notions of *libertas*, *imperium*, and *ius* served as important conceptual building blocks for Florentine republicans in their project of forging a conceptual identity for their city, fashioning it into a modern equivalent of its great ancestor, the ancient Roman republic.

How deeply entrenched the tie between justice and empire was in Florentine political imagination is suggested by the frequent inclusion

[34] Ibid., p. 150.
[35] Dati, "Istoria," p. 271: "... E tutto facevano i Fiorentini perché avevano la ragione secondo le leggi del mondo, ché volevano la loro possessione, la quale avevano comperata da colui di cui era di ragione ..."
[36] Ibid.: "... avevano i Fiorentini mandati loro ambasciadori a dimostrare la giusta impresa e compera legittima ..."
[37] Ibid., p. 238: "Puossi aggiugnere alla ragione naturale questo detto: che sia [per] divino giudicio, però che niuno bene si può acquistare sanza la grazia di Dio ... se genti sono al mondo dove queste virtù sieno, sono i Fiorentini ..." Cf. ibid., pp. 237 and 261.
[38] Bartolomeo Cerretani, *Storia fiorentina* (Florence: Olschki, 1994), pp. 380–381.

of empire among the fruits of justice in the highly conventional *protestationes de iustitia*. In one of the extant speeches, Simone Canigani extols justice as "the first principle of this flourishing empire" and exhorts the incoming magistrates to recall how much sweat, blood, toil, and danger their Florentine ancestors had had to endure in founding this empire (*inperio*) and in fighting for "the health of the patria."[39] Similarily, Filippo Pandolfini claims that the dictatorships of Sulla and Julius Caesar, and the subsequent fall of the Roman republic, show that justice is the only thing that "maintains, increases and exalts glorious empires and republics."[40] Bono Boni pushes the argument a step further by claiming that "the virtue of justice is a mean and a reason for expanding, governing and maintaining our republic." Boni goes on to celebrate the early Roman monarchy and the early republic for their devotion to justice, which had helped to make Rome "the queen of the world (*regina mundi*)."[41] This view is echoed by Francesco Rinuccini, who in his *protestatio* reminds us of how numerous countries, empires, and kingdoms have from small beginnings risen to become great and prosperous powers (*monarchie*) thanks to their commitment to justice. Yet again, the rise and fall of Rome serves as the admonishing lesson. As long as Rome was governed justly by its own citizens, it had continued to enjoy fame and glory and to prosper from its succession of victories, but as justice fell into neglect, it began to suffer calamities before finally being destroyed and completely devastated. As these examples suggest, the pairing of justice and empire was an integral part of the conventional political language of fifteenth-century Florence. Justice was not exclusively linked to liberty and the task of regulating the relations between citizens; it was also adduced to legitimate conquest, territorial growth, and the building of a growing and sustainable empire.

[39] Santini, "La *protestatio de iustitia*," 64: "... il primo principio di questo florentissimo inperio et reduciamci a memoria gli amirabili portamenti et excellentissime virtù de' primi auctori di quello, et vedremo quanti pericoli, quanti affanni sopportorono, quanto sudore, quanto sanghue sparsono per salute della patria."

[40] Ibid., 73: "... La qual cosa chiaramente si mostra che solo la iustitia è quella che mantiene, accresce et exalta gl'imperii gloriosi et rep[ubliche] ..."

[41] Ibid., 82: "Et secondo che universalmente affermano tutti gli autori sine summa iustitia respublica regi no posse et perché ella è virtù singulare, madre e regina di tutte l'altre, intendendo io la virtù della giustitia esser uno mezo e una chagione ad ampliare, regiere e mantenere la nostra replubicha, io intendo di quella brevemente tractare ..."; ibid., 83: "Inperò che, mentre che questa sacrosanta virtù della giustitia in quella monarchia rengniò, e dominarono e mari e lle terre e a tanta grandeza et exciellentia di istato divenne quella republicha mediante questa virtù della giustitia, che ella fu chiamata regina mundi, la reina del mondo; ma da poi che questa sacrosanta virtù fu isprezata, abattuta e vilipesa e la giustitia fu convertita in ingiustitia ..."

In short, justice belonged to both sides of Florentine republicanism, both to the language of liberty and to that of empire.

Before we attend to the question of why this conceptual framework based upon liberty, empire, and justice did not appeal to Machiavelli, there is another important aspect of the Florentine stance on justice and empire that needs to be addressed. As it would seem, the city's Roman identification inspired Florentine humanists to believe, or at least to claim, that Florentine justice was unique and attractive also to non-Florentines, and that many of the neighboring peoples looked upon the prospect of coming under Florentine rule with hope rather than apprehension. The general appeal of Florentine just rule had, during the Milanese wars, been an important aspect of Coluccio Salutati's defense of Florence's claim to exercise rightful dominion over its subject peoples. A similar view was expressed by Cino Rinuccini, who accused the Visconti dukes of ruling tyrannically and praised his compatriots for their benign, liberal, and most just way of treating their subject peoples.[42] An even more forceful evocation of Florentine justice is found in Leonardo Bruni's *Laudatio*, where we learn that "Florence not only protects its own citizens …, but it extends the same protection to foreigners." Justice is rendered to everyone, regardless of whether they are citizens or foreigners. No one is "allowed to suffer harm," and Florence "strives to ensure that each is given his due" (L 174). As a consequence, Florence has come to serve as a model of good and just government for other peoples as well.[43] This message continued to be broadcast throughout the fifteenth century, and if we are to believe Alamanno Rinuccini, writing in 1479, there had indeed been a time when the Florentine republic was "well known for justice, and men from distant countries brought cases to be tried in Florence."[44] But this vision could also be projected into the future, as when Girolamo Savonarola held out his promises for a new and glorious Florentine empire. In his *Treatise on the Constitution and Government of Florence* (1498), the Dominican friar discloses that after the Florentines have undergone their spiritual awakening and reformed their republic according to the principles of divine justice

---

[42] Cino Rinuccini, "Risponsiva alla Invettiva di messer Antonio Lusco," text in Lanza, *Firenze contra Milano*, pp. 187–197; quote from p. 190: "Viva viva il Comune di Firenze … Così benignamente, così liberamente, così giustamente viviamo coi nostri sudditi …"

[43] Bruni, "Panegyric," p. 124.

[44] Alamanno Rinuccini, "Liberty," text in English translation in *Humanism and Liberty: Writings on Freedom from Fifteenth-Century Florence*, ed. R. N. Watkins (Columbia: University of South Carolina Press), pp. 193–224, at p. 205.

good men, wanting to live where there is justice, will congregate there in great numbers. God, for justice also, will increase the city's empire, as he did that of the Romans. Because the Romans exercised strict and severe justice, He gave them imperial power over the whole world. He wanted justice to make his people righteous.[45]

In Savonarola's script for the future, Florence was to serve as a divine instrument of justice just as God in the past had used the Romans for similar ends. Attracted by Florentine justice and by the Florentine republic's elect status, he stated, neighboring peoples would seek its protection and welcome it as their overlord.

The conclusion to be drawn from this overview is that in the Florentine republican tradition the concepts of liberty, empire, and justice constitute such a close-knit unity that at times they appear to be used almost interchangeably. As we have seen, both empire and liberty are the so-called fruits of justice. However, justice can also be defined as the companion to republican liberty and as the consequence of a lasting and stable empire. Love of liberty is not merely defensive in character, but seeks its expression also in the pursuit of empire, while imperial expansion can be seen as a necessary precondition for the maintenance of liberty and the exercise of justice. The unity of the three concepts can also be said to reflect the general view of human nature that underlies this tradition. According to Florentine patriotic writers, man, or at least the citizen and the political man, is endowed with three natural desires. First, they argue that man has an inherent love of liberty, which, in the words of Salutati, is "completely natural" to him and, according to Alamanno Rinuccini, is natural not only to man but also to animals.[46] Second, they claim that it is in accordance with human nature to desire power, to acquire, to rise above others, to dominate, and to hold on to what one has conquered and regard it as one's own.[47] Third, they maintain that man has a natural inclination toward justice, or as Filippo Pandolfini puts it, we appear to have been born to "acquire and perform" this virtue.[48] In a similar vein, Salutati claims that "citizens in every popular republic desire justice, abhor theft

---

[45] Girolamo Savonarola, "Treatise on the Constitution and Government of Florence," text in English translation in Watkins, *Humanism and Liberty*, pp. 231–260, at p. 255.

[46] Baldassarri and Saiber, *Images of Quattrocento Florence*, p. 7; De Rosa, *Coluccio Salutati*, p. 92: "Tutti gli uomini, per natura, desiderano la libertà …"; Rinuccini, "Liberty," p. 200.

[47] Matteo Palmieri, *La presa di Pisa* (Naples: Mulino, 1995), p. 77.

[48] Santini, "La *protestatio de iustitia*," 69: "iniustamente et contro alla natura"; "apare l'uomo esere nato per acquistare et operare iustitia." See also ibid., 71.

and exalt the good," while Palmieri argues that all available sources – nature, human and divine law, ethical and theological writings – exhort us to act according to justice.[49] This would suggest that the conceptual unity of liberty, empire, and justice at the core of the humanist republic could be seen as an attempt to give political expression to an analogous unity of human desires rooted in the natural order of things. According to this tradition, the republic is, in other words, not to be conceived as an arbitrary creation or construct, but as a natural and rational ordering of desires.

To summarize our argument so far, the Florentine republican tradition was built around the general notion of liberty at home and empire abroad. Linked to this dual aim were two ideological vocabularies, one inward-looking, centered on liberty, and the other outward-oriented, clustered around the republic's quest for empire. Within this ideological framework, liberty and empire existed in a complementary but tense relationship, held together, on the one hand, by the paradigmatic example of the ancient Roman republic and, on the other, by the concept of justice, which, as we have seen, plays a crucial role in both the language of liberty and that of empire.

Having thus established that justice belongs to both sides of Florentine republicanism, we are now in a position to address the second problem raised at the beginning of this chapter. For if it is true that Machiavelli shared his Florentine predecessors' commitment to the dual objectives of liberty at home and empire abroad, as I have argued at great length elsewhere, we are faced with the question of why the author of *The Prince* and the *Discourses* did not also adopt their view of justice as the all-embracing and overarching principle holding these values and pursuits together. As we will see, Machiavelli had several weighty reasons for turning his back on the civic humanist tradition of combining liberty, empire, and justice.[50]

---

[49] Quoted from Ronald G. Witt, *Coluccio Salutati and His Public Letters* (Genève: Librairie Droz, 1976), p. 56 with slight adaptation; Palmieri, *Vita civile*, p. 199.

[50] The dominant scholarly view is that Machiavelli in his treatment of justice departs from the established conventions of medieval political thought and Renaissance republicanism. As Leo Strauss, Harvey Mansfield, and others have pointed out, there are no references to natural law or natural justice in Machiavelli. See Leo Strauss, "Three Waves of Modernity," in *Political Philosophy: Six Essays by Leo Strauss*, ed. H. Gildin (Indianapolis: Bobbs Merrill, 1975), p. 88; and Harvey Mansfield, *Machiavelli's Virtue* (Chicago: University of Chicago Press, 1996), pp. 21–22, 180–181, and 296. According to Mansfield, the objective of law in Machiavelli is to "secure order rather than justice" (p. 257) at the same time as fear in his theory "replaces justice as the ground for politics" (p. 303). Also, Quentin Skinner stresses Machiavelli's nonconformist position on justice.

To begin with, there are a number of general objections that Machiavelli could have raised against the humanist teaching of justice if he had chosen to challenge it head on. For the civic humanists the ideology of justice was intimately linked to the humanist program of classical learning, the *studia humanitatis*. Assuming that all men are rational and equally gifted with virtue, Renaissance humanists viewed liberal education, based on a combination of theoretical study and practical application, as the chief vehicle in their quest of human perfectibility. Leonardo Bruni articulates the general outlook underlying this program in the *Isagogue of Moral Philosophy* when he lays down the Aristotelian and Ciceronian doctrine of our natural receptivity to moral virtue: "we are, in a sense, naturally created with the potentiality for justice, fortitude, and liberality, but it is usage, training, and habituation that form us ... so that what by nature was disordered is in time made perfect by practice."[51] On the basis of such assumptions, Renaissance humanists developed a didactic and edifying discourse intent on persuading princes and rulers of republics that private goods should be subordinated to the public good, that the rule of justice is the most stable form of government, and that virtuous ends are best gained by virtuous means.[52] On the rare occasions when Machiavelli speaks of education, it is, for all we can tell, not this humanist ideal that he has in mind, but rather a form of mental and physical training designed to instill fear of God, military discipline, and strict obedience to the laws in citizens and subjects alike. In his work in general, and in *The Prince* and the *Discourses* in particular, the more than century-long classically inspired project to educate princes and republican magistrates in the art of justice is completely abandoned. As has often been observed, Machiavelli's break with this tradition went hand in hand with his

In Skinner's view, Machiavelli's notion of virtue involves the practice of only three of the conventional moral virtues: courage, temperance, and prudence. Justice, on the other hand, is excluded from the requirements and at times is even seen as an obstacle to the practice of virtue. On the basis of this observation, Skinner draws the conclusion that Machiavelli's virtue calls for "a willingness to discount the demands of justice" ("The Idea of Negative Liberty: Philosophical and Historical Perspectives," in *Philosophy in History: Essays on the Historiography of Philosophy*, ed. R. Rorty, J. B. Schneewind, and Q. Skinner [Cambridge: Cambridge University Press, 1984], pp. 193–221, at p. 216). A different view is taken by Anthony Parel, who argues that Machiavelli considers force, prudence, and justice to be "the foundations of the political order" ("Machiavelli's Notions of Justice: Text and Analysis," *Political Theory*, 18 [1990], 530–536, at 532). According to Parel, Machiavellian power politics, which largely operates outside or above the law, must be seen in relation to justice, since its aim is the creation of the conditions of positive law.

[51] G. Griffiths, J. Hankins, and D. Thompson, eds., *The Humanism of Leonardo Bruni*, p. 279.
[52] See, for example, Palmieri, *Vita civile*, pp. 65–66 and 132.

outright rejection of the humanist philosophy of man. For the Florentine
thinker, all men are *not* rational, human nature is diverse but fixed, and
virtue is *not* inherently persuasive. Consequently, the good man cannot
rest content with rational discourse and the teaching of virtue, but must
at times resort to other, more circumspect ways and venues to influence
those in power and the political community in general.

But Machiavelli had also other, more specific, reasons for dispensing
with the traditional linking of justice, liberty, and empire. In the following, we will concentrate on three aspects of this implied critique that
have a more direct bearing on Machiavelli's theory of empire. As we have
seen, justice was in the Florentine tradition considered to be the foundation upon which cities, republics, and kingdoms are erected. Machiavelli
repeats this traditional view in the preambles to his drafts for a new mili-
tia law of 1506, the *Cagione dell'ordinanza* and the *Provisioni della ordinanza*, where he argues that wherever power is exercised, the determining
factors are "justice and arms," and that all republics that have maintained
themselves and expanded have had as "their principal foundation two
things, that is, justice and arms."[53] Although Machiavelli here appears
to employ the conventional humanist language of justice, the meaning
he attaches to the term comes closer to that of the jurists, who tended
to equate justice with the rule of law and efficient legal procedure, as in
the expressions "to do justice *(fare giustitia)*" and "the administration
of justice *(l'administratione della giustitia)*."[54] This shift in significance
clearly anticipates his later treatment of the foundation of states in the
theoretical works, where he disposes of justice altogether by substituting
for it good laws. For example, in *The Prince* he claims that "good arms
(buone arme)" in combination with "good laws *(buone legge)*" serve as
the foundations of all states. Laws are subordinated to arms since there
"cannot be good laws where there are no good arms, and where there
are good arms there must be good laws."[55] Apart from a brief passage
based on Polybius, justice is in the *Discourses* completely omitted from
Machiavelli's extensive discussions on the foundations of states in general
and on the founding of Rome in particular.[56] Rome had not been founded

---

[53] Niccolò Machiavelli, *Opere*, 3 vols., ed. C. Vivanti (Turin: Einaudi, 1997–2005), I, pp. 26
and 31.

[54] Quoted from Gilbert, "Florentine Political Assumptions," 212. In the *Discourses* III.49,
Machiavelli refers to justice in this sense when he claims that the ancient Romans could
order the execution of a whole legion "per via di giustizia." See *Opere*, I, p. 524.

[55] *Il principe* 12, quoted from Machiavelli, *Opere*, I, p. 150.

[56] In the *Discorsi* I.2, Machiavelli gives a subtle twist to Polybius's account of the birth of
the notion of justice (Polybius, VI, 6, 6–7). While Polybius seems to place the origin of

on justice, but on Romulus's most unjust and cruel fratricide, which, in Machiavelli's view, had been necessary because founders must always act alone in order to gain sole authority over their subjects. Other prudent founders like Moses, Lycurgus, and Solon introduced laws conducive to the common good, but nowhere does Machiavelli let us believe that these laws were just or even aspired to justice. This shift from justice to law is highly significant, since good laws, in Machiavelli's understanding, do not, at least not necessarily, entail justice. Laws are "good (*buone*)" when they are effective in compelling obedience, in preserving the liberty of the republic, and in promoting future expansion.[57] Justice does not enter into the equation, at least not at this stage.

Second, Machiavelli must, in the light of the recent rebellions in the Florentine dominion, have had little patience with claims of Florentine justice being a model and an ideal for neighboring cities queuing up to seek the protection of the republic on the Arno.[58] In his view, back in the fourteenth century, Florence had had the opportunity to strengthen its power base in Tuscany by adopting a policy of friendship, humanity, and liberality in relation to its neighbors. Instead, the republic had adopted a shortsighted policy of half-measures, including broken promises, inconclusive wars, and halfhearted punishments, which had won it few friends and many enemies. The conquest of Pisa in 1406 had not become the hoped-for springboard to further expansion, and the ill-conceived wars of the 1410s and the 1420s had put enormous strains on the city's economy without yielding any concrete benefits. In 1430 Florence attacked the neighboring city of Lucca, but was forced to settle for peace without having achieved the subjugation of its neighbor. Lucca had under the first Medicean regime (1434–1494) continued to be an impediment to Florentine aspirations, and in 1479 Alamanno Rinuccini could write that the city had "seemed like a dragon that annually devoured Florentine money and blood."[59] At the time Machiavelli took office as secretary of the Second Chancery in 1498, the effects of Florence's failure to pursue a

---

justice in the judgment of the ruler, who in the eyes of the people will come to appear like a true king, Machiavelli relates how justice developed out of the subjects' partisan support for their benefactor (*benifactore*). In Machiavelli's account there is no question of the ruler's judgment being just. Instead, the idea of justice seems to follow from self-interest, fear of injuries, obedience, gratitude, and the need for institutionalized protection against evils (*male*). See Machiavelli, *Opere*, I, p. 204.

[57] Cf. Mansfield, *Machiavelli's Virtue*, pp. 256–257 and 312.

[58] In the *Cagione dell'ordinanza* of 1506, Machiavelli had actually claimed that Florence currently was almost devoid of justice. See Machiavelli, *Opere*, I, pp. 26–27.

[59] Rinuccini, "Liberty," in *The Earthly Republic*, p. 208.

grand imperial strategy had begun to show. The French invasion of Italy in 1494, which came to mark the beginning of the Italian Wars, brought sixty years of Medicean rule and almost ninety years of Florentine domination over Pisa to an abrupt end. The Florentine dominion was in a state of turmoil, and as fighting broke out in Pistoia and rebellions began in Arezzo and the Valdichiana region, the crisis deepened. Although the uprisings were quenched and Pisa was regained in 1509, the political landscape had undergone a dramatic change that had fundamentally altered the position of Florence vis-à-vis its neighbors. In Machiavelli's view, the new situation meant that there could no longer be any question of Florence winning over its neighbors through friendly and peaceful means. The only imperial strategy now remaining for Florence in relation to its unruly dominion, he insinuates in the *Discourses*, is direct rule and an undisguised form of repression designed to once and for all stamp the republic's authority on willing and unwilling subjects alike.[60]

This brings us to Machiavelli's third point of disagreement with his Florentine predecessors: the question of just means. In the humanist teaching on justice, the belief that good or just means are conducive to good ends plays a central role. This doctrine, which is at the core of the humanist moral treatise, the republican orations on justice as well as the mirror-for-princes genre, is clearly stated by Petrarch when he, in his *speculum principis* addressed to Francesco of Carrara, ruler of Padua, quotes Cicero's *De officiis*: "Nothing can be useful that is not at the same time just and honorable."[61] Matteo Palmieri agrees with this view by claiming that there exists a "subtle science (*sottile scientia*)" that teaches that the honorable and the useful are so linked together that they cannot be separated.[62]

While Machiavelli would hardly have denied that arguments that portray unjust and tyrannical methods as self-defeating might be rhetorically

---

[60] On Machiavelli's view of Florentine republicanism, see Hörnqvist, *Machiavelli and Empire*, pp. 113–147.

[61] Francesco Petrarch, "How a Ruler Ought to Govern His State," in *The Earthly Republic*, pp. 25–78, at p. 63. Cf. Marcia L. Colish, "Cicero's *De Officiis* and Machiavelli's *Prince*," *Sixteenth Century Journal*, 9 (1978), 81–93, at 89.

[62] Palmieri, *Vita civile*, p. 63: "l'honesto et l'utile essere insieme coniuncti, né potersi in alcuno modo dividere." It is worth noting that both Petrarch and Palmieri in this connection bring up the so-called Scipio's Dream, the *Somnium Scipionis*, from Cicero's *De republica*, according to which God has reserved a special place in heaven for rulers who have dutifully served their fatherland and ruled in justice. See Petrarch, "How a Ruler Ought to Govern His State," in *The Earthly Republic*, p. 41; and Palmieri, *Vita civile*, pp. 54–55.

effective and fulfill the purpose of discouraging republican magistrates and princes from unnecessarily oppressing their people, he would nonetheless have objected that the premises underlying this view are false. In this criticism, he could have expected conditional support from Christian theologians, who were equally aware of the fact that in this lowly world good acts are not always rewarded, while evil deeds often go unpunished. But whereas the Christian tradition solved this dilemma with the promise of justice meted out by God in the afterlife, chastising wrongdoers and bestowing eternal bliss on the righteous, Machiavelli's this-worldly philosophy offers no such assurances. If there is justice to be had, it must be of human making. The Florentine addresses the conflict between means and ends on several occasions in his work. In the famous chapter 15 of *The Prince*, he states that princely prudence consists in part of realizing that a ruler at times must embrace the vices, since good, or allegedly good, means may lead to his ruin, while evil, or seemingly evil, means could result in his security and well-being. In the *Discourses* 1.18, he puts the quandary in slightly different terms as he argues that reforming a corrupt republic requires the unlikely combination of either a good man (*uomo buono*) who makes himself prince by evil means (*vie cattive*) or an evil man (*uomo cattivo*) who, after having seized power, uses his authority for good ends (*operare bene*). Although Machiavelli never explicitly discusses the separation of the honorable and the useful, the good and the effective, in relation to the unity of liberty and empire under justice, it is evident that his demystification of Palmieri's "subtle science" must have far-reaching consequences for the doctrine of the republic's two ends. If justice is to be seen as only one of many instruments for maintaining liberty and achieving empire, and at times even is judged to stand in the way of this pursuit, the conceptual triad of liberty, empire, and justice is bound to dissolve.

But if justice cannot perform its traditional role as the mean or the unifying element holding the contrasting ends of liberty and empire together, what, if anything, can take its place? Or, put differently, what strategies does Machiavelli propose for controlling or balancing the potentially conflictual relationship between liberty and empire? And is there, his rejection of the humanist teaching on justice notwithstanding, still a place for justice in his theory?

To approach an understanding of Machiavelli's position on justice, we should begin by taking a closer look at the underpinnings of his theory of the republic's dual pursuit of liberty and empire. According to the Florentine thinker there exist, broadly speaking, two categories of men or two humors (*umori*), those who desire not to be oppressed, but to live free, and those who want to command and dominate others. The former group Machiavelli calls the "people" (*popolo*) and the latter the "great" (*grandi*).[63] How are these contrasting desires, or appetites (*appetiti*), to be satisfied or accommodated? The answer offered by Florentine republicanism, but never explicitly stated, is to guarantee the liberty of the people while opening up the road to empire and to glorious military undertakings for the great. This would result in a divided republic consisting of, on the one hand, inward-looking liberty lovers and, on the other, expansive and outward-looking glory seekers. These two groups, or humors, are obviously opposite, and they correspond neatly to the republic's two ends as well as to the two ideological vocabularies identified at the beginning of this chapter. However, viewed from a different standpoint, they are remarkably similar. Exclusively focused on one, and only one, of the republic's two ends, they are both too self-absorbed to perceive anything beyond their own immediate concerns and too fiercely partisan to care about the common good of the republic. Viewed from this angle, both parties reveal themselves as single-minded, self-interested, shortsighted, and one-dimensional. Their struggle for hegemony knows no compromises, and their inability to see the bigger picture causes them to define the republic exclusively in terms of liberty or empire, respectively. Consequently, there is an imperative need to balance the interests of these two potentially destabilizing forces and to keep them in check.

However, in focusing on the people and the great, we should not forget about a third category of citizens, whom Machiavelli seems to exempt from his division of the republic into two contrasting humors: the *prudenti*, or the prudent ones. This group, or category, does not only figure prominently in the *Discourses*; it could also be argued that this work as a whole is written from the viewpoint of the *prudente* and with the intent of imparting this perspective to its readers. In his analysis of the constitutional development and the expansion of the ancient Roman republic, Machiavelli rises above the partisan bickering of the great and the people, the few and the many, and takes a critical view of the quest for empire and the love of liberty. Warning that cities that "live free" tend to err either out of excessive thirst for acquisitions or out of too much love of liberty, he argues that the great have a propensity to engage in overambitious expansionist projects, overextending the republic's resources, while the people, anxious to maintain their freedom, are liable to reward unworthy men

---

[63] *Il principe* 9 and *Discorsi* I.4; *Opere*, I, pp. 143–146, 208–210.

and to distrust the virtuous, paving the way for corruption and tyranny.[64] It could be argued that Machiavelli here is speaking neither as a partisan of liberty nor as a champion of empire, but as a *prudente*.

The desire of the prudent man cannot be reduced to either liberty or empire. Instead, it would appear, it is directed at something resembling the common good. The task of the *prudenti*, as Machiavelli conceives it, is to balance the republic's two interests and aspirations, love of liberty and the pursuit of empire, but the balance sought after here differs sharply from the conventional Aristotelian doctrine of the mean, so dear to the Florentine civic humanists. In Machiavelli's view, virtue is not the mean between two extremes or vices, but consists instead in the capacity to use both extremes and the ability to combine and encompass them. Therefore, the prudent man cannot limit himself to act only on the "good" side of the ethical scale, but must also be able and willing to "enter into evil (*entrare nel male*)" when the gravity of the circumstances so requires.[65] His role is to mobilize the two parties, the people and the great, by exploiting their natural inclinations, turning the great's desire for domination outward toward the republic's external end – growth, acquisition, and glory – while placing the people in charge of guarding the liberty of the republic, curbing the tyrannical impulse of the great.[66] As we have begun to see, then, in Machiavelli's theory it is the virtue of prudence, and not that of justice, that takes on the role of binding liberty and empire together. Not being a partisan of either the people or the great, of either liberty or empire, the prudent man, it could be argued, is the only member of the Machiavellian republic who acts for the common good.

Where does this leave us with regard to Machiavelli's view of justice? Is it meaningful to speak of justice in connection to his theory? The answer must be a qualified yes and no. As we have seen, Machiavelli turns his back on the traditional view of justice as the foundation of states, replacing it with good arms and good, or functional, laws. Nor is there any room in his theory for justice as a standard by which laws can

---

[64] Machiavelli, *Discorsi* I.29: "Perché, avendo una città che vive libera duoi fini, l'uno lo acquistare, l'altro il mantenersi libera, conviene che nell'una cosa e nell'altra per troppo amore erri." Quoted from Machiavelli, *Opere*, I, p. 262.

[65] *Il principe* 18. Quoted from Machiavelli, *Opere*, I, p. 166.

[66] On the people as guardians of republican liberty, see John P. McCormick, "Machiavellian Democracy: Controlling Elites with Ferocious Populism," *American Political Science Review*, 95 (2001), 297–313. Cf. Mansfield, *Machiavelli's Virtue*, pp. 82–99; and J. G. A. Pocock, *The Machiavellian Moment: Florentine Political Thought and the Atlantic Tradition* (Princeton, N.J.: Princeton University Press, 1975), pp. 196–198.

be judged. Laws are either good or bad, depending on to what extent they serve the interest of liberty and contribute to the imperial aspirations of the republic. In this dual project, justice cannot provide an appropriate guide to what means should be employed, since allegedly good or just means are bound at times to have detrimental effects on liberty and at times to stand in the way of well-considered expansionist designs. So, where does justice enter into the picture?

From what has emerged in this study, it should be clear that in Machiavelli's republican theory, justice has no place at the beginning or during the process leading up to the establishment of world rule by a hegemonic republic similar to the ancient Roman republic. However, this leaves the possibility of justice, or a political order embodying justice, being the outcome or the end product of the previously mentioned process. Although Machiavelli never addresses this issue or explicitly considers the possibility, there are in his work implications pointing in this direction. On one of the rare occasions when the Florentine thinker brings up justice in the *Discourses*, he offers us a picture, or perhaps a marble relief, to contemplate. In a passage that has not received sufficient scholarly attention, the former secretary paints or sculpts what could be seen as a literary equivalent to Ambrogio Lorenzetti's frescoes of Good Government and Bad Government in the Sala dei Nove in the Palazzo Pubblico in Siena. The beholder who contemplates the image of the good times when virtuous emperors ruled

will see a prince secure in the midst of his secure citizens, and the world full of peace and justice (*ripieno di pace e di giustizia il mondo*); he will see the Senate with its authority, the magistrates with their honors, the rich citizens enjoying their wealth, nobility and virtue exalted, he will see every quiet and every good; and on the other side, every rancor, every license, corruption and ambition extinct; he will see golden ages (*tempi aurei*) in which everyone may hold and defend whatever opinion he wishes. In the end, he will see the world in triumph: the prince full of reverence and glory, the people full of love and security.[67]

Since this passage appears in a chapter in which Julius Caesar is condemned and Marcus Junius Brutus praised, it should definitely not be

---

[67] *Discorsi* I.10: "Perché in quelli governati da' buoni vedrà un principe sicuro in mezzo de' suoi sicuri cittadini, ripieno di pace e di giustizia il mondo: vedrà il senato con la sua autorità, i magistrati co' suoi onori; godersi i cittadini ricchi le loro ricchezze, la nobilità e la virtú esaltata, vedrà ogni quiete ed ogni bene; e, dall'altra parte, ogni rancore, ogni licenza, corruzione e ambizione spenta: vedrà i tempi aurei, dove ciascuno può tenere e difendere quella opinione che vuole. Vedrà, in fine, trionfare il mondo, pieno di riverenza e di gloria il principe, d'amore e sicurtà i popoli." Quoted from Machiavelli, *Opere*, I, p. 227.

interpreted as a defense of the Principate, but rather seen as a portrait of the city of Rome enjoying the fruits of the conquests made under the republic. This is the ancient Roman Empire at the height of its power before corruption came to permeate its whole social fabric, weakening the authority of the Senate and marking the end of Roman *libertas*. As it would seem, Machiavelli is here turning Aristotelian and Ciceronian republicanism on its head. Instead of liberty and empire being seen as the fruits of justice, it is the latter category that is defined as the fruit of the prudential strategy of combining the maintenance of liberty and the quest for empire. Instead of being the foundation of the republic or the standard by which political means can be judged, justice would thus turn out to be the result, or to use Machiavelli's own terms, the effect, or *effetto*, of this process. Since the ancient Romans had achieved this full cycle of power, there was in Machiavelli's view no reason why the modern Florentines would not be able to accomplish the same result. But to enter the process at the end of which a world "full of peace and justice" awaits them, Machiavelli's compatriots would have had to forget about justice and begin to practice prudence.

2

Conquest and the Just War

The "School of Salamanca" and the "Affair of the Indies"

Anthony Pagden

THE CATHOLIC MONARCHY

There never was, in either name or fact, a *Spanish* empire. There was, of course, the Holy Roman Empire, whose emperor was, for a while, also the king of the separate kingdoms of Spain. There was, too, for some three centuries a vast sprawling mass of territory spanning the Atlantic and Pacific oceans that was ruled over by a ruler in Castile. This was generally referred to as the "Spanish Monarchy" (at a time, it should be said, when the word "monarch" carried the implication of universal kingship). Between 1580 and 1648, when the kingdoms of the Iberian Peninsula were under one ruler, there was the "*Monarquía católica*," the most extensive political unit the world had ever seen, which reached from Messina to Macao and where, as the Spanish poet Bernardo de Balbuena, nicely phrased it in 1604, "Spain is joined to China, and Italy to Japan."[1]

On occasion, the kings of Castile and of Aragon (and sometimes also the kings of Portugal) assumed universalist poses, styling themselves – or at least allowing themselves to be addressed as – "lords of Christendom" or, less modestly, as "lords of all the world." There was even a rumor, spread by the Venetian ambassador in 1563, that Philip II proposed to have himself made "Emperor of the Americas" to compensate for the fact that his father had failed to secure for him succession to the Holy Roman Empire.[2] But Philip never took the initiative in any of this, and nothing ever came of it.

---

[1] Serge Gruzinski, *Les quatres parties du monde: Histoire d'une mondialisation* (Paris: Editions de la Martinière, 2004), p. 49
[2] See Anthony Pagden, *Lords of All the World: Ideologies of Empire in Spain, Britain and France c. 1500–c. 1800* (New Haven, Conn., and London: Yale University Press, 1995), p. 32.

This conglomerate, or "composite monarchy," over which the Hapsburgs and later the Bourbons ruled, and which has since the late eighteenth century been referred to as the "Spanish empire," was sustained imaginatively as the embodiment of the person – the *persona ficta* – of the monarch himself. But powerful though this unitary image clearly was, and despite such projects as the Count Duke of Olivares's "Union of Arms" of the 1620s, no Spanish monarch before Charles III ever made any sustained attempt to mold the various culturally heterogeneous realms of which the monarchy was composed into anything resembling the single unitary state, the *état unifié* that Louis XIV had attempted to impose upon France. The monarch himself acted as an agent of distribution and communal justice rather than as the undisputed political authority, and despite the centralizing efforts by successive Castilian rulers from Philip II to Charles III, constitutionally the monarchy more often resembled a federation of quasi-independent states than a single legally undivided *imperium*. As the diplomat Diego Saavedra Fajardo observed in 1639, what Spanish jurists liked to refer to as "provinces" (*provincias*) were in fact what in other regions of Europe were more properly designated "nations" (*naciones*) or "kingdoms" (*reinos*).[3] This was, of course, particularly true of the European dominions. Naples and Sicily remained sovereign kingdoms – as indeed did Aragon – Milan an independent duchy, and the Netherlands a conglomerate of counties and principalities. When in 1539 the great Dominican theologian Francisco de Vitoria – to whom I shall return – in a lecture on the origins of civil power wished to provide his audience with examples of what the Aristotelians called "perfect communities" – those, that is, that were politically self-sufficient – he chose as his example "Castile, Aragon, and other of their like" – one of which was Venice.[4] Even the Americas, although formally incorporated in the crown of Castile in 1523, enjoyed a large measure of independent political authority and were invariably described, before the late eighteenth century, when the word "colony," borrowed from the English, began to creep into the official discourse as "Kingdoms of the Indies," *Reinos de*

[3] *Empresas politics: Idea de un príncipe político-cristiano*, ed. A. Vaquero (Madrid: Editorial nacional, 1976), pp. 75–76.
[4] *De iure belli*, 1.2., in Francisco de Vitoria, *Vitoria Political Writings*, ed. Anthony Pagden and Jeremy Lawrance (Cambridge: Cambridge University Press, 1991), p. 301. All future references will be to this edition. The best available version of the Latin texts of Vitoria's *relectiones* is to be found in *Francisco de Vitoria Vorlesungen: Völkerrecht Politik Kirche*, ed. Ulrich Horst, Heinz-Gerhard Justenhoven, and Joachim Stüben, 2 vols. (Stuttgart: Kolhammer, 1997).

Indias. Charles V listed them separately among his many titles, and from 1680 they were governed by a separate code of laws.[5]

It was, of course, these *Reinos de Indias* that presented the most persistent (although by no means the only) ideological problem to their Spanish rulers. From 1511, when a Dominican named Antonio de Montesinos delivered a sermon to the incredulous settlers of the island of Hispaniola, in which he condemned them for violating the humanity and the rights of the Indians, until the late seventeenth century, a debate raged in Spain over the legitimacy of the "conquest" of America. The most original contributors to this debate were a group of theologians who have come to be known as the "Second Scholastic" or, more parochially, as the "School of Salamanca." These were, for the most part, the pupils, and the pupils of the pupils – from Domingo de Soto (1494–1560), Vitoria's successor in the Prime Chair of Theology at Salamanca, to the great Jesuit metaphysician Francisco Suárez (1548–1600) – of Francisco de Vitoria, who held the Prime Chair of Theology at Salamanca between 1526 and his death in 1546. Although they are often described vaguely as "theologians and jurists," they were all, in fact, theologians.[6] The discussion of the Roman law played a large role in their work, and their influence can be seen in particular in canon lawyers such as Diego Covarrubias y Leyva (1512–1567) and in the civil lawyer Fernando Vázquez de Menchaca (1512–1569).[7] But jurists were members of a distinct and, in the opinion of most theologians, inferior faculty. In the early modern world, theology, the "mother of sciences," because it dealt directly with first causes, was considered to be above all other modes of inquiry, and covered everything that belongs to what today is called "jurisprudence," as well as most of moral and political philosophy and what would later become the human sciences.[8]

---

[5] The *Nueva Recopilación de leyes de los reynos de las Indias*, compiled by the jurist Juan Solórzano y Pereira in the 1650s but only printed in 1680 after his death.

[6] Antony Anghie, for instance, describes Vitoria as a "theologian and jurist," as did the great James Brown Scott, the international lawyer who was responsible for the revival of interest in the School of Salamanca in the Anglophone world in the early twentieth century and for the reedition of many of their works. Antony Anghie, *Imperialism, Sovereignty and the Making of International Law* (Cambridge: Cambridge University Press, 2005), p. 13.

[7] See Annabel Brett, *Liberty, Right and Nature* (Cambridge: Cambridge University Press, 1997), p. 245. "Vázquez should be read neither in isolation from, nor as a continuation of, the School of Salamanca, but rather as a positive response to its achievements, and particularly to that of Soto."

[8] See the discussion in Francisco Suárez, *Tractatus de legibus ac Deo Legislatore* [1612], 8 vols., ed. Luciano Pereña (Madrid : CSIC, 1971), I, pp. 2–8.

Their involvement in the struggle over what Vitoria called the "affair of the Indies" had a wide and long-lasting resonance, sufficient even for that staunch anti-imperialist, Dr. Samuel Johnson, to remark as late as 1763: "I love the university of Salamanca, for when the Spaniards were in doubt as to the lawfulness of their conquering America, the University of Salamanca gave it as their opinion that it was not lawful."[9] Johnson was being overenthusiastic. The University of Salamanca never went that far. But on occasion, some of its members came perilously close.

The Scholastics' denial of the initial lawfulness of the conquest of America might also seem starkly incongruous with what we know of the actual practice of the Spanish in America. Certainly none of the arguments against colonization and settlement expressed by the School of Salamanca had much direct impact on colonial practice or even on colonial legislation. The two major acts of legislation covering the new settlements in the Americas, the Laws of Burgos of 1513 and the far more radical New Laws of 1542 (which the Council of the Indies largely repealed in 1545 rather than face a full-scale settler revolt), were aimed at limiting the abuses of the settlers and, more importantly for the crown, at curbing their territorial rights. They never raised in any explicit manner the question of the legitimacy of the occupation itself. Nor did anyone ever seriously propose that the Spanish should actually withdraw from the Americas, although a number of the settlers in Mexico appear to have believed that Charles V was seriously contemplating such a move.[10] The arguments of Vitoria and his successors were moral ones, and as Vitoria himself knew full well, rulers rarely did or indeed could act on moral principle alone. All kings, he once told a correspondent, are driven to think "from hand to mouth."[11] Politics was always, and necessarily, a pragmatic affair. Theology and philosophy should be confined to professional discourse. "I sometimes think how very foolish it is for one of my kind to think, let alone speak, about government and public affairs," he once wrote. "It seems to me even more absurd than a grandee pronouncing on our philosophies."[12] Yet there is something disingenuous in

[9] *Boswell's Life of Johnson*, ed. G. B. Hill, 2 vols. (Oxford: Oxford University Press, 1934), I, p. 45

[10] See Anthony Pagden, "Dispossessing the Barbarian: The Language of Spanish Thomism and the Debate over the Property Rights of the American Indians," in *The Languages of Political Theory in Early Modern Europe*, ed. Anthony Pagden (Cambridge: Cambridge University Press, 1987), pp. 79–98.

[11] "Letter to Bernardino de Vique," Vitoria, *Vitoria Political Writings*, p. 334.

[12] "Letter to Pedro Fernández de Velasco," ibid., p. 337.

this disclaimer. The theologians may have seen their role as that of moral advisers, but the range of topics on which the various members of the School of Salamanca gave their advice was very wide indeed. Vitoria was asked about the justice of the Portuguese slave trade, the validity of clandestine marriages, and the legitimacy of increasing the price of corn during a poor harvest, to name but a few. Melchor Cano (1509–1560) advised Philip II in his struggle with Pope Paul IV and was even consulted on how best to defend the Canary Islands against attacks by French pirates. Some – Vitoria himself, Cano, and Domingo de Soto – were taken away for long periods from their lecture halls to become diplomats (Soto was a member of the Spanish delegation at the Council of Trent), diplomats and councilors, or members of that select body of spiritual-cum-political advisers, the royal confessors.

It was, however, their views on the legitimacy of their sovereign's conquest of the Americas and, more broadly, on the nature of the polity that has come to be called the Spanish Empire for which they were best known by later generations. Carl Schmitt's claim that during the "four hundred years from the sixteenth to the twentieth centuries" the entire course of European international law (*Völkerrecht*) had been "determined by a fundamental course of events; conquest of a new world," may be an exaggeration.[13] It is evident, however, that the debate over the legitimacy of the conquest of the first of these "new worlds" did mark a decisive turn in the development of what would later come to be called "international law." It is also the case that Vitoria's discussion over what today would be called "sovereignty" was to have lasting influence on later understanding of universal rights and on the relationship between "civilized" and "uncivilized" societies.

ON CONQUEST AND INTERVENTION

The debate that lasted on and off from 1511 until the early seventeenth century was initially, as Francisco de Vitoria phrased it, an attempt to find an answer to the question "By what right (*ius*) were the barbarians subjected to Spanish rule?"[14] By asking this question in the first place, Vitoria

[13] *The Nomos of the Earth in the International Law of the Jus Publicum Europaeum*, trans. and ed. G. L. Umen (New York: Telos Press, 2003), p. 69. I have modified the translation slightly. See "L'impérialisme entre inclusion exclusive et exclusion inclusive: Carl Schmitt lecteur de Vitoria," in Christian Lazzeri and S. Nour, eds., *Reconnaissance, identité et intégration sociale* (Nanterre: Presses Universitaires de Paris Ouest, 2009), pp. 339–359.
[14] "On the American Indians," I, Introduction, Vitoria, *Vitoria Political Writings*, p. 233.

was also, as he seems to have been aware, raising a far wider, and for his royal master potentially far more damaging, doubt about the nature and the possible legitimacy not only of the Spanish monarchy in the Americas but of all empires everywhere.[15] He was also raising questions about what right, if any, a state had to make war against another state that had not caused it any direct harm. More generally, Vitoria pointed to issues that have still not been resolved about the right of any people to impose upon others what it believes to be the natural rights of all humankind or to intervene in affairs of another state in the defense of those whom it believes to be oppressed.

The key term, as Dr. Johnson had seen, was "conquering." For most of the other Habsburg possessions that had been acquired either through dynastic succession – "Tu felix Austria nube," as the saying went – or, in the case of Charles V's acquisition of Milan, by the assertion of imperial titles that had long been neglected.[16] America, however, was another place altogether. It clearly, despite ingenious attempts to prove that it had once been occupied by stranded Carthaginian sailors, had never formed part of the ancient Roman Empire – whose legitimate heirs the Holy Roman Emperors claimed to be – nor could any of its territories, unlike much of the Middle East, be said to be a part of the Christian world fallen into infidel hands. The Indians, in Vitoria's words, "were previously unknown to our world."[17] Whatever else they might be, they could clearly not, therefore, be "subjects by human [civil] law."[18]

The Spanish occupation of what was before 1492 a wholly unknown landmass had been the outcome of what, in particular after Hernán Cortés's seizure of the "empire" of Montezuma in 1519–1521, had been a highly publicized conquest. The word, as we shall see, caused the Spanish crown, as it was later to cause the English, considerable legal anxiety.[19] For all the triumphalism involved, the studious comparison with ancient

---

[15] "It may first of all be objected that *this whole dispute is unprofitable and fatuous* not only for those like us who have no warrant to question or censure the conduct of government in the Indies irrespective of whether or not it is rightly administered, but even for those whose business it is to frame and administer their government." "On the American Indians," I, Introduction, Vitoria, *Vitoria Political Writings*, pp. 233–234.

[16] *Bella gerant alii, tu felix Austria nube* ("Let others wage wars. You, happy Austria, marry").

[17] "On the American Indians," I, Introduction, Vitoria, *Vitoria Political Writings*, p. 233.

[18] Ibid., p. 238.

[19] For the English case, see Anthony Pagden, "Law, Colonization, Legitimation, and the European Background," in *The Cambridge History of Law in America*, vol. 1, ed. Michael Grossberg and Christopher L. Tomlins (Cambridge: Cambridge University Press, 2008), pp. 1–31.

Rome demonstrated that a "conquest" could only be justified if it were the outcome of a just war.[20] Such a war conferred upon the aggressor a right to wage war – the *ius ad bellum* – and was governed by a set of agreements about how the war should be conducted and the benefits that the victor was entitled to derive from it – the *ius in bello*.[21] In general, the Roman jurists had maintained that war could only be just if it was waged defensively and in pursuit of compensation for some alleged act of aggression against either the Romans themselves or their allies. "The best state," Cicero observed, "never undertakes war except to keep faith or in defense of its safety."[22] War was thus only a means of punishing an aggressor and of seizing compensation for damages suffered. Wars, said St. Augustine, in one of the most frequently cited passages on the subject

are just which revenge the injuries caused when the nation or *civitas* with which war is envisaged has either neglected to make recompense for illegitimate acts committed by its members, or to return what has been injuriously taken.[23]

How could such conditions possibly apply to wars against a distant people who had manifestly caused no harm to any European prior to their arrival and then had only apparently acted in self-defense? One possible answer was that, for some reason, they had not been in legitimate public and private possession of the territories they occupied before the Europeans arrived, in which case their lands might be considered "empty." The Indians' refusal to make way for the Spanish would then constitute grounds for a just war under the law of nature.

If this argument were to apply, it would have to be shown that *either* the Indians were in some sense less than fully human (or fully adult), in which case they could not be said to be true masters either of themselves or of their goods, *or* that, although both fully human and fully adult, they

[20] For the comparison with Rome, see the remarkable study by David A. Lupher, *Romans in a New World: Classical Models in Sixteenth-Century Spanish America* (Ann Arbor: University of Michigan Press, 2003).
[21] See, in general, S. Albert, *Bellum Iustum*, Frankfurter Althistorische Studien 10 (Kallmünz: Lassleben, 1980); Frederick H. Russell, *The Just War in the Middle Ages* (Cambridge: Cambridge University Press, 1975); and Jonathan Barnes, "The Just War," in *Cambridge History of Later Medieval Philosophy*, ed. Norman Kretzmann, Anthony Kenny, and Jan Pinborg (Cambridge: Cambridge University Press, 1982), pp. 775–778.
[22] *De Republica* 3.34.
[23] *Quaestionum in Heptateuchem*, VI. X. and cf. "War should be waged only as a necessity, and waged only that God may by it deliver men from necessity and preserve them in peace. For peace is not sought in order to kindle war, but war is waged in order that peace may be secured.... So it should be necessity, not desire, that destroys the enemy in battle." Epist. 189.6 [to Bonifatius], *Patrologia latina*, XXXIII, col. 856.

had somehow failed to fulfill the necessary conditions by which human beings were believed to acquire ownership over land.[24] In the first case, they would have to be either mad or in some other way irrational. It is under this heading that perhaps the most contentious attempt to deny the Indians their natural rights – Aristotle's theory of natural slavery – was introduced. A "natural" slave is one who, rather than being defined by his legal status, is defined by his psychological identity, since he is one who, contrary to the norm, possesses no independent autonomous self and thus lacks the capacity for deliberation or moral choice.[25] He is said to be capable of understanding but incapable of practical wisdom (*phronesis*), for "practical wisdom issues commands … but understanding only judges."[26] What this meant for Aristotle was that the slave was a kind of useful automaton – "almost an animated instrument of service," as Saint Thomas Aquinas said later[27] – and literally a "living but separate part of his master's frame."[28] Slaves are, for Aristotle, a feature of the natural world and a necessary requirement for the proper functioning of the only true political form, the *polis*, since "a *polis* cannot be administered without them."[29] There could never, however, exist a *polis* composed only of slaves – just as there could not be one made up solely of women and children.[30] If therefore the Indians could be shown to be such slaves, they clearly could not be said to have "true dominion, public and private."

With the somewhat dubious exception of an attempt by the Knights Templar in the early fifteenth century to justify their attacks upon the pagan Prussians of Poland's eastern frontiers, Aristotle's assertion that

---

[24] The term *dominium* employed by all the Spanish scholastics described, in Soto's definition, "a faculty and right [*facultas et ius*] that [a person] has over anything, to use it for his own benefit by any means that are permitted by law." *De iustitia et iure* (Salamanca, 1556), p. 280. The term "sovereignty," which I have used here rather loosely and which did not enter the language until later, translates as *dominium iurisdictionis*, that is, the "faculty and right" that a sovereign has over jurisdiction or government.

[25] For the most compelling modern discussion of the implications of Aristotle's views see Bernard Williams, *Shame and Necessity* (Berkeley, Los Angeles, and Oxford: California University Press, 1993), pp. 110–116.

[26] *Nicomachean Ethics* 1143a11.

[27] *In decem libros Ethicorum Aristotelis ad Nicomachum expositio*, ed. R. M. Spiazzi (Turin: Marietti, 1964), p. 1447 (*lectio*, 7.I.9).

[28] *Politics* 1254a8. For a more extensive and more nuanced account of Aristotle's views on this, see Benjamin Isaac, *The Invention of Racism in Classical Antiquity* (Princeton, N.J.: Princeton University Press, 2004), pp. 175–176.

[29] *Politics* 1283a14–23.

[30] In *Politics* 1252b5, however, the *barbaroi* are said to be made up entirely of slaves. But then such peoples do not live in *poleis*, and are merely biding their time until they will be enslaved and thus put to their proper use.

some men are by their very nature slaves had never been used before to justify territorial expansion. It could claim, therefore, to be a new theory to suit a new political situation.[31] The idea had considerable appeal, in particular among the settler populations in the Americas. But to most impartial observers, including Vitoria, it was not only ethnographically implausible – peoples such as the Aztecs and the Incas clearly constituted true civil societies[32] – it also suggested that if these Indians were such a race, they must be defective – and on a massive scale – which would clearly imply that God himself had created some kind of imperfection. For, said Vitoria, "our intellect is from God, and if it were to have a nat-ural inclination toward error or falsehood then this would have to be attributed to God."[33] It would also, of course, imply that the Indians did not possess the capacity to understand the teachings of the Gospels. This so alarmed the papacy that in May 1537 Paul III issued a bull, *Sublimis Deus*, denouncing the idea that "the Indians of the West and South, and other people of whom We have recent knowledge should be treated as dumb brutes created for our service" as the invention of the devil, and confirming their rationality, their humanity, and thus "that they may and should, freely and legitimately, enjoy their liberty and possession of their property."[34]

All of the Spanish scholastics rejected the natural slave argument to some degree. Vitoria was prepared to adduce from the related argument that *if* the Indians were all truly mad, they could make no more claim to be able to govern their own affairs than a group of children, in which case the Spanish king would possess a highly constrained right to take "them into his control." But since this would be due under the terms of the obligation we all have to our neighbors, it could only be done "for the benefit and the good of the barbarians and not merely for the profit of the Spanish."[35] This would seem to imply, at least, that the gold and silver that the Spaniards had extracted in massive quantities from the mines in

[31] Pawel Czartoryski, *Wczesna recepcja Polityki Arystotelesa na Uniwer sytecie Krakowskim* (Wroclaw: Zaklad Narodowy im. Ossolinskich – Wydawnictwo, Polskiej Akademii Nauk, 1963), p. 132. I am grateful to Dr. Christopher Ligota for this information.

[32] On this see Anthony Pagden, *The Fall of Natural Man: The American Indian and the Origins of Comparative Ethnology* (Cambridge: Cambridge University Press, 1982), pp. 68–79.

[33] *Comentarios a la Secunda Secundae de Santo Tomás*, 6 vols., ed. Vicente Beltrán de Heredia (Salamanca: Universidad de Salamanca, 1932–1952), III, p. 11.

[34] Lewis Hanke, "Pope Paul III and the American Indians," *Harvard Theological Review*, 30 (1937), 65–102.

[35] "On the American Indians," 3.8, Vitoria, *Vitoria Political Writings*, pp. 290–291.

Mexico and Peru could not legitimately be shipped back to Europe to pay for costly wars fought against other Christian princes. This argument, although it occurs right at the end of the text, and is advanced "merely for the sake of argument," was translated by later jurists into an embryonic theory of "trusteeship." Following the creation of the Mandate System by the League of Nations after 1918, international lawyers struggling to find some place for what was in effect – and in law – a "suspension of sovereignty" turned to Vitoria's claim as a way of challenging the arguments of nineteenth-century positivists that "uncivilized" peoples might legitimately be appropriated by "civilized" ones, because only the latter could claim to constitute states and thus to exercise sovereignty. There is indeed hardly any book written on the status of the mandates that does not, at some point, refer to Vitoria.[36]

It was also the case, as another of Vitoria's pupils, the Dominican theologian Melchor Cano, argued in 1546, that even if it were true that the Indians were some kind of children in need of civic education, the Christians would not be entitled to "take them into their care" if they had to conquer them in order to do so. For any act whose purpose is to secure the good of another is a precept of charity, and no act of charity can ever involve coercion. The position of the Castilian crown, Cano concluded, somewhat unflatteringly for his monarch, was like that of a beggar to whom alms may be due but who is not empowered to extract them.[37]

Vitoria's other argument maintained that in order to be in true possession of a land, it had to be "occupied," which generally meant that it had to be either enclosed or in some way modified by human hand, or as the English in America constantly insisted, "improved." This claim, although it was later used by many of the champions of the Virginia Company, the poet John Donne among them, and plays a significant role in John Locke's argument in favor of the English settlements in America, was, at best, a slippery one.[38] There was no general consensus on what constituted occupation, and the *terra nullius* argument made no proper distinction between possession and sovereignty. For even if an area of land was unoccupied and unused, it might still be under the jurisdiction

---

[36] Anghie, *Imperialism, Sovereignty and the Making of International Law*, pp. 144–145.

[37] *De Dominio indorum*, printed in Luciano Pereña, *Misión de España en América* (Madrid: Consejo Superior de Investigaciones Científicas, 1956), p. 107. For a more extensive reading of Cano's *relectio*, see Lupher, *Romans in a New World*, pp. 85–93.

[38] For a wider discussion of this position, see James Tully, "Aboriginal Property and Western Theory: Recovering a Middle Ground," *Social Philosophy and Policy*, 11 (1994), 153–180.

of a legitimate prince. Even the great sixteenth-century jurist Alberico
Gentili, who although a firm proponent of the claim that "God did not
create the world to be empty," and generally prepared to concede extensive rights to Europeans over non-Europeans on the grounds of their
greater technical capacities, was certain that although the occupation
of lands formally under the jurisdiction of the Ottoman state would be
licit, the settlers would, nevertheless, be bound to accept the sovereignty
of the sultan.[39] The fact that the "barbarians" had failed to develop their
territories might be adduced in support of the argument concerning their
mental capacity, but, Vitoria concluded, of itself "it provides no support
for possession of these lands, any more than it would if they had discovered us."[40]

Vitoria also employed two more natural law arguments in favor of
the conquests, both of which make broad general assertions that were to
have a lasting impact on all subsequent thinking about the legitimation
of the intervention of one state in the affairs of another.

The first was what might be broadly described as the "humanitarian
argument." It could be said, Vitoria wrote, that "either on account of
the personal tyranny of the barbarians' masters toward their subjects or
because of their tyrannical and oppressive laws against the innocent," the
Spanish have a right to intervene "even without the pope's authority."
The Roman law of vicinage, to which Vitoria alludes here, required that
"neighbors" support each other in times of crisis. The Spanish, therefore,
have an obligation to come to the "defense of the innocent," and this
applied even if the innocent were willing participants in the crimes committed against them. The crimes Vitoria had in mind were human sacrifice and cannibalism, and in such extreme cases, "It makes no difference
that all the barbarians consent to these kinds of rights and sacrifices, or
that they refuse to accept the Spaniards as their liberators in the matter." For prolonged habit is capable of obscuring every human being's
understanding of the natural law, and no man may "deliver himself up to
execution" (unless justly convicted of a crime) for the same reason that
he may not commit suicide, because possession of his own body (*dominium coporis suuis*) belongs not to him but to God. Clearly, if the rulers of
the barbarians refuse to abandon their crimes against their people, then
"their masters may be changed and new princes set up."[41] In other words,

---

[39] *De Iure belli*, 2 vols., trans. R. C. Rolfe (Oxford: Clarendon Press, 1933) I, XVII, para. 131.
[40] "On the American Indians," 2.3. Vitoria, *Vitoria Political Writings*, pp. 264–265.
[41] Ibid., 3.5.15, pp. 287–288. This is the fifth "just" title.

since the norms of the Christian civil community were universal, they therefore represented those that all peoples, no matter what their beliefs, should attempt to emulate. Any who actively resisted this claim, arguing that their own laws and customs compelled them to behave otherwise, provided grounds for a just war. The Spanish were here merely acting on behalf of, and by the authority of, a supposed international community. They were in America – or in those parts of America where human sacrifice and cannibalism were supposedly practiced – by historical contingency, and the task thus fell to them. But it could just as easily have been assumed by any other ruler, Christian or, indeed, non-Christian, so long as his own civil laws were in accordance with the law of nature.

Vitoria's conception of war "in defense of the innocent," in common with all attempts to justify armed intervention in the interests of "others," fails, of course, to specify very clearly what would count as "tyranny" and "oppressive laws." It was, too, an innovative move since, in general, theories of the "just war" avoided claims made on behalf of third parties unless these were specifically involved as "allies" (*socii*).[42] The Indians might, for instance, quite reasonably have sought the assistance of the Europeans in their (legitimate) struggles against other Indians. This had indeed, as Vitoria points out, happened in the case of the Tlaxcalans, who – at least in Hernán Cortés's account of events – had sought Spanish aid in their struggle against the Aztecs.[43] But few would accept that any state could intervene in the affairs of any other without the express request of at least a legally recognized representative body from that state. Fewer still would have accepted that one ruler had the authority to decide what constitutes an "offense against the innocent" in another state.

In the case of the American Indians, the humanitarian argument for conquest, and the subsequent imposition of "new princes" and hence in effect the creation of new states – "regime change," as it is now called – was fairly circumscribed. In other, less specific contexts, however, Vitoria substantially broadened the possible applications of the same argument. "It should be noted," he wrote,

that the prince has the authority not only over his own people, but also over foreigners to force them to abstain from harming others; this is his right by the law of nations and the authority of the whole world. Indeed, it seems he has this right by natural law: the world could not exist unless some men had the power and authority to deter the wicked by force from doing harm to the good and the innocent.

[42] See Barnes, "The Just War," 775–778.
[43] "On the American Indians," 3.7, Vitoria, *Vitoria Political Writings*, p. 289.

Furthermore, since in Vitoria's opinion the "commonwealth," in the person of the prince, clearly had the authority "in natural law" to "punish those of its own members who are intent on harming it with execution or other penalties," it followed that

[i]f the commonwealth has these powers against its own members, there can be no doubt that the whole world has the same powers against any harmful and evil men. And these powers can only exist if exercised through the princes of the commonwealth.[44]

There were, in addition, further, and somewhat more sinister, ways in which it was possible to extend the range of this injunction. One maintained that if it was legitimate for a ruler to right a wrong on behalf "of the whole world," then it might also be legitimate for a prince to wage war in order to prevent any future, or further, deterioration in the status quo. In the view of Francisco Suárez, perhaps the most influential neo-Thomist writer on the justice of war in the seventeenth century, this would, for instance, have constituted a cause for a just war against Henry VIII of England. For England, because of the offenses Henry had caused its peoples, was already, or so Suárez claimed to believe, in disarray and might therefore legitimately be attacked to prevent further collapse.[45] "War," as Suárez phrased it, "is permitted so that the state may preserve the integrity of its rights," even if that war had been initiated by a foreign power.[46]

This, however, posed the question of how, in the case of America, the Spanish crown had acquired the authority of "the whole world that is a commonwealth." On this occasion, Vitoria seems to have simply identified the natural law with the law of nations. But the *ius gentium*, which had originally been the law used by the Romans in their dealings with the *gentes* – that is, non-Roman citizens – had in the hands of the Scholastics been transformed into a complex theory of international law. It was held to constitute a series of rules and norms to which all reasonable people could, under the proper circumstances, be brought to agree.

[44] "On the Law of War," 1.4.19, Vitoria, *Vitoria Political Writings*, p. 305. The term used by all the Spanish scholastics was, of course, *respublica* – literally, the "common thing"; since, however, the English term "republic" has come to denote a particular constitution, the now archaic term "commonwealth" seemed a more appropriate translation.

[45] See Anthony Pagden, *Spanish Imperialism and the Political Imagination* (New Haven, Conn., and London: Yale University Press, 1990), p. 31.

[46] *Disputatio xii. De Bello*, from *Opus de triplice virtute theologica, fide spe et charitate* [Paris, 1621], printed in Luciano Pereña Vicente, *Teoria de la guerra en Francisco Suárez*, 2 vols. (Madrid: Consejo Superior de Investigaciones Científicas, 1954), II, pp. 126–127.

For some this meant that it was a reflection of the natural law or, in the most commonly used formula, a "secondary" natural law. For most of the Spanish Scholastics, however, including Vitoria himself on most occasions, the *ius gentium* was part of the human or civil law, which, in Suárez's words, "had been introduced not by evidence but by the probable and common estimation of men" and enacted, if only *ex hypothesi*, by what Vitoria described as "the whole world which is in a sense a commonwealth."[47] How then, it might be asked, did this world-commonwealth confer *dominium iurisdictionis* on the prince who was to defend its integrity against the "tyrannous and barbarous" since there clearly existed no body empowered to legislate on its behalf? (One answer might have been the pope if his claim to exercise jurisdiction over the entire world were accepted, but as we shall see, neither Vitoria nor any of his successors did accept it.)

There was a further problem with this line of argument as a justification for *conquest*, for although it might provide grounds for initial intervention, it offered no charter for effective colonization. Since anything resembling "humanitarian" intervention could only be for the good of those supposedly afflicted, once the "integrity of the state" had been established, the invading power should logically withdraw. According to Augustine, however, Cicero had also argued in Book 3 of *De Republica* that wars might be waged "in defense of faith." This clearly widened the possible application of both the Ciceronian and the Augustinian grounds for the *ius ad bellum*. If "fides" is understood here, as Augustine understood it, to mean religious belief, then for the neo-Thomists this comes dangerously close to the argument, which Vitoria associated with the Englishmen Richard FitzRalph and John Wycliff, the Bohemian reformer Jan Huss, and the "modern heretics" Luther and Calvin, that sovereignty (*dominium iurisdictionis*) depended upon God's grace, rather than God's laws, and that no "ungodly" person could be a legitimate ruler.[48] For

---

47 Suárez, *De legibus ac deo legislatore* II. Xix, 4, and Vitoria, "On Civil Power," 3, 4, Vitoria, *Vitoria Political Writings*, p. 40. See also Heredia, *Comentarios a la Secunda Secundae de Santo Tomás*, III, pp. 89–90. For a more detailed account see Daniel Deckers, *Gerechtigkeit und Recht: Eine historisch-kritische Untersuchung der Gerechtigkeitslehre des Francisco de Vitoria (1483–1546)* (Freiburg: Universitätsverlag Freiburg, 1991), pp. 345–394. Domingo de Soto was even more direct in claiming that "the law of nations is distinct from the natural law and is included in the positive law." *De iustitia et iure* Lib. 3 q. I art 3.

48 See "On Civil Power," 3.1–6, Vitoria, *Vitoria Political Writings*, p. 42. This is the so-called Calvinist Theory of Revolution, although both Calvin and Luther themselves insisted that "ungodly princes" had been placed in power as a punishment by God and might not, therefore, be resisted. See in general Quentin Skinner, *The Foundations of*

the neo-Thomists, however, all forms of *dominium* derived wholly from
the natural law. "For he maketh his sun to rise on the evil and on the
good," they were fond of saying after St. Matthew (5.45), meaning that
the *laws* of nature did not change in accordance with a person's behavior or beliefs. All legitimately constituted rulers – even Muslims – were,
therefore, true *domini*.

Furthermore, as Suárez observed, it was not man's task to vindicate
God. If God wished to take revenge upon the pagans for their sins, he
remarked acidly, "he is capable of doing so for himself."[49] But "fides"
could also be interpreted, as Cicero himself would have done, to stand
for a way of life, in this case, of course, the way of life practiced within
the Roman *civitas*. It could, therefore, be claimed that an offensively
un-Christian lifestyle, which meant an offensively non-European lifestyle, did, in effect, constitute a violation of nature's laws. And if that
lifestyle involved the legal and social sanctioning of such practices as
human sacrifice and cannibalism, then it might be held to pose a threat to
the continuing existence of the entire "world-commonwealth" and thus
a threat not merely to a single group, but to the integrity of humanity
itself. In that case, the Christian prince might go to war on the grounds
that St. Augustine had endorsed elsewhere in the *City of God*, namely, to
"acquire peace," peace in this context being defined as a "work of justice"
(*opus justitiae*) for the restoration of the "tranquility of the order of all
things."[50] In such circumstances, argued Suárez, "the natural power and
jurisdiction of the human republic" could be mobilized as a "reason for
universal conquest."[51] Since Suárez was also prepared to consider that
any attempt to "impede the law of Christ" might constitute legitimate
grounds for such action, the scope of the jurisdiction exercised by the
"human republic" could, potentially at least, be very wide indeed.[52]

What this implied, in effect, was that a European ruler could claim to
make war upon an otherwise harmless adversary in order to establish
what later generations of colonizers would call "civilization." Since, however, the purpose of such a war was still only to remedy ills, the victor
was only entitled to seize such movable goods as he deemed necessary
to compensate for the losses he had incurred. He might also seize goods,

Modern Political Thought, 2 vols. (Cambridge: Cambridge University Press, 1978), II,
    pp. 189–238.
[49] *Disputatio xii. De Bello*, pp. 149–152.
[50] *De Civitate Dei*, XIX. 13.
[51] *Disputatio xii. De Bello*, p. 238.
[52] Ibid., pp. 158–161.

and even persons, as punishment for wrongdoing. But what were termed "immovable goods" – that is, territory, cities, and, crucially, what lay beneath the land – were another matter. Vitoria accepted that

it is sometimes lawful to occupy a fort or town, but the governing factor in this case must be moderation, not armed might. If necessity and the requirements of war demand that the greater part of enemy territory or a large number of cities be occupied in this way, they ought to be returned once the war is over and peace has been made, only keeping so much as may be considered fair in equity and humanity for the reparation of losses and expenses and the punishment of injustice.[53]

Once again, the Spanish scholastics were faced with the uncomfortable truth that while the behavior of the Indians prior to their discovery might have provided the Spanish crown with justification for an invasion, it could not provide it with any grounds for subsequent conquest and occupation.

CREATING A UNIVERSAL IMPERIUM

The second of Vitoria's arguments, and it was to have a long subsequent history, was based upon the – somewhat dubious – claim that the division of things (*divisio rerum*), that is, the carving up of the world into autonomous (and sovereignty-bearing) nations that had taken place after mankind's departure from the state of nature (or the Garden of Eden) had not obscured certain natural rights, which remain the common property of all human beings.[54] Among these were what he called – and he seems to have been the first to do so – "the right of natural partnership and communication" (*ius naturalis societas et communicationis*).[55] This phrase describes a complex set of claims divided into five propositions. At the core, however, lies an allusion to the ancient obligation to offer hospitality to strangers. This Vitoria transformed from a Greek custom into a right under the law of nations – which, once again for the sake of this argument he assumes, somewhat evasively, "either is, or derives from

---

[53] "On the Law of War," 3.7, Vitoria, *Vitoria Political Writings*, p. 324.
[54] See Anthony Pagden, "Stoicism, Cosmopolitanism and the Legacy of European Imperialism," *Constellations*, 7 (2000), 3–22.
[55] "On the American Indians," 3.1, Vitoria, *Vitoria Political Writings*, p. 278. As he defines it, this seems to have been Vitoria's own creation. St. Augustine had suggested that denial of a right of passage might be sufficient *injuria* for a just war. But this has none of the structure of Vitoria's argument (*Quaestiones in Heptateuchum*, IV. 44; *Decretum* C.23. 2.3).

the natural law."[56] "Amongst all nations," he wrote, "it is considered inhuman to treat travelers badly without some special cause, humane and dutiful to behave hospitably to strangers." "In the beginning of the world," he continued,

> when all things were held in common, everyone was allowed to visit and travel through any land he wished. This right was clearly not taken away by the division of property; it was never the intention of nations to prevent men's free mutual intercourse with one another by its division.

The right to hospitality, and in particular to assistance in moments of danger, is, of course, based upon the supposition of a common human identity. It was this that, in the famous passage in Virgil's *Aeneid*, makes Aeneas, outraged at being denied shelter by the kings of Latium, exclaim:

> What men, what monsters, what inhuman race,
> What laws, what barbarous customs of the place,
> Shut up a desert shore to drowning men,
> And drive us to the cruel sea again![57]

"Nature," added Vitoria, now quoting Roman law, "has decreed a certain kinship between all men" (*Digest* I.i.3). Man is not a "wolf to his fellow men – *homo homini lupus* – as the comedian says, but a fellow."[58] All of this brings with it an obligation to friendship, for "amity between men is part of the natural law."

Vitoria's point is that a right to travel peacefully, and to be granted hospitality, is precisely a right that survives from man's primitive condition, and as such, it cannot be abrogated by merely human legislation. It is also the case – and this he takes to be self-evidently a principle of the natural law – that "the Spaniards are the barbarians' neighbors, as is shown by the parable of the Samaritan (Luke 10: 29–37); and the barbarians are

---

[56] "On the American Indians," 3.1, Vitoria, *Vitoria Political Writings*, p. 278, citing Justinian *Institutes* I.2.1, "what natural reason has established among all nations is called the law of nations," which would just as well describe a positive law that also derived similarly from reason in that sense; *ratio scripta* ("written reason") is how the Roman jurists described the civil code.

[57] *Aeneid*, I, 539–540. The translation is by John Dryden.

[58] "On the American Indians," 3.1, Vitoria, *Vitoria Political Writings*, p. 280. Schmitt offers a curious distortion of this passage, transforming "Non enim *homini homo lupus* est, ut ait comicus, sed homo" into an aphorism of Vitoria's own, "homo homini homo." "This threefold *homo*," he admits, "sounds rather tautological and neutralizing," but he assumes it to be a ploy on Vitoria's part to assert that the Indians do not forfeit their rights by being non-Christians, since they are still human and "the general quality of being human need not level out the social, legal and political distinctions developed in the course of human history." Schmitt, *The Nomos of the Earth*, p. 105.

obliged to love their neighbors as themselves," which meant that they could not "lawfully bar them [the Spaniards] from their homeland without due cause."[59] (This did not mean, however, that the Indians and the Spaniards were neighbors in the sense that either the theologians or the Roman jurists would have understood the term.)

The same argument Vitoria rather more dubiously extended to commerce. By the terms of the law of nations, travelers (*peregrini*) may not be prevented from carrying on trade "so long as they do not harm the citizens." Therefore, "they [the Spaniards] may import the commodities which they [the Indians] lack and export the gold and silver and other things which they have in abundance." This was, Vitoria recognized, a two-way argument: if the barbarians could not interfere with the right of the Europeans to travel among and trade with them, then no European state could prevent another from doing the same thing. The French, for instance, could not lawfully "prevent the Spaniards from traveling to or even living in France and vice versa."[60]

One thing is clear from this analogy, and of related comments made elsewhere by Vitoria and by Soto. For the School of Salamanca in general there existed no distinction, as far as rights – in particular sovereignty – were concerned, between the European Christian world and the non-European pagan and barbarian world.[61] Such a distinction played an important role in the positivist international law of the nineteenth century, and some traces of it can be found in Hugo Grotius. But although Vitoria, Soto, and Suárez all allow that certain kinds of behavior, which constitute violations of the natural law, will deprive a people of its natural dominium, they always insist that they would do so even if those responsible were Christians. The natural law must apply to all peoples equally.

The crucial component of Vitoria's argument was his assertion that the right of communication, and of sociability, because it had survived the division of lands after the creation of civil society, was what Fernando Vázquez de Menchaca would call a *liberrima facultas, ius absolutum,*

---

[59] "On the American Indians," 3, Vitoria, *Vitoria Political Writings*, p. 279.
[60] Ibid., p. 280.
[61] Anthony Anghie's assertion that "Vitoria bases his conclusion that the Indians are not sovereign on the simple assertion that they are pagan" is false. Had Vitoria held any such position he would, on his own account, have fallen prey to the heresy of deriving *dominium* from grace, not law. Anghie, *Imperialism, Sovereignty and the Making of International Law*, p. 29. And see Martti Koskenniemi, *The Gentle Civilizer of Nations: The Rise and Fall of International Law, 1870–1960* (Cambridge: Cambridge University Press, 2001), pp. 98–178.

that is, an absolute right that could not be interfered with by any human society.[62] Vitoria's claim that all humans have a right of free (peaceful) access to all parts of the world draws upon a long ancient and humanist tradition, and was seized upon in 1609 by the Dutch humanist Hugo Grotius in his own celebrated attack on the Portuguese claim to have exclusive sailing rights in the Indian Ocean.[63] It also resurfaces much later, in another form and without any apparent indebtedness to Vitoria's formulation, in Immanuel Kant's celebrated "Cosmopolitan Right" (*ius cosmopoliticum*).

The problem with the argument, however, as the great Saxon jurist Samuel Pufendorf pointed out in 1672 in a rebuttal of both Vitoria and Grotius, was that it confused a mere right of transit with rights of property. This "natural communication," he wrote scathingly, "cannot prevent a property holder from having the final decision on the question, whether he wishes to share with others the use of his property." It was also, in his view, "crude indeed" to claim that everyone, irrespective of "the numbers in which they had come" or "their purpose in coming," possessed such a right. In 1546, another of Vitoria's pupils, the Dominican theologian Melchor Cano, had made much the same point. The Spaniards might have natural rights as travelers or even as ambassadors, but they had gone to America as neither. "We would not," he concluded dryly, "be prepared to describe Alexander the Great as a 'traveler.'"[64]

For both Cano and Pufendorf, however, the key issue was the power of the state. It was, Cano argued, clearly absurd to suggest that there might exist a law that would forbid a prince from controlling the passage of foreigners over his own territories. Such a law would, as Vitoria had recognized, prevent the Spanish king from forbidding the French to enter Spain if he so wished, which was contrary to actual practice and a violation of the civil laws of Castile. Did it mean, then, that the civil laws of Castile were contrary to natural law? If so, then the French would have as perfect a right to wage war against Charles V as he had to make war on the Indians. Implicitly at least, for both Cano and Pufendorf, it was clear that there simply could be no right that had somehow mysteriously survived the *divisio rerum*. "Most writers," concluded Pufendorf, "feel that the safest reply to make is this: Every state may reach a decision, according

[62] See Brett, *Liberty, Right and Nature*, pp. 205–206.
[63] All are quoted by Grotius, *The Free Sea*, trans. Richard Hakluyt, edited with an introduction by David Armitage (Indianapolis: Liberty Fund, 2004), pp. 10–12.
[64] *De Dominio indorum*, 142, "nisi vocetur Alexander peregrinus."

to its own usage, on the admission of foreigners who come to it for other reasons than are necessary and deserving of sympathy." Refugees clearly possessed some kind of right of permanent settlement. But refugees had no right to behave as conquerors, and they certainly did not have any prior claim over any portion of their land of adoption. "Such persons must recognize the established government of that country, and so adapt themselves to it so that they may be the source of no conspiracies and revolts." And this again could hardly apply to the Spanish.[65]

Pufendorf, who shared Hobbes's vision of the absolute sovereignty of the state, clearly found the idea that private rights – such as the *ius peregrinandi* – might trump state rights obnoxious. He might have added that Vitoria's claim elsewhere that "any person, even a private citizen, may declare and wage a defensive war" – which Grotius had found most useful – in effect conceded to the largely unauthorized bands of freebooters that roamed the Americas the right to wage war in pursuit of their own interests against groups who were, nominally at least, recognized to constitute true civil communities.[66]

While these arguments were to have considerable influence on subsequent thinking about empire, none of them could confer upon the Spanish crown what it most needed: grounds for true sovereignty – *dominium iurisdictionis* – over the Indians, much less undisputed rights over their property. The Spanish monarchs, however, had always maintained that the Indians were neither slaves nor overgrown children, but adult rational subjects of the crown and free, if not quite equal to, say, the people of Milan. And to make good on this presumption, the crown had to have a far more substantial claim to sovereignty than any that the neo-Thomists could provide it in natural law.

Until at least the mid-eighteenth century, the Spanish monarchs never wavered in their conviction that they did indeed possess such a claim. It was based not upon any supposed natural law right, but upon the assertion that, unknown to them, the Indians had already been subject to the Spanish monarchy *before* their conquest. And this assertion derived not from any consideration of the Indians' mental status, or of

---

[65] *De iure naturae et gentium libri octo*, 2 vols., trans. C. H. Oldfather and W. A. Oldfather (Oxford: Clarendon Press, 1934), II, pp. 364–366. I would like to thank Theodore Christov for drawing my attention to this text.

[66] "On the Law of War," 1.2, Vitoria, *Vitoria Political Writings*, p. 299. On Grotius's use of this claim, see Richard Tuck, *The Rights of War and Peace: Political Thought and the International Order from Grotius to Kant* (Oxford: Oxford University Press, 1999), pp. 81–83.

the condition of their societies prior to their discovery. It derived from a donation.

Ever since the ninth century, the canon lawyers in the service of the Curia had held that the pope, as vicar of Christ, enjoyed both spiritual and secular authority over all the peoples of the world, whatever their religious beliefs. If this were the case, then the pope could grant sovereignty over a non-Christian people to a Christian prince. Acting on this belief, in 1454 Pope Nicholas V had granted to Afonso V of Portugal rights of settlement over all "provinces, islands, ports, places and seas, already acquired and which you might acquire in the future, no matter what their number size or quality" in Africa from Cape Bojador and Cape Nun, "and thence all southern coasts until their end."[67] After Columbus returned from his second voyage in 1493 and it became clear to all – except Columbus himself – that what he had discovered was not the outer fringes of "Cathay," but some new world whose size and potential wealth were as yet unknown, the Castilian crown hastily secured from Pope Alexander VI the famous Bulls of Donation to the Americas, which granted territorial rights over all those lands "as you have discovered or are about to discover"[68] and that were not already occupied by another Christian prince.

One year later, Spain and Portugal signed a treaty at Tordesillas that divided the entire globe, of which they then possessed only the most primitive geographical knowledge, into two discrete spheres of jurisdiction along a line set at 370 leagues west of the Cape Verde Islands. (This corresponded approximately to $46°$ $30'$ W, although at the time, before the invention of the marine chronometer, it could not be established with any accuracy.) The western half of the globe went to Castile, which believed that it now controlled an unhindered route to Asia. The eastern half went to Portugal, intent mainly on keeping its Castilian rivals out of the South Atlantic, which thereby came into possession of Brazil.

The treaty was a purely civil agreement between two states – and as such was granted some respect even by the Protestant powers, who, of course, ridiculed the idea that the papacy might be able to make land grants to secular rulers. But its very existence relied on the idea that the

---

[67] *Romanus pontifex*, in *Monumenta hericina* (Coimbra: Comissao Executiva das Comemoracoes do V Centenario da Morte do Infante D. Henrique, 1960–1974), XII, pp. 71–79.

[68] There were five bulls in all. They are printed in Manuel Giménez Fernández, "Nuevas consideraciones sobre la historia y el sentido de las letras alejandrinas de 1493 referentes a las Indias," *Anuario de estudios américanos*, I (1944), 173–429.

pope was the monarch of the world. Since both the Bulls of Donation and the Treaty of Tordesillas were cast in the future tense, they also assumed that the actual inhabitants of all those territories had no legitimate claim to them. They were, so to speak, caretakers, biding their time until the arrival of their true owners. Any attempt to resist could, therefore, be met with legitimate force.

Despite the absurdities involved, on which all the Spanish scholastics dwelt at length, the Bulls of Donation remained the main prop of Spanish arguments in defense of their claims over the Americas until well into the eighteenth century. What William Paterson, first governor of the Bank of England, contemptuously dismissed in 1701 as "certain imaginary mathematical lines between heaven and earth" remained the main point of ideological dispute between Spain and its European rivals in America.[69] There is almost no French or English attack on the claims to Spanish sovereignty overseas that does not begin with a rejection of the validity of both the Bulls of Donation and the terms of the Treaty of Tordesillas. The papal bulls are also the only justification for the Spanish presence in America offered by the Historiographer Royal, Antonio de Herrera, in his massive *Historia general de los hechos de los Castellanos en las islas y tierra firme del Mar Océano* of 1601–1615, from which, given Herrera's place in the royal household, it is safe to assume that this was a position with which the Castilian crown wished to be associated.[70] Even Bartolomé de las Casas, the celebrated "Defender of the Indians," never once questioned the legitimacy of the papal donation, despite his contempt for the ways in which it was implemented.[71]

But the doctrine of papal plenitude of power, on which the legitimacy of the bulls depended, raised serious difficulties. For whereas it might be acceptable to grant the Church some measure of precedence over the secular authority on spiritual and even moral grounds, the idea that the papacy could make grants of sovereignty ran directly counter to the hallowed, if often abused, injunction of Jesus himself to "Render ... unto Caesar the things which are Caesar's; and unto God the things that are God's" (Matthew 22:21), and it raised questions about the spheres of

[69] *The Writings of William Paterson, Founder of the Bank of England*, 2 vols., ed. S. Bannister (London: Effingham Wilson, 1858), I, p. 121.
[70] See David Brading, *The First America: The Spanish Monarchy, Creole Patriots, and the Liberal State, 1492–1867* (Cambridge: Cambridge University Press, 1991), pp. 205–210.
[71] *Aquí se contiene treynta proposiciones muy jurídicas*, in *Fray Bartolomé de las Casas, Obras Completas*, ed. Ramón Hernández (Madrid: Editorial Alianza, 1992), X, pp. 201–214.

jurisdiction shared by pope and emperor, both of whom, at one time or another, made mutually incompatible claims to universal sovereignty.

One of the key arguments proposed by the canon lawyers, which had been advanced most forcefully by the decretalist Hostiensis in the thirteenth century, was that the pope – who, in the canonist's view, was the true heir of the Roman emperors – enjoyed not only sovereignty over the entire world, Christian and non-Christian, but also the right of ownership (*dominium ac proprietatem bonorum omnium*), on the authority of Justinian's decree *Bene a Zenon*, which reserves exclusive rights of property in "the world" to the Roman emperor, who had then bequeathed those rights to the papacy.[72] This then allowed the papacy to distribute that property among its subjects as it so wished. It was on this presumption that Pope Alexander VI had given Ferdinand and Isabella not only jurisdiction, but also property rights, over one-half of the world. Clearly, however, only the most committed champion of papal supremacy could find any reason for endorsing such a claim. It was, said Soto bluntly, nothing other than a prescription for tyranny. In practice, only the Turks had ever exercised such a right. A Christian prince, by contrast, whose rule was absolute but not arbitrary, could not make use of the goods (*bona*) of his subjects "except where it is necessary for the defence and government of the community."[73]

Furthermore, the essentially Augustinian argument on which all of this ultimately rested – that the pope could deprive infidels of their rights, and even of their property, because they were unbelievers – raised once again the specter of the Lutheran and Calvinist claim that the ungodly monarch might legitimately be removed from power by any of his more godly subjects or, indeed, by any other godly prince.

To exercise universal *dominium* the pope would, as Vitoria points out, have had to have acquired it through one of the three forms of law: divine, natural, or civil. Clearly, on the canon lawyers' own evidence, papal *dominium* could not derive from either civil or natural law. And, "as for divine law, no authority is forthcoming"; hence, "it is vain and willful to assert it."[74] All the references to secular authority in the Bible would indeed seem to suggest a clear distinction between the domain

---

[72] *Codex*, VII, 37, 3.
[73] *De iustitia et iure*, p. 301.
[74] "On the American Indians," 2.2, Vitoria, *Vitoria Political Writings*, p. 260. Vitoria uses the same arguments in I, "On the Power of the Church," 5.1, Vitoria, *Vitoria Political Writings*, pp. 83–84.

of Christ and that of Caesar. The pope's authority, as Innocent III had decreed, was confined to spiritual rather than secular matters, except where strictly moral issues were involved.[75] "It is clear from all that I have said," concluded Vitoria, "that the Spaniards when they first sailed to the lands of the barbarians carried with them no right at all to occupy their territories."[76]

Papal claims to plenitude of power over the whole world, furthermore, like all universalist claims, supposed the existence of a stable and recognizable cosmos. If, as Soto argued, the Latin term *terra* (or *orbis terrarum*) was taken to describe nothing more than the territorial limits of the jurisdiction of the Roman people, and if "Christendom" was deemed to be coextensive with the empire, there were grounds for supposing that the pope might be in a position to act as an adjudicator between Christian rulers, and such rulers "are bound to accept his judgment to avoid causing all the manifold spiritual evils which must necessarily arise from any war between Christian princes."[77] (It was precisely this claim, widely accepted by all Christians before the Reformation, that was effectively abandoned by the Treaty of Westphalia in 1648.)

There was, however, as Soto pointed out, some confusion in the various uses that both the papacy and the Roman Empire had made of the word *terra* or *orbis terrarum*. The papal donation to both Afonso V and Ferdinand and Isabella had been clearly intended to encompass literally the entire globe, not merely what the Greeks had called the *oikoumene*, the "inhabited world." Since the end of the fifteenth century, however, it had become obvious that this world, as an inhabited space, was no longer fixed but was continually expanding and, despite the limits imposed by God on all space, might do so for some considerable time to come. The word *terra* should therefore, argued Soto, be understood, in the indefinite (or subjunctive) mode, as limited in its application to a condition that was still only potential.[78] And if this were the case, then no claim to possession of it could be made at a future time. For Soto, and even more forcibly for Soto's contemporary Vázquez de Menchaca, the Bulls of Donation had thus been rendered void by the very facts they were intended to bring under control, for clearly no man – not even a pope – can have *dominium*

[75] See Brian Tierney, *The Crisis of Church and State 1050–1300* (Toronto: Toronto University Press, 1988), pp. 127–138.

[76] "On the American Indians," 2.2, Vitoria, *Vitoria Political Writings*, p. 264.

[77] *De Iustitia et iure*, p. 262.

[78] Ibid., p. 306.

over what is potential, since he would have no means of knowing just what it was he was claiming power over.[79] So long, that is, as the full extent of the inhabited world was unknown, any claim to universal sovereignty could only be based upon a tacit assumption that each new society, as it came to light, would have to conform to a rule – the juridical concepts of Western Europe – that had been devised with no prior knowledge of its existence. Furthermore, if such a rule were to be at all legitimate, it would also have to be one that had been created for the "exclusive use" of peoples whose particular needs were as yet unknown to those who had drafted it. And that, concluded Vázquez, would be "worthy of laughter and mockery."[80] The idea that in an ever-expanding world, one ruler, no matter how mighty the source of his authority, might be "superior in dignity to all other princes" was, declared Vázquez, "to be compared to the tales of children, to the advice of the aged and to the shadows of an unquiet sleep."[81] It is something of an irony that the "discoveries" in Africa, America, and Asia, and the recognition following Magellan's circumnavigation of the globe in 1519–1522, that the "Antipodes" was also probably inhabited should have shattered the stable notion of universal rule and with it the possible existence of a single universal culture on which the Roman world, and subsequently much of the medieval Christian world, had founded its conception of itself.

A similar argument could be applied to the analogous claim of the rulers of the oxymoronic "Holy Roman Empire of the German Nation," of which Charles V was, of course, one, to exercise *dominium* over all the world as the heirs of Augustus.[82] It was Soto who first addressed this question in a *relectio* of 1534.[83] On the first argument, he pointed out that the Romans had certainly never in fact exercised jurisdiction over the entire world, for "many nations were not then subjugated as is attested by Roman historical writing itself; and this point is most obvious with regard to the other hemisphere and the lands across the sea recently

---

[79] *Controversiarum illustrium aliarumque usu frequentium, libri tres* [1563], 3 vols., ed. Fidel Rodriguez Alcalde (Valladolid, n.p., 1931–1935), II, p. 30.

[80] Ibid., II, p. 29.

[81] Ibid., I, p. 17.

[82] As Vitoria, who similarly rejected the claim, pointed out, Charles V styled himself "Divine Maximilian or Eternally August Charles Lord of the World (*orbis dominus*)." "On the American Indians," 2.1, Vitoria, *Vitoria Political Writings*, p. 252.

[83] In a *relectio, De dominio.* Lupher makes much of this text and chastises me on several occasions for having paid scant – indeed, no – attention to it. Much of the argument that applies to America, however, was, *pace* Lupher, reworked in the fourth book of Soto's great treatise *De iustitia et iure* (*Romans in a New World*, pp. 344–347, passim).

discovered by our countrymen." And if that were the case, then clearly they could have no a priori jurisdiction over these places, and if that were indeed the case, then they could not claim to have exercised sovereignty over the entire world.[84] And even if the Romans had had exact geographical knowledge of what they freely called the *orbis terrarum*, they could not have claimed on those grounds alone to have any jurisdiction over any parts of it other than those that they actually administered.

The frequently cited (Christian) supposition that "God handed the world over to the Romans on account of their virtues" implied, Soto claims, that all the nations of the world "willingly handed themselves over to the Romans on account of their zeal for justice." In historical fact, however, "From their own historians we learn that their right was in force of arms (*ius era in armis*) and they subjugated many unwilling nations through no other title than that they were more powerful, and one cannot find where God gave them such a right."[85] Furthermore, the collective *virtus* of the Romans (assuming it to have existed at all) had been constituted by purely secular and civil qualities, such as justice and fortitude, which retain their intrinsic merit even when they are pursued for the wrong reasons. The Romans might have had the capacity for instructing the less able in the path of secular virtue, but that did not make their empire a divinely sanctified state. The supposition that had underpinned so much Christian thinking about the pagan empire was clearly false. It had been a purely human creation limited, like all such creations, in both time and space. As such, of course, its historical existence offered no possible legitimization for future imperial projects, especially those supposedly pursued in the interest of evangelization.[86]

But for Soto, there was a further, and in the long run far more compelling, reason why there could exist in the world no ruler of any kind with universal sovereignty. All the neo-Thomists insisted that civil power could only be transferred by society acting as a single body. What was known as the "efficient power" of the commonwealth, since it was "founded upon natural law," ultimately derived from God. But the "material cause" of

[84] Quoted in Lupher, *Romans in a New World*, p. 63. The argument is made again in Soto, *De Iustitia et iure*, p. 304.

[85] Quoted in Lupher, *Romans in a New World*, p. 65. As Lupher points out, what he calls the "starkly paradoxical phrase" *ius erat in armis* could not be read as meaning that the Roman Empire had been based, independently of divine decree, on the pursuit of the *ius belli*, merely that the Romans owed their success, as did the Spanish, to "brute military superiority."

[86] *De Iustitia et iure*, p. 305. A more detailed analysis of Soto's argument on this point is in Lupher, *Romans in a New World*, pp. 64–65.

civil power – that is, the actual task of administration and of the choice of who is to rule – must rest with the commonwealth, for, in Vitoria's words, "in the absence of any divine law, or human elective franchise (*suffragium*), there is no convincing reason why one man should have power more than another."[87] To create a truly *universal* empire, therefore, it would be necessary, said Soto, for "a general assembly to be called on which at least the major part consented to such an election." No one, however, could possibly imagine a general assembly of literally all the world. Even if, as the prehistory of civil society seemed to require, some such meeting had once been called, the new discoveries would have subsequently nullified its decisions, if only because, as Soto reiterated, "neither the name nor the fame of the Roman Caesars reached the Antipodes and the islands discovered by us."[88]

The Roman Empire itself, however exceptional it might have been, was merely, in fact – although this is not how any of the neo-Thomists phrased it – a very large state. Soto was prepared to accept that "the imperial authority … surpasses all others, [and] it is the most excellent of all," but only because it involved the rule of more than one people (*natio*). It did not, however, he continued, "follow from this that it is the only one to dominate the world."[89] The legitimacy of the emperor Antoninus Pius's claim to be *dominus totius orbis* rested, in the first instance, on the assumption that the Romans, unlike any of their predecessors, had indeed ruled over the entire inhabited world.[90] Charles V, then, had acquired his title to universal rulership by simple descent. In this case, however, what applied to the papacy also applied to the papally sanctified empire, with

---

[87] This is Vitoria's formulation, but the other members of the School of Salamanca were in broad agreement. Indeed, it is a conventional Thomist explanation of the sources of political power and the basis of the scholastic distinction between power and authority, which Hobbes ridiculed. "On Civil Power," I.3, 4, Vitoria, *Vitoria Political Writings*, pp. 10–12.

[88] *De Iustitia et iure*, p. 304.

[89] Ibid., p. 305.

[90] Antoninus's assertion, however, occurs in the *Lex Rhodia* (*Digest* XIV, 2. 9), where in reply to a complaint from one Eudaemon of Nicomedia that he had been robbed by the people of the Cyclades after being shipwrecked, he said, "I am lord of the world, but the law of the sea must be judged by the sea law of the Rhodians when our law does not conflict with it," which implicitly, at least, recognizes the existence of spheres of jurisdiction other than the Roman civil law (as, of course, does the mere existence of the *ius gentium*). Justinian similarly excluded the sea from his jurisdiction (*Institutes*, II, 1. 1), which led to considerable debate in the seventeenth century. Justinian's law, *Bene a Zenone* (*Codex* VII, 37, 3), which reserves exclusive rights of property to the emperor, and subsequently to the papacy, was frequently cited together with the *Lex Rhodia*.

the additional complication that the emperor, as a purely secular ruler, had to be elected, whereas the pope was chosen directly by God himself. The origins of the Christian Empire could be traced to the Roman republic's oath of allegiance to Augustus. From this initial moment, its jurisdiction passed to Constantine and thence to the Western Empire. Thus, by a process of continuing but limited historical transfer, there might exist a legitimate emperor of all *Christians*. Limited sovereignty of this kind, however, could not be extended to the whole world.

That he [the emperor] should be lord of all the world can be sustained by neither reason nor right (*ius*) since the part over which he ruled was very small in respect of the whole world. Thus this small part could not, in contradiction to natural law, impose a ruler upon its antipodes and other regions.[91]

Furthermore, and this was to become a crucial component of many later arguments against all extended empires, even if the emperor were able to *claim* universal sovereignty, he could not possibly exercise it in practice. And for Soto, as for most of the Roman jurists, *dominium* was for use. "Those things," he wrote,

which do not change, have fixed limits to their size, for an ant cannot reach the height of a man, nor a man the size of an elephant. It therefore follows that neither can a prince spread his warmth throughout a commonwealth which extends across all regions and all peoples, so that he can know, emend, correct and dispose of what happens in each individual province.... Consequently, as power exists in order to be exercised (*potestas sit propter usum*), and its exercise is impossible over such extended territory, it would follow that such an institution is vain. But God and nature never do anything in vain (*nihil fecit frustra*).[92]

The crucial claim here was that political authority had to be active if it were to be valid and the related argument that civil power existed for the good of *all* those caught up in it. The laws that governed extended states – empires – could be no different from those that governed single ones. All the peoples of the Indies, Europeans and Indians, were in this

---

[91] *De Iustitia et iure*, p. 306.

[92] Ibid., 306. The phrase "*nihil fecit frustra*" derives from an oft-repeated Aristotelian axiom. See, e.g., *On the Generation of Animals*, 741b4. In reply to this argument, royal apologists such as Gregorio López de Madera, a member of the *Consejo supremo* of Castile, argued that "what Father Domingo de Soto says about the most extended republics and kingdoms" could only apply to those "who do not possess the sufficient force to govern and preserve themselves, and since they are so dispersed, some parts are defective in administration, justice and good government." And those clearly did not include the Spanish Empire (*Excelencias de la monarquía y regno de España* [Madrid, 1625], pp. 74–75).

sense what Vázquez interestingly dubbed *cives et subditi* – "citizens and subjects"[93] – and the Spanish crown was responsible for their collective defense: this was the recognized function of every modern state.

None of this, of course, addressed the original question concerning the legitimacy of the conquest in the first place. In the end, most members of the School of Salamanca could see that if their arguments were to be taken to their proper conclusion, then, as Vitoria phrased it, "the whole Indian expedition and trade would cease." As Vitoria himself had pointed out, if the only unassailable argument in favor of the retention of the Spanish colonies – other than the presumed good will of the Spanish monarchs – was the purely realist one, then more damage would be done by withdrawal in particular, since, in theory at least, most of the indigenous populations had now converted to Christianity, than by continued occupation. Otherwise, there could be little economic reason for remaining, since the Portuguese crown had gained as much as the Castilian crown out of licit trade "with the same sorts of people without conquering them."[94]

Only a realist – or strongly existential – argument of this kind could have any force by the end of the sixteenth century, when the older indigenous societies in the Americas had, in fact, been replaced by new hybrid ones, ruled over by Europeans but composed of a large number of ethnic groups, not only Spanish and Indian, but also now African and the huge and growing mestizo community that would eventually come to account for the bulk of the population. In 1629, Juan de Solórzano y Pereira (1575–1654), judge (*oidor*) of the Court of Appeal (*Audiencia*) of Lima, published a work entitled *Disputatio de Indiarum iure sive de iusta Indiarum Occidentalium Inquisitione, acquisitione et retentione.*[95] Solórzano had been one of the architects of the *Nueva Recopilación de leyes de los reynos de las Indias* compiled in 1625 (although this was promulgated only in 1680 after his death), a text that was intended to do for America what the *Digest* – the main component of Roman civil law – had done for the Roman Empire, and his *Disputatio* was clearly meant to be both a history of the entire debate over the "affair of the Indies" and a conclusion.

For Solórzano, unsurprisingly perhaps, the entire dispute over the natural origins of the Spanish crown had been in vain. It was, he was

---

[93] *Controversiarum illustrium*, II, pp. 23–24.

[94] "On the American Indians," Conclusion, Vitoria, *Vitoria Political Writings*, p. 291.

[95] *A Disputation on the laws of the Indies, or on the just discovery acquisition and retention of the West Indies.* A shorter, and far more precise, Spanish version with the title *Politica Indiana* was published in 1647.

convinced, now only "of antiquarian interest" and was raised only by "certain heretics out of envy of our nation."[96] He also broadly endorsed Soto's rejection of any argument that the Holy Roman Emperor might have inherited, via Augustus, sovereignty over the entire world.[97] Like most royal apologists, Solórzano insisted that the only possible legitimate claim the Spanish crown had in the Americas was based upon the Bulls of Donation. But his take on this was very different from that of previous generations. For Solórzano it was no longer a matter of concern whether the papacy possessed universal *dominium* or not. What now mattered was that those at the time had clearly believed that it did. The bulls might, he was prepared to concede, have subsequently been shown to be "insufficient." At the time, however, they had provided legitimate grounds for conquest. It was not, in the end, the moment of founding that conferred legitimacy upon a society; it was its survival over time. In making this argument, Solórzano had introduced into the debate what was to become one of the most enduring arguments for the appropriation of territory: the Roman law of prescription. Indeed, many of those who had invested most in arguments from conquest and natural rights of occupancy were prepared to accept that these could only be sustained over time by the fact of prolonged occupation. The law of prescription was – and remains – a powerful weapon in the internationalists' armory, and it had been employed by all the European powers (as well as by more recent creations such as the State of Israel) at one time or another.[98] It claims very simply that continuous de facto occupation of a particular thing (*preascriptio longi temporis*) could be recognized de jure as a case of *dominium*. Long-term occupation could thus be employed to confirm retrospective rights of property and even – although this was more dubious – of jurisdiction. For, argued Solórzano,

even a dominion which has been acquired less perfectly or legitimately, it is sufficient to re-assert it and purge it of its defects, in particular when the peoples

---

[96] *Politica Indiana, sacada en lengua castellana de los dos tomos del derecho i govierno municipal de las Indias occidentales,* 3 vols., ed. Francisco Tomás y Valiente and Ana María Barrero (Madrid: Biblioteca Castro, 1996), I, pp. 143–144. The principal heretic he had in mind was Hugo Grotius, who had used many of the arguments of Vitoria and Vázquez – whom he labeled "the pride of Spain" – against the Portuguese claim to exercise *dominium* over the Indian Ocean. See *The Free Sea,* pp. 14–15 and xv.

[97] For Solórzano's position on the Roman Empire, see Lupher, *Romans in a New World,* pp. 186–188.

[98] It was also a notoriously slippery one, since, as Grotius pointed out, no one could establish with certainty just how long a "long time" might be. In *The Free Sea,* he claims – overstating the case – that "such a time is required of whose beginning there is no memory" (p. 48).

possessed do not object *and there has intervened a long space of time* [emphasis added] with which even tyranny is transformed into a perfect and legitimate monarchy, as happened in the case of the Romans, and in others of the greatest [peoples] who have been known to the world, in which this common law is established amongst all peoples.[99]

For Solórzano – who was also aware of the role given by sixteenth-century humanist jurists to custom (*consuetudo*) as the means by which prescription could render cases which existed de facto into ones de jure – it was always the objective condition that conferred legal rights and, in the end, it was legal, not natural, rights that were under discussion.[100] Any right the Spanish crown had to rule in the Americas had come to it via the law of nations, understood, as the School of Salamanca most often did, as a purely civil, if also universally accepted, body of law.

This brought the whole argument back to the place where Soto had, in effect, left it in 1556. The legitimacy of the original "conquest" – a word the Spanish crown outlawed in 1625 – was now no longer the issue. The real concern for the crown was now how to justify its continuing rule as a good for all of its various subjects and how to "purge of all its defects" the original occupation. An empire, Livy had declared at the end of the first century B.C., "remains powerful so long as its subjects rejoice in it."[101] If the empire of the Spanish monarchy was to become a reality and to survive, this, in the end, was the message it most needed to take to heart.

---

[99] *Politica Indiana*, I, pp. 142–143. Lupher quotes the same passage in *Romans in a New World*, p. 187.

[100] The most important source for the significance of prescription to such cases – and the one cited by Solórzano – was Bartolus's discussion (*repetitio*) on the law *Quominus*, under the title *De fluminibus* (*Digest* 43, 12.2), discussing the possibility of acquiring rights over a public river. See Brett, *Liberty, Right and Nature*, pp. 280–281.

[101] 8.13.16.

3

Alliances with Infidels in the European Imperial Expansion

Richard Tuck

We are accustomed to thinking about the spread of European empires in the sixteenth and seventeenth centuries in terms of military power and conquest and the occupation of allegedly unowned lands by European settlers. Most discussions of the political theories that accompanied this imperial expansion have accordingly concentrated on ideas either of just war or of legitimate settlement on uncultivated territory, and this material has now become a familiar part of the standard history of imperialism. But there was another aspect to imperial activity, which may in the long run have been just as important but which has, by comparison, been rather neglected by historians.[1] It too threw up difficult issues for the theorists of the time, and the different ways in which they resolved the issues may have contributed to striking differences between the behavior of the European powers in the non-European world. This was the willingness of European states to enter into a variety of agreements and alliances with non-European peoples and to intervene in the internecine warfare on new continents. The patchwork of empire in fact emerged from these alliances much more than from straightforward acts of conquest: from Cortés's agreement to fight the Aztecs on behalf of the people of Tlaxcala,[2] through the complicated arrangements of British India, and

[1] Recent exceptions to this are Peter Borschberg and Martine van Ittersum, from whose work and conversation I have learned a great deal.

[2] Charles Gibson argued that there was no formal agreement between Cortés and the Tlaxcala people, and indeed no formal alliances between the Spaniards and any American peoples, and that may be true ("Conquest, Capitulation, and Indian Treaties," *The American Historical Review*, 83 [1978], 1–15), but it was generally believed in sixteenth-century Europe that there had been such alliances; see, for instance, Vitoria on the Tlaxcalas, *Relectio I III.17*, and Juan de la Peña on Pizarro's war in *Quaestio 40 De Bello*

on to Lugard's "indirect rule," the most distinctive features of European empires were based on treaties and understandings of various kinds with local populations. Surprisingly, this was by no means a straightforward issue as far as many Europeans of the sixteenth and seventeenth centuries were concerned: a powerful tradition of hostility within Europe to such alliances had to be overcome before imperial expansion could continue in this form. In this chapter, I want to trace the history of this argument and suggest some of its implications for the shape and character of the different European empires.

The principal stumbling block for European treaties with non-European peoples was very clear: the Old Testament contained a number of passages that seemed to preclude any substantial agreements between the faithful and infidels. Exodus and Deuteronomy have many verses in which God orders the Israelites to "make no covenant" with their neighbors, lest (in the words of Deuteronomy VII.4) "they will turn away thy son from following me, that they may serve other gods."[3] And the historical books recount many instances in which indeed disaster fell on Israel because its kings had made military alliances with infidel rulers: thus, in II Chronicles XVI and I Kings XV, Asa allied with Ben-hadad, king of Syria, and God turned against him, while in II Kings XVI and II Chronicles XXVIII, Ahaz "provoked to anger the Lord God of his fathers" by allying with Tiglath-pilneser, king of Assyria. The Old Testament does allow the settlement of boundary disputes between faithful and infidel, as in the story of Laban and Jacob in Genesis XXXI.44–53, and in its account of the league between Solomon and Hiram, king of Tyre, it seemed to endorse a military alliance (I Kings V.12–14); but the tenor of its narratives was undeniably hostile to the kinds of alliance that European powers entered into with the rulers of the non-Christian world from the sixteenth century on. This continued into the New Testament: Paul's second letter to the Corinthians, chapter VI, appeared to condemn alliances with infidels: "What fellowship hath righteousness with unrighteousness? and what communion hath light with darkness? And what concord hath Christ with Belial? or what part hath he that believeth with an infidel? And what agreement hath the temple of God with idols? for ye are the temple of the loving God.... Wherefore come out from among them, and be ye separate, saith the Lord, and touch not the unclean thing."

20, in Juan de la Peña, *De Bello Contra Insulanos*, ed. L. Pereña et al. (Madrid: Corpus Hispanorum de Pace IX, Consejo Superior de Investigaciones Científicas, 1982), p. 454.
[3] See in particular Exodus XXIII.32 and XXXIV.12, Deuteronomy VII.1–4, and Judges II.2.

More or less as soon as rulers became Christian, however, they began to make alliances with non-Christian societies around them, and in particular to enter into military alliances with "infidels" against other Christians. As we shall see, this issue – alliances against Christians – became the central concern in the sixteenth- and seventeenth-century debates, and it was, of course, in practice often the most significant kind of alliance that the rival imperial powers contracted with non-Europeans. In the early Middle Ages, the circumstances of Anglo-Saxon England, the Viking North, or the Mediterranean during the progress of Islam all necessitated alliances and treaties of every kind between Christians and non-Christians, but it seems that contemporary theologians were usually wary and disapproving of such behavior. Bede, for example, bitterly condemned the action of the Welsh Christian King Ceadwalla of Gwynnedd in allying with the pagan King Penda of Mercia against the Anglo-Saxon Christian King Oswald of Northumbria, and Oswald was treated as one of the great martyrs of the English church when he fell in the resulting battle. Similarly, Pope John VIII warned Anastasius, bishop and dux of Naples, in 876, when Anastasius was contemplating a league with the Arabs of southern Italy against the Christian city of Salerno, that "non diligere Deum, qui mandata eius participando cum perfidis non custodit" and excommunicated him when he disregarded the warning.[4] When the crusades began, there was further scope both for Christian alliances with Moslem rulers and for the denunciation of them by ecclesiastical authorities. The Decretals contain a condemnation of any Christian who supplied materiel to the Saracens; the gloss added succinctly, "Note that Christians who attack other Christians in alliance with Saracens, either by supplying help or by participating themselves, are worse than Saracens. By canon law they are condemned to slavery and can be repeatedly excommunicated."[5] But the case that most alarmed the papacy was the alliance between the thirteenth-century Hohenstaufen rulers of southern Italy (Frederick II, Manfred, and Conradin) and the Moslems of the Apulian city of Lucera; this alliance was repeatedly condemned as an

---

[4] Fred G. Engreen, "Pope John the Eighth and the Arabs," *Speculum*, 20 (1945), 318–330, at 319 n. 4. See also Giulio Vismara, *Impium Foedus. Le origini della "Respublica Christiana"* (Milan: A. Giuffrè, 1974), p. 17. It should be said that John VIII himself struck an armistice with the Arabs, but this was a very different matter from the offensive league that Anastasius contracted.

[5] "Nota quod Christiani qui cum Sarracenis impugnant Christianos auxilio vel facto, deteriores sunt quam Sarraceni. Item servitus his inducitur iure canonico. Item excommunicatus potest iterum excommunicari." Gloss to Decretals 5.6.6, *Ita quorundam*; *Decretales D. Gregorii Papae IX … una cum glossis restitutae* (Rome, 1582), col. 1658.

impium foedus, and a crusade was declared against the Hohenstaufen.[6]
There is no suggestion in the great thirteenth-century canon law discussions of war against the infidels that alliances with infidels might ever be legitimate.[7]

This situation had changed, however, by the early fourteenth century, when the papacy itself began to consider allying with infidel rulers. First, there was the repeated possibility of some kind of agreement with the Mongols to drive the Moslems from the Holy Land; and second, the papacy supported Charles of Anjou in his conquest of southern Italy and his campaign in Sicily against Frederick of Aragon, a war in which Charles used the same Moslem assistance that had led to the excommunication of the Hohenstaufen. In Naples and at the Avignon court of the popes there was now active discussion of the question, and at least two writers defended the legitimacy of alliances with infidels. One was Oldradus de Ponte, a canon lawyer at Avignon, who (probably in the 1320s) put together a set of his *consilia* from the previous decade or so. He was particularly interested in Christian–infidel relations, and *consilium* 71 concerns the question "May a Christian, without sinning, use the help or assistance of infidels in his own defense?" Oldradus argued that "what

[6] See Vismara, *Impium Foedus*, p. 125, and Christoph T. Maier, "Crusade and Rhetoric Against the Muslim Colony of Lucera: Eudes of Châteaurouxs *Sermones de Rebellione Sarracenorum Lucherie in Apulia*," *Journal of Medieval History*, 21 (1995), 343–385.

[7] For these discussions, see Frederick H. Russell, *The Just War in the Middle Ages* (Cambridge: Cambridge University Press, 1975), and James Muldoon, *Popes, Lawyers, and Infidels* (Philadelphia: University of Pennsylvania Press, 1979). Concerned about the possibility of Christian–infidel alliances in thirteenth-century Spain, Innocent III ordered the bishops of Toledo and Compostella to intervene "auctoritate nostra tam ipsis regibus quam aliis Christianis omnibus sub poena excommunicationis et interdicti firmiter inhibentes ne se praesumant iungere Saracenis, vel contra Christianos illis consilium vel auxilium impertiri" (April 5, 1215; Vismara, *Impium Foedus*, pp. 93–94). It should be said that Islamic jurisprudence came to broadly similar conclusions about the legitimacy of alliances with Christians: the default situation between the Dar-al-Islam and the Dar-al-Harb was one of war, but temporary truces could be concluded (at first for up to ten years, but by the eighteenth century the Ottomans were willing to make truces for twenty-five years). Interestingly, the Ottomans were much more willing to conclude such treaties than the Moghul rulers in India (C. H. Alexandrowicz, *An Introduction to the History of the Law of Nations in the East Indies* [Oxford: Clarendon Press, 1967], pp. 90–96). But such truces could be unilaterally broken: for example, Selim II invaded Cyprus in 1570, breaking an agreement made with Venice three years earlier, on the advice of a jurist who argued that "Peace may be made with the infidels only when it is to the interest of all the Muslims to do so. If, after peace, permanent or temporary, has been made, it then appears more profitable to break it, then it is obligatory to break it" (V. L. Menage, "The English Capitulation of 1580: A Review Article," *International Journal of Middle East Studies*, 12 (1980), 373–383, at 378). Knowledge that this was the Islamic position informed Christian attitudes, and no doubt vice versa.

anyone does in defense of his body is considered to have been done as a matter of right" and that "not only can we make war upon our enemies [in alliance] with infidels and deceivers, but we can use deceit in doing so." He dismissed the Old Testament examples as not giving rise to general principles, but as having to do with specific features of the Israelite kings' relations with their neighbors. But Oldradus's discussion makes it clear that what he had in mind was predominantly alliances with infidels against other infidels – "quarrels and strife should be sown amongst the wicked, for (as St. Gregory says in his Moralia) it is just as harmful when the virtuous are disunited as it is pernicious when the wicked are not.... Because of this, the Saviour in Luke 12[:51] says that he did not come to bring peace to the nations, but rather division" – and he did not distinguish between these cases and those in which a Christian allied with infidels against another Christian.[8]

The second author, the Dominican theologian John of Naples, provided a much fuller discussion of the issue, though it was less influential than Oldradus's,[9] largely because it was couched in the form of an answer to the more limited question "if he lacks the necessary number of believers bearing arms, can a Christian king, who is a believer, use unbelievers for the just defense of the commonwealth (for example, Saracen mercenaries who come to him for the aforementioned just defense)?" This was, of course, the relevant question in the politics of Naples, and it raised in acute form the problem of alliances with infidels against other Christians. John's answer went into great detail about the general issue before concluding that in a situation of necessity a Christian ruler could indeed use the military assistance of infidels, even against other Christians.

Although unbelievers are wicked with respect to their faith, they can still be morally good with respect to an act that is good in its general character, such as fighting in a just war. As far as such an act is concerned, therefore, it is not a sin to make use of their assistance when there is a pressing necessity.... A war between believer and unbeliever can be just and permissible on the part of the unbeliever, namely, when it is unjust on the part of the believer.[10]

---

[8] Norman Zacour, *Jews and Saracens in the Consilia of Oldradus de Ponte* (Toronto: Pontifical Institute of Mediaeval Studies, 1990), Latin text on pp. 78–79, English translation on pp. 44–46.

[9] He is, however, cited in the very well-known *Summae Sylvestrinae* of Silvester Mazzolini da Prierio (1456–1527): *Summae Sylvestrinae* (Venice, 1601), I, p. 68r ("bellum" I.9).

[10] *The Cambridge Translations of Medieval Philosophical Texts*, ed. Arthur Stephen McGrade, John Kilcullen, and Matthew Kempshall (Cambridge: Cambridge University Press, 2001), II, p. 346. For details of John's life and political context, see the introduction to the text, pp. 326–328.

He warned, however, that this would not be licit if there was any risk that, as a consequence, the infidels might take power over Christians or subvert their faith.

The views of Oldradus and John held sway for much of the following two centuries. For example, they were repeated by their contemporary, the canonist Johannes Andreae,[11] by the fifteenth-century canonist Panormitanus in an influential commentary on the Decretals,[12] and by the late-fifteenth-century theologian John Mair in his commentary on Peter Lombard's Sentences.

> I say that a believer can seek help from an infidel against another infidel, as the Maccabees did, and as the Christians of our time sought help from the warlike Tamerlane, King of Persia, against Bayezid the ruler of the Turks. The faithful can even in some cases seek help from infidels against other members of the faith, though they must take care that this does not lead to the abandonment of the Christian republic.[13]

Nevertheless, there remained a certain anxiety about this latter case; Rodrigo Sánchez de Arévalo, writing in the first half of the fifteenth century, argued that in general, alliances between Christian and infidel were forbidden unless they were directed against an infidel ruler or unless a Christian state faced destruction at the hands of another Christian state if it did not use the assistance of infidel arms[14] – that is, there had to be a much more stringent standard of necessity than John of Naples had supposed. This anxiety redoubled when Francis I of France and Suleiman the Magnificent of Turkey concluded their famous alliance against the Hapsburgs in 1536;[15] lecturing on Aquinas in the mid-sixteenth century, the Spaniard Juan de la Peña concluded (with this example specifically in mind) that while it was legitimate

---

[11] See Andreae's additions to Guilelmus *Durandus's Speculum Iuris, De Iudaeis & Saracenis.* *Speculum Iuris* (Frankfurt, 1592), II, p. 472.

[12] On Decretals III.xxxiv.8 n.15; *Super Tertio Decretalium* (Lyons, 1531), fol. 178.

[13] "Dico quod fidelis potest querer opera ab infidel conta infidelem: quemadmodum Machabei, et nostri Christiani imploraraverunt opera Tambelanis Persarum regis pugnacissimi contra Pazaitem Turcarum principem. Possunt etiam fideles in aliquo eventu implorare opera infidelium contra fideles: cavendo ne id cedat in iactura reip. christianae." In 4 Sent. d.15. q.21. *In quartum Sententiarum questiones vtilissimæ* (Paris, 1521), fol. lxxxix r. and lxxxix v.

[14] Robert H. Schwoebel, "Coexistence, Conversion, and the Crusade against the Turks," *Studies in the Renaissance*, 12 (1965), 164–187, at 167.

[15] See De Lamar Jensen, "The Ottoman Turks in Sixteenth-Century French Diplomacy," *The Sixteenth Century Journal*, 16 (1985), 451–470. Joint military action began almost immediately, and during 1543–1544 the Turkish fleet wintered at Toulon.

per se to use infidel allies in any war, *per accidens* it could not be right for a Christian "because of the evils which follow for the Christian religion."[16] Iberian writers were reluctant to condemn alliances with infidels in general, as they had, of course, played a significant part in the creation of both the Portuguese and the Spanish empires;[17] Vitoria, for example, insisted that the Spaniards had been justified in allying with the Tlaxcalas against the Mexicans, and that this alliance could be seen as a principal justification for the conquest of America, though he did not discuss the issue of alliances against Christians. Molina and Suarez, too, continued to defend alliances with infidels, though both warned about the dangers of "scandal" to Christianity if the alliances were turned against other Christian states.[18] But away from Spain, Pierino Belli, a military jurist for the Hapsburgs and the House of Savoy in Italy, while agreeing that Christians could join with infidels in wars against infidels, criticized Oldradus and his followers and argued that it was never licit for Christians to ally with infidels against other Christians. "When there is war between the orthodox, I think that such alliance and support should be left severely alone."[19]

But already by the time Belli's book was published, Protestant writers had gone much further in their repudiation of the late medieval

---

[16] De la Peña, *De Bello Contra Insulanos*, p. 456 (example of the rex gallorum, p. 454). For some of the debate surrounding the alliance, see Michael Heath, "Unholy Alliance: Valois and Ottomans," *Renaissance Studies*, 3 (1989), 303–315.

[17] For example, in 1522 the Portuguese allied with the Hindus of western Java against the local Moslems. See George Masselman, *The Cradle of Colonialism* (New Haven, Conn.: Yale University Press, 1963), p. 219. For these early Portuguese treaties in East and South Asia, see also C. H. Alexandrowicz, *The European-African Confrontation: A Study in Treaty Making* (Leiden: A. W. Sijthoft, 1973), p. 15.

[18] See Luis de Molina, *De Iustitia et Iure* (Antwerp, 1615), I, p. 188 (Tom. I, Tract. II, disp. 112); *Selections from Three Works of Francisco Suarez*, trans. Gwladys L. Williams, Ammi Brown, and John Waldron (Oxford: Clarendon Press, 1944), II, p. 853.

[19] Pierino Belli, *De Re Militari et Bello Tractatus*, ed. Arrigo Cavalieri, trans. Herbert Nutting (Oxford: Clarendon Press, 1936), II, p. 93 (first published 1563). See p. 94 for his criticisms of Oldradus. As a councillor to Emmanuel Philibert of Savoy, Belli opposed an alliance between his prince and Suleiman to recover Cyprus for the House of Savoy; see Arrigo Cavalieri's introduction, II, pp. 11a–12a. The same position was taken up by another of Emmanuel Philibert's councillors, Octavianus Cacheranus of Osasco (sometimes called Octavianus Osascus) in his pamphlet *Disputatio an principi Christiano fas sit, pro sui suorumque bonorum tutella foedus inire, ac amicitia infidelibus iungi, ab eisque auxilium adversus alios principes Christianos petere* (Turin, 1569). Cacheranus concluded that it could not be licit to call on the Turks for aid against Christians "etiam pro rerum suarum defensione" (fol. 4r), though he did distinguish between Turks and other infidels (fol. 4v). He refers appreciatively to Belli's book (fol. 7r).

view. We find the beginnings of this movement in Calvin's commentary on Ezekiel XVI.26.

If any one raises the question whether it is lawful to enter into an alliance with the impious, the answer is easy, that we must beware of all alliances which may couple us under the same yoke; for we are naturally enough inclined towards all vices: and when we invent fresh occasions for sin we tempt God. And when any one joins himself in too great familiarity with the impious, it is just like using a fan to inflame his corrupt affections, which, as I have said, were already sufficiently flagrant in his mind. We must take care, therefore, as far as we can, not to make agreements with the impious.

Calvin accepted that Abraham was right to enter into an agreement with his neighbors in order to settle boundaries and live in peace. But Israel was protected by God and needed no alliances: "nothing, therefore, is better than to reef our sails, and to look to God alone, and to have our minds fixed on him, and not to allow any kind of alliance, unless necessity compels us."[20]

Calvin's remarks were systematized by the great Italian Protestant theologian Peter Martyr Vermigli (d. 1562) in his commentary on the Books of Kings. Dealing with the treaty between Asa and Ben-hadad (I Kings XV), Martyr accepted that "some pacts and agreements with infidels are not prohibited, in particular those concerning boundaries": it was licit to live in peace with one's neighbors, as the Venetians did with the Turks and the Poles with the Tartars. "But those treaties which involve common expeditions and mutual help are not permitted.... We despise them like dogs, and they treat us like dogs.... If they do not keep faith with the true God, how should we expect them to keep faith with us?"[21] No military alliances with infidels, even against infidel rulers, were to be allowed. This became the absolutely standard Protestant view for the next hundred years. Thus, the famous Elizabethan jurist Alberico Gentili (so similar, as has often been said, in other respects to Grotius) on this matter was firmly in the Protestant camp.

Commerce with infidels is not forbidden; the law of God does not bid us withdraw from the world, and the law of man commands commerce among all men.

[20] *Commentaries on the First Twenty Chapters of the Book of the Prophet Ezekiel*, trans. Thomas Myers (Edinburgh: T. Constable, 1849), II, pp. 128–129.
[21] "Non prohibentur certa pacta & conventiones cum infidelibus, praesertim de finibus.... Sed ea foedera, quae habent communes expeditiones & auxilia mutua, no sunt permittenda.... Nos illos ut canes dispicimus, atque ill nos ut canes habent.... Si Deo vero fidem non servant,quomodo speramus illos nobis fore fideles?" Peter Martyr, *Melachim id est Regum libri duoposteriores cum commentariis* (Zurich, 1571), p. 130v.

We are here inquiring about a treaty, a special union, and what has been said above does not convince me that this is lawfully contracted with men of a different religion.... [We are dealing with] an equal treaty and one of arms, which ought to be considered under two heads; for either a Christian joins arms with an infidel against another infidel or against a Christian. Against infidels the Maccabees did this and the kings of Judah, and in modern times the Portuguese. And such an alliance does not seem to me lawful; for, as you know, those kings of Judah are censured, one because he summoned the King of Syria to his aid against an attack from the King of Israel; the other because he had gone to the aid of the King of Israel against the Syrian. Therefore it is lawful neither to lend aid to infidels nor to accept aid from them against other infidels. And if it is not lawful to do this against infidels, how much less will it be allowed to do it against the faithful?[22]

Similarly, in France, the Huguenots strongly opposed the Valois alliance with the Turks. François de la Noue devoted one of his *Discours politique et militaires* to the topic, agreeing that there could be treaties for trade, but anything more was an offense to God.

In all such leagues as wee make with these destroiers and scourges of the worlde, in whom *treason, impietie, uniustice* and *crueltie,* have their continuall habitation, there is always *errour*, especially if we exceede certaine bounds prescribed by reason, because it is in no case lawfull to confederate with them, except for matter of small importance, and such as bindeth not the hearts with any strict amitie, neither the persons in anie great bond.[23]

Some Protestants went so far as to say that there should be no alliances even with the members of a different Protestant church: thus, the Lutheran Johann Tarnow (1586–1628) in his *Quaestio num et quae foedera cum diversae religionis hominibus et praecipue Lutheranis cum Calvinianis salva iniri possint conscientia* (1618) argued that although "it is said by many, it is licit to repel unjust violence with force, and thus even with these an alliance may be made," the end never justifies the means and Lutherans should not form alliances with Calvinists.[24] This was still a burning issue in the English Civil War, and one of the most complete

---

[22] *De Iure Belli Libri Tres,* ed. Coleman Phillipson and John C. Rolfe (Oxford: Oxford University Press, 1933), II, pp. 401–402 (first published 1589). See also, e.g., Andrew Willet, *Hexapla in Exodum: that is, A sixfold commentary vpon the second booke of Moses called Exodus* (London, 1608), p. 550.

[23] *The Politicke and Militarie Discourses of the Lord De la Noue* (London, 1587), p. 238 (first published as *Discours politiques et militaires* [Paris, 1587]).

[24] "Multis etiam in ore est, licere vim injustam vi repellere, & hactenus tamen cum his posse foedus sanciri." Johannes Tarnovius, *Quaestio num et quae foedera cum diversae religionis hominibus et praecipue Lutheranis cum Calvinianis salva iniri possint conscientia* (Rostock, 1618), sig. C2v.

treatments of the Protestant position, with copious references to the entire Protestant literature, was produced in the 1640s by the ablest of the Scottish Covenanting theologians, George Gillespie, in an attempt to persuade his fellow Covenanters not to to form any alliance with the "Enemies of Truth and Godlinesse" in England.[25]

A further twist to the Protestant view in England was provided by the most authoritative figure in the early seventeenth-century common law, Sir Edward Coke. In his judgement in Calvin's case (1607), Coke had to deal with the status of aliens under English law (the case turned on whether a Scotsman born after the accession of James to the English throne was still an alien in England). He declared that "Everie alien is either a friend that is in league, &c. or an enemie that is in open warre, &c. Everie alien enemie is either *pro tempore*, temporarie for a time, or *perpetuus*, perpetuall, or *specialiter permissus*, permitted especially." A temporary enemy alien might become a friend, and thereby acquire the right to bring legal action in England or to own property there, but

a perpetuall enemie (though there be no warres by fire and sword betweene them) cannot maintaine any action, or get any thing within this Reame. All Infidels are in law *perpetui inimici*,[26] perpetuall enemies (for the law presumes not that they will bee converted, that being *remota potentia*, a remote possibilitie) for betweene them, as with the divels, whose subiects they bee, and the Christian, there is perpetuall hostilitie, and can be no peace: for as the Apostle saith 2. Cor. 15. *quae autem conventio Christi ad Belial, aut quae pars fideli cum infideli*, and the law saith, *Iudaeo Christianum nullum serviat mancipium, nefas enim est quem Christus redemis blasphemum Christi in servitutis vinculis detinere.*[27] Register 282. *Infideles sunt Christi & Christianorum inimici.*[28] And herewith

---

[25] *An usefull case of conscience, discussed, and resolved. Concerning associations and confederacies with idolaters, infidels, hereticks, or any other known enemies of truth and godlinesse* (London, 1648) (Thomason picked it up on January 25, 1649). This was apparently a sermon originally delivered in 1640, at the time of the Bishops' War, in defense of separation from the English Church; it was reissued with a covering letter from Gillespie (who was on the point of death) denouncing the treaty made between Charles I and the Scots delegates at Carisbrooke in December 1647. It was reprinted several times and was included in Gillespie's *Treatise of miscellany questions* (Edinburgh, 1649). Gillespie was critical of Tarnovius (see sig. A4r), but only because he thought it was "strange" to regard Calvinism as a false religion.

[26] Interestingly, this is a phrase from Machiavelli's *Discorsi* I.13 used to describe the relationship between the Romans and the Equi and Volsci; it is Italian, not Latin.

[27] See Decretals 5.6.1.

[28] This is a characteristically misleading reference to William Rastell, *Registrum Omnium Brevium* (London, 1595), fol. 282v, which includes a writ of protection to the Hospital of St. John at Jerusalem "in tuitionem & defensionem universalis sacrosanctae ecclesiae contra Christi & christianorum inimicos institutum."

agreeth the booke in 12. H.8. fol.4[29] where it is holden, that a Pagan cannot have or maintaine any action at all.[30]

Coke repeated this in his posthumously published *Fourth Institutes*, where he asserted that the law of England on treaties was the same as the standard Protestant view.

There be four kinds of leagues. 1. *Foedus pacis*, and that a Christian Prince may have with an Infidel. *Si fieri possit, quod ex vobis est, cum omnibus hominibus pacem habeatis* [Romans XII.18]. 2. *Foedus congratulationis sive consolationis*; and this may a Christian Prince make with an Infidel, as David did with Haman.... 3. *Foedus commutationis mercium sive commercii*; and this also may be made with an Infidel, as King *Solomon* did with *Hiram* an Infidel, and *Joshua* did with the *Gibeonites*. 4. *Foedus mutui auxilii*; and this cannot be done with an Infidel or an Idolater. *Jehosophat* King of *Juda* made *foedus mutui auxilii* with *Achab* King of *Israel*, an Idolater: ... in which war *Achab* was slain, and *Jehosophat* was in extream danger. And after, as the Text saith, *Reversus est autem Jehosophat rex Judae in domum suam pacifice in Jerusalem, cui occurrit Jehu filius Hanani, & ait ad illum, Impio praebes auxilium, & his qui oderunt Dominum amicitia jungeris, & idcirco iram quidem Domini merebaris* [2 Chronicles XIX.2]. And the laws of England concerning these four leagues are as you perceive grounded upon the Law of God.[31]

So, by the beginning of the seventeenth century, Protestant Europe was more or less united in denying legitimacy to any military alliance contracted with an infidel ruler, and this view was to be found at the very heart of at least the English government. Catholic Europe still clung to the doctrine that such alliances could be contracted in order to make war on other infidels, but it was noticeably warier about using an infidel alliance against Christians than had been the case two hundred years earlier. These changed attitudes had begun to effect policy: Franco–Turkish military operations more or less ceased in the second half of the sixteenth century,[32] and negotiations between the French and the Ottomans

---

[29] See *Cy ensuist le Report de tout ceux cases, queux fueront collect en le Raigne de ... Henry le huistesme* (London: Richard Tottell, 1591), sig. B1 (Trinity Term 12 H8 fol. 4): outlaws, traitors and pagans are barred from bringing actions (Sir Richard Broke).

[30] Coke, *La sept part des reports* (London, 1608), fol. 17r–17v. He went on to say that because of this, if a Christian sovereign conquered a pagan country, the laws of that country were immediately void even if the sovereign did not expressly supersede them with his own. On the implications of this remark, see Robert A. Williams, Jr., *The American Indian in Western Legal Thought* (New York: Oxford University Press, 1990), pp. 199–200.

[31] Coke, *The Fourth Part of the Institutes of the Laws of England: Concerning the Jurisdiction of Courts* (London, 1644), p. 155.

[32] De Lamar Jensen, "The Ottoman Turks in Sixteenth-Century French Diplomacy," *The Sixteenth Century Journal*, 16 (1985), 451–470, at 459.

concentrated largely on trade issues. There were no new military treaties between the Portuguese or the Spaniards and non-European peoples, and there was an increasing unwillingness on the part of both empires to use indigenous help.[33] In the acute crisis of the 1580s there was a flurry of interest in England in the possibility of alliances of all kinds against Spain: negotiations were conducted at Constantinople about a joint Anglo–Turkish expedition against Spain,[34] and Richard Hakluyt in his *Discourse of Western Planting* (1584) urged the formation of "leagues" with indigenous victims of Spanish oppression in the New World.

> If wee (being thereto provoked by spanish injuries) woulde either joyne with these Savages [he was referring to the Chichimeca of northern Mexico], or sende or give them armour as the Spaniardes arme our Irishe Rebells, wee shoulde trouble the kinge of Spaine more in those partes, then he hath or can trouble us in Ireland.[35]

But nothing came of either scheme, even in the most serious danger that England faced in the course of the century.[36]

The country that broke with this view, and that forced a general change in European attitudes to these alliances, was the United Provinces. Facing an even greater threat to their survival than the English faced in 1588, the Dutch (as is well known) determined to carry the war against Spain first into the Far East and then into the Americas. In February 1603 the sultan (or king) of Johore, in the Straits of Malaya, asked for Dutch assistance in his struggle with the Portuguese; the result was the famous attack by

[33] See C. R. Boxer, "Portuguese and Spanish Projects for the Conquest of Southeast Asia 1580–1600," in his *Portuguese Conquest and Commerce in Southern Asia 1500–1750* (London: Variorum Reprints, 1985), III, pp. 135–136.

[34] See the material collected in Edwarde Barton and Edwin Pears, "The Spanish Armada and the Ottoman Porte," *English Historical Review*, 8 (1893), 439–466. In British Library Cottonian MS Titus. C. VII, among the papers of Sir Robert Cecil and his father (fol. 183), there is a manuscript copy of Cacheranus's book, *An principi Christiano fas sit, pro sui suorumque bonorum tutela, foedus inire cum infidelibus*, which presumably belongs to this period and which, as we have seen, was strongly opposed to such alliances.

[35] E. G. R. Taylor, ed., *The original writings & correspondence of the two Richard Hakluyts* (London: The Hakluyt Society, 1935), II, p. 241. See also chap. 11 (ibid., pp. 257–265). The discourse also contains a classic statement of intervention in local wars: any English settlement in the Americas should "enter into league with the petite princes their neighbours that have alwayes lightly warres one with an other, and so entringe league nowe with the one, and then with the other wee shall purchase our owne safetie and make ourselves Lordes of the whole." Ibid., p. 275.

[36] Though it was rumored in 1596 that the English attack on Cadiz was accompanied by "five galleys from Barbary." Nabil Matar, *Turks, Moors and Englishmen in the Age of Discovery* (New York: Columbia University Press, 1999), p. 20.

Jacob van Heemskerk on the Portuguese vessel the *Sancta Catarina* and its seizure as a prize.[37] The younger brother of the king was present on Heemskerk's ship during the operation. In November of the following year Steven van Hagen, the admiral of the Dutch fleet in the East Indies, made a formal treaty with the samorin or "keijzer" of Malabar, which included the ambitious provision that they would "drive [the Portuguese] out of all the lands of His Majesty, and also out of the whole of the Indies,"[38] and in 1605 Dutch forces joined with the king of Ternate to attack Portuguese Tidor. A whole host of treaties and alliances with the native rulers of East Asia followed in the next few years.[39] The Twelve Years Truce signed between the Dutch and the Spaniards in 1609 precluded any extension of these military alliances, but when it expired the Dutch began again to arrange them with indigenous opponents of Spain around the world; one of the most striking examples is the fleet that the United Provinces sent into the Pacific in 1623 with orders to offer "letters of alliance" to the native peoples of Chile and Peru.[40]

It should be emphasized that at the point at which the Dutch government under Jan van Oldenbarnevelt embarked on this policy, it was flying in the face of conventional opinion within the whole of international Protestantism. Theorists with influence in the United Provinces in these years, such as Johannes Althusius at Emden (a city with a Dutch garrison and a substantial role in Dutch politics) or Willielmus Zepperus at Herborn, in the lands of the Orange-Nassau family, all insisted that military alliances with infidels were illicit. As Zepperus said, though commercial treaties were permissible,

[s]ome treaties involve common expeditions and extensive military collaboration with infidels and the impious, like the treaties of Asa, Josaphat and Amasia. These are illicit and idolatrous. When there is such a mingling of armies, the people of God are always rubbing up against something evil and impious. In such camps

---

[37] See Peter Borschberg, "Hugo Grotius, East India Trade and the King of Johor," *Journal of Southeast Asian Studies*, 30 (1999), 225–248, and "The Seizure of the Sta. Caterina Revisted: The Portuguese Empire in Asia, VOC Politics and the Origins of the Dutch–Johor Alliance (1602–c. 1616)," *Journal of Southeast Asian Studies*, 33 (2002), 31–62.

[38] "verdrijven uyt alle de landen van Sijne Mayesteijt en ook uijt geheell Indien." J. E. Heeres, ed., *Corpus Diplomaticum Neerlando-Indicum* ('s-Gravenhage: Martinus Nijhoff, 1907), I, p. 30.

[39] See, e.g., the formal agreements in May 1606 for an offensive and defensive alliance with Johore (ibid., p. 43) and in January 1607 with Aceh (p. 50).

[40] A similar expedition was mounted in 1643. For these ventures, see Benjamin Schmidt, "Exotic Allies: The Dutch–Chilean Encounter and the (Failed) Conquest of America," *Renaissance Quarterly*, 52 (1999), 440–473.

the impious invoke their idols, ascribe victories to them and swear by them: God is strongly offended by such things.[41]

There was, however, one Dutch theorist who was willing to defend such alliances, and to do so in the most far-reaching terms. This was, of course, Hugo Grotius, who was commissioned by the East India Company to defend Heemskerk's seizure of the *Sancta Caterina*. The work that resulted from this commission, the so-called *De Iure Praedae*,[42] has long been recognized (since it was recovered in 1864) as a major work of political philosophy, in which Grotius put forward a remarkably complete version of the new kind of rights theory that was to dominate European intellectual life for the next two centuries. But (with the notable exception of Peter Borschberg) most scholars have concentrated either on the account Grotius gave in the *De Iure Praedae* of the right possessed by private individuals as well as states to make war in defense of their own legitimte interests, or on his theory of private property and the impossibility of ownership in territory that could not be transformed by human labor. These are indeed striking and important ideas, of great significance in the history of imperialism as well as in the general history of political thought, but the *De Iure Praedae* also contained a defense of the Dutch treaties in terms that were completely new within Protestantism. It is often said that in part the East India Company was stirred to produce a defense of the seizure by opposition from some of its more radical Protestant shareholders to its new belligerence;[43] this may be true, but one did not need to be a Mennonite or Anabaptist in the early-seventeenth-century United Provinces to be anxious about treaties with Moslem or Hindu nations against the Portuguese.

---

[41] "Quaedam enim communes habent expeditiones, & auxilia multa cum idolatris & impiis, qualia fuerunt Asae, Josaphati, Amasiae. Illa illicita sunt & idolatrica. Semper enim in tali exercituum commixtione, aliquid mali & impietatis affricatur populo Dei. In talibus castris impii idola sua invocant, illis victorias adscribunt, per illa jurant: quibus rebus vehementer Deus offenditur." *Legum Mosaicarum Forensium Explanatio* (Herborn, 1604), IV.6, p. 306. Althusis said the same in his *Politica Methodice Digesta* (Herborn, 1614), XXXIV.51, p. 780.

[42] There is still some argument over when the manuscript was composed; Martine van Ittersum and Peter Borschberg have argued cogently in some unpublished work that Grotius worked on it over a number of years, quite possibly (in the relevant sections) down to 1608.

[43] For example, the Mennonite Pieter Lijntgens, who approached Henry IV of France about creating a new East India Company that would not engage in warfare with Portugal. See Robert Fruin, "Een onuitgegeven werk van Hugo de Groot," in *Robert Fruin's Verspreide Geschriften* III (The Hague: Martinus Nijhoff, 1901), pp. 400–401.

A general discussion of the law of war (Prolegomena and chapters I to X) was followed by a chapter on the facts in the case, and then by two chapters devoted to the justice of the seizure if it took place in a "private" war (chapter XII) and to its justice in the context of a "public" war (chapter XIII). The final two chapters argued that the seizure was in addition both "honorable" and "beneficial." Chapter XII was published in 1608 as *Mare Liberum*, but Grotius refrained from publishing the rest of the work; a defense of the United Provinces' public war against Spain was inappropriate at the time of the peace negotiations that ended in the Twelve Years Truce (though it should be said that Grotius, while in the government at the time, was rather hesitant about the wisdom of the truce). The defense of the treaties occurs primarily in chapter XIII, and so was unknown to a readership beyond the Dutch government and the East India Company; not until Grotius returned to these issues in his *De Iure Belli ac Pacis* in 1625 did a wider European audience understand his position. The importance that Grotius ascribed to the possibility of alliances with infidels is illustrated by the fact that his papers contain both a separate esssay on the question, which was probably part of the *Vorabeiten*, the preliminary work, for *De Iure Praedae*,[44] and drafts of a number of letters to various rulers of East Indian states offering military assistance in return for trading privileges:[45] he was himself in the forefront of the Dutch attempts in these years to build a network of alliances with infidels against the Portuguese.

Grotius argued as follows in chapter XIII:

There is in India a kingdom called Johore, which has long been considered a sovereign principality, so that its ruler clearly possessed the authority necessary to conduct a public war. This ruler asked for help in warfare, from the Hollanders who had come to his land with their ships. Now, we have shown in another passage how well it accords with nature's plan and with human brotherhood that one person should give aid to another,[46] and therefore we readily see that the entrance of the Dutch into the war as allies of the King of Johore was permissible.

---

[44] So far unpublished; see an account of it by Peter Borschberg, "*De Societate Publica cum Infidelibus*: Ein Frühwerk von Hugo Grotius," *Zeitschrift der Savigny-Stiftung für Rechtsgeschichte*, Romanistische Abteilung, 115 (1998), 355–393.

[45] For a sample, see Hugo Grotius, *Commentary on the Law of Prize and Booty*, ed. Martine van Ittersum (Indianapolis: Liberty Fund, 2006), Appendix II.ix, pp. 553–555 (to the king of Tidore, winter 1606–1607). Others are to the queen of Patani, the samorin of Malabar, the seigneuries of Banda and Ambon, and the kings of Johore, Siau, Bantam, Ternate, and Tidore.

[46] In chapter VI, where he argued on general grounds that it is right to help other human beings in distress.

One may go farther and say that, since the Hollanders were well able to assist him thus, they could hardly have remained guiltless while withholding assistance....

Both the King of Johore and the [East Indian] nations elsewhere mentioned by us, are being ravaged by the Portuguese with slaughter and rapine on no other pretext than this, that the said ruler and nations granted admittance to the Dutch. In the light of these arguments, is there anyone who will deny that the injuries suffered by these East Indians are properly the concern of the Dutch?

Or do we perhaps believe that we have nothing in common with persons who have not accepted the Christian faith? Such a belief would be very far removed from the pious doctrine of Augustine, who declares (in his interpretation of the precept of Our Lord whereby we are bidden to love our neighbours) that the term *"neighbours"* obviously includes *every human being*. Moreover, the famous parable of the good Samaritan which is contained in the Gospels, teaches us that the obligations of humane conduct are not dispelled on grounds of religion. Accordingly, not only is it universally admitted that the protection of infidels from injury (even from injury by Christians) is never unjust, but it is furthermore maintained, by authorities who have examined this particular point,[47] that alliances and treaties with infidels may in many cases be justly contracted for the purpose of defending one's own rights, too. Such a course of action was adopted (so we are told) by Abraham, Isaac, David, Solomon, and the Maccabees....

Now, just as the King himself acted with excellent motives in striving to uphold his rights and protect his subjects, so the kindness of the Dutch in coming to his assistance was similarly laudable. In fact, there is nothing that serves the cause of the true religion better than such acts of kindness. Care must be taken to keep men safe, lest the hope of converting them (as the Church Fathers were formerly wont to say) should perish with their bodies. The Indian peoples must be shown what it means to be a Christian, in order that they may not believe all Christians to be as the Spaniards are. Let those peoples look upon religion stripped of false symbols, commerce devoid of fraud, arms unattended by injuries. Let them marvel at the faith which forbids that even infidels should be neglected. In achieving these ends, we shall be preparing men for God.[48]

Grotius had thus completely eliminated the specifically Christian anxiety about military alliances with infidels; indeed, if Christianity had any special purchase on the situation, it was to strengthen rather than weaken the natural justification for allying with any oppressed person or nation against the oppressor. When Grotius returned to the question in 1625, he argued that "the Right of making Alliances is common to all Men, and admits of no Exception on the Account of Religion. The Question is then, whether by the Law of GOD it be lawful or not? which has been

---

[47] Grotius cited Panormitanus, Vitoria, and Vitoria's contemporary, the Spaniard Franciscus Arias de Valderas.

[48] Grotius, *Commentary on the Law of Prize and Booty*, pp. 432–435.

the Subject of frequent Controversy" (II.15.8).[49] He then methodically worked through the Old Testament examples, dismissing each of them as having "their particular Reasons," and concluded that

the Gospel has made no Alterations in this Respect; nay, it gives a greater Encouragement to such Leagues, by Vertue of which, those who are not of the true Religion may be relieved in a just Cause; forasmuch as we are to do Good unto all Men, when an Opportunity offers; and this not only as a Thing commendable, and left to our Liberty and Discretion, but as what we are commanded and obliged to. For by the Example of GOD, who makes his Sun to arise on the Just and on the Unjust, and sends his Rain on the Wicked as well as the Righteous, we are taught to exclude no Man from the Benefit of our Kindness. (II.15.10)

Grotius now acknowledged that alliances with infidels did carry risks, which prudent Christian states would guard against; for example, "the Dwelling of such People should be in some separate Place" (II.15.11), and the alliance should not put the existence of Christendom in danger; but in general, he disregarded all the arguments against military cooperation with infidels that had been taken for granted within the Protestant tradition, and he went further than had usually been the case even within the Catholic tradition. Indeed, in the same year that *De Iure Belli ac Pacis* appeared, a Portuguese canonist, Seraphin de Freitas, published a long-delayed answer to *Mare Liberum* in which (though he was presumably ignorant of Grotius's own arguments in this area)[50] he dealt with the canonist tradition from Oldradus on, and concluded that

[i]t is agreed by the reckoning of everyone that it is not licit [to form such alliances] in an offensive war, as the previously cited authors in effect conclude. This is what the Dutch have done against the Portuguese, caring more (alas) that these places in the East should be occupied by Turks, Moors, and infidels, than by Catholics, and that the Koran of Mahomet should be taught rather than the gospel of Christ.[51]

Though Grotius's ideas were largely unknown until 1625, some Dutch Calvinists in the 1620s did begin to modify their opposition to the treaties,

---

[49] *The Rights of War and Peace*, ed. Richard Tuck (Indianapolis: Liberty Fund, 2005).
[50] The book was licensed in October 1624 (sig.¶ 3r). There is no indication in it that he had read *De Iure Belli*.
[51] "Omnium calculo receptum est id non licere in bello offensivo, ut in effectu sentient praecitati, quale inferunt contra Lusitanos Batavi, quorum interest (prodolor) illa in Orienti loca a Turcis potius, & Mauris, ac infidelibus, quam a Catholicis occupati, Alcoranumque Mahometis quam Christi evangelium promulgari." De Freitas, *De justo imperio Lusitanorum Asiatico* (Valladolid, 1625), XIII.52, fol. 147v. He quoted Cacheranus as an authority against the treaties (fol. 146v).

largely (no doubt) because of their obvious success in strengthening the Dutch position in the Far East. The theologian Antonius Walaeus (with whom Grotius had reasonably good relations, despite Walaeus's opposition to the government of Oldenbarnevelt) argued in a paper of c. 1620–1622 that since *pii principes* could in cases of necessity subject themselves to more powerful infidel rulers, a fortiori they could use their help.[52] Another theologian, Andreas Rivet, published a commentary on Hosea in 1625 in which he also defended the treaties, though with the less far-reaching argument that Christians were entitled to make alliances with infidels against other infidels, and therefore against those who "usurp the name of religion, and are worse and more cruel than any infidel" and are "idolaters and persecutors of us," but even then only in a situation of urgent necessity.[53] Nevertheless, despite this movement on the part of two leading Calvinist theologians, there were still many others in the United Provinces who remained unhappy about military alliances with infidel states; for example, William Ames, a professor at Franeker from 1622 to 1632, included a discussion of the question in his *De conscientia et eius iure* of 1631 and remarked that using the aid of infidels or helping them in war "fals out so often to bee unlawfull, that it ought not indeed to be tried without special heed.... [I]t beares a kind of show of diffidence, and inclination to compasse our ends either by right or wrong, and also of an unlawfull union with the wicked."[54]

Furthermore, the example of the Dutch was by no means followed promptly by other European states. In the East Indies, the English were very hesitant about joining with native rulers in military action: in 1614, for example, the English commander of the East India Company fleet refused to join with the Moghul forces in an attack on the Portuguese, though only a few days later he had to engage the Portuguese fleet

---

[52] *Opera Omnia* (Leiden, 1643), II, pp 428–430. The undated paper was printed among Walaeus's "Consilia et Epistolae" for 1620–1622. Walaeus gave as examples of legitimate treaties those of the Portuguese and Dutch in the East Indies and the attempts by the English to use treaties with gentiles in America against the Spaniards, "ut ex earum itinerariis liquet, in primis Gualteri Rali ante annos circiter 20, ex itinerariis Draci, Thomae Candisch, &c. circa Virginam, &c." – a reference to Gotthard Arthus's *Americæ pars VIII. Continens primo, descriptionem trium itinerum ... Francisci Draken, ... Secundo, iter ... Thomæ Candisch ... Tertio, duo itinera ... Gualtheri Ralegh* (Frankfort: Theodor de Bry, 1599). This would also date it c. 1620.

[53] *Opera Theologica* (Rotterdam, 1652), II, p. 640 (originally published as *Commentarius in Hoseam Prophetam* [Leiden, 1625]). See also his commentary on Exodus XXIII.32 (written after his commentary on Hosea) (*Opera Theologica*, I, p. 1096).

[54] *Conscience with the power and cases thereof* ([Leiden], 1639), p. 188 (first published as *De conscientia et eius iure* [Amsterdam, 1631]).

unilaterally. In 1622 an Anglo–Persian force ejected the Portuguese from their fort at Ormuz, but again the Company had first told the shah that it was unable to participate in a joint operation. It then agreed to do so on the condition that it would receive a factory on Ormuz in return, but James I's government disclaimed any involvement in the action and fined the Company; Ormuz was not maintained under English rule.[55] In the negotiations between the English and the Dutch between 1613 and 1618 about collaboration in the East Indies, the English consistently opposed any involvement in the kinds of military alliances that the Dutch had constructed (an opposition perhaps emphasized by the presence of Sir Edward Coke among the English delegates for the final round).[56] Not until the War of the Austrian Succession and the fall of Madras to the French in 1746 did the English call on the assistance of local states; thereafter, of course, there was a succession of military alliances against the French, which eventually led to the complex pattern of government in British India.

In the West Indies and America it was a similar story. Europeans were willing on occasion both to give and to receive assistance in wars with native Americans: famously, Samuel Champlain helped the Hurons in a battle with the Mohawks in 1609, and the English of Connecticut used Mohegans in the war with the Pequots in 1637. Sir Edward Andros also relied on the Mohawks to defend the English settlers from the Algonquins in "King Philip's War" in 1675–1676. But it was not until the war with France in the 1680s that the first of the "French and Indian" wars began, in which both European powers used a network of native allies; indeed, it can be argued that it was the alliance between the English and the Iroquois nations that was crucial to their eventual victory over France. As in other areas of imperial history, a technique pioneered by the Dutch was eventually taken over and applied with greater thoroughness and success by the English.

This relatively late use of military alliances with non-Europeans by states other than the United Provinces is paralleled by the surprising persistence in European theoretical discussions of hostility to the idea of military

---

[55] See Abdul Aziz M. Awad, "The Gulf in the Seventeenth Century," *Bulletin (British Society for Middle Eastern Studies)*, 12 (1985), 125–127.

[56] See G. N. Clark and W. J. M. van Eysinga, eds., *The Colonial Conferences Between England and the Netherlands in 1613 and 1615*, *Bibliotheca Visseriana* XV and XVII (Leiden: Brill, 1940, 1951); for the 1618 conferences, see *Berigten van het Historisch Gezelschap te Utrecht* VII.ii (1862), 81ff., and *Codex diplomaticus Neerlandicus: uitgeven door het Historisch Gezelschap te Utrecht*, 2nd series, III.ii (1856), pp. 127ff.

treaties with infidels. In Germany, in particular, it remained a familiar part of Protestant theology: for example, Polycarp Lyser, in his thesis at Leipzig, *Disputatio Politica de Foederibus cum Infidelibus* (1676), and the Jena jurist Johann Heinrich Pott, in his thesis *De Foederibus Fidelium cum Infidelibus* (Jena, 1686), both reiterate the line that Protestants had taken since the mid-sixteenth century: that while commercial treaties were acceptable, military alliances, especially against other Christians, were not.[57] In this respect the theologians continued to oppose the position taken in Germany by Samuel Pufendorf, whose work took for granted the correctness of Grotius's view. But even in England a thoroughly Grotian approach was quite late in being generally adopted, again outside the obvious circles in which Grotius's ideas in general were picked up, such as those of Selden or Hobbes (neither of whom, it should be said, deigned to address the question). Edward Littleton, a friend of Selden, lecturing at the Inner Temple in 1632 on Edward III's Statute of Merchant Strangers, repudiated Coke's remarks about infidels being *perpetui inimici* with the eminently Grotian sentiment that "the enmity is between us and their Religion, not between us and their persons; for they are all God's creatures";[58] but other lawyers continued to treat Coke's view as authoritative.[59] The professor of civil law at Oxford in the mid-seventeenth century, Richard Zouche, was closer to Gentili than to Grotius in his *Juris et judicii fecialis* of 1651: answering the question "whether a treaty may be made with those who are strangers in religion," he replied that

so far as military alliance is concerned, it is well known that the Asmoneaeans made a compact with the Spartans and the Romans, with the approval of the priests and people. Yet an exception must be made if the heathen are likely to derive great increase of strength from such an alliance; much more if war is to be made on men of the same religon; thus Alexander says, in Arrian, that those who make war with barbarians against Greeks are guilty of a grave sin.[60]

[57] For these works, see Alexandrowicz, *An Introduction to the History of the Law of Nations in the East Indies*, pp. 87–88, though he confuses Polycarp Lyser with the respondent, his younger brother Friedrich Wilhelm: *Disputatio Politica de Foederibus cum Infidelibus ... Praeses M. Polycapus Lyserus, Respondens Fridericus Guilielmus Lyserus* (Leipzig, 1676).

[58] "Enmity est inter nous & leur Religion, mais neg. inter nous & leur persons; car ils touts sont les creatures de Dieu." British Library, Hargrave MS 372, fol. 62r. Though the notes on the lectures remained unpublished, this passage was quoted by William Salkeld in his report on a case in 1697 (*English Reports* 1, Salkeld 46).

[59] See, e.g., Edmond Wingate, *Maximes of Reason: or, The Reason of the Common Law of England* (London, 1658), p. 10.

[60] *Iuris et Iudicii Fecialis, sive, Iuris Inter Gentes, et Quaestionum de Eodem Explicatio*, ed. Thomas Erskine Holland (Washington, D.C.: Carnegie Institution of Washington, 1911), II (II.IV.28 [recte 24]), p. 101.

One of the last moments in England when Coke's remarks on infidels were taken seriously came in the unlikely setting of the principal court case (*East India Company v. Thomas Sandys*) about the legal status of the East India Company in 1683–1685. A number of London merchants tried to break the Company's monopoly on the East India trade, and the team of lawyers marshalled to defend the Company and sue the interlopers decided on what must still have seemed the plausible tactic of insisting that because all infidels are *perpetui inimici*, trade with them without a specific royal licence (which could take any form the king chose) was illegal under English law. Attorney-General Robert Sawyer (arguing for the Company) argued that it traded with the Indian rulers under the terms of commercial leagues, of the kind that were permitted, but that further alliances would not be licit. An infidel

is called a "perpetuus inimicus," from the practice of the kings of England, and other kings and princes, not to make leagues of friendship or alliance with infidel princes; whether restrained from making such leagues by the municipal laws of the several Christian countries, or the general rights of Christianity, is not to my purpose to determine.[61]

Each one of the lawyers briefed for the Company returned to this theme: John Holt (later lord chief justice), for example, said, "I do conceive that by the law of the land, no subject of England can trade with infidels, without licence from the king; ... and for this very reason, because infidels are by the law taken notice of, and the law hath adjudged them to be perpetual enemies; the law hath set a mark upon them, and they are used as all other enemies are."[62]

The astonished counsel for the merchants opposing the monopoly responded with ridicule. As Sir George Treby (later chief justice of common pleas) remarked, "[I] did not expect so much divinity in the argument." "I must take leave to say, that this notion of Christians not to have commerce with infidels is a conceit absurd, monkish, fantastical and fanatical."[63] And though Lord Chief Justice Jeffries gave judgment for the East India Company, he too dismissed the relevance of Coke's remarks to the case: "I do not conceive there is any difference (though much discussion hath been about Indians and Infidels) whether the East-Indies were, at the time of the grant of this patent, inhabited by christians

---

[61] The East India Company vs. Thomas Sandys, *Cobbett's Complete Collection of State Trials*, ed. T. B. Howell, X (London: R. Bagshaw, 1811), col. 488.

[62] Ibid., coll. 373–374.

[63] Ibid., coll. 386, 392.

or infidels."[64] Grotius was as widely and as respectfully cited in the case as Coke, and the *Sandys* case is probably the last time the old view about treaties with infidels was taken even half seriously in an English court. By 1774, in a case dealing with the constitution of Grenada, the attorney Francis Hargrave could say that the distinction between Christian and infidel "is now justly exploded"; the judge, Lord Mansfield, interjected, "Don't quote the distinction for the honour of Coke," and in his judgment remarked that the idea "in all probability arose from the mad enthusiasm of the crusades."[65]

So, a long period of debate had come to an end, and what had seemed clearly part of God's law in the sixteenth century seemed equally clearly mad in the eighteenth century. But the debate had a number of continued effects. First, it is reasonable to think that it delayed the wholesale adoption by other nations of the Dutch approach to colonial ventures, and thus delayed the extensive European involvement in the internal affairs of both the East Indians and the native Americans; it may also have impeded a Portuguese or Spanish response to the Dutch (and later the English or French) approach, in which they could have used a similar network of native alliances; de Freitas's refusal to countenance this in his reply to *Mare Liberum* exemplifies the difficulties the Portuguese found in responding in kind to the Dutch. Second, it may have contributed to the gulf between the Germans and the "commercial nations" that had become so apparent by the time of Kant. German Protestants, as we have seen, were more resolutely opposed to associations with infidels than were any other groups in Europe, and the hostility to the activities of the colonizing powers that we find in Wolff or Kant (and even, to an extent, in Pufendorf) may have grown to some extent out of this religious tradition.[66] And lastly, there may be a deep paradox underneath the debate, just as there was (I have argued in various places) under the use of the language of natural rights, of which Grotius was also a pioneer. Natural jurisprudence of the Grotian kind allowed the nonagrarian peoples of the world to be seen as unfairly hoarding resources that should be turned over to agriculture and that should therefore be appropriated by people willing to farm: an

---

[64] Ibid., col. 520. But he does seem nevertheless to have accepted the Company's lawyers' claim about the general character of the law in this area; see his characteristic sneer at the defendant, col. 537.

[65] Ibid., XX (London: R. Bagshaw, 1814), coll. 294, 323.

[66] For this hostility, see my *The Rights of War and Peace: Political Theory and the International Order from Grotius to Kant* (Oxford: Oxford University Press, 2000), pp. 164–165.

Enlightenment discourse of natural rights turned out to justify colonialism far more effectively than any pre-Enlightenment theory had done. Similarly, once Europeans were morally freed to become fully involved in the complex politics of the Indies (both East and West) and to compete with one another for the support of local rulers, purely commercial relations of the kind the English envisaged in the early seventeenth century became harder to maintain. Both the Indian empire of the eighteenth century and the annexation of North America from the Atlantic to the Mississippi after 1763 were made possible by this change in the moral climate: the infidels in both places may have come to regret that they were no longer treated as *perpetui inimici* by the English.

4

John Locke

Theorist of Empire?

David Armitage

Even twenty-five years ago, it might have been eccentric to ask whether
John Locke was a theorist of empire. In the shorthand histories of political thought, Locke was the grandfather of liberalism; in the standard histories of philosophy, he was the exemplar of empiricism. Liberalism had
long been assumed to be incompatible with empire, and the main links
between empiricism and imperialism were generally found in the work
of Francis Bacon and the seventeenth-century Royal Society. However,
a generation of recent scholarship has fundamentally revised understandings of liberalism's relation to empire and in particular of Locke's
relationship to settler colonialism in North America and beyond.[1] The
impact of this work has been so widespread that, alongside Locke the

[1] See especially James Tully, "Rediscovering America: The *Two Treatises* and Aboriginal
Rights," in Tully, *An Approach to Political Philosophy: Locke in Contexts* (Cambridge,
1993), pp. 137–176; Barbara Arneil, *John Locke and America: The Defence of English
Colonialism* (Oxford, 1996); Duncan Ivison, "Locke, Liberalism and Empire," in *The
Philosophy of John Locke: New Perspectives*, ed. Peter R. Anstey (London, 2003), pp.
86–105; David Armitage, "John Locke, Carolina, and the *Two Treatises of Government*,"
Political Theory, 32 (2004), 602–627; James Farr, "Locke, Natural Law, and New World
Slavery," *Political Theory*, 36 (2008), 495–522. On the more general turn to the study of
empire among political theorists and historians of political thought, see Chapter 13 by
Jennifer Pitts in this book.

For their detailed comments on earlier versions of this chapter, I am especially grateful to
Daniel Carey, Tim Harris, Karuna Mantena, Nagamitsu Miura, Sankar Muthu, Kiyoshi
Shimokawa, and Sonoko Yamada. It arises from my work on an edition of Locke's colonial writings for the *Clarendon Edition of the Works of John Locke*: I owe special thanks
to Mark Goldie, John Milton, and James Tully for their patient support of that project.
I am also grateful to Tom Leng and Kiyoshi Shimokawa for sharing work in advance of
publication.

alleged founder of liberalism and Locke the pivotal empiricist, we now find "Locke, the champion of big property, empire, and appropriation of the lands of Amerindians."[2] Locke has finally joined the canon of theorists of empire, but how much does he deserve his place there?

What it might mean to be a theorist of empire was profoundly shaped by the experience and practices of imperialism in the two centuries between roughly 1757 and 1960: that is, from the beginning of European military dominance in South Asia to the first great wave of formal decolonization outside Europe. James Tully has succinctly summarized the key features of the European imperial vision in this period:

It is "imperial" in three senses of this polysemic word. It ranks all non-European cultures as "inferior" or "lower" from the point of view of the presumed direction of European civilisation towards *the* universal culture; it serves to legitimate European imperialism, not in the sense of being "right" ... but, nevertheless, in being the direction of nature and history and the precondition of an eventual, just, national and world order; and it is imposed on non-European peoples as their cultural self-understanding in the course of European imperialism *and* federalism.[3]

Tully's immediate example here was Immanuel Kant viewed through the lens of Edward Said's *Culture and Imperialism* (1993), but accounts of the relationship between Locke and empire have shared many of the same assumptions. He has been held to be an imperial thinker in all three senses: because he placed the world's peoples in a hierarchical order with Europeans at the top of the scale; because he legitimated European imperialism within a progressivist vision of history; and because he proposed European capacities – specifically, Europeans' rationality – as a universal standard against which other peoples were to be judged and toward which they were to be led.[4] On these grounds, there would now be widespread

---

[2] Jonathan Israel, "Enlightenment! Which Enlightenment?" *Journal of the History of Ideas*, 67 (2006), 523–545, at 529; however, see Israel, *Enlightenment Contested: Philosophy, Modernity, and the Emancipation of Man, 1670–1752* (Oxford, 2006), pp. 546, 603–605, for a more moderate admission that "it is perhaps not entirely fair to depict Locke as an ideologist of empire": ibid., p. 604.

[3] James Tully, *Public Philosophy in a New Key: II, Imperialism and Civic Freedom* (Cambridge, 2008), p. 27 (emphasis Tully's).

[4] See especially Bhikhu Parekh, "Liberalism and Colonialism: A Critique of Locke and Mill," in *The Decolonization of Imagination: Culture, Knowledge and Power*, ed. Jan Nederveen Pieterse and Bhikhu Parekh (London, 1995), pp. 81–98; Uday Singh Mehta, *Liberalism and Empire: A Study in Nineteenth-Century British Liberal Thought* (Chicago, 1999). For acute questionings of the assumptions summarized here, see Daniel Carey and Sven Trakulhun, "Universalism, Diversity, and the Postcolonial Enlightenment," in *Postcolonial Enlightenment: Eighteenth-Century Colonialism and Postcolonial Theory*,

agreement that Locke has as much claim to be a theorist of empire as any other proponent of the "self-consciously universal ... political, ethical and epistemological creed" of liberalism, including Bentham, James and John Stuart Mill, and Macaulay (to take only British examples).[5]

The philosophical distance between Locke and Kant, or between Locke and the Utilitarians, should give pause before affirming that consensus, as should the differences between the forms and conceptions of empire found in the seventeenth century and the nineteenth century.[6] This chapter will argue that Locke was clearly a *colonial* thinker. However, it will also argue that the label "imperial" cannot be aptly applied to him because he did not espouse or elaborate a hierarchical ordering of populations, least of all one that placed Europeans above or even apart from other groups, because he saw rationality itself as evenly distributed among human populations and the usual markings of civilization as contingent and fragile. It will be concluded that some of the specifically Atlantic features of Locke's thought can be explained by his connections with English colonial activity, and that he provided only limited grounds on which later imperial thinkers could erect their justifications for European settlement and indigenous dispossession.

JOHN LOCKE, COLONIAL THINKER

There can be no doubt that Locke was a specifically colonial thinker, if by that we mean simply someone who devoted much thought and attention to the settlement and governance of colonies. He was in fact more deeply involved in the practical business of promoting and running overseas settlements than any other European political thinker between the early seventeenth century, when Hugo Grotius wrote legal briefs for

  ed. Daniel Carey and Lynn Festa (Oxford, 2009), pp. 240–280, and Vicki Hsueh, *Hybrid Constitutions: Challenging Legacies of Law, Privilege, and Culture in Colonial America* (Durham, N.C., 2010), pp. 1–24.

[5] Mehta, *Liberalism and Empire*, p. 1. For an illuminating critique of this reading of liberalism, see Jennifer Pitts, *A Turn to Empire: The Rise of Imperial Liberalism in Britain and France* (Princeton, N.J., 2005).

[6] On Kant and empire, see especially Sankar Muthu, *Enlightenment Against Empire* (Princeton, N.J., 2003), chap. 5; on the varieties of empire, see *Theories of Empire, 1450–1800*, ed. David Armitage (Aldershot, England, 1998); Andrew Porter, "From Empire to Commonwealth of Nations," in *Imperium/Empire/Reich: Ein Konzept politischer Herrschaft im deutsch-britischen Vergleich*, ed. Franz Bosbach and Hermann Hiery (Munich, 1999), pp. 167–178; and James Tully, "Lineages of Contemporary Imperialism," in *Lineages of Empire: The Historical Roots of British Imperial Thought*, ed. Duncan Kelly (Oxford, 2009), pp. 3–29.

the Dutch East India Company, and the nineteenth century, when the Mills worked for the British East India Company.[7] His first administrative position was that of secretary to the Lords Proprietors of Carolina from 1669 to 1675, when he was involved in drafting the *Fundamental Constitutions of Carolina* (1669 and later revisions).[8] Among the provisions of Carolina's first frame of government were the creation of a class of hereditary "leet men" who were tied to the land and the introduction of chattel slaves, over whom every "freeman of Carolina" had "absolute power and authority," that is, the power of life and death.[9]

Locke never dissented, publicly or privately, from the harshest provisions of the *Fundamental Constitutions*, although he may also have played some role in expanding Carolina's boundaries of religious toleration and the protection of indigenous people. The *Constitutions* enshrined toleration for all theists, including "heathens, Jews, and other dissenters from the purity of the Christian religion." There is also later testimony that Locke opposed another of its provisions establishing the Church of England in Carolina, and he may have been responsible for the supplementary laws added to the *Constitutions* in 1671 that banned the enslavement of local Indians.[10] The Proprietors clearly approved of Locke's work for, in April 1671, they made him a hereditary "landgrave" of the colony for his great wisdom, learning, and industry in drawing up its form of government and establishing it on the Ashley River in Carolina

---

[7] On Grotius, see Martine Julia van Ittersum, *Profit and Principle: Hugo Grotius, Natural Rights Theories and the Rise of Dutch Power in the East Indies, 1595–1615* (Leiden, 2006); on the Mills and their milieu, see especially Eric Stokes, *The English Utilitarians and India* (Oxford, 1959); Bart Schulz and Georgios Varouxakis, eds., *Utilitarianism and Empire* (Lanham, Md., 2005); and Chapter 9 by Pratap Bhanu Mehta in this book.

[8] The evidence for Locke's hand in the *Fundamental Constitutions* is assessed in J. R. Milton, "John Locke and the Fundamental Constitutions of Carolina," *The Locke Newsletter*, 21 (1990), 111–133; Armitage, "John Locke, Carolina, and the *Two Treatises of Government*"; and Philip Milton, "Pierre Des Maizeaux, A Collection of Several Pieces of Mr. John Locke, and the Formation of the Locke Canon," *Eighteenth-Century Thought*, 3 (2007), 260–265.

[9] *The Fundamental Constitutions of Carolina* (1669), §§22–23, 101, in John Locke, *Political Essays*, ed. Mark Goldie (Cambridge, 1997), pp. 166, 180.

[10] *The Fundamental Constitutions of Carolina*, §87, in Locke, *Political Essays*, ed. Goldie, p. 178; John Marshall, *John Locke, Toleration and Early Enlightenment Culture* (Cambridge, 2006), pp. 599–600; *A Collection of Several Pieces of Mr. John Locke, Never before Printed, or Not Extant in his Works*, ed. Pierre Des Maizeaux (London, 1720), p. 42 n.; The [British] National Archives, Kew (hereafter, TNA), CO 5/286, fol. 41r, Temporary laws for Carolina (December 1671), printed in [W. J. Rivers,] *A Sketch of the History of South Carolina to the Close of the Proprietary Government by the Revolution of 1719* (Charleston, S.C., 1856), p. 353. These "laws" are in Locke's handwriting.

(*magna sua prudentia, eruditione et industria tam in stabilienda regiminis forma, quam in Coloniis ad Flumen Ashleium collocandis*). Locke never took up his 48,000-acre land grant and at one point tried to sell his title, but he never repudiated his collaboration with the Proprietors and seems to have taken pride in the *Fundamental Constitutions* right up to his death in 1704.[11]

By virtue of his connections to Carolina, Locke became the first European philosopher since Michel de Montaigne over a century before to meet and interrogate Native Americans in Europe. In 1670, two sons of the "emperor" of the Kiawah Creek town of Cofitachequi in Carolina traveled to England by way of Barbados. They were named, by the English at least, Honest and Just. Little is known about their movements before they returned to Carolina in 1672, but it is clear that Locke spoke to them before he completed the second draft of his *Essay Concerning Human Understanding* in 1671.[12] In what is now known as "Draft B" of the *Essay*, he compared mathematical computation to human language and speculated that all counting consisted of only three operations: addition, subtraction, and comparison. If a number becomes so large that it cannot be redescribed using the names of smaller numbers, Locke argued, it becomes impossible to conceive the idea of such an enormous sum:

And this I thinke to be the reason why *some Indians I have spoken with*, who were otherwise of quick rationall parts could not as we doe count to a 1000. though they could very well to 20 because their language being scanty & accomodated only to the few necessarys of a needy simple life unacquainted either with trade or Mathematiques, had noe words in it to stand for a thousand. soe that if you discoursed with them of those great numbers they would shew you the hairs of their head to expresse a great multitude which they could not number.[13]

When Locke incorporated a revised version of this passage into the published *Essay* (1690), he compared the constraints on the mathematical knowledge of the "*Americans*" with the similar limits on Europeans'

---

[11] Bodleian Library, Oxford, Locke Manuscripts (hereafter, Bod. MS Locke), b. 5/9 (4 April 1671); Armitage, "John Locke, Carolina, and the *Two Treatises of Government*," 608–611.

[12] St. Julien R. Childs, "Honest and Just at the Court of Charles II," *South Carolina Historical Magazine*, 64 (1963), 27; Alden T. Vaughan, *Transatlantic Encounters: American Indians in Britain, 1500–1776* (Cambridge, 2006), p. 104; Farr, "Locke, Natural Law, and New World Slavery," 498; Farr, "Locke, 'Some Americans,' and the Discourse on Carolina," *Locke Studies*, 9 (2009), 19–77.

[13] John Locke, "Draft B" (1671) of the *Essay*, §50, in *Drafts for the Essay Concerning Human Understanding and Other Philosophical Writings*, ed. Peter H. Nidditch and G. A. J. Rogers, 3 vols. projected (Oxford, 1990–), I, p. 157 (my emphasis).

rational capacities: "I doubt not but we our selves might distinctly number in Words, a great deal farther than we usually do, would we find out but some fit denominations to signifie them by."[14] Such skepticism would be characteristic of his later writings on the subject. The encounter with Honest and Just helped to shape Locke's conception of Native Americans' rational capacities and prevented him from concluding that Europeans alone possessed any superior cultural self-understanding.

Between 1672 and 1676, Locke followed his patron, the first Earl of Shaftesbury, in becoming a stockholder and coproprietor in a company set up to trade between the Bahamas and the American mainland.[15] In September 1672, he was also named in the charter of the Royal African Company, the English monopoly for trading in slaves.[16] In 1673–1674, he became secretary and then also treasurer to the Council for Trade and Foreign Plantations.[17] Moreover, from 1696 until ill health forced him to relinquish office in 1700, Locke was among the first commissioners appointed to the English Board of Trade, the main administrative body that oversaw the commerce and colonies of the Atlantic world. While in that post, he assured a correspondent in Virginia that "[t]he flourishing of the Plantations under their due and just regulations [is] that which I doe and shall always aim at," and he was always as active in its counsels as his fragile health would permit.[18] His administrative

---

[14] John Locke, *An Essay Concerning Human Understanding*, ed. Peter H. Nidditch (Oxford, 1975), p. 207 (II. xvi. 6).

[15] Hampshire Record Office, Winchester, Malmesbury Papers, 7M54/232, Articles of Agreement of the Bahamas Adventurers (4 September 1672); British Library, London (hereafter, BL), Add. MS 15640, fols. 3r–8v, 9r–15r; K. H. D. Haley, *The First Earl of Shaftesbury* (Oxford, 1968), pp. 232–233. On Shaftesbury's colonial vision, see Tom Leng, "Shaftesbury's Aristocratic Empire," in *Anthony Ashley Cooper, First Earl of Shaftesbury, 1621–1683*, ed. John Spurr (Aldershot, England: Ashgate, 2011), pp. 101–126.

[16] TNA, C 66/3136/45, CO 268/1/11 (27 September 1672).

[17] Library of Congress, Washington, D.C., Phillipps MS 8539, pt. 1, Journals of the Council for [Trade and] Foreign Plantations, 1670–1674; Ralph Paul Bieber, "The British Plantation Councils of 1670–4," *English Historical Review*, 40 (1925), 93–106; Eva Botella-Ordinas, "Debating Empires, Inventing Empires: British Territorial Claims Against the Spaniards in America, 1670–1714," *Journal for Early Modern Cultural Studies*, 10 (2010), 142–168, at 142–150.

[18] Locke to James Blair, 16 October 1699, in *The Correspondence of John Locke*, ed. E. S. de Beer, 8 vols. to date (Oxford, 1976–), VI, p. 706; Peter Laslett, "John Locke, the Great Recoinage and the Origins of the Board of Trade 1695–1698," in *John Locke: Problems and Perspectives*, ed. John Yolton (Cambridge, 1969), pp. 137–164; Michael Kammen, "Virginia at the Close of the Seventeenth Century: An Appraisal by James Blair and John Locke," *Virginia Magazine of History and Biography*, 74 (1966), 141–169; Jack Turner, "John Locke, Christian Mission, and Colonial America," *Modern Intellectual History*, 8 (2011), 267–297.

duties and financial investments over the course of four decades earned Locke practical experience of English colonial and commercial activity in North America, from New York to Carolina, in the Caribbean, Ireland, and Africa.[19] By the time he resigned from the Board of Trade in June 1700, he had become one of the two best-informed observers of the English Atlantic world of the late seventeenth century. Only his rival on the Board of Trade, the career administrator Sir William Blathwayt, had a more comprehensive command of English colonial administration by that time.[20]

Locke's experience in colonial administration both widened his horizons and focused his interests. During the closing decades of the seventeenth century, when Locke was most involved in colonial affairs, "there is evidence of sharpening legal distinctions between the Atlantic and the Indian Ocean." The Board of Trade's activities concentrated almost entirely on the Atlantic world, and they considered affairs in the Indian Ocean only when they had implications for that arena, as in the case of global piracy, for example.[21] Locke's economic writings provide evidence that his imperial vision was similarly bounded by the Atlantic. There is a single reference to the Indian Ocean arena in his economic writings, when he implored an antagonist "please to remember the great Sums of Money … carried every year to the *East-Indies*, for which we bring home consumable Commodities."[22] And Locke mentioned the East India Company only once in print, in his *Second Letter Concerning Toleration* (1690), when he taxed an interlocutor with failing to see that "Civil Society" has different goals from other forms of human association: "By which account there will be no difference between Church and State; A Commonwealth and an Army; or between a Family and the *East-India* Company; all which have hitherto been thought distinct sorts of Societies, instituted for different

[19] Most of his practical writings relating to colonial matters will appear in *John Locke, Colonial Writings*, ed. David Armitage (Oxford, forthcoming).

[20] Barbara C. Murison, "The Talented Mr Blathwayt: His Empire Revisited," in *English Atlantics Revisited: Essays Honouring Professor Ian K. Steele*, ed. Nancy L. Rhoden (Montreal and Kingston, 2007), pp. 33–58, at pp. 33–34.

[21] Lauren Benton, "Legal Spaces of Empire: Piracy and the Origins of Oceanic Regionalism," *Comparative Studies in Society and History*, 47 (2005), 700–724, at 718; TNA, CO 324/6, fols. 160r–64v, 166v–71r, 175; CO 5/1116, fols. 11r–17v; compare Bod. MS Locke c. 30, fols. 62–63, endorsed "Pyracy 97."

[22] Philip J. Stern, "'A Politie of Civill & Military Power': Political Thought and the Late Seventeenth-Century Foundations of the East India Company-State," *Journal of British Studies*, 47 (2008), 253–283; John Locke, *Some Considerations of the Consequences of the Lowering of Interest*, 2nd ed. (1696), in *Locke on Money*, ed. Patrick Hyde Kelly, 2 vols. (Oxford, 1991), I, p. 333.

Ends."²³ He did not invest in the New East India Company until after he had left the Board of Trade. Even then, he held on to his bonds for less than a year and sold them at a small loss in the summer of 1701.²⁴

Locke's imperial vision was comparatively less wide-ranging than that of many contemporary English political economists. For example, Sir William Petty gradually expanded his range outward from the Three Kingdoms of Britain and Ireland to the Atlantic world and from there to a conception of an economically defined, globally dispersed polity in which all of England's interests – British, American, African, and Asian – would be equally represented.²⁵ No less comprehensive were the analyses of England's East India trade by Charles Davenant and Henry Martyn, who each saw Asian commerce as crucial to England's economic fortunes and to the elaboration of interoceanic and global trade more generally. On their analysis, bullion taken largely from the Americas could be exchanged in Asia both for luxury goods and for more widely affordable commodities such as the extremely popular calicoes that were exported from India to England and the American colonies. For Martyn, in particular, the importation of cheaper textiles from India may have undercut domestic English industry, but that was an unavoidable side effect of comparative advantage to which protectionism could provide no solution: "When we shall be reduc'd to plain Labour without any manner of Art, we shall live at least as well as the Wild *Indians* of *America*, the *Hottantots* of *Africa*, or the Inhabitants of New *Holland*," he remarked sardonically. Martyn drew heavily on Locke's comparison between the productive capacities of England and America in the *Second Treatise* (II. 41) to support his argument. This debt only pointed up the absence of the Asian trades in Locke's vision of political economy, an absence made all the more poignant by the fact that in 1696 Locke missed his chance to ask "a Japonese" visitor to London "whether the importation of gold and silver" was prohibited in his country.²⁶

---

²³ John Locke, *A Second Letter Concerning Toleration* (London, 1690), p. 51. It is therefore highly unlikely that the distinctive voting procedures of the East India Company inspired his conception of majority rule in the *Two Treatises, pace* Francesco Galgano, "John Locke azionista delle compagnie coloniali (una chiave di lettura del *Secondo trattato del governo*)," *Contratto e impresa*, 23 (2007), 327–341, at 327–333, 340–341.

²⁴ Bod. MS Locke c. 1, fols. 106, 107.

²⁵ David Armitage, *The Ideological Origins of the British Empire* (Cambridge, 2000), pp. 152–153; Ted McCormick, *William Petty and the Ambitions of Political Arithmetic* (Oxford, 2009), pp. 230–233.

²⁶ Istvan Hont, *Jealousy of Trade: International Competition and the Nation-State in Historical Perspective* (Cambridge, Mass., 2005), pp. 201–222, 245–258; Henry Martyn, *Considerations upon the East-India Trade* (London, 1701), pp. 58, 72–73; Locke to Hans

The limits of Locke's imperial vision become even clearer when we compare him with other seventeenth-century European contributors to the modern tradition of natural jurisprudence. For example, Grotius's fundamental writings on natural law sprang originally from his defense of the Dutch East India Company's activities in maritime Southeast Asia, most notably in his *The Free Sea* (1609), the *locus classicus* for arguments in favor of freedom of trade across the oceans of the world and a work Locke certainly knew.[27] Later in the century, Samuel Pufendorf's conception of human sociability implied a potentially global conception of commercial society linking together the peoples of the world through mutually sustaining systems of utility and exchange.[28] This "neo-Aristotelian" vision of commercial sociability found its closest parallel in late-seventeenth-century French Augustinianism, especially in the work of the French theologian and essayist Pierre Nicole. As Nicole put it in his "Treatise of Peace" (1671), using the example of Northern European trade with East Asia:

The world then is our citty: and as inhabitants of it, we have intercourse with all man kinde, And doe receive from them advantages, or inconveniencys [*de l'utilité & tantôt du dommage*]. The Hollanders have a trade with Japan, we [the French] with Holland; and soe have a commerce with those people, at the farthest end of the world.... They are linked to us, on one side, or other; & all entre into that chain, which ties the whole race of men togeather by their mutuall wants [*besoins réciproques*].[29]

Nicole's vision of global commerce appeared here only fleetingly, but it contrasted starkly with Locke's own conception of commerce, which was by default almost entirely confined to the Atlantic world. Locke certainly knew Nicole's work, for he translated the "Treatise of Peace" in the mid-1670s. However, his political economy and political theory remained

---

Sloane, 15 March 1697, in *Correspondence*, ed. de Beer, VI, pp. 35–36. Sloane thought the visitor was Chinese, from "Emoy" (present-day Xiamen): Sloane to Locke, 18 March 1697, ibid., VI, p. 56.

[27] Hugo Grotius, *The Free Sea*, ed. David Armitage (Indianapolis, 2004); Grotius, *Commentary on the Law of Prize and Booty*, ed. Martine van Ittersum (Indianapolis, 2006). Locke possessed Grotius's *Mare Liberum* (1609) in an edition of Grotius, *De jure belli ac pacis libri tres* (The Hague, 1680), Bod. Locke 9. 99.

[28] Richard Tuck, *The Rights of War and Peace: Political Thought and the International Order from Grotius to Kant* (Oxford, 1999), pp. 167–172.

[29] Hont, *Jealousy of Trade*, pp. 45–51, 159–184; Pierre Nicole, "Treatise Concerning the Way of Preserving Peace with Men" (1671), trans. John Locke, in *John Locke as Translator: Three of the Essais of Pierre Nicole in French and English*, ed. Jean S. Yolton (Oxford, 2000), pp. 115–260, at p. 117. See also Richard Cumberland, *A Treatise of the Laws of Nature* (1672), ed. Jon Parkin (Indianapolis, 2005), p. 318.

more limited than Nicole's and his universalism more constrained than either Grotius's or Pufendorf's in its range of reference. As we will see, this combination of cosmopolitanism and regional concentration characterized Locke's universalism, more broadly conceived.

THE LIMITS OF LOCKEAN UNIVERSALISM

Locke sometimes joked with friends about emigrating to New England or Carolina, but he never traveled farther west than his native county of Somerset. He did not even see the Atlantic Ocean until he was fifty-six years old, and then only from La Rochelle in France. In this regard, he can be compared to his friend Sir Isaac Newton, who lived an entirely landlocked life while also acting, like Locke, as "a fundamental link between the colonial information order and the empiricist knowledge regime forged in the final decades of the seventeenth century."[30] And yet, unlike Newton, Locke did spend long periods outside England, including almost four years traveling in France (1675–1679) and six in exile in Holland (1683–1689). His correspondence likewise comprised a nearly worldwide web: among the almost 4,000 letters from and to him that survive, there are items from the Caribbean, New England, Virginia, and Carolina, as well as from Bengal and China, not to mention extensive exchanges with friends and acquaintances in Scotland, Ireland, France, the Netherlands, Germany, and Sweden. Among the seventeenth-century correspondence networks, only those of the Jesuit Athanasius Kircher and the philosopher Gottfried Wilhelm Leibniz were both larger in size and comparably farflung in extent.[31] During his years in Europe, he collected numerous accounts of the extra-European world. By the time of his death, Locke's collection of travel literature was one of the largest ever assembled in Britain, and it comprised 195 books, many maps, and a portfolio of ethnographic illustrations "of the inhabitants of severall remote parts of the world espetially the East Indies," which included representations

[30] *Correspondence*, ed. de Beer, I, pp. 379, 590, II, pp. 27, 34, 40, 68, 95, 105, 132, 141, 147, 441, 444; Bod. MS Locke f. 28, fol. 19; *Locke's Travels in France, 1675–1679, as Related in his Journals, Correspondence and Other Papers*, ed. John Lough (Cambridge, 1953), p. 232: "This is the first time I ever saw the Ocean" (7 September 1678); Simon Schaffer, "Newton on the Beach: The Information Order of *Principia Mathematica*," *History of Science*, 47 (2009), 243–276, at 247.

[31] Mark Goldie, "Introduction," in *John Locke: Selected Correspondence*, ed. Goldie (Oxford, 2002), pp. viii, xviii; Paula Findlen, ed., *Athanasius Kircher: The Last Man Who Knew Everything* (New York, 2004); Paul Lodge, ed., *Leibniz and His Correspondents* (Cambridge, 2004).

of Laplanders, Brazilian "Cannibal[s]," "Hottentot[s]" from the Cape of Good Hope, and inhabitants of Java, Amboina, Macassar, Malaya, Ternate, Tonkin, Japan, China, and "Tartary."[32]

In the course of compiling his major published works, Locke mined his library and pressed his global connections for data about matters medical, theological, ethnographic, social, and political. Their greatest impact can be found in the first five editions of the *Essay Concerning Human Understanding* (1690–1706), in which information regarding the diversity of human beliefs provided crucial ammunition for his arguments against the supposed innateness of ideas. The key test case for innatism was the idea of God. If even that seemingly most fundamental idea could not be shown to be universal, Locke argued, then surely no other could be said to be inborn, "since it is hard to conceive, how there should be innate Moral Principles, without an innate *Idea* of a *Deity*." He offered evidence to the contrary from the accounts of what "Navigation discovered, in these latter Ages." Not content with one or two examples to combat innatism, he continued to add empirical material to this passage and other similar ones until, in the first posthumous edition of the *Essay* (1706), "the number of authorities he had cited had risen to 16.... The locations they described ranged from the Caucasus and Lapland to Brazil, Paraguay, Siam, China, the Cape of Good Hope, and elsewhere." In this way, Locke made greater use of ethnographic information than any other philosopher in Britain before the eighteenth century.[33]

Locke's knowledge of travel literature, and the information he gathered as a servant of English colonial ventures, encouraged his skepticism about human capacities and about the alleged superiority of Europeans. In the early lectures he gave at Oxford that are now known as the *Essays on the Law of Nature* (c. 1663–1664), Locke had judged the "primitive and untutored tribes [*barbaras ... et nudas gentes*]" harshly, "since among most of them appears not the slightest trace or track of piety, merciful feeling, fidelity, chastity, and the rest of the virtues." To this extent,

---

[32] BL Add. MS 5253; Locke to William Charleton, 2 August 1687, in Locke, *Correspondence*, ed. de Beer, III, p. 240.

[33] Locke, *Essay Concerning Human Understanding*, ed. Nidditch, pp. 87–88 (I. iv. 8); Daniel Carey, *Locke, Shaftesbury, and Hutcheson: Contesting Diversity in the Enlightenment and Beyond* (Cambridge, 2006), pp. 71–92; Carey, "Locke, Travel Literature, and the Natural History of Man," *The Seventeenth Century*, 11 (1996), 259–280, at 263. Locke had earlier invoked the atheism of the inhabitants of Brazil and Soldania Bay in the *Essays on the Law of Nature* (c. 1663–1664): Locke, *Essays on the Law of Nature and Associated Writings*, ed. W. von Leyden (Oxford, 1954), pp. 172–174/173–175 (Latin/English).

he did not distinguish between the peoples "of Asia and America who do not consider themselves to be bound by the same laws, separated from us as they are by long stretches of land and unaccustomed to our morals and beliefs [*nec moribus nostris aut opinionibus assueti*]."[34] This recognition of diversity served the purposes of Locke's evolving criticism of innate ideas, but his evaluation of that diversity would become more complex in his later writings, starting in the late 1660s and early 1670s. His developing arguments in this regard do not easily fit the stereotype of an imperial theorist who ranked the peoples of the world hierarchically and placed some within, but many outside, the pale of liberalism.

It is now a commonplace that liberalism of the kind often traced back to Locke was both inclusive and universal in *theory* but exclusionary and contingent in *practice*. As the most eloquent and subtle proponent of this view has put it, "as a historical phenomenon, the period of liberal history is unmistakably marked by the systematic and sustained political exclusion of various groups and 'types' of people."[35] Among the categories of persons denied the benefits and rights that liberalism theoretically promised to all human beings were, variously, indigenous peoples, the enslaved, women, children, and the mentally disabled, those whom Locke called "mad Men" and "Idiots." The main criterion used to exclude such persons was their lack of rationality, and it has been argued that "[t]he American Indian is the example Locke uses to demonstrate a lack of reason."[36] Yet, as we have seen, Locke did not charge Native Americans with irrationality even when he convicted them of impiety, mercilessness, infidelity, promiscuousness, and other vices in 1663–1664. Indeed, as we have also seen, in 1671 he wrote of the "quick rationall parts" of the Carolina Indians he had interviewed in England.

Only in the First *Treatise of Government* did Locke ever call indigenous peoples "irrational," and then solely as a means of praising their untutored wisdom over the sophistication of supposedly civilized nations: "He that will impartially survey the World ... will have reason to think,

---

[34] Locke, *Essays on the Law of Nature*, ed. von Leyden, pp. 140/141, 162/163 (Latin/ English).

[35] Mehta, *Liberalism and Empire*, pp. 46–47 (on exclusion, quoted), pp. 52–64 (on Locke); compare Mehta, "Liberal Strategies of Exclusion," *Politics and Society*, 18 (1990), 427–454; Andrew Sartori, "The British Empire and Its Liberal Mission," *Journal of Modern History*, 78 (2006), 623–642; Jack P. Greene, ed., *Exclusionary Empire: English Liberty Overseas, 1600–1900* (Cambridge, 2010).

[36] Barbara Arneil, "Citizens, Wives, Latent Citizens and Non-Citizens in the *Two Treatises*: A Legacy of Inclusion, Exclusion and Assimilation," *Eighteenth-Century Thought*, 3 (2007), 209–222, at 216.

that the Woods and Forests, where the irrational untaught Inhabitants keep right by following Nature, are fitter to give us Rules, than Cities and Palaces, where those that call themselves Civil and Rational, go out of their way, by the Authority of Example" (I. 58).[37] Locke generally found greater inequalities of capacity *within* particular peoples than he did *between* them. In this vein, he argued in *The Conduct of the Understanding* (1697), "Amongst men of equall education there is great inequality of parts. And the woods of America as well as the Schools of Athens produce men of severall abilitys in the same kinde."[38] The more fundamental difference between "Americans" and Europeans therefore lay not in their intellectual abilities but in their contingent circumstances, their education, and their needs as shaped by their environment.

Locke argued consistently throughout his works that God sends us into this world without innate ideas or any of the other physical "conveniencies of life" (to use a favorite Lockean turn of phrase). It was necessary for human beings to exercise their physical and mental labor upon the otherwise inert creation given to them by God, this being "the Condition of Humane Life, which requires Labour and Materials to work on" (II. 35).[39] Human beings could neither add to nor subtract from the divine creation, but they had a duty to construct it to their own devices, both mentally and physically. What we might call Locke's "constructivist" understanding of human labor was basic to his epistemology in the *Essay Concerning Human Understanding*:

The Dominion of Man, in this little World of his own Understanding, being much the same, as it is in the great World of visible things; wherein his Power, however managed by Art and Skill, reaches no farther, than to compound and divide the Materials, that are made to his Hand....[40]

It is up to us to furnish ourselves with a stock of ideas, just as we must transform nature into materials for our use: "it is want of Industry and Consideration in us, and not of Bounty in him, if we have them not" (*Essay*, I. iv. 16). Thus, even the idea of God himself could be lacking, just as physical constructions like bridges or houses will be, if humans do not

---

[37] John Locke, *Two Treatises of Government*, ed. Peter Laslett, rev. ed. (Cambridge, 1988), p. 183. All references in the text are to this edition, by *Treatise* and paragraph number, unless otherwise noted.

[38] John Locke, *Of the Conduct of the Understanding*, ed. Paul Schuurman (Keele, England, 2000), p. 156.

[39] Compare E. J. Hundert, "The Making of *Homo Faber*: John Locke between Ideology and History," *Journal of the History of Ideas*, 33 (1972), 3–22.

[40] Locke, *Essay*, ed. Nidditch, p. 120 (II. ii. 2).

act industriously, if they fail to seize their God-given opportunities, or if they are constrained by their own reduced circumstances like the people of the "West Indies":

[N]ature furnish[es] us only with the materials for the most part rough and unfitted to our uses it requires labour art and thought to suit them to our occasions, and if the knowledg of men had not found out ways to shorten the labour and improve severall things which seem not a[t] first sight to be of any use to us we should spend all our time to make a scanty provision for a poore and miserable life. a sufficient instance whereof we have in the inhabitants of that large and fertill part of the world the west Indies, who lived a poore uncomfortable laborious life with all their industry scarce able to subsist and that perhaps only for want of knowing the use of that stone out of which the Inhabitants of the old world had the skill to draw Iron[.][41]

The presence or lack of adequate tools or commodities could account entirely for the differential productivity of particular peoples. Such conveniences are accidental and external; they bear no relation to the supposedly innate capacities of individuals or groups.

Locke was a thoroughgoing species nominalist and did not argue for any inherent ethnic, let alone racial, difference. Any people could go up or down the scale of civility according to the materials nature had given to them: "were the use of *Iron* lost among us, we should in a few Ages be unavoidably reduced to the Wants and Ignorance of the ancient savage *Americans*, whose natural Endowments and Provisions come no way short of those of the most flourishing and polite Nations."[42] He also believed firmly in the rationality of Native Americans and thought that the advantages enjoyed by Europeans, even by philosophers like himself, were accidental: "had the *Virginia* King *Apochancana* been educated in *England*, he had, perhaps, been as knowing a Divine, and as good a Mathematician, as any in it."[43] The lack of those advantages could just as easily make the English as irrational as Native Americans had become

---

[41] John Locke, "Understanding" (8 February 1677), Bod. MS Locke f. 2, p. 44, printed in Locke, *Political Essays*, ed. Goldie, p. 261.

[42] Locke, *Essay*, ed. Nidditch, p. 646 (IV. xii. 11). On Locke's antiessentialism, see the discussions in Jeremy Waldron, *God, Locke, and Equality: Christian Foundations in Locke's Political Thought* (Cambridge, 2002), chap. 3, "Species and the Shape of Equality," and Peter R. Anstey and Stephen A. Harris, "Locke and Botany," *Studies in History and Philosophy of Biological and Biomedical Sciences*, 37 (2006), 151–171.

[43] Locke, *Essay*, ed. Nidditch, p. 92 (I. iv. 12). In "Draft B" of the *Essay*, Locke had made the same point using the example of another Virginia Indian leader, Tottepottemay: Locke, "Draft B," §12, in *Drafts for the Essay*, eds. Nidditch and Rogers, I, p. 120, drawing on [John Lederer,] *The Discoveries of John Lederer*, trans. Sir William Talbot (London, 1672), p. 7; Farr, "Locke, 'Some Americans', and the Discourse on 'Carolina,'" 40–50.

because they lacked certain human inventions: "perhaps without books we should be as ignorant as the Indians whose minds are as ill-clad as their bodies."[44] Locke's stress on the contingency and the reversibility of so much that later thinkers took to be the marks of higher civilization therefore makes it impossible to call him an imperial theorist on the grounds that he ranked cultures within a progressivist vision of human history.

LOCKE AND THE LEGITIMATION OF EMPIRE

Locke can only be described as a theorist of "empire" in a narrowly restricted definition of that term. In early modern usage, the meanings of "empire" clustered around two main referents: empire as sovereignty (*imperium*) and empire as a composite state.[45] Locke would certainly have recognized the meaning of "empire" as sovereignty or *imperium* and understood it to be territorial in application, as in the passage in the *Second Treatise* where he described how the "several States and Kingdoms" of the world "have, by positive agreement, settled a Property amongst themselves, in distinct Parts and parcels of the Earth" (II. 45). However, there is no evidence that he would have understood "empire" to refer to a composite state: for example, the terms "English empire" or "British empire" appear nowhere in his writings. Nor did Locke anywhere conceive of an empire in terms that later theorists might have recognized: as a territorially defined, hierarchically organized polity that suspends diversity within unity, usually for the benefit of a metropolitan or other central authority.[46] He was, in regard to his strictly political theory (particularly in the *Two Treatises of Government*), a theorist of the commonwealth, or state, and not a theorist of empire. How, then, might he have come to be identified as an imperial theorist?

Three answers might be given to that question, two historical and one more immediately textual. The first goes back to the eighteenth and early nineteenth centuries, when Locke's opponents identified him as a theorist indebted to the experience of empire. Critics at that time focused on two particular features of his political theory: the prominence of Native

---

44 Locke, "Of Study" (27 March 1677), in Locke, *Political Essays*, ed. Goldie, p. 367.
45 Armitage, *The Ideological Origins of the British Empire*, pp. 29–32.
46 Compare Charles S. Maier, *Among Empires: American Ascendancy and Its Predecessors* (Cambridge, Mass., 2006), pp. 20–21, on empire as "a system of rule that transforms society at home even as it stabilizes inequality transnationally by replicating it geographically, in the core and on the periphery."

Americans in his account of the state of nature and the centrality of slavery to the colonial system imagined in the *Fundamental Constitutions of Carolina.* In this vein, shortly after Locke's death, his former pupil, the third Earl of Shaftesbury, condemned "the credulous Mr. Locke with his Indian barbarian stories of wild nations."[47] Sixty years later, the Anglican apologist George Horne, later bishop of Norwich, similarly objected to Locke's appeal to the Native American example: "This is not a state of *nature*, but the most *unnatural* state in the world, for creatures made in the image of God. And does a polite philosopher, in these enlightened days, send us to study politics under Cherokee tutors!"[48] And during the American Revolution, the conservative Anglican dean of Gloucester, Josiah Tucker, argued repeatedly that the colonists' rebelliousness sprang from their attachment to Locke's political theory. Among his strategies for discrediting American revolutionary ideology was thus to attack the contractarian theories of "Mr. LOCKE and his followers" on the grounds that they misleadingly deployed "the Tribes of Savage *Indians*" as examples of human sociability in a state of nature: "Let them not din our Ears with the examples of the Savages of *America*, as being any Proofs and Illustrations of their Hypothesis; – which, when thoroughly discussed, and accurately examined, prove just the contrary." Locke and his disciples, Tucker continued, were either ignorant of the true nature of the Native Americans "or they must have acted a very disingenuous Part" in appealing to them.[49] Shaftesbury, Horne, and Tucker shared the prejudices regarding the capacities of indigenous peoples associated with the high imperial vision. The critical distance between them and Locke is further evidence of how only with difficulty can he be assimilated to later imperial theories.

Locke's critics also accused him of hypocrisy with regard to another subaltern people entangled in the experience of empire: enslaved Africans and African Americans. Tucker, again, noted that in the *Fundamental*

[47] Third Earl of Shaftesbury to Michael Ainsworth, 3 June 1709, in *The Life, Unpublished Letters, and Philosophical Regimen of Anthony, Earl of Shaftesbury,* ed. Benjamin Rand (London, 1900), pp. 403–404.

[48] George Horne, "*Mr. Locke,* Consideration on His Scheme of an Original Compact" (in an Oxford assize-sermon originally preached in 1769 and revised c. 1792), in *The Reception of Locke's Politics,* ed. Mark Goldie, 6 vols. (London, 1999), III, pp. 229–238.

[49] Josiah Tucker, *A Treatise on Civil Government, in Three Parts* (London, 1781), pp. 200–201; J. G. A. Pocock, "Josiah Tucker on Burke, Locke, and Price: A Study in the Varieties of Eighteenth-Century Conservatism," in Pocock, *Virtue, Commerce, and History: Essays on Political Thought and History, Chiefly in the Eighteenth Century* (Cambridge, 1987), pp. 167–179.

Constitutions, Locke "lays it down as an invariable Maxim ... 'That every Freeman of *Carolina* shall have ABSOLUTE POWER AND AUTHORITY over his Negro Slaves.' " How could this be reconciled with the statement in the opening lines of the *Two Treatises of Government* that "Slavery is so vile and miserable an Estate of Man ... that 'tis hardly to be conceived, that an *Englishman*, much less a *Gentleman*, should plead for't"? So much for "the humane Mr. LOCKE! the great and glorious Assertor of the natural Rights and Liberties of Mankind." Tucker thought that in this regard Locke was just like all "Republicans," or what we would call "liberals": that is, in favor of leveling all hierarchies above themselves while "tyrannizing over those, whom Chance or Misfortune have placed below them."[50] (This might be seen as an ancestor of the argument that liberalism as a creed is exclusionary by its very nature.) Half a century later, in 1829, Jeremy Bentham used the same feature of the *Fundamental Constitutions* to ridicule Locke for his attachment to private property. If property holding were the criterion for political participation, Bentham charged, then its *reductio ad absurdum* could be found among the slaveholders of the British Caribbean: "Property the only object of care to Government. Persons possessing it alone entitled to be represented. West Indies the meridian for these principles of this liberty-champion": that is, Locke himself.[51]

The second historical answer to the question of how Locke could be thought of as a theorist of empire would be that his arguments were in fact often used in settler colonies around the world, and by other theorists who promoted European settlement beyond Europe, to justify the expropriation of indigenous peoples. For example, in the early-eighteenth-century context of settler claims against the native title of the Mohegans of Connecticut, Locke's work could be excerpted to argue that the Indians were pre-civil peoples who had less right to the lands on which they lived than the more industrious English colonists.[52] This

[50] [Josiah Tucker,] *A Series of Answers to Certain Popular Objections, Against Separating the Rebellious Colonies, and Discarding them Entirely* (Gloucester, England, 1776), pp. 103–104; Tucker, *A Treatise on Civil Government*, p. 168; Locke, *Two Treatises of Government*, ed. Laslett, p. 141.

[51] Jeremy Bentham, "Article on Utilitarianism" (8 June 1829), Bentham Papers, University College London, XIV, pp. 432 (marginal note), 433.

[52] John Bulkley, "Preface," in Roger Wolcott, *Poetical Meditations, Being the Improvement of Some Vacant Hours* (New London, 1725), pp. xv–lvi; Tully, "Rediscovering America: The *Two Treatises* and Aboriginal Rights," in Tully, *An Approach to Political Philosophy*, pp. 166–168; Craig Yirush, *Settlers, Liberty, and Empire: The Roots of Early American Political Theory, 1675–1775* (Cambridge, 2011), chap. 4, "John Bulkley and the Mohegans."

so-called agriculturalist argument gained its greatest purchase in the version inflected by Physiocratic political economy propagated by the Swiss jurist Emer de Vattel in his *Droit des gens* (1758), which argued that peoples who, "to avoid labour, chuse to live only by hunting, and their flocks" pursued an "idle mode of life, usurp more extensive territories than ... they would have occasion for, and have therefore no reason to complain, if other nations, more industrious, and too closely confined, come to take possession of a part of those lands." From this argument, it followed that "the establishment of many colonies on the continent of North America might, on their confining themselves within just bounds, be extremely lawful."[53] Vattel's arguments were widely dispersed across the globe by the circuits of empire in the late eighteenth and nineteenth centuries; their force could be felt when, for example, the Sydney *Herald* proclaimed in 1838 that Australia was for the Aborigines only "a common – they bestowed no labour upon the land – their ownership, their right, was nothing more than that of the Emu or the Kangaroo."[54] This was a theoretical justification for the foundations of property holding in an imperial context; it was certainly Lockean in form but not directly Lockean in origin.

Like these imperial iterations of Locke's arguments, the third, textual answer to the problem of Locke's identification as a theorist of empire goes back to the *Two Treatises of Government*. The allusions to non-European peoples in the *Two Treatises* are almost exclusively drawn from the Americas. There are only two passing references to Asia in the *Treatises*, one to the Chinese as "a very great and civil People" (I. 141), the other to the deleterious consequences of absolute monarchy Robert Knox had portrayed in his "late Relation of *Ceylon*" (1680, II. 2), which Locke acquired in 1681.[55] Otherwise, the historical and ethnographic examples Locke uses referred to "*Americans*," meaning

---

[53] Emer de Vattel, *The Law of Nations* (1758), ed. Béla Kapossy and Richard Whatmore (Indianapolis, 2008), pp. 129–130 (I. vii. 81).

[54] Quoted in Duncan Ivison, "The Nature of Rights and the History of Empire," in *British Political Thought in History, Literature and Theory, 1500–1800*, ed. David Armitage (Cambridge, 2006), pp. 191–211, at p. 197; on the persistence of Vattelian arguments in nineteenth-century British imperial thought, see Gregory Claeys, *Imperial Sceptics: British Critics of Empire, 1850–1920* (Cambridge, 2010), pp. 16–18, 108–109, 140, 202, 238, 263, 284–285.

[55] Robert Knox, *An Historical Relation of the Island of Ceylon* (London, 1680), pp. 43–47; Locke, *Two Treatises of Government*, ed. Laslett, p. 327 n. 12; Anna Winterbottom, "Producing and Using the *Historical Relation of Ceylon*: Robert Knox, the East India Company and the Royal Society," *British Journal for the History of Science*, 42 (2009), 515–538.

Native Americans, accompanied by occasional references to the creole settlers. Thus, in the *First Treatise*, Locke drew on examples from Peru,[56] from the settlement of Carolina and the "little Tribe[s]" "in many parts of *America*," and from "our late Histories of the *Northern America*" to ridicule Sir Robert Filmer's patriarchalism (I. 57, 145, 154). And in the same work, he twice alluded to the "Planter," a "Man in the *West-Indies*, who hath with him Sons of his own Friends, or Companions, Souldiers under Pay, or Slaves bought with Money," to disaggregate two forms of authority Filmer had conflated, political sovereignty and the power to make war (I. 130, 131).

The even more frequent allusions in the *Second Treatise* were likewise almost entirely confined to the Native Americans. In that work, "an *Indian*" stands beyond the reach of positive law made in Europe (II. 9). When "a *Swiss* and an *Indian*" encounter each other "in the Woods of *America*," they do so in a state of nature and hence are bound in their dealings by the laws of nature alone (II. 14). The Indians' family structures are flexible, yet matrilineal: "in those parts of *America* where when the Husband and Wife part, which happens frequently, the Children are all left to the Mother, follow her, and are wholly under her Care and Provision" (II. 65). A system of absolute monarchy in Europe would not ameliorate the instincts of a tyrant from across the Atlantic: "He that would have been insolent and injurious in the Woods of *America*, would not probably be much better in a Throne" (II. 92). All political societies began not in natural hierarchy but in consent, "And, if *Josephus Acosta*'s word may be taken, he tells us … in many parts of *America* there was no Government at all" (II. 102). "Conformable hereunto we find the People of *America*," Locke went on, "who living out of the reach of the Conquering Swords and spreading domination of the two great Empires of *Peru* and *Mexico*, enjoy'd their own natural freedom" (II. 105). Such peoples had "no Temptation to enlarge their Possessions of Land, or contest for wider extent of Ground," and "the Kings of the *Indians* in *America*, which is still a Pattern of the first Ages in *Asia* and *Europe*," are "little more than Generals of their Armies" (II. 108). They did not lack a medium of exchange, but "the Wampompeke of the *Americans*" was as incommensurable "to an *European* Prince, [as] the

---

[56] Locke used the same example of Peruvian cannibalism from Garcilaso de la Vega in Locke, *Essay*, ed. Nidditch, p. 71 (I. iv. 9). On Locke and Garcilaso, see James W. Fuerst, "Mestizo Rhetoric: The Political Thought of El Inca Garcilaso de la Vega" (PhD thesis, Harvard University, 2000), pp. 349–405.

Silver Money of *Europe* would have been formerly to an *American*" (II. 184).[57]

Fully half of Locke's allusions to the "Americans" clustered in a single chapter of the *Second Treatise*, chapter V, "Of Property." His first image of the primal positive community God had bestowed on humanity before the invention of private property is the "Fruit, or Venison, which nourishes the wild *Indian*, who knows no Inclosure, and is still a Tenant in common" (II. 26). This is the same Indian upon whom the "Law of reason makes the Deer" his "who hath killed it" (II. 30). Such goods show that "[t]he greatest part of things really useful to the Life of Man, and such as the necessity of subsisting made the first Commoners of the World look after, as it doth the *Americans* now, are generally things of short duration" (II. 46). Accordingly, the "several Nations of the *Americans* are ... rich in Land, and poor in all the Comforts of Life" (II. 41), as can be shown by comparing "[a]n Acre of Land that bears [in England] Twenty Bushels of Wheat, and another in *America* ... of the same natural, intrinsick Value" but very different productivity (II. 43). Anyone who "plant[ed] in some in-land, vacant places of *America*" would not be able greatly to enlarge their possessions; even if they did, "What would a Man value Ten Thousand, or an Hundred Thousand Acres of excellent Land, ready cultivated, and well stocked too with Cattle, in the middle of the in-land Parts of *America*, where he had no hopes of Commerce with other Parts of the World, to draw Money to him for the Sale of the Product" (II. 36, 48)? From that very fact Locke drew his famous conclusion: "Thus in the beginning all the World was *America*, and more so than that is now; for no such thing as Money was any where known" (II. 49).

The prominence of these allusions to America in the *Two Treatises*, and their accumulation in the chapter "Of Property," were in part the product of Locke's continuing relationship with Carolina in the early 1680s. During the summer of 1682, Locke was staying at the Earl of Shaftesbury's London residence at just the moment when the Carolina Proprietors were campaigning to revive the colony's fortunes and revised the *Fundamental Constitutions* to make their provisions more attractive to a wider range of potential settlers. A printed copy of the January 1682 *Fundamental Constitutions* survives with Locke's corrections and

[57] On the comparability of currencies, including "*Wampompeak*," in a colonial context, see also Locke, *Further Considerations Concerning Raising the Value of Money*, 3rd ed. (1696), in *Locke on Money*, ed. Kelly, II, p. 426; William Molyneux to Locke, 6 June 1696, in *Correspondence*, ed. de Beer, V, p. 653.

annotations, and provides evidence that America – and, by extension, empire of a specifically settler-colonial kind – was much on his mind that summer.[58] The most detailed examination of the composition and the dating of the *Two Treatises* suggests that Locke had begun the *Second Treatise* late in 1680 or early in 1681, laid it aside for a while, and then took it up again in early 1682 before completing the manuscript later that year. It seems likely that "Of Property" was among the last chapters to be written, and that it was written separately from the rest of the *Second Treatise*, a speculation that would fit with the internal evidence of allusions to America in that chapter as well as the external evidence of Locke's involvement with the fortunes of Carolina.[59] It would also explain why there seems to be a discontinuity between "Of Property" and its surrounding chapters, "Of Slavery" and "Of Paternal Power," each of which treats nonpolitical power and authority.

In composing "Of Property," Locke needed to produce a justification of appropriation that would do double duty, both in England and in America. Locke contended that "God gave the World to Men in Common; but ... it cannot be supposed he meant it should always remain common and uncultivated. He gave it to the use of the Industrious and Rational, (and *Labour* was to be *his Title* to it;) not to the Fancy or Covetousness of the Quarrelsom and Contentious" (II. 34). Each person has an exclusive right to his own body and therefore also to the labor of that body: "Whatsoever then he removes out of the State that Nature hath provided, and left it in, he hath mixed his *Labour* with, and joyned to it something that is his own, and thereby makes it his *Property*" (II. 27). Only after land had been appropriated in this way could it be apportioned "by compact and Agreement" in those parts of the world where a monetary economy had been introduced and land had become scarce, just as the "several States and Kingdoms ... have, by *positive agreement, settled a Property* amongst themselves in distinct Parts and parcels of the Earth," leaving "*great Tracts of Grounds*" waste and lying in common, "the Inhabitants thereof not having joyned with the rest of Mankind, in the consent of the Use of their common Money" (II. 45).[60]

[58] *The Fundamental Constitutions of Carolina* (London, 1682), New York Public Library, call-number *KC + 1682; Armitage, "John Locke, Carolina, and the *Two Treatises of Government*," 614–615.

[59] J. R. Milton, "Dating Locke's *Second Treatise*," *History of Political Thought*, 16 (1995), 356–390, at 389, 372–374.

[60] More generally on these passages, see David Armitage, "John Locke's International Thought," in *British International Thinkers from Hobbes to Namier*, ed. Ian Hall and Lisa Hill (Basingstoke, England, 2009), pp. 33–48.

The peculiar form of Locke's labor theory in the chapter "Of Property" marked a shift in his own thinking on the legitimate method of individual appropriation from the original community of goods presented by God to humankind.[61] As late as 1677–1678, Locke had offered a broadly Grotian account of the process by which the primal positive community in the world had given way to the regime of exclusive private property. Locke argued that this process was contractual and that it was designed to prevent a state of anarchic competition for resources:

> Men therefor must either enjoy all things in common or by compact determine their rights[.] if all things be left in common want rapine and force will unavoidably follow in which state, as is evident happynesse cannot be had which cannot consist without plenty and security. To avoid this estate compact must determin peoples rights.[62]

Such a contractual account of the origins of property could only refer to the agreements made between parties equally capable of entering into compacts with each other. In the seventeenth-century context of relations between Amerindians and Anglo-Americans, the incomers did not always recognize the indigenous peoples' equal capacity with Europeans to determine rights by compact. However, the *Fundamental Constitutions of Carolina* had implicitly recognized the collective federative capacity of the Indians of Carolina when it twice mentioned "treaties … with the neighbour Indians" (§§35, 50), but it expressly banned settlers from holding or claiming any land by "purchase or gift" from native peoples (§112).[63] The Indians' sovereignty (*imperium*) in terms of the law of nations was thereby distinguished from their rights of property (*dominium*), which were acknowledged neither as an attribute of their *imperium* over their territory nor as individually transferable attributes.

Locke's argument in "Of Property" ensured, at the very least, that it would not be inconsistent with the justifications for appropriation upon which the Carolina colony was founded. A limited range of such justifications was available by the late seventeenth century. For example,

---

[61] On changes in theories of property, and in particular their relation to colonialism, see Kiyoshi Shimokawa, "Property in the Seventeenth Century: Conventionalism, Unilateralism, and Colonialism," in *The Oxford Handbook of British Philosophy in the Seventeenth Century*, ed. Peter R. Anstey (Oxford, forthcoming).

[62] John Locke, "Morality" (c. 1677–1678), Bod. MS Locke c. 28, fol. 140, printed in Locke, *Political Essays*, ed. Goldie, p. 268; Richard Tuck, *Natural Rights Theories: Their Origin and Development* (Cambridge, 1979), pp. 168–169.

[63] TNA, PRO 30/24/47/3, fol. 66r, printed in Locke, *Political Essays*, ed. Goldie, p. 180. This provision remained unaltered in all subsequent revisions of the *Fundamental Constitutions*.

Amerindian unbelief alone could not provide a justification for dominion because, as the *Fundamental Constitutions* specified, "Idollatry
Ignorance or mistake gives us noe right to expell or use [the Natives
of Carolina] ill." Locke himself later upheld that same argument in his
Letter Concerning Toleration (1685): "No man whatsoever ought ... to
be deprived of his Terrestrial Enjoyments, upon account of his Religion.
Not even *Americans*, subjected unto a Christian Prince, are to be punished
either in Body or Goods, for not imbracing our Faith and Worship."[64]
Arguments from conquest would also have been implausible, for reasons
Locke himself made clear in chapter XVI of the *Second Treatise*, especially because the right of conquest even in a just war "*extends only to
the Lives* of those who joyn'd in the War, *not to their Estates*" or to their
descendants (II. 182); to believe otherwise would be to deny the two basic
natural rights possessed by "Every Man": freedom in his own person and
"before any other Man, to *inherit*, with his Brethren, his Fathers goods"
(II. 191). For all these reasons, there could be no legitimate appeal to a
right of conquest in the Americas as the foundation for English *imperium*
or *dominium*.

The only remaining argument was the contention (derived originally
from Roman law) that dominion fell to those best able to cultivate the
land to its fullest capacity,[65] not least to fulfill the biblical command to
subdue the earth (Genesis 1:28, 9:1). Precisely that argument underlaid the
rights claimed by the Proprietors over the land of Carolina, according to
the terms of their grants from the English Crown. Thus, the original 1629
grant had called Carolina a region "*hitherto untilled* ... But in some parts
of it inhabited by certain Barbarous men," and Charles II reaffirmed this
description in his 1663 grant, which had charged the Lords Proprietors
"to Transport and make an ample Colony of our Subjects ... unto a certain Country ... in the parts of AMERICA *not yet cultivated or planted*,
and only inhabited by some barbarous People who have no knowledge
of Almighty God."[66] This agriculturalist argument was the best justification that could be given for colonial dispossession after arguments from

---

[64] [John Locke,] *A Letter Concerning Toleration* (London, 1689), p. 34.
[65] Anthony Pagden, "The Struggle for Legitimacy and the Image of Empire in the Atlantic
to c. 1700," in *The Oxford History of the British Empire*, I: *The Origins of Empire*, ed.
Nicholas Canny (Oxford, 1998), pp. 34–54, at pp. 42–47; Lauren Benton and Benjamin
Straumann, "Acquiring Empire by Law: From Roman Doctrine to Early Modern
European Practice," *Law and History Review*, 28 (2010), 1–38.
[66] Charter to Sir Robert Heath (30 October 1629) and Charter to the Lords Proprietors of
Carolina (24 March 1663), in *North Carolina Charters and Constitutions, 1578–1698*,
ed. M. E. E. Parker (Raleigh, N.C., 1963), pp. 64, 76 (my emphases).

contract, conquest, and grace had been gradually abandoned, and it was precisely this argument that Locke adopted in the *Second Treatise*.

Locke amplified the relevance of America to his arguments when he made a final set of manuscript revisions to the *Two Treatises* sometime after 1698. The most extensive changes and additions he made were to the chapter "Of Property" and sprang from his experience as a commissioner on the Board of Trade in the late 1690s. First, he expanded his assessment of the benefits provided by cultivation and enclosure of land: "he who appropriates land to himself by his labour does not lessen but increase the common stock of Man kind," by a factor of ten to one, or more likely "it is much nearer an hundred to one. For I aske whether in the wild woods and uncultivated wast of America left to Nature, without any improvement, tillage or husbandry, a thousand acres yeild the needy and wretched inhabitants as many conveniencys of life as ten acres of equally fertill land in Devonshire where they are well cultivated?" A few paragraphs later, Locke made a second addition that turned this observation into a tenet of economic reason of state for William III and his ministers. He had originally concluded a brief discussion of the multifarious forms of labor that go into the production of any commodity with a reflection on the relative unimportance of land to value: "So little, that even amongst us, Land that is left wholly to Nature, that hath no improvement of Pasturage, Tillage, or Planting, is called ... wast[e]." In his revision, he went on, "This shews, how much numbers of Men are to be preferd to largenesse of dominions and that the increase of lands [sc. hands?] and the right imploying of them is the great art of government. And that Prince who shall be so wise and godlike as by established Laws of liberty to secure protection and incouragment to the honest industry of Mankind against the oppression of power and narrownesse of Party will quickly be too hard for his neighbours."[67]

Such encouragement of industry was for Locke a matter of equal importance at home in Britain and across the Atlantic in America. Labor, he wrote in an essay on the English poor law for the Board of Trade in 1697, was "the burden that lies on the industrious." Genuine relief for

---

[67] John Locke, manuscript additions to [Locke,] *Two Treatises of Government*, 3rd ed. (London, 1698), pp. 193, 197 (II. 37, 42), Christ's College, Cambridge, call-number BB 3 7a; Locke, *Two Treatises of Government*, ed. Laslett, p. 297 n. For recent discussions of these passages (but that ignore the evidence of their dating and context), see Edward Andrew, "A Note on Locke's 'The Great Art of Government,'" *Canadian Journal of Political Science/Revue canadienne de science politique*, 42 (2009), 511–519, and Lee Ward, "A Note on a Note on Locke's 'Great Art of Government,'" *Canadian Journal of Political Science/Revue canadienne de science politique*, 42 (2009), 521–523.

the poor "consists of finding work for them, and taking care that they do not live like drones upon the labour of others." A strict regimen of labor would have the benefit of providing education for the children of the poor, who would be put to work in school, to ensure that they would no longer be "as utter strangers both to religion and morality as they are to industry," perhaps like those natives of Carolina who, nearly twenty years earlier, the *Fundamental Constitutions* had deemed "utterly strangers to Christianity" but who were not on that account to be dispossessed or ill treated.[68]

These links among the *Fundamental Constitutions*, the *Two Treatises*, and the "Essay on the Poor Law" suggest two conclusions regarding Locke as a theorist of empire that reinforce the evidence from his other works treated in this chapter. The first is that his was not a universalistic vision of English, British, or European superiority over the rest of the world and its peoples. It did not assume formal equality only for those deemed to be "civil" peoples. Indeed, as Locke argued in a little-discussed passage in the *Letter Concerning Toleration*, even a Christian people, uprooted from their domestic setting and placed in an unfamiliar and dependent position, would be even more vulnerable than the "pagans" among whom they settled:

An inconsiderable and weak number of Christians, destitute of every thing, arrive in a Pagan Country: These Foreigners beseech the Inhabitants, by the bowels of Humanity, that they would succour them with the necessaries of life: Those necessaries are given them; Habitations are granted; and they all joyn together, and grow up into one Body of People. The Christian Religion by this means takes root in that Countrey, and spreads it self; but does not suddenly grow the strongest. While things are in this condition, Peace, Friendship, Faith and equal Justice, are preserved amongst them.

Charity demands equal treatment for both pagans and Christians, and weakness leads to a fragile tolerance. However, the consequences of dominance and the assumption of religious rectitude bring not just intolerance but dispossession and destruction:

At length the Magistrate becomes a Christian, and by that means their Party becomes the most powerful. Then immediately all Compacts are to be broken, all Civil Rights to be violated, that Idolatry may be extirpated: And unless these innocent Pagans, strict Observers of the Rules of Equity and the Law of Nature,

---

[68] John Locke, "An Essay on the Poor Law" (September–October 1697), in Locke, *Political Essays*, ed. Goldie, pp. 184, 189, 192; TNA CO 388/5, fols. 232r–48v (26 October 1697); Bod. MS Locke c. 30, fols. 86r–87v, 94r–95v, 111; A. L. Beier, "'Utter Strangers to Industry, Morality and Religion': John Locke on the Poor," *Eighteenth-Century Life*, 12 (1988), 28–41.

and no ways offending against the Laws of the Society, I say unless they will forsake their ancient Religion, and embrace a new and strange one, they are to be turned out of the Lands and Possessions of their Forefathers, and perhaps deprived of Life it self.

The conclusion Locke drew was Atlantic in form yet more general in application: "For the reason of the thing is equal, both in *America* and *Europe*. And neither Pagans there, nor any Dissenting Christians here, can with any right be deprived of their worldly Goods ... nor are any civil Rights to be either changed or violated upon account of Religion in one place more than another."[69]

A second conclusion follows from the first: Locke's theory was non-hierarchical and inclusive to the extent that all adult humans possessed the same rationality because reason is likewise equal "both in *America* and *Europe*" (and China, for example). As Locke put it in the *Second Treatise*, God gave the earth "to the use of the Industrious and Rational," with labor as their means to earn title to it; yet the opposite of "the Industrious and the Rational" in this passage were not the "idle" and the "irrational" but rather "the Quarrelsom and Contentious": that is, anyone who exceeded "the *bounds*, set by reason of what might serve for his *use*" and unjustly "desired the benefit of another's Pains, which he had no right to" (II. 31, 34). The rational do have a right to possession, but only if they exercise their industry and do not invade the fruits of another's labor. Locke did not justify dispossession on the grounds of any incapacity, whether mental or otherwise: if accumulation were pursued within the bounds set by reason, "there could be then little room for Quarrels or Contentions about Property so establish'd" (II. 31).[70] Least of all did he associate rationality with Europeans and irrationality with indigenous peoples. If any later settler colonialists sought an argument for indigenous dispossession on the grounds of their assumed innate rational superiority, as opposed to their lack of industry, only with some theoretical and historical difficulty could they have extracted such a justification from Locke's *Second Treatise*.

This chapter has tried to provide an account of Locke's conceptions of empire based on a full survey of his writings, in line with other recent

---

[69] [Locke,] *Letter Concerning Toleration*, pp. 35–36.
[70] Compare Locke, *Some Considerations*, in *Locke on Money*, ed. Kelly, I, p. 292: "Nature has bestowed Mines on several parts of the World: But the Riches are only for the Industrious and Frugal. Whomever else they visit, 'tis only with the Diligent and Sober only they stay."

discussions of his views – on slavery, for example.[71] I hope to have shown that Locke's thought underwent change and that the historical Locke was necessarily more complex and often more conflicted than later Lockeans – whether his followers or those who have analyzed his work – have perhaps given him credit for being. The contextual and conceptual limits to Locke's theories should remind us that diverse circumstances generated, and necessitated, differing strains of what has sometimes been aggregated as a single imperial "liberalism" of which Locke is now held to be the progenitor. There is, for example, very little concrete evidence for the reception of Locke among Britons in the East Indies before the mid-nineteenth century: the *Essay* being read by an East India Company official in Sumatra in 1714; Locke's works in the baggage of Arthur Wellesley, the future Duke of Wellington, in 1796; and Philip Francis's knowledge of the economic writings may be about the sum of it. In 1769, Warren Hastings had expressed a hope for "Lockes, Humes and Montesquieus in Number sufficient for each Department" to govern India through the East India Company. He would have been disappointed, at least in his desire for idiomatically Lockean administrators.[72]

Yet, there can be no doubt that the shape of Locke's political theory owed decisive debts to his experiences as a colonial administrator and servant of the English state. Those experiences also placed limits on his universalism and ensured that later appropriations of his arguments would often have to reformulate them to fit later colonial contingencies. If indeed we are to use the anachronistic shorthand "liberalism" to describe Locke's political theories, then we must be aware that there have been different strains of imperial and colonial liberalism and that they have not necessarily been continuous with each other. And if liberalism itself is to have the traces of its complicity with empire exposed and expunged, that will have to be undertaken in diverse and historically sensitive ways

---

[71] Especially Waldron, *God, Locke, and Equality*, pp. 197–206; Farr, "Locke, Natural Law, and New World Slavery."

[72] Joseph Collet to Richard Steele, 24 August 1714, in *The Private Letter Books of Joseph Collet*, ed. H. H. Dodwell (London, 1933), pp. 99–100 ("Mr. Lock who first taught me to distinguish between Words and things"); Philip Guedalla, *The Duke* (London, 1931), p. 55; Joseph Parkes and Herman Merivale, *Memoirs of Sir Philip Francis, K.C.B.*, 2 vols. (London, 1867), I, pp. 51–52; Ranajit Guha, *A Rule of Property for Bengal: An Essay on the Idea of Permanent Settlement*, 2nd ed. (Durham, N.C., 1996), pp. 97–98; Warren Hastings to George Vansittart, 23 December 1769, BL Add. MS 29125, fol. 22r (my thanks to Robert Travers for this reference). On the trajectory of "liberalism" in India itself, see C. A. Bayly, *Recovering Liberties: Indian Thought in the Age of Liberalism and Empire* (Cambridge, 2012).

to create various postcolonial liberalisms, some of which may be able to draw robustly upon other Lockean legacies.[73] For, as Locke himself put it with characteristically overbearing humility in 1692, "you wonder at my *News from the West-Indies*, I suppose because you found it not in your Books of *Europe* or *Asia*. But whatever you may think, I assure you all the World is not *Mile-End*."[74]

---

[73] See Duncan Ivison, *Postcolonial Liberalism* (Cambridge, 2002), for one distinguished attempt.
[74] [John Locke,] *A Third Letter for Toleration* (London, 1692), p. 72.

5

Montesquieu on Empire and Enlightenment

Michael Mosher

Il n'est pas indifférent que le peuple soit éclairé.

Montesquieu, Preface, *De l'esprit des lois*

THE WORTH OF EMPIRE

The memory of Roman antiquity and of a beneficent Pax Romana has intermittently stirred the embers of nostalgia for empire in Europe. Pierre Manent acknowledges, for instance, that there was a gap between actual performance and idealized memory but nevertheless cites the "prestige" of empire, which he calls "a natural political idea." Manent invites the reader to separate the "conquering zeal" that led to domination from the potential for an ideal outcome. In "bringing together ... all the known world under a unique power," empire addresses the possibility of "men's unity" and gives form to the "universality of human nature which seeks to be recognized."[1] Anthony Padgen is more disposed to emphasize the

[1] Pierre Manent, *An Intellectual History of Liberalism*, trans. Rebecca Balinski (Princeton, N.J.: Princeton University Press, 1994), pp. 3, 6.

For critical readings and responses (marked by an asterisk * if written) to earlier drafts and for the uttering of provocative comments at the right moment, I wish to thank Sunil Agnani, Richard Bourke, *David Conti, Cecil Courtney, Raymond Geuss, Greg Hill, Istvan Hont, James Kloppenberg, *Catherine Larrère, Pratap Mehta, *Sankar Muthu, Joseph Paff, Jennifer Pitts, *Paul Rahe, Alan Ryan, *Michael Sonenscher, *Céline Spector, and *Cheryl Welch. Thanks as well to Istvan Hont for inviting me to deliver the argument at the King's College Cambridge Research Seminar on Political Thought and Intellectual History; to Sankar Muthu for leading a conference of contributors at the Rockefeller Foundation Bellagio Study and Work Center, and to Denis Lacorne and Riva Kastoryano for lending support for several stays at the Centre d'Etudes et de Recherches Internationales (CERI) at Sciences-Po, Paris.

predatory conduct of empire builders. Empires are "created by conquest," and the conquered have been forcibly maintained in "subservience" with the aid of various ideologies of "civilization." Nevertheless, he also recognizes a potential in empire that aligns with Manent's understanding. Not only has empire been "a way of life for most of the peoples of the world," but on occasion it points to something that might correspond to Manent's "unity" and "universality of human nature." On Pagden's account, empires have occasionally created positive "opportunities" for the governed that "they could not otherwise have imagined," citing on the subject none other than the founder of modern India, Jawaharlal Nehru:

A foreign conquest with all its evils has one advantage: it widens the mental horizon of the people and compels them to look out of their shells. They realize that the world is a more variegated place than they had imagined.[2]

The possibility of the widening of "mental horizons" describes almost exactly the temptation to empire of that otherwise fiercely anticolonialist Enlightenment philosophe the Baron de Montesquieu. It also describes the temptation to empire that seems to accompany some of those currents of thought that coalesced into the various European Enlightenments.

One should not be distracted by the contrast that Manent's empire reveals unity while Nehru's exhibits variety, since implied in the idea of variety is a commonly shared perspective, a species of universal enlightenment, that the world is multiple and plural. The possible unity that follows from this perspective is related to the political question of whether there is a solution to the problem of governance in such a world. Liberalism has sometimes presented itself as a natural answer to this question, but the liberal solution to diversity had first to displace empire, which, from Alexander's conquests to the multicultural Austro-Hungarian monarchy, had long been considered the paramount solution to the problem of diversity.

MONTESQUIEU'S PRELIMINARY UNDERSTANDING OF EMPIRE

Was empire for Montesquieu potentially a way of containing the particularities of human life and giving expression to its normative unity? A

---

[2] Anthony Pagden, *Peoples and Empires: A Short History of European Migration and Conquest from Greece to the Present* (New York: Modern Library, 2001), pp. xxi, xxiv. See also Sunil Khilnani, *The Idea of India* (New York: Farrar Straus Giroux, 1998), p. 118.

negative response appears to leap from nearly every page of his writings. The prestige of empire is ostensibly the last thing on his mind. The Pax Romana is a cruel joke. His little book *Considerations on the Grandeur and Decadence of the Romans*, in running through the whole destructive cycle of Roman history from republic to empire, manages simultaneously to evoke both stunned admiration and deep horror at the spectacle. His "Reflections on Universal Monarchy in Europe" is a carefully worded argument about the perils for Europe of any sort of continental empire and of the dangers for France itself in Louis XIV's imperial policies.

The typology of regimes in *Spirit of Laws* is even more telling. The three types of government – republic (subdivided into democratic and aristocratic republics), monarchy, and despotism – are each natural in the sense of "natural" conveyed by the famous opening line of *Spirit of Laws*: "Laws, taken in their largest sense, are the necessary relations deriving from the nature of things" (*Laws*, I, 1).[3] That is to say, each form of government arises from a constellation of causally explicable reasons. Yet despotism also has a normative – or rather an antinormative – dimension. Despotism is a species of political evil. The fear and terror that Montesquieu considers as the very principle of despotism render impossible either of the ordinary motives of a decent politics, namely, the sense of "honor" and personal dignity appropriate to monarchy or an engaged love of equality (i.e., "virtue") engendered in the republic. As Montesquieu realizes when he writes that "the principle of despotic government is endlessly corrupted because it is corrupt by its nature" (*Laws*, VIII, 10), there is a paradox about despotism. It is a part of nature, but it is also antinatural. It provokes endless rebellions and falls easily, but it is just as quickly reestablished. It tends toward chaotic permanence that defies all reform. In looking at actual despotic nations, however, Montesquieu often qualifies this indictment. Russia is reformable, for instance, and China has excellences that put in doubt whether it is ruled by fear. Indeed, the threats to the regime – famine and popular outburst – serve to temper and discipline China's rulers, creating a sort of moderated despotism.[4]

---

[3] All references in the text to *De l'esprit des lois* are to book and chapter number. *Laws*, Book I, chapter 1 is abbreviated I, 1. Occasionally, there will be a page reference to the standard English translation, Montesquieu, *The Spirit of the Laws*, ed. and trans. Anne Cohler, Basia Miller, and Harold Stone (Cambridge: Cambridge University Press, 1989). Beginning with the title – I prefer *Spirit of Laws* – I have occasionally adopted my own translations, using the standard Pléiade edition, Montesquieu, *Oeuvres complètes*, ed. Roger Caillois (Paris: Gallimard, 1949), vol. 2.

[4] On these themes, see Catherine Larrère, "L'empire, entre fédération et républic," *Revue Montesquieu*, 8 (2006), 111–136; Sharon Krause, "Despotism in the *Spirit of Laws*," in

More to the point for the topic under discussion, despotisms are almost always empires.[5] This is, Montesquieu thought, a simple deduction from a science of political geography. Book VIII, chapter 15, which announces the geography lesson, is exactly one sentence long: "I shall be able to be understood only when the next four chapters have been read." Having signaled the importance of the subject, Montesquieu sets out a territorial logic for regimes. Republics are small, monarchies are best suited to bigger territories, but despotisms are governments that typically preside over expansive spaces. Empire – by definition, rule over a great extent of territory – is (almost) always despotic. There is a physics to rule in the Newtonian spaces of empire: ruthless execution of orders is the "supplement" that compensates for distance. ("Il faut la promptitude des resolutions suppléés à la distance" [*Laws*, VIII, 19].) The hypothesis exhibits a lawlike precision: "Speed in executing his decisions must supplement the distance separating him from his domains; fear must be used to prevent negligence on the part of the distant governor or magistrate" (*Laws*, VIII, 19).

Montesquieu's epistolary novel *Persian Letters* already exhibits the territorial logic of despotic empire made explicit in the *Laws*. Two Persians, Usbek and Rica, travel from their homeland west toward Paris, ostensibly on the road to their own enlightenment. Their astute observations hold up the French to ridicule, thus reversing the standard trope whereby a Western traveler points out the foibles of faraway peoples to the relish of the European reader. There is, however, a domestic subplot. One of the traveling Persians, Usbek, possesses a harem, or *serail*, replete with multiple wives and retainers, the latter consisting of castrated slaves or eunuchs. From Paris, Usbek governs his household in Ispahan, sending his commands through a creaky postal service that results in half-year delays between writing and receiving and much confusion about who has intercepted a letter and its actual intent – which, along with corrupt administrator-eunuchs, delays by more than a year Usbek's orders to restore order, leaving the reader to contemplate the absurdity of every effort to govern at a distance. The ensuing ignorance, betrayal, and frustration, along with the dramatic climax (the betrayal of Usbek by Roxanne, his

Montesquieu's Science of Politics: Essays on the Spirit of Laws, ed. David W. Carrithers, Michael A. Mosher, and Paul A. Rahe (Lanham, Md.: Rowman & Littlefield, 2001), pp. 231–271.

5 For a useful commentary that brings together all of Montesquieu's references to empire in *De l'esprit des lois*, see Jean Ehrard, "Idée et figures de l'empire dans l'esprit des lois," in *L'Empire avant l'empire: état d'une notion au XVIIIème siècle* (Clermont-Ferrand: Presses Universitaires Blaise-Pascal, 2004), pp. 41–54.

favorite wife, and her virtuous suicide), all illustrate the central theme of the territorial logic: communication across vast space, that is to say, the circumstance of empire, is the setting natural to despotic relationships.

Usbek tries to govern his household with motives that are, on his own interpretation, benign. He is, however, delusional on the subject of his own goodness. Quite apart from this, the frustrations inherent in governing from afar turn him into a desperate and enraged man. The scene replicates the inevitable politics of the despot. Rulers who govern at a great distance from subjects become tyrants.

Usbek is a philosopher with the instincts of a despot. He is clear-sighted enough about Paris but blind about Ispahan. His apparent thoughtfulness does not save him from prejudices, which elsewhere Montesquieu defines as "what makes one unaware of oneself" (*Laws*, Preface). One of the striking messages of *Persian Letters* is that governing too wide a territory, even with good intentions, yields only tyranny or revolutionary upheaval.

"ORIENTAL" AND TROPICAL DESPOTISMS

There are two other additions to Montesquieu's theory of despotic empire. Empire has an Asian face in the lands of the East or it has the look of the South ("le Midi") where one finds peoples oppressed by a tropical climate.[6] Although despotism is the *summum malum*, an unnatural system of power, nevertheless in "Asia ... despotism is, so to speak, naturalized" (*Laws*, V, 14). Moreover, it "usually reigns" in "hot climates" (*Laws*, V, 15). The normative dimension in Montesquieu's political philosophy collides with his descriptive natural histories. There are natural causes that permit despotic rule to coalesce in some regions of the world more than in others. Even if in all regions of the world the despot is in the wrong, Montesquieu never quite explicitly answers the question of whether, where no other government is possible, despotic empire is better than no rule at all. In the case of the Chinese empire, the answer is a qualified yes. Its rule has benign effects, as, despite the overall tyranny of the regime, China's government had always staved off the mass starvation that was a constant threat in this populous nation.

Montesquieu never excludes any region of the world from despotism. It is possible anywhere and at any time. "Despotic government ... leaps

---

[6] Montesquieu has legions of critics on these issues. See, for instance, Frederick G. Whelan, "Oriental Despotism: Anquetil-Duperron's Response to Montesquieu," *History of Political Thought*, 22, no. 4 (Winter 2001), 619–647.

up, so to speak before the eyes … for it only requires passion to establish it and all the world is good for that" (*Laws*, V, 14, p. 63). The despot's sword hangs over Europe as well. The Spanish monarchy declined into despotism, and the France of Louis XIV nearly became one before the monarch finally died. Even though the Europeans generally have "*moeurs*" (customs) of a free people and a temperate climate, "if by a long abuse of power or by a great conquest, despotism established itself, neither customs nor climate would restrain it" (*Laws*, VIII, 8). The right sort of tyrant could change everything even in a Europe favored by geography and climate. The future history of the continent has repeatedly confirmed this prediction.

Asia's geography is more favorable to despotic rule. The continent possesses larger and wider plains unbroken by mountains or broad rivers. Conquerors typically never stop until they reach these natural barriers. If in the end what they attempt to rule is a large enough political space, the logic of despotic rule prevails. Absent terror, commands delivered from afar are unlikely to be obeyed (*Laws*, XVIII, 6).

Such an argument is strictly neutral regarding the character of the peoples involved. The oppressiveness of the tropical climate undermines everyone's incentive to work. The only governments that succeed in hot climates are therefore those that apply fear to overcome the laziness natural to enervating heat (*Laws*, XIV, 5–9). However, Montesquieu makes the argument more personal in claiming that climate imprints itself on the very soul of a people: "As you move toward the countries of the south, you will believe you have moved away from morality itself" (*Laws*, XIV, 2). In all the histories of Asian countries, Montesquieu writes, "it is not possible to find a single trait that marks a free soul." There is bravery and courage, but it is "the heroism of servitude" (*Laws*, XVII, 6).

Montesquieu recognizes that there are distinct differences between collective mentalities, what he calls "*les esprits*," and the unpredictability of individual characters. In his methodological essay "*Sur les causes qui peuvent affecter les esprits et les caractères*," Montesquieu distinguishes between the "particular education that forms each character" and a "general education" that comes from each society and that, he adds, affects some individuals more than others.[7] But in the passages on climate and character in the *Laws*, which move quickly from the alleged collective characteristics of a people trapped by natural conditions to each person's individual fate, he seems to lose the sense of methodological caution

---

[7] Montesquieu, *Oeuvres complètes*, tome 2, p. 58.

that would have acknowledged the potential for a gap between collective mentality and individual fates.

ANTICOLONIALISM IN *PERSIAN LETTERS*

Anti-imperial sentiments are a feature of all of Montesquieu's writings. *Persian Letters* summarizes the indictment. Letter 121 condemns colonization in general and the Spanish depredations in the New World in particular. "Men ought to stay where they are," the character Uzbek declares at the outset.[8] This is an ironic statement, as neither Uzbek, who travels from Persia to Paris, nor his correspondent Rhedi, who ends up in the equally distant Venice, manages to stay put. Uzbek and Rhedi come to Europe as philosophers, not as conquerors. But Montesquieu allies the imperial grandeur of philosophical ambition with despotic motives. Not altogether novel, this view of the theoretical motive and enterprise has been speculated about from Plato to Bacon and survives as a trope of discourse in figures as disparate as Rousseau and Foucault.

Montesquieu makes two points about colonization. It weakens or destroys the colonized, and it weakens or destroys the colonizer: a bad arrangement overall. Colonies suck the life out of the metropolis: "an empire can be compared to a tree with branches which if they spread too far take all the sap from the trunk." The colony bleeds the metropolis financially, and colonial domination will come to haunt the metropolitan country, endangering its civil and political liberties. We are familiar with the latter phenomenon under the heading of "blowback."

It is irrelevant whether colonization is rational or irrational for the colonizer. From the point of view of the victims, one need attend only to the "cruelty" and "barbarism" of imperial conquest. The separate fates of Portugal and Spain are instructive, for "nothing is better calculated [than these examples] to cure monarchs of their passion for making conquests in remote places." Both countries "conquered immense kingdoms with inconceivable rapidity." But faced with the Machiavellian problem of the "preservation" of conquest, and with the cruelty that this would have required, the Portuguese humanely backed off. Of course, they then promptly lost their grip. Such was the logic of governing from afar. "The Portuguese ... did not use any cruelty [and] were soon expelled from all

---

[8] I cite by letter in the text, using and sometimes changing the translation in Montesquieu, *Persian Letters*, trans. Christopher Betts (Harmondsworth, England: Penguin Books, 1973). For the original, consult Montesquieu, *Oeuvres complètes*, vol. 1.

the countries that they had discovered." This is one possible "destiny" for imperial characters: "heroes" who "ruin themselves in conquering countries that they abruptly lose."

Worse are the Spanish, whom Montesquieu never tires of excoriating, for this nation did not flinch from the cruelty called for by imperial conquest. The *philosophe* does not mince words. "The Spaniards ... chose to exterminate" the Indians of Mexico and South America. He adds: "Never has a wicked plan been more punctiliously carried out." As a result of conquistador intervention, Montesquieu writes, "a people as numerous as the whole population of Europe was seen to disappear from the earth at the arrival of these barbarians whose only thought, in discovering the Indies, seems to have been to reveal to mankind the ultimate limits of cruelty." Montesquieu had read the work of Las Casas and other documenters of the horrific scenes in the New World, and he consequently declares that the Spanish invasion was the "most destructive of which history has ever spoken."⁹ He regards the events with the same horror that we feel in contemplating the Holocaust or the gulag.

DESCARTES IN MEXICO

Letter 121 of *Persian Letters* poses a strange counterfactual question: "What would have happened to [the Spanish conquerors] if they had given the American tribes enough time to recover from their admiration at the arrival of these new Gods?" In *Persian Letters*, the question remains rhetorical, but four years later, in a lecture to the Academy of Bordeaux, Montesquieu offers a radical answer. The question, he argues, should be how these people – or similar victims elsewhere – could have immunized themselves in advance against the thought that would otherwise occur to the "superstitious," that heavily armed invaders could well be "gods." For the French philosopher, the answer is obvious. They could have done so in the same way that a portion of the educated European public had done so, by internalizing the lessons of Enlightenment ideas.

Montesquieu offers his listeners a thought experiment. Imagine that Descartes had somehow gone to Mexico before the arrival of the invaders. That is to say, what if European ideas had preceded European arms? Montesquieu does not conclude that the Amerindians would have then possessed the technology of European weapons. For Montesquieu pins

---

⁹ "Discours sur les motifs qui doivent nous encourager aux sciences," *Oeuvres complètes*, vol. 1, p. 53.

his hopes on the view that those who pursue natural reasoning and science are morally transformed. The threat of providential intervention, which at any moment would defeat the very idea of natural causality, moves into the remote background, if it does not disappear altogether. Descartes, as the expounder of the scientific method, would have prepared this people mentally and morally for invasion.

What would they have learned? Materialism and the scientific outlook would have given them skepticism about the gods and would have encouraged them to find only natural and not divine reasons for the appearance of the strange men who confronted them. The agnostic or atheist implications of the new science would have taught them the radical equality of all beings and subsequently given them courage in the face of those better armed. Descartes "might have taught these peoples that men, constituted as they are, cannot be immortal; that the springs of their machines get worn out like all machines; and that the effects of nature are nothing but the consequences of laws and of the communication of movement."[10] That is to say, Cartesian Enlightenment would have taught Indians that Europeans could be killed.

Descartes would have taught them not to believe that the invaders were an "effect of an *invisible power*" (emphasis added). Montesquieu's passage echoes Hobbes's famously skeptical remark about the consequences of rejecting science: "They that make little or no enquiry into the natural causes of things ... are inclined to suppose ... *Powers invisible*; and," Hobbes adds sarcastically, "to stand in awe of their own imagination" (emphasis added).[11] Had Descartes gone to Mexico, there would have been no such misjudgment on the part of the newly enlightened inhabitants. In what must be one of the earliest recommendations of terrorist insurgency or guerrilla warfare, Montesquieu concluded that "the vast extent of their empire gave the Mexicans [the Aztecs] a thousand ways of destroying the foreigners."

Montesquieu leaves another version of this mental experiment in the *Pensées*. In this fragment, the mistakes of the Indians are due to their "ignorance of philosophy." It is a story of "superstition" and of its destructive prejudices.[12] Because they regarded the Spanish as "irritated Gods," they lost heart. Montezuma and the Incas could have had the

---

[10] "Discours sur les motifs," vol. 1, p. 53.
[11] "Discours sur les motifs," p. 54. Thomas Hobbes, *Leviathan*, ed. Richard Tuck (Cambridge: Cambridge University Press, 1996), chap. 11, p. 75.
[12] *Pensée* 614 (125 in chronological order) in *Oeuvres complètes*, vol. 1, pp. 1134–1135.

invaders "starved to death," but instead they attacked them only with useless "prayers" and "sacrifices."[13]

Besides observing that a thinker, renowned for his advocacy of political moderation, is capable of having a distinctly immoderate and murderous fantasy, what other conclusions should we draw from these fervidly anti-Spanish and anti-imperialist remarks?

The reader might conclude that the idea of Cartesian science as a spiritual resource for political victims sets up a double-edged sword. One side has the Amerindians cultivating the sharp edges of Enlightenment science in order to slay their enemies from the land of (partially) enlightened Europe. However, given that the Mexicans did not have Descartes on their side and continued to abide by their "prejudices" – that is to say, by their religion and culture – the other side of this proffered sword just might cut the way for a justification of a new kind of invasion, one that would elevate peoples bereft of "light" to enlightenment. And who was better situated than the Europeans to make conquests for "enlightenment"?

Edmund Burke, for one, argues against this ideological justification for British interference in India and cites Montesquieu as a source for this erroneous understanding.[14] With this tale of Cartesian science among the Amerindians, Montesquieu leaves the Mexicans with an unhappy choice. Given the geopolitical prospects, either accept the destruction of your country or prevent it by the prior self-imposed destruction of your culture by means of the replacement of indigenous religion with a universal science. Montesquieu is, however, correct. An indigenous culture could be "irrational" from the point of view of its survival. Given the nature of predator nations, certain cultures are bound to disappear. This is because either they cannot meet the cultural challenge of preparing for the threat and are physically destroyed; or they are capable of meeting the challenge, but in this case they destroy their own past by undergoing a fundamental cultural self-transformation. (Meiji Japan illustrates the latter possibility.)

In the guise of a fantasy about Descartes in Mexico, Montesquieu gives the reader a picture of a European spiritual civil war between faith and enlightenment. In imagining the right sort of philosophical education for the colonized, Montesquieu chooses sides in the debate between religion

---

[13] *Pensée* 614, pp. 1135–1136.
[14] Edmund Burke, *Works of Edmund Burke* (Boston: Little, Brown, and Company, 1865–1871), vol. 11, p. 207. See also Michael Mosher, "The Skeptic's Burke," *Political Theory*, 19, no. 3 (1991), 391–418.

and the new science. Montesquieu transfers this conflict from Europe to Mexico, where the potential for revolutionary conflict in Europe between the enlightened (the fictional Cartesian-educated Mexicans) and the unenlightened (priest-led Spanish conquistadors) becomes in Mexico a dress rehearsal for the future European revolution.

WOMEN AGAINST EMPIRE

Were the Europeans, philosophe and cleric alike, deceived about the "soft power" of their ideas to non-Europeans? Or was the potential unity of dispersed humanity, to which Pierre Manent refers, capable of being expressed in the ideas on offer in the various European Enlightenments?

Let us return to the primal scene of intellectual self-deception, the *Persian Letters*. First-time readers are themselves typically deceived. One is slow to understand the connection between Usbek the searcher after universal truths and Usbek the delusional intellectual whose increasing grasp of the sciences of Enlightenment teach him nothing about himself or his relationship to others. In addition to being a thinker, Usbek is a figure of despotic authority, a jealous husband, and the target of a political rebellion organized by his favorite wife, Roxanne. Her organized revolt against the tyranny of the *serail* fails. In her final letter to her oppressor and husband, she announces the perfect strategy of the colonized regarding the colonizer: "We were both happy: you thought that I had been deceived, while I was deceiving you" (Letter 161). It is an implicit contract that cannot survive being made explicit.

Roxanne, the great heroine of the *Persian Letters*, is a French subject in rebellion against overbearing kingship, a Persian princess revolting against the court/harem of her husband and, just possibly, in an anticlerical reading, a Christian woman tortured by convent life. She is, above all, simply the figure of the sequestered woman who has much to say and no one to say it to. Montesquieu's typology of government is intertwined with this figure.[15] The civic sociability of women and the possibility of women communicating with men in a public setting, and not merely in a private setting, are for Montesquieu the distinguishing marks of a polity that had escaped despotic domination. In *Spirit of Laws* he argues that European men have made a distinctive discovery about women that

---

[15] For a fuller discussion of these issues, see Michael Mosher, "The Judgmental Gaze of European Women: Gender, Sexuality, and the Critique of Republican Rule," *Political Theory*, 22, no. 1 (1994), 25–44.

has gone beyond lust and beyond even love, neither of which confers on women a public standing. European men have discovered that women are "very enlightened judges on a part of the things that constitute personal merit" (*Laws*, XXVIII, 22). Beginning with the late medieval practices of chivalry that acknowledged female judgment, European women slowly came to have, Montesquieu seems to suggest, both public standing and a public voice. By contrast, the despot enforces silence: "One communicates less in a country where everyone, whether as superior or as inferior, exercises and suffers arbitrary power than in those where liberty reigns in all its conditions" (*Laws*, XIX, 12).

For Montesquieu, women are the natural agents of change. "In China manners are indestructible" because "the women are completely separated from the men" (*Laws*, XIX, 13). In despotic societies, "women are ordinarily enclosed." If it were otherwise, "manners would change every day" (*Laws*, XIX, 12). He adds that "everything is closely linked together: the despotism of the prince is naturally united with the servitude of women" (*Laws*, XIX, 15).

From these correlations, Montesquieu draws two contrary conclusions, one for the observer and one for the actor. In *Spirit of Laws* he uses the passive language of the social scientist. In *Persian Letters* he uses the active language of the rebel. Even though Montesquieu obviously believes that he has discovered in communicative women the very criterion of a free society, which he approvingly says is best illustrated in the French case (where men and women have a "facility in communicating their thoughts" [*Laws*, XIX, 5]), he nevertheless insists in the *Laws* that women ought to remain enclosed under despotic rule. "It is a maxim of capital importance that the manners and mores of a despotic state must never be changed," the reason being that "in these states there are no laws ... there are only mores and manners and if you overturn them, you will overturn everything" (*Laws*, XIX, 12). If women are the agents for opening a culture's eyes to change, in a country where there is no framework of law to handle social change, the women must be enclosed to prevent revolution.

In the *Letters*, however, Roxanne is fully justified in revolting against Usbek's imperial governance of the harem. Montesquieu twice has Usbek unwittingly make Roxanne's revolutionary argument. In Letter 104, Usbek rehearses Locke's argument without naming its source:

If a ruler wants ... to tyrannize ... [over his subjects,] the basis of obedience is lost; nothing unites them and they go back to their natural liberty ... unlimited authority can never be legitimate, because it can never have a legitimate origin

[f]or we cannot give someone greater power over us than we have over ourselves – for instance, we cannot take our own lives.

In Letter 76, Usbek announces a radical version of this argument by drop-
ping the provision against suicide. The questions Usbek asks on behalf of
those contemplating suicide are still recognizably Lockian: "Why am I
required to work for a society from which I consent to be excluded and
to submit against my will to a convention which was made without my
participation?" In revolt against the *serail* (Letter 161), Roxanne bravely
adopts just these arguments:

How could you have thought me credulous enough to imagine that I was in the
world only in order to worship your caprices.... No, I may have lived in servitude, but I have always been free. I have amended your laws according to those
of Nature and my mind [*esprit*] has always kept me independent.

Roxanne stands forthrightly with the Cartesian-educated Indian, both
figures of universal resistance to tyrannical power. There is for the French
philosopher a moral unity to human nature even when there is no political form to represent it. Despite his reputation for acknowledging the
moral diversity of peoples, here we see the place reserved for moral
universalism.[16]

ROME – REPUBLICAN "PROJECT FOR INVADING ALL NATIONS"

Montesquieu's second published work, *Considerations on the Grandeur
and Decadence of the Romans* (*Considérations sur les causes de la grandeur des Romain et de leur décadence*), contemplated the spectacle of
Rome as both an enduring republic and the most famous and long-lived
empire in the West.[17] The forms of government through which the Romans
passed were paradigm illustrations for Montesquieu of the whole typology of rule. "I am strengthened in my maxims when I find the Romans on
my side," he exclaims in *Laws*, Book VI, chapter 15. He adds: "one can
never leave the Romans" (*Laws*, XI, 13).

---

[16] For a somewhat different appreciation of Montesquieu on these issues, see the fine essay
by Tzvetan Todorov, *On Human Diversity: Nationalism, Racism, and Exoticism in
French Thought*, trans. Catherine Porter (Cambridge, Mass.: Harvard University Press,
1993), pp. 353–366.

[17] Montesquieu, *Considerations on the Causes of the Greatness of the Romans and Their
Decline*, trans. David Lowenthal (Indianapolis: Hackett, 1999), chap. 15, p. 138 (originally published 1965). Montesquieu, *Oeuvres complètes*, vol. 2, p. 150. The page references in the text are to the English translation.

In *Considerations*, Montesquieu has Machiavelli in his sights. For Machiavelli, the Roman Republic was the model precisely because it was expansionary and because its external energies had, he thought, aided the Romans in resisting internal political corruption. Montesquieu undertakes to deconstruct this argument for imperial expansion.

To be sure, the Rome of the *Considerations* follows Machiavelli's narrative, but for the author without much taste for Roman means and with no taste for the outcome. For Montesquieu, Rome was simply a military regime.[18] Since from the beginning "Rome was a city without commerce and almost without arts, pillage was the only means individuals had of enriching themselves.... Rome was therefore in an endless and constantly violent war" (p. 27). Its success depended on the energy of its people, which was, in turn, a consequence of political liberty. But Rome also depended on the resistance of its enemies, which prevented it from expanding too fast: "Always striving and always meeting obstacles, Rome made its power felt without being able to extend it, and, within a very small orbit, practiced the virtues which were to be fatal to the world" (p. 29). The "small orbit" to which Rome was confined was its school of virtue. Had it succeeded too soon, the republic would have slipped into the decadence of empire early, before its expansion had gotten underway.

War was a form of "meditation" for the Romans, peace a mere "exercise" (p. 37). This reversed the usual trope. War was ordinarily an onerous and unhappy exercise, peace the contemplative moment, but the Romans were attuned to existence only in the conduct of war. In lines that the Nietzsche of *Genealogy of Morals* could have written, Montesquieu exults:

Rome was not guided by experiences of good and evil. Only its glory determined its actions, and since it could not imagine itself existing without commanding, no hope or fear could induce it to make a peace it did not impose. There is nothing so powerful as a republic in which the laws are observed not through fear, not through reason, but through passion[.] (p. 45)

This is, to be blunt, the religion of strength. It is on display not only in Nietzsche's aristocratic morality but also in the social Darwinism of the late nineteenth century and in twentieth-century European fascism.

Chapter 11 of the *Considerations* invites the reader to judge the Romans against the standards of Machiavellian realism. When the philosophe describes the Romans' awful economy of violence, he has in mind

---

[18] For the distinction between a military and a commercial republic, see *Laws*, III, 6, p. 48.

(though he does not name the source) *The Prince*, chapter eight, on the uses of "cruelty." "Since they inflicted unbelievable evils on their enemies, leagues were hardly ever formed against them, for the country furthest from the peril did not want to venture closer." Rome knew how to play the fox as well as the lion: "since it was [Roman] custom always to speak as masters, the ambassadors they sent to peoples who had not yet felt their power were sure to be mistreated – which was a sure pretext for waging a new war." Or yet again, "since they never made peace in good faith and since universal conquest was their object, their treaties were really only suspensions of war, and they put conditions into them that always began the ruin of the state accepting them" (p. 68). "They abused the subtlety of the terms of their language. They destroyed Carthage, saying that they had promised to preserve the people of the city but not the city itself" (p. 72). They became "masters of the world … and assigned all its treasure to themselves…. A thousand crimes were committed just to give the Romans all the money in the world" (74). The republic became an empire long before it was called an empire: "all nations … disappeared little by little into the Roman republic" (p. 75).

The Romans sought *grandeur*. "In a rapid succession of victories … [Pompey] joined an infinite number of countries to the body of its empire." This "completed the *splendid* work of Rome's greatness [*grandeur*]." "Splendid" was, however, sarcasm. Montesquieu's tone was bitter. The "spectacle of Roman magnificence" had little to do with "true power." Imperial aggression endangered Roman freedoms, for after Pompey, "public liberty was only the more endangered" (p. 81). Machiavelli's expansionary formula for the preservation of republics was, in the case of Rome, a failure. Republics required stability, not high-stakes aggression: "what makes free states last a shorter time than others is that both the misfortunes and the successes they encounter almost always cause them to lose their freedom." In both domestic and foreign policy:

[a] wise republic should hazard nothing that exposes it to either good or bad fortune. The only good to which it should aspire is the perpetuation of its condition. (p. 92)

The record of Rome as an empire was not better. "Augustus … established order, that is, a *durable servitude*" (p. 121; emphasis added). Republican institutions, the senate and the magistracies, remained in place, but they were purely for show. The imperial policy of the republic left only the shell of democracy. Of this phenomenon Montesquieu says that "no tyranny is crueler than the one practiced in the shadow of the laws and under the color of justice" (p. 130).

Cruelty marked the spirit of the Romans from beginning to end. "The Romans were accustomed to making sport of human nature in the person of their children and their slaves." Therefore, "they can scarcely know the virtue we call humanity" (p. 136).

The history of Rome represented a defeat for the human spirit. "How did this project for invading all nations end – a project so well planned, carried out, and completed – except by satiating the happiness of five or six monsters?" (p. 138).

Such is for the philosophe the prestige of empire. In the eighteenth-century debate over the foundations of legitimate monarchy in France, Montesquieu was close to the advocates of the *thèse nobiliaire*, those who thought that its origin derived from the consent of nobles who were descended from the northern barbarian conquest of the Roman Empire and not, as his many *thèse royale* opponents imagined, in a direct line of monarchical descent from the ancient Roman imperium.[19] Unlike *nobiliaire* compatriots like Boulainvilliers, Montesquieu did not dismiss the bloodiness and brutality of the barbarian conquest, but he spied in the moral gestures of the conquerors and in their subsequent legislation an instinct for civil liberty that no one habituated to the authority of the Roman Empire could possibly have possessed.

In his history of Rome, Montesquieu tests the Roman political actors by the standards of *The Prince*. He appraises the model of the expansionary republic that Machiavelli extolled in the *Discourses*. In short, we can see written all over the *Considerations* the bon mot that Montesquieu waits until the *Spirit of Laws* to deliver: "We have begun to be cured of Machiavellianism, and we will continue to be cured of it" (*Laws*, XXI, 20).

THE COST OF MODERN EMPIRE

Modern European monarchies were also imperial aggrandizers, as the case of Spain exemplified. But in the little piece that was once expected to accompany the 1734 *Considerations*, "Reflections on Universal Monarchy in Europe," Montesquieu explains why empire was a losing proposition for the Europeans of his time. There will never be another Rome to exercise "a constant superiority over the others" (p. 18).[20] "Universal monarchy" – Dante's approving term – now expressed only a false anxiety.

---

[19] See Michael Mosher, "Monarchy's Paradox: Honor in the Face of Sovereign Power," in *Montesquieu's Science of Politics*, ed. Carrithers et al., pp. 159–229, at p. 165.

[20] Page references in the text refer to the French original, "Réflexions sur la monarchie universelle en Europe," *Oeuvres complètes*, vol. 2, p. 18.

Readers may assume that the entire message of the essay was to warn readers about the efforts of Louis XIV to unify the crowns of France and Spain, posing a threat of a unified Catholic Europe against a divided Protestant Europe. This conclusion is, however, arguably wrong.[21] Montesquieu denies that exposing the schemes of Louis XIV is his intention in section XVII, the only one of twenty-five sections devoted to the king. "The enemies of a grand prince who reigned in our day have a thousand times accused him, *more out of fear than reason*, of having formed and conducted a policy of universal Monarchy" (p. 33, emphasis added).

Since, however, there may be scope for reading "more out of fear than reason" as an evasion of the censor, let us turn to two related issues. The first concerns Louis's intentions and the doubts of contemporary observers. While Louis XIV's ambiguous plans to enforce a dynastic claim in favor of the Bourbons for the crown of Spain precipitated the War of the Spanish Succession, in which a coalition of European Protestant powers eventually defeated France, it was less clear that Louis XIV really intended to create a universal Europe-wide monarchy. What constituted Louis's intentions was one of the great debates of the day. His motives may have been those of the other contending sovereigns, self-preservation and self-defense. Montesquieu might well have been sincere and not simply trying to avoid the censor when he wrote that those more persuaded by their "fears" than by their "reason" had precipitated the war against France.

In *Just and Unjust Wars*, Michael Walzer returned to these debates and argued that the obscurity of French intentions indicated that the War of the Spanish Succession was a paradigm example of an unjustified

---

[21] For a contrary view, see the arguments of Paul A. Rahe, "Empires Ancient and Modern," *Wilson Quarterly*, 28, no. 3 (Summer 2004), 68–84, and "The Book That Never Was: Montesquieu's Considerations on the Romans in Historical Context," *History of Political Thought*, 26, no. 1 (Spring 2005), 43–89. Céline Spector also translates a resumé of this article, "Le livre qui ne vit jamais le jour," for the previously cited *Revue Montesquieu*, 8 (2006), 67–79. For Rahe, the defeat of Louis XIV in the battle of Blenheim at the hands of Winston Churchill's ancestor, the Duke of Marlborough, was an event as decisive for Europe as the fall of the Berlin Wall. On my view, Montesquieu did not regard this or any other battle of modern times as decisive, nor did modern leadership count for as much. (Ancient warfare and leadership were different.) Montesquieu found events too deeply embedded in multiple causal contexts (social, intellectual, economic, political), or, as he would have said, too deeply informed by esprit. On this account, it is implausible to isolate just one set of factors in order to claim, with Churchill, that "battles are the principal milestones of secular history." Rahe and I, however, agree on many interpretive issues. Our disagreements are interesting in that they may stem from differing views on the significance of recent U.S. foreign policy. Catherine Larrère as well is evidently concerned with U.S. foreign policy in "L'empire, entre fédération et république."

"preventive war." It was illegitimate because any attempt at justification depended upon speculative suppositions both about French intentions and about their remote potential consequence.[22] On this perspective, even if one granted that French intentions were malign, normative justification for entering into a preventive war against France required as well an empirical assessment of the probability of French success in carrying out such intentions. Montesquieu offered a paradigm case of just such a negative assessment that would condemn this and almost any other preventive war: "Plans which require a lot of time in order to be executed almost never succeed: the inconstancy of fortune, the changeability of human minds, the variety of passions, the continual changes in circumstances, and the diversity of causes [at play] give birth to a thousand barriers" (p. 22).

According to this standard account of the medieval Catholic heritage of just war theory, unjustifiable preventive war stood opposed to a justifiable "preemptive war," when, for instance, an adversarial army has moved to the border of another country, requiring the menaced country to act immediately or risk being overrun. In making this war, the very paradigm of an unjustified preventive conflict, Walzer cited contemporary English observers like Jonathan Swift, who in 1711 stated his opposition to the war with Louis XIV in *The Conduct of the Allies and of the Late Ministry in Beginning and Carrying on the Present War*. After the fact, Emer de Vattel, the Swiss jurist and author of *The Law of Nations*, argued that the British and their allies were wrong about French intentions. "The principal sovereigns of Europe, habituated ... to dread the power and designs of Louis XIV, *carried their mistrust so far* that they were unwilling to permit a prince of the House of France to sit upon the throne of Spain.... [The French prince] ascended the throne in spite of the efforts of those who feared so greatly his elevation; and *events have proved that their policy was too suspicious*" (emphasis added).[23]

---

[22] Michael Walzer, *Just and Unjust War: A Moral Argument with Historical Illustrations* (New York: Basic Books, 1977), pp. 76–79. When these contrasting ideas of justification entered the debate over the advisability of the second Iraq war, the terms were reversed and have stayed that way. "Preemptive war" now appears to mean what "preventive war" meant in Walzer's account, namely, a war that seeks justification by invoking hypotheses whose remoteness to the event in question renders it illegitimate by just war standards.

[23] Emer de Vattel, *Le droit des gens, ou principes de la loi naturelle, appliquées à la conduite et aux affaires des nations et des souverains*, book III, chap. III, paragraph 44, 1758. For an English translation, see *The Law of Nations*, trans. Charles G. Fenwick, in *The Classics of International Law*, ed. James Brown Scott, vol. III (London: Wiley & Sons 1902), p. 250.

A second issue concerns Montesquieu's intentions. Against the idea that Montesquieu thought Louis a danger to Europe instead of just a menace to the French themselves, we point to the main thesis of the "Reflections," namely, that a European empire was impossible in modern times. War, for Montesquieu, had become less significant in European affairs. The short section III focuses entirely on this point:

> If you recall history you will see that it had not been warfare that has changed Europe over the last four centuries; rather it has been marriages, successions, treaties, edicts, that is to say, civil dispositions that change and has changed Europe. (p. 21)

The author cited the example of Spain, which lost twenty-five successive battles with France and in the end only a tiny part of its territory (p. 22). The defeat of the French in the War of the Spanish Succession was not a decisive defeat, for in Europe there were no decisive battles. Even had the French won the great battle, "the work would have been so far from succeeding that it would barely have begun." The European balance of power would have come into play. French allies would have changed sides, and even neutral powers would have taken up arms. Moreover, for Montesquieu, defeat did not damage French power. French victory would have been worse than defeat. Universal monarchy, if that was Louis's intention, would have been "fatal to Europe," but it would have weakened France, too. "Heaven which knows true advantages has better served [Louis] by defeats than by what he could have done in victory; in place of making him the sole king of Europe, heaven favored him more by leaving him [still!] the most powerful of all [European kings]" (p. 33).

Empire in Europe has become less likely because there has been a change in "the law of peoples." When the Romans took a city in ancient times, it was sacked to enrich the army. Its lands and people were sold. Rome's victories gave it the wealth of the whole world, whereas today, Montesquieu exclaims, "nothing remains but a justified horror at this barbarism." As a consequence, because it must preserve and not destroy, a country now "ruins itself" in conquest:

> When a monarch sends an army into an enemy country it sends at the same time a part of its treasure in order to keep the country going; it enriches the country it has begun to conquer and very often puts it into a state to chase [the army] out. (p. 19)

The wealth that "commerce" has brought to Europe increases the needs and expense of armies (p. 20). Commerce has to be maintained and requires "wisdom" in government. A state that "appears victorious externally" ruins itself internally by not attending to the policies that maintain its commerce. The latter flourish in the absence of combat so that neutral nations prosper. Through enforced neglect of arms, the vanquished grow rich again. Moreover, "decadence begins especially in times of great success." An apparently victorious country discovers that it "can neither possess nor maintain [its conquests] except by violent means" (p. 20). If Machiavelli imagined that an expansionary republic warded off political decadence by keeping its citizens focused and special interests at bay, Montesquieu supposed that the very politics that conquest introduced led to paralysis and to the corruption that Machiavelli had hoped to avert.

For Montesquieu, the New World conquests of Spain were always instructive. Apparent external success hid inner decadence: "During this time the Spanish monarchy declined without stopping." By extracting gold from the Amerindians and paying them next to nothing, Spain destroyed the Amerindian population, ruined the colonial economy, and abandoned more "natural" ways of acquiring wealth, namely, through manufacture and commerce in the metropolis. Spain illustrated yet another disadvantage of empire. The illusion of finding wealth in the Indies distracted the Spanish from making money at home. The colonial tail wagged the colonizer dog. "The [West] Indies and Spain are two powers under the same master but the Indies are the principal power and Spain only an accessory" (p. 32). Montesquieu draws the obvious conclusion: "Great conquests" are "difficult ... vain ... [and] dangerous" (p. 36).

EMPIRE OF SECURITY: FIRST LOOPHOLE IN THE
CASE AGAINST EMPIRE

By the standards of the modern law of peoples, Roman conquests were barbarous. Similarly, for Montesquieu, the Spanish and the French were cruel colonizers. Quite apart from these legal and moral judgments, which nations easily ignored, there was, however, a powerful disincentive to colonization. Imperial victory abroad led directly to the interior decline of nations. "Expansion," Montesquieu reiterates in the *Laws*, is a "misfortune." "Rivers run together into the sea; monarchies are lost in despotism" (*Laws*, VIII, 17). Imperial expansion attempts to defy, without success, the lesson in geography that connects increasing size to unwanted transformations in the character of a polity. A form of government "change[s] its spirit to the degree to which its boundaries are narrowed or extended" (*Laws*, VIII, 20).

What, however, does one say about a republic or a monarchy that has not yet reached the limits of its appropriate territorial rule? Provided that it has a right to go to war, the warning against an expansionary policy that distorted internal political arrangements would simply not apply. There is only the complication of deciding when those territorial limits have been reached in any particular case. Montesquieu explicitly acknowledges this possibility in the case of monarchy: "*it should conquer only up to the limits natural to its government*" (*Laws*, X, 9, emphasis added). Book X, chapters six to eight, makes a similar case for republics.[24]

Furthermore, Montesquieu supposes that where there is a right to go to war, there is necessarily a limited right as well to temporary territorial conquest. Otherwise, the conquering nation would never have a duty to undo the mischief it has caused. "It is for the conqueror," he claims, "to make amends for part of the evils he has done." Accordingly, the "right of conquest" is "a necessary, legitimate," and, Montesquieu adds, "an unfortunate right, which always leaves an immense debt to be discharged if human nature is to be repaid" (*Laws*, X, 4, p. 142). The right to war is based on "the right of natural defense" that all "societies" possess, a right that "sometimes carries with it a necessity to attack" (*Laws*, X, 2, p. 138).

But when does self-defense confer a right and a "necessity to attack"? The answer depends upon how one reads the separable clauses in a sentence that marks out (1) the broader claim for preventive war and (2) the narrower claim for preemptive war. The sentence in question argues that a right to attack is established "when a people sees [1] that a longer peace would put another people in a position to destroy it and [2] that an attack at this moment is the only way to prevent such destruction" (*Laws* X, 2, p. 138). Montesquieu has either presented two independent justifications for going to war or, in my view, a single one whereby no preventive war would be justified in the absence of an immediate endangering provocation that requires preemptive action.

War, if successful, led to conquest. Montesquieu offered a list of occupation policies that moved from the reprehensible to the good and, he hoped, from cruel antiquity to a more progressive modernity. (1) Worst were the ancient Romans, who simply "exterminated all the citizens." Almost as bad was (2) the other ancient practice of destroying the society and dispersing its inhabitants (our ethnic cleansing). (Of course, Montesquieu was wrong: neither the first nor the second practice has

---

[24] See the section "Empires of Trade" in this chapter.

ever been fully disavowed.) Conquest could, however, aim at (3) the better policy of giving a country new civil and political government. This policy is not as good as (4) a manner of conquest that accords with "modern times, ... contemporary reasoning ... the religion of the present day ... our philosophy ... and ... our mores," namely, the practice of allowing the conquered state to govern itself according to its own laws, leaving the conqueror only with "the exercise of political and civil government" (*Laws*, X, 3). Distinguishing between (3) and (4) is not easy for the reader who assumes the legitimacy of only one form of government, namely, democracy. But for Montesquieu, the monarchy and the republic were both legitimate forms of rule. If a monarchy were imposed on a republic or a republic on a monarchy, this would illustrate the less good third solution to the problem of conquest and occupation. Leaving a conquered country as it was politically, as either a monarchy or a republic, was for the author the best policy.

The author adds, jarringly, that occupation implies a limited right to enslave the conquered: "One has the right to reduce a people to servitude only when it is necessary for the preservation of a conquest." But occupation/enslavement must have limits. "Slavery cannot be eternal." As a consequence, "the conqueror who reduces a people to servitude should always reserve for himself means ... for allowing them to leave it." There must be a plan by which the conquered can come to enjoy the same rights as the conquerors. Montesquieu refers vaguely to "a certain length of time." That this stretch of time might endure for generations is indicated by the long list of accomplishments that must take place before "servitude should cease," namely, only after "all the parts of the conquering states are bound to those of the conquered state by customs, marriage, laws, associations, and a certain conformity of spirit" (*Laws*, X, 3).

Montesquieu has a specific case in mind: the slow assimilation of the former subjects of the defeated Roman Empire into the barbarian nations that emerged from the conquest. Montesquieu identifies with the "German" conquerors. They are, he says, "our fathers." They wisely "softened the laws that they had made in the heat, impetuosity, and arrogance of victory." There was, to be sure, popular resistance in the German tribes to mild treatment of the Romans. "The Burgundians, the Goths, and the Lombards wanted the Romans to continue to be the vanquished people." But happily "the laws of Euric, of Gundobard, and of Rotharis made the barbarian and the Roman fellow citizens" (*Laws* X, 3, pp. 140–141).

EMPIRE OF HUMAN RIGHTS: SECOND LOOPHOLE
IN THE CASE AGAINST EMPIRE

For Montesquieu, Gelon, the king of ancient Syracuse, made "the finest peace treaty mentioned in history." It was exceptional because it
demanded only that the Carthaginians "abolish the custom of sacrificing
their children," which is to say that the treaty "exacted a condition useful
only to the" Carthaginians, not to the conquerors (*Laws*, X, 5, p. 142).
The conquerors from Syracuse have – Montesquieu is sure of it – unam-
biguously improved the people they had defeated in battle. This story is
a perfect ancient analogy to a modern human rights intervention. Since
the Treaty of Westphalia, however, doctrines of national sovereignty have
regarded as illegitimate all interventions that endeavor to correct the
internal abuses of another country. Only after the exceptional horrors of
World War II has this convention partially broken down so that human
rights abuses can sometimes be advanced as justifiable causes for intervention and war. Given that challenges to the doctrine of sovereignty are
relatively recent, it is surprising to find something like this justification
for intervention in the *Spirit of Laws*.

We should not, however, be altogether surprised to find, in the great
anti-imperial thinker, cases that point to military intervention on something like the grounds of human rights and, more particularly, on
grounds of a duty to promote enlightenment, because the very basis for
Montesquieu's opposition to imperial conquest stems from his concern
with both human rights and the eradication of prejudice through enlightenment. Montesquieu's defense of interventions on behalf of human
rights in other countries may suggest an alignment of his views with
those whom Jennifer Pitts identifies as nineteenth-century imperial liberals, such as Mill and Tocqueville.[25]

There is a prior epistemological presupposition at work. Imperial liberalism presupposes ease of access to a common rational outlook. In the
empire of rights, every person, of whatever attachments and loyalties, is
presumed to be capable (under one or another set of ideal speech conditions or other arrangements conducive to rational impartiality) of recognizing what constitutes abusive conduct and irrational prejudice and
what does not. This image of individuals as capable of rational agreement on norms of conduct works well for the most part in a reading of

---

[25] Jennifer Pitts, *A Turn to Empire: The Rise of Imperial Liberalism in Britain and France*
(Princeton, N.J.: Princeton University Press, 2005).

Montesquieu. But sometimes the author speaks as though all that could be said is that each people is in possession of a distinctive esprit and that the perspective of each individual member is necessarily attuned to the expectations of this esprit. If esprit were always the necessary communal focus for individual perception and judgment, the case for easy rational agreement among individuals who belong to different communities would be harder to make out. To the extent that scattered remarks in his writings combine to suggest this understanding of the collectivist background to individual perception and judgment, Montesquieu stands closer to Herder and to the possibility of at least partially incommensurable standards of assessment between communities.[26]

Herderian cultural nationalism owes a debt to Montesquieu's initial conception of the collective spirit of peoples and of its impact on individual judgment, for Montesquieu breaks with the prevalent rationalism of Machiavelli, Hobbes, Descartes, and others by arguing that one cannot make sense of individuals without placing them in the context of their belonging at a certain time and place to a people whose customs and habits ground individual judgment. But in contrast to thinkers like Herder, Montesquieu also resists the implications of this argument and holds out for a relative individuality in the making of judgments. One cannot make sense of a people, or of their habits and expectations, without making room for the independent perceptions of its individual members. It is open to the latter always to make self-reflexive and, to that extent, detached assessments on the collectivities to which they are attached. If Montesquieu points to Herder and to the partially incommensurable perspectives of distinct peoples (or to Durkheim and the collective consciousness), he also never ceases to be a Cartesian rationalist grounded in the possibilities of the expressive "I" whose capacity for thinking alone establishes the individuality of existence.

Recall the *Persian Letters*. Roxanne is a troubling figure for those who believe that standards for judging a way of life must come from within that life for the good reason that these standards must be justifiable to those who belong to the community in question. Roxanne is a Persian woman who finds an ethical standpoint outside the harem from which she claims to judge it. No effort to impose on her the conventions of the

---

[26] For a defense of the cultural pluralism inherent in an acknowledgment of "partial incommensurability" between societies or ways of life, see Sankar Muthu, *Enlightenment against Empire* (Princeton, N.J.: Princeton University Press, 2003). For Muthu, Diderot, Herder, and Kant synthesize, no less than I argue Montesquieu does, the perspectives of individualist rationalism and cultural pluralism.

harem can now possibly make sense on this principle – that arguments must make sense to those to whom they are applied – since Roxanne has already indicated that the novel standards do make sense to her. (Indeed, they make sense even to Usbek, who is a European-educated traditionalist!) Her Cartesian self-assertion not only trumps membership, it ultimately threatens to transform membership. One could argue that Roxanne is but a fiction in the mind of a European thinker, but this claim does not diminish the number or importance of those who have criticized their own community from within by invoking standards that were also new to the community.

Justification from within a community means in part justification to those like Usbek who speak for cultural norms. But it also means the justification of cultural norms to individuals like Roxanne who stand in opposition to these norms. The fact that Usbek unwittingly supplies her with the individualist Lockean arguments for resistance in his hapless efforts at enlightenment makes her case easier; he had already gone down the road to individualist rationalism, and it was simply up to her to show him its practical consequences. However, the two strands of Montesquieu's theory – one stressing the collective, the other the individual – are sometimes on a collision course. If Montesquieu's discovery that peoples are organized into varieties of esprit leads to the conclusion that each community perceives the world exclusively through its own esprit-informed paradigm, there could be no world of knowledge that rose above esprit. Then the spirit of a people could only express the (Kuhnian or other suitable) paradigm through which organized knowledge is made available.

Montesquieu invents this way of looking at organized communities, but he never goes so far as to think that individual judgment counts for little outside these organized communities of apperception. To judge the world by the standard of communal identity and to judge the world by the belief that there are standards that rise above every collective identity are two radically different things, two incommensurabilities struggling, as it were, for the soul of Montesquieu.

EMPIRE OF ENLIGHTENMENT: THIRD LOOPHOLE
IN THE CASE AGAINST EMPIRE

In Book X, chapter 4 of the *Spirit of Laws*, Montesquieu opens the door wider to transformative foreign adventures that are justified on the grounds that, to cite the chapter title, there may be "some advantages for the conquered people" in submitting to rule by others. Providing advantages to the conquered is part of "the immense debt to be discharged" by the conqueror (*Laws*, X, 4, p. 142). Montesquieu carefully adds, however, that such "advantages" are so little spoken of because they create endless justifications for war. Nevertheless, he does not disavow the legitimacy of these arguments, however dangerous they may be.

Earlier, we showed how, for Montesquieu, human rights violations prepare the way for liberal empire. Now Montesquieu pushes to a far bolder claim: "A conquest can destroy harmful prejudices, and if I dare speak in this way, put a nation under a better genius." That is to say, a certain sort of conquest promotes enlightenment.

Montesquieu expects that normally a people should reform themselves. Sometimes, however, reform is impossible. Could a people's incapacity justify external intervention? The philosophe's answer is decidedly strange. He suggests that a political community might suffer from a strange phenomenon, one he calls "*la tyrannie sourde*." This is an odd species: a tyranny that cannot be heard or seen. It is, in fact, "imperceptible." This characterization of oppression may well be a linguistic ancestor to a more familiar trope: false consciousness. A people in these circumstances cannot know or judge the character of their rulers and consequently cannot act to secure their own interests. But why would this justify the intervention of another state?

In the language of contemporary international relations, Montesquieu points in the direction of the "failed state." To be sure, this term is typically reserved for cases in which anarchy and chaos prevail, but a state may also "fail" if it is both incapable of either protecting the people or giving them a voice to protest. A great many otherwise orderly states and societies may in this sense be failures. A failed state is, for Montesquieu, defined by the language of the classical republic as one that succumbs to "corruption," one in which the laws are not executed and the government has become an oppressor. Rather than strengthening those in power, corruption enervates. The state does not possess "the force of its original institution," which is why it is therefore liable to suffer conquest and also why conquest ought to be its fate: "What would a government lose from being re-founded, if it had reached the point of being unable to reform itself?" (*Laws*, X, 4, p. 141). The language evokes Machiavelli's scenario of a republican re-founding that recaptures the force of the old constitution. But Montesquieu may go further than his Florentine predecessor. Machiavelli issued a call to a revolutionary re-founding from within a corrupted state. Montesquieu takes the language of internal reform and makes it an argument for external conquest. Machiavelli's muscular prescription for a failed state was designed to preserve its independence against conquest. It could be independent only if there were a political order capable of producing a representative of the people who could act for it. But if internal reform should fail and the people are left without a representative and therefore without a collective will, Montesquieu shows that the same argument can be adapted to justify external conquest.

In effect, Montesquieu raises the question of whether international law may require intervention in the case of peoples unable to help themselves, defined as those who suffer from *la tyrannie sourde*. The issue is not evidently restricted to the absence of political liberty. For Montesquieu, the absence of political liberty also implicates the social question, that is to say, the exploitation of the poor by the rich. The author's paradigm case is "a people where by a thousand ruses and tricks the rich *imperceptibly* [a translation of *la tyrannie sourde*] practice the usurpation [of the poor]." In a remarkable psychological portrait, Montesquieu describes the oppressed as being incapacitated by their own guilt in feeling cheated. Under *la tyrannie sourde*, the "unhappy people tremble, seeing what they believe to be abuses of power, and [yet] though being oppressed by them, they believe they are wrong to feel this way about it" (*Laws* X, 4, p. 141). Silence reigns, communication rendered impossible. The people are deaf to their own interests because they do not trust themselves. They may see, but they cannot articulate what they see, which leaves them miserable and unwilling to lift a finger for their country.

We are only changing the metaphor in saying that the argument for action in response to the condition of *la tyrannie sourde* is simultaneously an argument for the practical duties that follow from the acquisition of knowledge understood as *lumière*, or enlightenment. Deafness is replaced by blindness, which is cured only by those who can shine light on things. This is a dangerous argument even for internal reform. It invites one to reject what people actually say about themselves on the grounds that they are in the grip of disorders that prevent them from understanding their real interests. It is, as Montesquieu conceded, even more dangerous as a justification for conquest. But the author does not regard the argument as illegitimate.

Montesquieu concludes the chapter by turning to the negative example of Spain. What might have justified Spanish intervention in the Americas? It all comes down to the wish; if only the Spanish had been good liberals in both policy and religion, their foreign policy in the Americas might have been applauded: "What good could the Spanish not have done for the Mexicans. They had a gentle religion to give them; they brought them a raging superstition. They could have set the slaves free; and they made freemen slaves" (*Laws*, X, 4, p. 142). In the counterfactual hypothesis regarding what the Spanish *might* have done, Montesquieu establishes an important principle and, at least in the light of his anticolonialist sentiments, a surprising one: a colonization that spreads enlightenment could be morally sanctioned. He maintains a discreet silence on the further question of whether the duty to spread enlightenment would justify initiating a war or would only be a moral requirement for victors after a conquest in a war that had been entered into for other reasons.

ALEXANDER'S EMPIRE: MODEL FOR MODERNITY?

Alexander was the greatest of the ancient Western empire builders. He briefly united Europe and Asia and in so doing set the template for future East–West relations. One could suspect that his tale of pillage and destruction across Asia Minor into India would have aroused anticolonial indignation in Montesquieu to the same degree to which it was aroused by the story of Spain in the Americas. But instead Montesquieu viewed Alexander as a paragon of virtue in conquest.[27]

In the *Spirit of Laws*, Montesquieu distinguished between Alexander's conduct at home and abroad. At home, he was an oppressor of Greek liberties. This was not admirable. The conquest of Asia elicited, however, the same amazed admiration at Alexander's brilliant strategy and tactics that was stirred in Montesquieu's soul by the spectacle of Rome at war. It was not only the rationality of Alexander's mind at war that drew the baron de la Brède to him. Alexander's conduct at war evoked in Montesquieu an aesthetic appreciation even when his actions led to real evils. Alexander "did two things that were bad: he burned Persepolis and killed Clitus," but what happened then testified to his beautiful soul:

He made them famous by his repentance, so that one forgot his criminal actions and remembered his respect for virtue, so that these actions were considered misfortunes rather than things proper to him, so that posterity finds the beauty of his soul at virtually the same time as his ravings and his weakness, so that

[27] On the significance of Alexander to Montesquieu, see also the following two studies: Catherine Larrère, "Montesquieu on Economics and Commerce," in *Montesquieu's Science of Politics*, ed. Carrithers et al., pp. 354–357; and Catherine Volpihac-Auger, "Montesquieu et l'impérialism grec: Alexandre ou l'art de la conquête," in *Montesquieu and the Spirit of Modernity*, ed. David W. Carrithers and Patrick Coleman (Oxford: Voltaire Foundation, 2002), pp. 49–60.

one had to be sorry for him and it was no longer possible to hate him. (*Laws*, X, 14, p. 151)

Alexander's occupation policies were, however, what made him truly stand out. To put it anachronistically, Alexander governed as a multiculturalist. He assimilated the conquered into an empire of plural cultures. In doing so, Alexander resisted the advice, Montesquieu said, following Plutarch's account, of his teacher, Aristotle. Aristotle "wanted him to treat the Greeks as masters and the Persians as slaves." (Kant made the same accusation against Aristotle, whose views, he said, were typical of Greek prejudices.) Alexander "thought only of uniting the two nations and wiping out the distinction between conquerors and vanquished," but he did so by assuming "the mores of the Persians in order not to distress the Persians by making them assume the mores of the Greeks" (*Laws*, X, 14, p. 149). He took wives among the subject populations and insisted that his generals do likewise. "He left to the vanquished peoples not only their mores but also their civil laws.... He respected the old traditions and everything that recorded the glory or the vanity of these peoples." He rebuilt the temples of the "Greeks, Babylonians, and Egyptians [and] ... there were few nations at whose altars he did not sacrifice" (Laws, X, 14, p. 150). One could argue that these gestures were tactics that would have preceded an eventual unification of the empire under Greek cultural hegemony, but Alexander planted the seeds of diversity too deep, in marriage, family, and religion, to imagine that this was a merely symbolic politics.

The utility of each locale was also Alexander's preoccupation. He thought only in every country of what would enhance "its prosperity and power." He was the "monarch of each nation" but "the first citizen of each town." In sum, if "the Romans conquered all in order to destroy all, [*Alexander*] *wanted to conquer all in order to preserve all*" (*Laws*, X, 14, pp. 150–151, emphasis added).

For Montesquieu, Alexander evidently understood that living in accord with one's own mores, customs, and laws, and being a member of the collective esprit thereby established, was a priority for everyone. In order to preserve the conquests of alien national communities, one should do as much as possible to re-create their own feeling of solidarity across the boundary between conquerors and conquered. Montesquieu's admiration of Alexander for these achievements suggests that a Herder-like appreciation of the human capacity for belonging was as important to the French philosopher as his more salient approval of detached individual intelligence.

The tension in Montesquieu's work between belonging and detached intelligence suggests a sticking point, an ultimate issue of potential inconsistency between Montesquieu's *ère de lumière* individualist rationalism with its universally applicable standards and his fondness for multiple particular ways of life and their often equally worthy but differentiated, fundamentally at odds collective solidarities. There is an existential question to be faced. What is the detached intellect to do when it comes in contact with these multiple particular ways of life? One answer to this question is: write a book that looks much like the *Spirit of Laws*. But that, for the writer and the reader, only reinforces the intellect in its detachment. What would real contact look like? That is what is at stake in the admiration that Montesquieu expresses for Alexander's conduct in the following line:

After the conquest, [Alexander] abandoned all the prejudices that had served him in making it; he assumed the mores of the Persians. (*Laws*, X, 14, p. 149)

The prejudices of Alexander were those that Aristotle taught: the Greeks were superior to the barbarians. This was a view, moreover, that Montesquieu shared. The prejudices of Aristotle, Alexander, and Montesquieu regarding Asians can be stated roughly as follows. The Asians do not practice political freedom. Their polities hence could not capture and transform into military power the collective energy, social innovations, and individual initiative that political freedom brings in its train. The peoples who practiced political freedom could and even should conquer the Asians. It was a duty of enlightenment.[28] As Montesquieu laconically but decisively put it: "It is not a matter of indifference that the people be enlightened" (*Spirit of Laws*, Preface).

These pieces of orientalist savoir-faire were first given expression in Herodotus's reflections on the struggles of the Greek city-states with the Persian Empire. The dogma was then conveyed by Montaigne into modern European philosophy ("The inhabitants of Asia served one single man because they could not pronounce one single syllable, which is 'No'").[29] To his credit, Montesquieu was not always sure that Europeans knew how to practice freedom. Nevertheless, in taking the "oriental harem" as

[28] This West–East invidious comparison Montesquieu also transposed into a North–South comparison, with the ironic result that the Greece of political liberty then joined the South: "The Goth Jornandes called Northern Europe the fabricator of human kind. I would rather call the North the fabricator of those instruments which break the chains forged in the South" (*Laws*, XVII, 5).

[29] Michel de Montaigne, *The Complete Essays of Montaigne*, trans. Donald M. Frame (Stanford, Calif.: Stanford University Press, 1958), I, 26, p. 115.

a preferred image of unfreedom, Montesquieu continued in a new register the old Herodotean understanding of the East.

A prejudice is not necessarily false knowledge. To be useful to those
who would exploit it, it must in some sense be true. The falsehood that
lurks in the prejudicial application of knowledge is self-referential:
persons who exploit their knowledge of others against them lack self-
understanding.

Montesquieu says this explicitly in his singular reflection on the subject
cited above: "Prejudice is what makes one unaware of oneself" (*Laws*,
Preface). In "oneself," there is a kind of Cartesian "I think" being commended, an "it is 'I' who is thinking." Whatever the particular detail that
one could know about any individual "I," all one need know about it is
that it is "I."

The universal knowledge of the interests of humanity (the work of
enlightenment understood solely as knowledge) accords with the individualist and rationalist side of Montesquieu. These interests are potentially
knowable by every individual, whatever his or her collective esprit or
individual mentality. In this context, the Alexandrian acknowledgment
of other selves would seem to accord more with the Herderian potential awaiting release in Montesquieu's thought, the idea of there being
not fully comparable agonistic collective spirits. This makes relating to
another group less a matter of recognizing it as a type under knowable
standards and more a question of acknowledging the standing of another
and of the potential dignity in a human existence.

In saying that Alexander overcame a prejudice about the Asians he
conquered, Montesquieu did not, I think, mean that Alexander discovered something new about Asians that inclined him to think that
his earlier beliefs were wrong. His beliefs may well have been wrong,
but Alexander was not at this moment giving up on them. Rather, he
was setting them aside and shifting the ground of his standing with the
Asians. He acknowledged their existence and position not as an object of
knowledge, but as a form of subjectivity in confrontation with his own
subjectivity. This was at the same time Alexander's acknowledgment of
himself, an admission that he had been unaware of himself, which is what
Montesquieu tells us prejudice at bottom is.

Whatever the knowledge content of the universal message that
Alexander carried to Asia, it was necessarily tainted by its bearer's particular identity. Whatever the value of the proffered universal interest – or
"advantage" – for those Alexander conquered, it had in it nothing *for* them
because there was nothing *of* them in it. There was no acknowledgment

of who they were except as cognitive objects to which Greek "enlightenment" might be applied.

As we see in the cruel figure of Usbek, the enlightened rationalist unaware of himself, universal knowledge claims are sometimes dehumanizing. With Alexander, Montesquieu gives us the substance of that "virtue we call humanity" (*Considerations*, XV, p. 136). Alexander is a man out of his time, a figure from cruel antiquity, who nevertheless points the way to modernity – a modernity characterized not only by *doux commerce* but also, as we argue later, by conquest as well.

Montesquieu appreciated the beauty of Alexander's integrative conduct without quite explaining why it was admirable. He lacked the vocabulary that we invoke, a vocabulary that is in truth post-Kantian.[30] But in admiring Alexander's conduct, Montesquieu himself switched from *knowing* the Asians to *acknowledging* them. Knowing permitted him to place them into a natural history of the human species. Acknowledging invited him to assimilate their existence to his own. Too little of this latter way of standing with others survives in Montesquieu's *Spirit of Laws*, which is a book of knowledge, a natural history of the human species, not the book of acknowledgment that the *Persian Letters* becomes in Roxanne's last letter to her husband.

FORCE AND INTERNATIONAL COMMERCE

Alexander served as an ancient model to modernity not only because he practiced the politics of mutual acknowledgment, but also because he illustrated the potential for an alliance between the warrior and the merchant. However, this connection is alleged to have been famously repudiated in Books XX–XXII of the *Laws*, where the overall message could be taken as claiming that commerce, allied with liberty, softened the "barbarous mores" of warrior nations (*Laws*, XX, 2). In creating a network of interlocking interests, commerce undermined two kinds of temptations: an expansionary foreign policy abroad and violent rebellion at home. Far from being a potential ally, commerce is always on these grounds the alternative to imperial conquest:

> Commerce, sometimes impeded by conquerors, sometimes hampered by monarchs, wanders across the earth, flees from where it is oppressed, and remains where it is left to breathe. (*Laws*, XXI, 5)

[30] The specific form of post-Kantian or post-Hegelian philosophy invoked by this distinction arises in Stanley Cavell, "Knowing and Acknowledging," in *Must We Mean What We Say?* 2nd ed. (Cambridge: Cambridge University Press, 2002), pp. 238–268.

In the midst of this discourse on *doux commerce* the author returns, strangely enough, to two examples of an expansionary foreign policy: the conquests of Alexander and those of the Persian king Darius. Both drove their armies to the sea down the river Indus while conquering those who stood in the way. But unlike Darius, Alexander on the Indus saw into the future. His became a voyage of enlightenment that intimated an East and West united not by conquest, but by commerce and trade. By contrast:

> The voyage that Darius had [the Persians] make down the Indus and the Indian Sea was the fancy of a prince who wants to show his power rather than the orderly project of a monarch who wants to use it. This had *no consequence, either for commerce or for sailing*, and if one departed from ignorance [in making the voyage], it was only to return to it shortly. (*Laws*, XXI, 8, emphasis added)

Commerce may have been *doux* in consequence but not in origin. Hard and rationally enlightened conquest preceded soft and rationally enlightened trade. Alexander constituted an ancient precedent of what was occurring in eighteenth-century Europe: an Enlightenment-inspired alliance of conquerors and agents of commerce. The exceptional character of Alexander's empire-building lay, Montesquieu claimed, in his wanting "to conquer all in order to preserve all." Conquest for preservation established a benchmark for legitimate acquisition that was applied, fairly or not, by Alexander's modern successors who sat astride those "empires of trade and liberty" that arose in seventeenth- and eighteenth-century England and Holland (and in the other mainly Protestant powers of Northern Europe).[31]

The implantation of colonies in the New World and in the East Indies required impositions upon and, more often than not, the outright conquest of indigenous inhabitants. Furthermore, European states' mercantilist and zero-sum understandings of trade relationships led to wars and near-wars. Trade and war were not strangers even to the English and the Dutch, whom Montesquieu favored over the more aggressive Portuguese and Spanish invaders. The inclusion of Alexander in Montesquieu's books on *doux commerce* was thus not only an acknowledgment of how ancient trade routes were opened but also a recognition that similar factors were at play in modern Europe. Alexander was an exemplar from antiquity but also a precursor for modernity.

If, however, something like Alexander's sword (say, the English or Dutch fleet) ultimately stood behind the *doux commerce* of modern Europe,

---

[31] Pagden, *Peoples and Empires*, p. 86.

how did Montesquieu distinguish between the English and Dutch trading empires and the empires of Spain and Portugal? All of them rested on a foundation of military prowess and intimidation. Montesquieu's answer was equivocal. England and Holland gave empire a new look thanks to the invention of the quasi-private trading company, which did not require the military conquests or the same overt degree of coercion associated with older empires. Montesquieu did not want to invoke even the name of empire in describing such arrangements. Nevertheless, he did admit that "jealousy of trade"[32] confounded the relations between Holland and England. These pretexts for commercial war were always present. In addition, he could not avoid a second admission: England had acquired Ireland the old-fashioned way, by conquest.

Where did France fit into this scheme of things? For Montesquieu, French colonial failures were scarcely less devastating than Roman transgressions. According to French public opinion in the metropolis, the people of the colonies were too prone to violence. But colonial violence only revealed, Montesquieu countered, the malign character of French domination.

Can the ferocity we find in the inhabitants of our colonies come from anything but the punishments constantly inflicted on this unhappy portion of the human race? When we are cruel in the civil state, what can we expect from natural gentleness and justice. (*Considerations*, XV, p. 136)

EQUIVOCATION ON POLITICAL ECONOMY

European monarchs sponsored great voyages of discovery. They were motivated by both the vainglory of a Darius and the utilitarian vision of an Alexander. Montesquieu sometimes seems to have supposed, however, that monarchy in any of its forms was not suited to colonization. Who was left to carry on Europe's colonization? A particularly blunt statement on this question comes from one of his notebooks, a dossier called "Book on Confederations and Colonies": "Colonies are best suited to republican states."[33] A note in the dossier suggested that he might have planned on adding the book to the *Spirit of Laws*. It is unknown why the document was excluded.[34]

---

[32] For an in-depth study, see Istvan Hont, *Jealousy of Trade: International Competition and the Nation-State in Historical Perspective* (Cambridge, Mass.: Harvard University Press, 2005).

[33] Montesquieu, *Oeuvres complètes*, vol. 2, p. 1007.

[34] See "Confédérations et Colonies," in the "Dossier de l'Esprit des Lois," *Oeuvres complètes*, vol. 2, pp. 1004–1010; and Catherine Volpilhac-Auger and Claire Bustarret,

In support of this view, the author argues that democracies are typically overpopulated. When people leave for the colonies, there is no sense of loss in the metropolis. Colonization relieves the burdens on the poor. Since the poor are also citizens, this defuses potentially dangerous class conflict in the metropolis. Republican colonization establishes colonies of independent states. Colonies therefore tend to support the home country. This is because "the new republic is not ordinarily under the domination of the old republic." There is a further advantage. As it is disinclined to incorporate the colony, the old republic "consequently does not expand its empire nor change its form of government." (In a prescient note, Montesquieu wonders if this is always true.) Monarchies have none of these advantages in establishing colonies. These kingdoms are typically underpopulated. Furthermore, monarchy cannot tolerate a colony that seeks independence from the sovereign. Therefore, the monarchy that seeks an empire exhausts itself twice over, first in losing needed people to the colonies and then in spending resources to maintain the conquest in order to prevent the colony from establishing its independence. The dossier carries a final warning. Whether a colony is established for the relief of excess population, for maintaining a conquest, or for commerce, one should be on guard against colonists, for they could become those animals that eat their mothers.

In the *Laws* these sentiments are abbreviated into a single line: "the spirit of monarchy is war and expansion; the spirit of republics is peace and moderation" (*Laws*, IX, 2). After the voyages of discovery, the Spanish monarchy "treated the newly discovered lands as objects of conquest." There are, however, "more refined" peoples who see these lands not as objects of conquest but as "objects of commerce." It is relevant that Montesquieu does not name these peoples: they may or may not be citizens of a republic. But on this view, trade is a substitute for conquest; quasi-private trading companies, a substitute for state domination; republican commerce, a substitute for monarchical predation. There is still a hint that coercion plays a role: "Empire," he says, was granted to these companies, but by restricting themselves to trade, they may have nearly overcome the republican dilemma of governing "distant states" (*Laws*, XXI, 21, p. 391).

L'Atelier de Montesquieu: Manuscrits inédits de la Brède (Naples: Liguori Editore and Oxford: Voltaire Foundation, 2001), pp. 43–67. Thanks to Céline Spector for a discussion of these files. See Céline Spector, "Montesquieu, l'Europe et les nouvelles figures de l'empire," *Revue Montesquieu*, 8 (2005–2006), 17–42, especially 28–29.

Readers could be forgiven, however, if they were to complain of cognitive dissonance in contemplating this image of the peaceable republic, for in large parts of Montesquieu's oeuvre (all of the *Considerations*, big portions of the *Spirit of the Laws*) the republic was far from a peaceable regime. It was instead filled with impoverished (or at least definitively noncommercial) warriors bent on predation, with the prime example being republican Rome. Of course, both Athens and Carthage were commercial republics and must be given their due. But neither was purely commercial. Of Athens, Montesquieu admits that it "was more attentive to extending its maritime empire than to enjoying it" (*Laws*, XXI, 7, my translation).

What then are we to make of those rapturous interludes where the author speaks of the purely commercial potential of the republic? To which countries do these passages refer – ancient Marseille, modern Genoa? Quite apart from the issue of what Montesquieu has in mind, these passages are fascinating in their own right. Their descriptions of the internal discipline of which the practitioners of a market economy are capable foreshadow Weber:

When democracy is founded on commerce, it may very well happen that individuals have great wealth, yet that the mores are not corrupted. This is because the spirit of commerce brings with it the spirit of frugality, economy, moderation, work, wisdom, tranquility, order, and rule. (*Laws*, V, 6)

In the later two books on commerce (*Laws*, XX, XXI), he qualifies this message by suggesting that republican political economy is always in the grip of disruptive possibilities.[35] Indeed, even in the introductory passage of *Laws*, V, 6, the fatal dialectic appears: "the ill comes when an excess of wealth destroys the spirit of commerce and one sees the sudden rise of the disorders of inequality that had not made themselves felt before." But renewed threat requires the citizens of republics to redouble their efforts. The commercial republic calls for equal inheritance. In addition, it needs an income floor and an income ceiling that "makes each poor citizen comfortable enough to work as the others do and ... bring[s] each rich citizen to a middle level" (*Laws*, V, 6).

One could imagine these conditions being met in republics of suitably small scale, a Marseille or a Genoa, but is it possible that Montesquieu

---

[35] For a helpful discussion regarding the two types, see Catheine Larrère, "Montesquieu: commerce de luxe et commerce d'économie," in *Lectures de l'Esprit des lois*, ed. Céline Spector and Thierry Hoquet (Bordeaux: Presses Universitaires de Bordeaux, 2004), pp. 121–143.

has bigger examples in mind, such as Holland and England? If so, the argument would appear to be tripped up by his theory about the transformative character of size.

The promotion of the republic as the agent of modern colonization and international commerce flies in the face of several of the discernible conclusions in the *Laws* that tend to indicate why republics are not suitable regimes for modern conditions. First, there is the political problem that should act as a cautionary barrier against the expansion of the republic. The republic is, of course, too small to compete against larger states, but when it grows large, it is threatened with revolutionary instability. England in its revolutionary republican moment during the seventeenth-century civil war is Montesquieu's standard example of this instability. The possibility of establishing a federation of republics is obviously a hope. Given the dossier "Book on Confederations and Colonies," perhaps this is the direction in which Montesquieu thinks modern republics would tend.

There is also an economic problem. Republics and monarchies are each suited to different economic arrangements: the "commerce of economy" for republics, because it is based on the rough equality of the market participants and on competition over the essentials of sustenance; and the "economy of luxury" for monarchies, which reflects and is founded on the inequality and social hierarchy found in aristocratic societies, and also on the fact that the political elites (the judicial and military nobility) are noncommercial and at least theoretically animated by standards other than tough "commerce of economy" competition over prices (*Laws*, XX, 4). The two models stand opposed to each other not only in their values but also in their institutional arrangements. It is, however, not obvious which kind of political economy Montesquieu prefers, as each tends to create different sets of desirable and undesirable conditions.

Montesquieu sometimes thinks of a republican economy as a fragile institution. The very success of a republican "commerce of economy" implies that it will transform itself into its opposite, an economy of luxury, and thus provoke a constitution-altering transformation from equality to inequality. The most succinct expression of this dialectical self-transformation is found in Montesquieu's second book on commerce: "The effect of commerce is wealth; the consequence of wealth, luxury; that of luxury, the perfection of the arts" (*Laws*, XXI, 6). But even earlier, the fragility of egalitarian commerce is prophesied at the very moment it is first defined: "One commerce leads to another, the small to the middling, the middling to the great, and he who earlier desired to gain little arrives at a position where he has no less desire to gain a great deal" (*Laws*, XX, 4). Republican economic enterprises unravel in the same manner as do republican politics. Either the republic submits to rivals or it conquers them, grows to excessive proportions, and undermines its constitution: "If a republic is small, it is destroyed by a foreign force; if it is large, it is destroyed by an internal vice" (*Laws*, IX, 1).

Montesquieu was ambivalent about these prospects. Michael Sonenscher seized on one side of the ambivalence, namely, Montesquieu's argument for monarchical political economy. For Sonenscher, the narrative purpose of *Considerations* in its recounting the life cycle of Rome from republic to empire was to instruct modernity on just this issue of the fragility of republican political economy. On this account, the modern Europe of monarchical states was the political solution that lay beyond the grasp of the Roman Republic: "the key to understanding Rome's historical trajectory was its inability, despite its imperial government and the massive amount of wealth and power at its command, to escape from its republican origins and become a monarchy in anything like the modern sense."[36] The ancients, Montesquieu had always claimed, simply did not understand monarchy (*Laws*, XI, 8). Rome did not, however, illustrate the unraveling of egalitarian "economy" into an inegalitarian luxury economy. From the beginning, Rome was a typically predatory republic and not a commercial nation. Of the Romans at the height of the Republic's expansion Montesquieu wrote: "masters of the world, they assigned all its treasures to themselves, and in plundering, were less unjust as conquerors than as legislators" (*Considerations*, VI, p. 74). Montesquieu contrasted the Roman model unfavorably to the "Barbarian," his name for the original constitution that became the European monarchical state. The advantage of monarchy was its weakness as a state; the very strength of the Roman model was its disadvantage. Weak monarchy was more compatible with both the independence of citizens and the independence of allied states (*Considerations*, VI, p. 76).

On Sonenscher's characterization, Rome was paralyzed in its economic track: "the switch from republic to empire had not been matched by a corresponding switch from conquest to commerce," which would have required Rome to have pursued the developmental path that ended in the European economy of inequality.[37] In support of this position,

---

[36] Michael Sonenscher, *Before the Deluge: Public Debt, Inequality, and the Intellectual Origins of the French Revolution* (Princeton, N.J.: Princeton University Press, 2007), p. 49.
[37] Sonenscher, *Deluge*, p. 101.

Montesquieu was evidently a reforming monarchist. For him, monarchy could not have been the fragile institution that disappeared two generations later in the French Revolution. Even after the Revolution, Hegel could claim that monarchy was the regime for modern times: "The development of the state to constitutional monarchy is the achievement of the modern world."[38] This was also Montesquieu's view. Montesquieu offered the public a reform model of an evolving monarchy that centered on the royal courts, or the *parlements*, which on this account possessed an evolutionary potential that could lead from *parlement* to parliament. The *Laws* were read as support for a *parlement*-centered reform ideology that thrived from 1748 until 1771, when Chancellor Maupeou dealt the courts a fatal blow.[39]

EMPIRES OF TRADE

Despite the terminological confusion thus engendered, when Montesquieu claims in the previously mentioned dossier that "colonies are best suited to republican states," he has principally in mind the English kingdom as the paramount example of a modern state that is able to construct the republican equivalent of an empire. Even regarding its manner of colonization, England is still "the republic that hides itself in the form of the monarchy" (*Laws*, V, 19).

In Book XIX, chapter 27, the second essay on England (Book XI, chapter 6 being the first), Montesquieu cites two examples of conquest or colonization. The first concerns the English-speaking colonies in North America. Montesquieu does not regard them as conquests, though his manner of making the point offers him a hedge. Speaking in the subjunctive of an England he never explicitly names, he surmises: "If this nation sent colonies abroad, it would do so to extend its commerce rather than its domination." "Rather than" we may take as meaning that "domination" was not the primary motive. English practices are spoken of in the subjunctive because it is only the ideal potential of England that interests this observer, not the compromises inherent in its actual practices. As this ideal England gives these colonies a government modeled after its own parliamentary practices, Montesquieu sees

---

[38] G. W. F. Hegel, *Elements of the Philosophy of Right*, ed. Allen W. Wood (Cambridge: Cambridge University Press, 1991), para. 273, p. 308.

[39] Michael Mosher, "Monarchy's Paradox: Honor in the Face of Sovereign Power," in *Montesquieu's Science of Politics*, especially pp. 192–198.

nothing but "prosperity" and the "formation of great peoples" in the woods of North America (*Laws*, XIX, 27).

Montesquieu's second example, Ireland under the thumb of England, is unequivocally a case of conquest. It appeared to contradict the generalization that fit the political geography of England: "If the nation inhabited an island, it would not be a conquering nation because overseas conquests would weaken it." (And arguably, Ireland weakened England.) Montesquieu admitted that English motives were those of "jealousy," the outcome of the mercantilist conviction that international commerce was a zero-sum game. On the whole, however, the baron de la Brède found more that was good than was bad in the conquest of Ireland. The English at least gave the Irish the semblance of the English model without giving them the independence actually to use it: "the great dependence in which the nation [Ireland] was held was such that the citizens there would be free and the state itself would be enslaved" (*Laws*, XIX, 27).

Returning to an earlier document, we find at the heart of "Reflections on Universal Monarchy" a brief to the Europeans against military empire. It may also constitute a plea for the establishment of the one empire to which Montesquieu could give nearly full-throated approval. Its territorial reach would be roughly coextensive with the conquests of Charlemagne. This is an empire that Montesquieu does not label "empire" but rather "federation" – as he does in the case of England's overseas colonies – a federation that creates "one nation" based solely on trade. The lands that this trading empire might encompass are almost, if not quite, captured in the European Union of (at this writing) twenty-seven federated states. Section Eighteen of "Universal Monarchy" reads in its entirety:

> Europe is no longer but one nation composed of several; France and England having need of the riches of Poland and Moscow just as one of their provinces has need of the others: the state which believes it can enhance its own power by the ruin of one that borders it ordinarily weakens itself along with its neighbor. (p. 34)

Almost as good as this atypical (because apparently noncoercive) model of continental empire were the "empires of the sea," a classification that Montesquieu used to distinguish ancient land empires like those of Rome and Persia from sea empires like those of Carthage ("Carthage was principally attentive to preserving the empire of the sea" [*Laws*, XXI, 11]) and Athens. England and its North American colonies constituted the preeminent modern example of an empire of the sea, although it bears reiteration that the author resisted using the term "empire" to describe these "federations" of global trade.

Land, the author says in another context, belongs to the inhabitants of each nation. He has quite the opposite idea about "movable effects," that is to say, commodities:

Movable effects [commodities] ... belong to the whole world, which in this regard *comprises but a single state* of which *all societies are members*. (*Laws*, XX, 23, emphasis added)

This notion of a single global state is evidently similar to the European Union-like arrangement cited previously. But this formulation, in going further, also brings us back to the themes with which we began. By way of the mediation of global commerce, Montesquieu presents his readers with an idea of an empire capable of exhibiting the unity and universality of human nature in all its manifold and particular diversity.

However, just as Montesquieu's *doux commerce* was not in its origins so soft, one should not suspect that the author was naive in paying this early tribute to globalization. There was always an element of coercion. For instance, there were excellent reasons why a country might legitimately avoid trade and its global empire. Political elites in one or another nation could establish monopolies that would not only distort trade relationships but also impoverish the rest of the nation (*Laws*, XX, 19–22). Poland should have avoided international trade altogether, since the Polish nobility pursued external trade in such a rapacious manner that the peasants were left in poverty. To take an opposite example, Tokugawa Japan was mostly cut off from global trade but did not apparently suffer from its isolation, for the commerce that it carefully controlled was, Montesquieu thought, in the process of making it rich (*Laws*, XX, 6 and 23). These qualifications to the argument for commerce were to have a brilliant future as the intellectual bases for the rejection of this last great Enlightenment project, the empire of trade and industry.

Through its federated structure, global commerce was an empire whose institutional framework might avoid, on Montesquieu's understanding, the political despotism into which other empires had fallen. Federated sovereignties established competition between the sovereigns that decreased the dependence of commercial agents on any one state. If in addition, as in England or any other well-regulated monarchy, representative institutions and a separation of powers enhanced the competition between the factions that sought to control the state, the liberties of citizens or subjects were also accordingly preserved. Montesquieu, in a famous passage, extolled the English people because they had been best able to sort out the roles of "three great things: religion, commerce, and liberty" (*Laws*, XX, 7). He praised them because they had not permitted religion to interfere with English civil liberties; unlike the Poles (who provided a cautionary tale), they had not allowed commercial elites to undermine political freedoms; and they had not permitted political elites to dominate trade.

TWO CONCLUSIONS REGARDING EMPIRES OF TRADE

These happy prospects outlined previously more than justify the complacent conclusion at which Montesquieu arrives near the end of his second book on commerce:

> Europe makes the commerce and navigation of the other three parts of the world, just as France, England, and Holland make nearly all the navigation and commerce of Europe. (*Laws*, XXI, 21, p. 393, my translation)

However, Montesquieu's view of global arrangements was not always so cheerful. This bland account of global order was an evidently highly laundered version of a much grimmer and more foreboding remark on global trade borrowed from his unpublished *Pensées*:

> *Europe*, which makes the commerce of the three other parts of the world, *is the tyrant of these three parts*. *France, England, and Holland*, which have made the commerce of Europe, *are the three tyrants of Europe and of the world*. (p. 568, emphasis added)[40]

A writer is entitled to change his mind, but this is a pretty dramatic switch. From an accusatory view of the domination inherent in global commerce that points to the radical power inequalities among nations, Montesquieu reverses course and, while utilizing the same sentence in an act of self-plagiarization, leaves the reader with a benign view of globally harmonious, mutually beneficial cooperation. (The *Pensée* at least adds, prophetically, "but this will not last.")

The shadow of the coercive Alexandrian warrior stands nearly unnoticed in the two books on commerce in the *Spirit of the Laws*, but this figure, we have shown, is a necessary element in Montesquieu's account of the rise of federations, that is to say, the rise of the trading empires that underlie *doux commerce*. In his account of the global network that constitutes a single state, the Alexandrian shadow is excised altogether.

---

[40] Montesquieu, *Penseés, Le Spicilège*, ed. Louis Desgraves (Paris: Robert Laffont, 1991), *Pensée* 568, p. 320.

Nevertheless, even in the published argument, the author shows that he is aware of the role of domination in international commerce. Modern European colonization exhibits a degree of dependency never seen in antiquity. Unlike the ancient world, these colonies "belong to" a state or a private company. Montesquieu identifies it as a "fundamental law" of the Europeans that "any commerce with a foreign colony is regarded as a pure monopoly." Such a policy can only be maintained by force of arms and would appear to diminish the advantages of the relatively peaceable colonization that Montesquieu elsewhere holds up as the European republican model. Moreover, the Europeans assert rights over the sea lanes of their colonies: "when foreign commerce is prohibited with the colony, one can navigate its seas only when this is established by treaty" (*Laws*, XXI, 21, pp. 391–392). All of this illustrates the coercive arm of *doux commerce*. As Montesquieu acknowledges, England "would need an army on the sea" (*Laws*, XIX, 27, p. 329).

The author may hide from the reader the shadow of Alexandrian conquest that the extension of global commerce presupposes, but his writing is revealing enough in its own way. Arrogance and overreaching accompany empire even in its maritime form. The English and others who control empires of the sea are ever ready to "insult" other peoples: "The empire of the sea has always given to the people who possess it a natural pride because, feeling capable of insulting [everyone] everywhere, they believe that their power has no limit other than the ocean" (*Laws*, XIX, p. 27).

It may be that empires of the sea should be praised at the end of the day for (eventually) exporting their systems of representative rule to their colonies, especially when these systems of rule embodied liberties only weakly represented in the precolonial societies. Nevertheless, mindful of the "insults" of the British in the short term, that is to say, given the history of British colonial domination, neither the eighteenth-century American revolutionaries nor the twentieth-century Indian nationalists in revolt against England were likely to have taken Montesquieu's detached view of the benefits of seaborne colonization in the *longue durée* – although, as we have seen, Nehru came close to doing so.

6

Edmund Burke on Empire, Self-Understanding, and Sympathy

Uday S. Mehta

When viewed from Britain in the eighteenth century, the empire was still a distant matter, notwithstanding the numerous ways in which it already laced domestic life. Edmund Burke (1729–1797) reflected on that distance and the myriad attending issues with a moral seriousness unmatched in his times and perhaps since. A salient and persistent feature of those reflections was that he never took a one-sided view on that distance. His palpable and genuinely deep concern for those he had never laid eyes on in the far extremities of the globe was always tethered to his concern for what the empire did to Britain itself and what Britain owed to itself – "in order to prove that the Americans have no right to their liberties, we are every day endeavoring to subvert the maxims which preserve the whole spirit of our own."[1] The fact is that the most searching and profound reflection on empire in modern times stemmed from a moral and political stance that was at once a remarkable extension of sympathy into the unfamiliar and a sustained expression of attentiveness to the conditions of self-knowledge. Unlike the nineteenth- and twentieth-century revolutionary tradition in which the question "What is to be done?" had an abstract ideological referent, substantially unhinged from the constraints of selfhood, for Burke, individuals and nations were obligated to wrestle simultaneously with that question and the question "Who are we, and given that fact, what is becoming of us?" This mode of moral and political knowledge regarding the empire was constitutionally constrained by the precepts of self-understanding and the demands of a kind of national

---

[1] Burke, "Speech on Conciliation with America," in *Writings and Speeches of Edmund Burke*, 12 vols (New York: J.F. Taylor and Co., 1901), vol. 2, pp. 130–136.

integrity. Perhaps surprisingly, it was precisely such a constrained or narrow view, coupled, of course, with remarkable insight and prescience, that produced a profound and truly moral understanding of the empire and that absolved Burke from relying on the familiar nostrums such as progress, the necessity of expanding trade, and the quest for national glory. Moreover, it steered him clear of exonerating the moral and political license that allegedly flowed from the vexations of exercising power at a distance and in circumstances of great cultural complexity. As with his other writings, the depth and reach of Burke's insight into the turgid functioning of the empire had everything to do with the deployment of a moral imagination, which alloyed self-understanding and sympathy.[2]

Burke not only reflected on the complexity of the empire, he also expressed a sustained and deep reluctance toward it, whether in India, Ireland, or America.[3] Here again he was, for the most part, an exception among his contemporaries and those who followed him into the twentieth century. He did not demand, as did none of his major contemporaries and few in the century that followed, that the British dismantle the empire altogether. Nevertheless, no thinker or statesman of the eighteenth or nineteenth century expresses anything like the moral indignation that Burke voiced against the injustices, cruelty, and greed, along with the psychological and political pretentiousness of the empire. Similarly, no thinker recognized with the clarity that Burke did that the empire had already become an alibi for a narrow and self-evasive assertion of power, one that was substantially at odds with the extant and emerging basis of legitimate power and whose only warrant was as a humble, and thus moral, engagement with strangers and friends.

Burke wrote on all the major sites of the British Empire – Ireland, America, and India.[4] Implicit in these reflections was the awareness that

---

[2] I borrow the term "moral imagination" from David Bromwich, who in his many writings on Burke has consistently emphasized its unifying significance to Burke's thinking. In his recent essay "Moral Imagination," Bromwich in fact points to a connection between Burke's understanding of the term and how it functions in the thought of that other great moral critic of the empire, M. K. Gandhi. See David Bromwich, "Moral Imagination," *Raritan Review*, 27 (Spring 2008), 4–33.

[3] The claim that Burke was in fact a critic of the empire has been challenged by an examination of his writings on the West Indies. This is an important qualification, but it does not shift the main thrust of his thinking, which remains deeply skeptical of imperial practices in the eighteenth century. See Margaret Kohn and Daniel I. O'Neill, "A Tale of Two Indias: Burke and Mill on Empire and Slavery in the West Indies and America," *Political Theory*, 34, no. 2 (April 2006), 192–228.

[4] Several recent works have focused on the ways in which the idea of empire travels and acquires theoretical clarity in the eighteenth and nineteenth centuries. See Jennifer Pitts, *A

following the Seven Years War (1756–1763), the British Empire was neither predominantly Protestant nor Anglophone. It now included French Catholics in Quebec and millions of Asians who were neither Christian nor white. Burke was alone in asking how traditional British liberties could be reconciled with "that vast, heterogeneous, intricate Mass of Interests, which at this day forms the Body of the British Power."[5] He was largely alone in his time in anticipating what a century later J. R. Seeley believed his contemporaries were still hesitant to admit, namely, that by the eighteenth century, "the history of England [was] not in England but in America and Asia."[6] The left-wing critic Harold Laski rightly commented that "[on] Ireland, America, and India, he [Burke] was at every point upon the side of the future" and that "he was the first English statesman to fully understand the moral import of the problem of subject races."[7] He opposed the injustice of the system of Protestant control in Ireland, and recognized without regret the fated nature of American independence and the legal pedantry on which George III's hollow power relied. He saw through the dubious convenience of ideas such as civilizational hierarchies, racial superiority, and the assumptions of cultural impoverishment by which British power justified its territorial expansionism and commercial avarice in India and elsewhere. The British Empire and its principal early instrument, the East India Company, certainly had their critics. But

Turn to Empire: The Rise of Imperial Liberalism in Britain and France (Princeton, N.J.: Princeton University Press, 2005). Also see Sankar Muthu, *Enlightenment against Empire* (Princeton, N.J.: Princeton University Press, 2003); David Armitage, *The Ideological Origins of the British Empire* (Cambridge: Cambridge University Press, 2000); Seamus Deane, *Foreign Affections: Essays on Edmund Burke* (Cork, Ireland: Cork University Press, 2005). Also see the thoughtful and richly detailed accounts by Richard Bourke, "Liberty, Authority and Trust in Burke's Idea of Empire," *Journal of the History of Ideas*, 61, no. 3 (Summer 2000), 453–471; and "Edmund Burke and the Politics of Conquest," *Modern Intellectual History*, 4, no. 3 (2007), 403–432.

5 Burke, Sheffield Archives, Wentworth Woodhouse Muniments 9/23, quoted in David Bromwich, "The Context of Burke's *Reflections*," *Social Research*, 58, no. 2 (1991), 313–354, at 328. On changes occurring in the British Empire in the late eighteenth century, see Linda Colley, *Britons: Forging the Nation 1707–1837* (New Haven, Conn.: Yale University Press, 1992), pp. 101–193; P. J. Marshall, *"A Free Though Conquering People": Eighteenth-Century and Its Empire* (Aldershot, U.K.: Ashgate, 2003); and Jack P. Greene, *Peripheries and Center: Constitutional Development in the Extended Polities of the British Empire and the United States (1607–1788)* (Athens: University of Georgia Press, 1986).

6 J. R. Seeley, *The Expansion of England* (Chicago: University of Chicago Press, 1971), p. 13 (originally published 1883). Seeley was the most influential and most widely read historian of the British Empire.

7 Harold Laski, *Political Thought in England from Locke to Bentham* (Oxford: Oxford University Press, 1950), pp. 149, 153.

no such critic would have, as Burke did, press that criticism by calling
into question the very possibility of "drawing up an indictment against
a whole people."[8] Constructing such indictments of entire peoples and
continents was a minor cottage industry among eighteenth- and nineteenth-century European intellectuals. And certainly few had the moral
courage to express, as Burke did to his constituents in Bristol, solidarity
with people who he admitted were strangers, but who nevertheless exercised a moral hold on his imagination and sympathies: "I confess to you
freely, that the sufferings and distresses of the people of America in this
cruel war, have at times affected me more deeply than I can express....
Yet the Americans are utter strangers to me."[9] Similarly, no statesman or
thinker of his times expressed the pained embarrassment, the capacious
compassion, and the sustained moral revulsion for the cruelty, torture,
deprivation, and injustice that the East India Company was perpetrating.
Burke is virtually alone in owning up to this as an indictment of Britain's
moral and political rectitude.

It is, of course, true that Burke did not oppose the empire in the sense
of calling for its immediate dismantling. He had too deep a deference to
established practices to countenance their easy or cavalier removal. Much
of what he says about the British rule in the empire is squarely within the
framework of a plea for good government; none of it is a plea for self-
government. But to conclude from this that Burke was merely an enlightened imperialist, an apologist laboring to secure the empire on surer and
more sustainable foundations, would be to thoroughly miss the tenor of
his thought and the challenge that he presented to the empire and to ways
of thinking and acting that supported it.[10] The point is not whether Burke
was or was not an imperialist in a simple declarative sense. In the eighteenth century that question had not surfaced to self-consciousness and
had scarcely any of the associations that it acquired following the nationalist struggles and the decolonization of European empires in the twentieth century. After all, even in the case of American independence, which
most closely resembles twentieth-century nationalism, the announced

---

[8] Burke, "Speech on Conciliation with America," *Writings and Speeches,* vol. 2, p. 136.
[9] Burke, "Speech at the Guildhall in Bristol, Previous to Election," *The Works of Edmund Burke,* ed. James Prior, 2 vols. (London: George Bell and Sons, 1886), vol. 2, p. 153.
[10] Nicholas Dirks, *The Scandal of Empire* (Cambridge, Mass.: Belknap Press, 2006), see in particular chapter 5, "Sovereignty," pp. 167–207. Also see David Bromwich, "Introduction," in *Edmund Burke: On Empire, Liberty, and Reform,* ed. David Bromwich (New Haven, Conn.: Yale University Press, 2000), pp. 1–39.

anti-imperialism is muted, as is evident from the almost deferential tone of the Declaration of Independence.

Regarding the empire, the relevant questions in the eighteenth and nineteenth centuries were, what was the nature of the relationships that it was predicated on, and that it fostered, and how were these understood at both ends of the imperial connection? Did the empire rely on and entrench a worldview in which hypostasized conceptions of national and cultural destinies got braided with the exercise and purported legitimacy of imperial power? Was that power underwritten by a "progressive" view of history in which places like India, and more generally the East, got coded as ossified and confined by their "traditions" and therefore understood as "backward" or stunted in a presumed civilizational teleology? Did this conception of historical development underappreciate the coherence of extant lived social forms, and only thus make them appear unstable and provisional stages in the realization of a cosmopolitan moral and political ideal? Did the category "traditional," or "native" as Hastings and others deployed it, serve to blanket these distant parts of the world in a way that local life forms and institutions were bleached of their coherence, flexibility, and contingency – in brief, of their possible vitality? Did the advocates of the empire hold to an overly narrow conception of political order, which implicitly sanctions imperial interventions by obscuring or distorting alternative ways of being and living collectively? And finally, what were the moral stakes of linkages, which, on the typical view, could only be sustained through power and notions of superiority? Burke was attentive to these questions throughout much of his career, both as an integral part of his political philosophy and because the empire was a special worry whose troubling implications he foresaw and that make his insights of enormous contemporary significance.

THE BACKGROUND OF INVOLVEMENT

Burke's involvement with British–Indian affairs began in 1767, the year he first entered Parliament, and concluded in his public role in 1795, two years before his death. He was the principal and in many instances the sole author of several parliamentary reports on India. The breadth and depth of his knowledge of India were legendary and are plainly evident in his writings. He was also the author of numerous parliamentary bills regarding Indian affairs, including the famous Fox India Bill. Neither the French Revolution, his native Ireland, America, nor parliamentary reform – all causes about which he felt passionately – invoked the febrile intensity and gravity of purpose that India did for Burke.[11] Burke often simultaneously brought to mind the threat posed by the French Revolution and that of the British in India, and at these moments it is always the latter that provoked greater concern for its actual and potential effects. In 1796, Burke wrote to Lord Loughborough: "Our Government and our Laws are beset by two different enemies, which are sapping its foundation, Indianism, and Jacobinism. In some cases they act separately, in some they act in conjunction: But of this I am sure; that the first is the worst by far."[12] Again in 1796 and toward the end of his life, when the deservedness of a state pension that Burke had been granted was being challenged by the Duke of Bedford, he emphasized and prioritized a lifetime spent in dealing with public issues:

> In truth, the services I am called on to account for are not those on which I value myself the most. If I were to call for a reward, (which I have never done,) it should be for those in which for fourteen years without intermission I showed the most industry and had the least success: I mean in the affairs of India. They are those on which I value myself the most; most for the importance; most for labour; most for the judgment; most for constancy and perseverance in the pursuit. Others may value them most for the intention. In that, surely, they are not mistaken.[13]

What makes this statement remarkable is that it dates from a time when, in the popular imagination, many of his prophecies regarding the turns that the French Revolution would take had been vindicated, and when his reputation was most celebrated and associated with that event. Ten years earlier, while he was in the midst of the Hastings trial and as his unremitting intense focus on Indian matters began to be the subject of public caricature and party concern, he wrote to Mary Palmer: "I have no party in this Business ... but among a set of people, who have none of your Lilies and Roses in their faces; but who are the images of the great Pattern as well as you and I. I know what I am doing; whether the white people like it or not."[14] The contemporary familiarity of such an exposing remark as "whether the white people like it or not" muffles the incredible and complex sensibility from which alone, in the eighteenth century, it

[11] See the excellent study by Frederick Whelan, *Edmund Burke and India: Political Morality and Empire* (Pittsburgh: University of Pittsburgh Press, 1996).

[12] *The Correspondence of Edmund Burke*, ed. Thomas Copeland, 10 vols. (Chicago: University of Chicago Press, 1958–1978), vol. 8, p. 432.

[13] Burke, "Letter to a Noble Lord," *Writings and Speeches*, vol. 5, p. 192.

[14] Ibid., p. 254.

could stem and the thunderous effect it must have had on Mary Palmer at least.

There was, indeed, something excessive in the tenacity that Burke brought to bear on Indian issues. His opening speech to the House of Lords imploring them to impeach Hastings went on for seven days; his closing arguments went on for nine. A plausible case can be made that the reason the greatest British parliamentarian of the eighteenth century was offered a position only in the Privy Council and never in the cabinet, and that too as paymaster general, was his apparently inexplicable obsession with the link between his people and those who had neither lilies nor roses in their faces.[15] And yet, despite the price he had paid for this obsession, Burke was unrelenting. A few months before his death, he wrote to his young friend and literary executor, French Laurence:

Let not this cruel, daring, unexampled act of publick corruption, guilt, and meanness go down – to a posterity, perhaps as careless as the present race, without its due animadversion, which will be best found in its own acts and monuments. Let my endeavors to save the Nation from that Shame and Guilt, be my monument; The only one I ever will have. Let every thing I have done, said, or written be forgotten but this. I have struggled with the great and the little on this point during the greater part of my active Life; and I wish after my death, to have my Defiance of the Judgments of those, who consider the dominion of the glorious Empire given by an incomprehensible dispensation of the Divine providence into our hands as nothing more than an opportunity of gratifying for the lowest of their purposes, the lowest of their passions – and that for such poor rewards, and for the most part, indirect and silly Bribes, as indicate even more the folly than the corruption of these infamous and contemptible wretches.... Above all make out the cruelty of this pretended acquittal, but in reality this barbarous and inhuman condemnation of whole Tribes and nations, and of all the abuses they contain. If ever Europe recovers its civilization that work will be useful. Remember! Remember! Remember![16]

Such intense commitment to a largely lost cause in which one might say (as the House of Lords did) that even if every charge Burke was urging

---

[15] Conor Cruise O'Brien, in his monumental thematic biography of Burke, supplies the evidence for such a case, even though the thrust of his interpretation and his explanation of Burke's concern with India involve Burke associating India with his native Ireland. See Conor Cruise O'Brien, *The Great Melody: A Thematic Biography and Commented Anthology of Edmund Burke* (Chicago: University of Chicago Press, 1992), pp. 257–384, 579–592. Also see James Prior, *Life of the Right Honourable Edmund Burke* (London: H. G. Bohn, 1854), pp. 243–275; Fredrick Whelan, "Burke, India, and Orientalism," in *Edmund Burke: Fresh Perspectives*, ed. Ian Crowe (Columbia: University of Missouri Press, 2004).

[16] Burke, "Correspondence," *Writings and Speeches*, vol. 9, pp. 62–63. This letter is representative of Burke's intensified preoccupation with Indian matters in his last years.

was true, and acknowledged as such, one would have little more than one corrupt governor-general, who had embezzled from the most profitable company in the world, allowed some prisoners of war to be tortured, countenanced the humiliation of an Indian begum, and perhaps directed the murder of one local official; in brief, he had abused his high office. The gravity of the matter is not, at least obviously, commensurate with the efforts and consequences of the previous decade and a half. But Burke was too self-conscious a writer and a thinker for one not to take him at his word. In any case, the concern with India spans his entire career, and is intertwined and conceptually consistent with most of his other works.

What is clear is that his writings on India are a sophisticated and moving elaboration on the idea of sympathy – the means through which one develops in oneself a feeling for another person or collectivity of persons. Burke's writings on the empire are a poignant example of what Hume distinguishes as the "understanding" in its function as perceiving the relations between things and "moral sentiments" as the register of the feelings associated with the perception of such relations.[17] Burke's efforts can be seen as an extended tutorial to his compatriots to help them perceive certain relations both between things within India and between things in India and Britain, so that the moral sentiments appropriate to such relations would be awakened in them.[18] There is scarcely a page in the thousands that Burke wrote and uttered during the Hastings trial, in the speech on the debts of the nabob of Arcot, in the Fox India Bill speech, or in his numerous other writings on India, Ireland, and America in which a simple but piercing concern with brutality, exploitation, the humiliation of women, the avarice of the East India Company and its parliamentary patrons, the corresponding effect of destitution, and the arbitrary use of unjust power is not an illuminated feature of the background that he is aware of and the implications of which he is at pains to convey to his audience. Consider the following statement uttered in the House of Commons, where the very people to whom it referred surrounded Burke:

This was the golden cup of abominations; this the chalice of the fornications of rapine, usury, and oppression, which was held out by the gorgeous eastern harlot;

---

[17] David Hume, *A Treatise on Human Nature*, ed. L. A. Selby-Bigge (Oxford: Clarendon Press, 1975), Book III, secs. 1–2, pp. 455–480. Also see Sheldon Wolin, "Hume and Conservatism," *American Political Science Review*, 48 (1954), 999–1016.
[18] See Bromwich, "Moral Imagination," for a subtle analysis of the relationship between sympathy and the imagination.

which so many people, so many of the nobles of this land, had drained to the very dregs. Do you think that no reckoning was to follow this lewd debauch? that no payment was to be demanded for this riot of public drunkenness and national prostitution? Here! you have it here before you.[19]

The metaphor and imagery of the empire as a debased and coerced orgy is frequent in his writings, as are the sentiments with which Burke concluded this speech:

Whoever therefore shall at any time bring before you [i.e., the Commons] any thing towards the relief of our distressed follow-citizens in India, and towards a subversion of the present most corrupt and oppressive system for its government, in me shall find ... a steady, earnest, and faithful assistant.[20]

Burke's sympathy and ire, and ultimately his political ideas, are anchored in thinking through, feeling, and transmitting with tactile intensity specific episodes, replete with proper nouns, imagined habitation of real but distant places, and an engagement with vital traditions of those who were often complete strangers. It is what gives to his work a texture of great descriptive richness and, equally, a quality of profound imaginative extension that links his concern with Britain and India in a simultaneous moral sweep. This is what Raymond Williams meant in commenting that it is his "style of thinking" that is essential to understanding Burke's views on the empire.[21]

Burke was deeply moved by various aspects of Indian social order and civilization, but his concern centered on India as a site of British political adventure and expansionism. The crucial question in all of his writing on India is, what was the ground for Burke's concern for India and, because it is closely related, what were the grounds for his deep reservations about British imperial practices in India? Burke's views on this question are closely linked to his broader thoughts on political identity, the basis of legitimacy, and the practices through which both can be undermined.

In his writings on India, as in his work on the French Revolution, Burke was primarily concerned with communities that were threatened. The greed and financial corruption of the empire, the capricious brutality with which Governor-General Hastings and his associates abused their office and power, the arbitrary and feigned concern that Parliament occasionally showed towards these and other abuses – in all these and numerous other instances, Burke's ire and sympathy were provoked in

[19] Burke, "Nabob of Arcot's Debts," *Writings and Speeches*, vol. 5, p. 543.
[20] Ibid., p. 552.
[21] Raymond Williams, *Culture and Society* (London: Chatto & Windus, 1958).

large part by concern for a threatened community. Even when his attention was fastened on individuals, as in his famous description of Marie
Antoinette fleeing from her bedchamber or as in numerous descriptions
of Indian men and women, the pathos he invoked was through the relations and circumstances that coalesced in these individuals as members of
a besieged community. The same was true of those who were the objects
of his scorn and condemnation. Warren Hastings, Paul Benfield, the Duke
of Bedford, and the Jacobins were judged mainly as members and instruments of one community involved in unsettling the integrity and coherence of another.

Because Burke's primary sympathy was directed toward communities,
it is important to consider how Burke identified communities or, more
generally, what he saw social order as residing in. In the imperial context,
this concern had two distinct components. The first relates to the factors
that inclined Burke to the conclusion that India (and America) did constitute a political community, and the second relates to the practices in light
of which it was threatened by imperial practices.

Burke consistently drew attention to certain long-standing and prevailing locational attachments and historical associations by virtue of
which India constituted a political community and Indians had a sense
of themselves as individuals and as members of such communities. One
of the striking features of Burke's views, in part because it contrasts so
starkly with the classical liberal tradition, is the political and psychological significance he attaches to places. In the familiar formulations,
individuals "belong to," "come from," and live "in" places. For Burke,
these forms of speech captured a fundamental aspect of individual and
collective identity. They suggest that we both possess places and are possessed by them. For Locke and the classical liberal tradition only the
former was the case – a relationship that was captured in the view of
property as the mere extension of individual will via the value infusing
capabilities of labor working on a "worthless Nature." In contrast, for
Burke, places partially constituted who we are, and in doing so, they
were, at a minimum, normatively relevant to the institutions and social
arrangements that we envision. We do not simply live in places; rather,
we inhabit them in the sense that they supply, from the very outset,
the conditions for the experiences that become habitual to us. Burke's
valorization of the habitual was not merely an obeisance to practices
that derived from preestablished traditions and that, hence, facilitated
the reproduction of the past. Rather, the emphasis on habits, and by
implication on locational attachments as an important ingredient of the

habitual, represented Burke's commitment to the idea that political and moral theories were only as credible as the psychological account that undergirded them. The normative force of history and location stems from their psychological centrality to identity formation. And for this reason, they supply at least some of the desiderata on which political institutions and social practices must rely.

The contrast between the significance that classical liberals like Locke attached to place and Burke's view is indicative of a broader difference, one that is important in their differing assessments of the empire. By viewing place and history as constitutive of human identity, Burke took identity as something partially, though importantly, given, and hence not wholly an artifice constituted of individual choice. Moreover, that which was given was also shared, to the extent that places and history engender common sentiments and because individuals understood them as such. This sharing had an irredeemably historical aspect to it in that it preceded individual will formation by being a ground for it. In fact, for Burke, history and place have much the same psychological valence.

One implication that Burke drew from these claims was that the existence of political society did not turn exclusively on individual capacities such as having reason, will, or being able to choose, but also on the presence of a certain shared order on the ground. In the imperial context, this was of crucial significance. Admittedly, the idea of a shared order is somewhat vague and in all likelihood does not, by itself, give us determinate conceptions of institutional arrangements, or how power is to be exercised and a host of other important issues. Nevertheless, for Burke, this order was crucial to establishing or settling at least one important question: did a group of people form a political community, that is, did they have the requisite sense of sharing something in common, beyond the merely contingent sharing that overlapping individual interests or preferences may produce? With respect to India and America, Burke's answer to this question was emphatically affirmative. This is where Burke unmistakably parted company with classical liberals like Locke, the Mills, and Macaulay. The latter tradition was virtually unified in its view regarding the absence of political community in India and, more generally, in the colonies. This absence, and the redress that the empire purportedly supplied for it, was the mainstay of the liberal justification of the empire: India was in a condition of tutelage. Like Lockean children, it was born to freedom but not yet capable of exercising it. The empire was a promissory note of future release conditional on following a specific trajectory of development.

The critical mirror that Burke holds up to these views, especially in the imperial context, though elsewhere too, was both psychological and political. In terms of the former, he claimed that inheritances are in some crucial measure involuntary and that they bind us (which, of course, is different than being confined) in the present through the inescapable mediation of location and the past. Psychologically, we are always *in medias res*. In terms of the latter, Burke's point was that the existence of political society and the form of institutional arrangements must be conditional on it because of the force of the former point. By reference to these two claims, he sees political society and order in India, and not just the prospect of it through the tutored development of individual capacities.

The other issue on which Burke focused his attention involved the British practices through which the social and political coherence of India was being dismembered. As with his concern with the ways in which the Jacobins were destroying France by recombining it at will, he was always vigilant regarding the ways in which imperial dislocations affected India and Britain. For Burke, these questions ultimately related to how individuals and communities came to have a confident sense of themselves and thus secured the conditions for their freedom, and how, in the clutches of certain ways of thinking and behaving, they risked dispossessing themselves of this sense. Burke's communitarianism picks out the very concerns that have been salient to identifying nations and subsequent nationalist claims. His sympathy for India stemmed from his deploying concepts through which India's potential nationhood was evident to him centuries before it was known to most Indians. Given this fact, or rather what Burke prefigures would be a fact, he was anticipating what Ben Anderson has called the "inner incompatibility between empire and nation."[22] For Burke, this incompatibility was necessarily mutually debilitating to India's nationhood and to Britain's pretended imperial nationhood.

BRAIDED CONCERNS: BRITAIN AND INDIA

Burke's writings on India were marked by a constant duality of purpose: a concern, on the one hand, for the effects that imperial practices would have on Britain and, on the other, for the effects they would have on India. The two concerns are alloyed. The oppression of India rebounds with similar effects on Britain; the British delinquents of India will become the

---

[22] Benedict Anderson, *Imagined Communities: Reflections on the Origins and Spread of Nationalism* (London: Verso, 1983), p. 39.

Commons of Great Britain. In terms that resonate with the utterances of later nationalists, Burke constantly drives home the point that the empire is doubly implicated. At the beginning of his speech urging his fellow parliamentarians to pass the Fox India Bill, he says: "I am certain that every means, effectual to preserve India from oppression, is a guard to preserve the British constitution from its worst corruption."[23] At the end of the speech, he reiterates the coupled nature of his concern: "I am happy to have lived to see this day; I feel myself overpaid for the labors of eighteen years, when, at this period, I am able to take my share, by one humble vote, in destroying a tyranny that exists to the disgrace of this nation, and the destruction of so large a part of the human species."[24] Elsewhere, he speaks of the abuse of power exercised over Indians as leading to the "annihilation" of British liberties.[25]

Burke's reasons for believing in this mutuality of imperial consequences are more specific than a generalized view such as that oppression does not pay or that the weak have weapons that the strong would do well to acknowledge in the exercise of their power. No doubt Burke held such views, especially in a form that suggested some Christian notion of justice. Burke's more precise and urgent reason for being worried about this mutuality – and this is the heart of the matter – is that the conditions that secure British liberties are threatened by the extension of British power in India. Similarly, the exercise of that power undermines the conditions that are requisite for the expression of Indian liberties. The various specific objections to British behavior in India that Burke details – the peculation of East India Company officials, the political greed involved in making allies and enemies among Indian princes for the purpose of extending British dominion, the cavalier instrumentality that underlies respecting or overriding local traditions, and similar attitudes toward the hierarchies of Indian social structure – all provoke the same general concern. They are instances in which the secure and stable conditions that secure the liberties of two societies are threatened.

This braided concern is vivid in the collective biography that Burke sketches of British functionaries in India and the trajectory of their effects on British and Indian society. They are, we are told, "young men (almost boys)" who govern "without society, and without sympathy with the natives." This for Burke is more telling: "they have no more social habits

---

[23] Burke, "Speech on Fox's India Bill," *Writings and Speeches*, vol. 5, p. 385.
[24] Ibid., p. 451.
[25] Ibid., p. 468

with the people than if they resided in England."[26] They are commercial and political mercenaries, unmarked by the burdens and privileges of any society, but nevertheless called upon to exercise power over the natives. In a brilliant and horrifying image, Burke describes them as "birds of prey" that swoop down, "wave after wave ... [with] nothing before the eyes of natives but an endless, hopeless prospect of new flights ... with appetites continually renewing for a food that is continually wasting."[27] They make their fortunes long before either "nature or reason have any opportunity to exert themselves for remedy of the excesses of their premature power."[28] Having preyed on India, they return to England for another feeding frenzy:

> Their prey is lodged in England; and the cries of India are given to sea and winds.... In India, all the vices operate by which sudden fortune is acquired; in England are often displayed, by the same persons, the virtues which dispense hereditary wealth. Arrived in England, the destroyers of the nobility and gentry of a whole kingdom will find the best company in this nation, at a board of elegance and hospitality. Here the manufacturer and the husbandman will bless the just and punctual hand, that in India has torn the cloth from the loom, or wrested the scanty portion of rice and salt from the peasants of Bengal.... They marry into your families; they enter into your senate; they ease your estates by loans; they raise their value by demand; they cherish and protect your relations which lie heavy on your patronage; and there is scarcely a house in the kingdom that does not feel some concern and interest that makes all your reform of our Eastern government appear officious and disgusting; and, on the whole, a most discouraging attempt.... Our Indian government is in its best state a grievance.[29]

The empire exercises its power through the creation of a class of individuals who are rootless and who afflict the societies they touch with a similar contagion. Lacking society themselves, they unsettle the norms of both British and Indian society. Burke may have been thinking in terms of rather concrete historical facts. As evinced by the life and career of Robert Clive, who is commonly thought of as the founder of the East India Company's dominion in India, the colonies, and especially India, had become a place where men and boys of humble and dislocated roots went not just to make a fortune but also to "acquire British society." Having destroyed the nobility and gentry in India, plucked the rice and salt from the Bengali peasant, they return to England with the monetary and social profits of that endeavor and insinuate their mercenary

---

[26] Ibid., p. 402.
[27] Ibid.
[28] Ibid.
[29] Ibid., p. 403.

logic into the historically sanctioned estates that anchor British society. They make money the medium of social and political circulation and order; they buy power and social standing, and in doing so subvert what, for Burke, are the traditional and historically appropriate foundations of each. In this sense, they are like the Jacobins. Unlike the latter's explicit commitment to start anew, the British functionaries in India insidiously, and hence more dangerously, uproot and level out the conditions that make Britain whole.[30] Burke is always attentive to a social dynamic internal to the Company, which has far-reaching domestic implications in Britain:

> Another circumstance which distinguishes the East India Company is the youth of the persons who are employed in the system of that service. The servants have almost universally been sent out to begin their career in active occupation and in the exercise of high authority, at that period of life which, in all other places, has been employed in the course of rigid education. To put the matter in a few words, – they are transformed from slippery youth to perilous independence, from perilous independence to inordinate expectations, from inordinate expectations to boundless power. Schoolboys without tutors, minors without guardians, the world is let loose upon them, with all its temptations, and they are let loose upon the world with all the power that despotism involves.[31]

The theme of the youthfulness of Company officials is significant even beyond the specific points Burke makes in regard to it. It offers a vivid contrast with the familiar characterization of liberal theorists who spoke of the childlike nature of Indians. J. S. Mill's image of Indians as still in need of "leading strings"[32] – the strings used to help children learn to walk – is a theme that Macaulay and others lifted and amplified as

---

[30] Speaking of the French revolutionaries, Burke constantly identifies them as "totally abolishing hereditary name and office [and] levelling all conditions of men (except where money *must make a difference*)." Burke, *Further Reflections on the Revolution in France*, ed. Daniel E. Ritchie (Indianapolis: Liberty Fund, 1992), "Thoughts on French Affairs," p. 211. The image of the British as birds of prey is precisely the one that Burke uses to portray the French revolutionaries: "The Revolution harpies of France, sprung from Night and Hell, or from the chaotic Anarchy which generates equivocally 'all monstrous, all prodigious things,' cuckoo-like, adulterously lay their eggs, and brood over, and hatch them in the nest of every neighboring state. These obscene harpies, who deck themselves in I know not what divine attributes, but who in reality are foul and ravenous birds of prey, (both mothers and daughters) flutter over our heads and souse down upon our tables, and leave nothing unrent, unrifled, unravaged, or unpolluted with the slime of their filthy offal." Burke, "Letter to a Noble Lord," *Writings and Speeches*, vol. 5, p. 187.

[31] Burke, "Impeachment of Warren Hastings," *Writings and Speeches*, vol. 9, p. 357.

[32] J. S. Mill, *Considerations on Representative Government*, in John Stuart Mill, *Three Essays* (Oxford: Oxford University Press, 1975), chap. 2, p. 175.

a general warrant for the necessity and justification of the empire. The theme also recapitulates a terror that Locke in *The Thoughts Concerning Education* spoke of in regard to children who did not obey, who had an overdeveloped sense of their own difference, and whose will therefore had to be bent by force. For Burke, in contrast, the terror associated with youth is the abuse of power that can easily become despotic because it has not been chastened by an understanding of the needs of society.

Burke's examples may appear to exhaust and limit the point he is making. But they also point to a more general claim (more general than his commitment to a particular social order), which involves the centrality that Burke places on social order as being a requisite for individual liberty. It is this idea that unifies and gives coherence to the wide range of disparate and often apparently contradictory positions that he defends. It is the well-ordered realities in the American colonies, the sobriety that limits their liberal Enlightenment, the "spirit of religion" that confines the "spirit of freedom," as Tocqueville had put it, that leads Burke to support the colonists in their "revolutionary" desire for independence. The same idea, this time combined with the absence of those well-ordered realities, motivates his refusal to countenance the revolutionary schemes in France. It is also what leads him to describe the landed nobility and "grand families" of Britain as the "great oaks" of society and that also underlies his proud condescension toward the Duke of Bedford when the latter, with inflamed enthusiasm for the French revolutionaries, overlooks the service of men like Burke for the legitimate exercise of his power.

Burke's conception of social order is difficult to elaborate because it is the point at which myriad effects converge to create that illusive and yet very tangible sense of individual and collective wholeness: a people's beliefs, which themselves are related to circumstances, the institutions that have molded their habits and expectations, the spaces both physical and social that have channeled their attachments, the obligations and responsibilities that have defined their sense of choices, the prejudices that give coherence to their experiences and anticipations. For Burke, these are the felt constituents of social order.

There are two clear senses in which this conception, however imprecise its boundaries may appear, challenges the familiar Lockean sense of social order. First, at both an individual and a collective level, Burke's conception features an experience and a corresponding identity that are profoundly and thoroughly in the middle of things. Their significance is defined by the texture of inescapable constraints, circumstances, and relations. Strip society and individuals of these, and for Burke there is an emptiness that can generate the revolutionary hubris of a wholesale transformation of society. It is the mosaic of circumstances and the prejudices that cling to them that give situations their distinctive hue. As Burke puts it in *Reflections*:

> I cannot stand forward, and give praise or blame to anything which relates to human actions, and human concerns, on a simple view of the object, as it stands stripped of every relation, in all the nakedness and solitude of metaphysical abstraction. Circumstances (which with some gentlemen pass for nothing) give in reality to every political principle its distinguishing color and discriminating effect. The circumstances are what render every civil and political scheme beneficial or noxious to mankind.[33]

There is nothing in Burke's view that corresponds to the giddy exhilaration of Lockean individuals being there at the beginning, covenanting to form "a people" and "a Commonwealth." There are no abstract principles and natural human interests that carry over from the state of nature and prescribe individual obligations, institutions, and the norms of justice in political society. For Burke, as for his contemporary Hume, obligations and the norms of justice spring from the local and the conventional. But this departure from Locke is so only because it makes explicit what is in fact implicit in Locke. Locke's rational individuals, acting in conformity with the laws of nature, in fact deploy a reason that is saturated with the content of conventional hierarchies and expectations. What Burke makes explicit and raises to the level of prudential political credo, Locke tucks into the pedagogy that a child must submit to before being acknowledged as reasonable.[34] Second, Burke's conception of social order is deeply psychological in that it asks the question, what makes individuals and collectivities whole? The force of this point is easily obscured by a term such as "traditionalist" that is often used to characterize the historical emphasis of his thought. This term misses what for Burke is of decisive importance in traditions, namely, that they constitute preconceived channels in which human actions are at home, even when those actions are directed to changing the contours of those channels. When people act in ways that presume to deny their own reliance on such channels, or when they encourage the wholesale dismantling of

---

[33] Burke, *Reflections on the French Revolution* (London: Everyman's Library, 1971), p. 6.

[34] For a reading of Locke that emphasizes the significance of conventions through a detailed focus on the content of education, see my *Anxiety of Freedom* (Ithaca, N.Y.: Cornell University Press, 1992), especially chaps. 3 and 4. See also Anne Stoler's insightful article, "Sexual Affronts and Racial Identities and the Cultural Politics of Exclusion in Southeast Asia," *Comparative Studies in Society and History*, 34, no. 3 (July 1992), 514–551.

those channels, they risk their own survival or, at a minimum, they risk becoming what David Bromwich calls "monstrous."[35] They distort the dimensions of social and individual equipoise by presuming to be secure in utterly unfamiliar circumstances. The naturalist perspective that sees human beings as satisfying desires all too easily overlooks the extent to which some of those desires are refracted borrowings – refracted, that is, through a constellation of familial and social dispositions. Even when those dispositions stem from errors, or what the Enlightenment called "prejudice," they structure our needs and hence the requirements of our health. In a letter written in 1789, Burke tells his correspondent:

> You have theories enough concerning the rights of men; it may not be amiss to add a small degree of attention to their nature and disposition. It is with man in the concrete; it is with common human life, and human actions, you are to be concerned.... Never wholly separate in your mind the merits of any political question from the men who are concerned in it.[36]

The counterbalancing of theories concerning the rights of men with Burke's alternative focus on human beings in the concrete underscores the significance he attaches to specific and jagged dispositions – dispositions that are lost in the abstractions that concern themselves only with the rights of men. It is also for this reason that Burke's work is replete with attention to human feelings, habits, sensibilities, and prejudices. It is because of this attention that Burke, who in one sense is an outstanding critic of Rousseau, in another sense illuminates an essential preoccupation of Rousseau's social thought.[37]

The psychological component in Burke's notion of social order is really continuous with the historical emphasis. Precisely because we are always in the middle of things, we rely on what precedes us, both chronologically and spatially. No doubt, as the Enlightenment insisted, history is the

---

[35] David Bromwich, *A Choice of Inheritance* (Cambridge, Mass.: Harvard University Press, 1989), p. 48. Alfred Cobban, in his classic work *Edmund Burke and the Revolt against the Eighteenth Century* (London: George Allen & Unwin, 1929), also points to a similar reading.

[36] Burke, "Letter to Charles-Jean-Francois Depont," *Further Reflections*, p. 13. Later in the same letter he says: "There is by the essential fundamental constitution of things, a radical infirmity in all human contrivance; and the weakness is often attached to the very perfection of our political mechanism, that some defect in it – something that stops short of its principles, something that controls, that mitigates, that moderates it – becomes a necessary corrective to the evils that the theoretic perfection would produce." Ibid., p. 15.

[37] Burke's most extensive remarks on Rousseau are in "A Letter to a Member of the National Assembly," *Further Reflections*.

record of our prejudices. But – and this is a distinctly Burkeian contribution to the Enlightenment – these prejudices also give us a sense of continuity and hence a sense of ourselves. They protect us from constantly having to question our practices, and they protect us in those instances where practices are by will, necessity, or accident transformed. All of this is true even when the prejudices and the practices have been impugned. Finally, it is the psychological disposition of his thinking that underlies Burke's violently antirevolutionary impulse and his gradualist preference. The process of adaptation is always gradual. Even when circumstances change, as he acknowledges they always do, individuals and institutions for Burke retain traces of an investment in the past. And only gradual change can accommodate the needs and instincts that correspond to those traces. Burke summarizes this dialectic of history and the psychological reliance it generates:

History consists, for the greater part, of the miseries brought upon the world by pride, ambition, avarice, revenge, lust, sedition, hypocrisy, ungoverned zeal, and all the train of disorderly appetites which shake the public with the same.... These vices are the causes of those storms. Religion, morals, laws, prerogatives, privileges, liberties, rights of men, are the pretexts. The pretexts are always found in some specious appearance of a real good. You would not secure men from tyranny and sedition by rooting out of the mind the principles to which these fraudulent pretexts apply? If you did, you would root out everything that is valuable in the human breast.[38]

What is striking here is that Burke justifies a reliance on history while pointing to the dark record of history. The causes of miseries are constituents of our nature, and for that reason, they cannot be selectively erased through the redemptive pretexts of laws, religion, or rights. Only history, and by that Burke clearly means social order in an extensive form, can ameliorate and guide the effects of our passions. The role of the reformer is to constantly decipher and shape the social conditions through which these passions can be contained and expressed.

There is an obvious objection that this line of thinking invites. It is an objection that is leveled at many thinkers who appear to magnify the role of history and, in the process, become apologists for it. Stated simply, the objection is that a reliance on history or a view of the normative force of history gives us no critical leverage from which to adjudicate between historically possible alternatives, and it approaches the existing social arrangements with a presumption in favor of their legitimacy.

---

[38] Burke, *Reflections*, pp. 137–138.

At an extreme, it justifies everything that is settled and concrete, and in doing so denies the very reasons for which we might appeal to a thinker's counsel. Burke does not engage or anticipate this line of objection, but clearly, for him, all social arrangements draw on features of the past. But they do not, for that reason, necessarily result in orderly arrangements that secure the psychological health of individuals and the comity of society. Nothing in Burke's conception of history denies the possibility of our individually and collectively misinterpreting or incorrectly deciphering the range of stable alternatives. We always retain that possibility; indeed, there are events such as those in France and India where the vast mass of a people are set on establishing the detrimental effects of that possibility. The Jacobins in France overlook the entrenchment of the past when they abolish property and expand the franchise. For Burke, the Terror is the price that was paid for that oversight. Similarly, the East India Company officials, in exercising political power in India, overlook the historical limitations and obligations attached to that power. The massive infusion of money for buying parliamentary seats is the price that the British pay for that oversight.

The link between history or society and the passions also informs Burke's view of freedom. In his views on freedom, Burke once again brings to the fore something that is deep and fundamental in Locke by challenging a familiar surface characterization of Locke.[39] Just as for Locke, for Burke the "desire for liberty," as he calls it, is a constituent of our nature. But for Burke, this desire is itself an inheritance. It is not, as Locke so often has been interpreted to mean, a pre-given datum of our biological status. Of course, with Locke too, the exercise of this freedom turns on the capacity for reason, which itself is related to our ability to understand the limits that natural law puts on our freedom. Burke accepts all of this but gives it a distinct meaning. The reason that informs Locke's conception of freedom is for Burke thoroughly social, including social understood as something ineradicably historical. As he puts it:

I certainly think that all men who desire [liberty] deserve it. It is not the reward of our merit, or the acquisition of our industry. It is our inheritance. It is the birthright of our species. We cannot forfeit our right to it, but by what forfeits our title to the privileges of our kind. I mean the abuse, or oblivion, of our rational faculties and a ferocious indocility which makes us prompt to wrong and violence, destroys our social nature, and transforms us into something little better than the description of wild beasts. To men so degraded, a state of strong constraint is a

---

[39] Burke always claimed to be a "follower of Locke."

sort of necessary substitute for freedom; since, bad as it is, it may deliver them in
some measure from the worst of all slavery – that is, the despotism of their own
blind and brutal passions.[40]

Every idea in this passage is vintage Locke. The emphasis on the link
between freedom and reason, the negative association between freedom
and the despotism of uncontrolled passions, and even the link between
freedom and moderation (in contrast to "ferocious indocility") – all of
these are borrowings from Locke. And yet, Burke's meaning is substantially different. Where Burke speaks of "inheritance" and "birthright," he
should be understood as implicitly, though emphatically, privileging those
terms over the words "human nature."[41] Both inheritance and birthright
carry with them important historical and social attachments. It is not
simply our birth as a biological event; our birthright is the middle term
linking the past and the future. It is something that can be lost, destroyed,
or even stolen, as in the biblical story of Jacob and Esau. Freedom inheres
in us because our birth links us to the conditions that make it possible. Domestic choices, economic opportunities, communal experiences,
and political responsibilities – these and other preexisting constraints
and possibilities are what constitute the conditions for freedom. Burke
elaborates his meaning to his French correspondent: "It is not solitary,
unconnected, individual, selfish liberty, as if every man was to regulate
the whole of his conduct by his will. The liberty I mean is social liberty....
This kind of liberty is, indeed, but another name for justice; ascertained
by wise laws and secured by well-constructed institutions."[42]

Burke is quite specific about the conditions requisite for freedom. At
least in the societies that he considers in detail (Britain, France, America,
Ireland, and India), these conditions always include a hierarchy of social
classes, with corresponding titles and norms of courtesy. His views on
history make it easy to see why he believed in natural aristocracies who
had a prescriptive claim on political authority. But focusing on the hierarchy of classes leads us to miss Burke's more general underlying thought.
The source of our attachments, including the attachments we have to the
obligations we feel, are, at least at their source, local. For Burke, hierarchy is an implied feature of that recognition: "We begin our public affections in our families. No cold relation is a zealous citizen. We pass on to

---

[40] Burke, "Letter to Depont," *Further Reflections*, p. 7.
[41] See Sheldon Wolin, "Contract and Birthright," *Political Theory*, 14, no. 2 (May 1986),
179–195.
[42] Burke, "Letter to Depont," *Further Reflections*, pp. 7–8.

our neighborhoods, and our habitual provincial connections ... so many little images of the great country in which the heart found something which it could fill."[43] The leveling out of these distinctions is always to be viewed with the greatest suspicion. For Burke, such "experiments" invariably provoke the thought that they are motivated by an easy instrumentality that the concrete situation cannot sustain and that will ultimately exact a heavy toll.[44] Indeed, more often than not, Burke uses the term "Jacobinism" (and the term "Indianism") to designate an ideology and a set of practices that are reckless in their disregard for the extant order of the communities they operate in. They function in the manner of money, one of whose disturbing effects, Burke suggests, stems from the ease and uniformity with which it "circulates."[45]

Location or place and history are the two facets of social order most important to Burke. Their significance stems from the role they play in securing the conditions of freedom. Moreover, both are critical to understanding Burke's sympathy and apprehensions regarding the effect of British colonial practices on India and on Britain. Because place and history are aspects through which the continuity of the past, the present, and the future are experienced, they are vested for Burke with a special moral gravity. In his view, they both relate to the conditions that are requisite for the psychological and moral integrity of individuals and communities. People have psychological reliance on the places to which they belong and the position they occupy in a social system. But these reliances can be overlooked both by a failure of reflection (which for Burke is something wholly distinct from speculation) on the conditions that sustain us and by

---

[43] Burke, *Further Reflections*, p. 167.

[44] "I can never be convinced, that the scheme of placing the highest powers of the state in churchwardens and constables, and other such officers, guided by the prudence of litigious attornies ... and set in action by shameless women of the lowest condition, by keepers of hotels, taverns, and brothels, by pert apprentices, by clerks, shop-boys, hairdressers, fidlers, and dancers on the stage ... can never be put into any shape that must not be both disgraceful and destructive." Burke, "Letter to a Member of the National Assembly," *Further Reflections*, p. 30. He makes the same point with less objectionable language and details in *Reflections*: "After I had read over the list of the persons and descriptions selected into the Tiers Etat, nothing which they afterward did could appear astonishing. Among them, indeed I saw some of known rank; some of shining talents; but of any practical experience in the state, not one man was to be found. The best were only men of theory." Burke, *Reflections*, p. 38.

[45] Burke, "Thoughts on French Affairs," *Further Reflections*, p. 213. Bromwich rightly suggests that by the 1790s, for Burke the terms "money," "speculation," "philosophy," and "atheism" are "rough synonyms." See Bromwich, "The Context of Burke's *Reflections*," 331. I think Burke would have added the terms "East India Company" and "empire" to this list.

an overinvestment in expedited and convulsive change. The consequences of such failure are, according to Burke, invariably dire and extreme. We risk dispossessing ourselves, as in the case of the Duke of Bedford, and we risk dispossessing entire communities, as in France, India, and Britain: "when the subject of our demolition and construction is not breaking timber but sentient human beings, by the sudden alteration of whose state, conditions, and habits, multitudes may be rendered miserable."[46]

This account, which stems from the Burkean insistence on acknowledging our being in the middle of things, implies a posture not only toward place but also toward history. To have a sense of oneself on this account requires being conscious of our status as inheritors and as transmitters of an inheritance. At a social level, it involves imbuing institutions with a status appropriate to something that has, at least in part, made us who we are and on which we have a collective reliance:

> One of the first and most leading principles on which the commonwealth and the laws are consecrated, is lest the temporary possessors and life-renters in it, unmindful of what they have received from their ancestors or of what is due to their posterity, should act as if they were the entire masters; that they should not think it amongst their rights to cut off the entail or commit waste on the inheritance, by destroying at their pleasure the whole original fabric of their society; hazarding to leave to those who come after them a ruin instead of an habitation – and teaching these successors as little to respect their contrivances, as they had themselves respected the institutions of their forefathers. By this unprincipled facility of changing the state as often, and as much, and in as many ways as there are floating fancies or fashions, the whole chain and continuity of the commonwealth would be broken. No one generation could link with the other. Men would become little better than the flies of a summer.[47]

To act as though one were the "entire masters" of the institutions that circumscribe our existence is to act doubly against our nature. It is to deny that our institutions are an inheritance and to sever the transmission of an inheritance to future generations. That would amount to giving life a seasonal duration. It is what Burke associates with every kind of absolutism. If Burke in this passage sounds paternalistic, he means to endorse an attitude that is at least parental. The unprincipled facility of changing states has its analogue in parents who do not support their progeny.[48] Both break the chain of continuity that secures healthy human existence.

---

[46] Burke, *Reflections*, p. 144.
[47] Ibid., pp. 91–92.
[48] "Parents, in the order of Providence, are made for their children, and not their children for them." Quoted in Sir Philip Magnus, *Edmund Burke* (London: J. Murray, 1939), p. 268.

In this, Burke's defense of history is meant as a defense of the conditions
that make life whole. The recognition of our temporality is what facilitates respect for the institutions of our forebears and a concomitant concern for future generations.

Burke seems to be suggesting that only through the acceptance of
society as an ongoing, and hence historical, partnership can basic human
sentiments – such as those that parents naturally feel toward their children – be secure. The same instinct that stops us from consuming at
the expense of our children must give us pause in totally transforming
the extant order of society. Nothing Burke says here or elsewhere is an
indictment against any and every kind of change. It is a plea against only
that species of change that has uprooting as its initial motive. For Burke,
the impulse to start all over again, or to construct new foundations,
is much the same as the attitude that assumes that no one will follow
after me.

The British may have believed in the illusion of their permanence in
India.[49] At any rate, they were insistent on denying the fact that India had
a history of its own. They were especially insistent on denying that India's
past included the integuments of society and social order. What India had
was a long record of despotism with no society to limit or support it. As
Bryan Turner has suggested, the overwhelming thrust of orientalist writings was to suggest that the Orient was "all state and no society."[50] This
was a view of India that Burke was intimately familiar with. The core of
Hastings's defense was a variant on it. In assuming despotic authority,
Hastings claimed that he was merely conforming to local customs and
expectations. His use of power had not been arbitrary because it followed
a norm of arbitrary power.[51] Burke's argument is a frontal challenge to
Hastings's reading of India:

I must do justice to the East. I assert that their morality is equal to ours, in whatever regards the duties of governors, fathers, and superiors; and I challenge the

---

[49] This is a claim Francis Hutchins defends in his book *The Illusion of Permanence: British
    Imperialism in India* (Princeton, N.J.: Princeton University Press, 1967).
[50] Bryan Turner, "Orientalism and the Problem of Civil Society in Islam," in *Orientalism,
    Islam and Islamists*, ed. Asaf Hussain, Robert Olson, and Jamil Qureshi (Brattleboro, Vt:
    Amana Books, 1984), p. 39.
[51] "I had an arbitrary power to exercise: I exercise it. Slaves I found the people: slaves they
    are, – they are so by their constitution"; "The whole history of Asia is nothing more
    than precedents to prove the invariable exercise of arbitrary power." Warren Hastings
    quoted in Burke, "Impeachment of Warren Hastings," *Writings and Speeches*, vol. 9, pp.
    448, 451.

world to show in any modern European book more true morality and wisdom than is to be found in the writings of Asiatic men in high trust, and who have been counsellors to princes. If this be the true morality of Asia, as I affirm and can prove that it is, the pleas founded on Mr. Hastings's geographical morality is [*sic*] annihilated.[52]

Hastings's plea is interrogated in the hundreds of pages that constitute Burke's response. In rhetorically moving prose and with endless details, the House of Commons, and later the House of Lords, are told of Hindu and Muslim public and private law, religion, social structure, and commercial practices, of caste mobility and professional change, of the basis of political power and the limits placed on it, of social groups, the patriotism of men, the chivalry of warriors, the virtue of women, and the other empires that, unlike the British, settled and mixed their blood and inheritance with those of the natives. Burke is dismissive of Hastings's "geographical morality."[53] Hastings is a British governor-general, exercising the authority granted to him by the East India Company and indirectly by the king. He is bound by those norms and by the constraints that are attached to those norms.[54] The relativism Hastings invokes in his defense is only a "screen" through which he betrays his own history and that of the Indians by refusing to acknowledge that one is his and the other is not. It is this sort of self-betrayal, in which Hastings transposes the substance of his historical inheritance with its form, that compounds Burke's worry when he imagines the delinquents of India becoming the Commons of Great Britain. The prospect of an ancient commonwealth set on wasting its inheritance must have filled Burke with horror. For Hastings, geography was merely one of many instrumental ruses and not what, in Burke's view, it was for the rajah of Tanjore and the people of the Carnatic – a weighty index of who they were, a dwelling cemented by the changing though never wholly voluntary alloy of history and sentiments.

---

[52] Ibid., p. 476.

[53] "Let your Lordships know that these gentlemen have formed a plan of geographical morality, by which the duties of men, in public and in private situations, are not to be governed by their relation to the great Governor of the Universe, or by their relation to mankind, but by climates, degrees of longitude, parallel, not of life, but of latitudes: as is when you crossed the equinocial, all the virtues die, as they say some insects die when they cross the line." Ibid., pp. 447–448.

[54] "My Lords, we contend that Mr. Hastings, as a British governor, ought to govern on British principles, not by British forms, – God forbid! – for if ever there was a case in which the letter kills and the spirit gives life, it would be an attempt to introduce British forms and the substance of despotic principles together into any country." Ibid., p. 447.

The defense of India as having a history, a history with society, with laws, and with classes, is one of the most common postures that Burke assumes. Toward the end of the trial, Burke reiterates this defense:

On one side, your Lordships have the prisoner declaring that the people have no laws, no rights, no usage, no distinctions of rank, no sense of honour, no property – in short, they are nothing but a herd of slaves, to be governed by the arbitrary will of a master. On the other side, we assert, that the direct contrary of this is true. And to prove our assertion ... we have referred you to the Mahometan law, which is binding upon all, from the crowned head to the meanest subject – a law interwoven with the wisest, the most learned, and most enlightened jurisprudence that perhaps ever existed in the world.[55]

This is Burke's summary statement on behalf of a history that has been experienced by Indians. The statement recalls numerous passages from *Reflections* and his other writings on the French Revolution. The categories that are significant are all the same – laws, rights, usage, distinctions of rank, honor, and property. There is no contradiction here. The categories Burke points to are the categories that are relevant to the claim he is making here and in the French context. It is the historical evidence for these categories, and not any and every history, that validates the point he is making in both of these contexts. Society and social order are not identical to history, even though they do require having a history. Correspondingly, the sympathy that Burke feels for India is not merely sympathy for an oppressed people; it is sympathy for a people who constituted a threatened community and one that he also believed was oppressed. He makes this clear in his speech on the Fox India Bill when he says, "this multitude of men [Indians] does not consist of an abject and barbarous populous; much less of gangs of savages like the Guaranies and the Chiquitos, who wander on the waste borders of the Amazons, or the Plate."[56] Burke's defense of Indian history vindicates a social order in which freedom would not be "solitary, unconnected, individual, selfish liberty, as if every man was to regulate the whole of his conduct by his own will." It vindicates what subsequent nationalists

[55] Burke, "Impeachment of Warren Hastings," *Writings and Speeches*, vol. 11, p. 219.
[56] Burke, "Speech on Mr. Fox's East-India Bill," *Writings and Speeches*, vol. 5, p. 389. Also note the following: "In a state of rude nature there is no such thing as a people. A number of men in themselves have no collective capacity. The idea of a people is the idea of a corporation. It is wholly artificial; and made, like all other legal fictions, by common agreement. What the particular nature of that agreement was, is collected from the form into which the particular society has been cast." "Appeal from the New to the Old Whigs," *Writings and Speeches*, vol. 3, p. 82.

might have called the conditions appropriate for self-determination and, therefore, for independence.

CONCLUSION: EMPIRE AND NATION

Alessandro d'Entrèves, in his classic book *The Notion of the State*, makes the point that "ideas of nation and nationality are entirely absent from the definition of the state" in the writings of Machiavelli, Hobbes, and Bodin.[57] He could have added Locke to that list. The reason he offers for this omission is straightforward. All these theorists broadly start with individuals with defined needs and interests, and they ask, in light of these needs and interests, and given some other constraints, what set of political arrangements would conduce to their survival and well-being? Given this line of inquiry, it is difficult to see where considerations of territoriality and history as grounds of individual and group identity could be accommodated. Either they are altogether extraneous to the enterprise or – and with Locke, at least, this is more evident – they are being presupposed and are hence almost irrecoverably implicit. What follows is that considerations of individual identity that turn on the affections of territoriality and the processes of history are similarly displaced. One might say that liberals have theorized the state while either ignoring or presuming the coherence of the nation.

The contrast with Burke is obvious. In his "Speech on the State of Representation of the Commons in Parliament," he states:

Our Constitution is a prescriptive Constitution; it is a Constitution, whose sole authority is that it has existed time out of mind.... Prescription is the most solid of all titles, not only to property, but, which is to secure that property to Government. They harmonize with each other, and give mutual aid to one another. It is accompanied with another ground of authority in the constitution of the human mind, presumption. It is a presumption in favor of any settled scheme of government against any untried project, that a nation has long existed and flourished under it. It is a better presumption even of the choice of a nation, far better than any sudden or temporary arrangement by actual election. Because a nation is not an idea only of local extent, and individual momentary aggregation, but it is an idea of continuity, which extends in time as well as in numbers, and in space. And this is a choice not of one day, or one set of people, not a tumultuary or giddy choice; it is a deliberate election of ages and of generations.[58]

---

[57] Alessandro d'Entrèves, *The Notion of the State: An Introduction to Political Theory* (Oxford: Clarendon Press, 1967), p.170.

[58] Burke, "Speech on the State of Representation of Commons in Parliament," *Writings and Speeches,* vol. 7, pp. 94–95.

A nation is more than the choice that people express in consenting to their government. It is more than the aggregate of individuals contracting to form a state, as Hegel importantly pointed out. A nation goes beyond the giddy exhilaration that may accompany changing government. It is something that stands as a foundation to all of this, but it can serve as this foundation only because it represents continuity in time and in space of a certain social order that has a sanction in the human mind. It is this continuity that nationalists spoke on behalf of as they challenged empires. And it is this that Burke anticipated.

There is one final aspect of Burke's thought that informs the entire tenor of his writings on the empire and that also pertains to the nation. It is the perspective of Burke as a spectator – concerned, at points sympathetic, at others critical – but always mindful of a distance, not simply physical but more importantly emotional, that separates him from those whose story he is recounting. It is a history he had studied with great diligence and passion. But Burke seems always aware that neither quality makes it his history, nor does he presume that it will be transparent to him. History as experienced is more than the knowledge of that experience. Burke is always conscious of this. Acknowledging a history and a set of concerns of which he has no part, or rather only a spectatorial part, has significant implications. First, it suggests that inheritances are specific and bounded. Second, the spectatorial perspective indicates a position from which something can be viewed without sanctioning, touching, or meddling with it. It encourages the idea of restraint on the use of power, especially when the view is from a distance. Burke will not countenance power, even when backed by knowledge, arrogating to itself the ready right to meddle with other peoples' histories, especially when those histories have produced a social coherence of their own. There is a hesitance in Burke, just as there is an impatience in so many of his adversaries and contemporaries. It is a moral hesitance. He will not allow power to become the connective tissue that links everything. Something of this idea is suggested in a remark Burke makes in Parliament: "if we are not able to contrive some method of governing India well which will not of necessity become the means of governing Great Britain ill, a ground is laid for their eternal separation, but none for sacrificing the people of that country to our constitution."[59] Burke appears to be saying that there is more to morality than the imperative to govern.

---

[59] Burke, "Speech on Fox's India Bill," *Writings and Speeches*, vol. 2, p. 438.

There is an almost reverent humility that Burke feels when faced with cultural, economic, and political differences. That humility touches and surrounds his thought in a way that permits him to accept those differences as lived possibilities even when they sharply contrast, as the norms in India no doubt did, with the practices with which Burke is at home. Here Burke expresses a tolerance that is grounded on an acceptance of his own limitations and his own possible obtuseness to other practices. It is therefore a deeper tolerance than that of his liberal compatriots, even when they made toleration the focus of their theoretical attention. In contrast to the darkness that James Mill and others ascribe to India, Burke sees and accepts that darkness as perhaps stemming from the limits of his own circumscribed vision.

The term "nation" and its cognates are scarce in Burke's writings. It would be wrong to view Burke's thought as though it were concerned with theorizing the nation or explicating its underlying basis. That was not the emphasis of his thought. And yet, Burke did understand the basis of nations and the sentiments and the energy that they drew on. He understood that ultimately it was these sentiments, of place, belonging, and history, that empires violated and for which they attempted to substitute a form of power that only aggravated that violation. But also, and for Burke this was crucial, empires manifested a profound lack of self-understanding in the conceit with which they viewed sentiments as subservient to power. In this he was prescient and clearly remains so.

7

Adam Smith in the British Empire

Emma Rothschild

Approximately one-third of the *Wealth of Nations* is about empire, or at least about the long-distance commerce that was so intricately entangled, in Smith's description, with the eighteenth-century empires. Of the two quarto volumes of the first edition of 1776, the first begins with an elogy to long-distance exchange, including the commerce between London and Calcutta. The second volume is largely concerned with the regulation of overseas commerce and with government policies, especially in relation to commerce, taxes, and foreign wars. The *Additions and Corrections* that Smith published in 1784 as a slim separate volume, and that begins abstractly and audaciously – "Wealth, as Mr Hobbes says, is power" – is almost entirely about overseas commerce, including bounties, elephants' teeth, and East India companies.[1]

These disquisitions on commerce are not easy to read, and they are not often read. There have been distinguished studies of Smith's colonial writings, particularly in relation to the Atlantic colonies.[2] But the pages in which he describes the sealskins of the British Greenland fishery, or the importation of undressed flax, or *Memoirs of Wool*, or the constitution of the Turkey Company, are among the most obscure corners of the overgrown forest of Smith's mind. As Jean-Baptiste Say wrote in 1803, the *Wealth of Nations* is a "vast chaos of just ideas, pell-mell with pieces

---

[1] *Additions and Corrections to the First and Second Editions of Dr. Adam Smith's Inquiry into the Nature and Causes of the Wealth of Nations* (London, 1784), p. [1].

[2] See Richard Koebner, *Empire* (Cambridge, 1961); Donald Winch, *Classical Political Economy and Colonies* (Cambridge, Mass., 1965); Donald Winch, *Adam Smith's Politics: An Essay in Historiographic Revision* (Cambridge, 1978); Jennifer Pitts, *A Turn to Empire: The Rise of Imperial Liberalism in Britain and France* (Princeton, N.J., 2005).

of positive knowledge," over-full of historical digressions and from time to time "lacking in interest for anyone other than the English" (or at least for the adminstratively minded Lowland Scots.)[3]

What I would like to suggest, in this chapter, is that a view of Smith "in the British Empire" – as an individual who was preoccupied with the political difficulties of empire, who was intensely conscious of the public dramas of the times in respect of the British, French, and Moghul empires, and who lived, in London and Scotland, in a milieu of hectic imperial connections – can illuminate some important aspects of his political thought and of the political scene of the late eighteenth century. It may even illuminate the position of Smith in modern political and philosophical debates, including debates over the modernity of empire; it is with these questions that I will conclude.

Smith described the *Wealth of Nations* in a celebrated letter of 1780, to an old friend who had become a commissioner of the Danish–Norwegian commercial college, as the "very violent attack I had made upon the whole commercial system of Great Britain."[4] The commercial system, in this epitome, was the system of long-distance commerce; of exports and imports; and of the taxes, bounties, monopolies, forts, and fleets by which they were regulated. The expression "commercial system" was itself relatively recent, having come into use in the mid-1750s. But its meaning was closely connected to, first, the sale of goods for use in distant places, or at least in places with different political institutions ("commerce"), and second, the political and administrative arrangements (the "system") by which the sales were protected or encouraged or impeded.

Smith's idyll of opulence was founded, as in the elogy at the beginning of the *Wealth of Nations*, on a vista of the long-distance division of labor. The difficulty with the idyll, which was Smith's principal subject in Book Four of the *Wealth of Nations*, and in the *Additions and Corrections*, was that long-distance commerce was insecure in multiple respects. This insecurity inspired a demand on the part of commercial men for government protection. The commercial connections of European merchants had expanded, in the course of the eighteenth century, over extremely long distances in space, time, and political institutions. The commerce with

---

[3] "Discours préliminaire," in Jean-Baptiste Say, *Traité d'Economie Politique, ou simple exposition de la manière dont se forment, se distribuent, et se consomment les richesses* (Paris, 1803), pp. vi, xxv.

[4] Letter from Smith to Andreas Holt of 26 October 1780 in *The Correspondence of Adam Smith*, ed. E. C. Mossner and I. S. Ross, 2nd ed. (Oxford, 1987), p. 251.

the two Indies, in the expression that for the abbé Raynal encompassed the Atlantic from the Arctic to the Antarctic and the Indian Ocean eastward from the Cape of Good Hope to the Straits of Magellan, was even more insecure than the older European or Levantine trade. The empires of the times, which are the principal subject of Book Five of the *Wealth of Nations*, with their far-flung wars and their fiscal imprudence, were correspondingly even more imposing.

Smith is at his most sublimely contemptuous in his denunciations of commercial enmity, as his earliest biographer observed in 1793; they are "expressed in a tone of indignation, which he seldom assumes in his political writings."[5] The projectors of speculative banks have "golden dreams" of profit; Sir Walter Raleigh had "strange delusions" about the golden city of Eldorado; Britain's Atlantic empire is a "golden dream" of politicians, "not an empire, but the project of an empire; not a gold mine, but the project of a gold mine." The "mean rapacity, the monopolizing spirit of merchants and manufacturers," leads them to aspire to be "the rulers of mankind." The "sneaking arts of underling tradesmen" are expressed with "all the passionate confidence of interested falsehood." They influence relationships between countries and between peoples; "mercantile jealousy is excited, and both inflames, and is itself inflamed, by the violence of national animosity."[6]

Colonies and empires were in general, for Smith, monuments to unreason. The motives for their establishment, in modern times, were "avidity," "folly and injustice," and the "sacred thirst of gold"; "a great empire has been established for the sole purpose of raising up a nation of customers."[7] They encouraged the African slave trade, in which a cruel fortune "subjected those nations of heroes to the refuse of the jails of Europe."[8] In India and the East Indies, the "arts of oppression" had become most "perfectly destructive." The elaborate commercial economy of Bengal, a country "remarkable for the exportation of a great variety of manufactures," in which "the Mahometan government" had been "extremely attentive to the making and maintaining of good roads and navigable

---

[5] Dugald Stewart, "Account of the Life and Writings of Adam Smith, LL.D" (1793), in Adam Smith, *Essays on philosophical subjects*, ed. W. P. D. Wightman and J. C. Bryce (Oxford, 1980), pp. 263–332, at p. 316.

[6] Adam Smith, *An Inquiry into the Nature and Causes of the Wealth of Nations*, ed. R. H. Campbell and A. S. Skinner (Oxford, 1976), pp. 310, 493, 496, 563, 947.

[7] Ibid., pp. 562, 563, 588.

[8] Adam Smith, *Theory of Moral Sentiments*, ed. D. D. Raphael and A. L. Macfie (Oxford, 1976), p. 206.

canals," and to the maintenance of "a very moderate" land revenue, had been overthrown.[9]

There is something idiosyncratically disagreeable, Smith suggested, in the circumstances whereby companies come to be "the sovereigns of the countries which they have conquered." They have the power of sovereigns. They are possessed by "the spirit of war and conquest." But they continue to think of themselves as merchants, and they "regard the character of the sovereign as but an appendix to that of the merchant." The trading spirit makes them bad sovereigns, and the "spirit of sovereignty seems to have rendered them equally bad traders." They are indifferent to the "happiness or misery of their subjects." Their interest is to acquire a share in "the appointment of the plunderers of India." They are engaged in "the pleasure of wasting, or the profit of embezzling."[10]

The whole expense of the "late war" – the Seven Years War, in Europe, India, and America, which had ended in 1763 – was in Smith's account incurred in support of the monopoly of colonial trade; it was "altogether a colony quarrel." The wars of the times were for Smith the clearest illustration of the "profusion of government." They were also an illustration of the frivolity of British sovereigns, who "amused the people with the imagination that they possessed a great empire on the west side of the Atlantic." This was not security, but childishness. The people in the capital were not in danger of violence, but "enjoy, at their ease, the amusement of reading in the newspapers the exploits of their own fleets and armies.... They are commonly dissatisfied with the return of peace, which puts an end to their amusement, and to a thousand visionary hopes of conquest and national glory."[11]

Even Christopher Columbus is an absurd and sinister figure in the *Wealth of Nations*, who on his return from his first voyage to America was welcomed with a "solemn procession" consisting of little gold ornaments, "some bales of cotton," and "some stuffed skins of the huge alligator and manati; all of which were preceded by six or seven of the wretched natives, whose singular colour and appearance added greatly to the novelty of the show." To the abbé Raynal's enthusiastic observation that "the discovery of America, and that of a passage to the East Indies by the Cape of Good Hope, are the two greatest and most important events

---

[9] Smith, *The Wealth of Nations*, pp. 636, 683, 838, 839.
[10] Ibid., pp. 637, 749, 752, 753, 819.
[11] Ibid., pp. 345, 615, 920, 947.

recorded in the history of mankind," Smith added a far more sombre conclusion: "To the natives however, both of the East and West Indies, all the commercial benefits which can have resulted from those events have been sunk and lost in the dreadful misfortunes which they have occasioned."[12]

Smith has been celebrated or execrated, during most of the period since his death in 1790, as the inspiration of one or more great abstractions: free trade, the national economy, self-interest, sympathy, the "essentially utilitarian framework," in Akeel Bilgrami's expression, of a "desacralized world," or a world without enchantment.[13] It is easy to see why his writings on empire should have seemed so unimportant within this vast posthumous renown. They are extremely detailed (all the passages about the herring buss fishery and the value of an ounce of fine gold in the Calcutta mint); they are related to the ephemeral disputes of a particular time and place ("in all these additions, *the present state of things* means always the state in which they were during the year 1783 and the beginning of the present year 1784," Smith observed dispiritingly in the "advertisement" to the third edition of the *Wealth of Nations*).[14] "It is too much like a publication for the present moment," Smith's friend Hugh Blair wrote in 1776, of the passages in the first edition on the crisis of the British Atlantic empire.[15] Smith's diatribes against colonial oppression have fitted only awkwardly, in a more general sense, into the posthumous politics of *Smithianismus* and empire.

To see Smith in his own times, I would like to suggest, is by contrast to see these criticisms of empire as at the very center of his concerns. The context of the *Wealth of Nations* in the "high" political thought of the time provides one illustration. The politics of distance was critical to David Hume's *Political Discourses* of 1752, the only one of Hume's works, in his own description, "that was successful on the first publication" and the immediate inspiration for Smith's economic writings.[16] The peaceful exchange of commodities and ideas in which "commerce is extended all over the globe" was in deadly peril, in Hume's account, from the spirit

---

[12] Ibid., pp. 561, 626.
[13] Akeel Bilgrami, "Gandhi, Newton and the Enlightenment" (Delhi University, 2006: Sukhamoy Chakravarthi Lecture), pp. 12, 46.
[14] Smith, *The Wealth of Nations*, p. 8.
[15] Letter from Hugh Blair to Smith of 3 April 1776 in *The Correspondence of Adam Smith*, p. 188.
[16] "My Own Life," in David Hume, *Essays Moral, Political, and Literary*, ed. Eugene F. Miller (Indianapolis, 1987), p. xxxvi.

of conquest and empire. "War is attended with every destructive circumstance"; it tended, if funded by public borrowing, to "dissolution and destruction." The freedom of government was itself at risk: the Roman Empire had declined not because of luxury but because of the "unlimited extent of conquests." The last paragraph of the *Political Discourses*, like the last paragraph of the *Wealth of Nations*, was an excoriation of imperial conquest: "extensive conquests, when pursued, must be the ruin of every free government."[17]

The politics of empire was central, too, to the other great influence on Smith's political and economic thought, the French economic theories with which he was so preoccupied in the 1760s. Smith lived in France, from 1764 to 1766, at a time of intense interest in the political economy of colonies, a reevaluation of empire that engaged all the theorists whom Smith most admired. François Quesnay and A. R. J. Turgot have been seen, like Smith, as the inspiration for the great abstractions of free trade and the national economy. But they, too, were concerned with theories of conquest and dominion. The supposed national objective in the colonies was, in Quesnay's description, a "confusion, disorder and absurdity" of the interests of traders and shippers, colonists and sovereigns, a "confusion and obscurity of ideas" in which the "State, the nation, the metropolis, the shippers have been confounded under the name of *metropolis*."[18]

Turgot's intention, as a young man, had been to investigate the "inequality of power" in relation to colonies, the oppression of conquered peoples, and the "route of money around the globe." He denounced Spartan slavery (a violation of "all the rights of humanity") and American slavery ("what scenes of horror and of cruelties"); when he himself became minister, initially of the navy and colonies, he anticipated, in Condorcet's later account, that "he could produce a revolution in commerce; destroy this tyrannical avidity which desolates Asia in order to dishonour and corrupt Europe," encourage the revolt of all American colonies, and bring about "the disappearance, little by little, by wise laws, of this slavery of negroes, the opprobrium of modern nations."[19] André Morellet and Dupont de

---

[17] Hume, *Essays*, pp. 276, 351, 363, 529.

[18] [François Quesnay], "Remarques sur l'opinion de l'auteur de l'esprit des lois concernant les colonies" (1766), in *François Quesnay et la physiocratie* (Paris, 1958), vol. 2, pp. 782–790.

[19] Condorcet, *Vie de M. Turgot* (1786), in *Oeuvres de Condorcet*, ed. A. Condorcet O'Connor and M. F. Arago (Paris, 1847–1849), vol. 5, p. 49; "Discours aux Sorboniques" (1750), "Plan d'un ouvrage sur la géographie politique" (1751), in A. R. J. Turgot, *Oeuvres de Turgot et Documents le Concernant*, ed. Gustave Schelle (Paris, 1913–1923), vol. 1, pp. 204, 207, 261, 263.

Nemours, Smith's less eminent friends among the French economists, were active, by the end of his period in France, in the controversies that led to the abolition, in 1769, of the French East India Company.[20]

The political history of the times – the "medium" political and economic thought, or the thoughts that were expressed in parliamentary reports and speeches (in England) and in pamphlets and periodicals (in France or Scotland) – provides a second illustration of Smith's imperial setting. The interlude between the end of the Seven Years War in 1763 and the beginning of the American Revolutionary War in 1775 was a period of intense political dispute, in France and in Britain, over the North American disturbances, the Atlantic slave economy, and the commerce of the East India companies. It was in the course of this interwar period that Smith wrote the *Wealth of Nations*, his very violent attack on the commercial system.

Smith's rhetoric, in his criticisms of modern empires, is strikingly close to the language of the political debates. "One and forty times did the House sit upon this business," Edmund Burke said in December 1772, in a debate in the House of Commons on the English East India Company and its "rapacity and tyranny" in India; "books upon books, and papers upon papers were brought up and piled upon your table." The phrase a "golden dream," which Smith used so effectively, was ubiquitous in the debates. Smith's detailed description of Bengal drew upon one of the most polemical of the books, by William Bolts. His denunciation of the East India Company was the echo of Morellet's earlier polemics against the "expenses of sovereignty" of the French Compagnie des Indes; a "company which is both commercial and conquering is a monster which cannot survive for long." It was an echo, too, of the British parliamentary rhetoric of 1772 and 1773: in the words of Colonel, later General John Burgoyne, at the time the chairman of a select committee on the East India Company, "if by some means sovereignty and law are not separated from trade ... India and Great Britain will be sunk and overwhelmed, never to rise again."[21]

---

[20] See Emma Rothschild, "Global Commerce and the Question of Sovereignty in the Eighteenth-Century Provinces," *Modern Intellectual History*, 1, no. 1 (April 2004), 1–25.

[21] See House of Commons debates of 13 April, 18 May, and 18 December 1772 in *The Parliamentary History of England, from the Earliest Period to the Year 1803* (London, 1813), vol. 17, cols. 458–459, 474, 652, 663, 671; Burgoyne speech, cols. 458–459; Abbé Morellet, *Examen de la réponse de M. N** au mémoire de M. l'Abbé Morellet, sur la compagnie des Indes; Par l'Auteur du mémoire* (Paris, 1769), pp. 71, 83; Jacques Necker, "Réponse au mémoire de M. l'abbé Morellet sur la compagnie des Indes" (1769), in *Oeuvres Complètes de M. Necker* (Paris, 1820), vol. 15, p. 142.

Smith's own milieu provides a third sort of illustration. Smith was sur-rounded, from his earliest childhood, by families with commercial and colonial connections. James Townsend Oswald, his closest friend in his home town of Kirkaldy, was commissioner of the navy and an expert on East Indian affairs; Oswald's son was the secretary of the Leeward Islands in the West Indies. David Hume worked as a young man for the Bristol sugar trading company of Michael Miller and set out, in 1746, to make his fortune in America (he was detained in the English Channel by unfavorable winds). One of Smith's favorite students, William Johnstone, later Pulteney, was the third of seven sons who included three officials of the East India Company, a governor of West Florida, and three propri-etors of sugar plantations in Grenada; another student, Robert Cullen, was an expert on the cosmopolitan law of slavery.[22]

Smith's Danish-Norwegian friend, Andreas Holt, was an official of the Danish commercial college at a time of extensive reform in Danish over-seas commerce, with a new charter of the Asiatic Company, in 1772, and a period of almost entirely free trade to India, overseen by the college.[23] Holt's two pupils, Peter and Carsten Anker, who were Smith's other Danish acquaintances, were closely involved in colonial commerce, one as a director of the Asiatic Company and the other as governor of the Danish colony of Tranquebar in South India.[24]

The connections of lowlands Scotland to the East and West Indies expanded throughout the eighteenth century and provide a fascinating subject of economic history and of the prosopography of enlightenment. In the new world of the 1760s and 1770s, the world in which Smith composed the *Wealth of Nations*, these connections extended virtually everywhere in the intellectual milieus of Edinburgh and Glasgow. Their advantages, for Smith's friends, consisted both in office and in recognition,

---

[22] On David Hume's and James Townsend Oswald's commercial and colonial connec-tions, see Emma Rothschild, "The Atlantic Worlds of David Hume," in *Soundings in Atlantic History: Latent Structures and Intellectual Currents, 1500–1830*, ed. Bernard Bailyn (Cambridge, Mass., 2009), pp. 405–450, at pp. 405–448, 409–410, 428; on the Johnstone-Pulteney family and Robert Cullen, see Emma Rothschild, *The Inner Life of Empires: An Eighteenth-Century History* (Princeton, N.J., 2011).

[23] *Den danske civile centraladministrations embedsetat, 1660–1848* (Copenhagen, 1889), p. 192; A. Rasch and P. P. Sveistrup, *Asiatisk Kompagni i den florissante periode 1772–1792* (Copenhagen, 1948), pp. 69–82.

[24] Letter of 26 October 1780 to Peter Anker, in *The Correspondence of Adam Smith*, pp. 253–254; *Norsk Forfatter-Lexikon, 1844–1880*, ed. J. B. Halvorsen (Kristiania, 1885), vol. 1, pp. 67, 72; Ole Feldbaek, *India Trade under the Danish Flag 1772–1808: European Enterprise and Anglo-Indian Remittance and Trade* (Odense, 1969), pp. 13–45, 130–151.

the opportunity of being consulted. Smith himself was recommended (by William Pulteney) for a position as adviser to the East India Company in London or Bengal; the philosopher Adam Ferguson and Smith's close friend Andrew Stuart actively sought such positions; James "Ossian" Macpherson, who had earlier been an official in West Florida, was employed in London by the nabob of Arcot. Robert Cullen was the legal counsel to the owner of Joseph Knight, the slave brought from Africa to Jamaica and from Jamaica to Scotland, whose suit to secure his freedom, in Perth and Edinburgh, ended slavery in the British Isles.[25]

The connections to the empire were particularly intense, it seems, in the most obscure of the many lost periods in Smith's long and uneventful life, or the "four years" he spent in London between 1773 and 1777, during which he "finished and published" the *Wealth of Nations*.[26] There are only four letters from Smith that survive from the period in London (with the exception of a detailed exchange about Adam Ferguson's pension). But it is clear that he lived in a scene that was intensely political and was involved, in particular, in the politics of empire. He was himself involved in the solicitation of East Indian positions, including for the son of his friend the inventor John Roebuck, in March 1776, a request sent on to Madras by James Macpherson on behalf of "Dr Adam Smith, one of my best friends."[27]

The sense of connectedness to the new world of commerce – of being "in the British Empire" – was not even, in Smith's milieu, a question of distant connections. There were relationships of expectation, as when Hume, or Ferguson, or Andrew Stuart determined to set out for the empire, or when the nieces and nephews of the Macphersons or the Johnstones learned that they were to be the beneficiaries in their uncles' wills. But there were also far more immediate connections. Of the seven Johnstone brothers, five became owners of slaves; at least two of them, including William Pulteney, owned slaves who were brought to the United Kingdom; John Johnstone, who was the member of Parliament for Adam Smith's home borough, lived a few miles from Kirkaldy with two slaves

---

[25] See Rothschild, *The Inner Life of Empires*.
[26] Letter to Andreas Holt of 26 October 1780, in *The Correspondence of Adam Smith*, p. 252. Smith was in Edinburgh in April 1773, went to live in London, and returned to Scotland in June 1777; in 1776, he spent the period from April to December on an extended visit to Scotland; *The Correspondence of Adam Smith*, pp. 168, 194, 223, 429–430.
[27] Letter of 25 March 1776 from James Macpherson to John Macpherson, Macpherson Papers, Oriental and India Office Collections, British Library, Mss Eur F291/122.

from Bengal; Joseph Knight, who was brought to Perth, was the slave of one of the Johnstone sisters' son-in-law.

A final illustration of Smith "in the British Empire" has to do with the reception of both the *Wealth of Nations* and the *Theory of Moral Sentiments*. It is interesting that the earliest publications that were actually *about* Smith were concerned, in general, with his writings on empire. The first work in which Smith was named in the title was a defense of the continental colonies by the American publicist Arthur Lee, published in London in 1764. Adam Smith had "exalted into heroes" the African slaves, Lee wrote, and "debased into monsters" the American colonists. But the Africans were characterized by "universal depravity and barbarism," "a race the most detestable and vile that ever the earth produced," and the American savages were "atrocious," "perfidious," "cowardly and cruel." The colonists of Virginia, Maryland, and the Carolinas were, by contrast, and despite the oppressions of colonial policy, "descended from worthy ancestors, from whom he has not proved them to have degenerated."[28]

The second work in which Smith was named in the title was a *Letter to Adam Smith*, published in 1776 by Thomas Pownall, the former governor of Massachusetts Bay. Pownall, like Lee, sought to defend the colonial system against Smith's contempt and his supposed support for a "dismemberment of the empire." The American monopoly is not an "*invidious and malignant project* (as you stile it)," from which "Great Britain derives nothing but loss," Pownall wrote. "I do not see the malignancy of the principle of a monopoly" even in respect of commercial opulence, he concluded, and in respect of "sovereign power" it was "indispensible."[29]

The third publication in the title of which Smith is mentioned was the response in 1777 by George Horne, at the time the vice-chancellor of the University of Oxford, to Smith's account of the tranquil death of David Hume.[30] The fourth work, a *Candid Examination of the East-India Company ... with Strictures on some of the Self-Contradictions and Historical Errors of Dr. Adam Smith*, which was published by the poet

---

[28] [Arthur Lee], *An Essay, in Vindication of the Continental Colonies of America, From A Censure of Mr Adam Smith, in his Theory of Moral Sentiments. With some Reflections on Slavery in General. By an American* (London, 1764), pp. iv, v, 13, 30.
[29] Thomas Pownall, *A Letter from Governor Pownall to Adam Smith, L.L.D. F.R.S. Being an examination of several points of doctrine, laid down in his "Inquiry into the nature and causes of the wealth of nations"* (London, 1776), pp. 7, 27, 37, 39.
[30] [George Horne], *A Letter to Adam Smith LL.D. on the Life, Death, and Philosophy of his friend David Hume Esq., By one of the People called Christians* (Oxford, 1777); Nigel Aston, "Horne, George (1730–1792)," *Oxford Dictionary of National Biography* (Oxford, 2004).

William Julius Mickle in 1779, was once again a criticism of Smith's views of global and colonial commerce and a denunciation of the "sovereign brow of contempt" with which modern philosophers "look down from their lofty dictatorial chairs." Smith's error, for Mickle, was to have sought the abolition of the East India Company, and to have promoted a system of "voluntary, unconnected settlers" and a "free trade with Asia." Smith was ignorant, in Mickle's account, of the insecurity of the commerce with the Indies. His schemes of reform would either resign the East India merchants to the political protection of Indian sovereigns themselves or require the establishment of an elaborate political-military establishment in India by the sovereign of Great Britain. "It is, according to the Doctor, as safe to settle in, and trade with India, as to take a counting-house near London-bridge, or to buy a peck of peas at Covent-Garden."[31]

So to what extent, in conclusion, does the view I have been describing, of Adam Smith in the British Empire, help to illuminate his ideas, either in his own times or in ours? It points, I would like to suggest, to two profound difficulties of Smith's system or systems. The first has to do with the political conditions for the flourishing of free trade, and in particular with those conditions that necessarily involve the political institutions of more than one society, because the trade itself extends across the frontiers of societies or states. Smith believed that long-distance commerce was the source of increases in opulence and that "order and good government" – the "equal and impartial administration of justice," "the liberty of every individual, the sense which he has of his own security" – were the most important conditions of such opulence.[32] But long-distance commerce required at least one of three sorts of "order" if it was to be tolerably secure. The first was the order that is provided, in distant societies, by the political institutions of those societies themselves; this was the abbé Morellet's recourse when he recommended French merchants trading with the East Indies to the protection of the "Indian princes."[33] The second was the order provided by the sovereigns of the merchants' own society; this was the recourse of empire in a military and political

---

[31] [William Julius Mickle], *A Candid Examination of the Reasons for Depriving the East-India Company of its Charter, contained in "The History and Management of the East-India Company, from its Commencement to the Present Time." Together with Strictures on some of the Self-Contradictions and Historical Errors of Dr. Adam Smith, in his Reasons for the Abolition of the said Company* (London, 1779), pp. 8, 17, 26.

[32] Smith, *The Wealth of Nations*, pp. 405, 610, 722–723.

[33] Abbé Morellet, *Mémoire sur la situation actuelle de la Compagnie des Indes* (Paris, 1769), pp. 155, 160.

sense. The third was the order provided by institutions that transcend the frontiers of existing political societies; this was the utopia of an oceanic government, or a world assembly, with which so many eighteenth-century figures, including Smith, were so intrigued.[34]

William Julius Mickle's book is a work of the moment, full of misrepresentations and misquotations. But it points to a serious difficulty in Smith's system, which is that he does not choose any of these three possible orders. He is respectful of the "Mahometan government" of Bengal without being prepared to confide to it the orderliness of British commerce. He is in favor of an expansion of the role of the British sovereign in India without considering the extent to which this would bring with it all the ills of empire that he elsewhere denounces – the American system, as Mickle pointed out.[35] He is intrigued by systems of government across frontiers but identifies them as no more than utopias. It is interesting that the very first extended debate about free trade after the publication of the *Wealth of Nations* was in fact the debate that Mickle entered, in a long historical introduction to his translation of the Portugese epic *The Lusiad* and in his *Candid Examination* of a "free trade with India."[36] It was not a debate in which Smith was in any evident sense the victor.

The second difficulty with Smith's system is more profound. To see Smith "in the British Empire" is to see him, as I have suggested, as an eloquent critic of the ills of empire, including the ills of slavery in which so many of his friends were inculpated. The passage in the *Theory of Moral Sentiments* to which Arthur Lee so objected, about magnanimous slaves and their sordid masters, is an example of Smith's own philosophical method of sympathy, of seeing moral choices with the eyes of other

[34] On the absence of a "common superior" to resolve disputes between neighboring countries, see Smith, *The Theory of Moral Sentiments*, p. 228; and on the prospect of a "states-general of the British Empire," see *The Wealth of Nations*, p. 933.

[35] See Robert Travers, "British India as a Problem in Political Economy: Comparing James Steuart and Adam Smith," in *Lineages of Empire: Proceedings of the British Academy, 155*, ed. Duncan Kelly (London, 2009), pp. 137–160; and Sankar Muthu, "Adam Smith's Critique of International Trading Companies: Theorizing 'Globalization' in the Age of Enlightenment," *Political Theory*, 36, no. 2 (April 2008), 185–212.

[36] "A *free trade* in the Indian seas was a disgrace to commerce," Mickle wrote in his introduction to *The Lusiad*; William Julius Mickle, "The History of the Rise and Fall of the Portugese Empire in the East," in *The Lusiad; or, the discovery of India. An epic poem. Translated from the original Portuguese of Luis de Camöens*, 2nd ed. (Oxford, 1778), pp. lxix–clxxxvi, clxv. Mickle's *Candid Examination*, published the following year, was an extended inquiry into the difficulties of a "free trade with India," "free trade with the Eastern World, "free trade with the East," and "free trade with Asia" (pp. 12, 13, 15, 17, 20, 24, 26).

people, or "changing places in fancy."[37] So is the passage in the *Wealth of Nations* in which he inverts Raynal's enthusiasm for commerce; "to the natives however, both of the East and West Indies, all the commercial benefits ... have been sunk and lost." There is no question in the case of Smith, unlike in the case of David Hume, that the universal human nature to which he alludes so frequently is the human nature of all individual human beings, including the individuals whom he describes as "natives" or "savages."[38]

But Smith's system of seeing oneself through other people's eyes, or from other positions, or in other situations – the system that Philip Kitcher has called a "hall of mirrors" – is not, in any straightforward sense, a system that has room for extremely distant and different people. There are passages, certainly, in the *Theory of Moral Sentiments* that have been taken to indicate that Smith in his many references to "other people," including people who see our sentiments "at a certain distance from us," intended to extend the universe of reflection to persons who are very unlike "ourselves." Smith was himself highly conscious of the difficulty, as in his observations on the different senses in which a man might sympathize with a woman in "child-bed," or on the "man of humanity in Europe," who hears the terrible news of an earthquake that destroys the empire of China.[39] But the system of sympathy cannot easily be both a system of continuing conversation and a system that includes very distant individuals. This is the problem, again in Kitcher's terms, of "how large the population of these others is to be," or of who it is we see in the many mirrors of the self. It is a problem that is particularly poignant if Smith is set in his own world of friendship in the new British Empire.[40]

To return, then, to Smith's ideas in our own times. Smith was, in his own terms and in the terms of his early opponents, an effective critic of empire. He was not a consistent critic, and his rhetoric of oppression and rapacity was little more, from time to time, than the conventional idiom of one side or the other in the unending disputes over the constitution of the East India Company (or the Compagnie des Indes). But he described the inhabitants of India, at least, as very unchildlike, with a "great variety

---

[37] Smith, *The Theory of Moral Sentiments*, p. 10.
[38] Smith, *The Wealth of Nations*, pp. 559, 561, 626. On Hume's racism, see Rothschild, "The Atlantic Worlds of David Hume," pp. 422–429.
[39] Smith, *The Theory of Moral Sentiments*, pp. 110, 112, 136, 317.
[40] Philip Kitcher, "The Hall of Mirrors," 2004–2005 Romanell Lecture, *Proceedings and Addresses of the American Philosophical Association*, 79, no. 2 (November 2005), 67–84, at 69.

of manufactures," a "very moderate" land tax, and "extremely attentive" to roads and canals; "civilized, inoffensive and industrious," in the
words of his source, William Bolts, or a "commercial country" of "mild,
civilized, and polite people" with an "ancient constitution."[41] His own
dilemmas of empire, or of the insecurity of long-distance commerce and
long-distance imagination, are very similar to the dilemmas, still, of our
own times.

The vista of Smith in the British Empire may also cast some light on
an even more momentous charge that has been laid against him within
the culture wars or enlightenment wars of the twenty-first century. This
is the charge, in Akeel Bilgrami's words, of having been the hero of a
"thick notion of scientific rationality," the consequence of which, for very
large numbers of individuals, is a "pervasive and long-standing disenchantment of their world," a false direction, with its origins in the earlier
false choices of the seventeenth century.[42] It is an awesome charge, and it
is in at least one regard well justified. Smith, like Hume, had a less than
respectful view of the activity of reasoning (and of Sir Isaac Newton's
astronomical system, which he described as having acquired "the most
universal empire that was ever established in philosophy").[43] But he was
a devastating critic, again like Hume, of the "superstition" that ascribes
"the irregular events of nature" to "intelligent, though invisible beings –
to gods, demons, witches, genii, fairies." The dream of enlightenment, in
the sense of emancipation from the "reverence that approaches to fear,"
was at the heart of his own system or systems.[44]

The interesting question, it seems to me, is of the extent to which the
dream was itself a new enchantment of the world. The idea of a universal
human nature – a nature that is the nature of everyone without exception, savages and East India Company officials and slaves – is not (or at
least was not for Smith) a scientific idea. It was the idea of a value that
is in nature; that is the foundation for one or more sciences of mankind,
but that is not itself a value to be discovered by science. The metaphysical
character of these ideas was observed by the conservative critics of the

---

[41] Smith, *The Wealth of Nations*, pp. 683, 838, 839; William Bolts, *Considerations on
India Affairs; particularly respecting the present state of Bengal and its dependencies.
With a map of those countries, chiefly from actual surveys* (London, 1772), pp. 37, 90,
206, 228.

[42] Akeel Bilgrami, "Occidentalism, the Very Idea: An Essay on Enlightenment and
Enchantment," *Critical Inquiry*, 32 (Spring 2006), 381–411, at 406–407.

[43] "The History of Astronomy," in Smith, *Essays on philosophical subjects*, p. 104.

[44] Ibid., pp. 48–49.

French Enlightenment in their insight that it was man who had become the deity of the French Revolution. But it was evident, I think, to Smith and his friends as well – to the philosopher John Bruce, for example, in his evocation of the "Rights of Mankind as the proper Objects of the Moral Faculty."[45] To see Smith in the British Empire is to see the difficulties of this dream, and its grace.

---

[45] As Smith wrote in a recommendation for John Bruce's *Elements of the Science of Ethics*, "he and I differ a little, as David Hume and I used to do.... It is as free of Metaphysics as is possible for any work upon that subject to be. Its fault, in my opinion, is that it is too free of them." Letter of 7 May 1786 from Smith to Thomas Cadell in *The Correspondence of Adam Smith*, p. 296; John Bruce, *Elements of the Science of Ethics, on the Principle of Natural Philosophy* (London, 1786), p. 153.

8

Conquest, Commerce, and Cosmopolitanism in Enlightenment Political Thought

Sankar Muthu

In modern European political thought generally, and by the time of the "long eighteenth century" in particular, there is a striking awareness of the *global* reach of social, commercial, and political institutions and practices, as well as a belief that traditional moral categories might have to be rethought and transformed for the purposes of attending to such global concerns. Immanuel Kant noted the historical circumstances that made the idea of cosmopolitan justice politically relevant rather than absurdly utopian, and he suggested along these lines that "the community of nations of the earth has now gone so far that a violation of justice on one place of the earth is felt in all."[1] This awareness of the interconnectedness of societies and the formation of a transcontinental community of humankind has a long history that precedes, and is then greatly enhanced by, the European oceanic voyages in the 1490s westward to the Americas and eastward directly to India by way of the Cape of Good Hope.

[1] Immanuel Kant, *Toward Perpetual Peace* (1795), in *Practical Philosophy*, ed. and trans. Mary Gregor (Cambridge: Cambridge University Press, 1996), p. 330; Immanuel Kant, *Kants gesammelte Schriften, herausgegeben von der Preussischen Akademie der Wissenschaften zu Berlin* (Berlin: Walter de Gruyter, 1902–), vol. 8, p. 360. References to Kant in the text are to this German edition, cited by volume and page number. With occasional modifications, quotations are from the previously cited *Practical Philosophy* and from Immanuel Kant, *Toward Perpetual Peace and Other Writings on Politics, Peace, and History*, ed. Pauline Kleingeld and trans. David L. Colclasure (New Haven, Conn.: Yale University Press, 2006).

Many thanks to the participants at workshops and to the members of audiences at lectures who commented on portions of this chapter. I would like to dedicate this chapter to the memory of Terence Moore for his support of this volume and, more generally, for his life-long service to scholarship in the humanities.

In European political thought, these interconnections were often discussed in terms of the concept of commerce. The Latin concept of *commercium*, and the French, English, and German understandings of commerce that derive from it, refer not only to market trade and economic arrangements, but also to communication, exchange, and interaction more generally. One central feature of many modern theories of global interaction is the idea of a universal (and fundamentally sociable) community of humankind that either exists or can be brought into being by viewing oceans as connecting the peoples of the world. This is a key Enlightenment ideal of global commerce in part because of the view, held by many in this period, that humans are constitutively commercial beings – that is, they are fundamentally social and communicative, and they desire to engage in exchange and interaction with other humans generally and not just within their particular tribe or society. Nonetheless, these forms of contact were thought to be deeply problematic by many of the very thinkers who supported the idea of a global interactive community across borders. Such views about global connections in the eighteenth century were often rooted in concerns about empire, slavery, and transnational commercial domination. For some thinkers, these problems made it clear that there was no fundamental value to global communication and exchange; along these lines, Johann Gottlieb Fichte endorsed a form of national isolationism and autarky. Most Enlightenment thinkers, however, wanted to achieve what Fichte had concluded was both theoretically and practically impossible: preserving the benefits of global communication and exchange while making global domination and injustice less likely in the future. The political writings of (among others) Denis Diderot, Abbé Raynal, Adam Smith, Kant, and many eighteenth-century antislavery activists constitute an ambivalent strand of Enlightenment thought about global society, world citizenship, and transcontinental commerce, one that justifies and encourages global connections but that also counsels resistance against imperial and commercial exploitation and domination.

OCEANIC TIES AND THE UNIVERSAL SOCIETY OF HUMANITY

While the history of seaborne and oceanic trade is extensive, as Diderot, Smith, and Kant acknowledge in their many references to ancient seafaring trading routes, in many writings before the sixteenth to eighteenth centuries, oceans were described as providentially disruptive of contact, communication, and trade. That is, oceans were sometimes thought to keep distant peoples apart for good reason. Such views existed alongside sometimes flourishing transnational and distant trade, but they persisted in many writings and kept alive the idea, however much in tension with the actual practice of ancient and medieval societies, that contact with the customs, ideas, practices, and goods of foreign peoples could be corrupting or degrading, and could in addition lead to political instability and threats to communities' safety and security.[2]

Sometimes these concerns were raised while, at the same time, acknowledging the widespread seaborne trade that existed in ancient times. Thus, a verse in one of Horace's odes states: "All to no avail did God deliberately separate countries by the divisive ocean [*Oceano dissociabili*] if, in spite of that, impious boats go skipping over the seas that were meant to remain inviolate."[3] In a discussion of the founding of Rome that has some parallels with Plato's arguments in the *Laws*, Cicero inveighed against the mixing of peoples and the openness to outsiders that maritime cities made possible; thus, it was wise, in his view, for Rome to be situated close enough to the sea to gain material benefits without being on the sea itself. The "lust for trafficking and sailing the seas" disperses some of the citizens of maritime cities and exposes those who remain to "a certain corruption and degeneration of morals; for they receive a mixture of strange languages and customs, and import foreign ways as well as foreign merchandise."[4] For precisely such reasons, in presentations of political utopias, both classical and modern, the limits imposed by oceans and seas were usually thought to be sacrosanct. As J. G. A. Pocock has noted, "Since its dawn in Athens, Hellenic and European political philosophy had shown an occasional but powerful bias against seafaring and trade, a preference ... for keeping societies enclosed within the conditions it had devised for keeping them utopian communities."[5] Strikingly, in the long history of utopian reflections, the conception of an imagined perfect society was often that of a closed society.

[2] For a classic discussion of this feature of premodern thought and its eclipse, see Jacob Viner, *The Role of Providence in the Social Order* (Princeton, N.J.: Princeton University Press, 1972), pp. 27–54.

[3] The Latin reads: "nequiquam deus abscidit/ prudens Oceano dissociabili/ terras, si tamen impiae/ non tangenda rates transiliunt vada." Horace, *Odes and Epodes*, ed. and trans. Niall Rudd (Cambridge, Mass.: Harvard University Press, 2004), bk. I.3, pp. 30–31.

[4] Marcus Tullius Cicero, *De Re Publica, De Legibus*, trans. Clinton Walker Keyes (Cambridge, Mass.: Harvard University Press, 1928); *De Re Publica*, bk. II, iv.7–9 and v.10, pp. 117–121. Cf. Plato, *Laws*, IV, 704a–705b.

[5] J. G. A. Pocock, *Barbarism and Religion*, vol. 4: *Barbarians, Savages, and Empires* (Cambridge: Cambridge University Press, 2005), p. 307.

While such concerns never disappear, they are very much under assault for a wide variety of intellectual and political reasons in early modern Europe. The idea that oceans exist not to keep peoples apart, or to make it more difficult for them to interact with one another, but rather to allow and even to encourage them to engage in commerce and communication by providing a neutral expanse along which voyagers can traverse is given a strong defense and an extensive justification in early modern writings of the 1500s onward. Indeed, such commentaries in the sixteenth century can perhaps be seen as early articulations of what would eventually (and retrospectively) be deemed the "cosmopolitanism" of modern or Enlightenment thought.

A number of the earliest comments about the ethics of transnational, and especially transcontinental, contact and communication in the modern period occur in the context of imperial acquisition and the resulting debates over the legal and moral basis, if any, of European conquests. Thus, Francisco de Vitoria, the Dominican theologian of Salamanca, in a lecture about the Spanish conquests of the Americas, delivered in 1539, argues in favor of a right to engage in partnership and communication with others throughout the globe and across the oceans.[6] Vitoria argues that the norms of hospitality toward strangers and travelers would fail to have much force if "travellers were doing something evil by visiting foreign nations" (278). They most certainly are not, Vitoria argues, and in part because some vestigial traces of what was once the common ownership of the earth still remain. As he puts it, "in the beginning of the world, when all things were held in common, everyone was allowed to visit and travel through any land he wished. This right was clearly not taken away by the division of property; it was never the intention of nations to prevent humans' free mutual intercourse with one another by this division" (278). In particular, Vitoria goes on to note, "the open sea, rivers, and ports are the common property of all" (279). All this makes possible – in language that Vitoria draws from Roman law, in particular from Justinian's *Digest* – "a certain kinship among all humans" (280).

Arguing in a different imperial context – not about the Americas, but instead about European trading activities in the "Spice Islands" (southeast

---

[6] Francisco de Vitoria, "De Indis," in Vitoria, *Political Writings*, ed. Jeremy Lawrance and Anthony Pagden (Cambridge: Cambridge University Press, 1992), pp. 233–292. For contrasting interpretations of this aspect of Vitoria's thought, see the chapter by Anthony Pagden in this book; Georg Cavallar, *The Rights of Strangers* (Aldershot, England: Ashgate, 2002), chap. 2; Antony Anghie, *Imperialism, Sovereignty, and the Making of International Law* (Cambridge: Cambridge University Press, 2004), chap. 1.

Asia) – Hugo Grotius offered a rousing and influential defense of the *mare liberum*, the free seas. In 1609, Grotius made these arguments, we should recall, not to promote universal brotherhood – although he does refer to the "most praiseworthy bond of human fellowship" that makes possible engaging in reciprocal, mutual service to one another as humans across borders (8) – but as part of a legal brief in order to defend the interests of the Dutch East India Company, in particular the Company's aggressive seizure of a Portuguese ship in the straits of Singapore, a vessel that held an astonishingly valuable imperial cargo.[7] This lawyerly argument, however, ended up becoming, almost word for word, a chapter in *De Jure Praedae Commentarius*, one of Grotius's philosophical works, and it thus informs more broadly his treatment of the *ius gentium* (the law of nations or international law).[8]

In *Mare Liberum*, Grotius argued that it was God's will to bring peoples together in mutual commerce. "He wished human friendships to be engendered by mutual needs and resources, lest individuals deeming themselves entirely sufficient unto themselves should for that very reason be rendered unsociable" (7). Thus, we find here what is often at work in later Enlightenment arguments along these lines: a view of human sociability and the idea that oceanic commerce and mutual interchange and communication across borders put into effect the sociable character of humanity itself. These ties that exist across borders are characterized by Grotius as fundamentally in accord with nature itself, for the so-called trade winds make oceanic contact possible. As he asks, "doesn't the ocean, navigable in every direction with which God has encompassed all the earth, and the regular and the occasional winds which blow now from one quarter and now from another, offer sufficient proof that Nature has given to all peoples a right of access to all other peoples?" (8).

In the same period, in 1593, Richard Hooker makes some of the same arguments, but with an even greater emphasis on the idea of a *universal fellowship of humanity*. This was thought to be a community of humans not united by a single sovereign, but nonetheless still a recognizable body of sociable and interacting individuals bound together by the oceans and by what oceans made possible: contact, communication, the trade

---

[7] Hugo Grotius, *The Freedom of the Seas*, ed. James Brown Scott, trans. Ralph Van Deman Magoffin (New York: Oxford University Press, 1916). See also Hugo Grotius, *The Free Sea*, ed. David Armitage, trans. Richard Hakluyt (Indianapolis: Liberty Fund, 2004).

[8] Hugo Grotius, *Commentary on the Law of Prize and Booty*, ed. Martine Julia van Ittersum (Indianapolis: Liberty Fund, 2006), chap. XII. See Richard Tuck, *The Rights of War and Peace* (Oxford: Oxford University Press, 1999), pp. 78–94.

of goods, the exchange of ideas, the enlarging of our sensibilities, and the cultivation of our sociable capacities. Part of the basis of this view is the idea that human sociability knows no bounds in practice and ought to know no bounds; it is not, and it should not be, limited by language, customs, or sovereign borders.

In the *Laws of Ecclesiastical Polity*, Hooker writes that it is "a natural delight which man hath to transfuse from himself into others, and to receive from others into himself especially those things wherein the excellency of his kind doth most consist. The chiefest instrument of human communion therefore is speech, because thereby we impart mutually one to another the [concepts] of our reasonable understanding" (96–97). One might think that this need to interact, and especially to exchange speech and ideas, with others could be satisfied simply within the bounds of a civil society. But Hooker takes it as his task to argue precisely against that view, and instead to affirm a larger global society (again, not a sovereign one – that is, not a world state – but a society nonetheless), and he echoes here some of Cicero's more cosmopolitan arguments about the fellowship of humanity as a whole.[9] As Hooker argues, "notwithstanding" the sociability and communion that we can foster within a civil society, humans

are not satisfied but we covet (if it might be) to have a kind of society and fellowship even with all mankind. Which thing Socrates intending to signify professed himself a Citizen, not of this or that commonwealth, but of the world. And an effect of that very natural desire in us ... appeareth by the wonderful delight men have, some to visit foreign countries, some to discover nations not heard of in former ages, we all to know the affairs and dealings of other people, yea to be in league of amity with them: and this not only for traffic's sake, or to the end that when many are confederated each may make other the more strong, but for such cause also as moved the Queen of Sheba to visit Solomon.[10]

In the multiple (and nearly identical) versions of that biblical story, the queen of Sheba (of Arabia) traveled what was then taken to be a vast distance to see King Solomon simply, we are told, to learn about his society, the ways of his people, and the nature of his celebrated political

[9] Marcus Tullius Cicero, *De Officiis*, trans. Walter Miller (Cambridge, Mass.: Harvard University Press, 1975), bk. I, 49–53; see Cicero, *On Duties*, ed. M. T. Griffin and E. M. Atkins (Cambridge: Cambridge University Press, 1991), pp. 21–23: "the fellowship of the entire human race ... its bonding consists of reason and speech, which reconcile men to one another, through teaching, learning, communicating, debating and making judgements, and unite them in a kind of natural fellowship" (p. 21).
[10] Richard Hooker, *Of the Laws of Ecclesiastical Polity*, ed. Arthur Stephen McGrade (Cambridge: Cambridge University Press, 1989), p. 97 (bk. I, chap. 10).

rule.[11] Having tested Solomon on these issues and engaged in a dialogue about these political and social matters, and having exchanged various goods in trade, she then returned to Arabia – and, importantly, no conquest, civilizing mission, or commercial corruptions ensued. Such is the ideal type, then, as it is envisioned and elaborated by many defenders, of far-flung (and ultimately oceanic and transcontinental) contact, trade, and communication.

ENLIGHTENMENT ANXIETIES ABOUT GLOBAL INTERCONNECTIONS

This vision of universal fellowship was predictably attractive to many Enlightenment thinkers, and indeed, many of them believed that their own intellectual activities were helping to bring into being such a community, or at least one small version of it: what they so often referred to as the "republic of letters" that spanned multiple societies. Nonetheless, in the eighteenth century, there were strong concerns about global interconnections. The ideal of universal fellowship across borders and the belief that oceans (and deserts) could bring far-flung peoples together in exchange and interaction were still widely held, but the violence, exploitation, slavery, conquest, and occupation of societies that so often followed global voyaging created a deep ambivalence about the historical development, and the ongoing problems, of global commerce and communication. Indeed, the fact that Grotius's arguments about global commercial relations were made precisely to justify the Dutch East India Company's imperial activities, and the possibility that Vitoria made his own arguments about universal fellowship in ways that (whether he intended to or not) could be used to support conquest and the occupation of foreign lands, raise the question of whether Enlightenment norms of commerce could celebrate the idea of an interactive and universal community of humanity without, at the same time, legitimizing forms of exploitation and imperial rule that often followed these global voyages.

After Britain's decisive victories in the Seven Years War (perhaps the first truly world war), what we sometimes encounter even in British political thought, including in the writings of some of Britain's most eminent and widely read political thinkers, is not triumphalism but,

[11] 1 Kings 10:1–10:13; cf. 2 Chronicles 9:1–9:12. There are also brief references to the queen of Sheba's visit "from the ends of the earth" to King Solomon in Matthew 12:42 and Luke 11:31.

instead, notably, a tremendous sense of anxiety about global commerce and empire. It had been a standard part of many early modern ideologies of empire that a commercial and maritime empire was consistent with maintaining liberty at home, and thus that the traditional Roman and neo-Roman concerns about the great tensions between *imperium* and *libertas* could be kept at bay by this new form of modern commercial empire.[12] In the French intellectual context as well, some of the most influential theorists of transnational commerce, such as Montesquieu, argued that the sovereign practitioners of modern oceanic commerce, however aggressive and acquisitive, might be able to avoid the tendency toward despotism that usually plagued territorial empires of past ages. (It should be noted, however, that Montesquieu argued that commercial empires might also be characterized by the dangerous combination of taking offence too easily from other nations and cultivating a strident arrogance about the extent of their power abroad.[13]) It is striking, then, that the idea of maritime empire and commerce as congruent with liberty has much less hold over European political thinkers of the late eighteenth century.

Some of the criticisms of the global commercial order that we find in the late eighteenth century were especially concerned with the corrupting effects of far-flung transcontinental commercial and imperial depredations upon Europe itself. For example, Richard Price's commentary on global connections, in an addition made in 1777 to his tracts on civil liberty, was principally concerned with how the corrupting, exploitative, and imperial nature of global ties undermines the ability of European societies to rule themselves justly. In many such commentaries, the image of a corrupted or fallen Rome, and more broadly comparisons of modern voyaging and conquests with ancient empires, recur frequently. This was precisely the association that was meant to be severed by some early modern British and French ideologies of empire, but they reemerge in many late-eighteenth-century British and French writings. As Price notes:

---

[12] See David Armitage, *The Ideological Origins of the British Empire* (Cambridge: Cambridge University Press, 2000), chap. 4.

[13] As Montesquieu argues in Book 19 of the *Spirit of the Laws*, ed. and trans. Anne M. Cohler, Basia Carolyn Miller, and Harold Samuel Stone (Cambridge: Cambridge University Press, 1989), pp. 328, 329: "A commercial nation has a prodigious number of small, particular interests; therefore, it can offend and be offended in an infinity of ways. This nation would become sovereignly jealous and would find more distress in the prosperity of others than enjoyment in its own.... A naval empire has always given the peoples who have possessed it a natural pride, because, feeling themselves able to insult others everywhere, they believe that their power is as boundless as the ocean."

I cannot help mentioning here the addition which has been lately made to the power of the Crown by throwing into its hands the East-India Company. Nothing more unfavourable to the security of public liberty has been done since the Revolution. And should our statesmen, *thus strengthened by the patronage of the East, be farther strengthened by the patronage of the West*, they will indeed have no small reason for triumph and there will be little left to protect us against the encroachments and usurpations of power. Rome sunk into slavery in consequence of enlarging its territories and becoming the center of the wealth of conquered provinces, and the seat of universal empire. It seems the appointment of Providence that free states, when, not contented with self-government and prompted by the love of dominion, they make themselves masters of other states shall lose liberty at the same time that they take it away [from others] and, by subduing, be themselves subdued.[14]

When East and West are linked together by Europe, both oppression abroad and moral and political corruption within are thought to occur as a result of the flows of commerce and power that result from such extraordinary global connections. Imperial domination leads to self-domination and consequently imperils self-government. Whatever the concerns about the domination of peoples outside of Europe that Price expressed at such moments, his primary motivation, it seems, concerns the impact that such global interconnections have upon Europe itself.

Richard Price and Edmund Burke, who famously held such starkly opposed beliefs about the French Revolution (Burke's *Reflections on the Revolution in France* was occasioned by Price's defense of the Revolution), were on the issue of global connections, at least, remarkably similar in their views. Burke assessed the state of global commerce in 1793 in the following manner:

Can we say, that even at this very hour we are not invidiously aggrandized? We are already in possession of almost all the commerce of the world. Our Empire in India is an awful thing. If we should come to be in a condition not only to have all this ascendant in commerce, but to be absolutely able, without the least controul, to hold the commerce of all other Nations totally dependent upon our good pleasure, we may say that we shall not abuse this astonishing, and hitherto unheard of power. But every other Nation will think we shall abuse it. It is impossible but that sooner or later, this state of things must produce a combination against us which may end in our ruin.[15]

[14] Richard Price, "Two Tracts on Civil Liberty, the War with America, and The Debts and Finances of the Kingdom: with A General Introduction and Supplement," in *Political Writings*, ed. D. O. Thomas (Cambridge: Cambridge University Press, 1991), p. 99 (emphasis added).

[15] Edmund Burke, "Remarks on the Policy of the Allies," in E. Burke, *Three memorials on French affairs written in the years 1791, 1792 and 1793 by the late Right Hon. Edmund Burke* (London: F. and C. Rivington, 1797), p. 182.

This is nothing less than what Enlightenment thinkers were so often fearful of: the threat of universal monarchy (or universal empire) and the wars and oppression that would result from trying to achieve it and from attempting to combat it. But this is a distinctive, if not an entirely novel, twist on an old idea: a form of empire that results from global commerce and interconnections, from commercial practices and commercial ties that were thought to be enlightened, and yet that might lead to the ruin of Britain and, by implication, to the ruin of European civilization itself. Global commerce, then, could place the very possibility of building and maintaining moderate and peaceful (or "enlightened") societies at risk.

As noted earlier, in early modern British and French political thought up to and including the early and mid-eighteenth century, the idea of empire as maritime and commercial could be used to assuage the fear that imperial and trading activities abroad would lead to a loss of liberty at home. By the late eighteenth century, however, that narrative of commercial and seaborne empire would no longer be comforting for at least some of the political thinkers who reflected upon global connections, transcontinental commerce, and far-flung imperial power that extended across the oceans to lands in every quarter of the globe. Early modern ideologies of empire at times sought to extinguish traditional Roman and neo-Roman concerns about the tensions between *libertas* and *imperium*. Reflections upon the global dimensions of commerce and empire in the late eighteenth century seem to bring back these older concerns that were at least somewhat successfully displaced by earlier ideologies of empire, but not, it seems, in a way that amounted simply to a revival of the classical and neo-classical concerns. Despite Price's invocation of Rome, oceanic trade and *imperium* in the late eighteenth century could foster a distinctive set of anxieties and ideologies about global connections that concerned not the military threat to self-governance at home, but rather the transcontinental flows of moral and political corruption and aggrandizing power from which powerful navies and oceanic distances would offer little protection.[16]

---

[16] As J. G. A. Pocock notes about Raynal's *Histoire*: "The whole enterprise of commerce begins to look self-defeating when viewed in an oceanic and global setting." J. G. A. Pocock, *Barbarism and Religion*, vol. 4: *Barbarians, Savages and Empires* (Cambridge: Cambridge University Press, 2005), p. 255. Cf. Sunil Agnani's insightful analysis: S. Agnani, "*Doux Commerce, Douce Colonisation*: Diderot and the Two Indies of the French Enlightenment," in *The Anthropology of the Enlightenment*, ed. Larry Wolff and Mario Cipolloni (Stanford, Calif.: Stanford University Press, 2007), pp. 65–84.

Enlightenment thinkers could have responded to the horrendous injustices and corruption that global interconnections gave rise to by returning to the isolationism of those who had decried voyaging and transcultural contact and who had pointed to the seas and oceans as useful impediments to human arrogance. One Enlightenment thinker to defend such a view at length was J. G. Fichte in his treatise of 1800, *The Closed Commercial State*, in which he asserted that political societies should aim for complete self-sufficiency, and that in such a world, "the members of ... [each] closed nation ... will live only among one another, and will have extremely little contact with foreigners; hence that nation will retain by these measures its own peculiar mode of life, institutions, and customs, and it will love with a strong attachment its fatherland."[17] As one would expect, the strategy of endorsing national isolationism and autarky is not how most Enlightenment thinkers responded to the challenges of global commerce; indeed, for most of them, proposals like Fichte's were not only unworkable in practice but also, in some fundamental sense, dehumanizing. Among most writers whom we retrospectively describe as Enlightenment thinkers, there was a deep commitment to the cosmopolitan connections that were thought to follow from a belief in the centrality of sociability and communication to humanity itself. Those who saw themselves as members of a kind of republic of letters (whether radical or reformist) that stretched across borders were often motivated by an intellectual sensibility that embraced an openness to flows of ideas and goods across borders and thus to some vision of transnational commerce and communication.

Ultimately, though, this created something of a paradox. In the late Enlightenment, it was becoming increasingly clear that the process of "enlightenment" – of enlightened reform of social and political institutions, practices, and mores – depended in part upon commerce, and the connections across societies that it made possible, but that *global* commerce especially was destroying any possibility that societies (both

---

[17] J. G. Fichte, "The Closed Commercial State," in *The Political Thought of the German Romantics*, ed. H. S. Reiss (Oxford: Blackwell, 1955), pp. 86–102, at p. 102. On this fascinating and understudied work, see Isaac Nakhimovsky, *The Closed Commercial State: Perpetual Peace and Commercial Society from Rousseau to Fichte* (Princeton, N.J.: Princeton University Press, 2011). Clearly, Fichte had moved away from his earlier sympathetic engagement with Kant's cosmopolitan right; see J. G. Fichte, *Foundations of Natural Right According to the Principles of the Wissenschaftslehre*, ed. Frederick Neuhouser (Cambridge: Cambridge University Press, 2000), pp. 332–334. For an interpretation of this shift, see David James, "Fichte's Reappraisal of Kant's Theory of Cosmopolitan Right," *History of European Ideas*, 36 (2010), 61–70.

European and non-European) would become truly enlightened. Putting this in terms of the concept of commercial humanity, what was needed to bring about the flourishing of this humanity – its communicative and sociable nature – was itself destructive and corrupting of humanity. Humanity was thus enabled (at least potentially) by global commerce and communication, and yet in practice was degraded by it. There was an awareness of this fundamental tension among many late-eighteenth-century political thinkers, who were consequently deeply disturbed by this paradox and who responded to it in different ways.

RESPONDING TO THE PROBLEMS OF GLOBAL COMMERCE

The Enlightenment historiography of global travel, trade, contact, communication, and indeed often conquest, occupation, and slavery, includes many works that deal with some aspects of these developments and practices, but only in some key late Enlightenment writings can one find philosophically informed and empirically detailed accounts of the wide array of transcontinental connections from the 1490s onward. The two most significant texts along these lines, both initially published in the 1770s, are Adam Smith's *An Inquiry into the Causes of the Wealth of Nations* and Abbé Raynal's *Philosophical and Political History of European Settlements and Commerce in the Two Indies* (a massive multivolume work published under Raynal's name but composed anonymously by many philosophes, including Diderot, who wrote many of its antislavery and anti-imperial passages).[18] Both of these works offer trenchantly

---

[18] [Abbé] Guillaume-Thomas Raynal, *Histoire philosophique et politique des établissements et du commerce des Européens dans les deux Indes*, 10 vols. (Genève: Jean-Leonard Pellet, 1780). The *Histoire* was first published in 1772. All of Diderot's contributions can be found from the 1780 edition onward. Anthony Strugnell and a team of scholars whom he has commissioned are now at work on a modern critical edition of the *Histoire* that will be published by the Voltaire Foundation. Since this edition is in its early stages, there is no standard edition that is used to cite the *Histoire*; moreover, volume and page numbers differ from edition to edition. Thus, I have cited Raynal's *Histoire* by book and chapter (the *Histoire* is divided into nineteen books, a division that is consistent across many editions). I have used the following editions: [Abbé] Guillaume-Thomas Raynal, *Histoire philosophique et politique des établissements et du commerce des Européens dans les deux Indes* (Genève: Jean-Leonard Pellet, 1780), 10 volumes; and [Abbé] Guillaume-Thomas Raynal, *A Philosophical and Political History of the Settlements and Trade of the Europeans in the East and West Indies*, trans. J. O. Justamond (London: W. Strahan and T. Cadell, 1783), 8 volumes. A small selection of Diderot's contributions to the *Histoire* is available in a contemporary English translation; see Denis Diderot, *Political Writings*, ed. John Hope Mason and Robert Wokler (Cambridge: Cambridge University Press, 1992), pp. 169–214. The passages from the *Histoire* that I quote in this

critical analyses of global relations in the modern world, but they also offer some brief reflections about how a deeply unjust global system of commerce and interaction might be reformed in future generations.

Notably, Raynal, Diderot, and Adam Smith believed that Europe had become too corrupted by global interconnections to undertake serious reform itself, and so it would be resistance from the non-European world over time that would help produce the conditions for at least some semblance of global justice. This resistance, they believed, might come about precisely because of global commerce and communication, as a result of the very processes that, in their day and in their view, were so deeply unjust. Global connections could be made more just in the future, then, only if non-European nations gained power over time from commercial connections and used that power to create conditions of equity.

In the *History of the Two Indies*, Diderot calls upon his readers to restore what he calls the "happy fraternity that constituted the delight of the first ages," which presents some sense of his ideal of commerce:

Let people, in whatever country fate has placed them, under whatever government they live, whatever religion they practice, communicate as freely with each other as the inhabitants of one hamlet with those of a neighbouring one ... that is to say, without duties, without formalities, without predilections. (XIX, 6)

This idyllic vision of an open commerce, broadly understood to signify the free trade not only of goods, but also of ideas and sentiments, already exists, in his opinion, in small and fragmented ways throughout the globe. Diderot's hope is that global commerce might, in part, create and sustain the crucibles for future reform and perhaps even revolution. The islands of liberty sustained by commercial interactions, as ideas and goods exchange and circulate, could ideally be used over many generations to resist, to battle against, and ultimately to reform other aspects of global commerce that are oppressive, that enervate political energies, and that deny liberty both to those in European nations and to those abroad.

Ultimately, then, global commerce on this Enlightenment view is a double-edged sword. For Diderot, political reform depends crucially upon

chapter have all been checked against the 1780 Pellet edition. The issue of the authorship of each passage and the possibly contrasting views of the contributors are complex matters that I do not address here. In this chapter, I refer sometimes to Diderot and Raynal together and at other times I focus exclusively upon Diderot's contributions. On these matters, see Yves Benot, "Diderot, Pechmeja, Raynal et l'anticolonialisme," *Europe*, 41 (1963), 137–153; and Michèle Duchet, *Diderot et l'Histoire des deux Indes ou l'Écriture Fragmentaire* (Paris: François Maspero, 1971).

individuals becoming sensible of their own freedom in order to break free from the psychological "chains" that limit their ability to assess critically their own conditions. He suggests that "humans are only sensible of their freedom when they engage in commercial interaction" (V, 33). Rather than the material gains and luxuries that commerce yields, and the productivity behind them, the genuine improvement to human welfare that global commerce and communication enable lies instead in their potential to change individuals' sense of their own condition, a condition that in part is corrupted and oppressed by commerce but that could nevertheless be reformed by the communicative and material interactions that global commerce itself makes possible. Diderot's disposition toward global commerce – one that led him to draw out the diverse strands of commercial practices and their varying social consequences – makes possible the view that some such strands could be set in opposition to others. But all of this would be most likely to occur not in European societies that had thoroughly corrupted and degraded themselves, and that had set up wealthy and powerful elites who seemed determined never to yield to policies that would be in the best interests of both their societies and humanity as a whole; rather, the non-European world would have to be humanity's hope for progress in the future.

Diderot's views about combatting slavery illustrate this well. In the *Histoire*, he argues that Europeans have become so corrupted by the wealth and the luxuries that the global system of slavery provides that they will never dismantle such a system voluntarily. Ultimately, slaves will have to use the arts of oppression of their masters against them in order to achieve liberty. Diderot asserts that slaves will thus rise up violently, break their chains, slaughter their former masters, and form their own societies. Along these lines, what would become a celebrated prophecy of the *Histoire* stated that a "Black Spartacus" would emerge to liberate slaves and to promote true freedom in the New World (XI, 24).

Adam Smith, as a result of his intensively critical analysis of the modern development of global commerce, was also deeply pessimistic about whether international trading companies and the vast system of global inequality and corruption that they helped to build in league with their client states could ever be challenged effectively from within European countries.[19] Smith argues emphatically that the public interests of both

---

[19] In the following few paragraphs, I draw upon Sankar Muthu, "Adam Smith's Critique of International Trading Companies: Theorizing 'Globalization' in the Age of Enlightenment," *Political Theory*, 36, no. 2 (April 2008), 185–212.

European and non-European nations have been "sacrificed to the interest of *those* merchants," namely, the merchants of the international joint stock companies. (IV.vii.b.49; emphasis added).[20] Smith understood, therefore, that such international companies and their corporate and governmental allies would not easily be reformed. In his view, eliminating the colonial context within which they operated would be a significant improvement. Smith states explicitly that European powers should simply stop engaging in imperial fantasies and focus instead on their own societies' problems. But he realized that such hopes were, in his day, wildly utopian, even though the freeing of all colonies would be not only just but also beneficial for all concerned.

In addition, establishing treaties of commerce that would genuinely bring about transnational exchanges, with truly open and fair competition, would no doubt be "more advantageous to the great body of the people, though less so to the merchants" (IV.vii.c.66), and he thus was fully aware that any proposal to shore up the economic and political health of even only European countries, which had ravaged *themselves* by their imperial exploits and mercantilist policies, would have to take on powerful company, merchant, and state interests. Smith's analysis made it clear that this was extremely unlikely. Even with regard to Britain specifically, the country that Smith believed had made the most progress domestically toward instituting a system of natural liberty, the corruption of powerful company and merchant interests made the goal of a truly free commerce impossible. As Smith puts it:

> To expect, indeed, that the freedom of trade should ever be entirely restored in Great Britain, is as absurd as to expect that an Oceana or Utopia should ever be established in it. Not only the prejudices of the publick, but what is much more unconquerable, the private interests of many individuals, irresistibly oppose it. (IV.ii.43; 471)

Ultimately, for Smith, the idea that European countries and international companies would reform themselves is a notion that only a "visionary enthusiast" could seriously entertain.

In Smith's view, we should look not to economic reform as such or to more enlightened ideas taking hold among the powerful classes of Europe

[20] Adam Smith, *An Inquiry into the Nature and Causes of the Wealth of Nations*, ed. R. H. Campbell and A. S. Skinner, textual ed. W. B. Todd, 2 vols. (Indianapolis: Liberty Fund, 1981; Oxford: Clarendon Press, 1976). Citations from the *Wealth of Nations* are in the main text and follow the standard practice of listing book, chapter, section, and paragraph numbers; I have also cited the page number(s) from the Oxford/Liberty Classics edition.

(both of which are unlikely to happen, in his view); rather, he argues, we should look to possible changes in political power in the international sphere. In the final analysis, then, Smith believed that only greater equality of power among nations throughout the world could yield conditions of respect and foster global justice. Smith's hope, as he states explicitly, is that Europe will grow weaker and non-European countries will grow stronger, thereby creating with *mutual fear* the conditions that the norms of justice themselves cannot bring about. Intriguingly, Smith believed that further global commerce itself, even within a corrupt mercantilist system of international political economy, would help over time to empower the weak. As Smith writes:

> [N]othing seems more likely to establish this equality of force [among European and non-European nations] than that mutual communication of knowledge and of all sorts of improvements which an extensive commerce from all countries to all countries naturally, or rather necessarily, carries along with it. (IV.vii.c.80)

Smith's hope, then, offered in just a couple of sentences in the context of an otherwise unremittingly grim account of international political economy, was that global commerce over many centuries (or perhaps over millennia) would yield greater equality of political power internationally that could begin to realize, however imperfectly, what he took to be the sacred right of commercial and communicative liberty exercised globally across borders.

   This is still a rather severe vision because it is the prospect of mutual fear, rather than mutual friendship, that does much of the work of ensuring that nations will exploit one another less often and less severely in the future. In an ideal world, Smith writes, "commerce ... ought naturally to be, among nations, as among individuals, a bond of union and friendship." As we have seen, this is the vision of the universal community of humankind. However, in a nonideal context – more specifically, in the nonutopian world of Smith's own time and even in his imagined future – he notes bluntly that commerce is instead "the most fertile source of discord and animosity," and thus presumably the greater equality of force among nations that he envisions in the future would produce not a union of friendship, but a second-best alternative that depends upon the *countervailing animosities* that geopolitical equity would make possible (IV.iii.c.9; 493). Peoples might hold each other in check if non-European nations, in particular, become more powerful over time.

BRITISH ANTISLAVERY ACTIVISTS AND THE SUGAR BOYCOTT

A contrasting vision of how to reform global relations was offered by British antislavery activists in the late 1780s and 1790s. The history of the abolitionist movement, the movement to end the British slave trade, which was seen by most of its proponents to be the first stage in what would be the eventual emancipation of slaves, and thus the end of the institution of slavery itself, is often symbolically viewed as having been launched by a now celebrated meeting that took place on May 22, 1787. A small committee of citizens (just a dozen people) formed itself that day into an antislavery group and drew up a plan to oppose Britain's participation in the slave trade. At the time, there was virtually no organized resistance to the slave trade in Britain; indeed, only a relatively small number of mostly Quakers (themselves a Dissenting group, and thus marginal to British society) had written against both the trade and the institution of slavery itself, though (up to that point) without any discernible effect. But what was in May 1787 a fringe movement became within a few years a widespread national mass movement, largely organized and run by that very committee, and ultimately involving hundreds of thousands of Britons, most of whom had never participated directly in politics before.[21] The writings of some of these activists constitute significant and distinctive contributions to Enlightenment discourses of transnational commerce and global interconnections.

Unlike Raynal, Diderot, and Adam Smith, who were read and regularly cited and quoted by antislavery pamphleteers, the most radical of the abolitionist activists in this period argued that the system of global commerce could indeed be reformed by Europeans themselves, if only they came to the realization that they were morally implicated in the oppression and exploitation of these global ties as a result of their consumption of slave-produced goods, such as sugar, which had rapidly become one of the staple items in most British households. In contrast,

---

[21] For a narrative history of the British abolitionist and antislavery movement, see Adam Hochschild, *Bury the Chains: Prophets and Rebels in the Fight to Free an Empire's Slaves* (New York: Houghton Mifflin, 2005). For recent scholarly accounts of the national and imperial dimensions of the British abolitionist movement, see Christopher Leslie Brown, *Moral Capital: Foundations of British Abolitionism* (Chapel Hill: University of North Carolina Press, 2006); David Brion Davis, *Inhuman Bondage: The Rise and Fall of Slavery in the New World* (Oxford: Oxford University Press, 2006), chap. 12; and Seymour Drescher, *Abolition: A History of Slavery and Antislavery* (Cambridge: Cambridge University Press, 2009), chap. 8.

Diderot and Smith focused their moral criticisms primarily upon elites: monarchs, states, plantation owners, international trading companies, wealthy merchants, and manufacturing and professional associations. This was a group that stretched across borders from the plantations of the West Indies, to Britain, to continental Europe, to India, and to the Spice Islands – and this powerful network of merchants and state officials had, in Smith's and Diderot's view, collectively captured European state power and were dictating the terms of domestic and foreign policy to their own narrow, private advantage, and against the true interests of both European and non-European societies.

While this concentrated moral responsibility among a relatively small group of individuals and institutions, simultaneously it disempowered most others. Diderot and Smith both thought that it would be nearly impossible for most Europeans to challenge or to dislodge this power. The reform would have to come from without, from the non-European world. Antislavery activists, however, argued that the moral responsibility lay with the mass of people who bought blood-soaked goods, to use their imagery, and while this was a shocking and distressing thought to many Britons at the time, it was also empowering, for it meant that the people as a whole had the power to reform the system of global commerce through morally informed choices about consumption.

The most influential pamphlet to make these arguments was by an antislavery activist named William Fox. His "Address to the People of Great Britain" was published in 1791 and sold an extraordinary 70,000 copies in four months.[22] Fox notes that both the slave trade and slavery itself constitutes "a system of cruelty which it is painful even to recite" (155). He hopes for a time when Britons "shall no longer range the world to increase the misery of mankind." That extensive reach from Britain to all quarters of the globe yields a set of injustices that both oppresses others and barbarizes Britain itself, ironically in the very so-called age of Enlightenment. As Fox writes, "we, in an enlightened age, have greatly surpassed, in brutality and injustice, the most ignorant and barbarous ages: and while we are pretending to the finest feelings of humanity, are exercising unprecedented cruelty" (155). Fox argues that legislative means to end the slave trade and then to abolish slavery itself could not

---

[22] William Fox, *An Address to the People of Great Britain, on the Propriety of Abstaining from West India Sugar and Rum* (London: M. Gurney, 1791), reprinted in *Slavery, Abolition and Emancipation: Writings in the British Romantic Period*, vol. 2: *The Abolition Debate*, ed. Peter J. Kitson (London: Pickering & Chatto, 1999).

be counted on for the simple reason that many members of Parliament were either investors in the West India trade or were themselves plantation owners at a distance. In addition, he argues that colonial societies often saw themselves as largely independent of parliamentary decisions, so that even if legislation could be proposed and passed in London, it might not take effect in the Caribbean or on the western coast of Africa. "The Legislature," Fox writes, "having refused to interpose, *the people* are now necessarily called on" to act (155, emphasis added).

The main reason, in Fox's view, that the people should act is that they themselves are morally to blame for the injustices of global commerce and of slavery in particular. As he argues,

let us not think, that the crime rests alone with those who conduct the traffic, or the legislature by which it is protected. If we purchase the commodity we participate in the crime. The slave-dealer, the slave-holder, and the slave-driver, are virtually the agents of the consumer ... [the consumer] is the original cause, the first mover in the horrid process. (155–156)

The global connections of the eighteenth century include the moral ties and the moral guilt of transnational commerce, but also, as a result, the ability to exonerate oneself by acting as an enlightened consumer. Fox calls upon consumers to boycott West India sugar and rum, and he offers the economic analysis that this will create a glut of sugar on the world market, thereby reducing the price and the profits from sugar, which will ultimately limit the ability of planters to purchase and import slaves. In making this case, Fox deals with the most popular counterarguments that were already circulating: that there is a moral right to consume goods as long as one does not directly engage in injustice. Fox asserts that because consumers are the prime movers of this branch of global commerce, they are, in his terms, "partners in crime." To those who argue that the vast distance between Britain and Africa and the Caribbean means that Britons have no special duty to African slaves, Fox responds that degrees of connection and geographical distance make no difference in morality. "The offices of humanity and functions of justice" are not "circumscribed by geographical boundaries" (160). African slaves, Fox argues, are our brethren – fellow members of a society larger than simply the British nation. Thus, in another political context, we encounter the reemergence of the ideal of the universal community of humankind. Moreover, while the ties of global commerce might be vast in terms of distance and the number of middlemen, this is still a chain of criminality that, in Fox's view, is rooted in theft, robbery, and often murder. Thus, simply by consuming sugar, we are "accessaries to the murder before the fact; as by receiving the produce of [slave] labour, we are accessaries to the robbery, after the fact" (159).

Fox's pamphlet helped to convince large numbers of Britons to abstain from sugar and rum. Historians estimate that roughly 400,000 Britons at the height of the boycott had stopped purchasing sugar.[23] These were impressive numbers to be sure, but far more people would have had to boycott in order to produce Fox's intended effect. In the end, Diderot's concern may well have been insightful: luxuries from global commerce had either blinded people to their connections to the sources of such goods or, worse, had made them immune to the sufferings of distant others, even in those cases when Europeans could be enlightened as to their global and moral connections to oppression abroad.

Still, the sugar boycott helped strengthen the antislavery movement, and it publicized the deep connections that Britons now had to many millions of people in different continents. Ultimately, legislative action was essential, but Parliament was in part responding to a large-scale public movement. Thus, the idea that the people as such had acted was, in some respects, accurate. The slave trade was ended by an act of Parliament in 1807, although slavery itself would not be abolished in all British territories until 1833.

In the interim, the larger issue for many antislavery activists was to set forth a plan for the future that would make it clear how global slave systems of commerce could be replaced by trade among free nations, including independent African and Caribbean nations. Thus, they rejected the possibility of less trade or fewer ties with other continents. Their vision for what had earlier been described as a universal society of humankind, however, was by no means thoroughly egalitarian. This was the side of the antislavery movement that could treat commerce as a kind of civilizing agent and that aimed to transform what were taken to be traditional African societies into commercial societies. A program directed largely by European activists could easily shift, in this way, from an egalitarian movement to a hierarchical project in which Britons, in this case, would play a paternal role in cultivating African societies to fully realize their commercial spirit.

Thomas Clarkson, the most influential of the antislavery activists (and one of the dozen individuals at the 1787 antislavery meeting), was

---

[23] For example, see Seymour Drescher's analysis of the evidence in *Capitalism and Antislavery: British Mobilization in Comparative Perspective* (Oxford: Oxford University Press, 1987), pp. 79ff.

legendary for traveling across England on horseback to convince his fellow countrymen of the injustice of slavery. He carried with him a bag that contained samples of iron slave shackles and instruments of torture that slave-ship captains and slave owners had used. Yet he also carried, in the same bag, samples of African agricultural goods and textiles to show that Britain could carry on a profitable trade with free African peoples. In his writings, he argued both that Africans possessed the spirit of commerce, thus treating African societies as fundamentally no different than European societies, but also that indigenous African peoples are "at best ignorant" of the various "mechanical arts," so their tremendous potential as commercial peoples would have to be brought into being with European help and oversight.[24]

No European figure of the eighteenth century could plausibly be deemed more humanitarian or considered a greater hero of the antislavery movement than Thomas Clarkson, and yet, replacing slave commerce with free commerce meant, in his view, "introducing" Africans to commerce. Global commerce, understood in this sense, was a civilizing agent, one that would not buttress but instead *replace* slavery and far-flung empire. Such an idea would soon be theoretically elaborated by one of the most implacable opponents of slavery and empire in French Enlightenment thought: the marquis de Condorcet. As Condorcet argues in his *Sketch on the Progress of the Human Mind*, if one were to survey the history of European activities in the non-European world, then what would emerge is "how our trade monopolies, our treachery, our murderous contempt for men of another colour or creed ... have destroyed the respect and goodwill that" – as he goes on to note – "the superiority of our knowledge and the benefits of our commerce at first won for us in the eyes of the inhabitants" of the non-European world.[25] Thus, in addition to presenting a blistering and heartfelt criticism of European empires and commercial enterprises, Condorcet argues that global commerce, without slavery and territorial empires, could be and should be a civilizing enterprise undertaken by Europeans trading and living abroad.

Condorcet suggests that corrupt military enterprises, imperial regimes, and international trading companies in the non-European world should

---

[24] Thomas Clarkson, *An Essay on the Impolicy of the African Slave Trade* (London: J. Phillips, 1788), p. 8.

[25] Jean Antoinne Nicolas de Caritat, marquis de Condorcet, *Sketch for a Historical Picture of the Progress of the Human Mind* [*Equisse d'un tableau historique des progrès de l'esprit humain*, originally published 1795], trans. June Barraclough (New York: Noonday Press, 1955), p. 176.

be replaced by communities of European merchants who engage in commerce as part of a nonimperial civilizing mission. Hence, "what have been no better than the counting-houses of brigands will become colonies of citizens propagating throughout Africa and Asia the principles and the practice of liberty, knowledge and reason, that they have brought from Europe" (177). At the very end of the eighteenth century, Condorcet's understanding of the replacement of conquest, slavery, and monopolistic trading companies with free transnational commerce offers an antislavery, (arguably) an anti-imperialist, and yet a paternalistic and hierarchical civilizing narrative of commercial development. This would be a different kind of global connection, certainly not one based upon slavery, but one that by the mid-nineteenth century would become mutatis mutandis the basis of renewed European imperial ideologies that justified conquest and rule throughout much of Africa and beyond.

KANT: COSMOPOLITAN CONNECTIONS AND PRODUCTIVE RESISTANCE IN GLOBAL RELATIONS

Thus far, we have encountered three distinct Enlightenment perspectives on how best to counter the imperial and domineering corruptions of global connections: (1) a view that denies any fundamental value to global commerce and that accordingly endorses national isolationism and autarky; (2) an account of global commerce as a (putatively) nonimperial, European-led civilizing mission that will spread the ideals of liberty abroad; and (3) an affirmation of a cosmopolitan vision of global exchange and communication but by means of a future balance of power among peoples that would be brought about by non-European resistance against European commercial, military, and political power.

Immanuel Kant's arguments in favor of cosmopolitan right, against conquest and empire, and in favor of a plurality of political communities (and, accordingly, against a world state) place him, broadly speaking, within the third Enlightenment tradition of theorizing global commerce. Although Kant's political thought is often presented as strongly internationalist (indeed, sometimes as naively so), Kant affirms cosmopolitan and global commercial norms by endorsing the idea of rival communities and, accordingly, he values resistance by non-European nations – both by countries such as China and Japan and by hunting and pastoral ("nomadic") nations.[26] In this sense, Kant's approach to theorizing

---

[26] For a nuanced reading of Kant as an imperial civilizationist – one that is based, in my view, on mistaken interpretations both of Kant's view of civilization (discussed further

global connections has much in common with the particular strand of Enlightenment thought on these issues that includes Raynal, Diderot, and Adam Smith, a view that could be characterized as a "cosmopolitanism of countervailing powers." An appreciation of the international and cosmopolitan features of Kant's thought requires, first, an analysis of his arguments about what is valuable about global exchange; second, an account of the problems that have arisen, in Kant's view, as a result of increasing global connections; third, an examination of Kant's Rousseauian concerns about civilization, and thus an analysis of why Kant did not favor commerce among individuals and peoples because of any commitment to increasing or spreading civilization, along the lines of what Condorcet had recommended, for example; and fourth, an interpretation of Kant's arguments in favor of rival communities, and of a certain kind of antagonism among peoples, that is, of a "productive resistance" between nations.

The notion of commerce as interaction is bound up, for Kant, as it was so often in Enlightenment writings, with the exchange of goods; as we have seen, understandings of communication and of trade tend to run together and to inform one another very closely in this period. The importance of communication as such is emphasized by Kant in a number of writings: he argues in *Theory and Practice*, for example, that "it is a natural calling of humanity to communicate with one another, especially in what concerns people generally" (8:305). Among the things that tend to concern people generally is their survival and sustenance, which can be greatly aided by trade. In *Toward Perpetual Peace*, he asserts that the various articles of trade, such as salt, probably first brought together peoples in sustained communicative relations with one another. As Kant writes, "the first articles, everywhere in demand, of a trade among various peoples ... first brought [them] into a peaceable relation to each other

---

later on) and of the function of Kant's theory of progress and philosophy of history within his broader political philosophy (as I have argued in *Enlightenment against Empire* (Princeton, N.J.: Princeton University Press, 2003), pp. 162–169), as well as a lack of recognition of Kant's explicit defense, in *The Metaphysics of Morals*, of "non-civilized" nomadic ways of life as no less valuable than other collective ways of life (discussed later) – see James Tully, "The Kantian Idea of Europe: Critical and Cosmopolitan Perspectives," in *The Idea of Europe*, ed. Anthony Pagden (Cambridge: Cambridge University Press, 2002), pp. 331–358, reprinted in James Tully, *Public Philosophy in a New Key*, vol. 2: *Imperialism and Civic Freedom* (Cambridge: Cambridge University Press, 2008), pp. 15–42. Intriguingly, the analysis of Kant's theory of global connections that I offer here has something in common with – and thus could be seen as an early, Enlightenment theorization of – what Tully persuasively and insightfully analyzes as the contemporary practice of "glocalisation" (ibid., p. 300).

and so into understanding [and], community ... with one another, even with the most distant" (8:364, emphasis added). In the *Metaphysics of Morals*, he speculates – again, in common with many earlier defenders of commercial interaction – that while the seas and oceans "might seem to remove nations from any community with one another, they are [in fact] the arrangements of nature most favouring their commerce by means of navigation" (6:352). Kant also famously contends, as Montesquieu and others had argued, that the "spirit of commerce" creates a mutual self-interest among nations not to go to war and to resolve international conflicts as often as possible by mediation, not due to moral aims but because of what he calls "the power of money"; this too can help to unite nations (8:368).

In Kant's view, there is potentially another kind of commercial check, as it were, on states' warlike and conquering activities, and this can be seen as a complementary effect of the power of money. While the power of money can lead to a sense of mutual self-interest that might cause nations to mediate conflicts peacefully, it can also compel states to avoid war when they have become bankrupted by debt. National debt and the relationship between debt and warmaking were central topics in Enlightenment debates about transnational commerce; in this context, Kant argues that perpetual peace can only exist if no states continue to raise national debts to finance war. He contends that the kind of easy money that debt makes possible fuels wars in the most pernicious manner, since the subjects of states do not pay the cost of the wars themselves. Thus, their estimation of the cost of war is hidden by a national debt that only later generations will confront. Debt financing of wars might, however, in Kant's view, be undone through the overuse of debt. Kant argues, in the *Idea for a Universal History*, that "the ever-growing burden of debt" will lead to situations in which "the repayment of [such a debt will] become immeasurable," and that this will produce the upheaval of a severe debt crisis; if that happens, Kant writes, "in any one state in our part of the world, [which is] so linked in its commercial activities to other nations, [this] will have [reverberations] in all other states" (8:28). As a result, he contends that many states would likely offer themselves as judges or mediators for international disputes to try to put an end to the ceaseless wars that produce a series of financial shocks and debt crises, which can now never be contained in one or a few nations given the close commercial connections of so many nations throughout the world. These "structural revolutions," as Kant calls them, might be the first early steps toward the ultimate formation of a voluntary congress of states. Thus, here, too, Kant theorizes the power of money, but in a negative form: not to enhance short-term profits, but to avoid recurring global debt crises and financial collapses (8:28).

All of this needs to be balanced against the injustices and violence that Kant also notes are brought about in part by commerce, by increasing connections among peoples. The agents of commerce can also be the agents of slavery, of conquest, of the expropriation of goods and lands, and of mass exploitation. This is yet another side of the power of money; overall, then, Kant offers a nuanced understanding of modern global commerce that has much in common with the arguments of Adam Smith, Raynal, and Diderot. Kant's political thought is similarly ambivalent toward the rise of global commerce: the growing interconnections among peoples might provide in the future the incentives for trying to overcome war, yet they also provide the occasions for the most extraordinary forms of injustice and violence. Indeed, the primary violators of cosmopolitan right, in Kant's view, are "the civilized, *especially* [*the*] *commercial*, states in our part of the world" (8:358, emphasis added). It is the *commercial character* of many European countries that provides them the opportunity to engage in the most gruesome forms of injustice, in Kant's opinion. In describing their activities abroad, Kant argues that

> the injustice they show in visiting foreign lands and peoples (which with them is tantamount to conquering them) goes to horrifying lengths. When America, the negro countries, the Spice Islands, the Cape, and so forth were discovered, they were, to them [to European commercial states], countries belonging to no one, since they counted the inhabitants as nothing. In the East Indies (Hindustan), they brought in foreign soldiers under the pretext of merely proposing to set up trading posts, but with them [came] oppression of the inhabitants, incitement of the various Indian states to widespread wars, famine, rebellions, treachery, and the whole litany of troubles that oppress the human race. (8:358–359)

The particular litany of troubles that Kant describes is precisely what Adam Smith investigates at such length in the *Wealth of Nations* vis-à-vis, in particular, the activities of European states and commercial trading companies. And, indeed, just as Smith had argued, Kant notes that considered as business enterprises, the ultimate irony is that such companies are not even profitable. They are all, Kant states, "on the verge of collapse," although, as Adam Smith had argued, they are never allowed to completely fail; rather, they are predictably and routinely bailed out by their states, which have increasingly come under these companies' influence and control. Kant's conception of the norms of cosmopolitan right was meant both to provide a normative critique and to offer moral guidance to those in his time who struggled to come to terms with the grave injustices that global commerce routinely engendered.

How, then, would the politically productive aspects of commercial connections across borders be maintained without entailing the destructive and unjust practices that global commerce makes possible? To begin with, it is important to note that, in Kant's view, increasing civilization – societies becoming civilized or becoming more civilized over time – will fail to create the conditions in which humans can approximate the goal of perpetual peace. What Condorcet proposes, for example, to achieve conditions of global justice in the future contrasts sharply with Kant's arguments. To be sure, in Kant's view, the initial formation in the past of some civilized societies produced great misery and injustice while also making possible the development of the arts and sciences. Yet, and here very much under the influence of Rousseau, this does not in and of itself constitute meaningful progress for humanity as a whole, and it fails to justify civilizing missions in Kant's own time or in the future. As Kant argues, humans who currently live in civilized societies – that is, sedentary, agriculturally based societies with centralized political power and an elaborate hierarchy of social strata – endure

the most severe ills deceptively disguised as external prosperity.... We are cultivated to a great extent by the arts and sciences. And we are civilized to a troublesome degree in all forms of social courteousness and decency. But to consider ourselves to be already fully moralized is quite premature. For the *idea* of morality *is* part of culture. But the use of this idea, which leads only to that which resembles morality in the love of honor and outward decency, comprises only *mere civilization*. (8:26, emphases added)

Kant notes that what is necessary, namely, "moral cultivation," "requires a long internal process in every commonwealth," and he warns that "[a]ll that is good but that is not based on morally good convictions is nothing but pure outward show and shimmering misery" (8:26). Strikingly, Kant's grim assessment of European societies leads him to conclude that "culture, according to true principles of the education as both human being and citizen, *perhaps has not even really begun*, much less been completed" (8:116, emphasis added). Overall, then, Kant's assessment of the state of civilization in its current form is that it consists of "manifold human misery" and oppressive, unjustifiable inequality (8:117).

Furthermore, the primary agents of global injustice are not "uncivilized" peoples (that is, hunting and gathering, or pastoral or other nomadic peoples), such as the Cree on the plains of North America or the Bedouins in the Sahara, but rather, in Kant's view, commercial European states: among others, Britain, France, Spain, Portugal, the Dutch Republic, and those linked closely to these states and benefitting from their global exploitation, including Prussia. Forcibly turning nomadic societies into sedentary ones is unjust in part, according to Kant, because nomadic peoples have as much legitimate claim to the land they use for their way of life as the claim that sedentary societies have over their own land. This in itself is a notable claim in the context of eighteenth-century debates; the influential Swiss jurist Emer de Vattel had argued, for instance, that nomadic peoples have no legitimate claim over large territories because they were irrationally failing to cultivate the land on which they roamed.[27] In addition, while some might claim that stealing a nation's land and murdering some of its people in the process is "to the world's advantage ... because these rough peoples will become civilized," Kant characterizes this argument as deeply problematic due both to the means *and* to the proposed end. That is, Kant concludes not only that such a defense of conquest and empire is immoral because of the proposed violent means, but also that the very goal of spreading civilization is "specious" [*scheinbar*; the root *Schein* = fictitious or pseudo] (6:353).

Why is it not to the world's advantage that all peoples become sedentary and practice agriculture? Referring to the collective lives led by hunting or pastoral peoples, and to the large open spaces of land that are required for such lives to be led, Kant argues that "as long as they keep within their boundaries the way they want to *live* on their land is up to their own discretion (*res merae facultatis*)" (6:266). *Res merae facultatis* (or *iura merae facultatis*) is a legal concept used both in the law of nations and more broadly in other modern jurisprudential texts; it refers to acts solely of the free will without any constraint, which one may or may not do at one's pleasure. Kant's use of it here is significant: this is precisely the term that he uses in his political philosophy when he defends *individual* autonomy against the power of the state, arguing that individuals should be free to pursue their own way of life, to practice their own religion, and to live in accordance with their own conception of happiness. A violation of that freedom is what Kant refers to as the greatest conceivable despotism that a state can commit. It is striking, then, that Kant also uses this concept with regard to *nations* and to their collective ways of life – most importantly to the crucial decision concerning how a people will gain its sustenance from the land: hunting and gathering or fishing or pastoralism

---

[27] On this aspect of Vattel's thought, see Richard Tuck, *The Rights of War and Peace* (Oxford: Oxford University Press, 1999), pp. 195–196.

or settled agriculture. To interfere with that decision, which shapes the life of a whole people, to conquer and to settle colonies or trading outposts on that basis – that is, to build empires in order to spread civilization by means of imperial commerce and domination – is, therefore, by Kant's own logic, the greatest conceivable despotism committed by states on the global scale.

How, then, should the salutary effects of global exchange and interaction be balanced against the forms of injustice and oppression that global commerce makes possible? Kant clearly has no sympathy for what might be termed the "civilizationist solution," and so he offers instead a defense of the norms of hospitality and just commerce, which he uses, as we have seen, negatively to condemn colonialism and exploitative trading practices and, as we will see, positively to describe an equilibrium between the separateness and distinct identity of nations as well as attempted (and sometimes actual) communicative and commercial connections among them. Global justice consists of that balance rather than an open and always unimpeded free exchange and trade among nations. Kant makes a defense only of possible attempted commerce with other peoples, and his description of a global society makes it clear that the bond of amity among all peoples is not the goal of a properly construed conception of global justice: such a global society will be a "peaceful, *even if not friendly*, thoroughgoing community of all nations on the earth" (6:352). It is crucial to appreciate, then, the vision of rival communities and even of a certain antagonism among nations that is part of Kant's ideal conception of global relations.

Some reflection upon Kant's understanding of unsocial sociability, as well as an examination of his arguments against a world state, make clear Kant's dual commitment to fostering connections among peoples and yet simultaneously to encouraging a productive resistance between and among peoples.[28] Kant introduces the idea of unsocial sociability in

[28] It is sometimes argued that Kant's theory of progress underwrites (not normatively, but sociologically or historically) an imperial mission or that it treats Europe as a vanguard for global progress. (For a sophisticated version of this argument, see Thomas McCarthy's fine book, *Race, Empire, and the Idea of Human Development* [Cambridge: Cambridge University Press, 2009].) The full range of the textual evidence both from Kant's writings on history and politics and from his theory of teleological judgment suggests, instead, that Kant's philosophy of history is a narrative of hope; that is, it is meant to instill hope in humans who otherwise would be numbed into complacency by the injustices of the world. Indeed, Kant does not provide a developmental or sociological justification of any aspect of civilized society (including empire) in light of his philosophy of history; rather, his philosophy of history is meant to convince his readers that they should view "nature"

The Idea for a Universal History from a Cosmopolitan Perspective to reflect upon both individual human behavior and the behavior of states. He offers a defense of the positive effects of the *un*sociable quality of human nature, in particular, not only because it helps to impel some humans toward the formation of civil unions and, in the future, he hopes, toward an international federation – in other words, it is not simply temporarily valuable toward some end at which point unsociability is no longer productive – but also because, even within such ideal institutions, the antagonism that comes from this unsociability is socially and politically valuable. Kant introduces this understanding of antagonism in the following way:

> I take antagonism to mean the *unsocial sociability* of human beings, that is, their tendency to enter into society, a tendency connected, however, with a constant resistance that continually threatens to break up this society. This unsociable sociability is obviously part of human nature. Human beings have an inclination to associate with one another because in such a condition they feel themselves to be more human.... But they also have a strong tendency to isolate themselves, because they encounter in themselves the unsociable trait that predisposes them to want to direct everything only to their own ends and hence to expect to encounter resistance everywhere, just as they know that they themselves tend to resist others. (8:20–21)

This resistance, and the tendency to isolate oneself, the desire to direct (one might even say to dominate others), and correspondingly the expectation to meet resistance elsewhere, and hence to desire one's own protected space, all constitute essential aspects of Kant's ideal account of

as being on their side when they fight against war, against conquest and empire, against the injustices of civilized life, and in favor of republican self-governance for their own communities. They will likely lose most of their battles in convincing political elites to stop conquering and in their efforts to foster republicanism, but Kant's philosophy of history is meant to sustain them, to provide them with hope, even in those dark times when it seems that any real progress is unattainable. Thus, when humans lose a battle to convince their political elites that they should not engage in a particular conquest, they can restore their sense of hope by realizing that that conquest or that war might nonetheless yield some progress. They should still continue to fight the next possible war or conquest, but when they lose various battles, they ought to hope that real progress is still possible. Otherwise, as thinking, critically minded individuals, who are thus aware of the grave and deep-set injustices in the world, they will give up in their struggle to create better societies and to improve their social and political conditions. Kant's theory of progress and history, I have argued, was intended to enable humans' agency and to embolden humanity to fight against war, conquest, and empire and for the republican goal of independent, equal, politically self-governing communities. Kant's philosophy of history is thus part of his arsenal of rhetorical and philosophical weapons, as it were, against empire, war, and conquest and the hierarchy of peoples that they imply. For more on this aspect of Kant's thought, see my *Enlightenment against Empire*, pp. 162–171.

global commerce and global justice. Hence, Kant argues in favor of hunting or pasturing peoples actively (and, if necessary, violently) *resisting*
others' attempts to change or to civilize their societies, and Kant in that
context uses the language of resistance (6:266). Similarly, Kant justifies
the wisdom of the reaction of China and Japan to European incursions,
and he applauds their attempts to limit their peoples' interactions with
European merchants, missionaries, and others.[29] These are precisely
examples of what Kant describes as the productive resistance that global
justice requires.

At the global level, our goal, Kant writes, should be "to discover a law
of equilibrium with regard to the *in itself productive resistance* between
many states[.]" As he goes on to note, a "cosmopolitan condition of public security is thus introduced, which is not completely free of *danger* …
but also not without a principle of the equality of their mutual *actions and
reactions*, so that they do not destroy one another" (8:26). This delicate
balancing act between our communicative and commercial bonds, on the
one hand, and the danger and productive resistance between peoples, on
the other – this equality of actions and reactions (what Kant at one point
describes as ideally "a peace that is produced and secured … by means
of … [the] equilibrium [of peoples] in liveliest competition" [8:367]) – is
also at work in Kant's analysis of why humans ought to reject, and how
humans might avoid, the formation of a world state.

In the 1790s, Kant begins to argue that a sovereign world state is deeply
problematic, in part because states would not voluntarily give up sovereign power, and thus a world state could only be created by conquest and
empire, which itself would be unjust.[30] The unlikelihood of creating such

---

[29] See Peter Niesen, "Colonialism and Hospitality," *Politics and Ethics Review*, 3, no. 1
(April 2007), 90–108.

[30] This is one of the many significant transformations in Kant's social and political thought
that occurred in the 1790s. Perhaps most notably, while Kant clearly held a hierarchical
view of superior and inferior peoples in his account of race, it is striking that he dis-
carded his theory of race in the mid-1790s and replaced it with a nonbiological, sociological account of how peoples distinctively used their territory for their sustenance (for
example, by hunting, by pastoralism, or by sedentary agriculture). He had already begun
to develop such an account in some slightly earlier writings, such as the *Conjectural
Beginning of Human History* (1786). I offered a brief account of the chronological
shift in Kant's thinking about the diversity of human peoples in *Enlightenment against
Empire*, pp. 180–186. Since then, Pauline Kleingeld has argued at greater length and
with far more precision than I offered in my book that there was, indeed, a shift in Kant's
thinking along these lines. See Pauline Kleingeld, "Kant's Second Thoughts on Race,"
The Philosophical Quarterly, 57 (2007), 573–592. Kleingeld argues that the key period
during which Kant drops hierarchical race thinking is the mid-1790s, which is precisely

a global state, and the unjust means that would therefore be necessary to attempt to create it, are only part of the problem with such a concept, in Kant's view. In common with many eighteenth-century thinkers who were outright republicans or who integrated elements of republicanism into their theories, such as Montesquieu and the Federalist framers of the American Constitution, Kant assumed that the governance of very large territories (let alone the whole earth) would over time necessitate despotic rule. Moreover, given the impossibility of effectively governing such large territories, a world state could even lead to the dissolution of republican self-rule or, indeed, of any state-governed rule at the global level (6:350). In that case – given that local forms of sovereignty would have been destroyed in order to produce a world state – throughout the world, in every society, human relations would ultimately consist of nothing but brute force, of the rule of the strong over the weak.[31] In Kant's terms, a "soulless despotism ... finally deteriorates into anarchy" (8:367; cf. 6:350).

One of the primary challenges that humans face, Kant argues, is that political elites crave world domination (or "universal monarchy," to use the Enlightenment term) – peace only on their own terms and achieved by means of war – and are willing to use cunning and force toward that end. Happily, Kant writes, differences in language and in religion create a kind of friction among peoples; there is less intermingling among peoples than there would have been as a result, and a certain sense of separation

---

the period during which Kant writes and publishes his key works in political philosophy, including his anti-imperialist theory of cosmopolitan justice (*Toward Perpetual Peace* [1795], *Metaphysics of Morals* [1797]), and it is also, importantly, the period during which Kant argues that nomadic and other "non-civilized" peoples do not practice inferior ways of life and that they can legitimately resist any attempt to force them to become civilized (i.e., to become sedentary and agricultural peoples).

[31] Cf. Pauline Kleingeld, "Approaching Perpetual Peace: Kant's Defence of a League of States and His Ideal of a World Federation," *European Journal of Philosophy*, 12, no. 3 (2004), 304–325; and, more generally, Pauline Kleingeld, *Kant and Cosmopolitanism: The Philosophical Ideal of World Citizenship* (Cambridge: Cambridge University Press, 2011). See also Georg Cavallar, *Imperfect Cosmopolis* (Cardiff: University of Wales Press, 2011). Kant's concern about the lawless savagery of the strong taking advantage of the weak informs his accounts of the state of nature, including his analysis of the natural condition in the international arena, where the most dangerous savages by far, in Kant's view, were "European savages" – that is, powerful European states (see 8:354; cf. 8:357). In such conditions, Kant believes that lawful, respectful relations among peoples would come about *partly* through antagonistic mutual coercion. As he writes, in "a state devoid of justice ... in which when rights are in dispute ... there would be no judge competent to render a verdict having rightful force. Hence each may impel the other by force to leave this state and enter into a rightful condition" (6:312; cf. 8:349).

among peoples becomes established. This is a passage that sometimes astonishes Kant's readers, but we should recall here the desire for isolation that is part of the unsociable antagonism that he values. This in itself, to be sure, is potentially problematic, for as Kant himself notes, a "propensity to mutual hatred" could thereby be fostered, and such animosity could serve as "pretexts for war" (8:367). Thus, Kant cautions in the *Metaphysics of Morals* that the idea of a right of nations "involves *only* the concept of an antagonism *in accordance with principles of outer freedom* by which each can preserve what belongs to it, but not a way of acquiring, by which one state's increase of power could threaten others" (6:347, emphasis added). Hence, this is an antagonism rooted in a commitment to self-preservation rather than conquest, and it thus helps to ensure the separateness of peoples and the plurality of communities that global justice requires. Ideally, Kant argues, the resistance and friction between peoples ought to be balanced against attempted commercial and communicative connections among peoples, which in part are likely to ensue for profit-oriented goals, if not for mutual understanding or out of friendship.

Eventually, Kant hopes, this would be supplemented by the peaceful mediation of disputes that a voluntary congress of states would make possible, an institution that would come about partly by the emergence and growth of culture – not civilization, but moral cultivation. As we have seen, in Kant's view, a moral culture had not even begun to be developed in the eighteenth century, for only "mere civilization" had come into existence; thus, no country or continent possessed in his own time even some modicum of what genuinely counted as moral culture that could be spread to other societies. Rather, in the future, such cultivation would finally begin to be fostered collectively by humankind "gradually coming within reach" of mutual understanding and of the principles concerning what can approximate true conditions of peace – that is, peace among societies without despotism or empire (8:367). It should be noted that, even as part of Kant's ideal theory of global justice, such a condition would both come about and would depend for its continuation upon the balancing forces of attempted and actual commercial and communicative connections, on the one hand, and a productive antagonism and resistance between peoples, on the other. Kant's writings, then, exhibit – and, indeed, Kant explicitly theorizes – an ambivalence toward global connections that, in many respects, carries on a distinctive Enlightenment intellectual tradition about global commerce, communication, and justice, one rooted in a deep antipathy toward conquest and empire.

Diderot, Smith, and Kant asserted that non-Europeans would have to dictate the terms of a renewed global commerce and a reformed set of global interconnections to combat and ultimately to lessen transnational forms of exploitation and oppression. These thinkers shared a grim and well-founded pessimism about the willingness of Western European governments and trading companies – that is, the willingness of the most powerful states and commercial institutions of their time – to forge a less brutal system of global affairs. As noted earlier, the *History of the Two Indies* had prophesied a Black Spartacus. Diderot died before the beginning of the Haitian revolution, and thus could never know that Toussaint L'Ouverture, the former slave and rebel leader, had read the *Histoire* and proclaimed himself in his speeches to be precisely this foretold Black Spartacus. As Diderot, Smith, and Kant theorized, fostering even a semblance of what might count as a universal community of humankind would require an equality of rival countervailing forces emanating from different quarters of the globe, rather than a set of reforms directed by Europeans, whether ill or well intentioned. In their view, the formation of a nonimperial global society would require genuinely cosmopolitan foundations.

9

Liberalism, Nation, and Empire

The Case of J. S. Mill

Pratap Bhanu Mehta

The relationship between John Stuart Mill's political thought and imperialism has, in the literature, been approached in three different ways. The first approach is straightforwardly historical. Mill was not just a thinker. He was an important interlocutor in thinking about imperial power. He worked for the East India Company, whose approach to imperial governance he defended. He also weighed in on almost all of the important controversies surrounding the colonies in his time, from India to Ireland, from Jamaica to Australia. This approach documents his views on *specific* colonial entanglements.[1] The second approach looks more specifically at his *political* theory, in particular the ways in which ideas of liberty and autonomy are deployed in the context of the empire.[2] The third approach looks more closely at Mill's *social theory*, his account of the evolution of societies and his assessment of the causal mechanisms

---

[1] Works in this genre include Lynn Zastoupil, *John Stuart Mill and India* (Stanford, Calif.: Stanford University Press, 1994); Katherine Smits, "John Stuart Mill on the Antipodes: Settler Violence Against Indigenous Peoples and the Legitimacy of Colonial Rule," *Australian Journal of Politics and History*, 54, no. 1 (2008), 1–15; David Theo Goldberg, "Liberalism's Limits: Carlyle and Mill on the Negro Question," in *Utilitarianism and Empire*, ed. Bart Schultz and Georgios Varouxakis (Lanham, Md.: Lexington Books, 2005), pp. 125–135.

[2] The most impressive work in the genre is Uday Singh Mehta, *Liberalism and Empire* (Chicago: University of Chicago Press, 1999). For a critique of Mehta, see Mark Tunick, "Tolerant Imperialism: John Stuart Mill's Defense of British Rule in India," *Review of Politics*, 68 (2006), 586–611.

I would like to acknowledge the profound debt I owe to Alan Ryan for getting me interested in Mill; to Uday Mehta for probing conversations on Mill and empire; to Glyn Morgan for skeptical questioning; and to Jennifer Pitts, Karuna Mantena, and Sankar Muthu for setting new benchmarks in thinking about the relationship between political theory and empire.

by which social change occurs.[3] In practice, many good works combine all three approaches. But the presence of these distinct strands in Mill's entanglement with the question of empire poses a formidable interpretive challenge. First, what is the connection between Mill's specific historical judgments, say on India, and his social and political theory? Second, what is the connection between his social and political theory? To what extent do concepts central to his political theory – liberty, democracy, autonomy, and progress – rely upon concepts central to his social imagination, such as civilization, barbarism, power, and nation? Which of these connections is important to thinking about his entanglement in empire? While much of the literature has powerfully explored several of these connections, this chapter argues that Mill's conception of the "nation" is central not only to his political and social theory, but also to his thinking about empire. I also argue that his entanglement with the question of empire is interesting in two directions. In a very familiar manner, we are prone to ask the question: what implications do Mill's political and social theories have for empire? But there is also a reverse question: to what degree does the entanglement with questions of empire reveal certain assumptions in Mill's social and political theories? This chapter examines both of these questions. It has three principal parts. After some brief remarks on Mill's historical sensibility, I first examine how it came about that a collectivity had to be a nation of a particular kind to have its rights acknowledged. Second, I show the degree to which Mill's understanding of the legitimacy of colonial power rests on an understanding of national character. Finally, I suggest how the discipline of commerce and the state are central to Mill's understanding of empire.

MILL'S HISTORICAL SENSIBILITY

Before we approach the central argument, a few preliminary remarks about Mill's historical sensibility are in order. One of the abiding curiosities of Mill's liberalism is his defense of imperialism – the idea that one set of people may justifiably exercise sovereignty over another in view of some feature or set of features that make them superior to others. The

---

[3] The best work on this subject is Jennifer Pitts, *A Turn to Empire* (Princeton, N.J.: Princeton University Press, 2005). While Pitts's work straddles the distinctions I am making, it is particularly powerful on Mill's deployment of the scales of civilization argument. Another excellent essay is Karuna Mantena, "Mill and the Imperial Predicament," in *J. S. Mill's Political Thought: A Bicentennial Reassessment*, ed. A. Zakaras and N. Urbinati (Cambridge: Cambridge University Press, 2007), pp. 299–315.

simplest justification for this belief stems from his philosophy of history, his account of progress whereby peoples would, gradually and collectively, develop their capacities and characters to the fullest extent possible. Some societies were further along this path than others, and as a matter of right and a matter of duty, they needed to help create the preconditions that would help other, less fortunate societies on the same path by whatever means appropriate. For most "barbarians" some form of imperial subordination – a good, stout, reliable despotism – was appropriate.[4] What remains puzzling and embarrassing to Mill's readers is the antipathy toward and lack of appreciation of other civilizations and cultures that this account rested on. His official doctrine sees very little of value in other civilizations and cultures. Mill seldom gives a sense that some loss might be associated with the onward march of progress that transforms or destroys some cultures in its wake; seldom gives a sense that some significant part of the human experience might be instantiated in different cultures and might be in danger of being lost; seldom gives a sense that a single culture may not possess a monopoly on human achievement and good. For someone who so eloquently painted pictures of the many-sidedness of the human character, for someone who attributed Europe's progress to its diversity, and for someone whose official methodological doctrine required him to empathically acquire knowledge of the human condition, this feature of Mill's thought remains puzzling.[5] Indeed, Uday Mehta has noted that the problem with Mill's approach to difference is just this: he lacks the humility to appreciate how peoples' historical investments matter to them.[6]

This is even more puzzling in light of the fact that there was nothing in his character that usually impeded such imaginative judgments. Mill was emphatically no racist in any conventional sense of the term.[7] He held that any deficiency that societies or peoples exhibited was a result of the

---

[4] John Stuart Mill, *Collected Works* (hereafter CW) (Toronto: University of Toronto Press, 1963–), XVIII, p. 224.

[5] Mill frequently advocated an imaginative hermeneutic. For just two of many instances, see CW, I, pp. 333 and 459. Mill praised Ware for "the power of throwing his own mind, and of making their readers throw theirs, into the minds and the circumstances of persons who lived far off and long ago." Ware had the power to make "us see things as those persons in distant time and space saw or might have seen them" and, therefore, could make us "*feel* with them and in some measure understand them." He chided Hume and Bentham for lacking the quality of sympathetic imagination. For his critique of Hume, see CW, XX. p. 135.

[6] Mehta, *Liberalism and Empire*, p. 82.

[7] For a contrary view, see David Goldberg's "Liberalism's Limits," 127, which argues that Mill is a more dangerous racist that Carlyle.

institutional configurations of their society rather than the innate limits of their capacities.[8] His position on these matters was clearly perceived to be hostile to the racialist presumptions of Victorian anthropology.[9] His letters also display a degree of generosity that is unexpected in light of his official doctrine. His declaration that the Bengales[10] were civilized after all, and his defense of the character and governing capacities of Indian women who acted as de facto rulers more often than anywhere in Europe,[11] does not seem to have led him to any degree of self-doubt about his cultural judgments. The ease, self-confidence, and vehemence with which Mill developed his hierarchies of people that were so central to the self-representations of imperialism still remains puzzling for any-one who finds his political philosophy genuinely attractive.[12]

As Jennifer Pitts has argued, Mill's account of progress is central to understanding his sensibility.[13] Mill's analysis of progress, his under-standing of its aims and preconditions, accounts for this aspect of his sen-sibility. Progress has two meanings in Mill's account: one denotes facts of an external or sociological nature, like increasing complexity, increasing division of labor, and so on. It is a sociological theory of modernization. The other meaning of progress denotes the attainment of human perfect-ibility, the gradual coming into being of societies where noble characters of the Millian sort would flourish. The first sense of progress greatly facil-itated the second but did not guarantee it. Indeed, many of Mill's anxi-eties stem from the fact that emerging sociological progress might even impede the development of human capabilities and character. And much of his effort is devoted to ensuring that it did not.

The peculiarity of his account of progress stems from the fact that he seems to have consistently believed in two propositions. First, all the features and dispositions that would make a character attractive or noble would be instantiated simultaneously: the intelligent would also be

[8] For an indignant personal expression of this view, see CW, XVII, p.1767.

[9] See, for example, the Victorian anthropologist Knox's critique of Mill in "Race Legislation and Political Economy," *Anthropological Review*, 13 (1866), 246–263.

[10] Ibid.

[11] See the letter to Charlotte Speir Manning of 14 January 1870. "As the native states were in my department at the India House I had opportunities of knowing all that was known about the manner in which they [Native States] were governed and during many years by far the greater number of instances of vigorous and skilful administration which came to my knowledge were by Ranees and Raees as regents for minor chiefs." CW, XVII, p.1686.

[12] For a succinct account of these, see Bhikhu Parekh, "Superior Peoples," *Times Literary Supplement* (25 February 1994), 11–13.

[13] Pitts, *A Turn to Empire*, p.135.

sensitive, public-spirited, and benevolent, for example. Second, various modes of life that were worth living would all be compossible within a single social system. To take a common example: for Mill, a society could be both achievement oriented and benevolent, embody a vigorous clash of contrary viewpoints yet achieve a sense of wholeness. There is seldom a sense in Mill that any one of the poles of these contrasting pairs might in the end be incompatible with the other. His belief that any one of the poles of these contrasts could be balanced by another rather than be out-done by it seems more like an article of faith than a well-argued position. I suspect that it is partly this belief in the compossibility of various good things that gives his liberalism a sense that the world is indeed without significant loss and that, therefore, the passing away of different cultures is not a matter of regret. Mill has a keen sense of the many sides of human character and the requirements that sustain them, but seldom a sense of the ultimate incompatibility of their various constituents. This is perhaps what gives his liberalism less of a tragic cast than, say, Isaiah Berlin's or, to a lesser degree, Tocqueville's.

Having made this preliminary claim about Mill's historical sensibil-ity, I will, in the rest of this chapter, discuss some further elements of Mill's imperial imagination. As the late Eric Stokes put it, imperialism contained within it "an unformulated philosophy of life and politics."[14] I will discuss aspects of this unformulated philosophy in the work of John Stuart Mill. First, however, some disclaimers are in order. My aim is not to provide details of Mill's career with the East India Company, nor is it to give an exhaustive account of Mill's imperial ideology.[15] I follow Pagden's lead in viewing imperial ideologies as being constituted by a constellation of themes, and I have selected some themes in Mill's work: the manner in which conceptions of nation, national character, and civ-ilization operate in Mill's political philosophy and their implications for imperial discourse.[16] I have selected the following elements in the belief that, first, these are some of the underappreciated elements of imperial

---

[14] Eric Stokes, *The Political Ideas of English Imperialism* (Oxford: Oxford University Press, 1955).

[15] For convenient summaries, see Lynn Zastoupil, *John Stuart Mill and India* (Stanford, Calif.: Stanford University Press, 1994); R. J. Moore, "John Stuart Mill at India House," *Historical Journal*, 20, no. 81 (1983), 479–519; Eileen Sullivan, "Liberalism and Imperialism: J. S. Mill's Defense of the British Empire," *Journal of the History of Ideas*, 44 (1983), 599–617.

[16] An advantage of Pagden's survey, *Lords of All the World* (New Haven, Conn.: Yale University Press, 1995), is that it deals with myriad interrelated themes that go into the making of the imperial imagination rather than with a set of juristic concepts.

ideology; second, that they shed an interesting light on the character of Mill's political theory; and third, that these assumptions shaped the functioning of postimperial politics to a significant degree.

NATION AND NATIONALITY IN MILL'S THOUGHT

Nationality looms large over Mill's writings; he was one of the most ardent supporters of the principle of self-determination. As much as he hoped that the principle of nationality would one day be transcended, and as much as he regretted that the sentiment could be "grievous," so long as the sentiment existed, it was "practically of the very first importance."[17] The assumption that peoples are divided into distinct territorial entities whose inhabitants *identify* with each other is for Mill a precondition of representative government. The content of the principle of nationality can be stated quite simply: "a portion of mankind may be said to constitute a nationality, if they are united among themselves by common sympathies, which do not exist between them and any others."[18] The sources that sustain this principle are also plainly listed. These sources rely on "prepolitical elements": identity of race or descent, a community of language, or a community of religion. The advantages of a common nationality are also palpable: besides allowing people to be better organized to defend their independence, the possession of a nationality contributes to the stability of a society. It contributes to social stability by creating conditions whereby one part of the community does not consider themselves as foreigners with regard to another part; they set value on their connection. They feel that they are one people, that their lot is cast together, that any evil done to any of their fellow countrymen is evil done to themselves, and they do not desire to selfishly free themselves from their share in any common inconvenience by severing the connection.

A few points should be noticed about Mill's conception of nationality. The first is that for Mill "the boundaries of governments should in the main coincide with those of nationalities." He is not unaware of the complications of this position. He recognizes that there are many areas, even in Europe, where these nationalities are so comingled, that it would not be practical for them to set up separate governments.[19] In such situations, these nationalities should comingle and attempt to live under equal

[17] CW, XX, p. 347.
[18] CW, XIX, p. 380 ("Considerations"); see also CW, X, p. 135 ("Coleridge").
[19] CW, XIX, p. 549, where Mill discusses the Hungarian situation.

laws and rights. The striking feature of Mill's discussion is that these instances never lead him to consider the difficulties and costs implicit in the formation of nations. So insistently does Mill describe the principle of nationality in terms of unity and identity that there is a striking absence of any conceptual space for granting corporate recognition to groups as anything other than unitary nations defined in his terms.

The particularities that set nations apart from one another carry no moral weight; yet, these elements mark out a people as separate. The term "nation" and its cognates, "nationality" and so forth, are used ambiguously in Mill's writings as both descriptive and evaluative terms. In the descriptive sense, "nation" is simply a placeholder that denotes distinct peoples and comes closest to the premodern use of the term as referring to peoples who share a common culture, language, customs, or traditions but are not yet necessarily integrated into distinct political communities.[20] In an evaluative sense, it refers to those peoples who have organized themselves into a distinct kind of *political* society. When Mill writes that barbarians have no rights as nations, he means nations in the latter sense, although they are nations in some sense in that they possess marks of particularity that distinguish them from others.[21]

The crucial point for Mill – and one of the sources of tension in his political philosophy – is that both contractual and cultural requirements are braided together in his understanding of nationhood. What I mean is this: Mill thinks that a sense of nationhood can be sustained, on the one hand, by a free association of individual wills that coalesce around a set of shared values or publicly proclaimed principles, usually arrived at through free discussion. On the other hand, this sense of cohesion also relies on determinants (like history, memory, language, etc.) that lie beneath the surface of shared *values* provided by the nation's laws. In

[20] The political sense of the term "nation" is, of course, credited to the French Revolution, which transformed the prepolitical meaning of the term into a constitutive feature of the identity of citizens of a democratic polity and aligned it with the concept of sovereignty. See Istvan Hont, "The Permanent Crisis of a Divided Mankind: 'Contemporary Crisis of the Nation State' in Historical Perspective," in *Crisis of the Nation State*, ed. John Dunn (Oxford: Blackwell, 1992), pp. 447–528. Liah Greenfeld argued in *Nationalism* (Cambridge, Mass.: Harvard University Press, 1992) that the political meaning of the term can be traced back to seventeenth-century England, but the alignment of nation with sovereignty is not as clear in the English tradition as it is in the Jacobin tradition, which made the idea of popular sovereignty constitutive of the idea of the nation. Even Mill was somewhat skeptical of the idea of popular sovereignty. See CW, XXII, p.150.
[21] Both uses continued long into the nineteenth century. J. Seeley, for example, in his *Expansion of England* (London: Macmillan, 1883) used the term both as a substitute for race (to include America and Australia) and to refer to the English political nation.

a sense, the first aspect refers to questions of legitimacy – what form of political organization it is legitimate for a nation to have; the second to questions of identity – what marks distinguish one nation from another. It is perhaps a credit to Mill's understanding that he at least recognized that questions of legitimacy do not exhaust the domain of identity.

In a sense, the tension between the descriptive and evaluative was one of the enduring tensions of imperial discourse that has continued to shape postimperial politics as well. On the one hand, Mill had to denigrate the elements that *presently* constituted the sense of nationality – the elements that constituted its identity, as it were – that some of the peoples of the colonies possessed. It was these very elements that marked out their *separate identity as peoples* and made them candidates for recognition as distinct territorial entities in the *future*. The boundaries and mutual cohesion of all the examples of nations that he gives – be they advanced nations capable of self-government or backward ones – are formed by some elements of these particularities of race, language, religion, and so on. The sense of distinctness of these nations *was* constituted by these "prepolitical" elements – race, shared tradition, history. They are the necessary background to the formation of nationality and the securing of difference. Yet, not only did the colonies' aspirations to "identity" have to remain subordinate until they had fulfilled what in Mill's view were the requirements of legitimacy,[22] the imperial process had to systematically violate the claims of that identity. This might not be such an incongruous position were it not for the fact that, for all the advanced nations, Mill recognizes the claims of both identity and legitimacy. The problem Mill faces is this: these particularities – identity of race, religion, or shared memories – themselves do not, on Mill's account, carry moral weight or require recognition in the colonies. But these are, as I shall argue, given their due weight in the recognition of advanced nations.

This can perhaps be seen in some aspects of Mill's discussion of assimilation. For Mill, not all "nationalities" in the descriptive sense would form political nationalities. For one thing, they had to be sufficient in size and number ("extensive aggregate"), like the Irish or Indians. Some, like the Bretons, the French Canadians, the Basque, or the Welsh and Scottish, were better off assimilating into larger nationalities.[23] But on closer inspection, it turns out that all of those smaller nationalities for

[22] For example, Mill regretted consistently that the Irish had acquired a sense of nationality – mutual cohesion and distinctness – before reaching maturity. See CW, X.
[23] CW, XIX, chap. 16.

whom he advocates assimilation assimilate not only to "advanced political principles" but also to the particularities, like language, that constitute the larger nationality they assimilate to. The French Canadians were
to assimilate to Anglo-Saxon particularities. The ostensible normative
argument was that assimilation into a wider culture would be normatively better.

Further, Mill's demarcation of the hierarchies of peoples along the
lines of race, language, and so on seems, apart from other things, an odd
piece of moral psychology. He seems unaware of the *effects* that creating
subordination along these lines would have on members of those groups.
A striking and ironic example of this is his treatment of the French
Canadians, whose "so much talked of nationality" Mill would advocate
using all "legitimate means to destroy."[24] What better way of ensuring
that the French Canadians would retain their sense of nationality! By
establishing inferiority and superiority along these particular lines and
then privileging some over others, Mill was helping to ensure that those
very boundaries would continue to shape politics in significant ways. The
"politics of recognition," to use Charles Taylor's phrase, may be less a
consequence of the dismantling of medieval hierarchies, as Taylor himself
supposes, than a product of the hierarchies instituted in imperialism.[25]

Mill's principle of nationality is imbued with what Hobsbawm calls
"a deep horizontal comradeship" among those who belong to it, and is
in this sense democratic and egalitarian. The sources of stability do not
derive from fidelity to a "constitution" in the eighteenth-century sense of
the term – a particular ordering of ranks and classes with vertical principles of hierarchy and subordination of the kind one finds in Burke. For
Burke, the existence of privileged classes and a historic constitution was
enough to confer nationhood; indeed, that was his definition of a nation.
Any society that possessed such features was for Burke a candidate for
nationhood. What Burke saw violated in the imperial annexations of
Poland and Corsica,[26] the Jacobin usurpation in France, and the British

---

[24] CW, VI, p. 459 ("Lord Durham's Return").
[25] See Charles Taylor, *The Politics of Recognition* (Princeton, N.J.: Princeton University
Press, 1992), for the argument that the politics of recognition is a consequence of the
breakdown of medieval hierarchies.
[26] For Burke's defense of Poland and Corsica as "oppressed nationalities," see *Annual
Register*, 1768, p. 44; ibid., 1769, p. 32. For Burke's definition of a nation, see "Speech on
a Motion Made in the House of Commons ... for a committee to Inquire into the state
of Representation of the Commons in Parliament" (1782) in *The Works of the Right
Honorable Edmund Burke* (Boston: Little, Brown, and Company, 1871), vol. 7, p. 95.

rule in India had this in common: they constituted a violation of historic constitutions and an ongoing system of ranks and orderings.

Further, Mill's principle of nationality is a forward-looking one in that its value derives not from its antiquity, or the emotive significance associated with being part of an ongoing tradition, but from its being a prerequisite for a forward-looking political order. This was part of the reason that Mill felt less compunction than Burke in denying that the presence in India of a long-standing social fabric, with its own historical associations, memories, and principles of subordination, its own set of geographical attachments, gave it certain rights as a *nation*.

Curiously enough, Mill did take a feature of the Burkean sensibility seriously.[27] In his critique of Bentham he argued:

He [Bentham] has, I think, been, to a certain extent, misled in the theory of politics, by supposing that submission of the mass of mankind to an established government is mainly owing to a reasoning perception of the necessity of legal protection, and of the common interest of all in a prompt and zealous obedience to the law. He was not, I am persuaded, aware, how very much of the really, wonderful acquiescence of mankind in any government which they find established, is the effect of mere habit and imagination, and therefore depends upon the preservation of something like the continuity of existence in the institutions and identity in their outward forms; cannot transfer itself easily to new institutions, even though in themselves preferable; and is greatly shaken where there occurs anything like a break in the line of historical duration – anything which can be termed the end of the old constitution and the beginning of a new one.[28]

There were "collateral influences" that held society together, a lesson Mill claimed to have learned from the "Germano-Coleridgeans" but was really the means by which eighteenth-century Whig doctrines, especially Burkean ones, made their way into nineteenth-century liberalism.[29] The extent to which these sentiments sit well with the seemingly unbridled combativeness and rationalism of a text like *On Liberty* is an interesting question to which there is still no compelling answer. One strategy is to minimize the import of these ideas and suggest that Mill's assimilation of

"A nation is not only an idea of local extent and individual momentary aggregation, but it is an idea of continuity which extends in time as well as in numbers and in space...; it is constitution made by what is ten thousand times better than choice: it is made by the peculiar circumstances, occasions, tempers and dispositions and moral, civil and social habitude of the people, which disclose themselves only in a long space of time. It is a vestment which accommodates itself to the body."

[27] Mehta, in *Liberalism and Empire*, accuses Mill of just this.
[28] CW, X, p. 17 ("Remarks on Bentham's Philosophy").
[29] See J. W. Burrow, *Whigs and Liberals: Continuity and Change in English Political Thought* (Oxford: Clarendon Press, 1988).

these ideas is largely cosmetic, a sign of his intellectual generosity rather than of his political theory. A second, more fruitful response would be to ask to what extent the kind of liberty that Mill envisioned elsewhere presumed, as a backdrop, these collateral conditions and indeed needed to be tempered by a regard for them. If one takes the second view, one I am inclined toward, then Mill's denial of the status of his colonies as corporate entities is puzzling still.

But this Burkean assessment mattered to Mill's historical judgments. In the 1860s he made a concession to "Rajput nationality." His advocacy of indirect rule of the Rajputs, despite misgivings, rested on a fleeting appreciation of the sentiments expressed earlier. He wrote:

> I approved of all Lord Dalhousie's annexations, except that of Kerouli which never took effect, having been at once disallowed from home and indeed Lord D. himself gave it up before he knew of its being negatived. My principle was this. Wherever there are really native states, with a *nationality, historical traditions and feelings,* which is emphatically the case with Rajput states, there I would on no account take the advantage of any heirs to put an end to them.[30]

It was precisely these sentiments that had made Burke so mindful of the conduct of the British in India. By violating long-standing traditions in India, the British were being unmindful of the very sources on which the Indian sense of nationhood rested. Why Mill is not able to extend this generosity to other parts of India, not to mention other colonies more generally, may be easily explained. Part of the reason stems from his suspicion of any sense of nationality founded on a hierarchical ancient regime; part from the fact that he and Burke vehemently disagreed on whether the rest of India had any long-standing constitutions, that is, indigenous institutions that could provide these elements of continuity at all. He saw, unlike Burke, the rest of India being subject simply to a series of despotisms, and even his recognition that the despotic tendencies that did exist were partly a consequence of colonialism[31] seems to have, in the final analysis, done nothing to shake his conviction that the despotism

---

[30] CW, XVI, pp.1202–1203. It is perhaps no coincidence that the English appreciation of Rajputs began and lasted only so long as the Marathas, a "people" who Mill thought were as foreign to the kingdom they ruled as the British, were still an implacable threat. Zastoupil, *Mill and India,* chaps. 3 and 4, contains a good discussion of Mill's moderation toward these states.

[31] CW, XXX, p. 227, where Mill acknowledges that the mere appearance of the English government in India destroys the balance of social relations and leads to further rigidities. Also, in chap. 18 of *Considerations,* he acknowledges that the East India Company's presence greatly exacerbated the local despotisms that existed.

of the British was unquestionably vastly superior. But how these crucial ingredients of nationality that he himself identified in his critique of Bentham were to be created, or restored once they had been ruptured by colonialism, is a question he seems to have been less mindful of.

Of course, one can argue that these ingredients of nationality were in many instances created by colonialism. The first was in a way Mill did anticipate: the creation of modern state structures around which the conception of a nation could coalesce. The second was in a way Mill did not anticipate: the creation of a shared history of subordination that would itself be the impetus to develop a political sense of nationhood. But if the experience of postcolonial nationalism is any guide, both of these factors had to be supplanted by the very elements of continuity that Mill fleetingly recognized as contributing to a sense of nationhood and order. The fact that postcolonial nationalists saw it as one of their ideological functions to claim continuity between elements of the precolonial past and the modern states they sought to build may be a tribute to the insight contained in Mill's critique of Bentham; that he acted less on it than Burke may be an indication of the extent to which he underestimated the force of many of his own presuppositions when they were applied to the colonies.

To understand more fully the basis on which the colonies were denied the status of nations and the paradoxical implications of Mill's view, one needs to understand more fully the basis of his arguments. Three distinct but overlapping sets of orderings constitute Mill's hierarchical ranking of societies: the first is the contrast between stationary and progressive societies; the second is a contrast between savages and barbarians, on the one hand, and civilized societies on the other; the third is the hierarchy of national characters within "civilized societies."[32] Although the terms "barbarian" and "savage" were often used interchangeably by Mill, they stood for a set of distinct categories whose theoretical provenance can be traced to the Scottish Enlightenment. "Savage" referred to primitive tribes with transient social organizations, while "barbarian" referred to a phase of society with permanent political institutions, some system of property, and a principle of subordination.[33] Adam Ferguson was the first

---

[32] The best discussion of this is Pitts's *A Turn to Empire*, pp. 135ff.

[33] See Adam Ferguson, *An Essay on the History of Civil Society*, ed. Fania Oz-Salzberger (Cambridge: Cambridge University Press, 1995). For reasons not entirely clear, the *Oxford English Dictionary* seems to suggest that the distinction was made clearly for the first time by Matthew Arnold in 1838. Robert Young, *Colonial Desire* (London: Routledge, 1994), is misled by this attribution. Of course, in France, the distinction is due to Montesquieu.

theorist to make this contrast central to his argument and may indeed have been the first theorist to use "civilization" as a theoretical term to refer to a distinct mode of social organization defined in contrast to both savages and barbarians.[34] The range of meanings that came to be associated with the term remained somewhat indeterminate throughout the subsequent period. James Mill complained that in the orientalist William Jones's writing, the "term civilization was ... as by most men attached to no definite assemblage of ideas." James Mill's editor, Horace Wilson, duly turned the complaint back on him.[35] It is also worth mentioning that the term "civilization" was used in the singular, and it was only in the late nineteenth century that its plural form came into use. The indeterminacies and difficulties of the concept of civilization are reflected in Mill's strategy for defining it.

Mill holds on to the two associations of this term: civilization was associated with perfectibility, but it was more often defined through what it was not: barbarian or savage. Mill lists a series of contrasts: savage societies are thinly settled, consist of wandering tribes, and have no systematic political arrangements for their security and no property. Civilized societies are, by contrast, more densely settled, in villages or cities, and have settled political arrangements, better security of property, and so on.[36] But the civilized also exhibit additional features: most importantly, the capacity for cooperation. The essential requisites for cooperation are the ability to restrain one's will, the ability to sacrifice and make future-oriented plans – in short, the ability to be disciplined. The theme of discipline looms large in Mill's historical imagination. But the significant example that he uses to demonstrate the barbarians' incapacity to cooperate and be disciplined is their weakness in the craft of war. The sign of discipline and the ability to cooperate create the ability to wage war successfully; defeat itself is a marker of being less civilized, of an incapacity to handle complexity (make alliances, for example) and discipline. Examples of societies that exhibit these traits are the native states of India and the Spanish, both of which had succumbed to other powers.[37]

[34] The term "civilization" was of juridical origin, which began to be widely used in the eighteenth century to denote a distinct kind of society almost at the same time that the term "progress" acquired great currency. For an interesting survey of the concept in France, see J. Starobinski's essay "The Word CIVILIZATION," in his *Blessings in Disguise or the Morality of Evil* (Cambridge, Mass.: Harvard University Press, 1993), chap. 1.
[35] See James Mill's *History of British India* repr. (New York: Chelsea Publishers, 1968), bk. II, p.110.
[36] CW, XVII, pp.119ff ("Civilization").
[37] CW, XVIII, p.122.

This characterization of the barbarians serves as a theoretical prelude to the argument of "A Few Words on Non-Intervention," where Mill proclaims barbarian societies to be exempt from the normal laws that govern intervention among the civilized nations. This essay was an attempt to delineate the conditions under which intervention was permissible. Mill dissented from Cobden's unequivocal defense of the principle of nonintervention and argued that there were times when a free government should intervene even if this was inconsistent with the nonintervention principle. If the liberty of a people had been interfered with by other powers, intervention was justified; intervention in civil wars was to be avoided unless it was a protracted one in which there was no "probability of a speedy issue"; if a people were struggling against a native tyranny upheld by foreign arms, intervention could redress the balance. Mill's ambition was to lay the foundations for a new "law of nations" that would be congruent with the changing interests of "civilized nations." He argued that such foundations for the law of nations as had been provided by Pufendorf and Vattel were seriously outdated, because they had been designed for an age when the interests of civilized states were those of "territorial attack and defence."[38] Now these interests are "liberty, just government and sympathy of opinion."[39] For Mill, nationality was a necessary means for the attainment of liberty; hence, movements and wars of national self-determination, under these new foundations, needed to be sympathized with and supported.[40]

The rules that govern intervention, however, do not apply to barbarians. Mill gives two sets of grounds for their preclusion, and the examples again are similar. First, barbarians are incapable of restraining their present desires, they are not under the influence of far-reaching motives, and hence they cannot be considered capable of abiding by treaties. Second, barbarians are not yet ready for liberty; indeed, such elements of nationality as they possess (the marks that distinguish them from others) make

---

[38] CW, XX ("Vindication of the French Revolution of February 1848"), p. 346. The reference to Pufendorf and Vattel is on p. 345. It is ironic that Mill read Vattel to argue for the strictest principles of nonintervention. Edmund Burke had famously used Vattel's authority to argue for intervention after the French Revolution. Burke saw Vattel as arguing that it was legitimate to intervene in a civil war if it was not clear that deposing a monarch had the authority of the nation behind it. In this case, the war was against a principle, not a nation. See Edmund Burke, appendix to the "Remarks on the Policy of the Allies," *Works* (London: Henry G. Bohn, 1854–1889), vol. 3, pp. 458–466, where Vattel is quoted profusely to justify intervention.

[39] CW, XX, p. 346.

[40] Ibid., p. 348, for Mill's defense of the Italians and Poles.

their nationality an impediment to liberty and progress. "The sacred duties which civilized nations owed to the independence and nationality of each other are not binding towards those to whom nationality and independence are either a certain evil, or at best a questionable good."[41] The consequence was that "barbarians have no right as a *nation*, except a right to such treatment as may, at the earliest possible period fit them for *becoming one*."[42]

"*Barbarians have no right as a nation.*" The assumptions that this terse statement embodied were of momentous consequence. First, it suggested that groups could not claim rights as corporate entities unless they were constituted as nations in the proper political sense of the term. Second, by defending the nation-state and the idea of unity that it embodied, Mill was foreclosing the space in which distinct peoples could be granted some recognition as *corporate* entities without all the political trappings that Mill associated with a proper sense of nationhood.[43] Finally, the possession of nationhood became a mark of civilization. That and only that could entitle a people to any sort of recognition. By making nationality in the political sense a mark of civilization, Mill helped shaped one of the enduring features of post-nineteenth-century politics. The claim to being a nation became the form in which groups sought recognition. When Dr. Martin Delaney, writing in 1859 after a visit to Niger, wrote "that the claims of no people are respected until they are presented in a national capacity,"[44] or when Benjamin Kidd complained in 1920 that one of the spectacles of the modern world is that "more of tribal or local egotisms ... have expressed themselves under the form of nationality – claiming, in this respect alone, the rights and tolerance of our civilization,"[45] they were describing a structure of discourse whose main assumptions were not only congruent with Mill's, they were in part legitimized by him. By tying the nation to civilization, Mill was also aligning it with self-esteem and all the consequences that follow from a politics of self-esteem.

[41] CW, XXI, p.119.

[42] CW, XXI, p.119 ("A Few Words on Non-Intervention").

[43] One practical instance of this foreclosure was Mill's endorsement of the Durham Report. All of Mill's assumptions about the uniformity of the nation-state, the superiority of certain races, and the desirability of imperial expansion converge in that endorsement. For a discussion of the report itself, see J. Tully, *Strange Multiplicity* (Cambridge: Cambridge University Press, 1995), pp. 158–162.

[44] Quoted in Basil Davidson, *The Black Man's Burden* (New York: Random House, 1992), p. 43.

[45] Benjamin Kidd, *Principles of Western Civilization* (New York: Macmillan, 1902), pp. 5–6, 99.

In crude military terms, Mill even tied nationality to the possession of power. Those nations that possess the feeling of nationality have been the most powerful countries in proportion to their territory and resources: England, France, Holland, and Switzerland; indeed, the woes of modern peoples spring, to a large extent, from the absence of this feeling of nationality. This was a doctrine that again, curiously enough, Burke had done much to legitimize during the late-eighteenth-century wars against the French. It was during those wars that Burke had suggested that "to do anything without raising a spirit (I mean a National Spirit) with all the energy and much of the conduct of a Party Spirit, I hold to be a thing utterly impossible." The curious idea that a unitary will, as embodied in the spirit of nationality, was a principal cause of success in war, and therefore the chief means of defending one's liberty, became one of the main ingredients through which the principle of nationality came to be legitimized. By aligning the languages of nationhood with both civilization and power, Mill was ensuring that the nation would continue to be the currency of self-esteem in the modern world.

THE QUESTION OF CHARACTER

What holds nations together? The feelings of unity and mutual cohesion derive from something more than a voluntary act of association. The sources of this unity and cohesion are diverse: they could be the identity of race, or community of language, or the possession of a national history or collective pride connected with the experience of that history. But these sources serve merely to demarcate peoples territorially. What holds nations together and describes them is a shared national character (a concept on which Hume's originating influence was important) – a commonality of opinions, feelings, and habits.

The concept of national character, as Stefan Collini has noted, had both descriptive and evaluative elements. It could refer to the sum of mental and moral qualities, or to the set of settled dispositions that distinguished a nation or a race viewed as a homogeneous whole, or it could refer to those of these traits that were particularly valuable.[46]

The idea of national character gradually supplanted the civic republican discourse on virtue in light of these features: First, the degree to which Mill thought that peoples *as collectivities* possess a character that

---

[46] See Stefan Collini, *Public Moralists* (Oxford: Oxford University Press, 1991), pp. 96–108.

distinguishes them from others is striking and was an essential premise in his ability to rank various nationalities. "National character" is an *objective* attribute of nations; it is not predicated upon any self-awareness on the part of those whom it describes. This can be usefully contrasted with a more contemporary term, "national identity,"[47] that carries a more reflexive dimension and is more a principle of subjective identification than of objective attributes. Mill's view of human diversity is therefore constructed from an objective "ethological" point of view, rather than one that gives credence to the way peoples subjectively understand their differences and create meanings. It is somewhat ironic that one of the foremost theorists of the way ideas relate to the subjective and inward should have missed so spectacularly the fact that the enduring power of differences does not always come from objective differences, but rather from subjective identifications that may be more recalcitrant than the substantial differences in character traits. Second, the concept of a national character was linked to Mill's idea of progress in a complex way. Mill, like many of his contemporaries, thought that the development or possession of a certain type of national character was as much an *index* of progress as it was its cause.[48]

Most importantly, the idea of a character collectively possessed is also deeply braided with Mill's moral psychology. Mill thought that we are motivated, in part, not only by a conception that we form of our own character, but also by a conception of the character of those around us.[49] The exertion of virtue or conscience depends entirely upon having faith in the actual existence of such feelings and dispositions in others.[50] In short, Mill thought that virtue was a "participable"[51] good. It is easier for me to be virtuous if I can be secure in the belief that everyone around me is virtuous in more or less the same sense as well. For Mill a shared national character was, therefore, a source of *moral* motivation, one of those collateral influences that society could not do without.

[47] For this contrast I am indebted to Perry Anderson, *A Zone of Engagement* (London: Verso, 1992), pp. 268ff.

[48] See Collini, *Public Moralists*, p. 108. For examples of Mill treating national character as a cause, see CW, XIX, p. 421 ("Considerations"), where he discusses the propitiousness of the English versus the French character for democracy.

[49] For this point I am indebted to Glyn Morgan, *The Idea of a European Superstate* (Princeton, N.J.: Princeton University Press, 2005).

[50] CW, X, p.15 ("Remarks on Bentham").

[51] The concept of "participable good" is taken from Cornelius Castoriadis, *Crossroads in the Labyrinth* (Cambridge, Mass: MIT Press, 1985). It refers to those goods, like virtue, that are easier to enjoy if more people around you do so as well.

This point is important for understanding Mill's theory of moral motivation, which is interesting here for two reasons. First, it is different from a Kantian theory of motivation in which the requirements of morality are sufficient to generate the motive that can elicit its own performance and therefore better defines why nationality may matter for moral purposes. Second, I think there is a deep unresolved tension in Mill's arguments that is worth highlighting. In order to see what he is up to, we need a brief digression on *Utilitarianism*.

One of the many oddities of that work (in light of Mill's arguments elsewhere) is his view that motives are always instilled by education, training, and discipline rather than being aroused by argument. Mill makes a distinction between "internal sanctions" and "external sanctions." The former refer to "a feeling in our own mind, a pain more or less intense, attendant on violation of duty which in the properly cultivated moral nature rises, in the more serious cases into shrinking from it as an impossibility." The latter refer to such things as reward and punishment, the love of God, the love of others, and the concomitant desire to please them. Mill argues, however, that internal sanctions, such as they exist, have no content because through "a sufficient use of external sanctions and the force of early impressions, the internal sanctions can be cultivated in almost any direction[.]" The upshot of the argument is that one can be *trained*, through external influences, to be a utilitarian, just as one can be trained to be almost anything else. Any internal sanctions that act upon us are, on this view, a product of our upbringing, not a product of our understanding of correct moral concepts.

This view, of course, raises all sorts of questions about Mill's arguments, not the least of which is whether Mill's own works can be reasonably expected to *persuade* those who did not have the right kind of upbringing or whether they are, like most arguments, more like ontological proofs for the existence of God: designed to persuade those who are already so inclined. Given his view of the malleability of human nature, any sort of confidence we might have in the possibility of morality is heavily dependent upon a convincing account of the mechanisms by which external sanctions can inculcate morality. Mill's writings are pervaded by a concern for what such mechanisms might be. Even *On Liberty* seems less a tract against the homogenizing effects of public opinion per se[52] than a tract on mobilizing the armory of public opinion, that most important of external sanctions, for liberal causes.

---

[52] See CW, XVIII, p. 228 ("On Liberty").

For Mill, a *collective* conception of ourselves as possessing characters of a certain sort was one of those collateral influences necessary to elicit the performance of moral actions. This conception, for reasons explained earlier, had to be collective and was partly self-fulfilling to the extent that a belief in it itself helped bring about the state of affairs it described. This is why, for Mill, it is important that a people be constituted as a *self-conscious collectivity.*

A self-conscious sense of being part of a collectivity (the feeling of nationality) is a precondition for moral action in that a sense of identification is prior to a sense of moral obligation. Mill takes it to be axiomatic that one effectively enacts moral obligations *only* if one identifies with those whom one's moral actions affect. One of the virtues of the nation was that it expressed this sense of identification with a group larger than one's family or locality and hence enlarged the domain of those to whom we effectively owed moral duties. Mill would have had no trouble conceding that, to a certain extent, the defense of the nation as the locus of identification was arbitrary, and he hoped it would be transcended. The level of identification for Mill could be secured gradually and only through a series of historical stages; it was not a consequence of a proper understanding of the requirements of the moral law. This was so for the simple reason that our moral behavior was secured by external sanctions, and the degree of our identification with others was limited by the extent to which the institutions we experienced had shaped us.

A striking feature of Mill's formulations is the acknowledgment that nationality, at least at a certain stage of human progress, partly performs the function of religion to seek that kind of affect that can elicit moral performance. Mill seems to have been keenly aware that however arbitrary the boundaries of any nation, and whatever their status as "imagined communities," they could braid themselves with moral motivation in a way that other possible imaginings seem less capable of doing.

In the context of imperial discourse, the idea of national character performs several functions in the argument. First, it gives a more complex typology of different societies and the institutions appropriate to molding their character. Mill never gave up the thought that political institutions could mold collective self-conceptions and "improve" the national character. But he believed that very different institutions are needed "to train to the perfection of their nature, or to constitute into a *united nation* or social polity, an essentially subjective people like the Germans, and an essentially objective people like those of Northern or Central Italy ... the one wanting individuality, the other fellow feeling; the one failing for want of exacting enough for itself, the other for want of conceding enough to others."[53] The kinds of institutions that a society needed had to be carefully modulated to its needs in a manner in which they could take that society to the next level of progress. For some societies, despotism was appropriate.

Second, the possession of a kind of national character made a people entitled to rule. This was the case in the familiar sense that a people more capable of exercising discipline, practicing liberty, and applying reason were better equipped to use their leading strings to walk the rest of humanity up the ladder of progress. But Mill's sense of the English entitlement to rule came from a much thicker description of their character. The two salient features of this conception were, first, that the English were least likely to themselves be absorbed by other races and, second, that they were the nation whose character was in part defined by the capacity to have moral scruples and dispositions of a disinterested and benevolent kind. It was these considerations that enabled Mill, as I shall suggest momentarily, to answer those critics who thought that empire was politically corrupting.

Ever since the 1750s, with the emergence of a different kind of empire based on conquest (India and Canada) and attempts to suppress the American colonists, the question of the extent to which an overseas empire was compatible with liberty at home had become an urgent one. The dominant view was that the possession of an empire did not subvert English constitutional liberties at home, although there was a consistent stream in British political thought, from Burke to Charles James Fox, through Cobden and J. A. Hobson, that consistently warned, in Hobson's words, that "it is a nemesis of Imperialism that the arts and crafts of tyranny, acquired and exercised on our unfree Empire should be turned against our liberties at home."[54] Indeed, the *political* worry about the corruptive effects of empire on English institutions and character were among the most persistent sources of doubt about the desirability of empire. Although Mill seems not to have directly participated in these debates, almost all of his proposals defending the East India Company as the governing structure of empire need to be understood as a response to these considerations.

The British Empire frequently invited comparisons with the Greek and Roman imperial experience. The invocation of these models usually had

[53] CW, X, p.105 ("Remarks on Bentham").
[54] J. A. Hobson, *Imperialism* (London: Hutchinson, 1902), p.160.

a political purpose. In the context of the American colonial disturbances, much hinged on the argument about whether the American colonies were to be regarded like the Greek colonies in which the settlers had exercised their natural right to emigrate and transplant Greek institutions without the parent city exercising any sovereignty over them, or whether the Roman model, in which the metropolis continued to exercise sovereignty over the colonies, was more appropriate.[55] In the early nineteenth century, the Greek–Roman comparison was again being used with a different purpose in mind. Many members of the group known as "colonial reformers," with whom Mill had aligned, argued against an empire on the ground that, as in Rome, such an empire served merely to enhance the power of the military and aristocratic classes at home and hence led to its corruption and decline. The colonial reformers instead proposed, in the case of Canada, New Zealand, and Australia, at any rate, the fostering of settlement colonies, much as in ancient Greece. The idea was to replicate English institutions and society in a manner in which they would not be dependent upon the parent country but would be self-supporting. This would ensure that the constitutional balance that preserved British liberties at home would not be subverted. It would also ensure that these colonies would act as autonomous societies, with their own checks and balances, rather than rely on the mother country to provide them. It was the distance of the control from home that had, the colonial reformers argued, provided opportunities for self-aggrandizement and lawlessness of Englishmen overseas. Giving the colonies the character of self-contained societies would therefore facilitate the maintenance of the character and habits of civilized Englishmen in environments that might not otherwise be propitious for such maintenance. It would also ensure that these colonists would not undermine liberties at home.

The category of "despotism" is a complex one in Mill's thought. As Nadia Urbinati has argued, Mill never made it entirely clear when a society would be ready to emerge from despotism.[56] But his worry about despotism worked in both directions. On the one hand, colonies could be subject to despotism. On the other hand, there was a danger that empire could produce despotism in the colonizer. It was to forestall the possible consequences of this despotism that Mill made the proposals in chapter 18 of *Representative Government*. He argued that the administration of

---

[55] For these debates in the context of the American empire, see Peter Miller, *Defining the Common Good* (Cambridge: Cambridge University Press, 1994), pp.198ff.
[56] Nadia Urbinati, "Many Heads of the Hydra," in Urbinati and Zakaras, *J. S. Mill*, p. 96.

India should be vested in a disinterested, virtuous, and benevolent elite, one that the East India Company was in a better position to provide, in a manner in which it could be insulated from the pressures of politics in Britain. Mill thought this insulation would serve a dual purpose: it would prevent officials and settlers in India from exploiting public opinion in Britain to pursue their more acquisitive and exploitive aims. It would also ensure that power would be vested in a disinterested elite, one better informed about the conditions in India and hence more capable of ruling. The model he invoked was that of the government of Prussia – "a most skillfully organized aristocracy of all the most highly educated men in the kingdom[;] the British government in India partakes (with considerable modifications) of the same character."[57]

As Karuna Mantena has shown, Mill's arguments deflate anxieties about British corruption in two ways.[58] First, he hopes that this institutional configuration would both prevent the corruption of the British polity and protect Indian subjects from the predatory designs of more speculative merchants. Second, he uses the concept of national character to argue for English incorruptibility. This might seem surprising in light of the fact that Mill was loath to contemplate any "admixture of races" in the Indian context for fear that a superior nationality might be absorbed into an inferior one. On numerous occasions, Mill describes the predatory and insolent character of the English in India.[59] He acknowledges the "insolence" of the English, which had become "a disgrace." He often speaks of the cruel treatment of the natives by the settlers, of their avarice and greed, of their capacity for despotism. Yet, these traits never seemed to cast any doubt on his imperial self-confidence; and, perhaps more damaging, they never led him to doubt the proposition that the most advanced peoples, those who best understand liberty and reason, would also have the more admirable character. When J. F. Stephens claimed to turn an Indian lantern on English problems, this was the first point he urged against Mill's doctrines: namely, that the connection between

---

[57] CW, XVIII, p. 23 ("The Rationale for Representation").
[58] Mantena, "Mill and the Imperial Predicament," 310.
[59] See, for example CW, XIX, p. 571 ("Considerations"). "When a country holds another in subjection, the individuals of the ruling people who resort to the foreign country to make their fortunes are ... armed with prestige and filled with the scornful overbearingness of the conquering nation. Among a people like that of India, the utmost efforts of the public authorities are not enough for the effectual protection of the weak against the strong; and of all the strong the European settlers are the strongest." See also the interesting letter to Charles Dilke, where Mill again talks about the insolence of the English in some detail. CW, XVII ("Letter to Charles Wentworth Dilke," 30 September 1870).

being an advanced people and possessing a more incorruptible character was tenuous. Stephens argued with relentless logic that what entitled the English to rule and what secured their rule was their power, not the fact of their being enlightened. On a charitable reading, this might suggest that Mill, for all his talk of character, believed in the end that it was the right degree of institutional control and incentives that secured virtuous behavior, not character itself. But it would perhaps be missing the flavor of mid-nineteenth-century confidence to press that view too far. After all, it was a mature Mill who wrote:

Perhaps the English are the fittest people to rule over the barbarous or the semi barbarous nations of the East, precisely because they are the stiffest, *and most wedded to their own customs,* of all civilized people. All the former conquerors of the east have been absorbed into it, and have adopted its ways, instead of communicating to it their own. So did the Portuguese, so would the French have done. Not so John Bull; if he has one foot in India, he will always have another on the English shore.[60]

The English entitlement to rule thus rested upon their being *secure* in their own customs – perhaps a rather ironic compliment from one who thought that being wedded to custom was about the worse sin one could commit. One is almost tempted to suggest that it is the sense of fragility associated with this ideal of national character that in the end leads Mill to place an even greater burden on his arguments concerning the inadequacies and decrepitude of other national characters. For what restores the self-confidence and coherence of this self-perception is an image of the other – or a set of others – one can define oneself against; this self-conception requires for its sustenance precisely the sort of unnuanced view of others that so marks Mill's writings and is so strikingly at odds with his best moral and intellectual instincts.

Could the possession of an empire itself have a salutary effect on national character? Could this itself help sustain the collective self-conception required for superior moral action? It is certainly the case that Mill was not an indiscriminate nationalist; for him, national pride, that spring of motivation, should always have its content examined. In a letter to Tocqueville, Mill conceded Tocqueville's claim "that the feeling of orgueil national [national pride] is the only feeling of a public spirited and elevating kind which remains and which therefore ought not to be permitted to go down. How true this is everyday makes itself perfectly evident." Later in the letter, Mill warns that the ideals in whose

[60] CW, XVII, p. 647.

service that feeling ought to be exercised should be better than "the low and grovelling ones" that the French seemed to have at present, that is, in the cause of Algeria's improvement. It is difficult, however, to shake off the sense that for Mill, the national character was sustained, in part, by a sense of mission that, in his context, a *well-governed* empire could supply. Later in his life, Mill seems to have placed increasing emphasis on the motivational consequences of prestige that an empire would bring. It bears repeating that this prestige was an instrument for humankind's improvement, yet it was prestige nevertheless. In a letter in 1862 he argues, against the separatists like Goldwin Smith, that "any separation from the colonies would greatly diminish the prestige of England, which prestige I believe to be in the present state of the world, a great advantage to mankind."[61]

It is interesting to ask about the extent to which, for Mill, having a collective conception of oneself as *being superior* can itself have a motivating function. After all, it was Mill who had argued, against Bentham, that people are motivated in part by a conception of themselves. This, of course, has disquieting consequences: it will then be the case that constructions of superiority will not, as an empirical matter at any rate, be an incidental part of moral motivation but crucial to it. By the same token, a collective perception of oneself as inferior will generate its own pathologies. Of course, how one defines the axes of superiority or inferiority remains important. But if Mill's account of motivation is correct, then his institutions of the hierarchies of superior and inferior peoples, secured by the operations of colonial power, may have had more portentous consequences than he was in a position to fathom.

DISCIPLINE AND COMMERCE

For Mill, the sentiment of nationality was a vehicle for moral development. And one of the implications of his conception was that the range of affairs on which practical reason could be exercised should also correspondingly expand. Mill appreciated some of the virtues that various local participatory forms of self-rule – like those in Italian republics and Asiatic villages – had exhibited. Indeed, Mill's account of these Asiatic villages is more generous than one would expect. They were not, as for Marx or Maine, repositories of immobilized custom, outdated production, or unbridled superstition, but instead exhibited commendable forms

---

[61] CW, XVII, p. 1767 ("Letter to Charles Wentworth Dilke," 30 September 1870).

of self-rule. Their chief defect, in the end, was the spirit of localism that they reflected. This impeded their development of the capacity to reflect upon a larger ambit of affairs or develop affective identification with a larger group of people. In the end, for Mill, there was no cause to lament the passing of this form of self-government. For all of his appreciation of Pericles as a paragon of virtue, it was the amalgamating functions of Alexander's empire that ultimately drew his approval. Mill was quite comfortable with the thought that the formation of the wider allegiances he cherished, especially those to the nation-state, could be forged only through the struggle to form larger states through illiberal means. Like many eighteenth-century thinkers, he credited the absolutist states with creating the preconditions for modern liberty: destroying smaller communities and destroying the intermediate orders that had been the sources of decentralized oppression. Like Adam Smith, he believed that the emancipation of serfs was the product of absolutist states or "irresponsible monarchies."

Libertarian readings of *On Liberty* have obscured an appreciation of Mill's sense of the preconditions for the exercise of liberty. One of these is the principle of nationality that I have discussed at some length. The second is a sense of restraining discipline. Discipline was for Mill itself a mark of civilization rather than its repressive potential. One of the principles of social order for him is education, whose main feature is a "restraining discipline." Discipline for Mill is the "suppression of personal impulses and aims." Whenever and in proportion to which the success of retraining discipline is relaxed, "the *natural tendency* of mankind to anarchy reasserted itself." Even a text like *On Liberty,* after acknowledging that a "man's desires and impulses are the expressions of his own nature," goes on to add the significant qualification "as it has been developed and modified by his own culture." I mention all this to establish the following thought: Mill saw civilization as an achievement that was more precarious than the optimism of his doctrine would suggest. What secured civilization was the disciplining power of the state. There is an astonishing toughness in Mill's liberalism that made him considerably less ambivalent about the costs of state formation than most twentieth-century liberals acknowledge. For Mill, in most cases, the discipline that makes a people capable of regular obedience and respect for the rule of law requires an immeasurably long process of struggle, gestation, and even "foreign force."

Nothing but foreign force would induce a tribe of North American Indians to submit to the restraints of regular and civilized government. The same might be said, though somewhat less absolutely, of the barbarians who overran the Roman Empire. It required centuries of time, and an entire change of circumstances, to discipline them into regular obedience even to their own leaders, when not actually serving under their own banner.[62]

In fact, James Fitzjames Stephens, ever the astutest of Mill's critics, pressed Mill's own historical sociology against his political theory: What reason was there to suppose that moral improvement and the cause of liberty were served by deliberation? What reason was there to suppose that deliberation led to moral improvement rather than stout discipline? Of course, Mill could and did historicize the need for such discipline: it applied only to the early stages of improvement.

It is in this context that Mill's remarks about the two other agents of civilization, commerce and property, and their relation to Mill's views on empire need to be understood. Mill's economic case for imperialism was straightforward. He followed the colonial reformers and Wakefield, in particular, in arguing that England suffered from a surplus of both population and capital, a combination that would lead to a declining rate of profit. A declining rate of profit would reduce investment, and England would reach a stationary state prematurely.[63] Mill suggested that England should rely more heavily on foreign trade and outlets for investment, both of which would be secured by colonization. "There needs be no hesitation in affirming that colonization in the present state of the world, is the best affair of business in which the capital of an old and wealthy country can engage."[64] Colonization solved the problem of excess population at home, while the flows of capital outward ensured a higher and more stable rate of profit. These arguments were formulated primarily in the context of white settler colonies. The uncivilized dependencies in India and Africa were also markets for English capital and suppliers of cheap agricultural products. But these benefits were possible only if the order and security of these countries were secured by maintaining an empire.[65]

Mill believed commerce to be a "necessary condition and indispensable machinery" of civilization. Like many of his eighteenth-century

---

[62] CW, XIX, p. 374 ("Considerations").

[63] For Mill's debt to Wakefield, see his letter to Gustave de Beaumont in CW, XVIII, p. 1992. I will not go into the details of the argument here. Donald Winch, *Classical Political Economy and the Colonies* (Cambridge, Mass.: Harvard University Press, 1965), remains the best work on the subject. A convenient summary is found in Sullivan, "Liberalism and Imperialism: J. S. Mill's Defense of the British Empire," p. 607. The relevant discussion in *Principles of Political Economy* is found in CW, III, pp. 735–741.

[64] CW, II, p. 963 ("Principles of Political Economy").

[65] Ibid., pp.186–187.

predecessors, he saw commerce as a medium through which ideas were exchanged, parochialism overcome, and the wealth and prosperity of *all* humankind regarded with goodwill. Commerce would, he suggested, make war obsolete by strengthening those interests that were opposed to it. Yet, this optimism about commerce, characteristic more of the eighteenth century than of the nineteenth, began to fade somewhat. In the 1860s, in the face of protectionist moves in Europe and the United States, Mill began to see the empire as the means of maintaining a free trade zone. In a reversal of two very influential nineteenth-century theses, he argued in effect that the empire was necessary for maintaining free trade and that power was necessary for wealth rather than the other way around.[66] This statement also reversed the astonishing hypothesis that thinkers like Diderot and Constant had entertained of commerce replacing war. "War then comes before commerce. The former is all savage impulse, the latter civilized calculation," Benjamin Constant had declared in 1813.[67] War and empire were, in Mill's estimation, necessary to secure commerce.[68]

Commercial civilization for Mill is not generated spontaneously but requires the discipline of well-formed states behind it. Mill thought that capitalism in the colonies could be established only through legislation. The price of land should be set sufficiently high that the immigrants would have to work longer to purchase it. In the absence of this restriction, or in conditions under which families could acquire farms for themselves quickly, two problems would follow. Individual farms could not be large enough because there would be a shortage of hired labor, and the dispersion of labor into smaller farms would deprive the colonies of the benefits of the division of labor and agricultural surplus.[69]

The proposition that the state would have to intervene massively in the affairs and social structures of the uncivilized dependencies began to form the cornerstone of Mill's recommendations on imperial policy. In both Ireland and India, Mill wanted to create a class of peasant proprietors whose small landholdings would be the best means of economic,

---

[66] CW, XIX, p. 565 ("Considerations").
[67] See Benjamin Constant, *Political Writings*, ed. Biancamaria Fontana (Cambridge: Cambridge University Press, 1988), p. 53. Pagden, *Lords of All the World*, chaps. 6 and 7, contains a good discussion of these themes.
[68] CW, XIX, p. 565.
[69] See CW, III, pp. 958ff. This was the proposal that drew Marx's wrath. Marx saw it as a case in which the socially productive power of labor, the use of machinery, and so on were impossible without the expropriation of labor and the corresponding transformation into the means of capital. See Marx, *Capital* (New York: Penguin Classics, 1981), vol. I, chap. 13.

social, and moral improvement in these countries. The kinds of economic agents that Smith valued – those capable of exercising effort, foresight, and prudence – had to be *created*. Economic legislation for Mill was palpably a form of education, a mechanism for disciplining desires and aspirations that would otherwise take an anarchic course. On these matters, his recommendations for the moral improvement of colonial subjects were of a piece with his recommendations for the English working classes. In his writings on Ireland, he argued that

without a change in the people, the most beneficent change in their mere outward circumstances would not last a generation. You will never change the people unless you make themselves the instruments, by opening to them an opportunity to work out for themselves all the other changes. You will never change the people but by changing the *external motives* which act on them and shape their lives from the cradle to the grave.... The real effective education of a people is given by the circumstances by which they are surrounded. What shapes the character is not what is purposely taught, so much as the unintentional teaching of institutions and social relations.... Nothing you can say will alter the state of his [the peasant's] mind, only something you can *do*.[70]

By arguing that the state would be the instrument of civilization, by producing in the colonies, especially India and Ireland, the conditions that would facilitate the production of economic agents who could exercise the necessary "effort, prudence and foresight" that civilization required, Mill was granting functional legitimacy to an institution whose moral and civilizing functions he had done much to recommend. Although Mill speaks of "advancing civilization," he knew better than most how much of that rested on "external sanctions" and how important the creation of nation-states would be in providing those sanctions. Although Mill hoped that one day both the principle of nationality and the nation-state could be transcended, the peculiar justification he gave for the nation-state and the imperial and civilizational hierarchies he aligned them with have made them a more recalcitrant phenomenon than even he would have anticipated. And it should also remind us of the extent to which, historically, liberalism has rested on a strong state and the principle of nationality – with all of the costs involved.

CONCLUSION

This chapter has argued that Mill's conception of nationality is central to understanding his entanglement in empire. Three familiar assumptions

[70] See CW, XXIV, p. 955.

characterize much of modern politics and have, among other assumptions, profoundly influenced its course. The first is the familiar claim that territorially separate peoples, whose populations understand themselves as constituting a people, are an essential precondition for representative government – that the nation-state is an essential backdrop against which representative government flourishes. The second, somewhat more surprising assumption of modern politics is that many, if not most, groups that seek recognition of their identities do so by claiming to be *nations*. The languages of nationhood now permeate the self-understanding of many groups that seek recognition, and being acknowledged as a nation is often constitutive of the identity, prestige, and self-understanding of these groups. The third assumption is that nation-states claim for themselves a civilizing function. They are one of the principal agents of modernity that transform smaller and perhaps more parochial identities into larger ones. They seek to produce not only citizens with allegiances to the nation-state, but also individuals with a set of attributes that enable them to function properly in a modern economy. It could indeed be argued that many of the other aspirations of the modern project – individuality, authenticity, self-government, and so on – function within the confines of, and are chastened by, these assumptions. All of these assumptions came together in Mill and shaped his view of the relations between societies. And it is one of history's supreme ironies that Mill's conception of nationality, while it legitimized colonial power, also became the principal language in which colonialism was resisted.

Republicanism, Liberalism, and Empire in Postrevolutionary France

Jennifer Pitts

Colonies (nos): s'attrister quand on en parle.

Flaubert, *Dictionnaire des idées reçues*

Writers on the Left in France, in publications such as the *Monde Diplomatique* and *Politis*, have voiced frustration in recent years at the country's long-standing neglect of France's colonial history.[1] Whereas post-colonial studies now has a history several decades old in the Anglophone world, it has come only lately to France; indeed, a recent volume starts by making "a case for Francophone postcolonial studies."[2] Broader public debates, too, have only reluctantly begun to attend to France's colonial history. This new attention has arisen in large part in reaction to the new presence of immigrants from the former colonies in public life, thanks to the struggles of the *banlieues* and the headscarf debate. Discussion of the Algerian war, long repressed, has also begun to intensify, in part because the generation that fought that war is aging and there has been a desire to capture their experience while interviews are still possible.[3] Still, these

---

[1] Several great critical historians of the French empire of an older generation, notably Yves Benot and Claude Liauzu, have recently died, and relatively few prominent French historians now study colonial history, though a much younger generation has taken up the subject.

[2] Charles Forsdick and David Murphy, eds., *Francophone Postcolonial Studies: A Critical Introduction* (New York: Oxford University Press, 2003). Also see Marie-Claude Smouts, ed., *La situation postcoloniale: Les* postcolonial studies *dans le débat français* (Paris: Sciences Po, 2007).

[3] Scholars are belatedly paying particular attention to the role of the *harkis*, the Algerian soldiers who fought on the side of the French, and of their subsequent marginalization in

Earlier drafts of this chapter were presented to audiences at Yale, Stanford, and New York University, to whom I am very grateful for comments and discussion.

discussions have been largely reactive and relatively defensive: so defensive, indeed, that the National Assembly passed a law in February 2005 requiring that history textbooks and teachers, and university researchers, "acknowledge and recognize in particular the positive role of the French presence abroad, especially in North Africa."[4] The law sparked an outcry among historians, but the National Assembly refused to consider a motion to repeal it, and then-President Chirac had to use extraordinary measures to have it rescinded.[5] A group of French scholars known as Achac has developed the idea of a *fracture coloniale* to describe this mutual mistrust and misunderstanding on the part of the various participants in debates over France's colonial past and postcolonial present.[6] The phrase *fracture coloniale* derives from *fracture sociale*, which became popular during Chirac's presidency (1995–2007) as a description of the various forces thought to be pulling French society apart. The popularity of the term *fracture* in France as a way to describe political problems suggests the degree to which national unity, or the unity of the republic, continues to represent a paramount goal in French political discourse.[7]

The republican tradition, that is to say, continues to frame French debates on empire, as it has done since the Revolution. Moreover, recent literature has stressed the degree to which nineteenth-century French liberalism had its roots in the distinctively republican discourse of the revolutionary period.[8] French republicanism and Anglophone liberalism have shared numerous features in relation to empire: both are egalitarian

France. See Tom Charbit, *Les Harkis* (Paris: La Découverte, 2006); and Gilles Manceron and Fatima Benaci-Lancou, *Les Harkis dans la colonisation et ses suites* (Paris: Editions de l'atelier, 2008).

[4] See Loi n° 2005–158 du 23 février 2005, http://www.admi.net/jo/20050224/DEFX0300218L.html. Also see Benjamin Stora's discussion of the law in *L'Humanité*, 6 decembre 2005, http://www.humanite.fr/2005-12-06_Societe_Debut-d-une-dangereuse-guerre-des-memoires.

[5] See Robert Aldrich, "Colonial Past, Post-Colonial Present: History Wars French-style," *History Australia*, 3, no. 1 (2006), 14.1–14.10.

[6] See Pascal Blanchard, Nicolas Bancel, and Sandrine Lemaire, *La fracture coloniale: La société française au prisme de l'héritage colonial* (Paris: La Découverte, 2005); Pascal Blanchard is president of the Association pour la connaissance de l'histoire de l'Afrique contemporaine (Achac).

[7] Emile Chabal, "La République postcoloniale? Making the Nation in Late 20th Century France," in *France's Lost Empires: Fragmentation, Nostalgia and la fracture coloniale*, ed. Kate Marsh and Nicola Frith (Lanham, Md.: Lexington Books, 2011).

[8] See Ira Katznelson and Andreas Kalyvas, *Liberal Beginnings: Making a Republic for the Moderns* (Cambridge: Cambridge University Press, 2008), and Andrew Jainchill, *Reimagining Politics after the Terror: The Republican Origins of French Liberalism* (Ithaca, N.Y.: Cornell University Press, 2008).

traditions of moral universalism, and both uphold an ideal of political emancipation that has tended to entail assimilation to a European political model. French republicanism, even more than Anglophone political liberalism, is committed to an abstract and ostensibly universal notion of citizenship, but one that in fact rests on a culturally particular history. This problem has been clear in the debates over headscarves, where a particularly French ideal of *laicité* has been taken by many in France to represent the universally valid approach to the place of religion in the public sphere.[9] And French republicanism shares some of the theoretical tensions that bedeviled British liberalism's support for empire: most important, that despite its universalist commitments, it long supported the domination of colonial subjects, as well as exceptional laws and institutions in the colonies. I would add that republicanism involves a particular temptation to empire: insofar as it is a tradition that celebrates political virtue and the political health of the republic, republicanism has at least since Machiavelli had a kind of affinity for militarism and territorial expansion when these are seen to contribute to the glory of the republic.[10] This aspect of the tradition is certainly visible among self-declared liberal republicans in nineteenth-century France. It led to an embrace of imperial expansion even among those like Tocqueville, who recognized the failure of European empires to serve universal values or to benefit their colonial subjects. Britain's national identity was, arguably, equally inextricable from its status as an imperial power, but British political thinkers were consistently far more circumspect than the French about drawing connections between political health at home and conquests abroad.

The first decade of the subjugation of Algeria marked a critical moment in French liberalism's evolving relation to empire. When France captured the city of Algiers from its Ottoman rulers in 1830, the elements of a thoroughgoing liberal critique of French imperial expansion were available: Benjamin Constant and other liberal republicans under Napoleon's empire and the Bourbon restoration had continued a tradition of thought, stretching back to the prerevolutionary Enlightenment,

---

[9] The law that banned conspicuously religious clothing was written in ostensibly universal terms: large crucifixes and kipas are also banned. And yet the law is clearly directed at headscarves worn by Muslim girls and women. See Olivier Roy, *Secularism Confronts Islam*, trans. George Holoch (New York: Columbia University Press, 2007), chap. 1; and Joan Scott, *The Politics of the Veil* (Princeton, N.J.: Princeton University Press, 2007).

[10] Republicanism also had the particular worry that empire would cause the death of republican liberty; Montesquieu's *Considerations on the Decline and Fall of the Romans* was the locus classicus for French revolutionary claims of this sort. I am grateful to Samuel Moyn for a conversation on this point.

that held that liberty and empire were incompatible, that conquest could
only be accomplished with barbarous levels of violence unbecoming a
modern nation, and that the right of peoples to independence and self-
government was universal. Not only was principled criticism of the
Algeria conquest muted, however, but the languages of both liberalism
and republicanism were invoked more often in support of the conquest
than against it. As in so many areas of domestic policy, the liberals who
came to power under the July Monarchy failed to live up to the promise
of their opposition politics under the Restoration.[11] What criticism there
was of the conquest was almost entirely restricted to claims, made by
liberal political economists during the conquest's earliest phase, that the
national interest lay in free trade rather than in conquest and colonization. These arguments soon caved before the embrace of a new colonial
mission by most thinkers from the Left and the liberal center, most prominently Alexis de Tocqueville.

The sputtering and then quick extinction, during the liberal July
Monarchy, of a critique of imperial expansion among the putative heirs
of Diderot and Constant was due in part to the long-standing anxiety
among French liberals and progressives about France's international stat-
ure.[12] During the Revolution, political discourse had been inflected with
a sense of entitlement to empire that stemmed from memories of France's
earlier status as a great colonial power and from the desire to erase the
long history of defeat by Britain that stretched back to the loss of the bulk
of French colonial territory in the New World and India at the end of the
Seven Years War. Debate about overseas colonies was muted, though
the Constitution of the Year III (promulgated after the emancipation of
the West Indian slaves) declared the French colonies to be "integral parts
of the Republic," subject to the same constitutional law.[13] But as Andrew
Jainchill has recently shown, the years between the Terror and the rise

[11] See G. A. Kelly, *The Humane Comedy: Constant, Tocqueville, and French Liberalism*
(Cambridge: Cambridge University Press, 1992), pp. 2–4; and Sudhir Hazareesingh,
*From Subject to Citizen: The Second Empire and the Emergence of Modern French
Democracy* (Princeton, N.J.: Princeton University Press, 1998), pp. 165–169.
[12] Perhaps, too, to the odd timing of the conquest: while the liberals opposed Charles X's
military expedition and might not have initiated it themselves, they inherited the conquest a few weeks later and were loath to give it up. Still, such a conquest had long
been contemplated; see Ann Thomson, "Arguments for the Conquest of Algiers in the
Late Eighteenth and Early Nineteenth Centuries," *Maghreb Review*, 14, no. 1–2 (1989),
108–118. On Diderot, see Sankar Muthu, *Enlightenment against Empire* (Princeton,
N.J.: Princeton University Press, 2003).
[13] See Jacques Godechot, ed., *Les constitutions de la France depuis 1789* (Paris: Garnier-
Flammarion, 1979), p. 104.

of Napoleon witnessed an impassioned debate, carried on in republican terms, about whether expansion into contiguous European territory was justifiable and advisable. Jainchill argues that during the Revolution critics of expansion, such as Robespierre, tended to argue from classical republican premises that empire threatens liberty, while advocates of annexation (of the Rhineland, the Austrian Netherlands, and other territories) tended to invoke the "modern" republican argument that representative government made territorial expansion safe for republicanism, though he recognizes that Constant later made his iconic critique of conquest precisely in modern terms.[14]

But despite efforts by various revolutionary governments to restore the colonial empire and to extend France's boundaries within Europe, France ultimately lost further territory during the Revolution.[15] Napoleon, in addition to his spectacular and disastrous expansion across Europe and his Egyptian expedition, nursed aspirations of global hegemony even more ephemeral and illusory. The "colonial madness" under Napoleon (his own and his supporters') included projects, all failed, to recover the prosperous West Indian sugar colonies, to retrieve "l'Inde française" (reduced since 1763 to five small outposts), and to acquire new colonies in Senegal, Madagascar, Java, and Cochinchina.[16] Criticism in this period was stifled: Napoleon made it illegal, for instance, to publish abolitionist arguments after he reinstated slavery in the French colonies in 1802.[17]

[14] Jainchill, *Reimagining Politics*, chap. 4; he cites especially Charles-Guillaume Théremin, a liberal republican, and a Prussian-born descendant of Huguenots whose political views under the Directory in other ways nearly anticipated the liberal republicanism Constant would develop in the 1810s.

[15] France lost its colonies in India and Canada to the British in 1763 after the Seven Years War and a number of its Caribbean colonies during the Revolution and empire, including most significantly Saint-Domingue, which became independent Haiti in 1804, though it was recognized by France only in 1825. France ultimately regained Martinique, Guadeloupe, and Guiana from the British in 1814, 1816, and 1817, respectively. See Yves Benot, *La Révolution française et la fin des colonies, 1789–1794* (Paris: La Découverte, 2004). Also see Paul Cheney, *Revolutionary Commerce: Globalization and the French Monarchy* (Cambridge, Mass.: Harvard University Press, 2010).

[16] See Yves Benot, *La démence coloniale sous Napoléon* (Paris: La Découverte, 1991).

[17] See *1802: Rétablissement de l'esclavage dans les colonies françaises*, ed. Yves Benot and Marcel Dorigny (Paris: Maisonneuve et Larose, 2003). The indefatigable revolutionary Abbé Grégoire was one of the few who continued to press the abolitionist cause (and did so through the 1820s); he evaded the censors by inserting his abolitionist arguments into a work apparently of literary scholarship; see Grégoire, *De la littérature des nègres ou Recherches sur leurs facultés intellectuelles, leurs qualités morales* (Paris: Maradan, 1808), and David Geggus, "Haiti and the Abolitionists: Opinion, Propaganda, and International Politics in Britain and France, 1804–1816," in *Abolition and Its Aftermath*, ed. David Richardson (London: Frank Cass, 1985), pp. 113–140, at p. 117.

Occasional tracts published under Napoleon kept up a weak current of
anticolonial argument, though there was little in this period that might
be described as a republican or proto-liberal critique of colonization. The
boldest rejection of empire came from the abbé de Pradt, an émigré archbishop who held in *Les Trois Ages des Colonies* that emancipation of the
colonies was simply the inevitable result of the Revolution and must be
accepted as such by postrevolutionary Europe.[18] Pradt exempted British
India, however, arguing that British rule there remained in Europe's interest until Europeans succeeded in instilling a taste for their products in
India, at which point colonial emancipation and free trade would be the
only sensible course. Notably absent under the Napoleonic Empire were
criticisms of colonization on moral grounds of common humanity or the
right to self-government of the kind articulated by Diderot in his contributions to Raynal's *Histoire des Deux Indes*.[19]

The early years of the Bourbon Restoration, in contrast, did see
a flourishing of self-consciously liberal and liberal-republican criticisms of conquest and colonization, beginning with Constant's *De
l'esprit de conquête*, first published in 1814, when Napoleon's (first)
fall appeared imminent. There was, too, a renaissance of abolitionist
argument and of critiques of French policy in the slave colonies among
leading liberals, including Constant and others in the Coppet group
such as Germaine de Staël and Sismondi; and indeed, during the later
years of the Restoration, political debate about France's colonies was
largely confined to debate over slavery and the slave trade.[20] Charles
de Rémusat, an aspiring liberal politician and a member with Constant
of the Société des morales chrétiennes, who later, as a liberal deputy,
was a supporter of the Algeria conquest, made an early impression on

[18] Dominique Dufour Pradt, *Les Trois âges des colonies, ou de leur état passé, présent et à
venir* (Paris: Chez Giguet, 1801–1802).

[19] See Benot, *La démence coloniale*. The two chief critics of colonization during the
Napoleonic era whom Benot discusses were by no means liberals: in addition to the émigré abbé de Pradt, there was Félix Carteau, an ultra *colon* and an enemy of the Société
des Amis des Noirs, who declared the sugar colonies detrimental to the prosperity of the
metropole and said that the only useful colonies were those that France no longer had:
namely, sparsely populated territories available for settlement; see Benot, *La démence
coloniale*, pp. 272–281.

[20] See Lawrence C. Jennings, *French Anti-Slavery: The Movement for the Abolition of
Slavery in France, 1802–1848* (Cambridge: Cambridge University Press, 2000); Nelly
Schmidt, *Abolitionnistes de l'esclavage et réformateurs des colonies, 1820–1851* (Paris:
Éditions Karthala, 2000); Serge Daget, "L'Abolition de la Traite des Noirs en France de
1814 à 1831," *Cahiers d'études africaines*, 41 (1971), 14–58.

liberal Paris society with an abolitionist play that excoriated the moral corruption of planter society.[21]

The great colonial (and anticolonial) historian Yves Benot has argued that the global vision of the early Restoration critics of empire rested on two ideas, twin reactions against Napoleon's project for global hegemony through war and conquest: first, the end of colonial rule, an idea nourished by Haitian independence and the movements for independence in Spanish America; and second, the idea of a peaceful and benevolent regime of global commerce.[22] These writers, as Benot notes, tended to place naive faith in the possibility of equal, noncoercive commerce among states at differing levels of economic and military development. This faith would give way among later liberals to the view that if trade required the development of backward nations, colonial rule might be a necessary prerequisite of free trade.

In a pattern that would persist into the July Monarchy, the dominant strand of anticolonial argument under the Restoration stressed on grounds of political economy that colonial regimes, and especially slavery, were detrimental to both colonies and metropoles. Jean-Baptiste Say and Victor Destutt de Tracy are representative figures; according to Say, colonies imposed an "enormous burden" (*énorme fardeau*) on European peoples, "an obstacle and not an aid [*auxiliaire*] to their prosperity," which would be furthered instead by the "complete emancipation of the world."[23] The abbé de Pradt, the legitimist archbishop cited earlier, remade himself as a liberal under the Restoration and in 1817 argued that the time had come for the separation of all colonies from their metropoles, for a "new world of relations" in which European states would have to

---

[21] The play, read aloud in Paris salons, remained unpublished; see Rémusat, *L'habitation de Saint-Domingue, ou l'insurrection*, ed. J. R. Derr (Paris: Editions du C.N.R.S., 1977).

[22] See Benot, *La démence coloniale*, p. 288; the following paragraph is indebted to chapter 9 of this book.

[23] See J. B. Say, *Cours complet d'économie politique pratique*, ed. Horace Say (Paris, 1852); pt. 4, chap. 23, "Résultats de la politique coloniale des Européens," quoted passage on p. 632. But Say also argued that "Asia is the birthplace of arbitrary and unlimited government," and that in India the "salutary influence of a civilized metropole" made itself felt in the administration of justice from Britain even if the colonial authorities could be abusive, as evidenced by the impeachment trial of Warren Hastings (pp. 649ff.). Say and Tracy were active opponents of slavery under the Restoration, again with an emphasis on political economy arguments from metropolitan interest; see Jennings, *French Anti-Slavery*. Also see Anna Plassart, "Un Impérialiste Libéral"? Jean-Baptiste Say on Colonies and the Extra-European World, *French Historical Studies*, 32, no. 2 (Spring 2009), 224–250.

accept all former colonies as sovereign powers.[24] "If the bloody opposition to the emancipation of America be cruel to that country," he argued, "it is equally fatal to the prosperity of the whole world," which could be pursued only when free commerce among sovereign states supplanted colonial monopolies.[25] The young abolitionist Civique de Gastine (ca. 1793–1822) departed from political economy to argue on more purely moral and political grounds that the principles of the Revolution, and indeed the survival of liberal government in the metropole, required colonial emancipation:

> The liberal, constitutional, and representative form of the new governments being established in Europe, and especially in the New World, absolutely necessitates the abandonment of the abominable policy that was the basis on which rested the system that subordinated colonies to metropoles, just as the slaves in Rome were subordinated to the patricians.... Humanity urgently demands, for the tranquility and happiness of the human race, that the governments of the Old World adopt the just and equitable system of the liberty of peoples.[26]

Gastine's works, published just a few years after Constant's seminal and multiply reprinted *On the Spirit of Conquest*, shared the latter's core idea that the liberal project of representative government at home was inextricable from an international politics of peaceful commerce and the mutual respect of sovereign states. Gastine arguably went further than Constant in not simply condemning conquest but in calling for the emancipation of all existing overseas colonies, something that Constant did neither in *On the Spirit of Conquest* nor in his many parliamentary speeches and

---

[24] See de Pradt, *Des colonies et de la revolution actuelle de l'Amérique* (Paris: F. Bechet, 1817), II, pp. 86–87. De Pradt stressed the historical inevitability of colonies' independence rather than Europeans' moral obligation to grant it (see, e.g., his chapter on British India, II, pp. 327–352).

[25] De Pradt, *Des colonies*, I, p. xxiv; quoted from the English translation, *The Colonies, and the Present American Revolutions, by M. de Pradt, formerly Archbishop of Malines* (London: Baldwin, Cradock, and Joy, 1817), pp. xvi–xvii.

[26] *Histoire de la République de Haiti* (Paris: Chez Plancher, 1819), pp. 263–264. He argued that the Haitians, with their peaceable respect for rights and treaties, had made far better use of their independence than European states had. The portrait of Haiti is far more sanguine than that in his slightly earlier book, *La liberté des peuples* (Paris: Chez les marchands des nouveautés, 1818), in which Gastine had acknowledged the charge that the Haitian government was despotic, arguing that it had to be so because the slaves in Saint-Domingue had regarded their masters, who lived under a similarly despotic monarchy, as free, and so knew no better; and that in addition, "they were not civilized enough to create for themselves a truly liberal government.... They have done all they can for the moment; later they will do the rest" (p. 57). See also the discussion in Benot, *La démence coloniale*, pp. 284–285.

other writings during the Restoration on French colonial policy in the West Indies.

CONSTANT AND CONQUEST

In *On the Spirit of Conquest*,[27] Constant provided the classic articulation of a liberal republican critique of empire and a powerful indictment of the peculiarly dangerous interplay between populist politics and imperial adventurism. Constant's immediate target was Napoleon's militarization of French society and his expansion across Europe and into Egypt, but the pamphlet's broader, biting condemnation of projects of global conquest suggests that he understood Napoleon's continental wars to be just one aspect of the emperor's larger fantasy of global hegemony. He writes of certain modern governments' desire to "conquer the world," "to acquire remote countries, the possession of which will add nothing to national prosperity," and he describes the conquering soldiers as "victims, doomed to fight and die at the far ends of the earth."[28] Constant, like Gastine a few years later, depicted conquest as the antithesis of, and the greatest threat to, liberal constitutionalism. One of Constant's achievements in the work was to perceive so early and so clearly the social dynamics, and the moral and political dangers, of expansionism by "modern nations."[29] Constant intertwined moral and historical arguments against what he identified as the "spirit of conquest," which had reached its apogee in Napoleon's empire but which, Constant believed, could be seen more broadly as a danger distinctive of postrevolutionary, indeed of all modern, politics. Though enthusiasm for Napoleonic militarism was, to be sure, at a low ebb when the work was published, Constant was sufficiently shrewd and farsighted to identify in advance many of the political and rhetorical strategies that the advocates of the Algerian conquest would use to sell that conquest to the French nation.

Against the spirit of conquest, Constant's pamphlet proposed a liberal counternarrative of postrevolutionary France, a redemptive story

---

[27] *De l'esprit de conquête et de l'usurpation dans leurs rapports avec la civilization euro-péene*, in *Oeuvres*, ed. Alfred Roulin (Paris: Pléiade, 1957). The passages cited are from *The Spirit of Conquest*, in Constant, *Political Writings*, ed. Biancamaria Fontana (Cambridge: Cambridge University Press, 1988).

[28] *Spirit*, in Constant, *Political Writings*, p. 67.

[29] Ibid., p. 54. See especially pp. 63–70 for Constant's analysis of conquest's corruption of public life. I discuss Constant's views on empire at greater length in *A Turn to Empire* (Princeton, N.J.: Princeton University Press, 2005).

according to which the nation might purge itself of its Napoleonic heritage and declare itself for peaceful, restrained commercial relations with its neighbors and the globe. The essay offers what at times seems a naive portrait of commerce as antithetical to war: commerce "rests upon the good understanding of nations with each other, it can be sustained only by justice; it is founded upon equality; it thrives in peace."[30] In its argument that commerce might make possible a new sort of mutuality among states, *On the Spirit of Conquest*, like so much of Constant's work, shows the mark of his Scottish Enlightenment education. But where Constant sometimes simplistically presented war and commerce as mutually exclusive modes of international interaction, eighteenth-century Scots such as Hume and Smith had been clear-eyed about the dangers of the common misalliance of modern commerce and war that Hume termed "the jealousy of trade."[31] They fully recognized the complicity of commercial motives in recent wars such as the Seven Years War. They sought, rather, to show that commerce *need* not provoke wars of expansion and rivalry and that commercial nations could benefit by adopting a politics of mutual encouragement rather than militarized competition.

Constant, with his penchant for making moral arguments in historical terms, often couched this dichotomy more deterministically, suggesting simply that commerce would "necessarily" replace war, that international commercial ties would make patriotism irrelevant and violence obsolete unless power-hungry men disrupted this natural course of events.[32] The essay thus seems to ignore commerce's role in sparking modern wars and imperial violence. But it also tells a more complicated story, for in insisting that the peaceful commercial spirit was a fragile achievement, and in detailing the ways in which modern governments co-opted their citizens for violent projects of expansion, Constant showed precisely that the spirit of conquest was far from obsolete. The essay suggests that modern self-interest may be seen to have moral value and moral purpose, but that this purpose is threatened by other tendencies of the age, and indeed by darker possibilities latent in self-interest itself. Much of the power of

---

[30] *Spirit*, in Constant, *Political Writings*, p. 65.

[31] See Hume, "Of the Jealousy of Trade" (ca. 1759), in *Essays Moral, Political and Literary*, ed. Eugene F. Miller (Indianapolis: Liberty Fund, 1985), pp. 327–331; Smith, *An Inquiry into the Nature and Causes of the Wealth of Nations*, ed. R. H. Campbell and A. S. Skinner (Indianapolis: Liberty Fund, 1976), IV.vii.c.85; and Istvan Hont, *Jealousy of Trade* (Cambridge, Mass.: Harvard University Press, 2005), esp. pp. 72–76.

[32] "The condition of modern nations thus prevents them from being bellicose by nature" (*Spirit*, in Constant, *Political Writings*, p. 54).

the essay comes from its persistent intimations that a moral direction to history can be perceived but that modern citizens must be prepared to struggle on its behalf.[33]

Constant had little occasion in later years to discuss conquest, for during the crisis-ridden Bourbon Restoration, France was not in a position to regain most of the territories lost over the years to the British or to expand into new ones. A staunch critic of French colonial policy regarding the slave trade, slaves, and free *gens de couleurs* in the colonies, he earned a reputation as one of the Chamber of Deputies' most eloquent abolitionists. In June 1830, six months before his death, Constant did denounce the Bourbon regime's effort to use the assault on Algiers to manipulate domestic politics, calling on the electors to "preserve the Charter from the repercussions [*contre-coup*] of Algiers" and to avoid succumbing to the regime's "illusions and seductions."[34] But Constant had also increasingly come to characterize Ottomans, and Muslims more generally, as alien and despotic. The Greek war of independence against the Ottoman Empire had occasioned his most virulent depictions of oriental despotism, in his 1825 pamphlet *Appel aux nations chrétiennes en faveur des Grecs*. And in the 1830 speech just quoted, he also offered a caricature of "barbaric" Algiers and a note of patriotic pandering: "Let us applaud the ruin of a den of pirates ... instead of respecting the quality of sovereignty in a barbarian. May the city of Algiers be flung into its port! Honor to the French soldiers. But let us demand a strict accounting of the disproportionate sacrifices" that those soldiers suffered for an affair of royal vanity. These tensions in Constant's thought presage many French liberals' vacillations and misgivings toward, and their ultimate embrace of, a French Algeria.

LIBERAL CRITICISM OF THE ALGERIAN CONQUEST

When Charles X's dying regime sent a military expedition to the city of Algiers in May 1830, partly in a failed effort to bolster its allies' prospects in the June election by inflaming national pride, the liberal opposition

[33] For a subtle discussion of the *Conquest* essay's paradoxes, see Stephen Holmes, "Liberal Uses of Bourbon Legitimism," *Journal of the History of Ideas*, 43, no. 2 (1982), 229–248, at 235.

[34] "Alger et les élections," *Le Temps*, 20 June 1830; reprinted in Constant, *Positions de Combat à la veille de juillet 1830: Articles publiés dans "Le Temps," 1829–1930*, ed. Ephraïm Harpaz (Paris: Campion-Slatkine, 1989), pp. 190–192. Constant insisted that the episode was "an affair of honor" between the dey of Algiers and Charles X.

opposed the expedition.[35] News of the troops' seizure of Algiers on July 5 reached Paris too late to influence the elections, which precipitated the Bourbons' downfall in the July Revolution. Just weeks later, the self-consciously liberal government of the July Monarchy inherited the new conquest along with the throne. Liberal deputies worried over this Bourbon provenance of the conquest for years afterward.[36] Still, soon after the liberals came to power, they became preoccupied by the old anxiety about France's international standing, and many concluded that this could be secured (especially against British hegemony) only through colonial possessions. Despite the flourishing of anticonquest texts immediately after Napoleon's fall, his exploits, especially in Egypt, were now remembered with nostalgia by those attempting to secure the new regime amid the polarizations of Left–Right politics. One of the July Monarchy's early symbolic gestures was its erection of an obelisk from the Luxor temple at the center of the Place de la Concorde, once home to the guillotine. The colossal monument's unifying message of French glory and superiority over the Orient helped to suppress the memory of the divisive politics of revolution and counterrevolution.[37] In placing the obelisk in that politically inflamed spot, these liberals were, oddly, echoing Napoleon's own decision to place another symbol of Eastern empire, a three-story-high elephant, in the Place de la Bastille.[38] And as the obelisk might have suggested, for all the bitterness of the debates over Algeria in the early years of the July Monarchy, there was soon a similar convergence on the desirability of preserving the conquest in some form.

It is difficult to judge whether Constant might have maintained his resolute opposition to conquest, as expressed in 1814, had he remained alive to witness the feverish expansion of French power in Algeria over the next two decades. His liberal heirs were split on the question. In the early years of the Algeria conquest, at least until the issuing in July 1834

---

[35] See, e.g., Louis Blanc, *History of Ten Years* (London: Chapman and Hall, 1845), I, pp. 80–85. Blanc, a leftist critic of the "bourgeois" July Monarchy, ridiculed the liberals' opposition to the Algiers expedition as mere "party rancor."

[36] See, e.g., the debate of 9 June 1836, in which Adolphe Thiers sought to explain his current support for a French Algeria in light of his earlier opposition to the Algiers expedition: "When the expedition was sent under the Restoration, I was among those who criticized it, and I think that was France's sentiment at that time. But when the expedition was successful and France's insult avenged, I was seized with joy." *Archives Parlementaires de 1787 à 1860* (Paris: 1902), vol. 105, pp. 155–157.

[37] See the superb account in Todd Porterfield, *The Allure of Empire: Art in the Service of French Imperialism, 1798–1836* (Princeton, N.J.: Princeton University Press, 1998), pp. 13–41.

[38] See Simon Schama, *Citizens* (New York: Alfred A. Knopf, 1989), pp. 3–5.

of the royal ordinance that has been called the birth certificate of French Algeria,[39] there was a vocal contingent of *anticolonistes* in the Chamber of Deputies who expressed horror at the barbarity of the conquest and called for the abandonment of any colonial project in Algeria. Leftist deputies argued that the conquest compared badly even with the folly of the crusades and the expedition to Egypt. They argued that the French had inexcusably violated the terms of the city's treaty of surrender; and that far from bringing civilization to Algeria, as they had pretended, the French had violated the fundamental principles of civilization – good faith, justice, respect for others – while failing to recognize precisely those qualities in the Algerians.[40]

It was telling, however, and perhaps ultimately destructive for the *anticoloniste* cause, that even the strongest French critics of the colony framed their arguments largely in terms of French interests and political economy. As Xavier de Sade, one prominent liberal critic of the conquest, argued, "I see perfectly the advantages we could gain from several provinces on the Rhine.... If someone can show us that we could gain the same fruits from our possession in Algiers, I will join the ranks of its most decided partisans."[41] His colleague André Dupin (aîné), a leader of the Center-Left "*tiers parti*" under the July Monarchy, ridiculed the idea, widespread on the left as well as the center and right, that to withdraw from Algeria would wound national pride. But he also argued that their only guide should be French interests: "If it is useful, we must keep Algiers, even if the Restoration did not intend to do so. If it is harmful, it must be abandoned."[42]

---

[39] Ruedy, *Modern Algeria* (Bloomington: Indiana University Press, 2005 [1992]), p. 54; the ordinance created a military colony named "les possessions françaises dans le Nord de l'Afrique."

[40] See the speeches of Xavier de Sade, Amédée Desjobert, and André Dupin in the *Archives Parlementaires*: de Sade, vol. 82, p. 190 (3 April 1833); Dupin, vol. 89, pp. 490–491 (29 April 1834); Desjobert, vol. 89, pp. 509–512 (29 April 1834).

[41] *Archives Parlementaires*, vol. 82, p. 190.

[42] Ibid., vol. 89, p. 491. Dupin did, however, criticize French abuses in Algeria since the conquest, including massacres, theft of indigenous property, and violations of religious sites: "while we lacked loyalty, justice, and respect for the indigenes, these were not lacking in their behavior toward us ... they have religion, equity, good faith; they know how to keep their word, and they don't deserve to receive from us what I would call lessons in barbarism" (p. 493). The following year, he rejected the idea that the French brought civilization to Algeria: "No ... We send there people who wouldn't dare show their faces in the metropole and who are legitimated when they are in foreign countries ... speculators who follow the armies to see what they can seize.... The rage for speculation has been pushed to the point of scandal in Algiers" (Chamber of Deputies, 20 May 1835, quoted by Liauzu, *Histoire de l'anticolonialism en France* [Paris: Armand Colin, 2005], p. 55).

A more emphatically anticolonial economic argument came from one of Dupin's critics on economic questions, a liberal journalist named Henri Fonfrède. As early as 1836, Fonfrède was calling for the "*décolonisation*" of Algiers: surely one of the earliest uses of the word, either in French or English.[43] Fonfrède, the son of a Girondin deputy to the Convention who had been executed in 1793, was a leading free-trader from Bordeaux, a journalist with ties to Constant, and, under the Restoration, an associate of the liberal opposition group Aide-toi, le ciel t'aidera. He opposed slavery and colonial monopolies, and he wrote a series of articles denouncing the occupation of the Algerian regency in his newspaper, *Le Mémorial Bordelais*. But although he condemned the conquest of Algeria as "un crime ... de lèze-humanité," Fonfrède's critique of the conquest also stressed its incompatibility with French interests: the conquest was a "parricide," "un crime de lèze-nation."[44]

A rare exception to the primarily interest-based approach was the deputy Amédée Desjobert, who joined the Chamber in 1833 and was a sharp critic of French colonial policy in parliamentary debates as well as in a raft of publications, beginning with the powerful *La Question d'Alger* of 1837, which called for an independent, Arab-governed Algeria.[45] Echoing Constant's argument that conquest corrupts democratic publics and destroys constitutional government at home, he argued that the July Monarchy had done with Algeria exactly as Napoleon had done with Egypt: forced a disastrous and unjust conquest on a corrupted and deluded public. He warned that in Algeria the French would quickly sacrifice, "in the form of a holocaust, the most important of our liberties!"[46]

---

[43] See J.-J. Hémardinquer, "Henri Fonfrède ou l'homme du Midi révolté (1827–38)," *Annales du Midi*, 88 (1976), 451–464; David Todd, *L'identité économique de la France: Libre-echange et protectionnisme, 1814–1851* (Paris: Grasset, 2008), pp. 125–38; and Todd, "A French Imperial Meridian, 1814–1870," *Past and Present*, 210 (2011), 155–186. I am grateful to David Todd for alerting me to Fonfrède's critique of the conquest and his early use of this term.

[44] Henri Fonfrède, *Oevures*, ed. C.-A. Campan (Bordeaux: Chaumas-Gayet, 1844–1847), vol. 8, p. 170.

[45] Desjobert knew the *Miroir* (discussed later) and cited the book's memorable image of the sale of bloodied jewelry at a market after the massacre of the tribe of El Ouffia. Amédée Desjobert, *La Question d'Alger* (Paris: P. Dufart, 1837), p. 219. I discuss Desjobert in *A Turn to Empire*, pp. 185–189.

[46] Desjobert, *La Question d'Alger*, pp. 43–44. On the corruption of public opinion, see pp. 6–7 and later his declaration that "we have received the mandate of the people to guard its interests, and we will defend them against everything, against the people itself, whose most generous passions are being excited. In time, it will be able to distinguish its true friends from its interested flatterers" (p. 15).

Desjobert was probably alone among French politicians on the left in the thoroughgoing nature of his critique: for Desjobert, economics, democracy at home, morality, and principles of international justice all demanded France's withdrawal from Algeria.

At this moment of early colonial ferment and vocal, if circumscribed, criticism of the conquest, Constant's anticolonial legacy was, arguably, most eloquently taken up by an Algerian businessman and legal scholar, Hamdan ben Othman Khodja (ca. 1773–1842). Indeed, Hamdan Khodja's *Miroir*, published in Paris in October 1833, announced its liberal filiation with an epigraph by Constant.[47] The first Algerian contribution to French public deliberation about the "question d'Alger," the *Miroir* self-consciously embodied both a liberal cosmopolitan and a Muslim perspective. Along with Desjobert, Hamdan Khodja was nearly alone in French debates in making a principled argument for a complete French withdrawal from Algeria – what he called a "liberal emancipation" of the country.[48] The *Miroir* sought to present to the French political imagination the idea of an independent Algeria that might take its place in a nineteenth-century Europe of emerging nationalities and engage with European states as a diplomatic equal.

The work indicates the critical possibilities of liberal discourse at a moment when liberalism was being marshaled in France and Britain in the service of empire. While sovereignty norms and membership in the international legal community were coming to be regarded by European liberals as inseparable from a distinctively European civilization, the *Miroir* offers an alternative conception, however fleeting its purchase on the French imagination, of a more expansive international order. "I see every free people interested in the Poles and in the reestablishment of their nationality ... and when my eyes return to the country of Algiers, I see its wretched inhabitants placed under the yoke of despotism, extermination, and all the scourges of war, and all these horrors committed in

[47] His book's complete title was *Aperçu historique et statistique sur la Régence d'Alger, intitulé en Arabe le Miroir* [*Historical and Statistical Survey of the Regency of Algiers, Entitled The Mirror in Arabic*] (Paris: Goetschy fils, 1833). The circumstances of its composition are obscure, and it is possible that Hamdan Khodja had French collaborators, though their possible identity remains unknown. I discuss Hamdan Khodja in "Liberalism and Empire in a Nineteenth-Century Algerian Mirror," *Modern Intellectual History*, 6, no. 2 (2009), 287–313.

[48] Hamdan Khodja, *Miroir*, 1833, p. 325. A pamphlet by an Englishman, S. Bannister, was another document to propose an indigenous government for Algeria; see *Appel en faveur d'Alger et de l'Afrique du Nord par un Anglais* (Paris: Dondey-Dupré, 1833).

the name of free France."[49] Conscious of Algerian vulnerability and the reach of French power, Hamdan Khodja sought to navigate within the imperial space in which the French political imagination was arguably coming to situate itself. But he also urged his French audience to conceive of itself and of Algeria in national and not imperial terms. While granting that the country had been placed, in the deferential language of his appeal to the king, under "Your Majesty's guardianship [*tutelle*]," Hamdan Khodja proposed that the king "emancipate the Algerians [and] restore harmony between the two peoples," for "Algerians, too, have rights that should permit them to enjoy liberty and all the advantages that European nations enjoy."[50]

We may consider *Miroir* as part of the global "liberal constitutionalist moment" proposed by C. A. Bayly as a context for the thought of the Bengali intellectual Rammohan Roy.[51] Like Rammohan, Hamdan Khodja repeatedly drew analogies between European events and ideas and those of his own locality and tradition. In doing so, he was both demonstrating European liberalism's compatibility with Islam and situating Algeria within a liberal European narrative from which his French contemporaries sought to exclude it. The *Miroir*'s repeated invocations of Greece and Belgium as models for an independent Algeria likewise suggest that what David Armitage has called the "contagion of sovereignty" was spreading to circles in the Maghreb at around the time that it was spreading among South American and Indian intellectuals.[52] Such gestures, however, proved sadly futile in the France of the July Monarchy, as establishment liberals, finally in power, quickly abandoned the vision of peaceful and mutually beneficial global commerce that had animated the earlier critiques of Napoleon.

In arguing that Algerians shared the principles of the law of nations that bound together Europeans, and in casting Algeria as a potential part of Europe, Hamdan Khodja may have exceeded the bounds of plausibility for a French audience of which even the more pluralist members,

---

[49] Here and unless otherwise noted, I cite the modern edition (which does not include the entire original text): Hamdan Khodja, *Le Miroir*, ed. Abdelkader Djeghloul (Arles: Sindbad/Actes Sud, 1985), p. 206.

[50] Réclamations, pièce 10, *Miroir*, 1833, p. 426.

[51] C. A. Bayly, "Rammohan Roy and the Advent of Constitutional Liberalism in India, 1800–1830," *Modern Intellectual History*, 4, no. 1 (2007), 25–41, and his "Afterword" in the same issue, 163–169.

[52] David Armitage, *The Declaration of Independence: A Global History* (Cambridge, Mass.: Harvard University Press, 2007); and see Bayly, "Rammohan Roy," 33.

such as Constant, were inclined to regard Muslims as fanatical barbarians.[53] But he also, perhaps, perceived that the July Monarchy, if not anticolonialist, did understand itself as having rejected the Napoleonic policy of total hegemony and as being committed to principles of an international rule of law. The Doctrinaire leader François Guizot, minister and ambassador under the July Monarchy, declared in his memoirs that the regime represented the antithesis of the "ambitious and bellicose fever," the "exploits gigantesques" and the "projets chimériques," of the Convention and empire. "From its birth and throughout the course of its life the government of 1830 fought against this posthumous passion for adventures and conquests." Even against the wishes of a population at times nostalgic for the glories of those earlier regimes, he wrote, it was "the fundamental character of the government of 1830 to have taken European public law for the rule of its foreign policy." Yet Guizot was also an unswerving supporter both of colonization in Algeria and West Africa and of Bugeaud's brutal methods of the 1840s; he boasted that "I did not merely seize but sought out occasions and means to extend in Africa the presence and the power of France."[54] Although Guizot was well to the right, in domestic politics, of the other *Algéristes* discussed here, his embrace of extra-European conquest even as he celebrated the July Monarchy's rejection of Napoleonic bellicosity was characteristic of liberal opinion and thus of Hamdan Khodja's intended audience. In the end, then, though the *Miroir* exposed some of the hypocrisies of the new liberal position on conquest, it had little hope of converting its French readers.

Some of the *anticolonistes*', and possibly Hamdan Khodja's, criticisms did find their way into the official reports of the two commissions of inquiry convened by the king in 1833 to examine the conquest.[55] The commissions' reports lamented the French military's violation of the terms of the capitulation treaty, their disregard of property rights, the violation of mosques and holy sites, and other offenses against Muslim

[53] "[O]ur law is founded only on the principles of the law of nations" (Hamdan Khodja, *Miroir*, p. 91).

[54] François Guizot, *Mémoires pour servir à l'histoire de mon temps, tome VII, 1832–1837* (*La question d'Orient*), ed. Clémence Muller (Paleo: Sources de l'histoire de France, 2004), pp. 6–7, 11, 28.

[55] Hamdan Khodja was one of two Algerians to testify before the commission in Paris; his testimony was acerbic and unsparing. *Procès verbaux et rapports de la Commission d'Afrique, instituée par ordonnance du Roi du 12 décembre 1833* (Paris: L'imprimerie royale, 1834), pp. 45–59 (*Séance du 23 janvier*).

mores.[56] The first commission's report included a scathing indictment of the methods of conquest:

We have sent to their deaths on simple suspicion and without trial people whose guilt was always doubtful and then despoiled their heirs. We massacred people carrying [our] safe conducts, slaughtered on suspicion entire populations subsequently found to be innocent; we have put on trial men considered saints by the country, men revered because they had enough courage to expose themselves to our fury so that they could intervene on behalf of their unfortunate compatriots; judges were found to condemn them and civilized men to execute them. We have thrown into prison chiefs of tribes for offering hospitality to our deserters; we have rewarded treason in the name of negotiation, and termed diplomatic action odious acts of entrapment.[57]

But even those commissioners who recognized the "barbarity" of the conquest persisted in the belief that the colonial administration could be reformed. They also declared their hands tied by the commitment of French public opinion to possession of Algeria.[58] The Commission d'Afrique decided by a vote of seventeen to two that "to abandon our conquests would be to offend the nation in its legitimate pride [and] to sacrifice the advantages of commerce and political power."[59] The metropolitan authorities thus allowed themselves to voice considerable discomfort with the conquest without repudiating it.

ALGERIA AND THE RISE OF IMPERIAL LIBERALISM

Moreover, powerful segments of liberal opinion had thrown themselves behind the conquest. The liberal republican Alphonse de Lamartine, in a speech brimming with poetic invocations of the nation's colonial mission, ridiculed the limited perspective of political economy, "a new science that often takes its axioms for facts, and its paradoxes for truths." While he

[56] See *Procès verbaux et rapports de la Commission nommée par le Roi, le 7 juillet 1833, pour aller recueillir en Afrique tous let faits propre à éclairer le Gouvernement sur l'état du pays et sur les mesures que réclame son avenir* (Paris, 1834). Also see Xavier Yacono, "La Régence d'Alger d'après l'enquête des commissions de 1833–34," *Revue de l'Occident Musulman et de la Méditerranée*, 1 (1966), 229–244, and "Comment la France décida de rester en Alger," *Atti del I Congresso internazionale di studi nord-africani* (Cagliari, Italy, 1965), pp. 321–337.
[57] Report by the deputy de la Pinsonnière; *Procès-Verbaux*, vol. 1, pp. 333–334. Translation from Ruedy, *Modern Algeria*, p. 50.
[58] *Procès-Verbaux*, vol. 1, p. 140; see also one member's protest against such "giving in to [public] opinion" (p. 116).
[59] Ibid., p. 405; also see Yacono, "Comment la France." The dissenters were Hippolyte Passy and Xavier de Sade.

agreed that Algeria would likely be a financial loss for France, he pointed to England's "system of universal existence, of colonial ubiquity" as the source of its dynamism and power and asked:

> Have nations nothing more to do than add up columns of figures? And have we descended to such a degree of social materialism that arithmetic alone shall preside over the councils of the Chamber and the government and alone determine the resolutions of this noble nation? ... If gold has its weight, do not politics, national honor, the disinterested protection of the weak, humanity – do they not also have theirs?[60]

Already in 1834, some defenders of the colony were insisting that Algeria *was* France.[61] Lamartine, for one, pronounced the idea of giving up the colony a "fatal thought ... an antinational, antisocial, antihuman thought." Lamartine's paean to national glory was echoed a few years later by another self-described liberal, Adolphe Thiers, president of the council of ministers (effectively the prime minister) as well as minister of foreign affairs, who excused the violence of the conquest as ordinary and inevitable: "I don't say that there will never be misfortunes, never mistakes, never excesses. What government could have the presumption to maintain that in using the means of war in foreign countries, everything will always be done wisely and humanely? That is impossible; we don't even accept such a condition for the defense of our borders. War is war."[62]

The republican *Dictionnaire Politique* of 1843, in its emphasis on France's great historic mission to colonize, epitomized the dominant leftist position on the conquest.[63] The work's article "Colonie," written by the liberal political economist Jean-Gustave Courcelle-Seneuil, argued that although "we recognize the abuses of [our colonial] regime and believe that it demands radical reforms," the "need to colonize is no passing fantasy for a great and strong nation.... Every people tends to

---

[60] *Archives Parlementaires*, vol. 89, pp. 676–677 (2 May 1834).

[61] See Desjobert's rejection of such claims; *Archives Parlementaires*, vol. 89, p. 510.

[62] *Archives Parlementaires*, vol. 105, p. 155 (9 June 1836). Thiers rejected the claim of some critics that there was no liberty in parliamentary debates over the question, that they had become "par trop impérial." Declaring that "we make no pretension to return to the imperial system," he nonetheless denounced the "furor of denigration against everything that is greater, more useful, more patriotic." The speech betrays his anxiety that the regime was perceived as both too Bourbon and too Napoleonic.

[63] Claude Liauzu has argued that the generation born after 1789 conceived France's colonial vocation in light of "the myth of revolutionary war in which it saw a fight between two principles rather than two countries or European peoples"; *Histoire de l'anticolonialism en France*, p. 48.

develop itself not merely by a rapid growth in population, but by this
instinctive sentiment of ambition and movement, which is the most noble
and eminent of the human soul.... Colonization is the most praiseworthy
and glorious form of conquest; it is the most direct means of propagating
civilization."[64] The *Dictionnaire*'s article on Algeria criticized the early
years of the enterprise as a period of violence and vacillation, characterized the war as one of high costs that benefited only speculators rather
than the national interest, and declared that the administration was "too
often beneath what [that of] the Turks had been." But it regarded the
preservation of Algeria as a "question of honor and national interest"
and expressed satisfaction that, despite all the mistakes of the early years,
public opinion was firmly in favor of the conquest.[65]

Concerns about the violence of the conquest were thus shared by critics and supporters of the colony. Defenders of the conquest, in appropri-
ating these worries and pledging themselves to reform, disarmed such
arguments as a basis for anticolonialism. The legislator Gaëtan de La
Rochefoucauld was among the most eloquent in denouncing the notorious 1832 massacre of the tribe of El Ouffia and the French failure to
punish such excesses. But he used this critique to argue for his own plan
of colonization, which would begin with legal pluralism and gradually
work toward civilizing and converting the Algerians: "Would it not be
the greatest and most glorious event for France, this mission she gives
a young prince to bring about the revolution that is unfolding at this
moment in Africa?" he asked. "France has, in Algiers, not a few military
posts to occupy nor a few commercial relations to extend, but a whole
continent to enlighten."[66] The narrow insistence by most critics that
France's interests should determine the question left them in a rhetorically weak position vis-à-vis such proposals. Their opponents, the liberal
and republican supporters of a French Algeria, could acknowledge and
disable criticisms of conquest's brutality while casting critics as cramped
economists oblivious to the claims of public opinion, national honor, and
France's international status, especially vis-à-vis England. Their arguments in these early years would be repeated and given particular force
by Tocqueville, who, throughout the 1840s, as the French were extending

[64] [Jean-Gustave] Courcelle-Seneuil, "Colonie," in *Dictionnaire politique*, intro. by Garnier-
Pagès (Paris: Pagnerre, 1843), pp. 233–235, at p. 234. Courcelle-Seneuil (1813–1892) was
a translator of Smith's *Wealth of Nations* and Mill's *Principles of Political Economy*.
[65] [J. J. O.] Pellion, "Alger, Algérie," in *Dictionnaire politique*, pp. 46–48.
[66] Gaëtan de La Rochefoucauld, speech of 29 April 1834; *Archives Parlementaires*, vol. 89,
p. 488.

and consolidating the conquest, was the Chamber of Deputies' most visible Algeria expert and supporter of the conquest.[67]

TOCQUEVILLE AND ALGERIA

Tocqueville's political career began after the brief period of vigorous debate over the conquest; he entered the Chamber of Deputies in 1839 as an avid proponent of a French Algeria, as well as a critic of what he regarded as the incompetence of the French authorities in pursuing it and of what he saw as the apathy of the French political classes toward such an important undertaking. Tocqueville was convinced for most of his political career that his colleagues undervalued French colonies and their political worth for France. He devoted such energy to the question of colonization because he felt he had grasped the historic importance of conquest as few Frenchmen in his day had done.

The question of Africa will be set decidedly on the path toward a good and great solution only when ... ministers fall or rise because of it. Then, the first minds of the country will be at its service, then the attention, the effort, the activity of men of state will turn that way. That moment has not altogether arrived, but it is very near. The sentiment of the chamber and of the government is already that Algeria is today our greatest affair.[68]

Much of the recent literature on Tocqueville and Algeria has dwelled on the question of how his liberalism can be reconciled with his support for empire, and perhaps more pointedly with his clear-eyed support for the violent domination of native Algerians, even as he acknowledged that colonial rule more often barbarized than civilized its subjects.[69] I would

---

[67] Tocqueville's "Letters on Algeria" of 1837 strongly resemble La Rochefoucauld's position described earlier; his later invocation of national honor and arguments that a country like France could not retreat from Algeria without signaling its decline to the world echo the Lamartine speech just quoted. See *Oeuvres Complètes* (hereafter OC), ed. J. P. Mayer (Paris: Gallimard, 1958–1998), III.1, and *Writings on Slavery and Empire*, ed. Jennifer Pitts (Baltimore: Johns Hopkins University Press, 2001), pp. 5–26 and 59.

[68] Letter to General de Lamoricière, 5 April 1846; in Tocqueville, *Lettres choisies*, ed. Françoise Mélonio and Laurence Gellec (Paris: Gallimard, 2003), p. 564.

[69] See Melvin Richter, "Tocqueville on Algeria," *Review of Politics*, 25 (1963), 362–398; Tzvetan Todorov, "Tocqueville et la doctrine coloniale," in *De la colonie en Algérie*, ed. Tzvetan Todorov (Brussels: Editions Complexe, 1988), pp. 9–34; Cheryl Welch, "Colonial Violence and the Rhetoric of Evasion: Tocqueville on Algeria," *Political Theory*, 31 (2003), 235–264; Jean-Louis Benoît, *Tocqueville: un destin paradoxal* (Paris: Bayard, 2005), pp. 264–279; Pitts, *A Turn to Empire*, chaps. 6 and 7; Margaret Kohn, "Empire's Law: Alexis de Tocqueville on Colonialism and the State of Exception," *Canadian Journal of Political Science*, 41, no. 2 (June 2008), 255–278.

suggest that the question should also be regarded as a broader question about the character of French liberalism at this formative moment. Tocqueville, though unique among his contemporaries in the philosophical and sociological richness of his liberalism, was strikingly in line with them in his judgments about conquest and colonization.[70]

Tocqueville consistently sought to represent a middle ground between the indiscriminate violence of Governor-General Bugeaud and those like his friend Claude de Corcelle, who, though not an *anticoloniste*, was earnestly concerned to prevent brutality toward the native Algerians. (In contrast, he was rather dismissive of the "polemics" of "Desjobert and company," who rejected the conquest altogether.[71]) His letters to Corcelle offer his most explicit, and most troubled, reflections on French relations with the Arabs in Algeria. From Algiers in 1846, he wrote:

> Not having you along, I tried at least to make up for your absence by asking a lot of questions to do with that great side of the African affair that occupies you so much, the maintenance of the indigenous race in the face of our own. I brought back this general notion, that, for the rest, I already had: that it is not only cruel, but absurd and impracticable, to try to force back or exterminate the natives; but through what means could the two races really be brought into contact? I confess with sorrow that my mind is troubled and hesitates.... Whatever happens, we can be sure that our proximity will create a social revolution among the Arabs, with painful effects.[72]

Though unsettled by Corcelle's worries, he also seized with some bravado the ground of realism: "From the moment that we committed that great *violence* of conquest, I think that we should not recoil from the small acts of violence [*violences de detail*] that are absolutely necessary to consolidate it."[73] And "[t]he quarrel is no longer between governments, but between races.... [I]n order for us to colonize to any extent, we must necessarily use not only violent measures, but visibly iniquitous ones."[74]

---

[70] Olivier Le Cour Grandmaison stresses this continuity between Tocqueville's views and those of his contemporaries: see the "Introduction" to *Coloniser, Exterminer* (Paris: Fayard, 2005).

[71] Letter to Beaumont, 9 August 1840, OC 18, pp. 420–421.

[72] Letter to Corcelle, 1 December 1846, OC 15, p. 224. He also described the famine and "extreme misery" among the Arabs and added that "the hatred which reigns between the two races ... is painful to see."

[73] Letter to Lamoricière of 5 April 1846, in *Lettres choisies*, p. 565.

[74] From the unpublished "Travail sur l'Algérie" of 1841, in OC 3.i, p. 242; Tocqueville, *Writings on Empire and Slavery* (hereafter *Empire and Slavery*), ed. and trans. Jennifer Pitts (Baltimore: Johns Hopkins University Press, 2001), p. 83. Also see the now infamous passage from the same essay: "I have often heard men in France whom I respect, but with whom I do not agree, find it wrong that we burn harvests, that we empty silos,

Although Tocqueville was both more nuanced in his analysis of the conquest's importance for France and more thoughtful about the costs of colonial violence than many of his contemporaries, he shared the widespread sense of imperial rivalry with Britain, the liberal-republican preoccupation with France's international standing as a great nation, and the willingness to carry out the conquest through the use of violence that would be considered unconscionable within Europe. And although his views, over two decades, about possible relations with native Algerians were more complex than those of many of his contemporaries, on this question he moved, with Guizot and others, rather quickly from early aspirations for mutual accommodation to a fairly implacable commitment to mere domination.[75]

In a brief but suggestive sketch, Tocqueville described what came to be called the "Eastern question" as central to the spirit of the age: it was characteristic of him, as indeed of many nineteenth-century European thinkers, to attempt to capture the movement of history and the essence of the moment.[76] The "movement of the European race into Asia" is the "movement of the century," Tocqueville wrote.[77] Tocqueville's first speech before the Chamber of Deputies, in 1839, was a passionate engagement in the Eastern question, in which Tocqueville took a resolutely, even belligerently, anti-British position. In his second major speech, on November 30, 1840, Tocqueville drew on the thoughts of his previous speech to suggest that, if France continued to lag behind in European colonial expansion, the country would not simply decline in importance but would become a sort of anachronism:

What is happening in Egypt and Syria is only part of an immense picture, only the beginning of an immense scene. Do you know what is happening in the Orient? An entire world is being transformed; from the banks of the Indus to the Black

---

and finally that we seize unarmed men, women, and children. These, in my view, are unfortunate necessities, but ones to which any people who want to wage war on the Arabs are obliged to submit"; OC 3.i, pp. 226–227; Tocqueville, *Empire and Slavery*, p. 70.

[75] For Guizot's shift, see his own claim that his early views were too "utopian": "experience has taught me … [that] I believed too much in the possibility of governing, with justice and peace, relations between French and Arabs, Christians and Muslims, settlers and natives." *Mémoires, tome vii*, p. 125.

[76] As J. S. Mill observed in his own essay "The Spirit of the Age," "The idea of comparing one's own age with former ages, or with our notion of those which are yet to come … never before was itself the dominant idea of any age"; Mill, *Collected Works*, ed. J. Robson and R. F. McRae (Toronto: University of Toronto Press, 1963–), XXII, p. 228.

[77] OC 3.ii, p. 279.

sea, in all that immense space, societies are crumbling, religions are being weakened, nationalities are disappearing, all the [old] lights are going out, the old Asiatic world is vanishing, and in its place the European world is rising. Europe in our times does not attack Asia only through a corner, as did Europe in the time of the crusades: She attacks ... from all sides, puncturing, enveloping, subduing.[78]

While it seems that the English liberals with whom Tocqueville corresponded believed much the same thing, they rarely stated so explicitly that to be a modern nation was to colonize. As the dominant colonial and maritime power, the British could carry out their intentions without agonizing, as French liberals so often did (to Desjobert's chagrin), about their national reputation or possible decline.

The combination of admiration and envy Tocqueville felt for Britain made him a perceptive analyst of the contradictions of the British imperial ideology of civilizing empire. Whereas a belief in progress and in the civilizing mission was an article of faith among the British liberals and philosophic radicals who dominated Indian policymaking after 1828, Tocqueville remained suspicious both of the rigid dichotomy between civilized and barbarous peoples employed by thinkers like James and J. S. Mill and of Europeans' confidence that their rule benefited and improved their non-European subjects.[79] Tocqueville regarded the British not only as hypocritical, but as self-deceiving, seduced by their myth that British rule was for their subjects' benefit despite much evidence to the contrary. "[W]hat I cannot get over," he wrote, "is their perpetual attempts to prove that they act in the interest of a principle, or for the good of the natives, or even for the advantage of the sovereigns they subjugate; it is their frank indignation toward those who resist them; these are the procedures with which they almost always surround violence."[80]

Because Tocqueville appreciated the complexity and the political character of Algerian society, as Mill never did that of India, and because he never succumbed altogether to the illusion that Europe's civilizing mission

---

[78] OC 3.ii, p. 290 (translation from Drescher, *Tocqueville and England* (Cambridge, Mass.: Harvard University Press, 1964), p. 156. Also see George Frederickson, *The Comparative Imagination: On the History of Racism, Nationalism, and Social Movements* (Berkeley: University of California Press, 1997), p. 113.

[79] On the civilizing idea in Mill, see J. M. Robson, "Civilization and Culture as Moral Concepts," in *The Cambridge Companion to Mill*, ed. John Skorupski (Cambridge: Cambridge University Press, 1998), chap. 9; Pitts, *A Turn to Empire*, chap. 5; and Alan Ryan, "Bureaucracy, Democracy, Liberty: Some Unanswered Questions in Mill's Politics," in *J. S. Mill's Political Thought*, ed. Nadia Urbinati and Alex Zakaras (Cambridge: Cambridge University Press, 2007), pp. 147–165.

[80] OC 3.i, p. 505.

provided a clear moral justification for despotic rule, Tocqueville's ambivalence about empire ran far deeper than Mill's. Tocqueville occasionally expressed enthusiasm for European imperialism on the grounds that it would contribute to progress among backward peoples, and he invoked the language of progress and barbarism, describing Algerian Arabs as "semi-barbarous"[81] and noting that "[i]t has been claimed that the peoples of India had already arrived at a very advanced state of civilization. I, for my part, am convinced of the contrary."[82] But he also preserved a suspicion that such arguments were disingenuous or delusional, and that imperial domination barbarized conquered peoples far more often than it improved them. In 1847 he concluded somewhat ruefully that Muslim society, although "backward and imperfect," had been far from uncivilized; it was the French who had made it barbaric.[83] Whenever he witnessed empire firsthand, he rejected outright the notion that imperialists had been a civilizing force.[84]

In his analysis of the rival British Empire, Tocqueville perceived and articulated the moral and political transgressions of imperial expansion in a way that he never did in the case of France. Tocqueville confided to his English friend Nassau Senior in 1857 that while he "rejoiced" at Britain's success in suppressing the Sepoy Rebellion, Britain's posture of arrogance had, not without reason, infuriated not only its subjects but the rest of the world as well. The striking absence of European sympathy for the British during the Sepoy Rebellion, he wrote, stemmed in part "from the conviction held by all the peoples of the world that England never considers anything but from the perspective of her greatness; that more than any other modern nation she lacks all sympathetic feeling for anyone else ... [that] she thinks only of herself, even when she seems the most occupied with them."[85] Tocqueville, who justified France's imperial expansion in Algeria on the basis of arguments about the importance

[81] "à moitié barbare"; "Essay on Algeria," OC 3.i, p. 229; Tocqueville, *Empire and Slavery*, p. 72.

[82] OC 3.i, p. 446.

[83] "First report," OC 3.i, pp. 322–323; Tocqueville, *Empire and Slavery*, pp. 140–141: "we can be accused sometimes less of having civilized the indigenous administration than of having lent its barbarity the forms and intelligence of Europe."

[84] Françoise Mélonio has argued that even if, for Tocqueville, national glory was the primary purpose of colonization, his belief in a *mission civilisatrice* and France's special revolutionary calling constituted an element in his justification: "the imperialist drift which he does not escape, but whose danger he has the merit of perceiving, demonstrates the ambiguity of his quest for grandeur"; "Nations et nationalismes," *The Tocqueville Review*, 18, no. 1 (1997), 61–75, at 72.

[85] 15 November 1857; OC 6.ii. p. 206.

of the conquest for French politics and the country's self-respect, never acknowledged that what he charged here of the British could be said of his own imperial program as well. In the end, the English hypocrisy that he captured with such clarity may have been too tempting for Tocqueville himself to resist.

Tocqueville's writings display deep and unresolved ambivalence about European empires. He expressed enthusiasm for the greatness and novelty of imperial conquest and rule (and, far less often, a belief in its goodness or justice), but also horror at its violence and occasionally disappointment at Europeans' consistent failure to realize their *mission civilisatrice*, although he also criticized defenders of such a mission as hypocritical. Tocqueville never forgot or denied the violence of imperial conquest, but his moral judgments about it vary wildly: from a sort of daring acceptance of the need for violence, which some readers have attributed to his "aristocratic" bent, to a belief that to repeat the depredations of the Spanish and Anglo-Americans in the New World would violate the laws of humanity. What is more, Tocqueville never explicitly confronted his own ambivalence or acknowledged the contradictions that his commitment to the conquest of Algeria imposed on his thought.[86]

Tocqueville held that French power and reputation within Europe would rely, increasingly, on its colonial possessions; a wide range of colonial actions were justified by this patent need. Tocqueville's concern for French glory and reputation in Europe, and his desire that the nation join in collective enterprises in order to preserve its liberty, lay behind his enthusiasm for the colonization of North Africa, even if Tocqueville himself never articulated the argument quite so explicitly.[87] Tocqueville felt deeply the imperatives of nation-building, and every one of his works attested to his fear that French liberty was fragile, far more vulnerable

[86] Cheryl Welch has offered a psychologically subtle reading of Tocqueville's "efforts to make colonial violence absent to his imagination" and of his violations or evasions, in his treatments of Algeria, of many of his own moral commitments and intuitions; Welch, "Colonial Violence and the Rhetoric of Evasion," p. 257. She argues powerfully that his strategies of evasion and modes of self-deception are characteristic of a weakness in liberalism more broadly, in that when liberals experience guilt over the commission of violence, having few means of justifying it explicitly, they resort to "more subtle means of psychic insulation."

[87] Michael Hereth argues that Tocqueville "never applied his knowledge of the evil consequences of foreign rule to Algeria" because in this context he adopted an "exclusively French viewpoint." Hereth, *Alexis de Tocqueville: Threats to Freedom in a Democracy*, trans. George F. Bogardus (Durham, N.C.: Duke University Press, 1986), pp. 161–162.

than the liberty of America or Great Britain. Tocqueville's fear that Frenchmen in his day were dangerously apolitical, preoccupied by their petty personal affairs, was exacerbated by the thought that there were no longer opportunities for glorious action. He saw large-scale empires – both glorious military conquest and prosperous settlement – as among the only arenas for grand political gestures in his day. Two pursuits that seemed to him worthy of a great nation were imperial expansion and the abolition of slavery in the French West Indies.[88] His fierce sense of rivalry with Britain, which competed with his admiration for the country's political and social institutions, encouraged his belief that national projects that earned British respect – as both empire and abolition were likely to do – would be of a particularly valuable kind.

In contrast to Constant's searing criticism of the military spirit, Tocqueville, despite some qualms, accepted the need for a dramatic increase of French troops for the sake of empire. Viewing a strong military presence in Algeria as a necessary condition of the settlement colony he sought (and often more sympathetic to the military than to the colonists, whom he often saw as greedy and self-absorbed), he devoted tremendous thought to the problem of civil–military relations in colonial society.[89] Tocqueville admired what he considered the military's displays of civic virtue in an otherwise apathetic nation.[90] Tocqueville thus repudiated Constant's claim, a modern liberal version of the classical republican fear that empire destroys liberty, that a strong military and the culture to which it gives rise are fundamentally incompatible with democratic liberty.

NATION AND EMPIRE

Frederick Cooper has argued that nineteenth-century Britain and France should be understood not, as they often are, as nation-states engaged in colonial conquest, but rather as empire-states in which the "space of

---

[88] Tocqueville cited the British abolition of slavery as one great event that suggested that the decadence of his age was not yet total. "The emancipation of slaves," OC 3.i, p. 79; Tocqueville, *Empire and Slavery*, p. 199.

[89] See especially the 1847 Reports (OC 3.i, pp. 314ff.; Tocqueville, *Empire and Slavery*, p. 133).

[90] In admiration of the French soldiers fighting in the Crimean War, he wrote to a friend, "Are you not astonished with me, Madame, upon seeing spring from a nation that appears so devoid of public virtues, an army that demonstrates itself to be so full of virtue? So much egoism here, so much self-sacrifice there"; Letter to Mme de Swetchine, OC 15.ii, p. 263.

empire" was a significant political framework in its own right.[91] Both
political leaders and those contesting expansion conceived of their political space as imperial, he states, noting that even those who argued that
colonies should be expressions of national power did so in the context
of centuries-old imperial rivalries, and that criticisms of empire on the
grounds of national independence were not the only, or even the most
important, ones.

This dual perspective of nation and empire, and a perception of the
tensions between these political forms, is evident in debates and political
texts at the time of the Algeria conquest, with regard to both France's
status as a nation and the disputed "nationality" of the Algerians. The
very notion of France as *la grande nation* in Napoleonic propaganda
had united the idea of the French nation with that of imperial expansion
within and outside Europe: "*la grande nation* is summoned to astonish
and console the world," as Napoleon put it in a speech to the army in
Italy in 1797.[92] Something of this idea was preserved in the thought of
self-professed liberals during the Algeria conquest, as Lamartine's yearn-
ing for "colonial ubiquity" as the nation's proper destiny suggests.[93]

As for the Algerians' nationality, many conceded that there was an
"Arab nationality" in the loose sense of cultural or ethnic association,
but it was widely denied that Algeria enjoyed the sort of affective or
political coherence that might underpin existence as a nation in a more
strictly political sense.[94] It was one of the founding myths of the conquest
that the French, having defeated the Ottoman dey, filled a political vac-
uum in Algeria, where a dizzying variety of races and tribes roamed the
countryside or jostled together in cities without forming a coherent social

[91] Frederick Cooper, *Colonialism in Question: Theory, Knowledge, History* (Berkeley: University of California Press, 2005), pp. 154–155.
[92] Henry Laurens, "Bonaparte, l'Orient et la Grande Nation," *Annales de la Révolution française*, no. 273 (July–September 1988), 289–301, at 297. Laurens argues that Napoleon adopted the expression from several Ottoman correspondents. Also see Jacques Godechot, *La Grande Nation, l'expansion révolutionnaire de la France dans le monde de 1789 à 1799* (Paris: Aubier Montaigne, 1983).
[93] Also see the discussion in the article "Nation" by Elias Regnault (a lawyer and, after 1848, minister of finance), in the *Dictionnaire Politique*. The article argues both that nations require "material" and "moral unity" and a degree of homogeneity, and that smaller nations will likely be incorporated into "superior" nations, asking, "Is there not something ridiculous in calling Belgium a nation?" It concludes that as humanity devel-ops, there will be a tendency toward ever greater concentrations until "all humanity is but one single Nation" (p. 625).
[94] For such a distinction between the looser and stricter senses of the term, see Regnault, "Nation."

or political body.[95] The Turks and their descendants were described as invaders who had never sunk roots in the country; urban elites, Muslim and Jewish alike, as no more true Algerians than the Turks; and the Berber and Arab tribes as groups irremediably hostile to one another who (falsely) did not even share the same religion.

That the "nationality" of Algeria was thought to be compatible with French rule is indicated by Thiers's 1836 speech, cited earlier. Thiers claimed not to "contest the [Arabs'] right to conserve their nationality" and promised that the government had no intention of "destroying the Arab nationality," as some deputies had charged. In his insistence on the term "nationality," Thiers was declaring himself in support of something further than simply the protection of individual Arab lives against the imputation of an exterminationist project. What this might be he left conveniently ambiguous, but by "nationality" he certainly did not mean political independence.[96] In contrast, when Amédée Desjobert argued that France should recognize "Arab nationality" in Algeria, he undoubtedly meant Algerian political independence. The Arabs and Kabyles formed, he argued, a single nationality "which must be aided along the paths of civilization. But it must walk them on its own; its steps will be more sure."[97] Desjobert considered Abd al-Qadir, the marabout who led the Arab tribes' military resistance to the French occupation and who established a rival state during the late 1830s, the "representative of Arab nationality." Desjobert maintained that the French had the moral duty to recognize him as the leader of the Algerian people and to abandon any plans for colonization.[98] France, Desjobert argued, should declare that

[95] See Patricia M. E. Lorcin, "Introduction," *Algeria and France, 1800–2000: Identity, Memory, Nostalgia* (Syracuse, N.Y.: Syracuse University Press 2006), p. xxiv; Jean-François Guilhaume, *Les mythes fondateurs de l'Algérie française* (Paris: Harmattan, 1992); and Lahouari Addi, "Colonial Mythologies: Algeria in the French Imagination," in *Franco–Arab Encounters*, ed. L. Carl Brown and Matthew S. Gordon (Beirut: American University of Beirut Press, 1996), pp. 93–105.

[96] Thiers, debate of 9 June 1836, *Archives Parlementaires*, vol. 105, pp. 159–160. He also argued that Algerians did not form a unified "national ensemble"; rather, there were a variety of populations – Turks, Koulouglis, Arabs in the towns, conflicting Arab tribes in the countryside – whose divisions could be manipulated by the French to entrench their power. As one whose newspaper was called *Le National*, Thiers was perhaps especially sensitive to the term's possible uses.

[97] Desjobert, *La Question d'Alger*, p. 324.

[98] Abd al-Qadir (Abd-el-Kader) was a religious leader or marabout and France's chief military opponent in Algeria at this time. Desjobert's remarks about Abd al-Qadir suggest, nonetheless, a belief in the superiority of European civilization: he writes that Abd al-Qadir "was the progressive man of his times.... His organizational genius began by centralizing Arab society, as much as it could be; he wanted to send all of the young

it would not recognize European colonists and that any Europeans who remained in Algeria did so at their own risk and as subjects of the indigenous government.[99] Like Hamdan Khodja, Desjobert called on the French to extend the same political standards to Algerians that they applied in Europe, pointing out the inconsistency of criticizing conquests in Europe while oppressing their own "Muslim Poland."[100]

In this context, Tocqueville's reflections a few years later on the political landscape in Algeria appear at once astute and cynical. Unlike those French analysts who simply dismissed Algerians' capacity for a national political life, Tocqueville clearly viewed the national consolidation of Algeria as an imminent possibility; he saw it as an event delayed not by the Algerians' barbarism or political immaturity, but just by the superior military power of the Ottoman Empire. He argued that the French, in their confusion and despite their heavy-handedness, had presented indigenous leaders with a chance for resurgence. Knowing nothing of the political organization developing among the local tribes, the French were unwittingly driving all the tribes into the arms of a single capable leader, Abd al-Qadir, and thus encouraging an Arab national unity that would make it impossible to subject the Arabs to French rule.[101] Now, "after 300 years [the Arab population] is reawakening and acting under a national leader."[102] He was deeply impressed by the speed with which Abd al-Qadir had emerged out of the anarchy and, within a few years of the Turkish defeat, established his national movement as the primary political and military force in western Algeria.[103] The French, Tocqueville

people of good families to France to be educated in our civilization, just as the Turks and Egyptians do"; Desjobert, *L'Algérie en 1846*, p. 114. See similar remarks in *La Question d'Alger*, pp. 324ff.

[99] Desjobert, *La Question d'Alger*, pp. 306ff. The advantages for France in his system would be, he claimed, continued suppression of piracy; peaceful possession of two or three coastal points that could be useful during a maritime war; greatly reduced expenses; the prospect of advantageous commerce in Africa; and "the glory for France, in propagating civilization, of doing something honorable for herself" (pp. 327–328).

[100] Desjobert, *L'Algérie en 1846* (Paris: Gillaumin, 1846), p. 91. In another of many echoes of the *Miroir*, Desjobert charged French oppression with having ravaged Algeria's potential futures: acknowledging that what he called "le système arabe" would be difficult to accomplish, Desjobert wrote, "we have nearly covered the Regency with impossibilities"; *La Question d'Alger*, p. 307.

[101] "Second letter," OC 3.i, p. 148; Tocqueville, *Empire and Slavery*, p. 22. He argued that no one had an "incontestable right" to rule after 300 years of Ottoman dominance, so that the task of the French was to get the Algerians used to, and dependent on, French power.

[102] OC 3.i, p. 145; Tocqueville, *Empire and Slavery*, p. 19.

[103] "Second letter," OC 3.i, pp. 143–144; Tocqueville, *Empire and Slavery*, pp. 17–18.

argued, should permit this renewed self-government in order to control it and put it to their own use. He argued that the French had to cultivate leaders such as Abd al-Qadir, since they could not possibly govern the country directly (the tribes disappeared into the desert whenever the French tried to control them), but they also had to encourage the rise of a number of rivals, for the national organization of Algerians under a single "national" leader would likely destroy French hopes of dominance.

Any worries, on the other hand, that the coherence or vitality of the French nation might be threatened by an imperial project – that conquest was alien to the modern nation and anathema to modern citizens, as Constant had argued – were outweighed by the conviction that the conquest was crucial for France's international standing, that the French nation was an imperial polity. That neither Tocqueville nor almost any other of his liberal or republican contemporaries could contemplate the emancipation, "abandonment," or political independence of Algeria attests to the great distance liberal thinking had traversed from the resolute criticism of Europe's imperial expansion articulated by their forbears, who wrote as members of liberal or proto-liberal oppositions to authoritarian regimes, under both the *ancien régime* and the Restoration. Deaf to the rare but eloquent protests from the metropole (Desjobert) and the colonies (Hamdan Khodja), as well as to the voices of their past, after 1834 French liberals and republicans with few exceptions committed themselves to a conception of national dignity that demanded an imperial politics. The distinctive stress that French republicanism has always laid on national unity and a national mission, which contributed to the mid-nineteenth-century colonial enthusiasm I have described, arguably continues to bedevil debates over the postcolonial present.[104]

---

[104] For self-declared republicans' claims that colonial guilt and multiculturalism threaten national unity, see Henri Peña-Ruiz, "Culture, cultures et laïcité," in *Hommes et Migrations*, no. 1259 (January–February 2006), 7, cited by Emile Chabal, "La République postcoloniale." Also see Daniel Lefeuvre, *Pour en finir avec la repentance coloniale* (Paris: Flammarion, 2006).

11

Colonies and Empire in the Political Thought of Hegel and Marx

Gabriel Paquette

Sidney Hook noted long ago that to treat G. W. F. Hegel and Karl
Marx together is not so much to express a well-established relationship
between the two men, but rather to raise a profound problem of intellectual lineage.[1] In spite of the formative and explicitly acknowledged
impact of Hegel's thought on Marx's development, the intellectual inheritance was uneven. One significant, if understudied, area of divergence
concerned colonies and empire. This chapter analyzes the imperial theme
in the thought of Hegel and Marx. It argues that Hegel was concerned
mainly with the creation of colonies of settlement as a response to poverty generated in European society by economic transformation, whereas
Marx's interest was drawn, first, to the decisive impetus of intercontinental trade in the formation of the global economy and, second, to the
role he believed contemporary European overseas empire would play in
hastening capitalism's maturation and demise.

For Hegel, colonies were a stopgap measure to alleviate a problem
endogenous to European society. The non-European world is incidental to his account.[2] For Marx, empire was a key exogenous variable in

[1] Sidney Hook, *From Hegel to Marx: Studies in the Intellectual Development of Karl
Marx* (London, 1936). For a deft summary of the scholarly literature concerning the
Hegel–Marx connection, see Ian Fraser and Tony Burns, eds., *The Hegel–Marx connection* (London, 2000).
[2] Of course, this is not to claim that the non-European world was irrelevant to his thought,
as even a casual reading of his *Philosophy of History* would reveal. Furthermore, Susan

An earlier version of the first two sections of this chapter was published as "Hegel's Analysis
of Colonialism and Its Roots in Scottish Political Economy," *Clio* [Ft. Wayne, Ind.], 32
(2003), 415–432. The author thanks Trinity College, Cambridge, for the material support
that enabled him to undertake this chapter.

the evolution of European society. It was indispensable to the process of "primitive accumulation" at the dawn of capitalism. It also served as a mechanism by which societies were drawn together into a single world market, an unavoidable way station on capitalism's road to self-subversion. For Hegel, colonies of settlement could restore the system of mutual interdependence essential to a flourishing civil society, a set of interlocking relationships undermined by the disparities of wealth endemic to capitalism. For Marx, who scoffed at the suggestion that colonization schemes could relieve the intractable social problems wrought by industrial capitalism, overseas empire facilitated the mutual interdependence of societies for the satisfaction of their needs, laying the groundwork for a higher form of social existence.

This chapter suggests that much of the divergence between Hegel and Marx on the imperial themes stems from the different intellectual influences as well as the disparate political contexts in which each operated. Hegel's analysis of colonies reflects its origins in Scottish political economy, whereas Marx's most sustained engagement with the subject of empire occurred during his stint as a journalist for the *New York Daily Tribune* in the 1850s. The judgments of both Hegel and Marx were influenced decisively by different phases of British overseas expansion. In Hegel's thought, British North America was a frequently invoked image; in Marx's writings, the consolidation of Britain's rule in India and its coercive diplomacy in China left an indelible imprint on his conception of empire's contribution to world history. By studying the place of colonies and empire in the thought of Hegel and Marx, this chapter aims to heighten scholarly appreciation of the extra-European dimension of their analyses of the development of European societies.

HEGEL'S ANALYSIS OF COLONIES IN THE *PHILOSOPHY OF RIGHT*

Hegel's most sustained treatment of colonialism is encountered in his *Elements of the Philosophy of Right* (1821). He presented colonialism, which he understood as overseas colonies of settlement,[3] as a potential

Buck-Morss has demonstrated convincingly that the Haitian revolution played a decisive role in the development of Hegel's dialectic of lordship and bondage in the *Phenomenology*. She argues that Hegel was not describing "slavery versus some mythical state of nature … but slaves versus masters, thus bringing into his text the present, historical realities that surrounded it like invisible ink." See Buck-Morss, *Hegel, Haiti, and Universal History* (Pittsburgh, 2009), p. 52.

[3] Edward Gibbon Wakefield's succinct 1849 definition of "colonization" accurately represents what Hegel meant when he employed the term. According to Wakefield, "of

solution to the conundrum of mass poverty generated in civil society. Hegel maintained that colonialism could meet the immediate material needs of the impoverished and also reintegrate them, perhaps circuitously, into the web of reciprocal relationships characteristic of civil society.

Hegel envisaged ethical life within the limits imposed by modern commercial society. He also sought to mitigate the destructive effects of unrestrained economic individualism and to incline members of society toward participation in communal institutions,[4] such as the corporation, that inculcate social values, accord recognition, and mediate the individual's relations with the state. Hegel's system, as a leading scholar has contended, is "a fragile accomplishment that is prone to corruption and collapse because of the individualism, indifference, and neglect of its citizens."[5] Colonies could reinstill a public-spirited disposition in the poor who had become alienated, "objectively cut off from participation" in civil society.[6]

Colonization represented a viable *political* solution within Hegel's framework and an *economic* one as well. Hegel proposed that the state should provide land, or private property, which would allow individuals to master external reality and imbue them with confidence in their capabilities. This awareness and responsibility, in turn, would provide membership in an estate, restore the "ethical objectivity"[7] suspended during prolonged periods of unemployment, and facilitate membership in the intermediary institutions of civil society. In this manner, colonization would reintegrate individuals into "a system of all-around interdependence" from which they were previously alienated. As a result of emigration and settlement abroad in countries that offered greater possibilities

---

colonization, the principal elements are emigration and the permanent settlement of the emigrants on unoccupied land. A colony therefore is a country wholly or partially unoccupied, which receives emigrants from a distance; and it is a colony of the country from which the emigrants proceed, which is therefore called the mother-country. The process by which the colony is peopled and settled, and to nothing else, I would give the name of colonization." See Wakefield, *A view of the art of colonization, with present reference to the British empire; in letters between a statesman and a colonist* (London, 1849), p. 16; for Marx's critique of Wakefield, see the third section of this chapter.

[4] Gareth Stedman Jones, "Hegel and the Economics of Civil Society," in *Civil Society: History and Possibilities*, ed. Sudipta Kaviraj and Sunil Khilnani (Cambridge, 2001), pp. 105–130, at 114.

[5] Alan Patten, *Hegel's Idea of Freedom* (Oxford, 1999), p. 38.

[6] Michael O. Hardimon, *Hegel's Social Philosophy: The Project of Reconciliation* (Cambridge, 1994), pp. 244–245.

[7] G. W. F. Hegel, *Elements of the Philosophy of Right*, ed. Allen W. Wood, trans. H. B. Nisbet. (Cambridge, 2000), §207 remark.

for subsistence, colonialism would also help individuals obtain the material subsistence that accorded with Hegel's requirement that people meet their own needs as a result of individual effort and work.

Some contemporary intellectual historians depict Hegel's advocacy of colonialism as a flawed solution to the problem of poverty for two reasons. First, it merely "displaces" and "duplicates" poverty in a "cruder and more brutal manner" in a new location, often accompanied by the "destruction of non-European peoples."[8] Second, colonies are a belated, futile, and desultory attempt to repair the "fiber of civil society that has disintegrated."[9]

Hegel's advocacy of colonialism has been seized upon as evidence of the incoherence of his overall vision of civil society, a weak link in his system. Avineri maintained that Hegel's unsatisfactory examination demonstrated his "basic intellectual honesty," a confession that he lacked a radical solution to the problem of poverty.[10] Hirschman, however, remained skeptical of the cogency of Hegel's argument, "the chain of unproven assertions and deductions" regarding colonialism. He was unconvinced that an "increasing maldistribution of income" results in a "shortfall of consumption in relation to production," which, in turn, logically instigates the search for external, undeveloped markets.[11] Neuhouser contended that colonialism "constitutes a serious blow to Hegel's theoretical ambitions" because it implies that civil society "is precisely not a stable

---

[8] Tsenay Serequeberhan, "The Idea of Colonialism in Hegel's 'Philosophy of Right,'" *International Philosophical Quarterly*, 29 (1989), 301–318, at 312; for reasons of scope, this chapter will not address the substantial literature on Hegel's negative depiction of non-European peoples and cultures, the major statement of which may be found in his *Lectures on the Philosophy of History*. Hegel did not explicitly connect his denigrating views with an advocacy of European imperialism. On Hegel's derogatory portraits of the non-European world, see Robert Bernasconi, "With What Must the Philosophy of World History Begin? On the Racial Basis of Hegel's Eurocentrism," *Nineteenth-Century Contexts*, 22 (2000), 171–201, at 190; and his more recent essay "With What Must the History of Philosophy Begin? Hegel's Role in the Debate on the Place of India within the History of Philosophy," in *Hegel's History of Philosophy: New Interpretations*, ed. David Duquette (Albany, N.Y., 2003), pp. 35–49.

[9] Joseph McCarney, *Hegel on History* (London, 2000), p. 144.

[10] Shlomo Avineri, *Hegel's Theory of the Modern State* (Cambridge, 1972), p. 154. This view has been echoed and expanded upon by Thomas A. Lewis, who argued that "despite both the numerous mechanisms Hegel recommends to combat poverty and his unambiguous claim that the poor have a right to subsistence, he never offers a solution he thinks will succeed." See his *Freedom and Tradition in Hegel: Reconsidering Anthropology, Ethics, and Religion* (Notre Dame, Ind., 2005), pp. 177–178.

[11] Albert O. Hirschman, "On Hegel, Imperialism, and Structural Stagnation," in his *Essays in Trespassing: Economics to Politics and Beyond* (Cambridge, 1981), pp. 167–176, at p. 168.

and self-sufficient system, but must instead rely on something outside of itself in order to achieve its ends."[12]

Few writers have issued sympathetic verdicts concerning Hegel's account of colonialism in the *Philosophy of Right*. Those who have insist that his writings on colonialism comprise but a minuscule theme in his thought, one whose importance must not be exaggerated. Walton, for example, held that colonialism is a solution that only England had exploited fully, but he insisted that Hegel did not regard England as a "paradigm instance of how civil society should be organized." Similarly, Bellamy observed that "if economic competition went unchecked then the only solution to overproduction would be the creation of new markets by colonization," but he inserted the caveat that Hegel did not advocate uninhibited market activity.[13]

Hegel analyzed colonialism in the context of his discussion of poverty, a condition in which individuals are "left with the needs" but "deprived of all the advantages of society," including education, health care, and "even the consolation of religion." Hegel's "universal authority" would not only address the "immediate deficiencies" of hunger, shelter, and material requirements for the indigent, but would also extirpate the deep-rooted "disposition to laziness, viciousness, and other vices" accompanying poverty.[14] Hegel explicitly recognized the "contingent character of almsgiving and charitable donation" and sought to alleviate publicly the "universal aspects of want" through "public poor houses, hospitals, and street lighting."[15]

---

[12] Frederick Neuhouser, *Foundations of Hegel's Social Theory: Actualizing Freedom* (Cambridge, Mass., and London, 2000), pp. 173–174. These arguments were anticipated by Robert Fatton, who argues that "the logic of imperialism implies that the resolution of the inherent problems plaguing civil society can be only temporary, since the conquest of new territories and new markets can only proceed ad infinitum," in "Hegel and the Riddle of Poverty: The Limits of Bourgeois Political Economy," *History of Political Economy*, 18 (1986), 579–600, at 596; for an excellent recent treatment of Hegel's conception of poverty, see Frederick Beiser, *Hegel* (New York and London, 2005), p. 250.

[13] A. S. Walton, "Economy, Utility, and Community in Hegel's Theory of Civil Society," in *The State and Civil Society: Studies in Hegel's Political Philosophy*, ed. Z. A. Pelczynski (Cambridge, 1984), pp. 244–261, at p. 254; Richard Bellamy, "Hegel and Liberalism," in his *Rethinking Liberalism* (London and New York, 2000), pp. 3–21, at p. 12. Ian Fraser offers a similar line of argument, insisting that Hegel never conceived of colonialism as a solution but was merely "observing and shedding light on" his contemporary society, in "Speculations on Poverty in Hegel's 'Philosophy of Right,'" *The European Legacy*, 1 (1997), 2055–2068, at 2060.

[14] Hegel, *Philosophy of Right*, §241.

[15] Ibid., §242.

Hegel acknowledged, however, that the unmitigated functioning of the market mechanism, "occupied internally with expanding its population and its industry," would produce inexorably "accumulation of wealth" and increased "specialization of labour," which "in turn leads to an inability to feel and enjoy wider freedoms, and particularly the spiritual advantages, of civil society."[16] Hegel argued that a "rabble" forms when a "large mass of people" lose "that feeling of right, integrity, and honour which comes from supporting oneself by one's activity and work" as a result of failing to achieve a "certain standard of living." Since no absolute benchmark of subsistence or deprivation exists, it is "the disposition associated with poverty, by inward rebellion against the rich, against society, against government," that produces a rabble.[17]

Hegel supported the colonization of empty lands overseas as an alternative to other forms of poverty relief. He believed that wealth redistribution, permanent income subsidies, and public employment are inadequate remedies for one of two reasons: first, individuals require "the mediation of work" and "the feeling of self-sufficiency and honour" in order to enter into the complex web of social interdependence that forms the basis of modern *sittlichkeit*; second, the economic predicament underpinning this social crisis, "overproduction and the lack of a proportionate number of consumers," precludes internal resolution because to employ displaced workers in production only would augment the surplus supply of unwanted goods. For this reason, civil society, conducted by the public authority, must "go beyond its own confines and look for consumers, and hence the means it requires for subsistence, in other nations which lack those means of which it has a surplus or which generally lag behind it in creativity." Indeed, Hegel portrayed overseas trade as the attribute of "all great and enterprising nations" in which "creativity has flourished," whereas nontrading nations have "stagnated internally and sunk into the most appalling and miserable superstition."[18]

Fully developed civil society is driven to colonize by the pressures of burgeoning population, overproduction, and underconsumption. Colonization would provide both a "new market and sphere of industrial activity" and what Hegel cryptically termed "a return to the family principle in a new country" for those relocated citizens.[19] It assumes two

---

[16] Ibid., §242 remark, §243.
[17] Ibid., §244, add. G.
[18] Ibid., §245, 246, 247 remark.
[19] Ibid., §248.

forms – sporadic and systematic – with the latter form initiated and regulated by the public authority to allay economic distress and provide a
new opportunity for poor members of society. He disparaged contemporary German emigration as haphazard and useless to the mother country
because it severed the link with the emigrant, who is "consequently of no
service." By contrast, he approvingly cited ancient Greek colonialism for
easing population pressure, producing new markets, and facilitating the
citizen's undivided attention to public affairs.

Toward the end of his life, however, Hegel cast doubt on the proposition that poverty could be permanently eradicated solely by a publicly
sponsored scheme of mass colonization. Hegel probably had the British
precedent in mind as he considered such a policy. In 1819, Parliament had
voted £50,000 to send 5,000 settlers to the Cape Colony. Furthermore,
economic distress in Ireland resulted in an allocation of £15,000 for
removing paupers to North America in 1823. Even larger sums were
granted for the same purpose in 1825 and 1827.[20] In "On the English
Reform Bill" (1831), Hegel disapproved of a "proposal to reduce the
surplus numbers of poor by establishing colonies [which] would have
to remove at least one million inhabitants to have any chance of success. But how could this be effected?" Hegel pinpointed the impracti-
cality of this scheme but conceded that a profound transformation was
required to prevent the repetition of this miserable scenario. "The empty
space thereby created," he warned, "would soon be filled in the same way
as before if laws and circumstances remained otherwise unchanged."[21]
Colonization was not, in Hegel's view, a remedy that could be prescribed
indefinitely. It could only function effectively as a safety valve amid acute
turmoil.

For most of his life, though, Hegel emphasized several factors that would
make recourse to colonization desirable. He initially pointed to population growth and chronic land scarcity, instead of overproduction-induced
poverty, as a trigger for colonization. Specific historical circumstances
probably led Hegel to address the topic of colonization in this manner. In
1815, 70 percent of the Prussian population inhabited rural areas and the
agrarian sector still dominated the economy. Industrialization had not yet
transformed the society; there were still twice as many artisans as factory

[20] British emigration and colonization policy discussed in Bernard Semmel, *The Rise of
Free Trade Imperialism: Classical Political Economy, the Empire of Free Trade, and
Imperialism, 1750–1850* (Cambridge, 1970), pp. 103–104.
[21] G. W. F. Hegel, "On the English Reform Bill," in Hegel, *Political Writings*, ed. Laurence
Dickey, trans. H. B. Nisbet (Cambridge, 1999), pp. 234–270, at p. 248.

workers. Most crucially, the population was steadily rising, doubling in Germany between 1815 and 1845, and reached an unsustainable level. Poor harvests in 1816 aggravated the situation and caused a sudden rise in food prices. This crisis encouraged thousands of Germans, primarily middle-class rural families, traveling as a unit, to emigrate, and the exodus cushioned the effects of rural pauperization;[22] 20,000 Germans emigrated in 1816–1817.[23]

In his early "Heidelberg" version of *Philosophy of Right* (1817–1818), written amid this unprecedented mass emigration from German-speaking states, Hegel argued that land scarcity had caused an agrarian crisis that precluded a "specific mode of life" for surplus inhabitants and compelled them to "earn a necessitous living at factory work without free independence or else the state must see to it that they are given some cultivated land." The public authority would facilitate colonization "where [the landless] can live in the same way as in the home country" and, reciprocally, colonists "forever remain citizens of their home country and are very useful to it." In this early version of the *Philosophy of Right*, Hegel referred to "emigration," instead of "sporadic" colonization, to signify the departure of a propertyless peasantry who "become assimilated into other peoples since their own country does not care for them."[24]

The Heidelberg *Philosophy of Right* contains an orientation that Hegel reversed in his subsequent Berlin lectures. Colonization was presented as a measure to alleviate rural land shortages precipitated by overpopulation. It was marked by an anti-industrial bias and suggested the need for a more expansive and paternalistic police role in the consolidation of a colony. Members of the new colony would form civil society afresh, but would be spared the industrial "factory work" that was becoming an indelible feature of the commercial society in which Hegel was living.

Hegel's proposed colonies would involve settlement, not conquest, the transplanting of a segment of the population to an uncongested place where they would be "granted the same rights as the inhabitants of the

---

[22] Brendan Simms, *The Struggle for Mastery in Germany, 1779–1850* (London, 1998), pp. 142–150 passim; James J. Sheehan, *German History 1770–1866* (Oxford, 1989), pp. 461–463.

[23] Figure cited in Klaus J. Bade, "German Transatlantic Emigration in the Nineteenth and Twentieth Centuries," in *European Expansion and Migration: Essays on the Intercontinental Migration from Asia, Africa, and Europe*, ed. P. C. Emmer and M. Mörner (New York and Oxford, 1992), pp. 121–155, at pp. 125–126.

[24] G. W. F. Hegel, *Lectures on Natural Right and Political Science: The First Philosophy of Right: Heidelberg, 1817–1818*, trans. J. M. Stewart and P. R. Hodgson (Berkeley, Calif., 1995), §120.

mother country."[25] In spite of its denigration of America's low "grade of civilization" and the "physically and psychically powerless" nature of its indigenous people, Hegel's account of European colonialism in the *Philosophy of History* emphasized the absence of brutal subjugation, the sheer availability of land, and its status as a historical phase of civil society.[26] In his comparison of European modes of overseas expansion, Hegel claimed that "South America was conquered, but North America colonized. The Spaniards took possession to govern it, and to become rich through occupying political offices, and by exactions."[27] Colonization, in Hegel's view, did not consist in a violent dispossession of the property of non-European inhabitants of a land designated for colonization. Instead, it was conceived of as a peaceful process of encroachment and settlement without expropriation.

More importantly, for Hegel, colonies represented an escape from the obstructive "burdens and imposts" of European society and offered a "sphere of action" to employ "independence of spirit" and "appliances and ingenuity … to realize some produce from the extensive and still virgin soil."[28] Yet, Hegel refused to abandon these settlers and held out hope for their reintegration into civil society. He intended for them to retain an "extended link" to the universal through overseas commerce and "forever remain citizens." Hegel recognized that the increasingly global nature of commerce rendered borders less significant. His advocacy of colonialism was not an admission, as Avineri and Neuhouser have claimed, that civil society is unable to resolve its own contradictions.

[25] Hegel, *Philosophy of Right*, §248 and §248 Add. G.

[26] It should be mentioned that in the 1817–1818 Heidelberg lectures, Hegel made much of the distinction between "civilised" and "uncivilised" peoples. He contended that "the civilised nation is conscious that the rights of barbarians are unequal to its own and treats their autonomy only as a formality"; furthermore, he argued that "insofar as uncivilised peoples have virtually no constitution, and the civilised people who live alongside them accordingly cannot rely on them and never feel secure, they take it on themselves to compel these rough people to accept a fixed constitution." Both quotes are taken from Colin Tyler, "Hegel, War, and the Tragedy of Imperialism," *History of European Ideas*, 30 (2004), 403–431, at 428.

[27] G. W. F. Hegel, *Philosophy of History*, trans. J. Sibree (New York, 1956), pp. 81–84 passim.

[28] Ibid., pp. 82, 86. Hegel's depiction of the Spaniards was not only the result of anti-Catholic prejudice, but also arose from the conviction that they were "not yet sufficiently cultivated" for advanced constitutions (*Philosophy of Right*, §274 Adds. H, G). M. J. Petry draws attention to a passage Hegel marked down from the *Morning Chronicle* in 1825 that claimed that the Spanish had "sunk into semi-barbarism" and are "weak, stupid, and tyrannical," in "Hegel and the *Morning Chronicle*," *Hegel-Studien*, 11 (1976), 11–80, at 30.

Hegel's approach nevertheless appears to suffer from its contradictory features, simultaneously espousing colonization as a panacea for poverty in some passages and as a temporary stopgap measure in others. It remains unclear how the inhabitants of new colonies will be reintegrated into the communal structures of civil society. A sustained link may be inferred, but the sequence by which colonies of settlement evolve from the "family principle" to civil society remains vague. It is only by examining the origins of Hegel's ideas on colonialism's advantages and disadvantages, particularly those that he inherited from eighteenth-century Scottish political economy, that some of these puzzles can be solved.

SCOTTISH POLITICAL ECONOMY AND HEGEL'S ANALYSIS OF COLONIALISM

Hegel partially inherited the ambivalence and inconsistency of his account of colonies from Sir James Steuart (1713–1780) and Adam Ferguson (1723–1816). These political writers had grappled with three issues pertinent to Hegel's account: the repercussions of extraterritorial expansion for commercial society and the social bonds uniting its citizens; the appropriate form of public intervention in a market economy when it produces poverty; and the social implications of population increase when it outstrips economic growth.

Scottish political economy had a "wide and marked reception" in late-eighteenth-century Germany. While it may be impossible to identify specific points of this transmission, it is clear that Hegel achieved competence in English by 1804 and purchased numerous English books in the 1790s during his Berne period. Hegel devoted three months in 1799 to digesting Steuart's *Principles of Political Oeconomy* (1767) and composing a commentary (that was subsequently lost).[29] It is manifestly odd, then, that Steuart's name goes unmentioned in the *Philosophy of Right* when Adam Smith, Jean-Baptiste Say, and David Ricardo are cited.[30] There is less direct evidence that Hegel read Ferguson, though the percolation of his

[29] Norbert Waszek, *The Scottish Enlightenment and Hegel's Account of "Civil Society"* (Dordrecht, Boston, Mass., and London, 1988), pp. 78, 108, 113, 115. As noted by Waszek, Rosencranz asserts that "all of Hegel's reflections about the nature of civil society" derived from Steuart; Waszek argues that Hegel's idea of a threat to man's "wholeness" posed by the unchecked mechanism of modern exchange economy derived from both Steuart and F. Schiller in *Letters on the Aesthetic Education of Man* (1794).

[30] Hegel, *Philosophy of Right*, §189 Remark. Note that apart from this reference, there is no textual evidence to support the claim that Hegel actually read Ricardo or Say; see Stedman Jones, "Hegel," p. 116n.

ideas in German intellectual circles is uncontroversial.[31] Though Hegel certainly read the *Wealth of Nations* and drew on it in other contexts, Smith's derisive depiction of colonial monopoly as a profligate burden on taxpayers and an impediment to industry bears no resemblance to Hegel's more positive account.[32]

Steuart's treatise enjoyed greater prestige than Smith's until at least 1800 in Germany because Steuart's emphasis on exchange and reciprocity, rather than labor value, rendered his ideas compatible with the tenets of Cameralism.[33] His insistence on the existence of a statesman to anticipate and correct instabilities also corresponded to the conventional function of the *polizei* in Germany, where the market was not treated as a self-regulating entity.[34] Hegel's discussion of colonies bears the imprint of these influences: a public authority must intervene to form a colony when economic trends collide dangerously and cause the bonds of social attachment to weaken.[35]

[31] Laurence Dickey notes that "scholars also have inferred from some of the excerpts in Hegel's *tagebüch* that he had read Ferguson while a schoolboy at Stuttgart" in his *Hegel: Religion, Economics, and Politics of Spirit, 1770–1807* (Cambridge, 1987), p. 192. While Fania Oz-Salzberger rejected a direct link between Ferguson's and Hegel's philosophies of history, she noted that Ferguson was elected as an external member of the Berlin Royal Academy of Sciences and Arts in 1793, mentioned the acclaim of both Ferguson's *Essay* and *Institutes* by German journals, and cited the impact of Ferguson's ideas on Herder, Hamann, Novalis, Jakobi, and Mendelssohn in her *Translating the Enlightenment: Scottish Civic Discourse in Eighteenth-Century Germany* (Oxford, 1999), pp. 255, 105, 130–133.

[32] Adam Smith, *An Inquiry into the Nature and Causes of the Wealth of Nations*, ed. R. H. Campbell and A. S. Skinner, 2 vols. (Oxford, 1976), II, pp. 590–610 passim. For Smith's influence on other aspects of Hegel's thought, see James P. Henderson and John B. Davis, "Adam Smith's Influence on Hegel's Philosophical Writings," *Journal of the History of Economic Thought*, 13 (1991), 184–204.

[33] Keith Tribe, *Governing Economy: The Reformation of German Economic Discourse, 1750–1840* (Cambridge, 1988), pp. 133, 139.

[34] Mark Neocleous, "Policing the System of Needs: Hegel, Political Economy, and the Police of the Market," *History of European Ideas*, 24 (1998), 43–58, at 45; Dickey, *Hegel*, pp. 197, 200.

[35] Other factors were decisive as well, of course, in leading Hegel to embrace Scottish political economy. It appealed to Hegel because he was disillusioned, according to Ritter, with the "abstractness and fundamentally inadequate one-sidedness" of the political thought of the French Revolution and aspired to establish a social system on the "inductive (hermeneutical) theory of the already existing, historically constituted social reality." See Joachim Ritter, "Hegel and the French Revolution," in *Hegel and the French Revolution: Essays on the Philosophy of Right*, trans. R. D. Winfield (Cambridge, Mass., and London, 1982), pp. 35–89, at p. 69. Furthermore, this influence was counteracted by the German Romantics' hostility toward the consequences of commercial society, whose division of labor condemned individuals to mind-numbing routine, dehumanized them, and corroded communal attachment. See Frederick C. Beiser, *Enlightenment, Revolution,*

More than the policy prescriptions of the political economists, Hegel was enamored of the extraction "from the endless multitude of details with which it is initially confronted the simple principle of things." He commended political economy for isolating the "laws underlying a mass of contingent occurrences." Pursuit of individual interest became, for Hegel, both transparent and predictable, opening up the possibility of rational interdependent relationships. Combined with the division of labor, Hegel imagined a system in which "subjective selfishness turns into a contribution towards the satisfaction of the needs of everyone else" and facilitates a higher form of freedom constructed on the basis of the autonomous pursuit of self-interest.[36]

Hegel's awkward and uneven treatment of colonies could partially stem from the Scottish civic humanist's uneasiness with territorial expansion in commercial societies. Adam Ferguson correlated the enlargement of a polity with the diminishment of civic awareness, contending that dispersed citizens "are disunited, and lose sight of their community" as "the greater part are thrown into a state of languor and obscurity, and suffer themselves to be governed at discretion." Conversely, however, high population density rendered citizens "profligate, licentious, seditious, and incapable of public affections."[37] Although war "tends to strengthen the bands of society" and promote "mutual attachment and courage,"[38] Ferguson argued that national enlargement attenuates the "common ties of society," leaving citizens with "no common affairs to transact, but those of trade." Because inhabitants "cease to perceive their connection to the state" due to the "distance from the seat of administration," political activism wanes and reduces them to passive subjects. Similarly, Ferguson was preoccupied with the "disorders to which a great empire is exposed" because the "prevention, vigilance, and quick execution" necessary to retain distant colonies drain national prosperity and invariably terminate in despotism.[39]

---

and Romanticism: The Genesis of Modern German Political Thought, 1790–1800 (Cambridge, Mass., and London, 1992), pp. 231–233 passim.

[36] Hegel, *Philosophy of Right*, §189 remark and adds. H, G, §199; Albert O. Hirschman, *The Passions and the Interests: Political Arguments for Capitalism Before Its Triumph* (Princeton, N.J., 1997), pp. 50–51; see also Mark R. Greer, "Individuality and the Economic Order in Hegel's Philosophy of Right," *European Journal of the History of Economic Thought*, 6 (1999), 566–568.

[37] Adam Ferguson, *Institutes of Moral Philosophy* (London, 1994), p. 265.

[38] Adam Ferguson, *An Essay on the History of Civil Society*, ed. Fania Oz-Salzberger (Cambridge, 2001), p. 99.

[39] Lisa Hill claimed that Ferguson believed civil society "contained the seeds of its own destruction." The division of labor's "specialization erodes martial and communal ardor,"

In contrast to Hegel, Ferguson did not link expansion to economic and demographic factors, such as price fluctuations and rapid population growth, because he conceded, according to the historian Istvan Hont, "no strictly economic bounds to the future of commercial society."[40] Like Hegel, however, he was aware of the ubiquitous risk of moral decline associated with commercial prosperity. Yet, Ferguson diverged from Hegel's viewpoint on the status of colonies. Whereas Hegel prophesied the beneficial repercussions of colonial emancipation, Ferguson vehemently rejected American independence from Britain in 1776. Because "no nation ever planted colonies with so liberal or noble a hand as England has done," Ferguson reasoned, the Americans should "repay us for all the blood and treasure we have expended in the common cause."[41] Unlike Hegel, he was unable to grasp the idea that "the liberation of colonies itself proves to be of the greatest advantage to the mother state."[42]

Ferguson also confronted poverty's tendency to erode the bonds of social attachment. Poverty was not a perturbation of commercial society but its defining feature, for "the exaltation of the few must depress the many." Ferguson postulated that society must "suffer the wealthy to squander, that the poor may subsist." When commercial society's benefit disappears entirely, however, "the charm of dominion is broken and the naked slave, as awake from a dream, is astonished to find he is free. When the fence is destroyed, the wilds are open and the herd breaks loose."[43] This dissolution follows the disenchantment caused by relative deprivation. Although he disparaged the "extreme meanness" of the "rude and uncultivated" classes, he recognized that an "admiration of

in "Adam Ferguson and the Paradox of Progress and Decline," *History of Political Thought*, 18 (1997), 677–706, at 681.

[40] Istvan Hont, "The 'Rich Country–Poor Country' Debate in Scottish Classical Political Economy," in *Wealth and Virtue: The Shaping of Political Economy in the Scottish Enlightenment*, ed. Istvan Hont and Michael Ignatieff (Cambridge, 1983), pp. 271–315, at p. 296; see also Anthony Brewer, "Adam Ferguson, Adam Smith and the Concept of Economic Growth," *History of Political Economy*, 31 (1999), 237–254.

[41] Adam Ferguson, *Remarks on a pamphlet lately published by Dr. Price, intitled 'Observations on the nature of civil liberty, the principles of government, and the justice and policy of the war with America'*, in a letter from a gentleman in the country to a member of Parliament (London, 1776), pp. 27, 19. For an analysis of Ferguson's views, see Richard B. Sher, "From Troglodytes to Americans: Montesquieu and the Scottish Enlightenment on Liberty, Virtue, and Commerce," in *Republicanism, Liberty, and Commercial Society, 1649–1776*, ed. David Wooton (London and Palo Alto, Calif., 1994), pp. 368–404, at p. 401.

[42] Hegel, *Philosophy of Right*, §248 Add. G.

[43] Ferguson, *Essay*, pp. 177, 225, 263.

wealth unpossessed" could lead to "corruption and baseness," a tendency to "rate our fellow citizens by the figure they make" and "to bow to the splendid equipage." Ferguson believed that public instruction, infused with martial vigilance, could offset these defects of civil society and help the poor recognize the necessity of social subordination. Wealth in civil society should be tolerated until it ceases to function as "the instrument of a vigorous spirit."[44]

Unlike both Hegel and Steuart, however, Ferguson would not countenance even well-intentioned government interference in commerce since it "only multipl[i]es interruptions and grounds of complaint." He warned that the "period of vision and chimera is near" when self-interested merchants pursue national goals. For each party, the consequences of such action would be chaos. His disdain for overlapping spheres also applied to colonies: Ferguson conceded that population growth rendered indispensable the "planting of a colony," but it should never be administered as a "palliative" to stimulate economic growth since this "arises from regards to [the] interest and personal safety" of individuals.[45]

Unlike Hegel, Ferguson neither conceived of colonization as an antidote to poverty's venomous consequences nor explicitly linked territorial expansion and economic fortune. Ferguson's predilection for the preservation of ardent civic activism and attachment, weakened by the atomism of commercial society, related to his views on colonial expansion. For this reason, he is a possible intellectual source for Hegel's ideas about colonialism. Like Hegel, Ferguson conceived of the market as an ethical sphere, but he did not maintain, as Hegel did, that it was subject to the interference of a public authority.

Hegel's justification of state intervention to combat poverty, however, derived primarily from Sir James Steuart, not Ferguson. Although Steuart argued that a statesman should neither "establish what oeconomy he pleases" nor "overturn at will the established laws of it," he maintained that the "principle [*sic*] object" of political economy is "to secure a certain fund of subsistence for all the inhabitants [and] to obviate every circumstance which may render it precarious."[46] Steuart contended

---

[44] Ibid., pp. 177, 239, 248.
[45] Ibid., pp. 139, 135.
[46] Sir James Steuart, *An inquiry into the principles of political oeconomy: being an essay on the science of domestic policy in free nations*, ed. A. S. Skinner with Noboru Kobayashi and Hiroshi Mizota, 2 vols. (London, 1998), I, pp. 20–21. It should also be noted that Steuart employed "statesman" as "a general term to signify the legislative and supreme power, according to the form of government," I, p. 20.

that failures were endemic to the market, were not self-correcting, and produced poverty requiring public action. Labeling chronic poverty "a disease which must be endured," Steuart defended the notion that "a state should provide retreats of all sorts, for the different conditions of her decayed inhabitants." He proposed public works in undeveloped regions as a response to structural unemployment.[47] Hegel placed less emphasis on the inevitability of market failure than Steuart, but permitted police "oversight and advanced provision" with regard to "the commonest necessities of life" and intervention to "moderate and shorten the duration of those dangerous convulsions" of market society.[48]

Steuart's statesman orchestrates, but does not unilaterally determine, intervention to eliminate poverty. Steuart insisted that "a good governor, by exposing the political state of certain classes of the people," should "prevail with men of substance to join in schemes for relief." In Steuart's framework, the rich and the poor are interdependent, as "the desires of the rich, and the means of gratifying them, make them call for the services of the poor," whereas "the necessities of the poor, and their desire of becoming rich, make them cheerfully answer the summons." Taxes further ensure the "public good, by throwing a part of the wealth of the rich into the hands of the industrious poor,"[49] as distinct from wealth redistribution to an indolent underclass. Steuart's emphasis on the necessity of work to mediate poverty resonates in Hegel's thought.

For Steuart, the advantages of industry, trade, and luxury compensated for defects, such as poverty, because they had gradually transformed the social ethos from "feudal and military" to "free and commercial." Poverty was only a transient problem because Steuart's system, like Ferguson's, perceived the potential for economic growth to be almost limitless in the long run.[50] While he lauded "schemes for recalling ancient simplicity and for making mankind honest and virtuous" as "beautiful speculations," they were not "practical in our degenerate age" of commercial society.[51] Like Hegel, but unlike Ferguson, Steuart acknowledged that the past was

[47] Ibid., pp. 71, 296–297.
[48] Hegel, *Philosophy of Right*, §§235–236, 236 Remark.
[49] Steuart, *Principles*, I, 293; II, all of chap. 26 passim.
[50] A. S. Skinner, "Sir James Steuart: The Market and the State," *History of Economic Ideas*, I (1993), 1–42, at 17.
[51] Steuart, *Principles*, II, p. 67; I, pp. 29, 69, 86. Steuart, like Marx in the middle decades of the following century, attributed a key role to "the discovery of America and the Indies" in European history because "modes changed and by turns enlivened the different branches of industry," I, p. 69. In this way, he acknowledged the importance of colonies to Europe's structural transformation.

irrevocable and the study of society required a modern basis. Unlike both Hegel and Ferguson, however, Steuart did not attempt to integrate economic relationships into a grand, all-encompassing vision of ethical life.

In Steuart's thought, colonies represent a specialized, but not necessarily desirable, intervention to solve the problem of overpopulation. Although "an increase in numbers in a state shows youth and vigour," Steuart alleged that population must be reduced "by degrees (either by encouragements given to leaving the country, or by establishing colonies & c.) until they be brought down to the just proportion of the growth of national subsistence." Colonies "check" population growth and enable the statesman "to preserve the wealth [a nation] has already acquired," a wealth jeopardized by the hazardous unreliability of foreign export markets.[52]

Hegel's reliance on Steuart's mechanics of colonization is transparent, but he also absorbed Ferguson's anxiety concerning expansion's corrosive impact on social attachment. There were alternative and more sophisticated models in political economy for understanding colonies at Hegel's disposal, including those proffered by Smith and Say. Hegel preferred Scottish writers of the eighteenth century because his chief concern was the manner in which a public authority could mend the frayed fabric of ethical life in commercial society. Hegel was preoccupied with the debilitating effects of population growth and land scarcity on participation in civil society, and it is only in this context that his encouragement of emigration to colonies of settlement can be properly understood.

MARX'S WRITINGS ON EMPIRE AND "MARXIAN" THEORIES OF IMPERIALISM: A TENUOUS RELATIONSHIP

The modern study of empire owes a tremendous debt to political writers, historians, and theorists working within the Marxian tradition. With the notable exceptions of Hobson and Schumpeter, the most influential theories concerning the forces underpinning European expansion emanate from writers with intellectual priorities and orientations derived, sometimes circuitously, from Marx. These include Rosa Luxemburg, V. I. Lenin, Frantz Fanon, Andre Gunder Frank, Immanuel Wallerstein, and, most recently, Antonio Negri.[53] It was often the case that Marx's successors

---

[52] Ibid., I, p. 87; II, pp. 18, 27.

[53] On the thinkers of the early and mid-twentieth century, see Tom Kemp, "The Marxist Theory of Imperialism," in *Studies in the Theory of Imperialism*, ed. Roger Owen and Bob Sutcliffe (London, 1972), pp. 15–34. For a survey of the postwar period, see Patrick

refined, expanded upon, radicalized, and, in some cases, rejected the insights gleaned from reading the master, a process further complicated by Marx's own shifting views on empire.[54] Furthermore, the peculiar historical circumstances of the twentieth century conspired to imbue the discourses of anti-imperialism, decolonization, and national liberation with political and economic language that was Marxian-inspired if not explicitly borrowed from Marx. It is difficult to imagine the speeches and writings of Mao Zedong and Fidel Castro, let alone those of the leaders of Nicaragua's Sandinistas, stripped of the vocabulary inherited from Marx.[55] To the contemporary mind, Marx and the critique of empire have become inseparable.

Two curious, perhaps paradoxical, aspects of Marx's engagement with colonial themes therefore deserve mention at the outset of this section. First, Marx never developed a full-fledged theory of empire. The lion's share of his most pertinent comments is encountered in his scattered newspaper articles from the 1850s, not in his major theoretical works.[56] Second, at least until the late 1850s, Marx favorably depicted the processes of intercontinental trade, the annihilation of distance through the employment of new technologies that facilitated communication, and the emergence of global interdependence that both presaged and underpinned European colonial expansion. In the twentieth and twenty-first

Wolfe, "History and Imperialism: A Century of Theory from Marx to Postcolonialism," *American Historical Review*, 102 (1997), 388–420. For a brilliant analysis of the theories of the past decade, see Philip Pomper, "The History and Theory of Empires," *History and Theory*, theme issue 44 (2005), 1–27.

54   For one fascinating example, take the case of Rosa Luxemburg. In her *The Accumulation of Capital* (1913), she disputed Marx's contention, in the second volume of *Capital*, that self-contained capitalist accumulation is possible. For Luxemburg, capitalism could neither exist nor survive as a self-contained system. Rather, it always had to appropriate from noncapitalist areas. For Lenin, "primitive accumulation" would continue so long as a noncapitalist area of the globe existed. For Marx, it occurred just at the very early stages of capitalism. For Luxemburg, however, primitive accumulation is happening all of the time. For a lucid analysis of this and other similar themes, see Bob Sutcliffe, "How Many Capitalisms? Historical Materialism in the Debates about Imperialism and Globalization," in *Historical Materialism and Globalization*, ed. Mark Rupert and Hazel Smith (London and New York, 2002), pp. 40–58, at pp. 47–48.

55   For an assessment of the pertinence of Marx's writings for the non-European world, particularly for the political-economic plight of the global South, see Umberto Melotti, *Marx and the Third World*, trans. Pat Ransford (New York, 1977).

56   As Chronis Polychroniov notes, "Marx's analysis of the capitalist mode of production makes no explicit reference to capitalist imperialism. Marx never developed a theory of imperialism," in his *Marxist Perspectives on Imperialism: A Theoretical Analysis* (London and New York, 1991), p. 33. Robert Young adds, however, that "it was Marx's writing that encouraged subsequent accounts of them as oppressive practices, subject to critical analysis"; see his *Postcolonialism: An Historical Introduction* (Oxford, 2001), p. 101.

centuries, these factors have been denigrated routinely as the bulwark of exploitative, neo-colonial relations between the industrialized North and the global South. Yet for Marx, at least the "early" and "middle" Marx, they were a prelude to a broader transformation.

The fragmentary nature of Marx's writings on empire, however, has not prevented them from attracting attention. In addition to being anthologized and serving as the fodder for innumerable scholarly articles, they were famously assailed by Edward Said in *Orientalism* (1978). "Marx's economic analyses," Said contended, "are perfectly fitted to a standard orientalist undertaking ... the idea of regenerating a fundamentally lifeless Asia is a piece of pure Romantic Orientalism."[57] With this attack, Marx's status as a guide for the non-European world was diminished, at least among those academics working within the paradigm of postcolonialism.

Said's critique has been, perhaps, more influential than it deserves to be.[58] While it is undeniable that Marx, in his writings before 1870 at least, adhered loosely (and not dogmatically) to a stadial view of the progress of civilization and consistently maintained that European societies were more advanced than their non-European counterparts, he did not make those judgments on the basis of some sort of derogatory notion of the limited capabilities of non-European societies. In fact, much of Marx's thought before 1870 is premised on the view that the convergence of societies is desirable, inevitable, and imminent. His philosophy of history offers a rather robust vision of the capacity of non-European peoples to innovate at an accelerated pace, even to outstrip Europeans once the stultifying straitjacket of tradition has been stripped away.

Furthermore, Marx reserved his most venomous attacks for European governments, some of which he categorized as "oriental despotisms." He claimed that "Spain, being but a superficial resemblance to the absolute monarchies of Europe in general, is rather to be ranged in a class with Asiatic forms of government. Spain, like Turkey, remained an agglomeration of mismanaged republics with nominal sovereignty at their head."[59]

---

[57] Edward W. Said, *Orientalism* (New York, 1994), p. 154.

[58] There is little doubt that, as D. A. Washbrook has observed, Said "represents European culture in ways which essentialize, objectify, demean, de-rationalize, and de-historicize it"; see Washbrook, "Orients and Occidents: Colonial Discourse Theory and the Historiography of the British Empire," in *The Oxford History of the British Empire*, ed. William Roger Louis (Oxford and New York, 1999), 5 vols., V (ed. Robin Winks), pp. 596–611, at p. 607.

[59] K. Marx, "Revolution in Spain [I]," *N[ew] Y[ork] D[aily] T[ribune]*, 9 September 1854, in Marx and F. Engels, *Revolution in Spain* (London, 1939), p. 26.

Of course, Marx is employing "Asiatic" and "oriental" as demeaning epithets. Yet, this usage cannot disguise (and should not distract from) his main point: the common despicable features of certain political institutions regardless of their provenance. No government was subjected to harsher treatment from Marx's pen than those of Prussia and the German princely states.[60] Even the political system of Britain, a nation that otherwise figures prominently in his thought as the most advanced society in whose historical wake other societies follow,[61] is ridiculed as pathetically anachronistic. "The British constitution," he wrote, "is just an old-fashioned, antiquated, and archaic compromise."[62] So, it is true that Marx had severely derogatory views of politics in Asia – characterized by supposedly despotic, self-indulgent, reckless kings who ruled over inert, innately reactionary peasantries – but non-European societies are hardly singled out or contrasted unfavorably with European states. Marx was, after all, an exile forced to flee from reactionary regimes. By casting doubt on the accuracy, or at least the severe limitations, of Said's interpretation of Marx, new vistas for further study of Marx's writings about empire are opened.[63]

While declaring, even celebrating, the world historical purpose of the European bourgeoisie, it is crucial to recall that Marx robustly despised the motives that had led to its interaction with the extra-European world. He refused to overlook the barbarism its agents employed. Marx unequivocally denounced British aims and methods in India: "the object was confessedly plunder by means of murder, in every respect as hideous

---

[60] In his essay "Marx on India: A Clarification," Aijaz Ahmad rightly observes that "Marx's denunciation of pre-colonial society in India is no more strident than his denunciations of Europe's own feudal past, or of the absolutist monarchies, or of the German burghers; his essays on Germany are every bit as nasty." See Ahmad, *In Theory: Classes, Nations, Literatures* (London and New York, 1992), p. 224. For an account of Marx's critique of German states, which he claimed had "shared the restoration of modern nations without having shared their revolutions," see David Leopold, *The Young Karl Marx: German Philosophy, Modern Politics, and Human Flourishing* (Cambridge, 2007), pp. 22–30.

[61] In the first edition of *Capital* (1867), Marx famously contended that "the country that is more developed industrially only shows, to the less developed, the image of its own future!", though in subsequent editions Marx shifted away from this claim.

[62] K. Marx (1855), quoted in Shlomo Avineri, *The Social and Political Thought of Karl Marx* (Cambridge, 1990), p. 42.

[63] As C. A. Bayly has rightly observed, "the faddishness of 'post-colonial' theorizing in the last two decades of the twentieth century caused many commentators to overlook the great body of work in British intellectual history which relates to questions of orientalism and imperial ideas. They saw only a tendency to create the other, rather than long-standing debates about commerce, virtue and polity"; see Bayly, "The Second British Empire," in *Oxford History*, V, pp. 54–72, at p. 70.

as the slave trade ... [it entailed] the infliction of all agonies on the poor, ignorant and helpless."[64] Britain's policy was premised on self-interest and executed with rapacity. "The ruling classes of Great Britain," he declared, "have had, till now, but an accidental, transitory and exceptional interest in the progress of India. The aristocracy wanted to conquer it, the moneyocracy to plunder it, and the millocracy to undersell it."[65] Britain was "activated only by the vilest interests and was stupid in her manner of enforcing them."[66] To pursue its ends, it stopped at nothing. "Torture," Marx reports in a subsequent dispatch, "formed an organic institution of [Britain's] financial policy" in India.[67] But the ultimate result of, and not the motivation for, British action mattered most to Marx. As he noted with a mixture of amusement and disgust: "has the bourgeoisie ever done more? Has it ever effected progress without dragging individuals and peoples through blood and dirt, through misery and degradation?"[68] And while asserting the inevitability of this process, he delighted in the Indian Mutiny of 1857, declaring that "England is, in fact, now expiating her long mismanagement of India."[69]

In considering Marx's favorable attitude toward European intervention in non-European societies, it is crucial to understand that Marx ridiculed crude, Palmerstonian-style gunboat diplomacy. He considered such action superficial interference in the affairs of a country for fleeting political advantage or economic gain. Marx disparaged this sort of action. "The contemplated intervention in Mexico by England, France, and Spain," he wrote in 1861, "is, in my opinion, one of the most monstrous enterprises ever chronicled in the annals of international history."[70] This episode aroused Marx's contempt because the powers of Western Europe were behaving as nothing more than "intruders" whose ambitions did not transcend petty dynastic politics. The principal features of Mexico's society and economy, in this case, would remain unmolested.

---

[64] K. Marx, "Parliamentary Debate on India," *NYDT*, 25 June 1853, in *Karl Marx on Colonialism and Modernization: His Despatches and Other Writings on China, India, Mexico, the Middle East and North Africa*, ed. Shlomo Avineri (Garden City, N.Y., 1968), pp. 77–78.

[65] K. Marx, "The Future Results of British Rule in India," *NYDT*, 8 August 1853, ibid., pp. 126–127.

[66] K. Marx, "The British Rule in India," *NYDT*, 25 June 1853, ibid., p. 88.

[67] K. Marx, "The Indian Revolt," *NYDT*, 16 September 1857, ibid., p. 212.

[68] K. Marx, "Future Results," ibid., p. 129.

[69] K. Marx and F. Engels, "The Crisis in England," *Die Presse*, 6 November 1861, in Marx and Engels, *The Civil War in the U.S.* (London, 1937), p. 87.

[70] K. Marx, "The Intervention in Mexico," *NYDT*, 23 November 1861, in Avineri, ed., p. 25.

Furthermore, Marx was painfully aware of how economic prosperity and relative political freedom in Britain itself drew strength from despicable practices abroad, both in other parts of Europe as well as in Asia. In 1858, Marx would rue that "the Ionian islands, like India and Ireland, prove only that to be free at home, John Bull must enslave abroad. Thus, at this very moment, while giving vent to his virtuous indignation against Bonaparte's spy system in Paris, he is himself introducing it in Dublin."[71] Marx was under no illusions about the pernicious effects of empire at home, the hypocrisy it often necessitated, and the compromises of political principles it routinely demanded.

MARX'S ANALYSIS OF COLONIES AND EMPIRE

Regardless of the uses to which Marx's writings were put by succeeding generations, an examination of his writings sheds an intense light on his intellectual development. In particular, empire played a crucial role in Marx's account of the evolution of the European economy, his understanding of capitalism's future trajectory, and his prophecy of the preconditions for its obsolescence.

Marx's newspaper articles on Britain's empire in India, with justification, have been the focus of much scholarly attention. Yet, even before he turned his gaze to India in the 1850s, the role of colonialism and empire in world history was discernibly embedded in his early thought. In the *Manifesto* (1848), the flowering of commerce associated with colonial expansion occupies a privileged station in his account of feudalism's demise. In fact, Europe's historical change – the transformation of its basic economic and social structures – was galvanized by its contact with, and growing dependence upon, non-European markets:

[T]he discovery of America and the voyages round Africa provided fresh territory for the rising bourgeoisie. The East Indian and Chinese market, the colonisation of America, the colonial trade, the general increase in the means of exchange and of commodities, all gave to commerce, to sea commerce, to industry, a boost such as never before, hence quick development to the revolutionary element in a crumbling feudal society.[72]

In the *German Ideology* (composed in 1845–1846), Marx explicitly privileged the transformative role of exogenous forces in Europe's historical

---

[71] K. Marx, "The Question of the Ionian Islands," December 1858, in Marx and F. Engels, *On Colonialism* (Moscow, n.d.), p. 202.
[72] K. Marx (with F. Engels), "Manifesto of the Communist Party," in K. Marx, *Later Political Writings* (Cambridge, 1996), p. 2.

trajectory. "The voyages of adventure, colonisation, and, above all, the expansion of markets into a world market ... all called forth a new stage of historical development."[73] In the first volume of *Capital* (1867), Marx used even stronger language. He emphasized the decisive role of forced migration, slavery, and the extraction of precious metals, instead of wealth derived from trade, as crucial episodes in the making of the modern economy.[74] Colonialism enabled nascent capitalism to flourish and, moreover, accelerated its development. Resorting to a botanical analogy, he observed that

the colonial system ripened, like a hot-house, trade and navigation ... the colonies secured a market for the budding manufactures, and, through the monopoly of the market ... increased accumulation. The treasures captured outside of Europe by undisguised looting, enslavement, and murder, floated back to the mother country and were there turned into capital.[75]

The importance of early European colonial expansion to the crucial stages in the creation of capitalism are laid bare in Marx's two accounts, in the *Manifesto* and the first volume of *Capital,* books whose respective publication dates were separated by two decades. If anything, in the latter work there is a discernible shift away from a disgusted astonishment with the passage to modernity ushered in by colonialism and toward a grudging recognition of the gruesome acts that propelled capitalism's global ascendancy.

Yet, common themes and assumptions may be detected in the two works. The first common feature is that contact with, and the deepening connection to, external markets were crucial moments in European society's transformation, a factor of "primitive accumulation."[76] They both presaged and led to the demise of Europe's imperfect social and economic arrangements that had asphyxiated the practices he associated with the early stirrings of capitalism. The second common feature is that social change is inseparable from destruction. Violence, exploitation, and

[73] K. Marx, "The German Ideology," in Marx, *Early Political Writings* (Cambridge, 1994), p. 161.
[74] "The discovery of gold and silver in America, the extirpation, enslavement and entombment of the aboriginal population ... the turning of Africa into a warren for the commercial hunting of black-skins ... these idyllic proceedings are the chief moments of primitive accumulation." See K. Marx, *Capital*, vol. I (1867), quoted in *Marx on Globalisation*, ed. David Renton (London, 2001), p. 50.
[75] K. Marx, *Capital*, vol. I (1867), quoted in ibid., p. 52.
[76] For the classic account, see part 8, "The So-Called Primitive Accumulation," in volume I of *Capital*. http://www.econlib.org/LIBRARY/YPDBooks/Marx/mrxCpA.html, accessed 28 August 2008.

conquistadors are historical change's handmaidens. Unsavory motives and distasteful, ruthless ambition are its unwitting yet inevitable accomplices, whose actions and practices produce unintended consequences that prod history along the trajectory imagined by Marx.[77] Recognition of these continuities in Marx's thought should enable a more accurate understanding of his newspaper articles of the 1850s.

Notwithstanding his low regard for non-European civilizations, Hegel had conceived of empire mainly in terms of settler colonies. Such offshoots would relieve European society of its most acute poverty, provide a vent for overpopulation, and mitigate some of the deleterious psychosocial effects of both proto-industrialization and the great disruption of rural life. For Hegel, as described in the first two sections of this chapter, colonialism represented an imperfect solution to the breakdown of the "system of needs" that was fundamental to a functioning civil society. Marx was not entirely dismissive of Hegel's understanding of poverty. Marx agreed that overcoming objective alienation would entail the coming into existence of certain social conditions that make it possible for people to actualize themselves both as individuals and as members of the community. Marx, however, rejected the assertion that the modern social world embodies those conditions.[78] This disagreement helps to explain the different appraisal of colonies of settlement encountered in the thought of Hegel and Marx.

Even in his earliest newspaper articles for the *New York Daily Tribune*, Marx was convinced that colonization, endorsed by Hegel, was merely a palliative for poverty. Such a scheme would not grapple with poverty's (and alienation's) underlying cause. Whereas Hegel conjectured that the maturation of colonies of settlement would create a herd of consumers for the metropolis's manufactured goods, Marx repudiated such logic as shortsighted. In an 1853 article on China, Marx mused that "notwithstanding California and Australia, notwithstanding the immense and unprecedented migration, there must even, without any particular accident, in due time arrive a moment when the extension of the markets is unable to keep pace with the extension of British manufactures, and this disproportion must bring about a new crisis, as it has done in the past."[79]

---

[77] For an excellent discussion of this theme, see Terence Ball, "History: Critique and Irony," in *The Cambridge Companion to Marx*, ed. Terrell Carver (Cambridge, 1991), pp. 124–142, at p. 134.

[78] Leopold, *The Young Karl Marx*, p. 76.

[79] K. Marx, "Revolution in China and in Europe," *NYDT* 14 June 1853, in *Karl Marx on Colonialism*, p. 65.

Emigration could only serve as a temporary antidote for a social ill that was bound to recur. Overpopulation, and the socioeconomic problems that accompanied it, were not easily remediable malfunctions, hiccups that would pass painlessly. They were, instead, symptoms of an underlying problem. The internal dynamics of capitalism augured its inexorable recurrence. Furthermore, Marx's observation of Britain's use of emigration inducement schemes after 1848 would have confirmed in his mind its intrinsically reactionary character. The transportation of prisoners to Britain's overseas colonies was, as historians Miles Taylor has pointed out, "the cornerstone of the British state's containment of Chartism and of post-Famine disorder in Ireland." Emigration increasingly came to be a solution for political dissent and petty crime, not merely a response to domestic overpopulation.[80]

Yet, there was another reason why Marx found the colonization schemes advocated by Hegel, Wakefield, and other contemporaries to be implausible and misguided. The vision of a colony in which, in Marx's words, the "bulk of the soil is still public property, and every settler can turn part of it into his private property and individual means of production, without hindering later settlers in the same operation" was anathema to the "capitalist mode of production." Marx argued that the "inveterate vice" of colonial production is its "opposition to the establishment of capital." He recalled that the "expropriation of the mass of the people from the soil" was the precondition of capitalism. For this reason, he prophesied, colonies of settlement were destined to recapitulate the pattern of the society from which the emigrants originally came. "Where the capitalist has at his back the power of the mother country," Marx predicted, "he tries to clear out of his way by force the modes of production and appropriation based on the independent labour of the producer."[81] While Marx favorably mentioned the colonization of the Antipodes and California, it was not because he interpreted, as Hegel did, such developments as offering succor to European civil society's most marginalized outcast members. Instead, he saw such colonists as the advance guard for the expansion of capitalism in virgin territory. Colonists would but

---

[80] Miles Taylor, "The 1848 Revolutions and the British Empire," *Past and Present*, 166 (2000), 153–159.
[81] All quotations are from Marx, *Capital*, I, pt. 8, chap. 33, "The Modern Theory of Colonisation" (http://www.econlib.org/LIBRARY/YPDBooks/Marx/mrxCpA.html; accessed 28 August 2008). In this chapter, Marx is not criticizing Hegel explicitly, but rather Wakefield, whose influential *Art of Colonization* was published to great acclaim in 1849.

fleetingly enjoy the position of "producer, who is the owner of the conditions of his own labour, [and] employs that labour to enrich himself instead of the capitalist."[82] The infestation of all the social ills that capitalism carries in its train would soon infiltrate and transform this bucolic precapitalist terrain.

Marx's attitude toward colonization schemes is consistent with his stance toward European imperial projects in extra-European lands and societies. He was most intrigued by empire's potential as a mechanism for the eradication of isolated, self-sufficient societies and the creation of global interdependence in which the satisfaction of the needs of each society relied on the rest. He envisaged the convergence and comingling of destinies of thousands of previously autonomous societies across the world.

Such a vision contrasted sharply with the one proffered by Hegel. In the *Philosophy of Right* and the *Philosophy of History*, Hegel never connected his assertion that the extra-European world was "un-historical" with a justification for European colonialism.[83] Marx did, and this attitude has stirred, if not infuriated, some scholars since its utterance. Yet, much of the fuss is unnecessary. It largely ignores Marx's understanding of historical change. The transformation of social and economic structures, as well as their orientation toward capitalist property arrangements and forms of economic production, was the lever of historical change.

Marx's writings of the 1850s and 1860s, as historian Gareth Stedman Jones has indicated, "inherited and reproduced these images of the passive mobility of the extra-European world."[84] Though the historical accuracy of Marx's claims must be assessed and deserves to be disputed (if not dismissed outright), the philosophy of history that underlies his views does not merit knee-jerk denigration. Colorful, even complex, political events, in Marx's judgment, are mere epiphenomena, the succession of dynasties a dazzling distraction from the absence of social and economic change. "All the civil wars, invasions, revolutions, conquests, famines, strangely complex, rapid and destructive as the successive actions in Hindustan

---

[82] For an essay that explores the connections between Wakefield and Marx, see H. O. Pappe, "Wakefield and Marx," *Economic History Review*, n.s. 4 (1951), 88–97.

[83] Though for evidence to the contrary from another, earlier work, see the passages cited in Tyler, "Hegel, War, and the Tragedy of Imperialism," 428.

[84] Gareth Stedman Jones, "Radicalism and the Extra-European World: The Case of Karl Marx," in *Victorian Visions of Global Order: Empire and International Relations in Nineteenth-Century Political Thought*, ed. Duncan Bell (Cambridge, 2007), pp. 186–214, at p. 195.

may appear," Marx argued, "did not go deeper than its surface."[85] For Marx, historical change is not a litany of power swaps, the ephemeral feats of conquerors, and the transient movement of peoples. Only in the context of Marx's broader project can the following remark, repugnant if read in isolation, become intelligible: "Indian society has no history at all, at least no known history. What we call history, is but the history of successive intruders who founded their empires on the passive bases of that unresisting and unchanging society."[86]

The historical accuracy of Marx's judgment should be indicted. It has long been established that Marx considered Asian societies as "stagnant, unchanging, non-dialectical, particularistic, limited, and devoid of societal mechanisms for change."[87] Yet, Marx's understanding of property relations and modes of production in India still deserve the attention of historians. As Avineri elucidated, Marx identified five characteristics of what he termed "Oriental society": first, the absence of private property in land; second, the state's position as the ultimate proprietor; third, at the local level, the holding of land in common; fourth, the integration of agriculture and manufactures into a closed system of an autarchic village economy; and, fifth, the existence of a centralized state that provides for public works, mainly irrigation and roads.[88]

Two further features underpinning India's economy precluded the economic dynamism that Marx considered indispensable to historical change. First, there had been no disaggregation of the individual's activity from that of the community. Marx claimed that such arrangements had been "founded either on the immature development of man individually, who has not yet severed the umbilical cord that unites him and his fellow men in a primitive tribal community, or upon direct relations of subjection."[89] Second, there had been no disentanglement of different types of economic

[85] Marx, "British Rule," p. 84.
[86] Marx, "Future Results," p. 125.
[87] Shlomo Avinieri, "Marx and Modernization," *The Review of Politics*, 31, no. 2 (1969), 172–188, at 181. On Marx's views on the "Asiatic" mode of production, see G. Lichtheim, "Marx and the Asiatic Mode of Production" [1963], reproduced in *Karl Marx's Social and Political Thought: Critical Assessments*, Vol. VI, *Modes of Production, the World System, Classes and Class Struggle*, ed. Bob Jessop with Russell Wheatley (London and New York, 1999), pp. 35–58.
[88] Avineri, "Marx and Modernization," 181–182. For a superb discussion of the origins of Marx's distinction between different forms of property in the German Historical School, see Gareth Stedman Jones, "Introduction," in Marx and Engels, *The Communist Manifesto* (London, 2002), pp. 156–157.
[89] Marx in *Capital*, vol. I, quoted in Stedman Jones, "Radicalism," p. 199.

activity; thus, the "circle of production is self-sustaining, unity of agriculture and craft manufactures etc."[90]

This analysis of Indian society pushed Marx to take a favorable attitude toward British imperial ambitions there. In Marx's view, developed
in a series of newspaper articles in the mid-1850s, British imperialism
in India would jump-start the motor of historical change. As he pithily
put it, "England has a double mission in India: one destructive, the other
regenerating – the annihilation of old Asiatic society and the laying of
the material foundations of western society in Asia."[91] The features that
British imperial rule would annihilate were precisely those that Marx
diagnosed as impediments to capitalism's modes of production. It would
"blow up the economical bases" of the "small semi-barbarian, semi-civi-
lised communities."[92] Just as Marx maintained that expansion of markets had precipitated the demise of feudalism in Europe, Marx held that
Britain's empire in India would pave the way for South Asia's integration
into the world market and lay the basis for the "universal intercourse
founded upon the mutual dependency of mankind."[93]

Marx conjectured that the 1850s were a peculiarly propitious time. In
the late 1840s, he had argued that "just as industry, commerce, sea trade
and railways have expanded, so the bourgeoisie has developed, increased
its capital, and pushed into the background all pre-existing classes from
the middle ages onwards."[94] Marx sought the universalization of the
market because it was, in his view, the precondition for the demise of
capitalism. In the *German Ideology*, he argued that "Communism is
empirically possible only as the act of ruling peoples, accomplished 'at
once' and simultaneously, which presupposes the universal development
of the productive forces and of the world commerce connected with it."[95]
This final stage of capitalism may be described as a radically globalized world. "Every civilised nation and every individual in them," Marx
argued, "becomes dependent on the entire world for the satisfaction of

[90] K. Marx, *Pre-Capitalist Economic Formations*, ed. E. Hobsbawm (London, 1964), p. 83.
   As Stedman Jones has pointed out, Marx was attuned to the methodological problems of
   the analysis of Asian societies that he developed: "the search for common features shared
   by societies and states allegedly defined by [the 'Asiatic'] mode of production turned out
   to be in vain; and it is notable that after 1859 Marx never again explicitly referred to the
   concept." See Stedman Jones, "Radicalism," p. 196.
[91] Marx, "Future Results," p. 125.
[92] Marx, "British Rule," p. 88.
[93] Marx, "Future Results," p. 131.
[94] Marx and Engels, "Manifesto," p. 3.
[95] Marx, "German Ideology," p. 133.

their needs, and destroy[s] the previous natural isolation of the separate nations."[96]

The creation of an interconnected world, whether by means of trade (regardless of its unequal terms) or through the collision of societies, would prevent certain societies from lapsing into older modes of economic activity. An interdependent world would provide insurance against historical contingency, against retrograde movements, against dizzying oscillation between modes of production. "Up till now," Marx declared, "violence, war, pillage, rape, and slaughter etc have been accepted as the driving force of history."[97] Yet, the new expansion of European capitalism, with empire as its vehicle, put an end to this state of affairs. The establishment of empire would guarantee the easy transmission of capitalist institutions. In fact, Marx intimated, there were certain advantages to be gained from disseminating new modes of economic life by conquest and through their imposition on a subjugated society.[98] Empire would ensure the durability and persistence of economic and social change.[99] Social and economic isomorphism on a global scale was, for the first time, a genuine possibility as the "interests, the circumstances of life within the proletariat become ever more similar," to borrow Marx's and Engel's phrase from the *Manifesto*.[100]

In the late 1840s and early 1850s, Marx believed that it was the bourgeoisie, acting through its respective national governments, that was driving this movement toward a universal market and the homogeneity of needs, aspirations, and tastes. As it strove to establish a "foothold everywhere, settle everywhere, establish connections everywhere," the bourgeoisie would make "underdeveloped and semi-developed nations dependent on the civilised ones, peasant societies dependent on bourgeois societies, the East on the West."[101] Marx put the matter bluntly to Engels in the late 1850s. "The specific task of bourgeois society," he argued, is

[96] Ibid., p. 164.

[97] Ibid., quoted in *Pre-Capitalist Economic Formations*, p. 123.

[98] Marx asserted that "when a form of interaction is brought ready made to a conquered country; while in its homeland it was still burdened with interests and relationships of earlier epochs, here, in the conquered land, it can and has to be imposed fully and without hindrance, if only to secure power for the conquerors." See Marx, "German Ideology," p. 177.

[99] "In early history," Marx pointed out, "each invention had to be made anew each day and independently in each locality.... Only when commerce becomes world commerce, with large industry as its basis and every nation drawn into the competitive struggle, is the continuance of the acquired productive forces secured." Ibid., pp. 158–159.

[100] Marx and Engels, "Manifesto," p. 9.

[101] Ibid., pp. 4–5.

the "establishment of a world market, at least in outline, and of production based on this world market."[102] In British imperial ambitions in India and beyond, Marx saw the bourgeoisie's handiwork and seems to have believed that its ambitions, marked by plunder and ephemeral political gain, were secondary to its world historical mission.

After the publication of the first volume of *Capital* in 1867, Marx revised his view of the correlation between colonialism, the economic development of the non-European world, and the advent of a globalized, interwoven civil society. This shift formed part of a broader revaluation of the historical sequence of capitalist development and the transition from one historical stage to the next. His intellectual evolution prompted Marx to revisit his earlier bleak depiction of Asian societies and to reconsider his ebullient endorsement of the swift eradication of "pre-capitalist" modes of production.[103] Even in *Capital*, the "Asiatic" mode of production came in for favorable comment and the village community was valued as a bulwark against social disintegration.[104]

Among the reasons for Marx's shifting attitude toward the non-European world, Marx's response to the emptiness of his youthful prophecy, that the crisis of capitalism was imminent, was undoubtedly one. Events, both in Europe and in the wider world, compelled him to reassess the relationship between empire, economic transformation, and the crisis of capitalism. He would note that "every time Ireland was about to develop industrially, she was crushed and reconverted into a purely agricultural land."[105] In the first volume of *Capital*, Marx vividly described "a new international division of labour, a division suited to the requirements of the chief centre of modern industry ... [that] converts one part of the world into a chiefly agricultural field of production, for supplying the other part which remains a chiefly industrial field."[106] He abandoned the earlier conviction, articulated in the *Manifesto*, that the bourgeoisie would "create the world in its own image" and would "drag all nations, even the most primitive ones, into civilisation ... force all nations to introduce

[102] Marx to Engels, 8 October 1858, in *Karl Marx on Colonialism*, ed. Avineri, pp. 438–439.
[103] For a full and rich treatment of this shift between 1848 and the early 1870s, see Stedman Jones, "Radicalism."
[104] Lichtheim, "Asiatic mode," p. 44.
[105] Marx, quoted in J. Larrain, "Classical Political Economists and Marx on Colonialism and Backward Nations" [1994], reproduced in *Karl Marx's Social and Political Thought*, ed. Jessop et al., pp. 178–179.
[106] Marx, quoted in Larrain, "Classical Political Economists," pp. 178–179.

so-called civilisation amongst themselves, i.e. to become bourgeois."[107] Marx's shift cannot be attributed to a mere crisis of confidence, but rather to the need to adjust his most cherished principles in response to the non-occurrence of long-awaited events.[108]

By 1877, most pointedly in a letter to his Russian admirers, Marx sternly warned against "metamorphosing my historical sketch of the growth of capitalism in western Europe into an historico-philosophical theory of the general path that every people is fated to tread, whatever the historical circumstances in which it finds itself."[109] In the 1870s, Marx appears to have embraced, in historian Teodor Shanin's phrase, "multi-directionality within a capitalist-dominated world of mutual dependence; indeed, of heterogeneity resulting from that very interdependence."[110] At the very end of his life, then, Marx softened his previously inveterate hostility to the peasantry's capacity to drive historical change. Certainly, as he observed developments in Western Europe in the 1830s and 1840s, his predisposition to disdain the peasantry had been confirmed by the reactionary clerical, feudal, or monarchist complexion of most rural movements.[111] In the late 1870s, however, Marx stopped

---

[107] Marx (with F. Engels), "Manifesto of the Communist Party," pp. 4–5. I would argue, with Eric Hobsbawm and Allan Megill, that the shift in Marx's thought may be exaggerated due to the tendency of some scholars to insist on the rigidity of Marx's linear view of historical development. As Hobsbawm has pointed out, "The statement that the Asiatic, ancient, feudal and bourgeois formations are 'progressive' does not therefore imply any simple linear view of history, not a simple view that history is progress. It merely states that each of these systems is in crucial respects further removed from the primitive state of man"; see Hobsbawm, "Introduction," in *Pre-capitalist*, p. 38; Furthermore, as Megill has noted, "it seems clear that we cannot take historical materialism seriously as any sort of general theory. We know this because of Marx and Engel's own willingness to diverge from important aspects of historical materialism, whether considered diachronically, as an account of historical sequence, or synchronically, as a statement as to which aspects of society are most fundamental ... it is also obvious that Marx modified his views of history and on social structure when confronted by what he took to be new evidence." See Megill, *Karl Marx: The Burden of Reason (Why Marx Rejected Politics and the Market)* (New York and Oxford, 2002), pp. 232–233.

[108] Yet, there is another plausible explanation for this shift in Marx's thought that deserves to be mentioned. As Donald R. Kelley has pointed out, it was Marx's engagement with new developments in anthropology that led him to revisit his earlier conceptions of the origins of private property and the merits of "primitive communism." See Kelley, "The Science of Anthropology: An Essay on the Very Old Marx," *Journal of the History of Ideas*, 45 (1984), 245–262 passim.

[109] Marx to the editorial board of *Otechestvenniye Zapiski*, November 1877, quoted in Avineri, "Marx and Modernization," p. 173.

[110] Teodor Shanin, "Late Marx: Gods and Craftsmen," in *Late Marx and the Russian Road: Marx and the "Peripheries of Capitalism,"* ed. Teodor Shanin (New York, 1983), pp. 5, 31.

[111] V. G. Kiernan, "Marx and India," in *Marxism and Imperialism* (London, 1974), p. 183.

depicting the peasantry and its primitive forms of property as antiquated and destined for extinction. Rather, he began to treat the "pre-capitalist" mode of production as the point of departure for a new form of social existence. Primitive communities were no longer portrayed as an unnatural and ephemeral stage on the road to capitalist development. Instead, they function as a precursor to a higher form of communal existence. The link in Marx's thought between despotic rule and communal property had been broken.[112] He now argued, at least in his famous 1881 letter to Vera Zasulich, that selective borrowing from capitalism could permit the modification of the village community without its obliteration. As Stedman Jones has noted, with reference to Marx's turn from placing his hopes in Western Europe's industrial, urbanized proletariat to Russia's besieged peasant commune, "what had started as the boldest of all post-capitalist theories had turned almost imperceptibly into the rebuilding of yet another precapitalist economic formation."[113] The consequence of this shift for his attitude toward empire was never explicitly articulated by Marx. But it is reasonable to conclude that the relatively narrow and parochial materialist perspective, which led him to favorably depict Britain's "double mission" in India, had been abandoned.

CONCLUSION

An analysis of the theme of colonies and empire in the political thought of Hegel and Marx suggests that the extra-European dimension is a crucial, if relatively neglected, feature of their thought and also facilitates unusual comparisons between them. In Hegel's case, his proposed recourse to colonies raises doubts concerning the self-sufficiency of the model of civil society he develops in the *Philosophy of Right*. Yet, it also demonstrates that Hegel addressed one of the most intransigent problems of his age, poverty, in a global context. It is also curious that Hegel's cultural imperialist attitudes were not necessarily a prelude to the genuine article, that

---

[112] Stedman Jones, "Radicalism," pp. 199–205 passim.
[113] Gareth Stedman Jones, "Marx's Critique of Political Economy: A Theory of History or a Theory of Communism?" in *Marxist History-Writing for the Twenty-First Century*, ed. Chris Wickham (Oxford, 2007), pp. 155–166. Moreover, by 1877, Marx would predict that the long-awaited revolution would begin in Russia, not in economically developed Western Europe. In a letter at the outset of the Russo-Turkish war, he stated, "This crisis is a new turning point for the history of Europe.... This time the revolution will begin in the East, hitherto the impregnable bastion and reserve army of counter-revolution." Marx, quoted in Stedman Jones, "Radicalism," p. 201.

his denigration of non-European cultures did not in any way prefigure advocacy of European overseas expansion. Instead, Hegel confined himself to a remarkably limited discussion of settler colonies as a strategic response to acute crises triggered by economic disruption.

Marx's engagement with the theme of empire was much more robust. On the one hand, unlike Hegel, he scoffed at the notion that colonies of settlement could do anything more than temporarily alleviate the structural problems afflicting European societies. On the other hand, the young Marx of the 1840s was fascinated by the extra-European midwife present at capitalism's birth, the "primitive accumulation" that mines, slaves, and transoceanic trade had engendered. Subsequently, in his newspaper articles of the 1850s, he would pin his hopes on the unintended beneficent consequences of European imperialism in Asia, speculating that it would galvanize and accelerate a global conjuncture that he contended must precede capitalism's collapse. Later, toward the end of his life, Marx would come to reappraise, and even place his hopes in, the "pre-capitalist" economic formations that he previously had scorned and deemed to be but debris best swept away by imperial rule. Analysis of the place of colonies and empire in the political thought of Hegel and Marx, then, suggests the pivotal role of extra-European affairs in it and also enables historians to better understand how political thought often emerges from political contexts that themselves have been shaped decisively by empire.

12

Social Theory in the Age of Empire

Karuna Mantena

INTRODUCTION

Although it has become axiomatic to associate the consolidation of the British Empire in the nineteenth century with the growth of ideologies of progress and civilization, the tendency to focus on the so-called civilizing mission as the crux of nineteenth-century justifications of imperial rule tends to obscure the fact that imperial ideology and governing strategies underwent fundamental transformations throughout the century. To be sure, the nineteenth century was the crucial period in which "liberal imperialism" came to be most clearly articulated and brazenly defended.[1] Yet, the surprising feature of nineteenth-century empire is how the period of its greatest geographic expansion in Asia and Africa – the period between 1857 and 1914 – directly coincided with a period of liberal retrenchment and the repudiation of central assumptions and imperatives underlying the civilizing mission. Where earlier liberal imperial ideologies often conceived of native societies as "backward, inefficient, despotic and corrupt"[2] and thus in need of radical reconstruction along Western lines, late imperial thinking questioned both the practicality and the theoretical underpinnings of such an interventionist agenda. In place of the transformative ambitions of liberal imperialism, a new emphasis on the potentially insurmountable differences between peoples came to

---

[1] See Uday Mehta, *Liberalism and Empire: A Study in Nineteenth-Century British Liberal Thought* (Chicago, 1999), and Jennifer Pitts, *A Turn to Empire: The Rise of Imperial Liberalism in Britain and France* (Princeton, N.J., 2006).

[2] The phrase is taken from David Cannadine, *Ornamentalism: How the British Saw Their Empire* (Oxford, 2001), p. 12.

the fore. Rather than modernized and assimilated, native societies would now be protected under the paternalist hand of the colonial state as they became inserted into the dynamics of imperial power, most notably in the theory and practice of indirect rule in colonial Africa.

This profound transition in imperial ideology was enabled by a series of interconnected political and intellectual developments. On the one hand, dramatic political crises such as the Indian Rebellion of 1857 became the occasion for important reassessments of past imperial policy. Significantly, these reassessments promoted new socio-theoretic accounts of native society as a way both to account for the fact of native dis-enchantment and resistance to imperial rule and to explain the failure of past imperial policy to modernize native society. Social theory made available a generic model of native society, newly defined as *traditional* society in opposition to modern society, that stressed the primacy of the "social" in understanding and explaining the nature of native society. By contrast to earlier conceptions of non-Western societies as politically dysfunctional (embodied in various theses on oriental despotism), these theories increasingly came to view native societies as apolitical functional wholes held together by stable bonds of custom and structures of kin-ship. This model of native society as an integral, but fragile, social whole would provide a theoretical foundation, and even a normative justifi-cation, for imperial ideologies of protection, preservation, and collab-oration. The intimate connection between the socio-theoretic model of traditional society and late imperial ideology emerges in its clearest and most influential articulation in the social and political theory of Henry Maine; thus, his work figures centrally in this story.

In exploring how social theory came to bear this causal imprint upon late imperial ideology, I want to draw attention to the imperial context of the origins of social theory, both in terms of how social theory influenced the theory and practice of nineteenth-century empire and how empire, in turn, shaped the central concepts of modern social theory. One of the most distinctive features of nineteenth-century social theory was its tendency to classify societies in dualistic terms, the modern–traditional dichotomy being the most prominent. Often in contrast to the dynamism of modern society, traditional society was construed as fundamentally static, dominated by nonrational forms of politics and economics, them-selves pervaded by religious, kin-based, customary ties. While it was in its model of traditional society that modern social theory elaborated its most deterministic model of social behavior, important strands of social theory also propagated a general view of society that emphasized the more nonrational bases of sociability. In important ways, social theory sought to project a model of the social as the privileged arena for understanding the nature and dynamics of society. By positing the social as primary in both a substantive and a methodological sense, social theory was contesting the priority that had been traditionally accorded to politics as the organizing force of society, the source of social cohesion and definition. In this sense, with the rise of social theory, the question of politics was reframed in a context that increasingly emphasized the limits of political action in relation to social, cultural, and historical imperatives. This shift toward a view of human behavior as a product of collective learning, social conditioning, and historically informed custom would have important legacies for twentieth-century social science. Not only is the modern anthropological concept of culture indebted to this model of society, but also the sociological tradition notably retained many of these elements in its general account of social integration.

THE ANCIENT AND THE MODERN: THE ORIGINS OF SOCIAL THEORY

The origin of modern social theory is often understood as primarily a methodological revolution, linked to the discovery of "society" as an organic and independent entity, whose inner lawlike dynamics can be discerned through scientific analysis. According to this view, the methodological innovation appears as a break from the idealism and individualism implicit in previous approaches to the study of society, especially as embodied in traditions of political philosophy. But to construe the specificity of social theory wholly in methodological terms would be to miss its substantive critique of political philosophy – especially of eighteenth-century political thought and the distinctive politics that it had spawned. Implicit in the logical priority claimed for the social was a substantive claim for preeminence as well. In conceptualizing the "social" in a way that revealed its pervasive role in the constitution of human action (and a central place as an explanation of action), political institutions and structures of authority were seen to express, rather than constitute, underlying social relations.[3] More specifically, notable strands of nineteenth-century

---

[3] See Sheldon Wolin, *Politics and Vision: Continuity and Innovation in Western Political Thought* (Boston, 1960), chap. 9. Political theorists such as Arendt, Strauss, and Wolin have construed the rise of the "social" and social science in the nineteenth century as a threat to the "political." Wolin's discussion in *Politics and Vision* comes closest to the analysis presented here. The conception of the political in Arendt (and Strauss), on the

social thought arose in opposition to, and as a critique of, the kind of political thinking that was considered to have nurtured the radicalism of the French Revolution. For what eighteenth-century revolutionary politics proposed, especially in the attempt to revive "ancient politics," was a view of the social world as eminently transformable and, indeed, perfectible through the agency of politics.

Commentators have noted the link between the rise of social theory and postrevolutionary debates about politics and society, noting the conservative origins of organic conceptions of society in the antirevolutionary thought of Burke, de Maistre, and Bonald, on the one hand, and the Romantic rediscovery of the medieval concept of the corporate group as a bulwark against atomized individualism and the growth of state power, on the other.[4] But while these accounts rightly highlight concepts that would become central to social theory – such as the prioritization of the concept of social order and the critique of the ideal of individualism, as well as an emphasis on pre- or nonrational belief as the foundation of authority – they do not account for the characteristic dichotomous form that modern social theory would come to take. In this respect, what seems of crucial importance is a related but distinct set of postrevolutionary debates that likewise were framed by a rejection of Enlightenment perfectionism and the ideals of the French Revolution but conducted in terms of a political, historical, and sociological reevaulation of ancient society. This nineteenth-century revival of the "quarrel of the ancients and the moderns" is a central, if overlooked, factor in the development of social theory's binary view of history. In fundamental ways, the dichotomy of the modern and the traditional was constructed upon an intensification of an earlier contrast between ancient and modern society. Moreover, in treating Greco-Roman societies as different and radically opposed to the

---

other hand, is one that construes politics as a certain kind of philosophical activity that itself has its roots in ancient politics. The notion of politics and political philosophy that I argue nineteenth-century social theory challenged was much more specific and more modern, defined in large part by the priority given to the state and political institutions as formative influences on society (and perhaps traceable to Hobbes). It is a view of politics that implies that politics can be an independent agent of change and creative reform, and thus positively accepts the possibility of a rational, willed transformation of society. The underlying universal assumption about the character of social actors, especially as objects of change, thus is one that emphasizes equality, mutability, and perfectibility.

[4] Robert A. Nisbet, "The French Revolution and the Rise of Sociology in France," *The American Journal of Sociology*, 49, no. 2 (September 1943), 156–164; Nisbet, "Conservatism and Sociology," *The American Journal of Sociology*, 58, no. 2 (September 1952), 167–175; Leon Bramson, *The Political Context of Sociology* (Princeton, N.J., 1961).

premises of modern commercial society, the quarrel of the ancients and the moderns was of crucial significance for the development of seminal, holistic conceptions of kinship, culture, and society.

Benjamin Constant's 1819 speech comparing ancient and modern liberty indicates some of the directions postrevolutionary reevaluations of the ancient world would take in the nineteenth century.[5] Constant's distinction between the collective political liberty of the ancient republics and the individual liberty of the moderns was put forward in the context of a defense of representative government, thus, in important ways, resuming a central eighteenth-century debate about the form of government most appropriate to modern commercial society. Constant considered ancient liberty to be intimately tied to a distinctive set of historical institutions – slavery, the structure of war and the citizen army, lack of commerce – that might be both impossible and undesirable to reproduce in modern times. For Constant, however, not only was achieving ancient liberty impractical, it was also a form of liberty that itself was far from ideal; it was in essence a *collective* freedom, one that often demanded sacrifices of individual freedom. Indeed, the fact that in Rome "the individual, almost always sovereign in public affairs, was a slave in all his private relations"[6] demonstrated, for Constant, that the ancients "had no notion of individual rights." It was a society in which the minutest customs were regulated by the law and private lives were always under strict surveillance. "Their social organization led them to desire an entirely different freedom," one that was compatible with "the complete subjection of the individual to the authority of the community."[7]

The important nineteenth-century twist that Constant gave to this more standard debate about the relative merits of ancient versus modern politics was the idea that it was in fact the experience of the French Revolution, its extravagances and disappointments, that demonstrated most forcibly the practical dangers of trying to re-create ancient politics. For Constant, the revolutionaries, "steeped in ancient views," had derived sanction for their unmixed admiration of ancient politics from philosophers such as Rousseau:

[B]y transposing into our modern age an extent of social power, of collective sovereignty, which belonged to other centuries, this sublime genius, animated by the

---

[5] Benjamin Constant, "The Liberty of Ancients Compared with That of the Moderns," Speech given at the Athénée Royal in 1819, in Constant, *Political Writings* (Cambridge, 1988), pp. 309–328.

[6] Ibid., p. 311.

[7] Ibid., p. 311.

purest love of liberty, has nevertheless furnished deadly pretexts for more than one kind of tyranny.[8]

The notion that advocates of the French Revolution had made a disastrous political error in attempting to re-create ancient institutions in modern times is an assertion that is repeated throughout the nineteenth century. The claim would, in the context of the study of ancient society, be closely tied to the argument that what had in fact laid the grounds for these political misadventures was a false picture of ancient society and politics. Whereas Constant could continue to admire aspects of ancient political liberty (its connection to virtue and self-development), later historians would present Roman life as so foreign and indeed so primitive as to be inimitable in any form. By midcentury, in the more conservative visions of Maine and Coulanges, a new interpretation of Greco-Roman societies highlighted those aspects that most differentiated ancient from modern society and, in the process, thoroughly ethnologized the ancients.[9]

Barthold Georg Niebuhr's *History of Rome*, covering the earliest periods of Roman prehistory, provided the nineteenth century's most influential historical-ethnological account of the origins of Roman political institutions.[10] Niebuhr's strategy in contesting the revolutionary interpretation of Roman politics was to emphasize the radical gulf between the ideas that animated Roman institutions and those of their modern imitators. "The ideas on which the institutions of the Roman state and its administration were founded," argued Niebuhr, were "no less different from ours, than Roman dwellings, clothing, and food."[11] Clear and accurate knowledge of the distinctiveness of ancient institutions would

---

[8] Ibid., pp. 317–320.

[9] Thomas R. Trautmann, *Lewis Henry Morgan and the Invention of Kinship* (Berkeley, 1987), p. 187.

[10] The central issue that spurred Niebuhr's interest in early Roman society (and that he considered his greatest achievement) was clarifying Roman agrarian history and landownership, specifically in relation to the much disputed agrarian law. Niebuhr feared a renewal in Prussia of the revolutionary fervor for land redistribution of the kind witnessed during the French Revolution; thus, he sought to stem the revolutionary idea of limiting property, especially as advocated by communist factions that justified the interference with property with ancient examples. The most dangerous example of this political use of ancient history was epitomized, for Niebuhr, by "Gracchus" Babeuf and his followers in their call to implement the so-called agrarian law in revolutionary France. Niebuhr turned to the historical study of the nature of agrarian law in ancient Rome and proposed a fundamental reinterpretation of its nature and function, one that overturned the account that had attained widespread acceptance, especially in republican political thought, since the Renaissance. See A. Momigliano, *Studies on Modern Scholarship* (Berkeley, 1994).

[11] Barthold Georg Niebuhr, *The History of Rome* (Philadelphia, 1835), I, p. xx.

thus serve to preclude "the silly desire of transferring out of ages totally different in character what would now be altogether inapplicable."[12] The most distinctive and fundamental institution of ancient society, for Niebuhr, was its *gentile* organization; this was the key to understanding the very nature of the ancient state. "When cities raise themselves to the rank of nations," argued Niebuhr, "we always find a division at first into tribes."[13] The Roman tribe was comprised of *curiae*, which in turn were made up of several *gentes*. The *gens* was a patrilineal community, comprised of all persons who could trace their descent to a common ancestor through the male line, that is, agnatically. The *gentes*, however, were not, for Niebuhr, families in any simple sense, but rather free corporations or self-regulating associations, each of which consisted of several families "united by a common chapel and a common hero."[14] The *gens* was thus simultaneously a social, religious, and political institution, which, most importantly, defined one's rights and duties as a citizen, for it was the very basis of "the relation in which individuals stood to the state."[15]

Niebuhr's conception of the Roman *gens* as the basis upon which political communities were first built would prove to be immensely influential.[16] For Niebuhr the *gens* was the exact counterpart of the Greek *genos* and could also be likened to the clan formation of the Scottish highlanders, the tribes of Arabia, and the *Geschlechter* of the medieval Germans. The discovery of *gentile* organization, organized by lineage and aggregated into larger groups such as the Grecian *phratry* or the Roman *curiae*, now understood as the earliest form of society, had a profound impact upon all of the original studies of kinship, from Maine's *Ancient Law* (1861) to Morgan's *Ancient Society* (1878). Between these two publications appeared all the classic studies of kinship: Bachofen's

---

[12] Ibid., I, p. xiii.

[13] B. G. Niebuhr, *Lectures on the History of Rome* (London, 1873), p. 80.

[14] Ibid., p. 101.

[15] Niebuhr intimated that the key to the transition from ancient to modern politics could be found in the transformation of genealogically ordered *gens* into local territorial groupings (which in Rome is associated with the reforms of Servius Tullius and in Greece with those of Cleisthenes). Thus, it is in Niebuhr's work that we glimpse the origins of the idea of a world-historical transition from kinship to locality as the basis of the state and political obligation that would be subsequently elaborated in the work of Maine, Morgan, and Marx/Engels. For Niebuhr's influence on Marx's analysis of ancient forms of collective property, see Norman Levine, "The German Historical School of Law and the Origins of Historical Materialism," *Journal of the History of Ideas*, 48, no. 3 (July 1987), 431–451.

[16] Niebuhr, *The History of Rome*, I, pp. 297–330 and Niebuhr, *Lectures on the History of Rome*, pp. 82–112.

Das Mutterrecht (1861), Fustel de Coulanges's *La cité antique* (1864), McLennan's *Primitive Marriage* (1865), and Morgan's *Systems of consanguinity and affinity of the human family* (1871). Taken together these works, all authored by lawyers/legal historians, initiated the first sustained theoretical discussion of kinship, thus constituting the central concept of modern anthropology.[17] The fact that kinship was discovered through the lens of studies of antiquity attests to the significance of the postrevolutionary legal histories of Rome and Greece as the basis for systematic comparison across societies. For these later works, sustained analyses of the origins and functions of the *gens* would not only help to explain certain peculiarities of ancient law and politics (the nature of ancient inheritance, the origin of the plebs, etc.), but would also serve as a way to conceptualize early human history – primitive societies – more generally. In other words, by designating the *gens* as the foundation of the ancient city-state, these works came to the view (and sought to demonstrate) that kinship structures – patterns of descent and lineage – were systematically bound up with the ideas and institutions of primitive society, especially the nature of hierarchy/power, property rights, and primitive religion.

Numas Denis Fustel de Coulanges's *La cité antique* and Henry Sumner Maine's *Ancient Law* are two seminal works in this vein. Both offer systematic theories about the origins and function of *gentile* organization in ancient society, which significantly point toward a more general sociological categorization.[18] Part of this drive for generalization appeared in their conscious application of the comparative method to the study of antiquity, in which the idea of a unity of Aryan peoples allowed the use of ancient Indian material to speculate on the remotest origins and obscurer aspects of Greco-Roman institutions. Moreover, both Coulanges and Maine, like Niebuhr, oriented their work against radical interpretations of ancient Rome (and thus also against the political implications of the French Revolution). Partisans of the Revolution "[h]aving imperfectly observed the institutions of the ancient city," argued Coulanges, "have dreamed of reviving them among us. They have deceived themselves about the liberty of the ancients, and on this very account liberty among

---

[17] See Trautmann, *Lewis Henry Morgan and the Invention of Kinship*; Adam Kuper, *The Invention of Primitive Society: Transformations of an Illusion* (London, 1988); George W. Stocking, *Victorian Anthropology* (New York, 1987).

[18] Numa-Denis Fustel de Coulanges, *The Ancient City* (Boston, 1874), originally published as *La cité antique* (Paris, 1864), and Henry Sumner Maine, *Ancient Law: Its Connection with the Early History of Society, and Its Relation to Modern Ideas* (Tucson, Ariz., 1986 [originally published in 1861]).

the moderns has been put in peril."[19] For Coulanges, there were "radical" and "essential" differences between ancient and modern peoples. Thus, when objectively observed, Greece and Rome should appear as foreign to us as "ancient India or Arabia" and thus "in a character absolutely inimitable; nothing in modern times resembles them; nothing in the future can resemble them."[20]

The rules of Greco-Roman society were fundamentally linked to the structure of the *gens*, or the ancient family. For Coulanges, ancient kinship marked out a community of worship, which in turn set the rules for marriage, laws of property, and laws of inheritance, as well as political institutions. This religion was the primeval cult of ancestors common to the Aryan family. Private property, *patria potestas*, and primogeniture were all institutions that, for Coulanges, had their origins in the protection and worship of ancestors. The focus on primitive religion and the centrality of its rites and beliefs to Roman life lent Coulanges's vision a conservative hue, one that was consciously defined to challenge constitutional and secular interpretations of the origin of Roman institutions. The conservatism went further in the sense that, for Coulanges, ancient religion was so imbricated in the foundation and maintenance of state institutions that "these two powers, associated and confounded, formed a power almost superhuman, to which the soul and body were equally enslaved."[21] In other words, following Constant's suggestion, Coulanges argued that the ancients "knew nothing of Individual Liberty";[22] indeed, all thought and action are seen to be deeply circumscribed by law. The imperative was always toward strict conformity with religious communal norms.

The ethnologizing of Rome in Maine's work also sought to stem the radical political implications that eighteenth-century invocations of republican Rome held. As opposed to liberty, Maine's Rome was defined by the oppressive strictures of *patria potestas* and submission to the patriarchal head of the ancient family. What Rousseau had idealized as primitive natural liberty – and what the revolutionaries had tried to re-create – stemmed, Maine argued, from a fundamental misconception of the uniformity of humanity in a supposed state of nature. For Maine, "Ancient Law knows next to nothing of Individuals";[23] rights and duties

[19] Fustel de Coulanges, *The Ancient City*, p. 9.
[20] Ibid., 10.
[21] Ibid., p. 220.
[22] Ibid., p. 219.
[23] Maine, *Ancient Law*, p. 250.

are exclusively conferred upon corporate family units, not individual citizens. The ancient patriarchal family is a corporate group (the unit of Niebuhr's *gentile* organization), organized under the archaic jurisdiction of *patria potestas*, the despotic power of the patriarch over dependent persons and property. Ancient society, then, is an aggregation of families, modern society a collection of individuals. For Maine, "this contrast is most forcibly expressed by saying that the *unit* of an ancient society was the Family, of modern society the Individual."[24]

In all of these original studies, "kinship" is conceived of as the key structural and comparative concept, a holistic marker signifying the unity and interdependence of social, political, legal, and domestic relations. Whether the structure of kinship and *gentile* organization is ultimately derived from political power (as in Maine), primitive religious rites (as in Coulanges), marriage classes (as in Morgan), or social structure (as in Durkheim), it is a unifying concept, one that is mirrored in every other major societal institution. In this way, Maine and Coulanges clearly stand in line with the burgeoning of modern social theory and a functionalist sociology that take as their methodological starting point the internal unity of social structure. And importantly, this recognition of the differences in social structure is dissolved into a dichotomous schema of radical opposites, the ancient versus the modern.

The reevaluation of Rome following the French Revolution demonstrates forcefully two characteristic propositions of modern social theory, both of which are simultaneously methodological and substantive theses. The distinctive features of ancient life are contrasted to the modern as another world in its entirety. It is not just one or two institutions of ancient life (such as slavery) that are singled out as foreign to modern sensibilities; instead, ancient culture – its fundamental ideas and institutions – is construed as opposed to the very premises of modern society. Furthermore, this radical difference is not only conceived of as systemic but is also depoliticized. That is, in the fundamental sense, the primacy of political institutions – forms of government or regime type – as having a formative power to shape social life is contested. Whereas in the work of Montesquieu, a century before, Roman law and *patria potestas* were ultimately related to the principle of government, namely, republican government,[25] for Coulanges political ideas and institutions are seen as

[24] Ibid., p. 121.
[25] In Montesquieu, *patria potestas* – a principle of power seemingly at odds with republican equality – is rendered an "auxiliary" power necessary to supplement the lack of repressive power in republics. Also, the domestic sphere, as the prime location for the

derivative of an elemental religious orientation. Likewise, even in Maine's more political characterization of ancient law and kinship, the autonomy of political life and imagination is precluded by its being strictly intertwined with social-structural imperatives.

It was a difference in the nature of society that could explain the irreconcilable differences between the ancient and modern worlds. The study of kinship, by unveiling a deep, even causal, logic to social organization, thus provided a substantive basis to the concept of the social as it came to be theoretically elaborated in classical sociology. Durkheim, in an early dissertation on Montesquieu and the foundation of social science – a thesis that was supervised by and dedicated to Coulanges – explicitly argued that the proper recognition of society as a real, natural "thing" went hand in hand with a rejection of claims of political philosophy. For Durkheim, political philosophers before Montesquieu tended to view aspects of social life, that is, laws, customs, and religion, as products of human will and thus amenable to alteration and perfection. Moreover, the defining features of social life – those features that distinguished one society from another – were ultimately associated with and categorized according to regime type. In this sense, both the central agencies of transformation and the most formative institutions were primarily political. For Durkheim, however, social science must begin at precisely that moment when the traditional project of political philosophy is abandoned, for

[i]f social [political] science is to exist, societies must be assumed to have a certain nature which results from the nature and arrangement of the elements composing them, and which is the source of social phenomena. Once the existence of such elements is granted, our lawgiver vanishes and his legend with him.[26]

This critique of the priority of politics as the vehicle for the radical reconstitution of society certainly resonates with a number of earlier, eighteenth-century arguments about the complexity of society, following Montesquieu, which emphasized the importance of the intricate play of manners and customs in the making of human sociability. It is also

reproduction of republican mores, is understood as justifiably constrained by patriarchal power. Thus, the tutelage of women, the institutional view of women as under the perpetual guardianship of either a father, a husband, or kinsmen, is construed as the appropriate counterpart to republican equality in the public sphere. See Montesquieu, *The Spirit of the Laws* (Cambridge, 1989), pp. 44–46, 50–51, 107.

[26] Emile Durkheim, *Montesquieu and Rousseau: Forerunners of Sociology* (Ann Arbor, Mich., 1965), pp. 11–13. In the original Latin dissertation, Durkheim specifically refers to the necessary foundation of "political science," which is rendered as "social science" in the French translation. See Emile Durkheim, *Montesquieu: quid secundatus politicae scientiae instituendae contulerit*, ed. W. Watts Miller, trans. Miller and Emma Griffiths (Oxford, 1997).

echoed in a general Aristotelian line of thinking that also emphasizes the need for forms of government to be made to fit the imperatives of social life. The distinctiveness of the nineteenth-century critique, I would argue, stems in part from a more rigid account of manners and customs, on the one hand, and a more holistic account of the social, on the other. The tendency of the nineteenth-century social theory was to insist on a great deal of systematicity to the social; society here emerges as a tightly knit, functional system. In Durkheim, the sui generis status of society implied that politics and forms of government were only ever epiphenomenal and/or merely contingently tied to social life; they were never constitutive of society. Maine, while more attentive to the dynamic interplay between externally imposed change and social progress, nevertheless viewed societies as having an internal coherence and logic that was prior to and independent of politics.

By the late nineteenth century, not only is re-creating Roman society seen as politically undesirable (as in Constant), it is also conceived of as impossible precisely because humanity is considered to be much more constrained by history and culture. The autonomy of politics is thus eclipsed as it is reduced to a derivative reflex of the more essential nature of society, however conceived. In contesting the eighteenth-century (Enlightenment) view of the political world and humanity's nature as essentially perfectible, social theory in these more conservative strands implied a more general theory of society in which both ancient and modern humans were seen to be much more constrained in the field of political imagination and action by their societal formations. In Durkheim's famous rendering of the distinctiveness of the modern social theory, social phenomena are "natural" things that, "like all other things in nature, which have their particular characteristics," do not "depend upon the human will."[27] Societies are natural equilibriums, and politics and political will no longer figure as determining elements, and people, one may add, are no longer free to imagine a world beyond these imposed constraints. The social thus emerges to mark the limits of politics.

INVENTING TRADITIONAL SOCIETY: MAINE AND THE COMPARATIVE IMAGINATION OF SOCIAL THEORY

From the discovery of the New World, to the encounter with oriental languages and civilizations, to the scramble for Africa, imperial encounters have engendered theoretical reflection on the nature of human diversity.

---

[27] Durkheim, *Montesquieu and Rousseau*, pp. 3–4.

These encounters generated new modes of comparison – new frameworks by which Europe would be related to other social and political forma- tions, and unfamiliar cultures and practices would be made scientifically (and morally) comprehensible. While eighteenth-century knowledge of other cultures was largely based on a handful of travelogues and amateur ethnographies, in the nineteenth century there was a veritable explosion of historical and anthropological research on the non-European world. In the heydey of empire, in addition to the work of scientist-explorers, there was the growth of official information provided by state function- aries, missionaries, and merchants who had sustained contact with native cultures in areas under European control. This information was more systematic in character, as it was tied to the mechanism and dynamics of imperial power and rule. In this period, the records and reports of expanding colonial bureaucracies ascended to the rank of evidentiary knowledge for the anthropologist and sociologist.

This expanding knowledge not only brought forth a variety of new facts to be confronted and comprehended, but also generated significant methodological innovations in the ways societies would be conceptual- ized, classified, and compared. Indeed, ideas about comparison and the "comparative method" were given a heightened investment in the nine- teenth century, as a subject for philosophical elucidation as well as a privileged model for attaining scientific certainty with a universal scope.[28] Two of the most ambitious theoretical endeavors to emerge in response to the challenge of universal or global comparison were nineteenth-cen- tury social theory (or classical sociology) and evolutionary anthropol- ogy. While classical social theory focused more squarely on analyzing the unprecedented nature and dynamics of industrializing societies, the attempt to chart the unique trajectory of Western modernity necessar- ily involved making large-scale and conceptually bold comparisons with other social formations, past and present. The birth of anthropology can be readily seen as intimately linked to the rapidly expanding scope of his- torical and ethnographical research, and its striking feature in its initial formation was the prominence of grand schemes of social evolution that attempted to enfold and categorize the radical diversity of social practices

---

[28] See John W. Burrow, *Evolution and Society: A Study in Victorian Social Theory* (Cambridge, 1968); John W. Burrow, Stefan Collini, and Donald Winch, *That Noble Science of Politics: A Study in Nineteenth-Century Intellectual History* (Cambridge, 1983); Stocking, *Victorian Anthropology*; Kenneth E. Bock, "The Comparative Method of Anthropology," *Comparative Studies in Society and History*, 8 (1966), 269–280.

across time and space.[29] Maine's work contributed to the development of both theoretical traditions, and he is often acknowledged as a "founding father" of both sociology and anthropology.[30] For, in many ways, it was one field of research with a common endeavor: to make sense of the prehistory (and future) of European humanity and society. In this sense, these prominent strands of nineteenth-century social science shaped a new vision of the relationship between past and present and contributed to a fundamental rethinking of the idea of the primitive.

Maine's famous generalization about the historical evolution of law as "a movement *from Status to Contract*"[31] can be seen as representative of the dualistic construction of traditional and modern societies typical of nineteenth-century social theory. Maine's contrast between the communal and corporate nature of ancient/primitive society versus the individualist focus of modern society not only directly shaped Ferdinand de Tönnies's evocative rendering of this binary conception in *Gemeinschaft und Gesellschaft*,[32] but also closely resonated with many of Durkheim's early formulations about the differences between mechanical and organic solidarity in simple and complex societies, respectively.[33]

[29] See Burrow, *Evolution and Society*.
[30] See Burrow, *Evolution and Society*; and Edward Shils, "Henry Sumner Maine in the Tradition of the Analysis of Society" and Alan D. J. Macfarlane, "Some Contributions of Maine to History and Anthropology," in *The Victorian Achievement of Sir Henry Sumner Maine: A Centennial Reappraisal*, ed. Alan Diamond (Cambridge, 1991), chaps. 7 and 8.
[31] Maine, *Ancient Law*, p. 165.
[32] Tönnies names Maine as one of three writers (the others being Gierke and Marx) who had "stimulated, instructed and corroborated" his work. See the "Preface" to Ferdinand de Tönnies, *Community and Civil Society (Gemeinschaft und Gesellschaft)*, trans. Jose Harris and Margaret Hollis (Cambridge, 2000 [originally published in 1887]).
[33] What is particularly striking about this austere mode of classification is how it differs quite markedly in its simplification from the most prominent early modern conceptual schemas for understanding the growth of human societies. Ever since Europe's dramatic encounter with the Americas, the tendency in modern comparative ethnologies and historical theories had been toward multiplying and diversifying the stages of social development, reaching a culmination of sorts in the sophisticated uses of a four-stage or stadial model of human progress in the eighteenth century. At that time, these successive stages were given a substantive conceptual formulation in the influential four-stage theory of development that linked modes of subsistence, types of property, and forms of government. The four stages were often defined as a series of successive epochs ranging from a savage stage linked to hunting-gathering societies, to a barbarian society of pastoral and shepherding peoples, to agricultural society, and finally culminating in modern commercial society. These theories were put to a variety of uses, ranging from analyses of socioeconomic development to complex historical accounts of the origins of feudalism and modern constitutional government after the demise of the Roman Empire. The last was

In Maine's work, the vivid account of the singular nature of ancient society initiated a generalized structure of contrast that would become foundational to the comparative imagination of modern social theory. In highlighting its difference from the dynamics of modern society, the newly ethnologized ancient world would be bracketed together with primitive, feudal-medieval, Eastern social forms as "traditional" societies defined through a common opposition to the unique trajectory of industrializing societies of the West. The impulse toward universal schemes of classification was bolstered by the ubiquitous enthusiasm for comparative methodologies in the nineteenth century. One of the key sources for this enthusiasm lay in the success of comparative philology and the dramatic impact of its proposition of an Indo-European language family linking Sanskrit to Greek and Latin.[34] The remapping of the historical relationship between languages and nations heralded by this discovery radically altered the context for the study of Greco-Roman antiquity, now firmly oriented eastward, with India as the privileged site of comparison. Indeed, the conceptual boldness of Coulanges's and Maine's reformulations of ancient society was made possible by their more systematic (and unprecedented) use of Indian evidence to make sense of ambiguous or unintelligible practices and beliefs of early antiquity. On the one hand, the Indo-European or Aryan idea functioned as an incorporative framework, used to extend the grounds of comparison globally; linguistic affinity could demonstrate institutional filiations between East and West and thereby elucidate what are taken to be general tendencies in human history. Yet, at the same time, a radical difference was also imputed to ancient customs, ideas, and institutions (especially Indian institutions), a

especially important given that a complex agricultural empire (Roman) had been overrun by nomadic, pastoral peoples. The four-stage theory would also be a prime reference with which to comprehend the unprecedented dynamics of contact, settlement, and colonization as they were unfolding with the global expansion of European empires. See J. G. A. Pocock, *Barbarism and Religion*, vol. IV: *Barbarians, Savages, Empires* (Cambridge, 2005).

[34] See Raymond Schwab, *The Oriental Renaissance: Europe's Rediscovery of India and the East, 1680–1880*, trans. Gene Patterson-Black and Victor Reinking (New York, 1984); Thomas R. Trautmann, *Aryans in British India* (Berkeley, 1997); Thomas R. Trautmann, *Languages and Nations: The Dravidian Proof in Colonial Madras* (Berkeley, 2006); Maurice Olender, *The Languages of Paradise: Race, Religion, and Philology in the Nineteenth Century*, trans. Arthur Goldhammer (Cambridge, Mass., 1992). The discovery of the Indo-European language family was also crucial in displacing eighteenth-century comparative models based upon forms of government and property by ones that sought affinities and contrasts in terms of geneaological connections between languages, races, and nations. On this see especially Martin Thom, *Republics, Nations, and Tribes* (London, 1995).

difference both subsumed and (chronologically) particularized in terms of a relegation to the "early history of society." In Maine's work, it was at first the ancient patriarchal family and then the agricultural village-community that were singled out as universal institutions that both bridge *and* entrench the divide between East and West, ancient and modern.

In *Ancient Law* Maine introduced the dictum "from Status to Contract" as a "law of progress" in which the "individual is steadily substituted for the Family, as the unit of which civil laws take." And "the tie between man and man which replaces by degrees those forms of reciprocity in rights and duties which have their origin in the Family ... is Contract."[35] The "Family" from which Maine believed our modern conceptions of rights and duties were distilled, or more precisely *disentangled*, was not the natural nuclear family, but rather the particular constellation of kinship and power embodied in the ancient patriarchal family. For Maine, research in comparative jurisprudence, again undergirded by the highly generative idea of an Indo-European language family, had demonstrated the widespread (perhaps even universal) existence of the ancient patriarchal family as the "the primeval condition of the human race." While the clearest delineation of the ancient family as a legal institution would be traced in Roman law, in later works Maine attempted to establish its generality and its varied articulation in institutions ranging from the Hindu Joint Family, to the East European (Slavic) House-Community, to its final transitional form in the Germanic (medieval) and Indian village-community. In proposing the patriarchal family as the original sociopolitical form of the (Indo-European) civilized world, Maine argued for the theoretical primacy of kinship as the ideological and institutional basis of early society. Modern society, then, begins to take shape in the interstices of the dissolution of the ancient family, leading to the emergence of the individual (as opposed to the corporate family) as the primary legal unit of society, and of territory (as opposed to kinship) as the primary grounds of political obligation.

For Maine, the ancient patriarchal family in all its forms was most importantly a corporate group, organized under something akin to the archaic jurisdiction of *patria potestas* – the absolute power of the patriarch over dependent persons and property.[36] It is a patriarchal or

---

[35] Maine, *Ancient Law*, pp. 165–166.
[36] "The group consists of animate and inanimate property, of wife, children, slaves, land, and goods, all held together by subjection to the despotic authority of the eldest male of the eldest ascending line, the father, grandfather, or even more remote ancestor. The force

patrilineal aggregate in that it is defined by agnatic consanguinity, its unity given by common obedience to the eldest male ascendant. The authority of the patriarch was supreme over "the life and death" of a whole host of dependents – mothers, siblings, wives, children, clients, slaves – and extended to (their) possessions, which he held in what Maine termed a "representative rather than in a proprietary character," a representative ownership that was coextensive with liability.[37] For Maine, it is precisely this *corporate* character of the ancient family that stamped itself on all areas of law in early jurisprudence. The transition from ancient to modern law would thus entail the continual restriction of the law of persons, that is, "the gradual dissolution of family dependency and the growth of individual obligation in its place." In this particular narrative of legal development, modern society reaches its telos in "a phase of social order in which all these relations arise from the free agreement of Individuals."[38]

Moreover, in a substantive sense, the corporate nature of the ancient family and the village-community was equated, in Maine, with a communal character and orientation. The family as a legal construct was explicitly modeled on the notion of a corporation sole, where the paterfamilias acted as the representative trustee of a unit, which was succeeded to universally and retained its personality intergenerationally. For Maine, kinship was its foundation, in that it was kinship rules that allocated legal/civil status and determined the status relations between persons. In this sense, importantly, kinship and kinship terminology were not just assemblages of customs and usages; they could not be reduced to a mere system of naming, a purely psychological guide to familial ties, or epiphenomenal residues of material relations, religious concepts, or biological drives. Rather, kinship rules were constitutive of social relations and thus of the social order itself; indeed, it was kinship that gave systematicity to social relations.

Maine's contrast between status and contract, which, in *Ancient Law,* was a formulation about the historical trajectory of Roman law (and, analogously, the development of Western legal systems), initiated a general classificatory framework, as the ancient was equated with other social systems in common opposition to the modern. The ancient family and, even more crucially, the village-community became nodal points of

---

which binds the group together is Power." Henry Sumner Maine, *Lectures on the Early History of Institutions* (London, 1893), p. 172.

[37] Maine, *Ancient Law,* p. 157.

[38] Ibid., pp. 165–167.

comparison through which Maine would weave together the histories of the various branches of the Aryan tree (i.e., India, Ireland, Rome, and Germany) into a continuous institutional history of the progressive development of private property, freedom of contract, and individual right. Yet, Maine's use of the comparative method, despite its expansive historical and geographical imagination, tended to reinforce the conceptual contrast between status and contract as structuring principles of radically opposed social formations. Status (or custom)[39] and contract not only defined the two endpoints of historical development but also determined the nature of all the intermediate stages that, in themselves, exhibited no distinct internal principle of organization not derived from the elementary construction of status or contract.

This contrast was further accentuated by the temporal horizon of the comparative method, which tended to conceptualize differences in social forms as differences in developmental states, that is, as differences in time. Maine's study of village-communities, for example, was premised upon and reinforced this kind of temporal and spatial contrast, especially along the lines of an East–West and traditional–modern dichotomy. In establishing historical affinities among English, Teutonic (German), and Indian (extending to Russian) agrarian histories, the framework produced a temporal equivalence between the institutions of the medieval West and contemporary Eastern phenomena, a process of comparison in which what lay *beyond* Europe was always already *before* Europe.[40] The ancient, medieval, and primitive are collapsed and subsumed under the generalizable category of "tradition," poised in common opposition to the uniqueness of the modern West. In this sense, the particularity of

---

[39] Although "Status to Contract" is Maine's most famous maxim, the term "status" appears rarely in Maine's works and, in later works, it disappears altogether. I would argue, however, that the opposition of status/contract continues to structure his thinking, metamorphosing into analogous binary formulations such as custom/market and custom/contract. Moreover, it is via these alternative formulations, that the notion of "custom" takes on a more anthropological and sociological resonance. Whereas, in the history of legal thought, custom was traditionally considered one among many sources of substantive law, in Maine's work it emerges to signify an entire legal and moral order at odds with a modern contractual and legislative system. The ideological roots of this opposition may perhaps be traced to European debates between defenders of common law/customary law and the advocates of natural law/codified law. But in Maine's more anthropological account, the difference between the two systems places less emphasis on the difference in sources of law than on the interplay and embeddedness of legal norms in the fabric of social and economic institutions.

[40] Bernard McGrane, *Beyond Anthropology: Society and the Other* (New York, 1989), chap. 3.

Western modernity was, thus, constructed through both an anthropological time frame and the consolidation of a unified and generalized category of tradition (as *premodern*).

MAINE AND LATE IMPERIAL IDEOLOGY

Like many British thinkers of the nineteenth century, Maine's life and work were intimately shaped by his interest in and professional connection to British India. As we have noted, Maine's first and still best-known work in the Anglophone world, *Ancient Law*, combined and juxtaposed research on ancient Roman, Greek, and Indian law to trace the evolutionary history of legal ideas from their classical foundations. Due in part to the popularity and reputation of *Ancient Law*, Maine was appointed to the Governor-General's Council in Calcutta, where he served as law member from 1862 to 1869. For the remainder of his life, Maine would maintain an active scholarly and political interest in Indian affairs. The majority of his late works, such as *Village-Communities in the East and West*, centered on the evolutionary and comparative history of Indian law and society.

As he was a highly visible member of the imperial administration and a preeminent scholar of Indian law and society, Maine's ideas would fundamentally shape the trajectory of late imperial ideology. As a critical conduit between emerging social theory and the imperatives of imperial governance, no intellectual was more influential in shaping the practical work of the late-nineteenth-century British Empire. Maine's tenure as law member of the Governor-General's Council coincided with an important transitional phase in the history of British rule in India, coming on the heels of the 1857 Indian Rebellion and the abolition of the East India Company with the assumption of direct rule by the Crown. And just as the long shadow of the French Revolution continued to shape nineteenth-century social and political thought, the Indian Rebellion was a watershed event in the transformation of British imperial ideology.[41]

For Maine, the so-called Indian Mutiny was "the greatest fact in all Anglo-Indian history."[42] According to Maine, the Mutiny came as a

---

[41] See Thomas R. Metcalf, *Ideologies of the Raj* (Cambridge, 1994); Metcalf, *The Aftermath of Revolt: India 1857–1880* (Princeton, N.J., 1964); Francis Hutchins, *The Illusion of Permanence: British Imperialism in India* (Princeton, N.J., 1967); Nicholas Dirks, *Castes of Mind: Colonialism and the Making of Modern India* (Princeton, N.J., 2001); D. A. Low, *The Lion Rampant: Essays in the Study of British Imperialism* (London, 1973).

[42] Henry Sumner Maine, "India," in *The Reign of Queen Victoria: A Survey of Fifty Years of Progress*, ed. Thomas Humphry Ward (London, 1887), I, pp. 460–528, at p. 470.

shock to the ruling power not only because of the speed and scale of its expansion into open rebellion but, more importantly, because it seemingly sprang from inscrutable sentiments, namely, religious and "caste" sentiment.[43] Maine declared this blindness to the strength and persistence of religious sentiments as arising from a "defect of knowledge or imagination which hides these truths from the English mind."[44] It was a defect, moreover, that had "a direct bearing on the structure of government which it may be possible to give to the Indian possessions of this country."[45] For Maine, it was

a question of the gravest practical importance for the rulers of India how far the condition of religious and social sentiment revealed by the Mutiny survives in any strength.... It is manifest that, if the belief in caste continues unimpaired or but slightly decayed, some paths of legislation and of executive action are seriously unsafe: it is possible to follow them, but it is imperative to walk warily.[46]

In tying together questions about the nature of native custom and belief to the exigencies of imperial governance, Maine was also advocating a fundamental reconceptualization of the nature of native society, one that would take more serious account of the supposed rigidity and strength of native beliefs. Maine's socio-theoretic reinterpretation of native society, and the innovations in relation to the study of Indian society it contained, in the context of imperial policy, provoked a profound change in attitudes regarding the scientific and practical basis of liberal ideologies of rule.

For Maine, previous accounts of Indian society suffered from a number of drawbacks. Substantively, as most colonial officers and European observers were based in the Presidency towns along the coasts, which had long histories of contact with the outside world, they were apt to view the urbanized (and more secularized) natives they encountered as representative of all of India. This led them to overestimate the possibility of

[43] Numerous explanations were proposed and debated as the various "lessons of 1857" rippled through imperial policy circles for decades to come. Victoria's Proclamation to the Princes, Chiefs and the People of India emphasized the religious aspects of revolt, an account that not only continues to dominate the popular historiography of 1857, but was the most prominent and most widely circulated explanation at the time. Religious explanations functioned at many levels, most evocatively as the proximate cause of the mutiny of the Bengal army. The mutiny began in response to a (true) rumor that the newly issued cartridges for Minié/Enfield rifles were greased with *both* pork and beef fats, thus offending both Muslim and Hindu sentiments. Maine himself concurred with this account and deemed "terrified fanaticism" the true, and not merely incidental, spark of revolt. See Maine, "India," p. 474.

[44] Ibid.

[45] Ibid., p. 476.

[46] Ibid.

reforming native belief along Western lines and thus underestimate the rigidity of native customs. A similarly mistaken view of Indian society, for Maine, was also inherent in utilitarianism, which had had an enormous impact in shaping the liberal agenda of colonial reform.[47] Utilitarian doctrines of political economy and jurisprudence, and the reforming doctrines in land tenure and legal reform they spawned, for Maine, tended to assume universal applicability, thus ignoring the very different logic of primitive or traditional society, of which the Indian village-community was a prime example. Thus, in emphasizing the sociological and historical conditions that separated traditional society from modern society, Maine argued that, methodologically, the study of primitive societies had to abandon abstract models of investigation that assumed that all societies could be subsumed analytically under universal definitions, laws, or maxims (especially deductive theories built upon theories of human nature). In his critique of utilitarianism, Maine argued that the abstract theories of political economy (as well as analytic definitions of law and sovereignty)

greatly underrate the value, power, and interest of that great body of custom and inherited ideas which ... they throw aside as friction. The best corrective which could be given to this disposition would be a demonstration that this "friction" is capable of scientific analysis and scientific measurement.[48]

Importantly, "custom" here is not understood as a way of describing a series of isolated phenomena. Nor is it given a substantive definition, that is, as a name for a particular set of ritual or religious practices. Rather, for Maine, custom is understood in structural and institutional terms, and as a customary *order*, an entire legal and moral order at odds with a modern contractual and legislative system.

Maine's methodological presumption toward viewing societies as social wholes was reinforced by and entangled with the substantive characterization of the structural integrity of primitive societies. Coupled with the classificatory framework that viewed ancient and modern societies as opposing ideal-typical societies, Maine's conceptualization of native

---

[47] See Eric Stokes, *The English Utilitarians and India* (Oxford, 1959). Although a consistent feature of all of Maine's work, his most important criticism of utilitarianism appears in *Village-Communities in the East and West* (London, 1876), "The Effects of Observation of India on Modern European Thought," The Rede Lecture of 1875 (reprinted in *Village-Communities*), and the last two chapters on sovereignty in *Early History of Institutions*.

[48] Maine, "The Effects of Observation of India on Modern European Thought," in *Village-Communities*, p. 233.

society was imbued with a new form of spatialization; custom and contract were animating features in a deeply *synchronic* account of social formations. Status/custom and contract were principles that rationally ordered and defined the internal relations that governed ideas, institutions, and practices. In this way, societies, whether defined through status or contract relations, were conceived of as functionally ordered, structured totalities: holistic societies where central principles animated and connected the different sets of relations and institutions.

The larger theoretical picture implicit in Maine's work, then, was less a temporalized ladder of civilization on which all societies are placed hierarchically than a spatial frontier where bounded societies live side by side, yet, significantly, in different temporalities. It is this spatial vision that is instantiated in the theory and practice of late imperial rule, especially in its most thorough incarnation in the development of indirect rule in Africa. As Maine wrote, "the British rulers of India are like men bound to make their watches keep true time in two longitudes at once.... If they are too slow, there will be no improvement. If they are too fast, there will be no security."[49] The metaphor of longitude aptly expresses this kind of spatialized conception of temporal difference and distance.

Maine's reconceptualization of Indian society provided an enormous fillip to the growth of "official anthropology" and its influence in crafting imperial policy.[50] Indeed, it directly spurred, in some quarters, a wholesale rejection of the liberal agenda of reform in favor of policies that sought the rehabilitation and protection of native customs and institutions. For many, protecting native traditions was a normative priority, and for them, Maine's evocative account of native society, where primitive custom rationally ordered social, political, and economic life, was particularly appealing. Others argued for a policy of protection and/or rehabilitation as a safeguard against instability, unrest, and rebellion. Indeed, in prioritizing the maintenance of order, liberal models of education, economy, and politics would all be limited because they were now considered to have inherently disintegrative effects on native/traditional society. Unlike liberal ruling strategies that construed traditional social structures, customs, and identities, such as those relating to caste and religion, as impediments to the project of improvement and thus good and

[49] Ibid., p. 237.
[50] See Clive Dewey, "The Influence of Sir Henry Maine on Agrarian Policy in India," in *The Victorian Achievement of Sir Henry Maine: A Centennial Reappraisal*, ed. Alan Diamond (Cambridge, 1995), pp. 353–375.

moral governance, the new ideologies of rule stressed the need for reconciliation with native institutions and structures of authority. In practical terms, this entailed a more conciliatory relation to the princely states, now seen both as bulwarks against radicalism and as authorities that commanded "natural" obedience.[51] There was also a notable shift away from the institution of the principles of laissez-faire and private property rights for the sake of protecting the traditional foundations of agrarian society, such as caste and the village-community.[52]

Yet, the linchpin for the consolidation of this new ideology of rule was a revised underlying account of what constituted threats to imperial rule. And in that respect, Maine provided one of the most important conceptual innovations to the theory of traditional society. The new account of threats stemmed in different ways from a generic characterization of a traditional society in crisis, that is, a society struggling to survive under the traumatic impact of contact with the West. Maine offered a provocative sociology of colonialism in which the bases of traditional society were seen as increasingly undermined by contact with the modern, where the collapse of traditional society was conceived of in terms of disruptions to a delicate social and cultural equilibrium.

Although primitive societies were functional wholes, in Maine's terms, self-acting and self-generating,[53] they were also, paradoxically, under the threat of imminent dissolution. The village-communities, whose observation was crucial for historical reconstruction, were everyday disappearing under the impact of imperial rule. Here lay the particular urgency in Maine's plea for comparative social science, for while British rule in India provided the conditions for sustained observation of these forms of ancient society, it was the very fact of that rule that was also undermining the social basis of these same archaic institutions. India must be studied at once, Maine argues, "[f]or this remarkable society, pregnant with interest at every point, and for the moment easily open to our observations, is undoubtedly passing away.... India itself is gradually losing everything which is characteristic of it."[54] And while Maine insisted that this disintegration of traditional Indian society was in large part produced *unwittingly* by the British, it was nevertheless a process that could not be reversed;

[51] Metcalf, *Ideologies of the Raj*, and Metcalf, *The Aftermath of Revolt*.
[52] Dewey, "The Influence of Sir Henry Maine on Agrarian Policy in India."
[53] Maine, *Village-Communities*, p. 101.
[54] Ibid., p. 24.

[w]e do not innovate or destroy in mere ignorance. We rather change because we cannot help it. Whatever be the nature and value of that bundle of influences which we call Progress, nothing can be more certain than that, when a society is once touched by it, it spreads like a contagion.[55]

Through the metaphor of contagion, Maine articulated a prescient account of the structural impact of colonial rule on native institutions and practices.[56]

The dissolution of the Indian village-community under the impact of British imperialism, for Maine, was a vivid example of the ways in which the colonizing process sets traditional and modern societies into a dramatic, living, and potentially devastating opposition. In this way, in Maine's work, the central historical contrast between modern and traditional societies, when transported to the imperial world, became ever more sharply drawn. For, in Maine's sociology of colonialism, the encounter between these opposed social forms necessarily led to conflict, a conflict that inevitably hastened the dissolution of ancient, customary forms of life. Moreover, in practical terms, the rapidity of the process of disintegration, for Maine, engendered grave consequences for the stability of imperial rule.

This warning about the potential "dissolution of society" under the imperative of empire served as the ideological linchpin of the theory and practice of indirect rule. For advocates of native institutions, Maine's cogent account of the disruptive structural impact of colonial/ modern institutions on native society vividly demonstrated the urgent need for protection. In this sense, the sympathetic portrayal of native society was coupled with a sociology of colonialism that not only identified avowed reform and intervention as causes of instability but also implied that everywhere traditional societies were inherently fragile in the context of modernity. The call for the protection or rehabilitation of native society was committed not only to the idea that native society contained within itself the resources for its maintenance and reproduction, but also to the idea that this unity was both threatened by and yet in need of imperial rule. For it was the portrayal of native society as

---

[55] Maine, "The Effects of Observation of India ...," in ibid., pp. 237–238.

[56] Maine detailed this process in reference to two key institutions: the Indian village-community and customary law; both accounts can be found in *Village-Communities*. I have analyzed Maine's account of the structural impact of imperialism in "Law and 'Tradition': Henry Maine and the Theoretical Origins of Indirect Rule," *Law and History*, ed. Andrew Lewis and Michael Lobban (Oxford, 2004), and in chaps. 3 and 4 of *Alibis of Empire: Henry Maine and the Ends of Liberal Imperialism* (Princeton, N.J., 2010).

simultaneously *intact* and *vulnerable* that underpinned the paternalistic impulse of late imperial rule.

More specifically, the idea that the reconciliation with authentically native institutions, rather than their eradication, would lead to stability was a dramatic reversal of earlier ideologies of imperial rule. This reversal of the goal of major transformation in native institutions, in practice, entailed a move to bolster, invent, and reinforce native authorities seen as traditional. The move was double-edged; on the one hand, it eulogized the stabilizing and inherently beneficial character of native rule, under native law, for native subjects. At the same time, imperial policy inscribed the native as naturally at home in his/her custom and thus resistant to reform, conversion, assimilation – in short, civilization. In this sense, the radical rethinking that occurred in the wake of the 1857 Rebellion not only reversed the main tenets of the civilizing mission, conceived of as a wholesale project of transformation of native society, but also rendered the native a slave to custom.

CONCLUSION

In India, what began as a principle of nonintervention or noninterference in native religious practices in the wake of the 1857 Rebellion had, by the turn of the twentieth century, metamorphosed into an array of arguments for the protection and rehabilitation of native institutions. Indirect rule, the rule through native institutions, became the foundational theory of late imperial administrative philosophy, articulated in different forms in Swettenham's vision for Malaya, Cromer's for Egypt, and Lugard's for Africa.[57]

The transition in imperial ideology inaugurated in the aftermath of the 1857 Rebellion was grounded in an intellectual reorientation in understandings of native society, a reorientation that was profoundly indebted to the model of traditional society taking shape in modern social theory. This apolitical model of a traditional society as a functional whole logically ordered by kin-based customary ties would be employed in a variety

---

[57] The most direct connection between Maine's work and later enactment of policies of indirect rule was his influence on Arthur Gordon, the first governor of Fiji, who sought to reconstitute Fijian society on the model of Maine's self-cultivating village-communities; see J. D. Legge, *Britain in Fiji, 1858–1880* (London,1958). See also Stokes, *The English Utilitarians in India*, pp. 309–310; C. A. Bayly, "Maine and Change in Nineteenth-Century India," in Diamond, *The Victorian Achievement of Sir Henry Maine*, p. 391; Mahmood Mamdani, *Citizen and Subject: Contemporary Africa and the Legacy of Late Colonialism* (Princeton, N.J., 1996), p. 49.

of ways to shore up a distinctively postliberal imperial order. On the one hand, with its emphasis on the stability and rigidity of native custom, the socio-theoretic model of traditional society enabled a redescription of native disenchantment with and resistance to imperial rule in social and cultural rather than political terms. That is, political rebellion, refracted through the imperial lens, appeared as a deep-seated cultural intransigence to modernization, assimiliation, and civilization (rather than as a contradiction inherent in any imperial project founded on the use of force to elicit societal transformation). On the other hand, in viewing traditional societies as functional yet threatened wholes, the burden of imperial rule was increasingly portrayed as a necessity emergent from the fragile nature of native societies themselves. In this manner, late imperial ideology came to rely upon socio-theoretic models of native society, both as the site of a new kind of legitimation and as the rubric through which to articulate distinct strategies of ruling imperial subjects.

The apolitical model of traditional society that became aligned with the imperatives of the nineteenth-century British Empire was a distinctive offshoot of the making of modern social theory. Maine outlined many of the central features of this model – kinship as a central structuring principle of society; the intermingling of law and religion in early jurisprudence; the predominance of ritual and rigid codes of conduct circumscribing individual action; the hold of custom on both modes of action and conceptual imagination; and, finally, the moral and functional priority of the community or the social whole – that would become commonplace assumptions about traditional society carried forward into twentieth-century anthropology and sociology, especially in theories of modernization. Twentieth-century anthropology, especially in British structural-functionalism, in which Maine's jural model of kinship was substantially revived, developed concepts of the social and of culture that were methodologically invested in notions of relativity, boundedness, and holism; they were (as in Maine) also premised upon substantive theses about the nature of traditional society, an intermingling that tended to reinforce at both levels assumptions about the internal cohesiveness and communal orientation of traditional societies, the cultural and social determination of individual action and behavior, and thus a deemphasis on (political) conflict, change, and agency.

In Maine's characterization of traditional society, an account of human action and behavior emerged that was profoundly shaped and limited by cultural and social norms. Maine's discussion of kinship as the central organizing principle of primitive society was meant to demonstrate the

slow and incremental generation of new legal ideas and practices. For
Maine, society is always in advance of the law (especially in progressive
societies). Legal transformation is thus a process of harmonizing essentially rigid and technical categories to new social relations. Thus, Maine
took as given the idea that Eastern ideas seemingly "move always within
a distinctly drawn circle of unchanging notions." The difference between
East and West was "really only a difference of degree." For even in the
most progressive Western societies, "there are more natural limitations
on the fertility of the intellect than we always admit to ourselves."[58] Thus,
for Maine, a fundamental fact of humans, primitive as well as modern,
was their inherent psychological resistance to change and innovation. In
this last conjecture, Maine took a psychological predisposition supposedly characteristic of primitive society and expanded it to a general feature of humankind.

Thus, a deterministic view of behavior was not only characteristic of
primitive or premodern societies, but was construed as a general feature
of human sociability. Therefore, while for Spencer the "tyranny of custom" was peculiar to the early stages of society, for Maine it was elevated
to the status of a sociological constant or maxim about human nature as
such. Human behavior was thus construed as a product of social learning,
institutional conditioning, and historically and culturally informed custom. By the end of the nineteenth century, it was precisely these elements
that constituted the core of the modern anthropological definition of
culture.[59] And as Margaret Archer has argued, it was this generalization
that produced a kind of inversion of the modern–traditional dichotomy,
in which the anthropological study of traditional society inaugurated a
view of culture that was then imported back into the sociological tradition as a general account of social integration and interdependency.[60]
The important methodological ramification of this translation is how the
structure/agency problem characteristic of modern social theory represents a doubling of and mirrors the culture/agency problem.

---

[58] Maine, *Early History of Institutions*, p. 128. The idea that humans are by nature "intensely
conservative," with a universal tendency to "abhor change," is a claim that Maine repeats
throughout *Popular Government* (Indianapolis, 1976 [originally published in 1888]).

[59] George W. Stocking, *Race, Culture, and Evolution: Essays in the History of Anthropology*
(Chicago, 1982).

[60] Margaret Archer, *Culture and Agency: The Place of Culture in Social Theory* (Cambridge,
1996).

13

Political Theory of Empire and Imperialism

An Appendix

Jennifer Pitts

The recent sustained attention to questions of empire and imperialism in political theory has at least two distinct sources: the turning, finally, of attention to a field of study that had occupied other scholars for over two decades; and the sense, shared by a broad global public, that contemporary global structural inequalities, and especially American unilateralism and militarism after 2001, demanded a reinterrogation of the idea of empire. As I will discuss (in the first section), a focus of the recent literature in the history of political thought has been on the place of empire in the work of political thinkers, many canonical, the imperial dimensions of whose thought had been relatively ignored prior to the last decade. Central to this conversation (the second section) has been the question of the relationship, theoretical and historical, of liberalism and empire, itself one of a broader set of questions about how universalisms have dealt with the moral, political, and legal inequalities inherent in empire. This chapter will return regularly to questions about liberalism and empire, which recur in the literatures on settler societies (the third section), contemporary neo-liberalism and American imperialism (the fourth section), global justice (the fifth section), and international law (the sixth section). Practitioners and historians of international law have begun to investigate thoroughly the imperial contexts and entanglements of their discipline. Public attention to the question of American empire has prompted a burst of scholarship about the nature of imperial polities and politics; partly in response to this conversation, a newer strand of scholarship

This chapter was previously published in the *Annual Review of Political Science*, 13 (2010), 211–235.

has begun to theorize imperial power (the seventh section), exploring its distinctive "political and ethical stakes" and asking to what extent, for instance, ideas in circulation in political theory, such as the republican conception of nondomination, can account for the dynamics of imperial power (Markell 2008). Finally (the eighth section), political theorists have belatedly begun to ask in a sustained way how their subject has been recast by the innovations and preoccupations of postcolonial studies (Persram 2007), even as postcolonial studies itself undergoes a prolonged moment of self-scrutiny (Scott 1999 and 2004, Loomba 2005).

Political theory has come slowly and late to the study of empire relative to other disciplines. In the 1970s, anthropology began a period of (some have said excessively) self-reflexive study in which anthropologists scrutinized their discipline's long complicity with and contributions to structures of imperial power (Geertz 1973, Asad 1975, Wolf 1982, Fabian 1983, Cohn 1987), and anthropologists continue to be among the most trenchant analysts of imperial and postcolonial politics as well as their intersections with global capitalism (Comaroff and Comaroff 1991 and 2009). The disciplines of literature and then history were rapidly, if incompletely, transformed by postcolonial studies, whose beginning is generally marked by the 1978 publication of Edward Said's *Orientalism* (reissued 2003; also see Said 1993). The histories of Britain and France, for instance, are now widely understood as imperial histories (for Britain, see Colley 1992, C. Hall 2000, 2002, and 2006, Burton 2003 and 2006, Wilson 2004; for France, see Clancy-Smith 1994, Conklin 1997, Lebovics 2004, Saada 2007). A central recent theme has been the ways in which European state structures and national identities were constituted in part through constructions of empire: historians have had to "rethink what it meant to study a continent called Europe" (Cooper 2005b, p. 401). German, Italian, and Russian historians have more recently also taken up imperial themes (Lieven 2000, Suny and Martin 2001, Burbank et al. 2007, Steinmetz 2007, Fitzpatrick 2008, Mazower 2008), and Latin American historians have perceived a new theoretical centrality for their too often peripheral region (Dussel 1995, Schmidt-Nowara and Nieto-Phillips 2005, Adelman 2006, Moraña et al. 2008). The imperial history of the United States, as both a settler society that conquered and absorbed vast continental territory throughout the nineteenth century and the ruler of unincorporated territories such as Cuba and the Philippines in the twentieth, is coming to be more widely studied as well as recognized as relevant background to contemporary events (Slotkin 1973, 1985, and 1998, Takaki 1979, White 1991, Blackhawk 2006, Kramer 2006,

Griffin 2007; Go 2008, Rana 2010). While renewed attention has been paid to non-European empires, such as the Chinese, the Mughal, and the Ottoman, *as* empires (Hevia 2003, Pollock 2006, Subrahmanyam 2006, Stoler et al., 2007, Duara 2009), the political-theoretic discussion has focused on European empires. More broadly, historical research has developed increasingly nuanced analyses of how empires govern, from Rome (Ando 2000) to the present (Maier 2006).

The newly dynamic field of world history has produced particularly sophisticated accounts of the asymmetrical interactions that brought about global modernity (Curtin 1984 and 2000, Bayly 1989 and 2004, Subrahmanyam 1996 and 2005, Benton 2001, Eley 2007). By comparison, political theory for much of the 1980s and 1990s was remarkably untouched by these powerful theoretical and thematic developments, although it clearly has a distinct interest in much of postcolonial studies' fields of analysis: the theorization of power, state formation, community and identity, and the historical study of such theorizations. (Rare exceptions in political science before the last decade included Doyle 1986, Mitchell 1991, Grovogui 1996.)

So, despite the late and relatively sparse attention that political theorists in a narrow disciplinary sense have paid to imperialism and its history, sustained, critical, and theoretically sophisticated analysis of empire has been widely available in other fields. Wendy Brown has argued that "[t]he work of thinking about political matters theoretically" has lately dispersed through a vast array of disciplines (2005, p. 66), for reasons that range from the receding of nation-state sovereignty (political theory's traditional purview) in the face of globalized capitalism to a reconceptualization of power's operation and circulation. Thanks in large part to Foucault, this rethinking has invited inquiries into power and politics from scholars of culture, language, and literature and from other forms of representation such as the visual arts. If all political theory has become cross-disciplinary, this is nowhere more true than in the study of empire. A proper understanding of the phenomenon of empire undoubtedly requires the contributions of disciplines including social and cultural history and theory; literary criticism; feminist criticism and history; and anthropology. Whether the subject is canonical political thinkers' reflections on conquest or the theorization of politics in the postcolonial present, much of the most innovative work, with which political scientists should engage far more than they do, takes place outside the confines of the discipline. Brown is entirely right to discourage us from policing political theory's boundaries or lamenting the dispersion of our subject, but we may still regret that political theory as a discipline has contributed less to the vigorous and significant scholarly conversation on empire than it might have been expected to do. This chapter will attempt both to critically assess the work done in the last decade by political theorists specifically and to gesture at the much broader and more diverse range of studies and debates beyond the discipline that undoubtedly constitute political theorizing about empire.

This chapter will not distinguish systematically between the imperial and the colonial. A working description of "empire" is "a political unit that is large and expansionist (or with memories of an expansionist past), reproducing differentiation and inequality among people it incorporates" – or, perhaps better, "annexes," since precisely a failure to incorporate is characteristic of empires (Calhoun et al. 2006, p. 3; also see Muldoon 1999). But since this description of an expansive and differentiated state might also be thought to apply to many large nation-states, we might add, with Lisa Wedeen, that "[i]n the age of nation-states, imperial states generally exercise [their extensive] dominion over populations that are perceived (by conqueror and conquered) as different from (in the sense of ineligible for incorporation into) the dominant state exercising control" (Wedeen forthcoming). The problem of managing difference is often seen as the perennial political challenge for empires, though it may be more accurate to say that empires *cultivate* forms of difference (see the seventh section). Charles Maier emphasizes the distinctive place of bloodshed in empires (with their "ambition ... territorial agenda, and ... problematic frontiers"), the transformation of the core society brought about by conquest, and the role of path dependency in the formation of empires, as even hesitant participants "cling ... to choices made early on whose reversal seems unthinkable" (Maier 2006, pp. 19, 21).

A commonly drawn distinction between imperial and colonial territories marks colonial territories (following the Latin *colonus*, or "farmer") as those that involve substantial settlement from the metropole, while the term "imperial" stresses extensive domination over others (see Kohn 2008). But official, popular, and even scholarly usage is unstable, and the terms "colonies" and "postcolonial" are applied equally to spaces of significant settlement and those without; indeed, the former now tends to be specified as "settler colonialism" (Elkins and Pedersen 2005). "Colonial empire" just as often refers to "exploitative economic relations between an imperial core and a subject periphery" (Subrahmanyam 2006, p. 220) or to "the occupation and annexation of regions beyond the global core and the seizure of foreign sovereignty," as in British India (Steinmetz

2006, p. 143). The term "imperialism" was, like most political "isms," a coinage of the mid-nineteenth century. Since its earliest usage, it has tended to be a term of opprobrium and one that emphasizes not only the extent but also the unaccountability of the power exercised (Connelly in Calhoun 2006, p. 19).

HISTORY OF POLITICAL THOUGHT

Recent work in the history of political thought has been concerned to show the centrality of empire to the theoretical and professional preoccupations of many of the key figures in the political theory canon, as well as to modern political languages and ideologies more broadly. This work has formed part of a broader new inquiry into what has begun to be called the "history of international thought" after a "fifty years' rift" between intellectual history and international relations (Armitage 2004a). Modern political thought since the European encounter with the New World has, not surprisingly, received most attention, but empire has proven an illuminating lens for the study of other thinkers, including Aristotle, whose *Politics* may be read as a response to the "depredations of [the Macedonian] empire" and as "problematizing the Greek polis" rather than idealizing it (Dietz 2007).

The study of empire as a theme in the history of political thought was pioneered by a few scholars working with a broadly Cambridge School approach, most prominently Anthony Pagden, James Tully, J. G. A. Pocock, Richard Tuck, and, more recently, David Armitage. Pagden's early seminal studies explored debates over the legitimation of Spanish rule in the New World, debates conducted in such languages as Aristotelian psychology (natural slave and child) and Roman legal and political thought (*imperium, dominium, orbis terrarum*) (1982, 1990, 1993). In illustrating the ways in which empires generated new states and political forms, and shaped modern political ideologies such as democratic republicanism, Pagden made a powerful case for the centrality of empire to political theory. His most recent books, written for more popular audiences, stress the possibly "insuperable future dilemmas" facing the polities created in the wake of formal empires (2001, p. 160) and, controversially, the "perpetual enmity" between Europe and Asia (2008). Tully placed questions connected to empire at the heart of both Locke's thought and modern constitutionalism, as I discuss further later on. Pocock insisted, from a professedly "antipodean" perspective, that British history and political thought must be understood in imperial and global terms (Pocock 2005, chap. 2 [1973]). More recently, his magisterial volumes on Enlightenment thought, by way of a study of the contexts of Gibbon's *Decline and Fall of the Roman Empire*, have emphasized the global orientation of the enlightened histories that were so prominent a feature of the intellectual landscape (1999–). He explores the wide range of meanings of "empire" at the time, as well as what he calls the era's "crisis of the seaborne empires" and the anxieties on the part of so many political and social thinkers of the time about the disorders of the global commerce that was supposed to succeed the age of conquests. As Richard Tuck has argued, early-modern theorists of subjective rights conceived the sovereign individual in terms of the sovereign state and vice versa. They worked out their theories, with "often brutal implications" for indigenous and non-European peoples, partly in response to two key practical problems arising from European commercial and imperial expansion: struggles over freedom and control of trade and navigation in Asia, and states' efforts to legitimate their settlement colonies in the New World (Tuck 1999, p. 108).

The importance of extra-European commerce and conquest to the development of European political thought is heightened, as recent scholarship has emphasized, by the active involvement as legislators, or employees or associates of trading companies, of so many key figures, including Grotius and Locke, Hobbes (Malcolm 2002), Burke (Whelan 1996, Burke 2000, Bourke 2007), Constant (Pitts 2008), Mill (Zastoupil 1994, Moir et al. 1999), and Tocqueville (2001, Richter 1963, Welch 2003, Pitts 2005). Recent work has explored, for instance, Grotius's sustained theoretical and legal efforts on behalf of the Dutch East India Company (Tuck 1999, Borschberg 2002, van Ittersum 2006) and has overturned the portrait of Grotius as the theorist par excellence of a modern international legal community of equal and independent sovereign states, illustrating instead his theorization of forms of divided or subordinate sovereignty for states outside Europe (Keene 2002). Locke's theory of property has long been associated with the colonization of America and more specifically with his role in drafting the *Fundamental Constitutions of Carolina* (1669), but recent scholarship has deepened our understanding of the extent of his involvement and its implications for his thought on property, sovereignty, and liberty (Tully 1993, Arneil 1996, Mehta 1999, Armitage 2004b, Farr 2008).

It is now widely agreed that a full understanding of these thinkers' ideas, as well as the broader traditions to which they contributed, requires attention to imperial and global contexts and concerns. Most fundamentally, such study makes it clear that the key concepts and languages of

European political thought – ideas of freedom and despotism, self-government, the autonomous individual – were imagined and articulated in light of, in response to, sometimes in justification of, imperial and commercial expansion beyond Europe. Ideologies of empire (Armitage 2000), from the republican (Fitzmaurice 2003; also see Hörnqvist 2004) to the utilitarian (Schultz and Varouxakis 2005), are being shown to have permeated political thought that had conventionally been studied either with little attention to its contexts or in European contexts alone.

As Tully has written, "European constitutional states, as state empires, developed within global systems of imperial and colonial law from the beginning" (Tully 2008, 2, p. 200). Just as we must understand modern Western constitutional democracy (and international law) as having emerged in an imperial context, so we must understand its exponents in the tradition of political thought, and those of other inherited political forms and concepts, in the same global and imperial context. Often this is to return thinkers to a context that they, too, saw as crucially significant, though it has been neglected by subsequent readers: this is especially the case for the thinkers of what is now being called the "global eighteenth century" (Nussbaum 2003; also see Manning and Cogliano 2008, Kelly 2009, Whelan 2009), including most prominently Smith (e.g., Muthu 2008) and Kant (e.g., Cavallar 2002), but also Hume (Rothschild 2004, 2008), Burke, Diderot, and less canonical figures such as the Abbé Raynal (Muthu 2003, Agnani 2004, Festa 2006). Other thinkers, such as Mill or Tocqueville, may have downplayed the theoretical significance of their imperial context; Mill's *Autobiography* depicts his nearly lifelong work for the East India Company as a comfortable day job that allowed him time to write and taught him something of public administration (Mill 1981, pp. 85–87). But both the reach and the limits of their knowledge and interests, and the truncated scope of apparently universal moral and political claims, are apparent only when we grasp the imperial dimensions of their careers and their thought.

LIBERALISM AND EMPIRE

A prominent theme has been the "mutually constitutive" relationship of liberalism and empire (Armitage 2004b, p. 602). Whether we apply the term "liberalism" strictly to theories developed after the 1810s, when "liberal" became a political category, or more broadly but conventionally to the languages of subjective rights and self-government stemming back to the early-modern period, the evolution of liberal thought coincided and deeply intersected with the rise of European empires. Liberalism arguably remains marked by features that rendered it often supportive of imperial domination, including a commitment to progress and a teleological view of history, a suspicion of certain kinds of cultural or ethical particularism, and a hospitable stance toward capitalism and the economic exploitation of nature (Parekh 1994 and 1995). European imperialisms were themselves decisively shaped by liberal preoccupations, including ideas of tutelage in self-government, exporting the rule of law, and the normativity of European modernity (for a critique of the last, see Chakrabarty 2000).

In response to an older tradition that assumed that liberalism, with its commitments to equality and self-government, must be anti-imperial (Berlin 1965), it has become increasingly common to argue that, on the contrary, the imperialistic "urge is *internal* to" liberalism (Mehta 1999, p. 20), that inherent in the very structure of liberal rationalism and abstraction is "a propensity for colonial domination" (Sartori 2006, p. 623, criticizing this idea). Postcolonial criticism of contemporary liberalism has stressed its *abstract rationalism*, which, though based on a culturally particular set of values, purports to articulate universal moral truths. Also criticized is liberalism's narrowly *rights-based* idiom of justice and the insufficiency of liberal distributive justice, particularly given liberalism's tendency to stress what Iris Young has called a "liability model" of injustice and to overlook structural injustices, or the ways in which "social processes put large categories of persons under a systematic threat of domination" even in the absence of harms traceable to responsible individuals (Young 2007, pp. 170ff.). Finally, liberalism's *moral individualism* is said to eclipse alternative "possibilities of human solidarity" and "narratives of connection" (Chakrabarty 2000, p. 23; see the summary of these criticisms in Ivison 2002, pp. 30–48).

Uday Mehta's influential *Liberalism and Empire* identifies as key culprits liberals' tacit presumptions of particular (European) social structures and anthropological characteristics behind ostensibly universalist moral claims, and the historicism and reformism of nineteenth-century liberals. He contrasts imperial liberalism's "judgmental" and "evangelical" qualities with Edmund Burke's keen grasp of the moral and political perils of empire and his "ability to view the unfamiliar from a perspective that does not a priori presume its provisionality" (1999, p. 214). Mehta's eloquent and theoretically rich discussion has been criticized (including by the present author) for offering an overly ahistorical and undifferentiated account of liberalism that understates the variety of its incarnations, and that overlooks critiques of and ambivalence toward conquest and empire on the part of eighteenth-century proto-liberals such as Diderot, Smith, Kant, and Bentham (Muthu 2003, Pitts 2005). Historians have also called for a corrective to the textual emphasis of such treatments through greater attention to material and social developments that conditioned liberalism's evolution (Cooper 2005b, Sartori 2006). Cooper criticizes flat accounts of European modernity and Enlightenment that ignore their "convoluted trajectory" and that, as a result, ironically render Europeans the "people without history" (2005a, p. 6). Rather than seeing liberalism since the seventeenth century as a theoretical unity, one that has consistently "prided itself on its universality and politically inclusionary character" (Mehta 1999, p. 46), these scholars urge us to see liberalism as an always changing ideology whose commitments at any given time result from contingent conjunctures of discourses (for instance, of rights or liberty), interests (such as those of merchants in an emerging commercial society), and institutions (the Bank of England, the East India Company).

Recent work has further explored liberalism's complicity with and constitution through empire as both have evolved since the early nineteenth century. The relationship between J. S. Mill's thought and his nearly lifelong career as a well-placed East India Company official has received particular scrutiny (Zastoupil 1994, Moir et al. 1999), given his status as iconic liberal and his sustained attention to all facets of the British Empire, from Ireland, India, and Jamaica to the settler colonies (Bell 2010). While much of this literature has been critical of Mill's crude and unsympathetic account of a "backward" India, his endorsement of "despotism" over "barbarians," and his belief that Europeans had no obligations under the law of nations to societies outside civilized Europe (Mehta 1999, Pitts 2005), others have defended his "tolerant" imperialism (Tunick 2006) or argued that he was a critical-minded supporter of British imperial rule who perceived its tendency toward systematic injustice (Kohn and O'Neill 2006). Yet, as Karuna Mantena has argued, Mill's thought exemplifies the "internal tensions" of liberal imperialism, which itself might be seen as merely one form of a family of imperial universalisms, projects of progressive reform that, when they encounter opposition or failure, commonly understand the fault to lie in the nature of the colonized societies rather than in the structure of imperial power, and too often give way to culturalist accounts of intransigent, illiberal others (Mantena 2007, 2010). Millian liberalism, however influential, did not, of course, exhaust British liberalism's posture toward empire in the later nineteenth century. If radical critiques of empire were rare (and remain underexplored), they did exist (Taylor 1991, Claeys 2007 and 2010). Imperial liberalism itself evolved and became bound up with various visions of global order (Bell 2007a and 2007b), often on the part of visionary internationalists whose aspirations for global peace and justice sat uneasily with their support for hierarchy and European dominance (Morefield 2005, Sylvest 2009).

The paradoxes of liberal imperialism explored in the historical literature remain instructive for political analysis in the age of American hegemony. The study of the history of American political thought has been less affected by the recent attention to empire (though recent studies include Shapiro [2006] and Ferguson [2008]). Michael Rogin, in groundbreaking essays from the 1970s on, argued that liberal ideology profoundly shaped America's imperial career and vice versa. "Liberal contractual relations diffused guilt" about the expulsion and extermination of native Americans, he argued. Rather than directly forcing Indians to abandon their land, Andrew Jackson's and later administrations insisted that their departures be formally voluntary; the expropriation, famines, and mass death that resulted could then be depicted as the unintended result of a complex set of individual (including Indian) actions and not the policy of the state (Rogin 1987, pp. 162–164; also see Rogin 1975). Rogin was concerned to explore the analogies with American actions in Vietnam, such as the refusal to accept responsibility for civilian deaths, but we might equally draw connections to more recent arguments that the United States can take no responsibility for the diffusion of violence in authoritarian or "failed" states around the globe, but that the only solution to that violence is for America to take up the burden of empire (e.g., Ignatieff 2003).

Liberalism is notoriously and inevitably a complex ideology whose exemplars share family resemblances rather than any strict doctrine. While its languages have contributed prominently to the articulation of imperial projects, and while the most powerful modern empires have, perhaps not coincidentally, been those of liberal states, liberal ideals have just as clearly furnished trenchant critiques of imperialism. As Fred Cooper has written, one could as easily argue that the urge to anti-imperialism is internal to liberalism (2005a, p. 413). Indeed, although it continues to be rare for political theorists to look outside European and American traditions of thought, new work has also emerged on liberalism's global dissemination, especially on various instances of what Christopher Bayly has called the "global liberal constitutional moment" in the early to mid-nineteenth century, when thinkers from India to North

Africa to the newly independent countries of Latin America adopted and adapted liberal language and categories for reformist or avowedly anti-imperial ends (Bayly 2007, Sartori 2008, Kohn 2009, Pitts 2009). While empire undoubtedly served as a vehicle for the imposition or spread of liberal ideas, it has been argued that the "global availability of [liberalism's] categories" also stemmed from social transformations around the globe that were related but not reducible to European imperial expansion (Sartori 2006, p. 640; also see Bayly 2004 and 2007). This work on global liberalisms joins a growing body of literature in "comparative political theory," which, while not necessarily concerned with questions of empire, has often engaged them in the course of addressing conjunctures between European political thought and those of other regions and traditions, especially Muslim (Parel and Keith 1992, Dallmayr 1999 and 2002, Euben 2006, Shogimen and Nederman 2009). This literature has explored conceptions and practices of translation as an alternative to the blithe assumption that a parochial European liberalism can successfully articulate universal values.

POSTCOLONIAL DILEMMAS IN SETTLER SOCIETIES

The possibilities, limits, and pathologies of liberalism also preoccupy the distinct political theory literature that has taken up the expropriation and subjugation of indigenous peoples in settler societies. These historical and ongoing injustices throw into question the legitimacy of such societies, and of the international society that recognizes them, as Paul Keal has argued (Keal 2003; also see Elkins and Pedersen 2005). Analysts of the settler-colonial past of the United States have argued that the country's "robust ideal of republican freedom emerged through practices of external coercion and control": that empire-building and the subjugation of noncitizens inside and outside the state's borders have been not simply unfortunate failures to live up to the country's liberal-democratic ideals, but instrumental in the production of the ideals themselves (Rana 2010). Political theory on such questions partly issues from and responds to recent legal and political developments in Canada, Australia, and New Zealand. The Australian High Court's 1992 decision in *Mabo* overturned the doctrine that Australia was *terra nullius* (land belonging to no one) at the time of European settlement and recognized indigenous title as part of Australian common law (see Fitzmaurice 2007 and, on the history of the idea of *terra nullius*, Benton and Straumann 2010), and the 1993 Native Title Act created controversial mechanisms to adjudicate indigenous groups' land claims. New Zealand law has increasingly recognized the 1840 Treaty of Waitangi and its principle of *tino rangatiratanga*, a complex concept that might be roughly rendered as Maori sovereign authority, as precursors to and conditions of national sovereignty (see Ivison et al. 2000, Pocock 2005).

Tully's *Strange Multiplicity* was an innovative work in the political theory of settler societies, with its argument that "the imperial culture embodied in most liberal constitutions" subverts rather than protects freedom and self-rule in culturally diverse postcolonial societies (1995, p. 7). Drawing on the "exemplary" struggles of aboriginal peoples, as well as methodological guidance from Wittgenstein, Foucault, and Quentin Skinner, Tully argues for a practice of "contemporary constitutionalism" that seeks a "mediated peace" and respect for difference rather than a comprehensive liberal justice (p. 211). Where Tully envisions practices of democratic *freedom* beyond liberalism, Elizabeth Povinelli has questioned the "hierarchy of values produced and institutionalized by the subject of freedom" and the imposition of this schema on postcolonial societies (Povinelli 2005, pp. 147, 159). She notes that mechanisms such as the Native Title Act impose "legal mandates on the form aboriginal culture must take" (Povinelli 2002, p. 39). Courts, she argues, have increasingly demanded that aboriginal subjects present themselves as unfree, as compelled by custom or culture, thereby "call[ing] on them to dehumanize themselves as the price of material reparation and public recognition." Povinelli imagines possibilities for justice through "an ongoing, critically oriented search for a better social life," rather than in terms of freedom or liberal agency; like Tully, she suggests that liberalism's idioms have continued to facilitate, rather than challenge, subjugation (2006, pp. 160, 163).

Duncan Ivison's *Postcolonial Liberalism* (2002) attempts to salvage and reform liberalism in response to such critiques. Ivison too draws on aboriginal laws, politics, and practices, if from an explicitly nonindigenous perspective. He is animated by kindred aims of "crafting a conceptual and discursive framework within which the argument between indigenous and non-indigenous people can be carried out on a more satisfactory footing" (p. 1). He imagines a "postcolonial liberal order" created out of the interactions between liberal constitutional structures and languages (rights, public reason, the idea of a modus vivendi) and avowedly indigenous political thought, as in the work of scholars and activists such as Taiaiake Alfred (1999) and Noel Pearson (2009), as well as indigenous practices of self-governance and land use. Given the supremacy of liberal discourse in the Anglo-American settler societies in question, it is perhaps inevitable that struggles for accommodation and coexistence will continue to take place substantially in and on liberal terms, as Tully, Povinelli (who describes her general project as a "critical theory of late liberalism"), and Ivison from their different positions within or outside liberalism all suggest. Whether liberalism retains emancipatory possibilities in the current global order, or whether its persistent limitations – perhaps, above all, its potential blindness to the ways in which liberal languages and practices mask operations of power as well as blindness to the provinciality and partiality of liberal commitments – should be explored are questions that should continue to occupy these debates at a theoretical level, while their participants engage as well with questions of contemporary politics and policy.

EMPIRE, NEO-LIBERALISM, AND THE LIBERAL STATE SINCE 2001

The mutual constitution of liberalism and empire, a subject of both history of political thought and postcolonial studies, has, along with the subject of empire more broadly, received exponentially greater attention since 2001, when the frank militarism and unilateralism of the Bush administration provoked a deluge of analyses of the category of empire and of the imperial nature of the American polity and the global order (Harvey 2003, Mann 2003, Khalidi 2004, Maier 2006, Hobsbawm 2008). The United States has been subject to steady criticism as an imperial power from the mid-nineteenth century on, and especially after the seizure of Cuba and the Philippines in the Spanish-American War; since decolonization in the 1950s and 1960s, critics on the left have regarded the global order more broadly as persistently imperial. And yet, except during the Vietnam War, these arguments were little taken up by broader scholarly and public debates. To those who have long analyzed global politics through the lens of empire, whether from postcolonial or Marxist or other perspectives, the spate of literature on American empire produced since 2001 often seems to misrecognize the phenomenon, to see novelty and exception in the American case where students of empire perceive reiterations of older patterns and tropes, or conversely, to seek too simple lessons from past empires (Calhoun et al. 2006, Tully 2008).

While some authors who have asked what lessons past empires may hold for America insist on their agnosticism regarding the desirability of American empire (Porter 2006), others have unabashedly and notoriously

called for America to acknowledge and embrace its imperial vocation and
to learn from the supposed successes as well as the weaknesses of past
models, above all the British Empire, in order to establish a duly liberal
or humanitarian empire (Ferguson 2003 and 2004, Ignatieff 2003, Lal
2004). Even as George W. Bush was protesting that "[w]e have no desire
to dominate, no ambitions of *empire*" (Bush 2004), these authors insisted
that America should accept, even embrace, its imperial power, which
they portrayed as inevitable (also see James 2006). In Ferguson's upbeat
account, the British Empire entrenched free trade, facilitated capital
export to the developing world, pioneered free labor, invested "immense
sums" in a global communications network, maintained an unequaled
global peace, and saved the world from fascism. The intense criticism the
book has prompted is partly a response to the shallowness and partiality of these historical claims. Despite occasional mention of episodes of
imperial brutality, Ferguson largely fails to address the British Empire's
systematic injuries: massive resource extraction, establishment of catastrophic systems of bonded labor, deindustrialization, entrenchment of
traditional structures of authority, and insertion of subsistence farmers
into often wildly unstable global market systems. Accounts of such phenomena need not deny, if motives matter at all, that imperial motives may
sometimes include good-faith intentions to bring stability and well-being
to the receiving populations. But myths of empire's benevolent effects,
particularly those of the British, have long demanded scrutiny. Recent
work has exposed the violence and death unleashed by the British, as in
the Indian and African famines and epidemics during what have been
called "late Victorian holocausts," or the British "gulag" in Kenya during the Mau Mau uprising (Davis 2001, Elkins 2005). Moreover, Fred
Cooper has argued, against myths of improving empire, that policies of
making colonies pay for themselves ("pay the costs of their own repression") and of relying on local elites to do the "dirty work" meant that
both the British and French empires largely eschewed development programs until belated efforts were made in the 1940s and 1950s to generate legitimacy for their rule. And when the French Empire's rhetoric of
inclusion was taken up by its African subjects in demands for full citizenship and economic equality after the Second World War, the French
government chose decolonization instead (Cooper 2005a, pp. 228–230,
Cooper 2006, p. 67).

A persistent failing of both imperial civilizing missions and their heirs
among "development" projects has been to see locals as objects for administration rather than as political subjects. Reformers with indifference to

local knowledge or contempt for the intellectual or political maturity of the intended beneficiaries of their projects can wreak economic and social havoc out of ignorance. When these failings are combined with other systematic vices of imperial rule – unaccountability to the subjects of power, policies driven partly by economic interests rooted in the metropole – the results of proletarianization, emiseration, chaos, and misrule have been frequently and predictably catastrophic. The same might be said of the American occupation in Iraq. A combination of overwhelming and unaccountable power, opportunism by private corporations, and abysmal planning caused by inattention and indifference have produced a landscape of perhaps irremediable misery and violence. Unaccountable imperial rule, as its eighteenth-century critics such as Burke well knew, is far more capable of destruction than of productive power.

Defenses of America's imperial presence as a vocation have tended to share a jaunty and even cynical tone combined with gestures at the "tragic" nature of imperial power. Michael Ignatieff's brief for "empire lite," characteristically of this literature, casts the United States as passive and vulnerable, a state "caught in the crossfire of a civil war raging within the Arab world," one that only belatedly "discovered" that its Middle Eastern allies were despotic or incompetent and that, sadly, is "damned if it does and damned if it doesn't" (Ignatieff 2003, pp. 8–9). Ignatieff ignores America's complicity in the creation of disorder and despotism in the Middle East, its history, in Rashid Khalidi's words, of "sowing crisis" (Johnson 2004, Mamdani 2004, Khalidi 2009). Key moments in this history include American and British sponsorship of the coup against Mossadegh in Iran in 1953 (Kinzer 2003 and 2006); support for authoritarian regimes such as that of Saudi Arabia throughout the post–World War II period; and proxy wars, as in Afghanistan in the late 1970s and 1980s, in which the United States armed the mujahideen fighting the Soviet-backed government. Ignatieff repeatedly describes the American empire's "enemies" as *the barbarians*, the absence of quotation marks around that loaded phrase leaving the reader in doubt as to whether he is quietly mocking those who think in such terms or uncritically adopting them himself. His larger purpose is to school the United States in the appropriate use of imperial power even as he expresses the moral anguish that he and Ferguson agree is characteristic of liberalism and so constitutive of liberal empire. As Jeanne Morefield has argued in an acute critique, Ignatieff's performance of anguish is cathartic rather than critical (Morefield 2008).

A particularly powerful volume of essays by scholars of empire questions this eye-catching literature's premise of seeking affirmative lessons *for* empire and instead proposes a critical investigation of the lessons to be learned *from* empires, as well as those lessons that have been learned *by* empires, asking what a critical anti-imperialism might mean today (Steinmetz in Calhoun 2006, pp. 139–140). Features widely assumed to distinguish the idiosyncratic American "empire" from its supposedly more typical predecessors turn out to be persistent, even ubiquitous imperial topoi. Among these are the self-reflexive quality of public debates in imperial polities, which have repeatedly dwelled on the questions "Are we an empire?," "What does it mean for us to be, or to have, an empire?," and "What does it mean to be the citizen of an empire?" When, during the notorious Don Pacifico affair in 1850, Lord Palmerston defended an aggressive British foreign policy with reference to the Roman tag "*Civis Romanus sum*," he was conjuring a vision of the British subject as one who could invoke the protection of the British state anywhere in the world and depicting Britain as an island of "liberty" and "order," but an island with global reach in a world of anarchy and insecurity (Palmerston 1850). Although the actions his speech defended were widely criticized as rash and provocative, his image of the imperial subject proved highly influential and is echoed today in American preoccupations with ensuring the security of the "homeland" through a global military presence.

The imperial self-scrutiny so characteristic of recent U.S. debates has also appeared in a number of Europe's old imperial powers, now reckoning with increased migration by inhabitants of their former colonies. Particularly fierce debates have raged in France, whose postcolonial reckoning comes very belatedly in comparison to Anglophone debates, despite iconic theorizations of empire during the period of decolonization by thinkers such as Fanon, Césaire, Memmi, and Sartre (Forsdick and Murphy 2003, Blanchard et al. 2005, Smouts 2007). This renewed attention comes in the wake of riots and police violence in the *banlieues*, spawned by poverty and social and economic exclusion among Muslims of North African origin, and following protracted controversy about whether the *foulard* or headscarf worn in public spaces such as schools violates the distinct French form of secularism known as *laïcité*. Scrutiny of the Algerian War, prompted in part by the aging of those who fought it (French and the pro-French Algerian soldiers known as *harkis*), have also contributed to this new literature. Scholars writing in both French and English have also produced sophisticated reinterpretations of slavery and abolition in the French colonies (Vergès 1999 and 2001, Dubois 2004).

GLOBALIZATION, COSMOPOLITANISM, AND GLOBAL JUSTICE

The dominant political theory literatures on cosmopolitanism and global justice have only glancingly and sporadically engaged with conceptual and historical continuities between formal imperialism and the current global (dis)order. Rawls's *Law of Peoples* (1999), which, like his *Theory of Justice* (1971), has spawned a large and often critical literature, is relatively indifferent to the history of Western domination and expropriation that contributed to the stratification of the world into, in his terms, "liberal" peoples (or those that aspire to or approximate liberal principles) and "rogue" states and "burdened" societies. With Rawls, the literature on contemporary cosmopolitanism has tended to ask how liberal states and societies should respond to the pathologies they encounter out there, and how they might intervene to promote democracy, rather than taking the prosperous and relatively stable societies of the global North and the impoverished and too often authoritarian states of the global South as products of the same long history of asymmetrical interaction and mutual constitution (e.g., Archibugi 2008; but see Pogge 2002). One might instead ask, with Iris Marion Young, how actors throughout the international system participate together in "structural injustice" and how they (we) might responsibly take ownership of such injustice (Young 2007).

Although the argument is not common among political theorists, even within the extensive literature on global justice, there is a powerful case to be made that the structural inequalities of the contemporary world cannot be understood without attention to their continuities, both historical and conceptual, with the major colonial empires. We should attend to the claim that "what passes for fair trade is neocolonial in structure and therefore exploitative in the extreme" (Harvey 2009, p. 46). One recent effort within the global justice literature seeks to take account of the colonial past by arguing that past colonial ties are a form of "associative relation" akin to common political membership, one that generates obligations of distributive justice well beyond duties of rectification for colonial wrongs (Ypi, Goodin, and Barry 2009).

James Tully has offered one of the latest and most fully articulated accounts in political theory of the imperial features of the current global order, what he calls an "informal and interactive" and "post-colonial" imperialism. The dismantling of formal empires, he notes, left in place "nominally sovereign, yet dependent Indigenous governments in a global

network of free trade imperialism" dominated by hegemonic great powers and their transnational corporations and governed through biased or
lopsided global financial institutions (Tully 2009, 2, p. 196). He argues
that our languages of political description are themselves imperial legacies (p. 130), so that the work of critique requires a thorough revisiting
of our theoretical categories and vocabularies. As Tully notes, mainstream political theory has tended to presume that imperialism ended
with decolonization and that the world after decolonization conforms to
a Westphalian model of a world of legally equal and independent states.
While the pervasive sense that Bush administration policies constituted a
new American empire has shaken this complacency, theoretical innovations of the sort Tully proposes remain rare. Tully's approach – which
aspires to a "new public philosophy for a [to be hoped for] de-imperi-
alising age" (p. 7) – draws on and responds to large literatures in cognate fields including anthropology, international law, and, more generally,
what always controversially goes under the name of "postcolonial studies," that have begun to undertake this theoretical work.

INTERNATIONAL LAW

Historians of international law have recently grappled with conceptual
and historical questions that parallel those preoccupying the scholarship
on liberalism or universalism and empire: Are the categories and formally
equal rules of the system of international law irredeemably bound up
with substantive inequality and European domination, or might they also
offer a means by which to combat that domination? In what ways are
international law's origins imperial, and to what extent has it been complicit with, or helped to legitimate, imperialism? How have legal practices
and imaginations – within Europe and the global North, in colonies and
postcolonial states, and transnationally – been bound up with the exercise
of imperial power and the construction of imperial sovereignty? As the
influential theorist of international law Martti Koskenniemi has argued,
there is reason to see international law as both "imperialist [and] anti-
imperialist": "sovereignty and international governance seem both good
and bad, liberating and threatening at the same time: neither provides a
recipe against domination" (2002, p. 198; also see 2001). Still, despite
what he sees as international law's theoretical ambivalence, Koskenniemi,
like many other recent scholars, has been concerned to demonstrate the
extent to which, as a historical matter, especially since the formative

period of the 1870s, it has been deeply complicit in European domination of the rest of the world.

A group of scholars known as TWAIL (Third World Approaches to International Law) has recently taken up the project, launched in the 1950s and 1960s among lawyers of the so-called new states after decolonization, of scrutinizing the ways in which the politics, practice, and scholarship of mainstream international law reproduce structures of global inequality and the subordination of third world peoples (Anghie et al. 2003). Antony Anghie's important book explores persistent patterns of exploitation in legal relations between Western and non-Western polities, from the fifteenth century to the present, under the rubric of the "dynamic of difference" (2004, p. 6; echoing Partha Chatterjee's notion of a "rule of colonial difference" [1986]; also see Burbank and Cooper 2010). Anghie argues that "sovereignty was improvised out of the colonial encounter." Relations of domination over non-Europeans, that is, were central to the formation of the system of international law, and not peripheral or irrelevant to a fundamentally European phenomenon. This argument constitutes a powerful rebuke to the standard understanding in legal scholarship since the nineteenth century that international law evolved through relations among sovereign European states and was then exported outside Europe as other states entered the family of nations (whether as they became civilized or as they attained statehood through decolonization). Contrary to the conventional view that decolonization marked the end of formal and legal inequalities (see, e.g., Jackson 1990), Anghie shows how international law has perpetuated the quasi-sovereign status of third world states, for instance through prejudicial rules governing natural resource extraction and agreements with multinational corporations (also see Miéville 2005).

The implications of such a revision are profound: debates over humanitarian intervention, for instance, share the assumption that such interventions constitute a rupture in a status quo of nonintervention and sovereign equality and that the challenge is to balance our respect for state sovereignty with a commitment to human rights. If we grasp the extent to which the sovereignty of third world states is always already deeply compromised through laws, institutions, and practices dominated by the great powers, our understanding of the challenges of intervention may radically change. This is certainly not to say that because various forms of intervention are already the norm, powerful states should be given the green light to intervene militarily whenever they see fit. But it is to argue that the choice between continuing to respect sovereignty or protecting human rights is a false one, that the world's powerful states bear considerable responsibility for the conditions producing the violence against which they then seek to intervene, and that if we want to protect the values of both political autonomy and human rights, we will subject the profound global inequalities and asymmetries of power to far greater scrutiny than they generally receive in debates over global justice. We will also, as Anne Orford urges, greatly expand the temporal frame in which we consider intervention, to consider not just the immediate crisis but also the widely shared responsibility for the broader conditions such as extreme poverty, a surfeit of weapons, and ecological crises that help to generate civil conflict, tyranny, and genocide (Orford 2003).

Recent literature has likewise undermined the "Westphalian myth" that the 1648 treaties established a narrowly European law of nations governing equal and independent sovereign states (Teschke 2003, Beaulac 2004). As Tully puts the point, "[t]he so-called Westphalian system is actually an imperial system of hegemonic and subaltern states constructed in the course of 'interactions' between imperial actors and imperialized collaborators and resisters" (Tully 2009, 2 p. 140). Much international relations theory and political theory more broadly continues to operate with a fairly reductive Westphalian image of legally equal and independent nation states, to pose the question of global justice as a conundrum about the tensions between sovereignty and human rights (principles recognized in the United Nations Charter). It tends to ask how liberal democracies should respond to violations "out there" by others not yet incorporated into the liberal global order, whereas revisionist accounts of the global legal order instead position global poverty, human rights violations, and other forms of subordination squarely as products of an imperial system (Rajagopal 2003, Falk et al. 2008). As we have seen, the standard view that regards imperialism as primarily a political relationship often assumes that decolonization ended imperial relations. On the Marxist view, in which imperialism denotes not primarily political but economic relations, formal decolonization simply marked an evolution in the forms of domination, for which Kwame Nkrumah coined the term "neo-colonialism" (Marks 2003, p. 452). Rereadings of international law through Marxist lenses have offered pointed criticism of recent strategies such as "good governance," structural adjustment, and conditionality (the imposition of conditions such as austerity or privatization regimes on developing countries for receipt of loans, development aid, or debt relief), by which international institutions controlled by dominant powers constrain third world and debtor countries to conform to economic and public policies that make them more amenable to the incursion of global capital (Marks 2003).

A vital new literature has examined broader intersections of law and empire, ranging from Rome; to the influence that Roman legal practices regarding war and conquest, though often ill understood, had on later empires (on that influence, see Lupher 2003, MacMillan 2006, MacCormack 2007); to the imperial traces in the early American constitutions (Bilder 2004, Hulsebosch 2005); to the importance for colonial conquest of the power to shape the legal frameworks governing land ownership (Banner 2005). As Clifford Ando has shown, Roman civil law was shot through with imperial language and categories; and the "languages and institutions of [Roman] Republicanism" – including citizenship itself, even as it was extended to provincials – were to a striking extent "developed in support of monarchical rule and imperial domination" (Ando 2008, 2010).

The circulation and translation of international law beyond modern Europe has also begun to receive sophisticated treatment, as in the literary critic Lydia Liu's account of Anglo-Chinese treaty relations and disputes over the nature of sovereignty (2004). Lauren Benton's pathbreaking *Law and Colonial Cultures* (2001) argued that the struggles of often peripheral actors in the plural legal spaces formed within and between empires – from British courts exercising jurisdiction in Mughal India to struggles over land title on the Uruguayan frontier – were central to the formation of the colonial state. It is to be followed by a study that further explores the porousness and irregularity of sovereignty in empire and by implication in European state formation, as a corrective to the traditional picture of sovereignty as above all territorial control (Benton 2009). Benton has insisted that we can only understand imperial law by attending to the actions of participants on the ground and at sea, as much as to the theoretical writings of the canonical jurists. She and others have begun to paint a far more variegated portrait of the discourses of political and legal theory deployed in the construction and defense of empires than has been available via the more elevated sources.

THEORIZING EMPIRE AS A POLITICAL SYSTEM

The fluidity and multifariousness of empires might furnish an object of study for political theory more than it has done. One fruitful course is taken by (the historian) Charles Maier's *Among Empires* (2006), which uses the question of American empire as an occasion for a broad analysis of imperial power and its characteristic forms, techniques, and dilemmas. Maier stresses the ways in which empires entrench and reproduce inequalities of power and wealth both among societies and within both metropole and colony, and the dynamics of social stratification such as the recruitment of elites in conquered societies or the cooptation of the subordinate classes in the metropole. While Maier's own analysis rightly takes account of the wide variety of imperial forms (noting, for instance, that distinctions between empire and hegemony are not very robust [pp. 62–64]), empires are too often treated as well-demarcated territorial entities on the model of nation-states with clear boundaries. As Ann Stoler has argued against the standard portrait, "architects of imperial rule," far from seeking to clarify borders and establish order, have often "invested in [and] exploited" the proliferation of "zones of ambiguity." Analysis should perhaps begin, she suggests, "not with a model of empire based on fixed, imperial cartographies" but instead with the recognition that "gradated variations and degrees of sovereignty and disenfranchisement" are typical, even definitive, of empire: from dependencies, protectorates, trusteeships, and mandates to the ambiguous status of Guantanamo Bay or American Samoa today (Stoler 2006, pp. 55–56). Legally and politically ill-defined or shifting spaces – places of partial, compromised, or vulnerable sovereignty; people with vague or unstable legal rights – are not a recent innovation or a derogation from some neater classical territorial form of empire with inhabitants sharply divided into rulers and ruled. Empires create and cultivate a variety of forms of political belonging, sometimes, as Clifford Ando puts it, "coopting local elites into (often derivative and defective) forms of membership and so alienating them in some fashion from the affective structures that might have tied them to their communities" (Ando, personal communication; also see Ando 2000).

If empires have often been analyzed in terms set by the nation-state, they have also too often been cast into a teleological history in which the imperial form precedes that of the nation-state and grows increasingly atavistic with the triumph of the nation-state model. Some scholars of historical empires have noted the resilience of imperial forms and suggested that the nation-state model, rather than representing the end of a historical trajectory, may prove remarkably ephemeral.

A further strand of debate has concerned the capacities of imperial power; some British historians especially have stressed the vulnerability and limitedness of British power even during the imperial heyday

(Colley 2002). If such accounts are right to insist that imperial states could not effectively project affirmative power very deeply into colonized societies, they sometimes appear to minimize the European empires' great capacity for destruction and their repeated tendency to wreak havoc in colonized societies – to deindustrialize them, render them less self-sufficient, emiserate rural populations, encourage famine, and truncate life expectancy – whether in deliberate campaigns of terror (Hochschild 1998, Elkins 2005) or through unaccountability and indifference to the welfare of local populations (Davis 2001). Debates have tended to suggest that empires are powerful versus powerless, rather than showing that they are powerless in certain ways but nonetheless capable of effecting dramatic and generally destructive change. The connections between imperial forms of power and the disruption of sustainable social systems merit further study.

Typical of imperial politics is a fascination with historical models, a concern to compare contemporary politics with previous empires and to insist on the newness, and, among modern European empires, the unprecedented benevolence and universalism, of the current imperial polity. Recent claims that the United States has inherited the challenges and opportunities of the British Empire might be seen as a modern version of the medieval *translatio imperii*, in which empires laid claim to the inherited authority of the Roman Empire (Pagden 1995). Sheldon Pollack has argued that the comparative history of empires, ancient and modern, and around the globe, shows that "it is only by looking at past empires that people have learned how to be imperial at all, since empire is a cultural practice and not some natural state" (Pollock 2006, p. 176). Indeed, central to the lives of all empires have been the ways in which they have been constituted through language and their own self-representations: the discourses that have arisen to describe, defend, and criticize them and the historical narratives that have been invoked to make sense of them. Ann Stoler notes that "[c]olonial empires were always dependent on social imaginaries, blueprints unrealized, borders never drawn, administrative categories of people and territories to which no one was sure who or what should belong" (Stoler 2006, p. 52). Scholars attempting a critical anti-imperialism have addressed not simply questions of which institutions can be considered imperial, but also the "discursive features" of empire: the "ceremonial trappings of U.S. power" or the militarization of the culture, such as the civilian fad for Humvees in the United States and the increasing presence of military recruiters and ROTC programs in high schools and universities (Steinmetz in Calhoun 2006, p. 139).

Students of empire and imperial histories are well placed to analyze such practices, beyond explicit talk of empire, that are also constitutive of imperial politics.

AFTER POSTCOLONIAL STUDIES

We have noted the vast influence of Said's *Orientalism* on literature and history; a distinct strand of postcolonial studies is subaltern studies, which began among South Asian historians in the 1980s (though key participants such as Ranajit Guha had been active since the 1960s), and of which it has been said that "no group has done more, by exhortation and practice, to stimulate research on colonial history" (Cooper 2005b, p. 419 n14). Political theory as a discipline has engaged only sporadically and belatedly with postcolonial studies; it is telling, for instance, that a volume on *Postcolonialism and Political Theory* was published only recently (Persram 2007). One of the most influential recent contributions of postcolonial thought has been the notion of "alternative modernities," an idea broached most pointedly by Dipesh Chakrabarty's *Provincializing Europe* (2000), and which has been taken up by theorists not usually attentive to questions of empire (see, for instance, Taylor 2004). Chakrabarty argues that European thought "is at once both indispensable and inadequate in helping us to think through the experiences of political modernity in non-Western nations" (2000, p. 16).

The field of postcolonial studies has itself recently undergone a new period of self-criticism and stock-taking in which scholars and critics have increasingly asked whether postcolonial studies as an intellectual movement has begun to "outlive [its] critical or political usefulness" (Loomba et al. 2005, p. 2) or whether, with its increasing theoretical sophistication and methodization, it has lost its critical purchase. A "familiar complaint" charges that "the postcolonial agenda is unduly set by Third World intellectuals who have emigrated to the First World, where they have adjusted to the workings of global capitalism"; a related charge has been that it is too much oriented to the needs and preoccupations of "Western theory" (Darby 2007, pp. 252–253). Postcolonial studies has arguably reached a juncture when the need to interrogate globalization's egregious structural injustices and their ideological supports remains as pressing as ever but postcolonial studies' historical emphasis on the decolonization of discourses – rather than on more direct forms of political critique, or criticism of global capitalism's exploitations – has come to seem inadequate to many. David Scott has identified the present as a transitional moment, "after postcoloniality," a moment that follows the periods of anticolonial nationalism and then postcolonial criticism and that demands a reorientation of the critical agenda: "With the collapse of the Bandung and socialist projects and with the new hegemony of a neoliberal globalization, it is no longer clear what 'overcoming' Western power actually means" (Scott 1999, p. 14). While the blatant American imperialism of the new millennium meant a return of some more blatant forms of Western power, Scott's questions about what postcolonial critique of neo-liberal hegemony should entail remain pressing. One particularly potent strand of new research challenges the limited neo-liberal models of democracy and civil society "on offer by the global leadership," as well as "the global politics of why societies should democratize" (Darby 2007, p. 256; Marks 2003 makes a similar argument). Lisa Wedeen's exploration of democratic practices and public spheres in authoritarian states, such as the deliberations and political contestations that occur in *qat chew* gatherings in Yemen, exemplifies such a challenge to the dominant, and reductive, models of democracy in political science and global policy circles (Wedeen 2008).

If political theory has been a late and muted voice in the postcolonial conversation, Scott (though, significantly, located in anthropology) offers another compelling model for its possible contribution. His work is informed by diverse influences including those of Foucault, Quentin Skinner, Reinhart Koselleck, Ian Hacking, and Hayden White. Scott combines a searching attention to what may be the critical demands of the present (e.g., the disaffection around sovereignty in the post-Bandung period) with a deeply informed historical sense of the myriad political and intellectual contexts of the works he engages, such as C. L. R. James's seminal text of anticolonial history, *The Black Jacobins* (1989 [1963]). Scott's *Conscripts of Modernity* (2004) exemplifies the continued vitality and critical potential of the kind of work that political theory might be said to be well equipped to perform: textual analysis that is theoretically incisive; attentive to social, cultural, and intellectual history and the ways in which these strands of history can inform each other; and engaged with the political dilemmas and critical demands, and responsive to the profound injustices, of the present. Such work is attuned to the continuities both historical and theoretical among different forms of imperial rule, but it avoids teleologies, whether triumphalist or declinist.

In the years after 2001, many scholars of empire noted how unaccustomed they were to the intense public, and even the broader scholarly, interest in their subject. Until then, many outside postcolonial studies had come to see empire as an archaic subject, even if others had all along insisted that formal decolonization in much of the world had neither vanquished imperial relations and politics nor rendered empire obsolete as an analytical framework. Some observers have been prepared to consider the danger of American imperialism over with the end of the distinctive form it took under the Bush administration, and they perhaps will have lost interest in the subject (Mann 2003, pp. 12–14, who hopes for "voluntary abandonment of the imperial project by Americans"; see Tully 2008, 2, p. 134). But the wider scrutiny of questions about empire, the renewed interest by those outside postcolonial studies in what was once considered by many an abstruse conversation that had run its course, and the revivified interest in the histories and legacies of the formal empires of the past will leave their mark. These developments have generated a fertile interdisciplinary exchange that should help to deepen and enliven political theory's hitherto sporadic conversations with precisely those cognate fields with which it shares so much intellectual labor and should be in closer, and ongoing, dialogue.

Works Cited

Adelman J. 2006. *Sovereignty and Revolution in the Iberian Atlantic.* Princeton, N.J.: Princeton University Press.

Agnani S. M. 2004. *Enlightenment Universalism and Colonial Knowledge: Denis Diderot and Edmund Burke, 1770–1800.* New York: Columbia University dissertation.

Alfred T. 1999. *Peace, Power, Righteousness: An Indigenous Manifesto.* Don Mills, Ontario: Oxford University Press.

Ando C. 2000. *Imperial Ideology and Provincial Loyalty in the Roman Empire.* Berkeley: University of California Press.

    2008. "Aliens, Ambassadors, and the Integrity of the Empire." *Law and History Review,* 26, 491–519.

    2010. "'A Dwelling Beyond Violence': On the Uses and Disadvantages of History for Contemporary Republicans." *History of Political Thought,* 31, 183–220.

Anghie A. 2003. *The Third World and International Order: Law, Politics, and Globalization.* Leiden: Brill Academic.

    2004. *Imperialism, Sovereignty and the Making of International Law.* Cambridge: Cambridge University Press.

Archibugi D. 2008. *The Global Commonwealth of Citizens: Toward Cosmopolitan Democracy.* Princeton, N.J.: Princeton University Press.

Armitage D. 2000. *The Ideological Origins of the British Empire.* Cambridge: Cambridge University Press.

    2004a. "The Fifty Years' Rift: Intellectual History and International Relations." *Modern Intellectual History,* 1, 97–109.

2004b. "John Locke, Carolina, and the *Two Treatises of Government.*" *Political Theory*, 32, 602–627.

Arneil B. 1996. *John Locke and America: The Defence of English Colonialism.* Oxford: Clarendon Press.

Asad T. 1975. *Anthropology and the Colonial Encounter.* London: Ithaca Press; Atlantic Highlands, N.J.: Humanities Press.

Banner S. 2005. *How the Indians Lost Their Land: Law and Power on the Frontier.* Cambridge, Mass.: Belknap Press of Harvard University Press.

2007. *Possessing the Pacific: Land, Settlers, and Indigenous People from Australia to Alaska.* Cambridge, Mass.: Harvard University Press.

Bayly C. A. 1989. *Imperial Meridian: The British Empire and the World, 1780–1830.* London and New York: Longman.

2004. *The Birth of the Modern World, 1780–1914: Global Connections and Comparisons.* Malden, Mass.: Blackwell.

2007. "Rammohun Roy and the Advent of Constitutional Liberalism in India, 1800–30." *Modern Intellectual History*, 4.

Beaulac S. 2004. *The Power of Language in the Making of International Law: The Word Sovereignty in Bodin and Vattel and the Myth of Westphalia.* Leiden and Boston: Martinus Nijhoff.

Bell D. 2007a. *The Idea of Greater Britain: Empire and the Future of World Order, 1860–1900.* Princeton, N.J.: Princeton University Press.

2007b. *Victorian Visions of Global Order: Empire and International Relations in Nineteenth-Century Political Thought.* Cambridge: Cambridge University Press.

2010. "John Stuart Mill on Colonies." *Political Theory*, 38, 1–31.

Benton L. 2001. *Law and Colonial Cultures: Legal Regimes in World History, 1400–1900.* Cambridge: Cambridge University Press.

2009. *A Search for Sovereignty: Law and Geography in European Empires, 1400–1900.* Cambridge: Cambridge University Press.

Benton L., Straumann B. 2010. "Acquiring Empire by Law: From Roman Doctrine to Early Modern European Practice." *Law and History Review*, 28, 1–38.

Berlin I. 1965. "The Thought of de Tocqueville" (review of *The Social and Political Thought of Alexis de Tocqueville*, by J. Lively). *History*, 50, 199–206.

Bilder M. S. 2004. *The Transatlantic Constitution: Colonial Legal Culture and the Empire.* Cambridge, Mass.: Harvard University Press.

Blackhawk N. 2006. *Violence Over the Land: Indians and Empires in the Early American West.* Cambridge, Mass.: Harvard University Press.

Blanchard P., Bancel N., Lemaire S. 2005. *La fracture coloniale: la société française au prisme de l'héritage colonial.* Paris: La Découverte.

Borschberg P. 2002. "The Seizure of the Sta. Catarina Revisited: The Portuguese Empire in Asia, VOC Politics and the Origins of the Dutch-Johor Alliance (1602–c.1616)." *Journal of Southeast Asian Studies*, 33, 31–62.

Bourke R. 2007. "Edmund Burke and the Politics of Conquest." *Modern Intellectual History*, 4, 403–432.

Brown W. 2005. *Edgework: Critical Essays on Knowledge and Politics.* Princeton, N.J.: Princeton University Press.

Burbank J., Cooper F. 2010. *Empires in World History*. Princeton, N.J.: Princeton University Press.

Burbank J., Von Hagen M., Remnev A. V. 2007. *Russian Empire: Space, People, Power, 1700–1930*. Bloomington: Indiana University Press.

Burke E., Bromwich D. 2000. *On Empire, Liberty, and Reform: Speeches and Letters*. New Haven, Conn.: Yale University Press.

Burton A. 2006. "New Narratives of Imperial Politics in the Nineteenth Century." In *At Home with the Empire: Metropolitan Culture and the Imperial World*, ed. C. Hall and S. O. Rose. Cambridge: Cambridge University Press, pp. 212–229.

Burton A. M. 2003. *After the Imperial Turn: Thinking with and through the Nation*. Durham, N.C.: Duke University Press.

Bush G. W. 2004. Address Before a Joint Session of the Congress on the State of the Union. The American Presidency Project http://www.presidency.ucsb.edu/ws/index.php?pid=2964#axzzlpgKprvbp.

Calhoun C. J., Cooper F., Moore K. W., Social Science Research Council (U.S.). 2006. *Lessons of Empire: Imperial Histories and American Power*. New York: The New Press (distributed by W. W. Norton).

Cavallar G. 2002. *The Rights of Strangers: Theories of International Hospitality, the Global Community, and Political Justice since Vitoria*. Aldershot, Hants, England, and Burlington, Vt.: Ashgate.

Chakrabarty D. 2000. *Provincializing Europe: Postcolonial Thought and Historical Difference*. Princeton, N.J.: Princeton University Press.

Chatterjee P. 1986. *Nationalist Thought and the Colonial World: A Derivative Discourse?* London and Totowa, N.J.: Zed Books for the United Nations University (U.S. distributor: Biblio Distribution Center).

Claeys G. 2007. "The 'Left' and the Critique of Empire c. 1865–1900: Three Roots of Humanitarian Foreign Policy." In *Victorian Visions of Global Order*, ed. D. Bell. Cambridge: Cambridge University Press, pp. 239–266.

2010. *Imperial Sceptics: British Critics of Empire 1850–1920*. Cambridge: Cambridge University Press.

Clancy-Smith J. A. 1994. *Rebel and Saint: Muslim Notables, Populist Protest, Colonial Encounters (Algeria and Tunisia, 1800–1904)*. Berkeley: University of California Press.

Cohen J. 2004. "Whose Sovereignty? Empire versus International Law." *Ethics and International Affairs*, 18, 1–24.

Cohn B. S., American Council of Learned Societies. 1987. *An Anthropologist among the Historians and Other Essays*. Delhi and New York: Oxford University Press.

Colley L. 1992. *Britons: Forging the Nation, 1707–1837*. New Haven, Conn.: Yale University Press.

2002. *Captives: Britain, Empire and the World, 1600–1850*. London: Jonathan Cape.

Comaroff J., Comaroff J. L. 1991. *Of Revelation and Revolution*. Chicago: University of Chicago Press.

Comaroff J. L., Comaroff J. 2009. *Ethnicity, Inc.* Chicago: University of Chicago Press.

Conklin A. L. 1997. *A Mission to Civilize: The Republican Idea of Empire in France and West Africa, 1895–1930*. Stanford, Calif.: Stanford University Press.

Cooper F. 2005a. *Colonialism in Question: Theory, Knowledge, History*. Berkeley: University of California Press.

2005b. "Postcolonial Studies and the Study of History." In *Postcolonial Studies and Beyond*, ed. A. Loomba. Durham, N.C.: Duke University Press, pp. 401–422.

2006. "Modernizing Colonialism and the Limits of Empire." In *Lessons of Empire: Imperial Histories and American Power*, ed. C. Calhoun, F. Cooper, and K. W. Moore. New York: The New Press, pp. 63–72.

Cooper F., Stoler A. L. 1997. *Tensions of Empire: Colonial Cultures in a Bourgeois World*. Berkeley: University of California Press.

Curtin P. D. 1984. *Cross-Cultural Trade in World History*. Cambridge: Cambridge University Press.

2000. *The World and the West: The European Challenge and the Overseas Response in the Age of Empire*. Cambridge: Cambridge University Press.

Curtis M. 2009. *Orientalism and Islam: European Thinkers on Oriental Despotism in the Middle East and India*. Cambridge: Cambridge University Press.

Dallmayr F. R. 1999. *Border Crossings: Toward a Comparative Political Theory*. Lanham, Md.: Lexington Books.

2002. *Dialogue among Civilizations: Some Exemplary Voices*. New York: Palgrave Macmillan.

Darby P. 2007. "Doing the Postcolonial Differently." See Persram 2007, pp. 249–270.

Davis M. 2001. *Late Victorian Holocausts: El Niño Famines and the Making of the Third World*. London and New York: Verso.

Dietz M. 2007. "Between Polis and Empire: Aristotle's *Politics*." Presented at the annual meeting of the American Political Science Association, Chicago.

Dirks N. B. 1992. *Colonialism and Culture*. Ann Arbor: University of Michigan Press.

2001. "Postcolonialism and Its Discontents: History, Anthropology, and Postcolonial Critique." In *Schools of Thought: Twenty-Five Years of Interpretive Social Science*, ed. J. W. Scott and D. Keates. Princeton, N.J.: Princeton University Press, pp. 227–251.

2006. *The Scandal of Empire: India and the Creation of Imperial Britain*. Cambridge, Mass.: Belknap Press of Harvard University Press.

Doyle M. W. 1986. *Empires*. Ithaca, N.Y.: Cornell University Press.

Duara P. 2009. *The Global and the Regional in China's Nation-Formation*. New York: Routledge.

Dubois L. 2004. *A Colony of Citizens: Revolution and Slave Emancipation in the French Caribbean, 1787–1804*. Chapel Hill, N.C.: Published for the Omohundro Institute of Early American History and Culture, Williamsburg, Va., by the University of North Carolina Press.

Dussel E. D., Barber M. D. 1995. *The Invention of the Americas: Eclipse of "the Other" and the Myth of Modernity*. New York: Continuum.

Eley G. 2007. "Historicizing the Global, Politicizing Capital: Giving the Present a Name." *History Workshop Journal*, 63, 154–188.

Elkins C. 2005. *Imperial Reckoning: The Untold Story of Britain's Gulag in Kenya*. New York: Henry Holt.

Elkins C., Pedersen S. 2005. *Settler Colonialism in the Twentieth Century: Projects, Practices, Legacies*. New York: Routledge.

Euben R. L. 2006. *Journeys to the Other Shore: Muslim and Western Travelers in Search of Knowledge*. Princeton, N.J.: Princeton University Press.

Fabian J. 1983. *Time and the Other: How Anthropology Makes Its Object*. New York: Columbia University Press.

Falk R., Stevens J., Rajagopal B. 2008. *International Law and the Third World: Reshaping Justice*. London and New York: Routledge-Cavendish.

Farr J. 2008. "Locke, Natural Law, and New World Slavery." *Political Theory*, 36, 495–522.

Ferguson K. E., Mironesco M. 2008. *Gender and Globalization in Asia and the Pacific: Method, Practice, Theory*. Honolulu: University of Hawaii Press.

Ferguson N. 2003. *Empire: The Rise and Demise of the British World Order and the Lessons for Global Power*. New York: Basic Books.

2004. *Colossus: The Price of America's Empire*. New York: Penguin Press.

Festa L. M. 2006. *Sentimental Figures of Empire in Eighteenth-Century Britain and France*. Baltimore: Johns Hopkins University Press.

Fitzmaurice A. 2003. *Humanism and America: An Intellectual History of English Colonisation, 1500–1625*. Cambridge: Cambridge University Press.

2007. "The Genealogy of *terra nullius*." *Australian Historical Studies*, 129, 1–15.

Fitzpatrick M. P. 2008. *Liberal Imperialism in Germany: Expansionism and Nationalism, 1848–1884*. New York: Berghahn Books.

Forsdick C, Murphy D. 2003. *Francophone Postcolonial Studies: A Critical Introduction*. New York: Oxford University Press.

Geertz C. 1973. *The Interpretation of Cultures: Selected Essays*. New York: Basic Books.

Go J. 2008. *American Empire and the Politics of Meaning: Elite Political Cultures in the Philippines and Puerto Rico during U.S. Colonialism*. Durham, N.C.: Duke University Press.

Goodman D. 2001. "Difference: An Enlightenment Concept." In *What's Left of Enlightenment? A Postmodern Question*, ed. K. M Baker and P. H. Reill. Stanford, Calif.: Stanford University Press, pp. 129–147.

Gould E. H. 2000. *The Persistence of Empire: British Political Culture in the Age of the American Revolution*. Chapel Hill, N.C.: Published for the Omohundro Institute of Early American History and Culture, Williamsburg, Va., by the University of North Carolina Press.

Griffin P. 2007. *American Leviathan: Empire, Nation, and Revolutionary Frontier*. New York: Hill & Wang.

Grovogui S. N. Z. 1996. *Sovereigns, Quasi Sovereigns, and Africans: Race and Self-Determination in International Law*. Minneapolis: University of Minnesota Press.

Hall C. 2000. *Cultures of Empire: Colonizers in Britain and the Empire in the Nineteenth and Twentieth Centuries: A Reader.* New York: Routledge.
2002. *Civilising Subjects: Colony and Metropole in the English Imagination, 1830–1867.* Chicago: University of Chicago Press.
Hall C., Rose S. O. 2006. *At Home with the Empire: Metropolitan Culture and the Imperial World.* Cambridge: Cambridge University Press.
Hardt M., Negri A. 2000. *Empire.* Cambridge, Mass.: Harvard University Press.
2004. *Multitude: War and Democracy in the Age of Empire.* New York: Penguin Press.
Harvey D. 2003. *The New Imperialism.* Oxford: Oxford University Press.
2009. *Cosmopolitanism and the Geographies of Freedom.* New York: Columbia University Press.
Hevia J. 2003. *English Lessons: The Pedagogy of Imperialism in Nineteenth-Century China.* Durham, N.C.: Duke University Press.
Hobsbawm E. J. 2008. *On Empire: America, War, and Global Supremacy.* New York: Pantheon Books.
Hochschild A. 1998. *King Leopold's Ghost: A Story of Greed, Terror, and Heroism in Colonial Africa.* Boston: Houghton Mifflin.
Hörnqvist M. 2004. *Machiavelli and Empire.* Cambridge: Cambridge University Press.
Hulsebosch D. J. 2005. *Constituting Empire: New York and the Transformation of Constitutionalism in the Atlantic World, 1664–1830.* Chapel Hill: University of North Carolina Press.
Ignatieff M. 2003. *Empire Lite: Nation Building in Bosnia, Kosovo, Afghanistan.* London: Vintage Books.
Ivison D. 2002. *Postcolonial Liberalism.* Cambridge: Cambridge University Press.
Ivison D., Patton P., Sanders W. 2000. *Political Theory and the Rights of Indigenous Peoples.* Cambridge: Cambridge University Press.
Jackson R. H. 1990. *Quasi-States: Sovereignty, International Relations, and the Third World.* Cambridge: Cambridge University Press.
James C. L. R. 1989 (1963). *The Black Jacobins: Toussaint L'Ouverture and the San Domingo Revolution.* New York: Vintage Books.
James H. 2006. *The Roman Predicament: How the Rules of International Order Create the Politics of Empire.* Princeton, N.J.: Princeton University Press.
Johnson C. A. 2004. *The Sorrows of Empire: Militarism, Secrecy, and the End of the Republic.* New York: Metropolitan Books.
Keal P. 2003. *European Conquest and the Rights of Indigenous Peoples: The Moral Backwardness of International Society.* Cambridge: Cambridge University Press.
Keene E. 2002. *Beyond the Anarchical Society: Grotius, Colonialism and Order in World Politics.* Cambridge: Cambridge University Press.
Kelly D. 2009. *Lineages of Empire: The Historical Roots of British Imperial Thought.* Oxford: Oxford University Press.
Khalidi R. 2004. *Resurrecting Empire: Western Footprints and America's Perilous Path in the Middle East.* Boston: Beacon Press.

2009. *Sowing Crisis: The Cold War and American Dominance in the Middle East*. Boston: Beacon Press.

Kinzer S. 2003. *All the Shah's Men: An American Coup and the Roots of Middle East Terror*. Hoboken, N.J.: John Wiley & Sons.

2006. *Overthrow: America's Century of Regime Change from Hawaii to Iraq*. New York: Times Books.

Kohn M. 2008 (2006). "Colonialism." *Stanford Encyclopedia of Philosophy*, ed. E. N. Zalta. Available at http://plato.stanford.edu./archives/fall2008/entries/colonialism/.

2009. "Afghānī on Empire, Islam, and Civilization." *Political Theory*, 37, 398–422.

Kohn M., O'Neill D. 2006. "A Tale of Two Indias: Burke and Mill on Empire and Slavery in the West Indies and Americas." *Political Theory*, 34, 192–228.

Koskenniemi M. 2001. *Gentle Civilizer of Nations: The Rise and Fall of International Law 1870–1960*. Cambridge: Cambridge University Press.

2002. "International Law and Imperialism." In *Contemporary Issues in International Law*, ed. D. Freeston, S. Subedi, and S. Davidson. The Hague and New York: Kluwer Law International, pp. 197–218.

Kramer P. 2006. *The Blood of Government: Race, Empire, the United States, and the Philippines*. Chapel Hill: University of North Carolina Press.

Lal D. 2004. *In Praise of Empires: Globalization and Order*. New York: Palgrave Macmillan.

Le Cour Grandmaison O. 2005. *Coloniser, exterminer: sur la guerre et l'état colonial*. Paris: Fayard.

Lebovics H. 2004. *Bringing the Empire Back Home: France in the Global Age*. Durham, N.C.: Duke University Press.

2006. *Imperialism and the Corruption of Democracies*. Durham, N.C.: Duke University Press.

Lieven D. C. B. 2000. *Empire: The Russian Empire and Its Rivals*. London: John Murray.

Liu L. H. 2004. *The Clash of Empires: The Invention of China in Modern World Making*. Cambridge, Mass.: Harvard University Press.

Loomba A., Kaul S., Bunzl M., Burton A., Esty J. 2005. *Postcolonial Studies and Beyond*. Durham, N.C.: Duke University Press.

Lupher D. A. 2003. *Romans in a New World: Classical Models in Sixteenth-Century Spanish America*. Ann Arbor: University of Michigan Press.

MacCormack S. 2007. *On the Wings of Time: Rome, the Incas, Spain, and Peru*. Princeton, N.J.: Princeton University Press.

MacMillan K. 2006. *Sovereignty and Possession in the English New World: The Legal Foundations of Empire, 1576–1640*. Cambridge: Cambridge University Press.

Maier C. S. 2006. *Among Empires: American Ascendancy and Its Predecessors*. Cambridge, Mass.: Harvard University Press.

Malcolm N. 2002. "Hobbes, Sandys, and the Virginia Company." In *Aspects of Hobbes*. Oxford: Clarendon Press, pp. 53–79.

Mamdani M. 2004. *Good Muslim, Bad Muslim: America, the Cold War, and the Roots of Terror*. New York: Pantheon Books.

Mann M. 2003. *Incoherent Empire*. London and New York: Verso.

Manning S., Cogliano F. D.. 2006. *The Atlantic Enlightenment*. Aldershot, UK: Ashgate.

Mantena K. 2007. "Mill and the Imperial Predicament." In *J. S. Mill's Political Thought*, ed. N. Urbinati and A. Zakaras. Cambridge: Cambridge University Press, pp. 298–318.

2010. *Alibis of Empire*. Princeton, N.J.: Princeton University Press.

Markell P. 2008. "The Insufficiency of Non-Domination." *Political Theory*, 36, 9–36.

Marks S. 2000. *The Riddle of All Constitutions: International Law, Democracy, and the Critique of Ideology*. Oxford: Oxford University Press.

2003. "Empire's Law." *Indiana Journal of Global Legal Studies*, 10, 449–466.

Marx K., Avineri S. 1968. *Karl Marx on Colonialism and Modernization; His Despatches [sic] and Other Writings on China, India, Mexico, the Middle East and North Africa*. Garden City, N.Y.: Doubleday.

Mazower M. 2008. *Hitler's Empire: How the Nazis Ruled Europe*. New York: Penguin Press.

Mehta U. 1999. *Liberalism and Empire: A Study in Nineteenth-Century British Liberal Thought*. Chicago: University of Chicago Press.

Miéville C. 2005. *Between Equal Rights: A Marxist Theory of International Law*. Leiden and Boston: Brill.

Mill J. S. 1981 (1873). *Autobiography*, ed. J. Robson and J. Stillinger. Vol. 1 of *Collected Works of John Stuart Mill*. Toronto: University of Toronto Press.

Mitchell T. 1991. *Colonizing Egypt*. Berkeley: University of California Press.

Moir M. I., Peers D. M., Zastoupil L. 1999. *J. S. Mill's Encounter with India*. Toronto: University of Toronto Press.

Moraña M., Dussel E. D., Jáuregui C. A. 2008. *Coloniality at Large: Latin America and the Postcolonial Debate*. Durham, N.C.: Duke University Press.

Morefield J. 2005. *Covenants without Swords: Idealist Liberalism and the Spirit of Empire*. Princeton, N.J.: Princeton University Press.

2008. "Empire, Tragedy, and the Liberal State in the Writings of Niall Ferguson and Michael Ignatieff." *Theory and Event*, 11. Available at http://muse.jhu.edu/login?/auth=0&type=summary&url=journals/theory_and_event/vo11/11.3morefield.html.

Muldoon J. 1999. *Empire and Order: The Concept of Empire, 800–1800*. New York: St. Martin's Press.

Muthu S. 2003. *Enlightenment against Empire*. Princeton, N.J.: Princeton University Press.

2008. "Adam Smith's Critique of International Trading Companies: Theorizing 'Globalization' in the Age of Enlightenment." *Political Theory*, 36, 185–212.

Negri A., Hardt M., Zolo D. 2008. *Reflections on Empire*. Cambridge and Malden, Mass.: Polity Press.

Nussbaum F. 2003. *The Global Eighteenth Century*. Baltimore: Johns Hopkins University Press.

Orford A. 2003. *Reading Humanitarian Intervention: Human Rights and the Use of Force in International Law*. Cambridge: Cambridge University Press.

Pagden A. 1982. *The Fall of Natural Man: The American Indian and the Origins of Comparative Ethnology.* Cambridge: Cambridge University Press.

1990. *Spanish Imperialism and the Political Imagination: Studies in European and Spanish-American Social and Political Theory, 1513–1830.* New Haven, Conn.: Yale University Press.

1993. *European Encounters with the New World: From Renaissance to Romanticism.* New Haven, Conn.: Yale University Press.

1995. *Lords of All the World: Ideologies of Empire in Spain, Britain and France c. 1500–c. 1850.* New Haven, Conn.: Yale University Press.

2001. *Peoples and Empires: A Short History of European Migration, Exploration, and Conquest from Greece to the Present.* New York: Modern Library.

2008. *Worlds at War: The 2,500-Year Struggle between East and West.* New York: Random House.

Palmerston H. J. T, Viscount. 1850. "Speech of 25 June 1850." *Hansard*, CXII [3rd Ser.], 380–444.

Paquette G. 2003. "Hegel's Analysis of Colonialism and Its Roots in Scottish Political Economy." *Clio*, 32, 415–432.

Parekh B. 1994. "Superior People: The Narrowness of Liberalism from Mill to Rawls." *Times Literary Supplement*, 25 February, 11–13.

1995. "Liberalism and Colonialism: A Critique of Locke and Mill." In *The Decolonization of Imagination: Culture, Knowledge and Power*, ed. J. N. Peterse and B. Parekh. London: Zed Books, pp. 81–98.

Parel A., Keith R. C. 1992. *Comparative Political Philosophy: Studies Under the Upas Tree.* New Delhi and Newbury Park, Calif.: Sage.

Pearson N. 2009. *Up from the Mission: Selected Writings.* Melbourne: Black Inc.

Persram N. 2007. *Postcolonialism and Political Theory.* Lanham, Md.: Lexington Books.

Pitts J. 2005. *A Turn to Empire: The Rise of Imperial Liberalism in Britain and France.* Princeton, N.J.: Princeton Unversity Press.

2008. "Constant's Thought on Empire and Slavery." In *The Cambridge Companion to Constant*, ed. H. Rosenblatt. Cambridge: Cambridge University Press, pp. 115–145.

2009. "Liberalism and Empire in a Nineteenth-Century Algerian Mirror." *Modern Intellectual History*, 6, 287–313.

Pocock J. G. A. 1999–. *Barbarism and Religion.* Cambridge: Cambridge University Press.

2005 [1973]. *The Discovery of Islands: Essays in British History.* Cambridge: Cambridge University Press.

Pogge T. 2002. *World Poverty and Human Rights: Cosmopolitan Responsibilities and Reforms.* Cambridge: Polity.

Pollock S. 2006. "Empire and Imitation." See Calhoun et al., 2006, pp. 175–188.

Porter B. 2004. *The Absent-Minded Imperialists: Empire, Society, and Culture in Britain.* Oxford: Oxford University Press.

2006. *Empire and Superempire: Britain, America, and the World.* New Haven, Conn.: Yale University Press.

Povinelli E. 2002. *The Cunning of Recognition: Indigenous Alterities and the Making of Australian Multiculturalism.* Durham, N.C.: Duke University Press.

2005. "A Flight from Freedom." See Loomba et al. 2005, pp. 145–165.

Rajagopal B. 2003. *International Law from Below: Development, Social Movements, and Third World Resistance.* Cambridge: Cambridge University Press.

Rana A. 2010. *The Two Faces of American Freedom.* Cambridge, Mass.: Harvard University Press.

Rawls J. 1971. *A Theory of Justice.* Cambridge, Mass.: Harvard University Press.

1999. *The Law of Peoples; with, "The Idea of Public Reason Revisited."* Cambridge, Mass.: Harvard University Press.

Richter M. 1963. "Tocqueville on Algeria." *Review of Politics*, 25, 362–398.

Rogin M. 1975. *Fathers and Children: Andrew Jackson and the Subjugation of the American Indian.* New York: Knopf.

1987. *Ronald Reagan, the Movie.* Berkeley and Los Angeles: University of California Press.

Rothschild E. 2004. "Global Commerce and the Question of Sovereignty in the Eighteenth-Century Provinces." *Modern Intellectual History*, 1, 3–25.

2008. "David Hume and the Seagods of the Atlantic." See Manning and Cogliano 2008, pp. 81–96.

Saada E. 2007. *Les enfants de la colonie: les métis de l'empire français entre sujétion et citoyenneté.* Paris: Découverte.

Said E. W. 1993. *Culture and Imperialism.* New York: Knopf (distributed by Random House).

2003. *Orientalism.* New York: Vintage Books.

Sartori A. 2006. "The British Empire and Its Liberal Mission." *Journal of Modern History*, 78, 623–642.

2008. *Bengal in Global Concept History.* Chicago: University of Chicago Press.

Schmidt-Nowara C., Nieto-Phillips J. M. 2005. *Interpreting Spanish Colonialism: Empires, Nations, and Legends.* Albuquerque: University of New Mexico Press.

Schultz B., Varouxakis G. 2005. *Utilitarianism and Empire.* Lanham, Md.: Lexington Books.

Scott D. 1999. *Refashioning Futures: Criticism After Postcoloniality.* Princeton, N.J.: Princeton University Press.

2004. *Conscripts of Modernity: The Tragedy of Colonial Enlightenment.* Durham, N.C.: Duke University Press.

Shapiro M. J. 2006. *Deforming American Political Thought: Ethnicity, Facticity, and Genre.* Lexington: University Press of Kentucky.

Shogimen T., Nederman C. J. 2009. *Western Political Thought in Dialogue with Asia.* Lanham, Md.: Lexington Books.

Slotkin R. 1973. *Regeneration Through Violence: The Mythology of the American Frontier, 1600–1860.* Middletown, Conn.: Wesleyan University Press.

1985. *The Fatal Environment: The Myth of the Frontier in the Age of Industrialization, 1800–1890.* New York: Atheneum.

1998. *Gunfighter Nation: The Myth of the Frontier in Twentieth-Century America*. Norman: University of Oklahoma Press.

Smouts M.-C. 2007. *La situation postcoloniale: les postcolonial studies dans le débat français*. Paris: Sciences Po.

Steinmetz G. 2006. "Imperialism or Colonialism? From Windhoek to Washington, by Way of Basra." In *Lessons of Empire: Imperial Histories and American Power*, ed. C. Calhoun, F. Cooper, and K. W. Moore. New York: The New Press, pp. 135–156.

2007. *The Devil's Handwriting: Precoloniality and the German Colonial State in Qingdao, Samoa, and Southwest Africa*. Chicago: University of Chicago Press.

Stoler A. L. 2006. "Imperial Formations and the Opacities of Rule." In *Lessons of Empire: Imperial Histories and American Power*, ed. C. Calhoun, F. Cooper, and K. W. Moore. New York: The New Press, pp. 48–60.

Stoler A. L., McGranahan C., Perdue P. C. 2007. *Imperial Formations*. Santa Fe, N.M.: School for Advanced Research Press; Oxford: James Currey.

Subrahmanyam S. 1996. *Merchant Networks in the Early Modern World*. Aldershot, UK, and Brookfield, Vt.: Variorum.

2005. *Explorations in Connected History*. New Delhi: Oxford University Press.

2006. "Imperial and Colonial Encounters: Some Comparative Reflections." In *Lessons of Empire: Imperial Histories and American Power*, ed. C. Calhoun, F. Cooper, and K. W. Moore. New York: The New Press, pp. 217–228.

Suny R. G., Martin T. 2001. *A State of Nations: Empire and Nation-Making in the Age of Lenin and Stalin*. New York: Oxford University Press.

Sylvest C. 2009. *British Liberal Internationalism, 1880–1930*. Manchester, UK: Manchester University Press.

Takaki R. 1979. *Iron Cages: Race and Culture in Nineteenth-Century America*. New York: Knopf.

Taylor C. 2004. *Modern Social Imaginaries*. Durham, N.C.: Duke University Press.

Taylor M. 1991. "Imperium et Libertas? Rethinking the Radical Critique of Imperialism during the Nineteenth Century." *Journal of Imperial and Commonwealth History*, 19, 1–23.

Teschke B. 2003. *The Myth of 1648: Class, Geopolitics, and the Making of Modern International Relations*. London and New York: Verso.

Tocqueville A., Pitts J. 2001. *Writings on Empire and Slavery*. Baltimore: Johns Hopkins University Press.

Tuck R. 1999. *The Rights of War and Peace: Political Thought and the International Order from Grotius to Kant*. Oxford: Oxford University Press.

Tully J. 1993. *An Approach to Political Philosophy: Locke in Contexts*. Cambridge: Cambridge University Press.

1995. *Strange Multiplicity: Constitutionalism in an Age of Diversity*. Cambridge: Cambridge University Press.

2008. *Public Philosophy in a New Key*. Cambridge: Cambridge University Press.

Tunick M. 2006. "Tolerant Imperialism: John Stuart Mill's Defense of British Rule in India." *Review of Politics*, 68, 586–611.

Van Ittersum M. J. 2006. *Profit and Principle: Hugo Grotius, Natural Rights Theories and the Rise of Dutch Power in the East Indies, 1595–1615.* Leiden and Boston: Brill.

Vergès F. 1999. *Monsters and Revolutionaries: Colonial Family Romance and Métissage.* Durham, N.C.: Duke University Press.

2001. *Abolir l'esclavage: une utopie coloniale, les ambiguïtés d'une politique humanitaire.* Paris: Albin Michel.

Wedeen L. 2008. *Peripheral Visions: Publics, Power, and Performance in Yemen.* Chicago: University of Chicago Press.

Forthcoming. "Scientific Knowledge, Liberalism, and Empire: Political Science in the Middle East."

Welch C. 2003. "Colonial Violence and the Rhetoric of Evasion: Tocqueville on Algeria." *Political Theory*, 31, 235–264.

Whelan F. G. 1996. *Edmund Burke and India: Political Morality and Empire.* Pittsburgh, Pa.: University of Pittsburgh Press.

2009. *Enlightenment Political Thought and Non-Western Societies: Sultans and Savages.* New York: Routledge.

White R. 1991. *The Middle Ground: Indians, Empires, and Republics in the Great Lakes Region, 1650–1840.* Cambridge and New York: Cambridge University Press.

Wilson K. 2004. *A New Imperial History: Culture, Identity, and Modernity in Britain and the Empire, 1660–1840.* Cambridge: Cambridge University Press.

Wolf E. R. 1982. *Europe and the People without History.* Berkeley: University of California Press.

Young I. M. 2007. *Global Challenges: War, Self-Determination and Responsibility for Justice.* Cambridge: Polity.

Ypi L., Goodin R. E., Barry C. 2009. "Associative Duties, Global Justice, and the Colonies." *Philosophy and Public Affairs*, 37, 103–135.

Zastoupil L. 1994. *John Stuart Mill and India.* Stanford, Calif.: Stanford University Press.

Index

Abbé de Pradt, 266, 267–268
Abbé Grégoire, 265n17
Abbé Raynal, 186, 187, 196, 200, 210, 211, 215, 223
Abd al-Qadir (Abd-el-Kader), 289, 289–290n98, 290–291
Aborigines, 101
Acciaiuoli, Donato, 11
Achac scholars, 262
Additions and Corrections to the First and Second Editions of Dr. Adam Smith's Inquiry into the Nature and Causes of the Wealth of Nations (A. Smith), 184, 185
"Address to the People of Great Britain" (Fox), 216–217
Aeneid (Virgil), 46
Afghanistan, 365
Africa, 220, 312, 313n74, 324, 348; colonial Africa, 325. *See also* North Africa; West Africa
African Americans, 99–100
Alexander VI (pope), and the Bulls of Donation to the Americas, 50, 50n68, 51–54, 59
Alexander the Great, empire of, 139–143, 144; occupation policies of, 140; prejudices of concerning Asians, 141, 142–143
Alfonso V (king of Spain), 53

Alfred, Taiaiake, 362
Algeria, 255, 288–289, 366; colonization of, 2; liberal opposition to the Algerian conquest, 271–278; and the rise of imperial liberalism, 278–281; subjugation of, 263–264. *See also* Tocqueville, Alexis de, and Algeria
Althusius, Johannes, 73
America, 41, 99, 187, 306n51, 312; colonists of, 193; discovery of gold and silver in, 313n74; as part of the British Empire, 156–157, 159
American Indians/Amerindians. *See* Native Americans
American Revolutionary War, 190
American Samoa, 372
Ames, William, 78
Among Empires (Maier), 371–372
Anastasius, 63
Ancient Law (Maine), 330, 339, 342
Ancient Society (Morgan), 330
Anderson, Benedict, 166
Ando, Clifford, 371, 372
Andreae, Johannes, 66
Andros, Edward, 79
Anghie, Anthony, 369
Anker, Carsten, 191
Anker, Peter, 191

CPSIA information can be obtained
at www.ICGtesting.com
Printed in the USA
LVHW101108041222
734547LV00001B/5